Data Mining and Analysis in the Engineering Field

Vishal Bhatnagar
Ambedkar Institute of Advanced Communication Technologies and Research, India

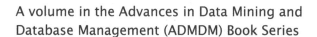

A volume in the Advances in Data Mining and Database Management (ADMDM) Book Series

Information Science REFERENCE
An Imprint of IGI Global

Managing Director:	Lindsay Johnston
Production Editor:	Jennifer Yoder
Development Editor:	Hayley Kang
Acquisitions Editor:	Kayla Wolfe
Typesetter:	Kaitlyn Kulp
Cover Design:	Jason Mull

Published in the United States of America by
   Information Science Reference (an imprint of IGI Global)
   701 E. Chocolate Avenue
   Hershey PA 17033
   Tel: 717-533-8845
   Fax: 717-533-8661
   E-mail: cust@igi-global.com
   Web site: http://www.igi-global.com

                    Library of Congress Cataloging-in-Publication Data

Data mining and analysis in the engineering field / Vishal Bhatnagar, editor.
     pages cm
  Includes bibliographical references and index.
  ISBN 978-1-4666-6086-1 (hardcover) -- ISBN 978-1-4666-6087-8 (ebook) -- ISBN 978-1-4666-6089-2 (print & perpetual access) 1. Data mining. I. Bhatnagar, Vishal, 1977-
  QA76.9.D343.D372 2014
  006.3'12--dc23
                              2014007990

This book is published in the IGI Global book series Advances in Data Mining and Database Management (ADMDM) (ISSN: 2327-1981; eISSN: 2327-199X)

British Cataloguing in Publication Data
A Cataloguing in Publication record for this book is available from the British Library.

For electronic access to this publication, please contact: eresources@igi-global.com.

Advances in Data Mining and Database Management (ADMDM) Book Series

David Taniar
Monash University, Australia

ISSN: 2327-1981
EISSN: 2327-199X

Mission

With the large amounts of information available to organizations in today's digital world, there is a need for continual research surrounding emerging methods and tools for collecting, analyzing, and storing data.

The **Advances in Data Mining & Database Management (ADMDM)** series aims to bring together research in information retrieval, data analysis, data warehousing, and related areas in order to become an ideal resource for those working and studying in these fields. IT professionals, software engineers, academicians and upper-level students will find titles within the ADMDM book series particularly useful for staying up-to-date on emerging research, theories, and applications in the fields of data mining and database management.

Coverage

- Cluster Analysis
- Customer Analytics
- Data Mining
- Data Quality
- Data Warehousing
- Database Security
- Database Testing
- Decision Support Systems
- Enterprise Systems
- Text Mining

IGI Global is currently accepting manuscripts for publication within this series. To submit a proposal for a volume in this series, please contact our Acquisition Editors at Acquisitions@igi-global.com or visit: http://www.igi-global.com/publish/.

)

Titles in this Series

For a list of additional titles in this series, please visit: www.igi-global.com

Biologically-Inspired Techniques for Knowledge Discovery and Data Mining
Shafiq Alam (University of Auckland, New Zealand)
Information Science Reference • copyright 2014 • 311pp • H/C (ISBN: 9781466660786) • US $265.00 (our price)

Data Mining and Analysis in the Engineering Field
Vishal Bhatnagar (Ambedkar Institute of Advanced Communication Technologies and Research, India)
Information Science Reference • copyright 2014 • 335pp • H/C (ISBN: 9781466660861) • US $225.00 (our price)

Handbook of Research on Cloud Infrastructures for Big Data Analytics
Pethuru Raj (IBM India Pvt Ltd, India) and Ganesh Chandra Deka (Ministry of Labour and Employment, India)
Information Science Reference • copyright 2014 • 570pp • H/C (ISBN: 9781466658646) • US $345.00 (our price)

Innovative Techniques and Applications of Entity Resolution
Hongzhi Wang (Harbin Institute of Technology, China)
Information Science Reference • copyright 2014 • 398pp • H/C (ISBN: 9781466651982) • US $205.00 (our price)

Innovative Document Summarization Techniques Revolutionizing Knowledge Understanding
Alessandro Fiori (IRCC, Institute for Cancer Research and Treatment, Italy)
Information Science Reference • copyright 2014 • 363pp • H/C (ISBN: 9781466650190) • US $175.00 (our price)

Emerging Methods in Predictive Analytics Risk Management and Decision-Making
William H. Hsu (Kansas State University, USA)
Information Science Reference • copyright 2014 • 425pp • H/C (ISBN: 9781466650633) • US $225.00 (our price)

Data Science and Simulation in Transportation Research
Davy Janssens (Hasselt University, Belgium) Ansar-Ul-Haque Yasar (Hasselt University, Belgium) and Luk Knapen (Hasselt University, Belgium)
Information Science Reference • copyright 2014 • 350pp • H/C (ISBN: 9781466649200) • US $175.00 (our price)

Big Data Management, Technologies, and Applications
Wen-Chen Hu (University of North Dakota, USA) and Naima Kaabouch (University of North Dakota, USA)
Information Science Reference • copyright 2014 • 342pp • H/C (ISBN: 9781466646995) • US $175.00 (our price)

Innovative Approaches of Data Visualization and Visual Analytics
Mao Lin Huang (University of Technology, Sydney, Australia) and Weidong Huang (CSIRO, Australia)
Information Science Reference • copyright 2014 • 464pp • H/C (ISBN: 9781466643093) • US $200.00 (our price)

www.igi-global.com

701 E. Chocolate Ave., Hershey, PA 17033
Order online at www.igi-global.com or call 717-533-8845 x100
To place a standing order for titles released in this series, contact: cust@igi-global.com
Mon-Fri 8:00 am - 5:00 pm (est) or fax 24 hours a day 717-533-8661

Table of Contents

Detailed Table of Contents

P. Vinod, SCMS School of Engineering and Technology, India
Jikku Kuriakose, SCMS School of Engineering and Technology, India
T. K. Ansari, SCMS School of Engineering and Technology, India
Sonal Ayyappan, SCMS School of Engineering and Technology, India

The authors in this chapter discuss different types of malware and their detection methods. They also propose a method of employing machine-learning techniques for the detection of metamorphic malware. This proposed method helps in selecting prominent features that could improve the classification accuracy of different malware. The malware type, the background of the different malware, and detection with the usage of data mining is very well presented in the chapter, which will definitely help young researchers to understand and pursue their work in this area. Experiment and results using TVF and WLLs have further strengthened the chapter. The authors conclude the chapter by stating the prospective research areas in the same domain, which will help researchers identify their own area and work in the same direction.

Tianxing Cai, Lamar University, USA

The author in this chapter present applications of data mining in the field of renewable energy and energy efficiency where data mining and analysis techniques are showing potential to solve the problems that arise in this area. The author describes the implementation procedures to demonstrate the application of curve fitting for renewable energy network design and optimization, which has the capability to handle the restoration during extreme and emergency situations with uncertain parameters. The motivation for the target audience is very well presented, which reflects the past and current research going in the field of renewable energy design and optimization. The prerequisite for the same is presented using the tabular data, which clearly indicates the ideal environment.

Chapter 3

N. K. Nagwani, National Institute of Technology, India
S. Verma, National Institute of Technology, India

The authors identify the statistical use of graphs in software repositories for revealing a wealth of information as knowledge. The authors argue for retrieving information available in software bug repositories, like the number of bugs priority-wise, component-wise, status-wise, developers-wise, module-wise, summary-terms-wise, which can be visualized with the help of two- or three-dimensional graphs. The authors state that visualization is a better source for identifying bugs in the software repositories. The authors generate two-dimensional and three-dimensional graphs using Java-based open-source APIs, namely Jzy3d (Java Easy 3D) and JFreeChart. The introductory section on visual data mining and visual analytics would encourage the young researchers to pursue their work in this emerging area. The authors emphasize the same by providing examples that clearly indicate the stated aim in an easily understandable method.

Chapter 4

Naveen Dahiya, MSIT, India
Vishal Bhatnagar, AIACT&R, India
Manjeet Singh, YMCAUST, India
Neeti Sangwan, MSIT, India

The authors demonstrate the real application of data mining tools and techniques for the complete SDLC. The crucial SDLC process is easily completed with the application of data mining in SDLC. The authors clearly state the research methodology in the form of a roadmap adapted, which allows all readers to understand the way the survey was carried out. The understandability is easy for the chapter, as the author identifies and demonstrates the research using a classification framework. This will enable identification of the future research areas.

Chapter 5

Pijush Samui, VIT University, India

The author demonstrates the application of data mining in civil engineering. The determination of pull out capacity (Q) of small ground anchor is a crucial task in civil engineering that can be solved using three data mining techniques (Genetic Programming [GP], Gaussian Process Regression [GPR], and Minimax Probability Machine Regression [MPMR]). The author also presents the comparison for all the three stated techniques. The work in this direction is very well presented in the form of a number of referenced papers. This effectively shows the real work that is progressing in this direction.

Chapter 6

Manish Kumar, IIIT, Allahabad, India
Shashank Srivastava, IIIT, Allahabad, India

The authors demonstrate the significance of the rules in various fields like weather forecasting, production, and sales, satellite communication, banks, etc. The author shows that rules may be extracted in different ways depending on the requirements and the dataset from which it has to be extracted. This chapter covers various methodologies for extracting such rules. It presents the impact of rule extraction for the predictive analysis in decision-making. The statistical techniques of hypothesis testing, linear regression, and nonlinear regression are presented by the authors. The adapted research methodology is shown by the authors at the end for better presentation and understandability. The section on tools for rules extraction will help young researchers understand the available tools in the market in a much easier and concise way.

Chapter 7

Jamie Godwin, University of Durham, UK
Peter Matthews, University of Durham, UK

The authors present a new paradigm using robust multivariate statistical methods to encapsulate normal operational behaviour—not failure behaviour—to autonomously derive unsupervised classifier labels for previously collected data in a rapid, cost-effective manner. The application of the same in mechanical engineering is demonstrated using two case studies. The authors explain the model development with a comparative evaluation of the metrics. The chapter is developed using the discussion on the problem background. This will help in better understandability. Future research directions are presented to enable the researchers to pursue research in the same domain.

Chapter 8

Gábor Hosszú, Budapest University of Technology and Economics, Hungary

The author shows the use of statistical techniques and clustering for relieving the hidden and unknown information from script relics. The author presents the application of clustering in the classification of rovash (pronounced "rove-ash") relics. The various Rovash scripts were used by nations in the Eurasian Steppe and in the Carpathian Basin as stated by the author. Considering the understandability problem of the same field, the motivation and literature review section is presented in a very effective way. The data mining technique of clustering is explained before the usage of the same for analysis. The chapter concludes with future research directions in the field of application of data mining in script relics.

Chapter 9

Understanding the need to classify objects of the universe based on the indiscernibility relation among them, the authors believe that rough set models would help. This chapter defines multigranulation rough sets for two universal sets, U and V. In addition, the algebraic properties, measures of uncertainty, and topological characterization that are interesting in the theory of multigranular rough sets are studied. This helps in describing and solving real life problems more accurately. The authors present a real world example for two universal sets on multigranulation to impart complete understanding of the concepts developed.

Chapter 10

The authors present the usage of data mining on unstructured data like the Weblog. The authors analyze frequent access patterns by applying the FP-growth algorithm, which is further optimized by using Genetic Algorithm (GA) and fuzzy logic. The solution for the effective analysis is proposed by the authors. The authors conclude with results that demonstrate that GA with fuzzy logic generates a higher number of optimized association rules as compared to GA. The time complexity of GA with fuzzy logic is higher as compared to GA, but the tradeoff is in favour of GA with fuzzy logic in terms of optimized outcomes.

Chapter 11

The authors discuss the most talked about topics of data mining. The authors discuss sentiment mining and opinion mining, which reveal hidden information from expressed opinions and sentiments. The authors survey the machine-learning approaches applied to sentiment analysis-based applications. The phases that are discussed in detail in this chapter for sentiment classification are feature extraction, feature weighting schemes, feature selection, and machine-learning methods. The authors show the evaluation method for sentiment analysis using the available free dataset. This would enable the target audience to better understand how to evaluate the available dataset. The authors also compare the various methods for sentiment analysis and conclude the chapter with future research directions.

Chapter 12

Elena Baralis, Politecnico di Torino, Italy
Luca Cagliero, Politecnico di Torino, Italy
Saima Jabeen, Politecnico di Torino, Italy
Alessandro Fiori, Institute for Cancer Research at Candiolo (IRCC), Italy
Sajid Shah, Politecnico di Torino, Italy

The authors discuss document summarization, which is a topic of current research. The authors present a novel strategy to combine ontology-based and social knowledge for addressing the problem of generic (not query-based) multi-document summarization of news articles. The authors analyze the social content acquired from real Twitter messages to understand the current interests of social network users for sentence evaluation. They show that the proposed summarizer performs better than the evaluated competitors on real news articles and Twitter messages. The related work is presented by the authors who helped in better understanding the overall growth in the said field.

Chapter 13

Shailendra Kumar Sonkar, National Institute of Technical Teacher's Training and Research,
India
Vishal Bhatnagar, Ambedkar Institute of Advanced Communication Technologies and
Research, India
Rama Krishna Challa, National Institute of Technical Teacher's Training and Research,
India

The growth of the social network is evident from the way all the current correspondence is done using the social medium only. This growth is further shown by the authors of this chapter. The authors identify key parameters for the identification of crucial information related to the use of social network by the users. The author proposes a framework for the use of data mining techniques on the key identified parameters, which will help later in quick and easy retrieval of information for the users. The related work and research methodology is presented in a clear manner, which helps in better understandability of the domain area. The authors present the advantages and disadvantages of the framework with the assumption for the developed framework. An empirical case example to better explain the underlying concept is done by the authors.

Chapter 14

Chellammal Surianarayanan, Bharathidasan University, India
Gopinath Ganapathy, Bharathidasan University, India

The authors argue for the use of data mining tools and techniques in revealing the hidden and unknown information from service-oriented computing. The authors present an overview of various issues of service discovery and composition and how they can be resolved using data-mining methods. Various research works that employ data-mining methods for discovery and composition are reviewed and classified by the authors. Adding the case study, which serves as a proof of concept for how data-mining techniques can enhance semantic service discovery, helps in better understanding of the concepts discussed.

Chapter 15

Abdulrahman R. Alazemi, Kuwait University, Kuwait
Abdulaziz R. Alazemi, Kuwait University, Kuwait

This chapter clearly states the underlying difference in theory for solving the confusion among the readers on usage of Business Intelligence and also usage of data mining. The chapter's inclusion in the book helps to show the use of data mining in revealing intelligent and crucial information from business data. This chapter strengthens the discussion on data mining analysis in various fields, as use of this technology is key when applied in business to get an effective ROI. The challenges in implementing the BI using data mining are clearly stated in this chapter.

Chapter 16

Seyed Jalaleddin Mousavirad, University of Kashan, Iran
Hossein Ebrahimpour-Komleh, University of Kashan, Iran

The diversified application of data mining and analysis is evident from this chapter. Classification of biomedical data plays a significant role in prediction and diagnosis of disease. The authors discuss feature selection without reducing the accuracy of the original set of features. The authors show the application of population-based feature selection to deal with issues of high dimensionality in biomedical data classification. The result found by the authors shows that population-based feature selection presents acceptable performance in biomedical data classification.

Chapter 17

Seyed Jalaleddin Mousavirad, University of Kashan, Iran
Hossein Ebrahimpour-Komleh, University of Kashan, Iran

The authors identify the use of the predictive data mining in medical diagnosis. They present a comparative study on medical diagnosis using predictive data mining. Data mining techniques, such as decision tree, neural networks, support vector machine, and lazy modelling are considered for predictive analysis. The authors show that data mining techniques can considerably help physicians.

Foreword

As digital businesses and society reinvent company processes and lifestyle behaviors, more information-based resources arise outside traditional information technology scenarios. Rapid growth of broadband connections elevates the number of connected people and connectable devices; the exigencies of living with online content and services has led to more than 2.7 billion people being connected to the Internet and 50 billion applications downloaded over all types of devices. Enterprises need to rapidly adjust more than one organizational or production layer to this new fast landscape; it is crucial to establish a novel analytical competitive advantage in order to not succumb to this tsunami of never-ending data generation. One of the main problems is trying to distill knowledge from this incredible source of information made of devices, people, processes, programs, and so on.

Beginning with the research around databases in the late 1980s, the field of data mining has acquired a leading role in the last decade, reinforcing the research community. Ranging from databases to machine learning, computational intelligence, statistics, visualization, and high-performance computing, the need to find synergistic approaches to the complex problem of adding value to data has been approached in various ways.

This book focuses on the analytical techniques of data mining, which are primarily classification, clustering, association rule mining, neural network, and genetic algorithms. These approaches are discussed considering many mathematical prerequisites and several useful application scenarios. The book is accessible to many potential readers, not strictly to those with experience in data mining.

Overall, this edited volume is a very welcome new publication in the arena of data mining, Dr. Vishal Bhatnagar has done an outstanding job by collecting timely and important contributions and opening new scenarios in the research and development of data mining systems.

Vincenzo Loia
University of Salerno, Italy

Vincenzo Loia *received the PhD in Computer Science from the University of Paris VI, France in 1989, and the bachelor degree in Computer Science from the University of Salerno in 1984. Since 1989, he has been a faculty member at the University of Salerno, where he teaches Operating Systems-Based Systems and Multi Agent-Based Systems. His current position is Professor of Computer Science. He was principal investigator in a number of industrial R&D projects and in academic research projects. He is the author of over 300 original research papers in international journals, book chapters, and in international conference proceedings. He has edited 5 research books about agent technology, Internet, and soft computing methodologies. He is Co-Editor-in Chief of Soft Computing, and founder and Editor-in-Chief of Ambient Intelligence and Humanized Computing, both published by Springer-Verlag. He serves as editor in a dozen international journals. His current research interests focus on merging soft computing and agent technology to design technologically complex environments, with particular interest in Web Intelligence and Ambient Intelligence applications.*

Preface

It is all about managing the bulk of the data available in various repositories. Currently, we rarely find a venture that does not have a bulk of data. The situation has come when the flow has gone above 1TB of data storage. The emergence of the data mining tools and techniques has helped in finding nuggets of information from the tera-bytes of data. Data mining is finding hidden and unknown information from large databases. The applications of data mining tools and techniques have grown. Each and every field has come up with uses for data mining tools and techniques. The narrow gap between the use of statistical techniques in data analysis and data mining has resulted in finding mixed applicability. The areas that have gained attention are:

- Software Engineering,
- Civil Engineering,
- Mechanical Engineering,
- Social Network and Mining,
- Web Mining,
- Sentiment Analysis/Opinion Mining,
- Data Labelling,
- Renewable Energy,
- Big Data Analytics,
- Visual Data Mining,
- Use of Data Mining in Fractals.

Data mining tools and techniques are helping to reveal hidden information from the databases. The various statistical and data mining techniques are helping to uncover valuable information from large databases. The major data mining techniques are:

- Classification,
- Clustering,
- Association Rule Mining.

The various statistical techniques are:

- Univariate and Multivariate Data Analysis,
- Hypothesis Testing,

- Use of Mean, Variance, and Standard Deviations in Data Analysis,
- Finding Randomness, etc.

These techniques are able to find widespread application in various engineering fields. The use of the large-scale algorithms has created a revolutionary aspect in the field of data analysis. The complex data analysis is now being eased using the technology of cloud computing, where the computational power of n-processors are used to analyze the data available. The technology of MapReduce and Hadoop has overcome all the hurdles, and now make complex and bulk data computation feasible.

The objective of this publication is to make researchers and other prospective readers aware of the latest trends and patterns in the inclusion of data mining tools and techniques in the engineering areas. The data mining application in the engineering fields of Software Engineering, Fractals, and Virtual Reality is gathered from eminent researchers across the globe. The mission of the publication is to come up with an edited book that discusses the latest and most advanced topic inclusion in contributions from renowned researchers whose work created a revolution in the area. The unique characteristics of the publication are that it:

1. Includes the work of eminent researchers in the application of data mining on emerging engineering areas like Software Engineering, Fractals, and Virtual Reality, which are current topics of research.
2. Is targeted towards providing quality, best, and latest research by eminent researchers considering how it affects common people in their everyday life, like the medical application of fractals or finding new metric and its importance in software engineering.
3. Will influence business users, common people, and society.

The impact of the contribution through this edited book is going to be widespread considering the very fact that areas like software engineering are established and growing fields and finding some significant impact of data mining in such a field will cause a great boom in the software industry, where they are constantly in search of novel and brilliant ways to make effective and productive software. Similarly, finding the data mining viability in the areas of mechanical engineering, which itself is gaining tremendous popularity, will add benefit from finding more and crisp output from the inclusion of data mining. The potential users of this book are:

1. The researchers will be able to know the latest application area of data mining in engineering.
2. The business users will get to know how inclusion of data mining can provide added advantages.
3. The common people will get the secure edge for their data, which is revealed in the social network analysis.

Intended audiences are:

1. Engineers,
2. Researchers,
3. Common People,
4. Business Users.

In my February 2013 call for chapters, I urged and sought contribution to this book from researchers, IT savvy professionals, and young engineers and industrialists across the globe with an aim to extract and accumulate the whole of modern research in the field of application of data mining and analysis using statistical techniques in various engineering fields. The beginning was overwhelming for me as I started to get many chapters with varied applications of the data mining tools and techniques in various fields. The authors whose chapters were selected were asked to include future research directions to enable young engineers and researchers to work in the domain.

The book is a collection of the seventeen chapters by eminent professors, researchers, and industry people from different countries. The chapters were initially peer reviewed by the editorial board members, reviewers, and industry people who themselves span many countries. The chapters are arranged so that all the chapters have the basic introductory topics and the advances as well as future research directions, which enable budding researchers and engineers to pursue their work in this area.

Chapter 1 by P. Vinod, Jikku Kuriakose, T. K. Ansari, and Sonal Ayyappan shows that malware or malicious code intends to harm computer systems without the knowledge of system users. These malicious softwares are unknowingly installed by naive users while browsing the Internet. Once installed, the malware performs unintentional activities like (a) steal username, password; (b) install spy software to provide remote access to the attackers; (c) flood spam messages; (d) perform denial of service attacks; etc. With the emergence of polymorphic and metamorphic malware, signature-based detectors are failing to detect new variants of these malware. The primary reason is that malicious code developed in new generation have different syntactic structures from their predecessor, thereby defeating any pattern matching techniques. Thus, the detection of morphed malware remains a complex open research problem for malware analysts. In this chapter, the authors discuss different types of malware with their detection methods. In addition, they present a proposed method employing machine learning techniques for the detection of metamorphic malware. The methodology demonstrates that appropriately selecting prominent features could improve the classification accuracy. The study also depicts that proposed methods that do not require signatures are effective in identifying and classifying morphed malware.

In chapter 2, Tianxing Cai discusses supply, which is characterized by its diversity, including traditional energy, such as fossil fuels, nuclear power, as well as renewable energy, such as solar, hydroelectric, geothermal, biomass, and wind energy. It involves a complex network system composed of energy generation, energy transformation, energy transportation, and energy consumption. The network does provide the great flexibility for energy transformation and transportation; meanwhile, it presents a complex task for conducting agile energy dispatching when extreme events have caused local energy shortages that need to be restored timely. One of the useful methodologies to solve such a problem is data mining and analysis. Their main objective is to take advantage of inherent tolerance of the imprecision and uncertainty to obtain tractability, robustness, and low solution-cost. The applications and developments of data mining and analysis have amazingly evolved in the last two decades. Many of these applications can be found in the field of renewable energy and energy efficiency where data mining and analysis techniques are showing a great potential to solve the problems that arise in this area. In this chapter, data mining and analysis techniques are briefly introduced. Then the implementation procedures are presented to demonstrate the application of curve fitting for renewable energy network design and optimization, which has the capability to handle the restoration during extreme and emergency situations with uncertain parameters.

Software repositories contain a wealth of information that can be analyzed for knowledge extraction. Software bug repositories are one such repository that stores the information about the defects identified during the development of software as argued by N. K. Nagwani and S. Verma. Information available in software bug repositories like number of bugs priority-wise, component-wise, status-wise, developers-wise, module-wise, summary-terms-wise, can be visualized with the help of two- or three-dimensional graphs. These visualizations help in understanding the bug distribution patterns, software matrices related to the software bugs, and developer information in the bug-fixing process. Visualization techniques are exploited with the help of open source technologies in this chapter to visualize the bug distribution information available in the software bug repositories. Two-dimensional and three-dimensional graphs are generated using java-based open source APIs, namely Jzy3d (Java Easy 3d) and JFreeChart. Android software bug repository is selected for the experimental demonstrations of graphs. The textual bug attribute information is also visualized using frequencies of frequent terms present in it.

Chapter 4 by Naveen Dahiya, Vishal Bhatnagar, Manjeet Singh, and Neeti Sangwan discusses that data mining has proven to be an important technique in terms of efficient information extraction, classification, clustering, and prediction of future trends from a database. The valuable properties of data mining have been put to use in many applications. One such application is Software Development Life Cycle (SDLC), where effective use of data mining techniques has been made by researchers. An exhaustive survey on application of data mining in SDLC has not been done in the past. In this chapter, the authors carry out an in-depth survey of existing literature focused towards application of data mining in SDLC and propose a framework that will classify the work done by various researchers in identification of prominent data mining techniques used in various phases of SDLC and pave the way for future research in the emerging area of data mining in SDLC.

Chapter 5 by Pijush Samui focuses on the determination of pull out capacity (Q) of small ground anchor is an imperative task in civil engineering. This chapter employs three data mining techniques (Genetic Programming [GP], Gaussian Process Regression [GPR], and Minimax Probability Machine Regression [MPMR]) for determination of Q of small ground anchor. Equivalent anchor diameter (D_{eq}), embedment depth (L), average cone resistance (q_c) along the embedment depth, average sleeve friction (f_s) along the embedment depth, and Installation Technique (IT) are used as inputs of the models. The output of models is Q. GP is an evolutionary computing method. The basic idea of GP has been taken from the concept of Genetic Algorithm. GPR is a probabilistic non-parametric modelling approach. It determines the parameter from the given datasets. The output of GPR is a normal distribution. MPMR has been developed based on the principal mimimax probability machine classification. The developed GP, GPR, and MPMR are compared with the Artificial Neural Network (ANN). This chapter also gives a comparative study between GP, GPR, and MPMR models.

Chapter 6 by Manish Kumar and Shashank Srivastava states rules are the smallest building blocks of data mining that produce the evidence for expected outcomes. Many organizations like weather forecasting, production and sales, satellite communications, banks, etc. have adopted this mode of technological understanding not for the enhanced productivity but to attain stability by analyzing past records and preparing a rule-based strategy for the future. Rules may be extracted in different ways depending on the requirements and the dataset from that has to be extracted. This chapter covers various methodologies for extracting such rules. It presents the impact of rule extraction for the predictive analysis in decision making.

Chapter 7 by Jamie Godwin and Peter Matthews explores how labelling of data is an expensive, labour-intensive, and time consuming process and, as such, results in vast quantities of data being unexploited when performing analysis through data mining. This chapter presents a new paradigm using robust multivariate statistical methods to encapsulate normal operational behaviour—not failure behaviour—to autonomously derive unsupervised classifier labels for previously collected data in a rapid, cost-effective manner. This enables traditional machine learning to take place on a much richer dataset. Two case studies are presented in the mechanical engineering domain, namely, a wind turbine gearbox and a rolling element bearing. A statistically sound and robust methodology is contributed, allowing for rapid labelling of data to enable traditional data mining techniques. Model development is detailed, along with a comparative evaluation of the metrics. Robust derivatives are presented and their superiority is shown. Example "R" code is given in the appendix, allowing readers to employ the techniques discussed. High levels of agreement between the derived statistical approaches and the underlying condition of the components can be found, showing the practical nature and benefit of this approach.

Chapter 8 by Gábor Hosszú presents statistical evaluations of script relics. Its concept is exploiting mathematical statistical methods to extract hidden correlations among different script relics. Examining the genealogy of the graphemes of scripts is necessary for exploring the evolution of the writing systems, reading undeciphered inscriptions, and deciphering undeciphered scripts. The chapter focuses on the cluster analysis as one of the most popular mathematical statistical methods. The chapter presents the application of the clustering in the classification of Rovash (pronounced "rove-ash," an alternative spelling: Rovas) relics. The various Rovash scripts were used by nations in the Eurasian Steppe and in the Carpathian Basin. The specialty of the Rovash paleography is that the Rovash script family shows a vital evolution during the last centuries; therefore, it is ideal to test the models of the evolution of the glyphs. The most important Rovash script is the Szekely-Hungarian Rovash. Cluster analysis algorithms are applied for determining the common sets among the significant Szekely-Hungarian Rovash alphabets. The determined Rovash relic ties prove the usefulness of the clustering methods in the Rovash paleography.

Chapter 9 by D. P. Acharjya and Mary A. Geetha explores the fundamental concept of crisp set has been extended in many directions in the recent past. The notion of rough set by Pawlak is noteworthy among them. The rough set philosophy is based on the concept that there is some information associated with each object of the universe. There is a need to classify objects of the universe based on the indiscernibility relation among them. In the view of granular computing, rough set model is researched by single granulation. It has been extended to multigranular rough set model in which the set approximations are defined by using multiple equivalence relations on the universe simultaneously. However, in many real life scenarios, an information system establishes the relation with different universes. This gave the extension of multigranulation rough set on single universal set to multigranulation rough set on two universal sets. This chapter defines multigranulation rough set for two universal sets U and V. In addition, the algebraic properties, measures of uncertainty and topological characterization that are interesting in the theory of multigranular rough sets are studied. This helps in describing and solving real life problems more accurately.

Chapter 10 by Manish Kumar and Sumit Kumar identifies Web usage mining which can extract useful information from Weblogs to discover user access patterns of Web pages. Web usage mining itself can be classified further depending on the kind of usage data. This may consider Web server data, application server data, or application level data. Web server data corresponds to the user logs that are collected at Web servers. Some of the typical data collected at Web server are the URL requested, the IP address from which the request originated, and timestamp. Weblog data is required to be cleaned, condensed, and transformed in order to retrieve and analyze significant and useful information. This chapter analyzes access frequent patterns by applying the FP-growth algorithm, which is further optimized by using Genetic Algorithm (GA) and fuzzy logic.

Chapter 11 by Basant Agarwal and Namita Mittal surveys on Opinion Mining or Sentiment Analysis is the study that analyzes people's opinions or sentiments from the text towards entities such as products and services. It has always been important to know what other people think. With the rapid growth of availability and popularity of online review sites, blogs', forums', and social networking sites' necessity of analysing and understanding these reviews has arisen. The main approaches for sentiment analysis can be categorized into semantic orientation-based approaches, knowledge-based, and machine-learning algorithms. This chapter surveys the machine learning approaches applied to sentiment analysis-based applications. The main emphasis of this chapter is to discuss the research involved in applying machine learning methods mostly for sentiment classification at document level. Machine learning-based approaches work in the following phases, which are discussed in detail in this chapter for sentiment classification: (1) feature extraction, (2) feature weighting schemes, (3) feature selection, and (4) machine-learning methods. This chapter also discusses the standard free benchmark datasets and evaluation methods for sentiment analysis. The authors conclude the chapter with a comparative study of some state-of-the-art methods for sentiment analysis and some possible future research directions in opinion mining and sentiment analysis.

Chapter 12 by Elena Baralis, Luca Cagliero, Saima Jabeen, Alessandro Fiori, and Sajid Shah overviews that with the diffusion of online newspapers and social media, users are becoming capable of retrieving dozens of news articles covering the same topic in a short time. News article summarization is the task of automatically selecting a worthwhile subset of news' sentences that users could easily explore. Promising research directions in this field are the use of semantics-based models (e.g., ontologies and taxonomies) to identify key document topics and the integration of social data analysis to also consider the current user's interests during summary generation. The chapter overviews the most recent research advances in document summarization and presents a novel strategy to combine ontology-based and social knowledge for addressing the problem of generic (not query-based) multi-document summarization of news articles. To identify the most salient news articles' sentences, an ontology-based text analysis is performed during the summarization process. Furthermore, the social content acquired from real Twitter messages is separately analyzed to also consider the current interests of social network users for sentence evaluation. The combination of ontological and social knowledge allows the generation of accurate and easy-to-read news summaries. Moreover, the proposed summarizer performs better than the evaluated competitors on real news articles and Twitter messages.

Chapter 13 by Shailendra Kumar Sonkar, Vishal Bhatnagar, and Rama Krishna Challa argues that dynamic social networks contain vast amounts of data, which is changing continuously. A search in a dynamic social network does not guarantee relevant, filtered, and timely information to the users all the time. There should be some sequential processes to apply some techniques and store the information internally that provides the relevant, filtered, and timely information to the users. In this chapter, the authors categorize the social network users into different age groups and identify the suitable and appropriate parameters, then assign these parameters to the already categorized age groups and propose a layered parameterized framework for intelligent information retrieval in dynamic social network using different techniques of data mining. The primary data mining techniques like clustering group the different groups of social network users based on similarities between key parameter items and by classifying the different classes of social network users based on differences among key parameter items, and it can be association rule mining, which finds the frequent social network users from the available users.

Chapter 14 by Chellammal Surianarayanan and Gopinath Ganapathy argues for implementation of data mining for service-oriented computing. Web services have become the de facto platform for developing enterprise applications using existing interoperable and reusable services that are accessible over networks. Development of any service-based application involves the process of discovering and combining one or more required services (i.e. service discovery) from the available services, which are quite large in number. With the availability of several services, manually discovering required services becomes impractical and time consuming. In applications having composition or dynamic needs, manual discovery even prohibits the usage of services itself. Therefore, effective techniques which extract relevant services from huge service repositories in relatively short intervals of time are crucial. Discovery of service usage patterns and associations/relationships among atomic services would facilitate efficient service composition. Further, with availability of several services, it is more likely to find many matched services for a given query, and hence, efficient methods are required to present the results in useful form to enable the client to choose the best one. Data mining provides well known exploratory techniques to extract relevant and useful information from huge data repositories. In this chapter, an overview of various issues of service discovery and composition and how they can be resolved using data mining methods are presented. Various research works that employ data mining methods for discovery and composition are reviewed and classified. A case study is presented that serves as a proof of concept for how data mining techniques can enhance semantic service discovery.

Chapter 15 by Abdulrahman R. Alazemi and Abdulaziz R. Alazemi explores the advent of information technologies brought with it the availability of huge amounts of data to be utilized by enterprises. Data mining technologies are used to search vast amounts of data for vital insight regarding business. Data mining is used to acquire business intelligence and to acquire hidden knowledge in large databases or the Internet. Business intelligence can find hidden relations, predict future outcomes, and speculate and allocate resources. This uncovered knowledge helps in gaining competitive advantages, better customer relationships, and even fraud detection. In this chapter, the authors describe how data mining is used to achieve business intelligence. Furthermore, they look into some of the challenges in achieving business intelligence.

Chapter 16 by Seyed Jalaleddin Mousavirad and Hossein Ebrahimpour-Komleh presents classification of biomedical data plays a significant role in prediction and diagnosis of disease. The existence of redundant and irrelevant features is one of the major problems in biomedical data classification. Excluding these features can improve the performance of classification algorithm. Feature selection is the problem of selecting a subset of features without reducing the accuracy of the original set of features. These algorithms are divided into three categories: wrapper, filter, and embedded methods. Wrapper methods use the learning algorithm for selection of features while filter methods use statistical characteristics of data. In the embedded methods, feature selection process combines with the learning process. Population-based metaheuristics can be applied for wrapper feature selection. In these algorithms, a population of candidate solutions is created. Then, they try to improve the objective function using some operators. This chapter presents the application of population-based feature selection to deal with issues of high dimensionality in the biomedical data classification. The result shows that population-based feature selection has presented acceptable performance in biomedical data classification.

Chapter 17 by Seyed Jalaleddin Mousavirad and Hossein Ebrahimpour-Komleh shows medical diagnosis is a most important problem in medical data mining. The possible errors of a physician can reduce with the help of data mining techniques. The goal of this chapter is to analyze and compare predictive data mining techniques in the medical diagnosis. To this purpose, various data mining techniques such as decision tree, neural networks, support vector machine, and lazy modelling are considered. Results show data mining techniques can considerably help a physician.

The applications of data mining are so diversified that it cannot be covered in single book. However, with the encouraging research contributed by the researchers in this book, we (contributors), EAB members, and reviewers tried to sum up the latest research domains, development in the business field, and applicable areas. This edited book will serve as a motivating factor for those researchers who have spent years working as data repositories, data analysts, statisticians, and budding researchers, as they will be able to get better response for their collected data irrespective of the domain/field, as data mining is applicable in each and every area. Engineers who are witnessing the never-ending competition in each and every field will get to know that by the application of data mining in their field, a new dimension will be added which will bring success in their field and business as they will replicate the knowledge sharing aspects in various business ventures.

Vishal Bhatnagar
Ambedkar Institute of Advanced Communication Technologies and Research, India

Acknowledgment

I would like to begin with a special note of thanks to the publishing team at IGI Global, whose contributions throughout the whole process have been invaluable. In particular, thanks to Vince D'Imperio and Christine Smith, whose continuous suggestions and valuable information kept me alarmed for timely completion of the book and whose input proved to be very valuable at every crucial stage of the development process. I would like to convey my heartfelt thanks to Kayla Wolfe for her initial support and necessary information. I would also like to thank Jan Travers for timely completion of the contract agreement and helping me to decide on the title of the book, which I feel is very essential for attracting the prospective contributors. I feel that in a crucial and long process, the role of each and every individual is important. I would also like to extend my sincere thanks to all other staff of IGI Global, who have been involved with the book.

I take this opportunity to extend my sincere gratitude to the most honorable Prof. L. A. Zadeh, whom I have troubled at every stage of this book's development. Indeed, I am fortunate that he is always ready and kind enough to help. The timely completion of the book is dependent on a crucial factor, which is the timely completion of the review of all the submitted chapters. I am indeed fortunate that my whole team of EAB members, reviewers, and authors helped to make this possible. I would like to extend my special thanks to Professor Vincenzo Loia for agreeing to write the foreword for the book and extending his full support and invaluable advice for improving the book.

The timely completion is also dependent on the environment that prevails around you. I would like to thank my college principal, Prof. Ashok Mittal, for his cordial support, valuable information and guidance, and above all, his motivation and concern for my health and progress. I would also like to thank my friends and colleagues for providing me necessary opinions and help all through the development process of this book.

I would like to take this opportunity to express my respect and love to my dear ones and my parents. Life is uncertain and full of hurdles. These I realized during the development of this book when I went through the rough patch as I met an accident. During this time, it was my parents who were with me and used to remind me to "not worry everything will come on track. Have patience and just do whatever you can do." I believe strongly that it is their belief and continuous love and affection that brought everything back on track. Thanks Mom and Dad! I would also like to extend my special thanks to my father-in-law for all his blessings and his positive opinion towards life, which he always shares with me. After so many years of marriage, I feel life is incomplete without the support and unbiased suggestions, which I get from my beloved wife. My life would be incomplete without her. Last but not least, my whole journey towards a bright career and research started when I received a blessing from God, a son who is like an angel for me. He, with his innocent thoughts, helped me many times and filled me with new energy for a new day in life.

Vishal Bhatnagar
Ambedkar Institute of Advanced Communication Technologies and Research, India
January 2014

Chapter 1
Optimal Features for Metamorphic Malware Detection

P. Vinod
*SCMS School of Engineering and Technology,
India*

T. K. Ansari
*SCMS School of Engineering and Technology,
India*

Jikku Kuriakose
*SCMS School of Engineering and Technology,
India*

Sonal Ayyappan
*SCMS School of Engineering and Technology,
India*

ABSTRACT

Malware or malicious code intends to harm computer systems without the knowledge of system users. These malicious softwares are unknowingly installed by naive users while browsing the Internet. Once installed, the malware performs unintentional activities like (a) steal username, password; (b) install spy software to provide remote access to the attackers; (c) flood spam messages; (d) perform denial of service attacks; etc. With the emergence of polymorphic and metamorphic malware, signature-based detectors are failing to detect new variants of these malware. The primary reason is that malicious code developed in new generation have different syntactic structures from their predecessor, thereby defeating any pattern matching techniques. Thus, the detection of morphed malware remains a complex open research problem for malware analysts. In this chapter, the authors discuss different types of malware with their detection methods. In addition, they present a proposed method employing machine learning techniques for the detection of metamorphic malware. The methodology demonstrates that appropriately selecting prominent features could improve the classification accuracy. The study also depicts that proposed methods that do not require signatures are effective in identifying and classifying morphed malware.

1. INTRODUCTION

Past few decades have shown tremendous increase in the use of computers that can invariably process small to big data. Likewise, we have also witnessed the popularity of Internet for usage for e-shopping, e-learning, e-reservation etc. In each of these applications online transactions is required to be performed. Vulnerabilities associated with the Internet, computer systems, softwares and operating systems are exploited by malware attackers and many black hat users to develop and launch sophisticated attacks. Mostly, attacks are created by recreating malicious programs (a.k.a

DOI: 10.4018/978-1-4666-6086-1.ch001

malware) using existing malware generation kits also known as *virus constructors*. Malware in general refer to all unwanted computer program (computer viruses, Trojans, rootkits, worms, adware, spyware etc.) that disrupt the normal functioning of the system. Emergence of free and open source software has shown increased market for malware writing which now have evolved into a profit making industry. The goal of these malicious software include activities like identity threats, consume system resources, and allow unauthorized access to the compromised systems. A common characteristics of malware is the capability to replicate and then propagate. Malicious programs make use of files, emails, macros, bluetooth or browser as a source of infection for its propagation.

Since the development of anti-virus (AV) software, signature scanning or pattern matching techniques are predominantly being used (Aycock, J 2006). Signature is a unique byte pattern or string capable of identifying a malicious code. Although, this method performs well in determining malware, however signature based scanning fail to detect unseen samples or *zero day malware attack*. Signature based techniques have some limitations on detection like (a) failure to detect encrypted code (b) lack of semantics knowledge of the programs (c) increase in the size of signature repository and (d) failure to detect obfuscated malware (Vinod et al, 2009). In order to circumvent the pattern based detection method, malware writers make use of complex obfuscation techniques to generate new strains. Obfuscation can take different forms (a) code packing (Yan, W. et al, 2008) (b) encryption of code using random decryptors (also known as *polymorphism*) and (c) complete code morphism which is referred as *metamorphism*. The basis of generating the metamorphic malware is to increase variability in the structure of code from one generation to another generation without affecting the functionality of programs.

Malware detection methods can be broadly classified as *static* and *dynamic*. With static analysis, the malware is detected by examining the code without its execution. Thus, static analysis is fast but may fail to detect parts of the malicious code that are executed only during runtime. During static analysis, the scanner checks for strings, file names, author signatures, system information, checksum etc. that differentiates malware from the benign program.

In dynamic analysis, samples are executed in a controlled environment. The scanners employing this method examine function/system calls, status of processor registers, flags, API parameters to determine if a program can be classified as malicious. Although, dynamic analysis is an improvement over static analysis where the detection time is usually very slow and therefore cannot be considered as the exclusive approach for malware detection. The main reason in dynamic analysis that the scanner tries to trace complete execution paths of the suspected sample. Infection of systems is the primary risk associated with dynamic analysis. To avoid this, malware scanners use virtualization or emulation based techniques. This reduces the efficiency as execution time is increased. Dynamic analysis may not succeed if malware incorporates *Anti-VM* and *Anti-emulation* checks.

Data mining methods are also gaining prominence in the detection of malware. In this method, a classification algorithm is used for modelling malware and benign behaviors/structure. The classifier is subjected to diverse malicious and benign patterns for the categorization of unseen samples (malware or benign). Recently machine learning techniques have gained popularity for the detection of malcode (Nir, N, 2012; Eitan, 2009; Asaf, S, 2009; Dima, S, 2009). Features of different category (Vinod, P., 2013) such as opcode *n-gram*, API call sequence, Portable Executable metadata or strings extracted from functions are used for the purpose of classification. In this chapter, we introduce different approaches encompassing data mining techniques for the identification of synthetic malware. For increased accuracy in the detection process, we discuss in detail the feature reduction methods. Later, in this chapter we discuss our proposed methods for malware analysis based on feature reduction known as Singular value decomposition (SVD) (Baker, K., 2013), term frequency variance (TVF), bigram distribution variance (BDV) and weighted log likelihood score (WLLS).

One of the bench mark dataset that is used in the domain of malware detection area is Next Generation Virus Kit (NGVCK). The viruses generated from NGVCK virus generators are transformed into complex obfuscated code by a morpher discussed in (Sudarshan, 2013). Authors in (Sudarshan, 2013) showed that the generated synthetic malware bypass Hidden Markov Model (HMM) based detector (Runwal, N, 2012; Lin D., 2011). Thus, we propose a similarity based detector designed to classify benign and metamorphic malware samples. Features are transformed in a new space using SVD, term frequency variance (TVF), bigram distribution variance (BDV) and weighted log likelihood score (WLLS) to reduce the feature vector length. Experiments are performed on imbalanced data set where the size of benign data set is kept two times the size of malware to replicate real world scenario. Our investigation depicted better detection rate for unseen malware and benign instances. Using our proposed method with strong feature reduction methods we could determine that the data mining approach based detectors are much superior in comparison to the HMM based detector proposed in (Sudarshan, 2013).

The main difference of our proposed methodology with similar approach lies in the fact that we unpack the samples before feature selection. This is owning to the fact that a packed sample is likely to be statistically different from benign (mostly present in unpacked state). If unpacking is not performed the approach may identify a packed benign as malicious or vice-versa. Other difference from the prior work is the difference in feature selection/reduction method.

2. MALWARE AND TYPES

Malware can be broadly classified based on their infection modes and propagation mechanisms. Modern malware are more sophisticated in terms of their complexity in behavior and appearance of code. A brief outline of different types of malware is presented in subsequent subsections.

2.1 Virus

A computer virus is a program which infects the system by replication. It uses a host program for infection and is propagated only by human intervention. Normally, computer viruses target auto-run files, executable system files and macros of document files for replication.

Virus may contain some module like (a) *a search routine*: to locate a program or file with specific file extension to infect and subsequently marks each file to avoid over infection (b) *copy routine:* copies the malicious code to a host file. This malicious code could be *prepended, appended* or *interleaved* at different locations of the host file (c) *anti–detection:* mechanisms to evade detection by antivirus products. These mechanisms can either be *encryption, code obfuscation* or *interrupt vector table modification* etc. (d) *payload:* which is primarily the main constituent of any virus used for self-replication.

2.2 Worms

Worms are self–replicating malicious programs like computer viruses. They spread via Internet without human interaction. Worms exploit two fundamental vulnerabilities (a) software bug and (b) security holes to propagate.

Worms attempt to scan open ports to launch different types of attacks. The most widely used mechanism to gain access to the target machine is by using network file sharing exploits, scanning for open ports or using chat and instant messaging software. Usually, worms propagate using infection vectors such as (a) electronic mail facility or (b) remote login and execution capability. The worm generally opens a backdoor and gives complete control of the target system to remote attackers and could result in denial of service transmission.

2.3 Trojans

A Trojan Horse is a non–self-replicating program. It enters the computer unnoticed and is usually disguised as a legitimate application. Once the system is infected by Trojan, it allows un–restricted access of the user system to attacker sitting in a remote location. Trojan Horse requires a host program in which it hides.

The basic component of a Trojan Horse is a *server* and *client* program. The server launches a malicious program which attracts the users. This malicious code is hidden in certain application, games, images, videos, songs etc. Malicious file are made to appear as legitimate by changing the name and extension of the program as normal files. After these applications are downloaded, Trojans create backdoors in the target machine that enable attackers to access systems remotely to collect sensitive information pertaining to ignorant users.

2.4 Backdoors

Backdoor is a program created by attackers to bypass network security checks to spy or interact with the victim machine. Backdoors are planted in softwares (open source or free ware) before their distribution and opens the channel for remote users to connect to the vulnerable machine. Softwares with backdoor sometime make use of Trojans for compromising a computer system. The user machine is victimized when an image or video consisting of backdoor is downloaded. Some backdoors allow an attacker to change root or

administrator privileges of target system, allowing remote execution of commands and monitoring activities of a target machine.

2.5 Logic Bombs

This category of malware can exist stand alone or can be interleaved inside a legitimate program. They have two basic components (a) payload: which is capable of performing malicious activities, like formatting hard disk or deleting system files (b) trigger: logic bombs can stay dormant for a specific event to occur delivering its malicious payload.

2.6 Adware

Adwares are malicious programs that appear in the form of pop-ups, flash and unsolicited advertisements while users are browsing the Internet. They are planted into freeware software or applications such as desktop themes, file sharing tools, fun games, mouse pointers and emotions/smiley etc. Sometimes adware are very dangerous as they redirect to unsolicited sites requiring users to register informations like password of email accounts, credit card or cvv numbers. Some adware work as spyware that collect keystrokes to gather valuable information and login credential pertaining to user.

2.7 Rootkits

Rootkit specifically hides itself by modifying applications pertaining to an operating system. The word rootkit is composed of root and kit. Root in Linux/Unix operating system refers to root or system administrator and kit refers to a set of applications or utility programs. By having the root user privilege, intruders can execute files, modify system configurations and monitor activities on the target machine. Rootkits are broadly classified as (a) *user mode rootkits:* such rootkits replace applications on top of the kernel with malicious code to achieve the required goal and (b) *kernel mode rootkits:* these rootkits modify the operating environment as they tend to receive calls coming to the system. Such rootkits create a process that responds to calls or requested services.

2.8 Bots and Botnets

Botnets are malicious programs, sometimes referred as software robots. Computers infected by botnets are known as zombies. The infected machines are under the control of a bot master or bot herder. Concealment of botnets usually occurs by making use of identical names of legitimate processes or system files. Generally, the bots contain a software that repeatedly performs the task of scanning IP and port to create more zombies. A botnet is mainly used for illegal purposes and the noticeable activities performed by bots are (a) distributed denial of service (DDoS) and (b) flood spam messages. Botnets that are used to launch DDoS attack, saturate bandwidth and resources of machines connected to Internet. Botnets propagate spam messages on victim machines and hijack contact list of users in the address book to launch a backdoor. One of the striking difference between worm and botnet is that worm does not have centralized control and therefore the collection of compromised machines is ineffectual whereas, with botnets the botmaster commands the zombies with the help of a central server (i.e. controller).

3. MODERN MALWARE

Polymorphic and metamorphic variants are structurally different in every new generation to thwart signatures based detectors. In the following subsections we briefly introduce polymorphic and metamorphic malware.

3.1 Polymorphic

Polymorphic malware encrypts its code with random keys to avoid detection. Polymorphic virus have a mutation engine which generate new keys for decrypting the encrypted malicious code. Once executed, the virus is again encrypted with different key. Subsequently the virus attaches itself to vulnerable application. Thus, each malware variant will have a different binary pattern as it is generated using new random keys. Such malware easily thwart signature based scanners. Figure 1 depicts structure of polymorphic malware.

3.2 Metamorphic Malware

Metamorphic malware are malicious software having the ability to transform their code during propagation. The change in the code is induced by *metamorphic engine*. Also, the metamorphic engine usually morphs its structure in every new generation to bypass detection (refer Figure 2).

Metamorphic malware employ different code transformation techniques such as *garbage code insertion, code rolling using branch instruction, equivalent instruction substitution, register reassignment and subroutine in lining and out lining* (refer Figure 3).

Generally, the malware writers keep the size of metamorphic engine small (Chouchane, 2006) with the intension that the antivirus would spent minimal time to scan the engine. Variants generated in successive generations are structurally dissimilar from their predecessors thus, signature based detectors fail to detect new malware specimens. Due to the very fact the detection of metamorphic malware is still a challenge for malware analyst. Even if there is substantial variation in

Figure 1. Polymorphic malware

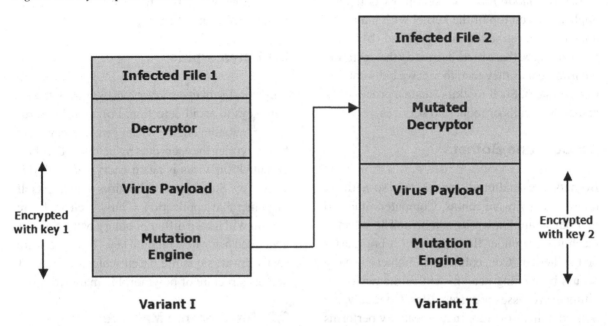

Figure 2. Metamorphic malware

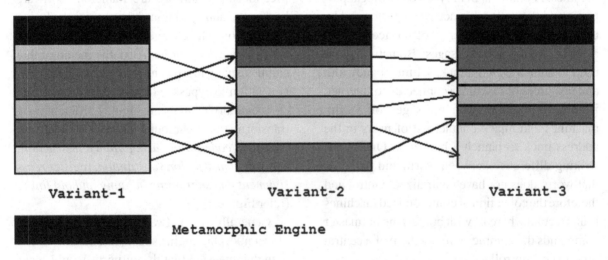

Figure 3. Obfuscation techniques used by metamorphic malware

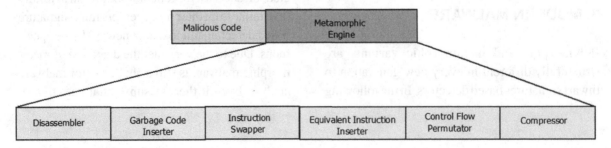

the code structure amongst the variants, massive variability cannot exists as it would affect the functionality of malicious executables. Hence, we feel that metamorphic malware exhibit similarity as genetic diversity. Following are different code obfuscation techniques

1. **Garbage Code Insertion:** In this method instruction such as NOP (No-operation) or those instructions which does not affect the functionality is inserted in the original program. Normally these instructions increase the overall execution time of the programs. Table 1 depicts certain *do-noting* statements instructions.

2. **Instruction Transposition:** Two instruction can be swapped *iff* the output of one instruction does not affect subsequent instruction or there exist no instruction dependency. Usually instructions are permuted by performing the data flow analysis so that the functionality of the program is not altered. Moreover, instruction transposition can be achieved by introducing *conditional/unconditional* branch instructions. Consider the following set instructions which can be permuted as they lack dependencies (also registers $R1 \neq R2 \neq R3 \neq R4 \neq R5$), here OP_i refers to different operation such as MOV, ADD, XOR etc.

Table 1. Garbage instruction

NOP	OR REG, 0
ADD REG, REG	XOR REG, 0
ADD REG, 0	MOV REG, REG
SUB REG, 0	PUSHFD POPFD
PUSH REG POP REG	PUSHAD POPAD
XCHG REG, REG	AND REG, 1

```
OP₁ R1, R2

OP₂ R3, [R4]

OP₃ R5, R5
```

3. **Equivalent Instruction Substitution:** Replacement of instructions are performed by maintaining a dictionary of semantically equivalent instructions. Instruction replacement can either expand or shrink the size of code. Following are some equivalent instructions.

```
ADD REG, 0 ↔ NOP

ADD REG, 1 ↔INC REG

MOV Reg,Reg ↔ NOP

SUB Reg,Imm ↔ ADD Reg,-Imm

SUB Mem,Imm ↔ ADD Mem,-Imm

AND REG, 0 ↔ MOV REG, 0 ; AND REG, REG

CMP REG, 0 ↔ JMP REG ;PUSH REG; RET

XCHG REG1, REG2 ↔ NOP ↔ PUSHFD; POPFD ↔ PUSH REG; POP REG

TEST Reg,Reg ↔ CMP Reg,0

LEA Reg,[Imm] ↔ MOV Reg,Imm
```

4. **Register Reassignment:** Is the simplest technique and can be detected by malware scanners using wild card matching techniques. The metamorphic engine replace a register with another register if the former is not used nor carries data. Suppose we

assume that register eax can be replaced be ebx, ebx by ecx and ecx by edx then the following two code fragments are equivalent (refer Figure 4).

5. **Subroutine in Lining/Out Lining:** In subroutine, a call to a subroutine is replaced by its definition. In this case the variant of the malware code contain few function definition/procedure. The code structure thus happens to be more linearized. Code outlining divides a block of code into subroutine(s) and inserts a series of subroutine call and its definitions resulting in increased number of functions definition in new variant.

4. METAMORPHIC MALWARE DETECTION METHODS

Prior research work in the domain of detection of metamorphic malware is discussed in (Vinod et. al, 2011a). Their research work also introduces detection of metamorphic malware variants using control flow graphs. In (Wing W, 2006) the author investigate the degree of metamorphism in different malware constructor such as Generation 2 (G2), Virus Creation Lab (VCL32), MPCGEN (Mass Code Generator), Next Generation Virus Creation Kit (NGVCK) obtained from (http://vx.netlux.org). They demonstrated that NGVCK constructor exhibited higher degree of meta-

morphism compared to all malware constructors considered in the study. Also, NGVCK generated variants depicted similarity in range of 1.5% to 21% with an average similarity of 10%. However, non-malware files exhibited similarity close to NGVCK. Thus, to detect metamorphic malware variants created with NGVCK tool Hidden Markov Model (HMM) based scanner was developed. Commercial antivirus failed to detect metamorphic malware variants developed with NGVCK. This shows that signature based detector actually fails to detect morphed malware. However, the experiment depicted that the HMM based detector could identify NGVCK variants. This proves that there existed opcode difference thus similarity method fairs well to classify malware and benign executables.

In (Vinod et al, 2010) proposed a method for detecting unseen malware samples by executing executable using STraceNTx in an emulated environment. Samples were generated with different malware kits like VCL32, IL_SMG, PS-MPC, MPCGEN and NGVCK. They extracted a common base signature from each malware constructor. It was found that unseen samples were detected using the base signature. Later, they investigated the degree of metamorphism amongst different constructors used in the study. Similarity amongst malware constructors were determined by computing proximity index. Inter constructor and intra constructor proximity was determined. The research depicted that all constructors showed

Figure 4. Code Snippet depicting register reassignment

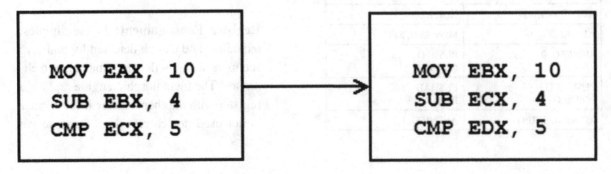

high intra constructor proximity except NGVCK. Unlike NGCVK constructor, code distortion was not significant indicating minimal degree of metamorphism. Also, inter constructor similarity was observed. Most of the samples was found to have higher proximity with other malware constructor. However, NGVCK generated variants depicted less intra constructor proximity. This indicate that metamorphic engine of NGVCK virus kit was observed to robust in comparison to other malware constructor used in the study.

Authors (Attaluri, S, 2009) used Profile Hidden Markov Models (PHMMs) from opcode alignment sequences obtained from morphed malware to create stronger detector for the classification of specimens (malware & benign). PHMMs are robust in comparison to standard HMM as the former capture positional information. The generated PHMM was tested on metamorphic malware samples generated from three malware constructors (VCL-32, PS-MPC and NGVCK). Detection rate of 100% was achieved for VCL-32 and PS-MPC samples whereas considering proper multiple aligned sequences of NGVCK malware a better detection rate was obtained to be considered for addressing the problem of virus detection. The study also highlighted that PHMMs were not effective if code block were permuted. However the primary disadvantage with PHMM is that they are computationally very expensive for constructing malware models.

(Vinod et al, 2009) created three malware samples and seven variants were generated from the base malware applying different code morphing techniques (equivalent instruction substitution, garbage insertion, code permutation using branch instruction). Code structure of variants were normalized with a custom built assembly code normalizer. Subsequently, control flow graph (CFG) of normalized code was created which resulted in normalized CFG. Later, from this normalized CFG, opcode sequence was extracted and compared with the opcode sequence of other variants using *Longest Common Subsequence*

(LCS). It was examined that variants of malware produced higher similarity. Moreover, morphed malware can be differentiated from benign files. The only drawback of using LCS method is it has computational complexity of $O(m.n)$ where m and n are the length of two opcode sequences extracted from malware/benign files.

(Lin D., 2011) developed a metamorphic engine that could evade HMM based detector. The idea of the study was to investigate as to what extent the base malware could be morphed so as to fail HMM based scanner. The metamorphic engine morphed the NGVCK generated malware code using elementary code obfuscation technique. More importantly the basic idea was to generate morphed malware copies that are structurally similar to benign files. In order to carry the experimentation Cygwin executables were considered as the benign samples (as they employ low level system functionality as malware specimens) and fragment of code from subroutines of these benign files were extracted, and inserted in malware samples without disturbing maliciousness. The experiment was conducted for different fraction of injected code (extracted from benign files) in range of 5% to 35%. It was observed that even 5% of benign code inserted as dead code in malware sample could thwart HMM detector. This research article opened a new door for malware analyst to understand that the metamorphic engine employing basic obfuscation method as insertion of dead code (from subroutine of benign files) could defeat both pattern based as well as spectrum based scanners.

In (M.E, Saleh, 2011) presented a novel method for the detection of metamorphic malware based on face recognition approach known as Eigenfaces. The premise were that eigenfaces differ from a basic face due to age, posture of face or conditions of light during image acquisition. These eigenfaces were generally abstracted using Principal component analysis. For each malware, binary set of vectors with significant variations were determined and these vectors were called eigenvectors. Likewise, the space was known as eigenspace. Such representation of viruses was termed as eigenviruses. One of the important property of the obtained eigenvector along with some determined weight was that they represents a general model of replicating malware specific to a family. An unseen binary sample was projected to eigen space. Subsequently, the distance of test specimen was computed with predetermined eigenvectors in the training set using Euclidean method. Computed distances were compared with the previously found threshold. If the distance was below some threshold the test sample was said to belong to a virus family or treated as non-family malware. Experiment was performed with 1000 metamorphic malware and 250 benign binaries. Detection rate of 100% was obtained with a false positive of 4%.

Metamorphic malware detection using control flow graph mining approach was proposed in (Mojtaba Eskandari, 2011). Portable executable malware sample were disassembled and after preprocessing step few instructions like jump (unconditional and conditional jump) with their target set of instructions, subroutine, API calls were retained. A control flow graph of the processed assembly code was generated and subsequently an API call graph was obtained. The sparse API graph was later converted into a feature vectors. Dimensionality reduction was performed to obtain optimal feature vector. Classification model was constructed and overall detection rate of 97.3% for unknown malware samples was achieved.

(Runwal N, 2012), devised a method for determining similarity between the files using opcode graphs (directed graph). An opcode graph is constructed from opcode extracted from malware files. Nodes are denoted as opcode and the directed edge between the nodes are represented as the probability of a successor opcode in a file with respect to a given opcode under consideration. The study depicted that the opcode graph similarity method outperformed HMM based detector and yielded no false positives or nega-

tives. While there existed good separation between the similarity scores of malware v/s malware and benign v/s benign. Hence, a threshold could be easily determined, based on this threshold, unseen samples can be classified as malware/benign. The authors also tested the effectiveness of the opcode graph model based on two attacks (a) removal of rare opcode and (b) transforming metamorphic engine into complex form (where junk code from benign samples are inserted into malware samples so that malware and benign samples appear structurally similar). The investigation highlights that metamorphic malware can be discriminated from benign executable even after the removal of uncommon opocodes. Also, the detection rate of HMM scanners and opcode graph based detector are comparable if benign code is injected in malicious files as dead code.

Studies in (Lin D., 2011) depicted that HMM based detector failed to detect strong metamorphic malware invariants generated through insertion of benign opcode as dead code. (Annie H, 2012) devised a method to improve the detection rate of HMM scanner by combining it with statistical methods such as chi squared test. It was observed from the experiments that HMM based detectors performed well if short sequence of benign opcode is added as junk code. Moreover, for a block of benign code added to malware file the detection rate of HMM based scanner degraded. Thus, chi-square based classification was produced. It was noticed that when a hybrid model was devised by integrating the outputs obtained from HMM and Chi-square classifier. This hybrid model depicted in improvement of classification accuracy.

In (Donabelle B, 2013) proposed a method for identification of metamorphic malware based on byte features using structural entropy and wavelet transform techniques. Byte entropies and wavelet transforms were applied on malicious files in order to segment them using different scaling parameter. Subsequently it was observed that the scaling parameter 3 and 4 segmented malware files appropriately. The segmented files were then compared based on edit distance. The entropy score depends on the length of malware files. Hence, in some cases the detector did not perform well as the NGVCK generated malware differed largely with respect to its length.

(Vinod et al, 2012b) created a probabilistic signature for the identification of metamorphic malware inspired by bio informatics multiple sequence alignment method (MSA). For each malware family single, group and MSA signature were constructed. Threshold were determined for different malware families. The results depicted promising outcome when compared to the detection rate achieved with 14 commercial antivirus scanners. Their study showed that the signatures generated using sequence alignment method were far superior in comparison to those generated by commercial AV. The proposed detector was found to have better detection rate (73.2% approximately) and was ranked third best compared to other commercial malware scanners.

5. DATA MINING TECHNIQUES FOR MALWARE DETECTION

The first major work in data mining for detecting malware was proposed in (J.O.Kephart, 1994). It is a signature based method that examines the source code of computer viruses and estimates the probability of instructions appearing in legitimate programs. The code sequence with minimum false positives is used as a signature for future detection. The authors in (Md.Enamul, K, 2005) proposed a "phylogeny" model, particularly used in areas of bioinformatics, for extracting information in genes, proteins or nucleotide sequences. The *n-gram* feature extraction technique was proposed and fixed permutation was applied on the code to generate new sequences, called *n-perms*. Since new variants of malware evolve by incorporating permutations, the proposed *n-perm* model was developed to capture instruction and block permutations. The

experiment was conducted on a limited data set consisting of 9 benign samples and 141 worms collected from VX Heavens (http://vx.netlux. org). The proposed method showed that similar variants appeared closer in the phylogenetic tree where each node represented a malware variant. The method did not depict how the *n-perm* model would behave if the instructions in a block of code are replaced by equivalent instructions which could either expand or shrink the size of blocks (with respect to number of instructions in a block).

The authors (Matthew et al, 2001) were the first to introduce malware detection using data mining method. Three types of features were extracted: PE Header, strings, and byte sequence features. To detect unknown computer viruses, classifiers like *decision tree* and *Naive Bayesian* network, *RIPPER* were used. The results showed that the machine learning method outperformed signature based techniques. The *boosted decision trees* show better classification with an area of 0.996 under the ROC curve.

Authors in (Kolter J.Z., 2006) extracted *n-gram* byte code from a collection of 1971 benign and 1651 malware samples. Top 500 n-*grams* were selected and evaluated on various inductive methods like Naive Bayes, decision trees, support vector machines and boosted versions of these classifiers. The authors indicated that the results obtained by them was better compared to the results presented by Schultz *et al* (Matthew et al, 2001). Better classification accuracy was obtained with boosted decision trees with area an under ROC curve of 0.996. In an extension to their study, the authors evaluated the effectiveness of earlier trained malware and benign models with new test data. It was found that the trained model were not good enough to identify unknown samples collected from the point after the training model was prepared. This study suggests that the training models also require updation for classification and identification of unknown malware samples.

(Robert M et al., 2009) proposed a method for malware detection using the opcode sequence obtained by disassembling executables. Opcode *n-grams* were extracted for *n = 1, 2,...., 6* from a large collection of malware and benign samples. Top *n-gram* was selected using three feature selection methods: *Document Frequency, Fischer Score* and *Gain ratio*. The malcode detection is based on the text categorization technique. The frequency of terms in documents are computed to prepare a vector representation of each term in a sample. The experiment was evaluated on different Malicious File Percentage (MFP) levels to depict the real scenario of the appearance of malware and benign samples. It was found that the 2-gram outperformed all *n-grams*. The feature selection method like Fischer score and Document Frequency were found to be better as compared to Gain Ratio. Top 300 opcodes *n-gram* was found to be effective in classification of the executable with an accuracy of 94.43%. The Boosted decision tree, decision tree, and Artificial Neural Network (ANN) produced low false positives compared to Naive and Boosted Naive Bayes. Also, the test set with MFP level of 30% was found to be better compared to other MFP levels with accuracy of 99%.

(Menahem et al, 2009b) proposed a method for improving malware detection using the ensemble method. Each classifier uses specific algorithm for classification as each classifier is suited for a particular domain. In order to achieve higher detection rate using machine learning technique, the authors combined the results of individual classifier using different methods like weighted voting, distribution summation, Naive-Bayes combination, Bayesian combination, stacking and Troika (Menahem et al, 2009a). The goal of this research was to evaluate whether ensemble based method would produce better classification accuracies as compared to individual classifiers. Since ensemble methods require high processing time, the experiment was performed on a part of initially collected data set (33%). From their experiments, it was observed that the Troika and Distribution function were found to be the best ensemble methods with accuracy of 95% and 93% respectively but suffered with high execution time overheads. All ensemble methods that outperformed in accuracies suffered in execution time. PE file header information, byte *n-grams* and function based features were extracted and binary, multiclass classification was performed. Troika was found to perform better for multiclass classification followed by Bayesian-combination. The authors suggest that since execution time is of prime concern, Bayesian combination would be a better choice for ensemble based classification of malware and benign instances.

Non-signature based method using Self-organizing maps (SOMs) was proposed in (Seon, Y., 2006). SOM is a feed-forward neural network for topological representation of the original data. This method is used to identify files infected by malware. Using SOM, it was observed in the study that the infected files projected a high density area. The experiment was conducted on 790 malware infected files. The proposed method was capable of detecting 84% of malware with false positive rate of 30%.

The authors in (Santos I, 2009) extracted *n-grams* from benign and malicious executables and used *k-nearest neighbour* algorithm to identify the unseen instances. In this method *n-grams* from malware and benign samples are extracted for *n = 2, 3, 4,...., 8* to form the training and test set. The number of coincidences of *n-grams* in the training set and test instance was determined. An unknown sample was considered as malware only if the difference of *k* most similar malware and benign instances was greater than a threshold *d*. The experiment was conducted on a data set collected from a software agency and the results depict that the detection rate for 2-gram was poor, 91% detection rate was obtained for 4-gram model.

Henchiri et al (Olivier, H., 2006) presented a method based on byte *n-gram* feature on different families of viruses collected from VX Heavens. For each family of viruses and inter-family, support threshold is computed and a maximum of 500 features that have higher frequency than that of threshold are retained. Likewise, features which have higher value than the inter-family support were retained and others were eliminated. The results were evaluated on the proposed classifier and compared with traditional classifiers like decision trees, Naive Bayes, and Support Vector Machine. From their experiments, it was observed that shorter byte sequences produced better detection rates between 93% to 96%. The performance degraded with feature length less than 200 features.

A non-signature based method using byte level file content was proposed in (Tabish, S.M, 2009). This method computes diverse features in block-wise manner over the byte level content of the file. Since blocks of bytes of a file is used for analysis, the prior information regarding the type of file is not required. Initially, each sample is divided into equal sized blocks and different information theoretic features are extracted. The feature extraction module extracts 13 different type of features for each *n-gram* (n = 1, 2, 3, 4). Thus, for each block 52 features are extracted. The experiments were conducted on malware data set collected from VX Heavens (http://vx.netlux.org) and benign samples consisting of different file types: DOC, JPG, EXE etc. Results depict that the proposed method is capable of achieving an accuracy above 90%.

The authors in (Igor, S., 2010) proposed a novel method for detecting variants of malware making use of opcode-sequences. This approach was based on determining the opcode frequency. The relevant opcodes were mined using mutual information and assigned with certain weights. The proposed method was tested on dataset downloaded from VX Heavens (http://vx.netlux.org) and was not tested for packed malware. The opcode sequence

of fixed length n = 1 or 2 was extracted for each malware and its variants. Proximity between the variants was computed using *cosine similarity* method. The similarity within malware data set was high as compared to benign set. Additionally, the similarity between malware and benign samples was low. Thus, it can be inferred that malware and benign samples are not as diverse as benign ones; a characteristics that can be used for discriminating it from benign instances.

Analysis and detection of malware using structural information of PE was proposed by authors in (Ronny, M., 2010). PE header fields were extracted from executables and top 23 features were extracted. The analysis was performed on two test sets: obfuscated malware and clean malware samples. A hypothesis based classification model was developed and the results were compared with WEKA classifiers. The detection rate of 92% was reported with obfuscated malware executables.

In their study (Vinod et al, 2011b) different features from both malware and benign files like instruction opcode (consisting of opcode and addressing mode), portable executable header fields and mnemonic *n-grams* was extracted. The primary objective was to understand the degree of obfuscation introduced by malware writers either by modifying the PE header, substituting equivalent opcode or modifying the addressing modes. Features were processed with *scatter criteria* and classified with classification algorithm implemented with WEKA. The experiments revealed that *Random Forest* outperformed all classifier in terms of classification accuracy. Also, accuracy of 98.1% was obtained if classification is performed considering PE Header information. It was noticed that obfuscation was predominantly performed by modifying instruction either by replacing a given opcode with equivalent opcode or modifying the addressing mode of instruction. Therefore, the classification accuracy did not fair well when these features were used for the identification of malicious executables.

Authors in (Vinod et al, 2012a) devised a method for the discrimination of malware samples from large collection of benign executables. *Bi-gram* features was extracted after unpacking packed malware samples provided by different user agencies using signature and dynamic unpackers. Reduced feature were obtained with *Principal Component Analysis* and *minimum redundancy and maximum relevance* techniques. Prominent features were extracted independently from malware and benign population. The objective of study was (a) to determine best feature (b) efficient classifier (c) appropriate feature selection methods and (d) optimal feature vector length that result in higher classification accuracy. They also investigated if the classification model performs well for imbalanced data set. Their results were also compared with previous literature and was found to produce detection rate of 97% with overall accuracy of 94.1%.

In (Vinod et al, 2013) proposed a novel method to create multicomponent feature (MCF features) composed of (a) opcode *bi-gram* (b) PE meta data (c) principal instruction code (opcode and addressing mode) and (d) prominent *uni-grams*. Features were reduced with *minimum redundancy and maximum relevance, principal component analysis* and extracting *eigen vectors*. They investigated different features and optimal feature vector length that yield higher classification accuracy. Experiments were performed on total 2217 malware and 3307 benign PE files. It was observed that *mRMR* feature selection method produced higher classification accuracy. Overall accuracy of 96.1% was obtained with this proposed technique.

George Dahl (2013) created a classification method from a very large data set consisting of 2.6 million malware samples belonging to 134 families. Sparse binary features constituting of strings, API trigram, parameter specific to an API were extracted from each specimen. Large feature space was reduced using Random projection to speed up and improve classification accuracy.

Training model was prepared using neural network with one or more hidden layer. The trained neural network produced reduction of 43% error rate. Also, higher accuracy was obtained with basic neural network in comparison to a neural network with two to three hidden layer. The degraded performance of neural network with hidden layer is due to the fact that there was not enough error to model hidden layer.

6. PROPOSED METHODOLOGY

In this section, we discuss our proposed methodologies for metamorphic malware detection. Dataset used for analysis contain thousands of attributes, most of which may be redundant and do not contribute to classification. Primary goal of feature reduction technique is to select minimum number of effective features such that the distribution of target class in reduced feature space is likely to be similar to the original dataset. Minimizing the attributes have the following benefits:

1. Reduces memory space and computation time involved during the training and testing phase.
2. Fewer attributes result in better knowledge of the data set. This is because prominent attributes demonstrate variation in features amongst different classes.
3. Fewer dimensions can be plotted and visualized easily.
4. Eliminates correlated features that do not contribute to classification.

Thus to develop detector that can discriminate samples accurately, we make use of feature selection methods, and thus propose two different schemes for metamorphic malware identification. In our first method, we propose a similarity based classifier were unseen malware samples are identified by computing the similarity with known files, which were utilized for determining threshold. In our second approach we use (a) term frequency variance (TFV) and (b) weighted log likelihood schemes (WLLS) and (c) *Bi-gram* Distribution Variance (BDV) to rank the bigram opcodes. Classification model was developed using these ranked features with classification algorithms such as Naïve Bayes, Instance based learner, J48, Boosted classifier and Random Forest implemented in WEKA (Mark Hall, 2009). In the following subsection we introduce our proposed malware scanner based on machine learning approach.

6.1 Applicability of SVD for Metamorphic Malware Detection

In this approach different steps used are data preprocessing, feature vector table creation, feature transformation using singular valued decomposition (SVD) (Baker, K., 2013) and similarity based classification (refer Figure 5). In Terrell et al. (2005) authors discuss methods to identify local anomaly such as denial of service attacks by capturing different features (packet size, source port/ destination port) by monitoring network packets for a duration of one hour. Large feature vectors were reduced using Singular Value Decomposition to identify anomalous traffic. Following are the various phases adopted by us in designing the detector.

1. The malware and benign portable executables (PE's) are first unpacked using signature based unpacker VMPacker and GNUPacker (www.woodman.com) and the disassembled with IDA-PRO disassembler, to generate ASM files (assembly code files).

2. The *.asm* files are then parsed with the developed parser to extract mnemonics which

are further stored individually in files with *.ins* extension. Consider the following set of instruction appearing in a file:

```
MOV EAX, EBX

PUSH EBX

POP ECX
```

After the preprocessing step each *.ins* file would contain MOV, PUSH, and POP statements.

3. These *.ins* files are used to prepare the dataset. Dataset are divided into train and test set where 80% of the processed malware and benign files (obtained from 2) are placed in a "train" and the remaining are placed in a "test" directory respectively.

4. *Bi-gram* opcodes were extracted from the training dataset motivated by the research work of authors in (Wei, J. 2005) were they observed that the prepared *n–gram* models outperformed in identifying infected files. Basically, *n–grams* are overlapping sub–strings of length *n* collected in a sliding window fashion. We extracted Opcode/mnemonic *n–gram* as they partially carry behavioral snapshot of each specimen. Let us consider some sequence of unigram as jmp, mov, add, inc, dec, jnz, call, int. The *bi-gram* equivalent generated are: jmpmov, movadd, addinc, incdec, decjnz, jnzcall, callint.

5. Later, a unique list of *bi-gram* opcode are independently determined from train set (malware and benign). This unique list is a structure of the form.

Figure 5. Applicability of SVD for metamorphic malware detection

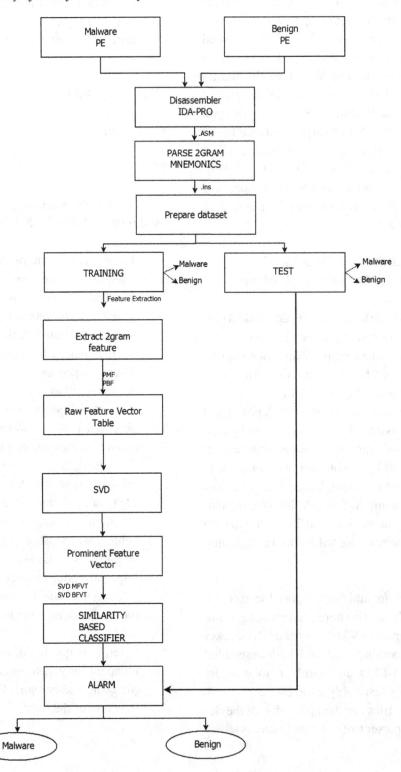

```
struct uniqueListElement{

char *bigramOpcode;

int totalFrequency;//Frequency of
each bi-gram in a

//malware or benign train set.

int howManySamples;//Number of sam-
ples a bi-gram is present (similar to
document frequency).

};
```

Initial processing is performed to extract those *bi-gram* that appear predominantly in most of the files. We selected *bi-grams* that appeared in at least 30% of malware or benign samples.

6. Using the pruned *bi-grams* obtained from step 5 Feature Vector Tables [$(M_i \cup B_i)$, F_m] and [$(M_i \cup B_i)$, F_b] is constructed where,
   a. $\mathbf{M_i}$: M_1, M_2..., M_p (malware files in the train data set).
   b. $\mathbf{B_i}$: B_1, B_2,..., B_q (benign files in the train data set).
   c. $\mathbf{F_m}$: The malware features.
   d. $\mathbf{F_b}$: The benign features.
7. SVD is applied on each feature vector table obtained from step 6 created with malware and other benign features. SVD generate robust features by eliminating components having less significant singular value. The mathematical representation for SVD of a matrix M is given by:

```
M= U .S. Vᵀ
```

The matrix *M* is decomposed into three other matrices *U, S* and *V^T*. Here *U* and *V* contain eigen vectors and *S* contains its square root of eigen values in decreasing order as diagonal elements.

U represents the relationship between the opcode (row) and the documents (column). *V^T* represents the relationship between the document (row) and the opcode (column). Eigen vector in column one of *U* corresponds to the largest eigen value in *S*, the eigen vector in column two of *U* corresponds to the next largest eigen value in *S* and so on. For a given document training file *d* we have $d = d^T.U.S^{-1}$. If only prominent *k* dimension are considered then we have $d_k = d^T.U_K.S_K^{-1}$.

Initially, for a given test (query) vector *q* ($q = q^T.U.S^{-1}$) we obtain $q_k = q^T.U_K.S_K^{-1}$. Ranking is performed based on *cosine similarity* method for each test file computed over samples in train set. Similarity metric are computed by considering opcode as the attributes. Normalized dot product of two vectors are determined. By computing the cosine similarity, we try to find cosine of the angle. For cosine similarities resulting in a value of 0, the files being compared do not have any opcodes in common because the angle between the files is 90 degrees. Given two vectors of attributes, *A* and *B*, the cosine similarity, $cos(\theta)$, is represented using a dot product and magnitude as

$$\text{Similarity} = \cos(\theta) =$$

$$\frac{A.B}{\|A\|\|B\|} = \frac{\sum_{i=1}^{n} A_i * B_i}{\sqrt{\sum_{i=1}^{n}(A_i)^2} * \sqrt{\sum_{i=1}^{n}(B_i)^2}}$$

We computed threshold which could identify a sample appropriately as malware or benign. We experimentally fixed threshold value of 0.45 to identify samples precisely. It means similarity of test sample is computed with each samples in the training set and if the computed similarity score is greater than 0.45 the sample is considered as malware otherwise treated as benign. Table 2 depict the similarity score of a test sample *G2_12.ins*

Table 2. Similarity of test document (G2_12.ins) with rest samples malware sample. Since top four samples depict malware thus, the test sample as assigned to class malware.

G2_12.ins	Rank/Cosine Similarity	Class
mpcgen_18.ins	0.856204	M
G2_49.ins	0.837805	M
mpcgen_35.ins	0.737201	M
G2_1.ins	0.637654	M
cleanup.ins	0.134863	B
G2_6.ins	0.897208	M
NGVCK_2.ins	0.756206	M

with malware and benign file. We can observe that the test file score high with all malware samples in train set and shows a very less similarity value with a benign file *cleanup.ins*.

6.1.1 Experiments and Results with SVD Features

The experiments was conducted on the same dataset as in (http://cs.sjsu.edu/~stamp/viruses). The malware files used were: NGVCK (Next Generation Virus Creation Kit), G2 (Malware Analyzer), MPCGEN (Phalcom Mass Code Generator), MWOR (Malicious Worm). The benign files were obtained from Internet sources. There are 150 malware and 2666 benign files. Experiments were performed on Intel ® Core ™ i5-2430m CPU @ 2.40 GHz 2.40 GHz with memory (RAM) of 4.00 GB. The parameters used for evaluation are:

1. **True Positive (TP):** The number of malwares correctly detected as malware.

2. **True egative (TN):** The number of benign files correctly detected as benign.

3. **False positive (FP):** The number of malware files wrongly classified as benign.

4. **False negative (FN):** The number of benign files wrongly classified as malware.

5. **Accuracy (ACC):** The accuracy can also be calculated as the ratio of the number of correctly classified instances. Defined as the ratio of number of true positives and true negatives to total number of classifications that is,

$$\text{Accuracy} = \frac{Tp + Tn}{Tp + Tn + Fp + Fn}$$

We created four imbalanced data set to investigate if malware samples can be correctly identified from a large collection of benign executable. Experiments is performed on features independently extracted from malware and benign samples. Tables 3 also shows the number of malware v/s benign files used for training and remaining samples are used for testing. Figure 6 depict the values corresponding to evaluation parameters.

An accuracy of 99.6% was obtained for dataset 1 using a malware feature space of length 563 (refer Figure 6). Similarly we performed the investigation of three other data set (refer Tables 4 to 6) and in

Table 3. Malware features for dataset 1

	#Samples	Ratio
Malware	30	30/563= 0.05
Benign	533	533/563 = 0.95

Figure 6. Classification accuracy obtained with malware features for dataset 1

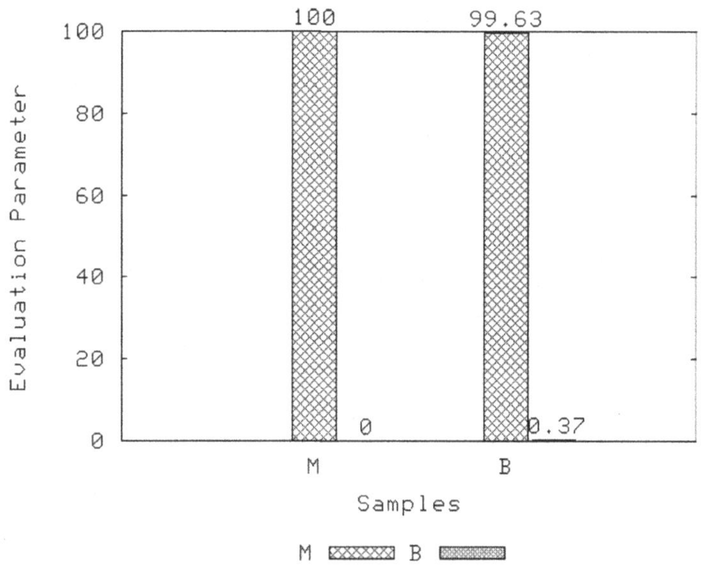

all cases we extracted malware *bi-gram* features. Accuracy is shown in following Figures 7 to 9.

An accuracy of 99.63% was obtained for dataset 2 using a malware feature space of length 563 (refer Figure 7).

An accuracy of 100% was obtained for dataset 3 using a malware feature space of length 563 (refer Figure 8).

An accuracy of 100% was obtained for dataset 4 using a benign feature space of length 564 (refer Figure 9 and Tables 7 to 10). Likewise, we extracted benign features from four different data set. Moreover, the number of malware samples considered are very less in comparison to benign samples. We record the overall classification accuracy also we determine the TPR, FPR, TNR and FNR values. From the result of all experiment we can observe that higher accuracy was obtained and our proposed methodology.

An accuracy of 98.22% was obtained for dataset 1 using a benign feature space of length 563. The malware database obtained has benign opcode inserted as junk code to defeat HMM based detector (http://cs.sjsu.edu/~stamp/viruses). The proposed classifier correctly classifies malware instances as malware. We also extracted benign features from remaining three data sets and recorded the classification accuracy (refer Figure 11 to Figure 13).

Table 4. Malware features for dataset 2

	#Samples	Ratio
Malware	30	30/563
Benign	533	533/563

Table 5. Malware features for dataset 3

	#Samples	Ratio
Malware	30	30/563
Benign	533	533/563

Table 6. Malware features for dataset 4

	#Samples	Ratio
Malware	30	30/564
Benign	534	534/564

Figure 7. Malware features for dataset 2

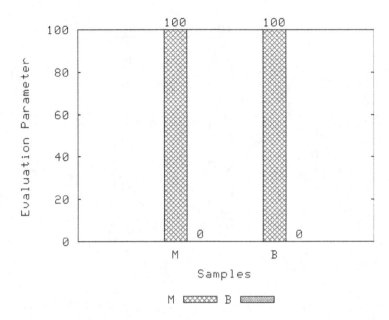

Figure 8. Malware features for dataset 3

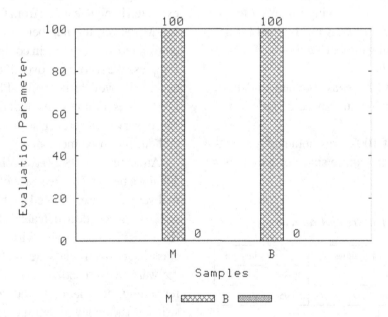

An accuracy of 98.69% was obtained for dataset 2 using a benign feature space of length 563.

An accuracy of 98.87% was obtained for dataset 3 using a benign feature space of length 563. The malware database obtained has benign opcode inserted as junk code to defeat HMM based detector. The proposed classifier correctly classifies malware instances as malware. Using robust feature reduction such as mRMR such rare opcodes can be removed to achieve better accuracy.

Figure 9. Malware features for dataset 4

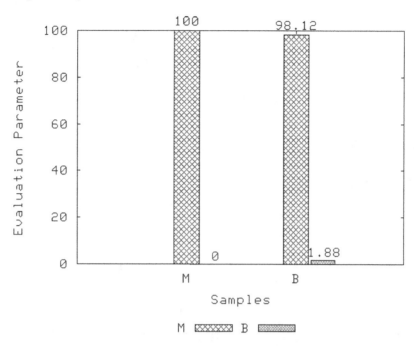

Table 7. Benign features for dataset 1

	#Sampled	Ratio
Malware	30	30/563
Benign	533	533/563

Table 9. Benign features for dataset 3

	#Samples	Ratio
Malware	30	30/563
Benign	533	533/563

Table 8. Benign features for dataset 2

	#Sampled	Ratio
Malware	30	30/563
Benign	533	533/563

Table 10. Benign features for dataset 4

	#Samples	Ratio
Malware	30	30/564
Benign	534	534/564

An accuracy of 98.58% was obtained for dataset 4 using a benign feature space of length 564.

6.1.2 Inference of Experiments

Our study on the strong metamorphic malware obtained from (http://cs.sjsu.edu/~stamp/viruses) depicted following outcomes.

1. *2gram* models were effective in capturing a program's temporal snapshot. It was also observed that the proposed method could classify benign samples with better accuracy using the *bi-gram models*.

2. The proposed system exhibit that the malware samples can be detected from an *imbalanced data set*. Such an imbalanced data set was

Figure 10. Benign features for dataset 1

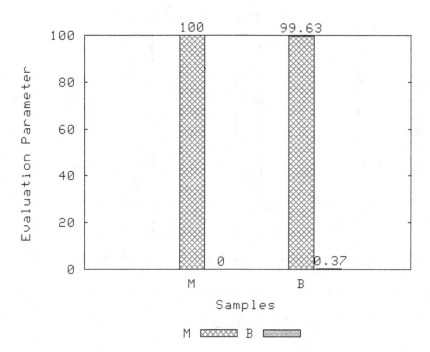

Figure 11. Benign features for dataset 2

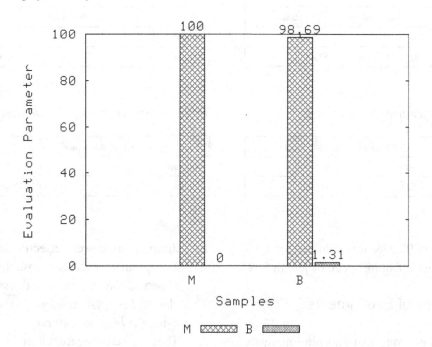

Figure 12. Benign features for dataset 3

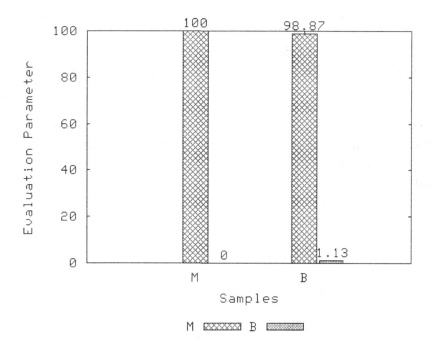

Figure 13. Benign features for dataset 4

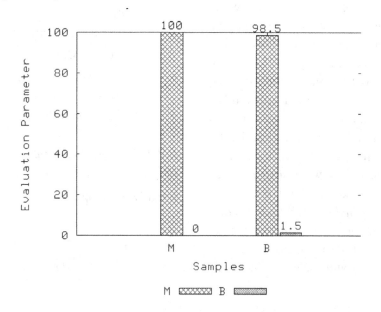

used to model the realistic scenario where benign programs exceed malicious ones.

3. It was also observed that the detection rate did not degrade even though the malware files were subjected to the insertion of be-

nign opcode to act as junk code. Malwares were morphed using benign junk code by dataset creator, to study if HMM based detector could be failed. We noticed that such uncommon opcode were eliminated by SVD. Classification accuracy in range 98.22% -100% was obtained.

6.2 Ranked BDV, TFV and WLLS Features for Malware Detection

In this proposed method, we develop classification models for identifying malicious and good samples (refer Figure 14). Similar to our previous method initially all samples are unpacked and disassembled using IDA Pro disassembler and subsequently we extract *bi-gram* mnemonics. In the next step, *bi-gram* dataset comprising of benign and malware samples are divided into training and testing set. Training and testing set are formed such that 50% of the dataset is used to prepare malware/benign model and remaining 50% is used for testing.

In the next phase, we investigate which *bi-gram* opcode can be used for differentiating malware and benign samples. To ascertain this we determine *bi*-gram opcode that are common to malware and benign training set. A total of 475 *bi*-grams were found to be common to both malware and benign executables in the training set. Histogram of common opcodes is determined in both the target classes, and *bi-gram* that existed with similar frequencies were eliminated (refer Figure 15).

The distribution of *bi-gram* opcodes clearly indicate that they can be used to classify unseen samples. Redundant feature were further eliminated using methods like (a) *Term Frequency Variance* and (b) *Weighted Log Likelihood Score* and (c) *bi-gram distribution variance* to create optimal feature vectors. In the following subsection we briefly discuss the feature selection methods used in this study.

6.2.1 Feature Selection

The original feature space is reduced using *Bi-gram* Distribution Varince (BDV), Term Frequency Variance (TFV) and Weighted log likelihood Score (WLLS). In this experiment we investigate the following:

- Effect of feature vector length on classification accuracy.
- Which feature selection method produced optimal feature vector.
- Finally, the classification algorithm that produced better result.

6.2.1.1 Term Frequency Variance (TVF)

For each feature t_i is obtained as,

$$T(t_i) = \sum_{C \in \{M,B\}} p(c_i) * [T_f(t_i, c) - T_f^\mu(t_i)]^2$$

where,

- $T(t_i)$: Term Frequency variance of each *bi-gram* t_i.
- $T_f(t_i, c)$: Frequency of each bigram t_i in class $C \in \{M, B\}$.
- $T_f^\mu(t_i)$: Average Frequency of bigram t_i with respect to both class.
- $P(C)$: Prior probability of classes.

6.2.1.2 Bi-Gram Distribution Variance (BDV)

For a *bi-gram* opcode op_i is defined as:

$$BDV\left(op_i\right) = \sum_{C = \{M,B\}} [P\left(op_i | C\right) - P^\mu \left(op_i\right)]^2$$

where,

- $BDV(op_i)$: *Bi-gram* Distribution Variance of each *bi-gram* op_i.

Figure 14. Proposed architecture for metamorphic malware detection using classification scheme

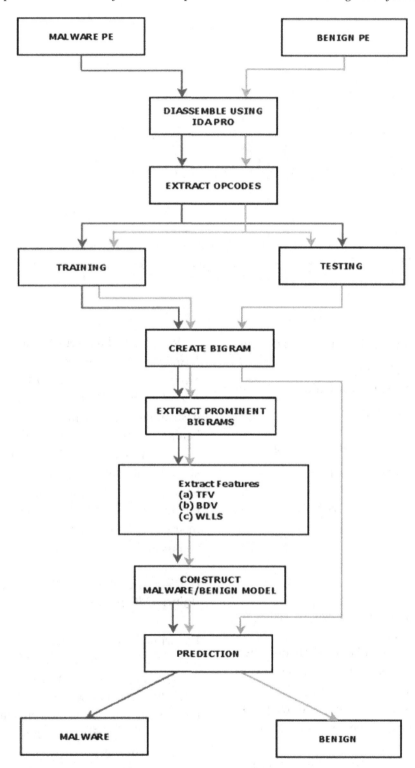

Figure 15. Histogram of bi-gram opcodes in malware and benign set

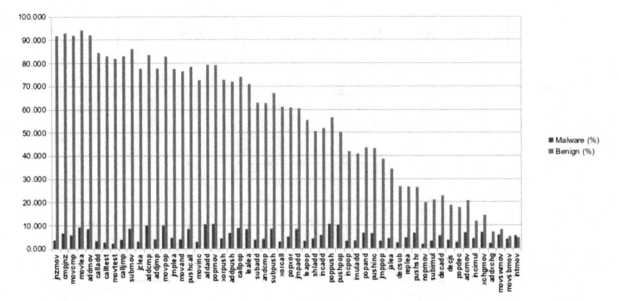

- $P\left(op_i \mid C\right)$: Probability of each bigram op_i in class $C \in \{M, B\}$.

- $P^\mu\left(op_i\right)$: Average distribution of bigram op_i with respect to both class.

6.2.1.3 Weighted Log Likelihood Score

WLLS for a feature f is defined as:

$$WLLS\left(f, C\right) = P\left(f, C\right) log \frac{P(f, C)}{P(f, \neg C)}$$

where,

- f: The *bi-gram* opcode whose score we wish to evaluate.
- C: The class (C is either malware or benign class) with respect to which the score is to be determined.
- $P(f, C)$: Ratio of feature f with respect to class C divided by the count of features in class C.
- $P(f, \neg C)$: Ratio of count of feature f in class $\neg C$ divided by the count of all features in class $\neg C$.

We obtain three set of features (a) *Bi-gram Distribution Variance (BDV)* (b) *Term Frequency Variance (TFV)* and with *(c) Weighted Log likelihood score. Bi-grams mnemonics* are sorted in descending order of these scores. Malware and benign models are prepared with different feature length considering top 100 and 250 features. Classification models are prepared individually for both feature length obtained with feature selection methods respectively. Model are evaluated using metrics such as accuracy, f-measure, precision and recall.

6.2.2 Experiment and Results using TVF and WLLS

Experiment was conducted on 867 metamorphic malware samples created using NGVCK constructor and 1318 benign samples collected from different Internet source. Before including the benign samples in experiment we scanned individual benign files using commercial antivirus scanner so that infected benign executables could be excluded from the benign data set which would otherwise result in false positives. Later, training data set constituting of 435 PE malware and 609 benign PE files is extracted from original data set as discussed previously and remaining samples is used in testing phase.

Classification model using different algorithms such as *Naïve Bayes, Instance based learner with 5 nearest neighborhood, J48, AdaBoostM1 with J48 as base classifier* and *Random Forest* implemented in WEKA is used for classification purpose. Evaluation metrics are tabulated in Tables 11 to Tables 16. We can observe that dimensionality reduction

Table 11. Evaluation metrics with top 250 BDV features

CLASSIFIER	ACCURACY	F-MEASURE	PRECESION	RECALL
NB	93.7%	92.9%	87.2%	99.3%
IBK-5	99.3%	99.2%	99.5%	98.8%
J48	99.9%	99.9%	100%	99.8%
ADABOOOSTMI(J48)	99.9%	99.9%	100%	99.8%
RANDOM FOREST	100%	100%	100%	100%

Table 12. Evaluation metrics with top 250 TFV features

CLASSIFIER	ACCURACY	F-MEASURE	PRECESION	RECALL
NB	93.7%	92.9%	87.2%	99.3%
IBK-5	99.3%	99.2%	99.5%	98.8%
J48	99.9%	99.9%	100%	99.8%
ADABOOOSTMI(J48)	99.9%	99.9%	100%	99.8%
RANDOMFOREST	99.9%	99.9%	100%	99.8%

Table 13. Evaluation metrics with top 250 WLLS features

CLASSIFIER	ACCURACY	F-MEASURE	PRECESION	RECALL
NB	93.9%	93.1%	87.6%	99.3%
IBK-5	99.3%	99.2%	99.3%	99.1%
J48	99.9%	99.9%	100%	99.8%
ADABOOOSTMI(J48)	99.9%	99.9%	100%	99.8%
RANDOMFOREST	99.9%	99.9%	100%	99.8%

Table 14. Evaluation metrics with top 100 BDV features

CLASSIFIER	ACCURACY	F-MEASURE	PRECESION	RECALL
NB	82.4%	82.4%	70.4%	99.3%
IBK-5	98.9%	98.7%	99.3%	98.1%
J48	98.1%	97.7%	96.8%	98.6%
ADABOOOSTMI(J48)	99.3%	99.2%	99.5%	98.8%
RANDOMFOREST	98.9%	98.7%	99.3%	98.1%

Table 15. Evaluation metrics with top 100 TFV features

CLASSIFIER	ACCURACY	F-MEASURE	PRECESION	RECALL
NB	81.0%	81.4%	68.6%	100%
IBK-5	99.0%	98.8%	99.1%	98.6%
J48	98.3%	97.9%	98.4%	97.5%
ADABOOOSTMI(J48)	99.3%	99.2%	99.1%	99.3%
RANDOMFOREST	99.0%	98.8%	98.6%	99.1%

Table 16. Evaluation metrics with top 100 WLLS features

CLASSIFIER	ACCURACY	F-MEASURE	PRECESION	RECALL
NB	92.8%	91.9%	86.1%	98.6%
IBK-5	99.0%	98.8%	98.8%	98.8%
J48	99.9%	99.9%	100%	98.8%
ADABOOOSTMI(J48)	99.9%	99.9%	100%	98.8%
RANDOMFOREST	98.8%	98.6%	98.6%	98.6%

improves the classification accuracy. Also, overall accuracy in range of 99.9% to 100% is obtained with classifier such as AdaBoost and Random Forest. AdaBoost is a meta classifier designed for boosting base classifier. In our proposed work, we have considered J48 as the base classifier. Boosting initially, assigns equal weights to training samples and individual classifiers are learned iteratively. Finally, a boosted classifier is built based on the votes gathered from all classifiers. Weights assigned is based on the performance of a classifier in terms of error rate. Lower the error rate, better the accuracy and higher the probability of its being selected for predicting the unknown tuples. A Random Forest is a collection of many decision trees. It is primarily used when the data set is very large. The decision tree is constructed by randomly selecting subsets of the training data and attributes that can partition the available data set. The final decision tree is an ensemble (i.e. a collection) of forest such that each decision tree contributes for classification of instances.

Also, the effect of feature length on classification accuracy is also investigated. We observe that there is a marginal change in the classification accuracy when the feature length is increased from 100 to 250. But a performance of a better malware scanner is based on the fact that the true positive rate should be higher also false positive rate should be lower. Accordingly we select top 250 TVF or WLLS features for identification purpose as there is negligible change in accuracy which could be ignored.

7. CONCLUSION

In this Chapter, we discussed a critical issue for the detection of *self-modifying* malware (a.k.a metamorphic malware). We introduced how metamorphic malware variants can created with varied obfuscation methods. Also, prior literature which address the detection of metamorphic malware along with the detection of malicious code using data mining methods are also discussed in this chapter. Later part of this chapter, we discussed our proposed methodology using data mining techniques for the detection of highly obfuscated malware invariants created with NGVCK constructors. The detection of metamorphic malware was performed using imbalanced data set. Results were promising and depicted that the malware generated with hacker developed tool can be identified with a higher accuracy. The experimental results depicts that as *bi-gram* can model metamorphic malware accurately. This is due to the fact that the code distortion or variations are not much pronounced in case of malware variants. Primarily the malware code is embedded with a small engine that mutates the base code to generate variants. Size of mutation engine cannot be too big to avoid detection and also there are limited number of replacements that are possible. Thus, it can be inferred that code variability cannot be too significant in malware samples.

The results obtained using mnemonic *n-gram* and instruction opcodes with very small feature lengths are better compared to prior work reported in literature. We also argue that better classification accuracies are achieved using better feature selection algorithms. Thus, for perfect detection system we feel that the selection of effective feature selection methods and inducer algorithms for classifier play a vital role in appropriate classification of the instances. In future, robust feature reduction methods can be used to further reduce feature length. This would eliminate the benign opcodes which appeared as noise in malware dataset considering them as redundant features. Also, multiple similarity measures can be used to test whether accuracy increases.

8. OPEN RESEARCH PROBLEMS

Following are some of the open issues that is required to be addressed.

1. Need for malicious & benign code development. This would help researchers understand the flow of function call based on different triggered events.

2. Identification and classification of prominent applications downloaded by users and inspect points of vulnerabilities.
3. Understand various sandboxes available for mobile malware detection and inspect different locations in system which are exposed to virtual machine (VM) installation. This is mandatory as the future malware would exploit these vulnerable infection vectors to launch virtual machine attack.
4. Determine *behavioural features* for malware and benign applications. Study the default permissions and modifications during series of time interval. This could help us develop strong benign and malware models.
5. Investigate robust feature selection and reduction techniques to extract prominent/discriminant features for classification of samples (suspicious or benign). Examine the applicability of method such as *Linear discriminant analysis, quadratic discriminant analysis etc.*
6. Identification of malicious APIs and prepare white, grey and blacklist for the same.

ACKNOWLEDGMENT

We would like to especially thank Prof. Mark Stamp, Department of Computer Science, San Jose State University, USA for sharing malware database for carrying out this study.

REFERENCES

Andrew, W., Michael, V., Matthew, H., Christopher, T., & Arun, L. (2007). *A: Exploiting similarity between variants to defeat malware: Vilo method for comparing and searching binary programs*. Academic Press.

Annie, H. T., & Mark, S. (2013). Chi-squared distance and metamorphic virus detection. *Journal in Computer Virology*, *9*(1), 1–14.

Asaf, S., Robert, M., Yuval, E., & Chanan, G. (2009). Detection of malicious code by applying machine learning classifiers on static features: A state-of-the-art survey. *Inf. Sec. Techn. Report*, *14*(1), 16–29.

Attaluri, S., McGhee, S., & Stamp, M. (2009). Profile hidden Markov models and metamorphic virus detection. *Journal in Computer Virology*, *5*, 151–169. doi:10.1007/s11416-008-0105-1

Aycock, J. (2006). Computer viruses and malware. *Advances in Information Security*, *22*, 1–227.

Baker, K. (2013). *Singular value decomposition tutorial*. Retrieved from http://www.ling.ohio-state.edu/~kbaker/pubs/Singular_Value_Decomposition_Tutorial.pdf

Baysa, D., & Low, R. M., & Stamp, M. (2013). Structural entropy and metamorphic malware. *Journal of Computer Virology and Hacking Techniques*.

Chouchane, M. R., & Lakhotia, A. (2006). Using engine signature to detect metamorphic malware. In *Proceedings of the 4th ACM Workshop on Recurring Malcode*. ACM.

Dahl, S. Deng, & Yu. (2013). Large-scale malware classification using random projections and neural networks. In *Proceedings of ICASSP 2013*. ICASSP.

Dima, S., Robert, M., Zvi, B., Yuval, S., & Yuval, E. (2009). Using artificial neural networks to detect unknown computer worms. *Neural Computing & Applications*, *18*(7), 663–674. doi:10.1007/s00521-009-0238-2

Eitan, M., Asaf, S., Lior, R., & Yuval, E. (2009). Improving malware detection by applying multi-inducer ensemble. *Computational Statistics & Data Analysis*, *53*(4), 1483–1494. doi:10.1016/j.csda.2008.10.015

Eskandari, & Hashemi. (n.d.). Metamorphic malware detection using control flow graph mining. *International Journal of Computer Science and Network Security*, *11*(12), 1-6.

Hall, Frank, & Holmes, Pfahringer, Reutemann, & Witten. (2009). The WEKA data mining software: An update. *SIGKDD Explorations*, *11*(1). doi:10.1145/1656274.1656278

Henchiri, O., & Japkowicz, N. (2006). A feature selection and evaluation scheme for computer virus detection. In *Proceedings of ICDM* (pp. 891-895). IEEE Computer Society.

Igor, S., Felix, B., Javier, N., Yoseba, P., Borja, S., Carlos, L., & Pablo, B. (2010). Idea: Opcode-sequence-based malware detection. [LNCS]. *Proceedings of Engineering Secure Software and Systems*, *5965*, 35–43. doi:10.1007/978-3-642-11747-3_3

Kephart & Arnold. (1994). A feature selection and evaluation of computer virus signatures. In *Proceedings of the 4th Virus Bulletin International Conference*. Virus Bulletin Ltd.

Kolter, J. Z., & Maloof, M. A. (2006). Learning to detect and classify malicious executables in the wild. *Journal of Machine Learning Research*, *6*, 2721–2744.

Lin, D., & Stamp, M. (2011). Hunting for undetectable metamorphic viruses. *Journal in Computer Virology*, *7*, 201–214. doi:10.1007/s11416-010-0148-y

Md.Enamul, K., Andrew, W., & Lakhotia. (2005). Malware phylogeny generation using permutations of code. *Journal in Computer Virology*, *1*(1-2), 13-23.

Menahem, E., Rokach, L., & Elovici, Y. (2009a). Troika-An improved stacking schema for classification tasks. *Journal of Information Science*, *179*, 4097–4122. doi:10.1016/j.ins.2009.08.025

Menahem, E., Shabtai, A., Rokach, L., & Elovici, Y. (2009b). Improving malware detection by applying multi-inducer ensemble. *Computational Statistics & Data Analysis, 53*(4), 1483–1494. doi:10.1016/j.csda.2008.10.015

Moskovitch, R., Nissim, N., & Elovici, Y. (2009). Acquisition of malicious code using active learning. In *Proceedings of Privacy, Security, and Trust in KDD* (pp. 74–91). Berlin: Springer-Verlag. doi:10.1007/978-3-642-01718-6_6

Nir, N., Robert, M., Lior, R., & Yuval, E. (2012). Detecting unknown computer worm activity via support vector machines and active learning. *Pattern Analysis & Applications, 15*(4), 459–475. doi:10.1007/s10044-012-0296-4

Olivier, H., & Nathalie, J. (2006). A feature selection and evaluation scheme for computer virus detection. In *Proceedings of the Sixth International Conference on Data Mining*, (pp. 891-895). Washington, DC: IEEE Computer Society.

Open Source Machine Learning Software Weka. (n.d.). Retrieved from http://www.cs.waikato.ac.nz/ml/weka/

Robert, M., Dima, S., Clint, F., Nir, N., Nathalie, J., & Yuval, E. (2009). Unknown malcode detection and the imbalance problem. *Journal in Computer Virology, 5*(4), 295–308. doi:10.1007/s11416-009-0122-8

Ronny, M., Tobias, H., Christian, K., & Jana, D. (2010). Statistical detection of malicious PE-executables for fast offline analysis. [LNCS]. *Proceedings of Communications and Multimedia Security, 6109*, 93–105. doi:10.1007/978-3-642-13241-4_10

Runwal, N., Mark, S., & Low, R. M. (2012). Opcode graph similarity and metamorphic detection. *Journal in Computer Virology, 8*(1-2), 37–52. doi:10.1007/s11416-012-0160-5

Saleh, Mohamed, & Nabi. (2011). Eigenviruses for metamorphic virus recognition. *IET Information Security, 5*(4), 191-198.

Santos, I., Penya, Y. K., Devesa, J., & Bringas, P. G. (2009). N-grams-based file signatures for malware detection. In J. Cordeiro, & J. Filipe (Eds.), *ICEIS* (Vol. 2, pp. 317–320). ICEIS.

Schultz, E. Zadok, & Stolfo. (2001). Data mining methods for detection of new malicious executables. In *Proceedings of the IEEE Symposium on Security and Privacy*, (pp. 38-49). Washington, DC: IEEE Computer Society.

Seon, Y., & Ulrich, U. N. (2006). Towards establishing a unknown virus detection technique using SOM. *Journal in Computer Virology, 2*(3), 163–186.

Sudarshan, M. S., & Mark, S. (2013). Metamorphic worm that carries its own morphing engine. *Journal in Computer Virology, 9*(2), 49–58.

Tabish, S. M., Shafiq, M. Z., & Farooq, M. (2009). Malware detection using statistical analysis of byte-level file content. In *Proceedings of the ACM SIGKDD Workshop on Cyber Security and Intelligence Informatics* (CSI-KDD' 09), (pp. 23-31). New York, NY: ACM.

Terrell, Jeffay, Smith, Zhang, Shen, Zhu, & Nobel. (2005). Multivariate SVD analyses for network anomaly detection. In *Proceedings of ACM SIGCOMM Conference*. ACM.

Vinod, P. Laxmi, Gaur, Kumar, & Chundawat. (2009). Static CFG analyzer for metamorphic malware code. *In Proceedings of the 2nd International Conference on Security of Information and Networks*. SIN.

Vinod, P. Jain, Golecha, Gaur, & Laxmi. (2010). MEDUSA: Metamorphic malware dynamic analysis using signature from API. In *Proceedings of the 3rd International Conference on Security of Information and Networks* (SIN 2010) (pp. 263-269). Rostov-on-Don, Russia: SIN.

Vinod, P. Laxmi, & Gaur. (2012a). Reform: Relevant features for malware analysis. In *Proceedings of 26th International Conference on Advanced Information Networking and Applications Workshops* (WAINA 2012) (pp. 738-744). Fukuoka, Japan: WAINA.

Vinod, P., Laxmi, V., & Gaur, M. (2011a). Metamorphic malware analysis and detection methods. In R. Santanam, M. Sethumadhavan, & M. Virendra (Eds.), *Cyber security, cyber crime and cyber forensics: Applications and perspectives* (pp. 178–202). Hershey, PA: Information Science Reference.

Vinod, P., Laxmi, V., & Gaur, M. S. (2011b). Scattered feature space for malware analysis. In *Proceedings of Advances in Computing and Communications* (pp. 562–571). Berlin: Springer. doi:10.1007/978-3-642-22709-7_55

Vinod, P., Laxmi, V., Gaur, M. S., & Chauhan, G. (2012b). Momentum: MetamOrphic malware exploration techniques using MSA signatures. In Proceedings of Innovations in Information Technology (IIT). IIT.

Vinod, P., Vijay, L., Manoj, S. G., Smita, N., & Parvez, F. (2013). MCF: Multi-component features for malware analysis. In *Proceedings of 27th IEEE International Conference on Advanced Information Networking and Applications* (AINA-2013). Barcelona, Spain: AINA.

VX Heavens. (n.d.). Retrieved from http://vx.netlux.org/lib

Wei, J. L., Wang, K., Stolfo, S. J., & Herzog, B. (2005). Fileprints: Identifying file types by n-gram analysis. In *Proceedings of the Sixth Annual IEEE SMC 4th Virus Bulletin Conference*, (pp. 64-71). IEEE.

Wong, W., & Stamp, M. (2006). Hunting for metamorphic engines. *Journal in Computer Virology*, 2(3), 211–229. doi:10.1007/s11416-006-0028-7

Yan, W., Zhang, Z., & Ansari, N. (2008). Revealing packed malware. *IEEE Security and Privacy*, 6, 65–69. doi:10.1109/MSP.2008.126

KEY TERMS AND DEFINITIONS

Classification: Assigning the target class labels to instances. Two approaches are popular (a) supervised where set of possible classes are known in advance and (b) unsupervised where the set of classes are not known in and thus we clustering is performed.

Feature Selection: Is also known as attribute selection, is process by which redundant variables or attributes are eliminated to construct precise model for classification.

Malware: Is a general term to refer to all potentially unwanted malicious software. They refer to computer virus, worms, Trojan, spyware, botnet etc.

Metamorphic Malware: Malicious programs which are have high diversity in structure but are functionally similar to each other.

Obfuscation: Obfuscation refers to hiding or concealing the details of the program or software. This is done for securing the software from being easily understood or cracked.

Chapter 2
Application of Data Mining and Analysis Techniques for Renewable Energy Network Design and Optimization

Tianxing Cai
Lamar University, USA

ABSTRACT

Energy supply is characterized by its diversity, including traditional energy, such as fossil fuels, nuclear power, as well as renewable energy, such as solar, hydroelectric, geothermal, biomass, and wind energy. It involves a complex network system composed of energy generation, energy transformation, energy transportation, and energy consumption. The network does provide the great flexibility for energy transformation and transportation; meanwhile, it presents a complex task for conducting agile energy dispatching when extreme events have caused local energy shortages that need to be restored timely. One of the useful methodologies to solve such a problem is data mining and analysis. Their main objective is to take advantage of inherent tolerance of the imprecision and uncertainty to obtain tractability, robustness, and low solution-cost. The applications and developments of data mining and analysis have amazingly evolved in the last two decades. Many of these applications can be found in the field of renewable energy and energy efficiency where data mining and analysis techniques are showing a great potential to solve the problems that arise in this area. In this chapter, data mining and analysis techniques are briefly introduced. Then the implementation procedures are presented to demonstrate the application of curve fitting for renewable energy network design and optimization, which has the capability to handle the restoration during extreme and emergency situations with uncertain parameters.

INTRODUCTION

Renewable energy is a socially and politically defined category of energy sources. Renewable energy is generally defined as energy that comes from resources which are continually replenished on a human timescale such as sunlight, wind, rain, tides, waves and geothermal heat. About 16% of global final energy consumption comes from renewable resources, with 10% of all energy from traditional biomass, mainly used for heating, and 3.4% from hydroelectricity. New renewable

DOI: 10.4018/978-1-4666-6086-1.ch002

energy (small hydro, modern biomass, wind, solar, geothermal, and bio-fuels) accounted for another 3% and are growing rapidly. The share of renewable energy in electricity generation is around 19%, with 16% of electricity coming from hydroelectricity and 3% from new renewable energy(Energy Information Administration,2013). These energy types have realized multiple choices to form a complex network system composed of energy generation, energy transformation, energy transportation, and energy consumption. The network should provide the great flexibility for energy transformation and transportation; meanwhile, it should also complete a complex task for conducting agile energy dispatching when extreme events have caused local energy shortages. Actually, any type of dispatched energy under certain emergency condition has its own characteristics in terms of availability, quantity, transportation speed, and conversion rate and efficiency to other types of energy. Thus, different types of energy should be dispatched through a superior plan. For instance, energy sources such as petroleum or coal can be directly transported to a suffered area; meanwhile, they can also be converted to electricity in a source region and then sent to the suffered area through an available electricity network. Sometimes, even the transportation of the same type of energy may have different alternative routes for selection, which needs to be optimally determined from the view point of the entire energy dispatch system.

One of the useful methodologies to solve such kind of problem is data mining and analysis (Fayyad, Piatetsky-Shapiro, Smyth, & Uthurusamy, 1996). Actually Data mining is an interdisciplinary subfield of computer science to discover the knowledge in the database process(Hand, 2007). It is the computational process of discovering patterns in large data sets involving methods at the intersection of artificial intelligence, machine learning, statistics, and database systems (Han,

Kamber, & Pei, 2006). The overall goal of the data mining process is to extract information from a data set and transform it into an understandable structure for further use. Aside from the raw analysis step, it involves database and data management aspects, data pre-processing, model and inference considerations, interestingness metrics, complexity considerations, post-processing of discovered structures, visualization, and online updating. Their main objective is to take advantage of inherent tolerance of the imprecision and uncertainty to obtain tractability, robustness and low solution-cost. The applications and developments of data mining and analysis have amazingly evolved in many applications in the last two decades (Fayyad, Piatetsky-Shapiro, & Smyth, 1996). It can also be used in the field of renewable energy and energy efficiency where data mining and analysis techniques are showing a great potential to solve the problems that arise in this area, such as energy network dispatch (Cai, Zhao, & Xu, 2012). In this chapter, several data mining and analysis techniques will be briefly introduced. Then the methodology framework and implementation procedures will be presented to demonstrate the application of artificial neural networks and curve fitting for renewable energy network design and optimization which has the capability to handle the restoration during the extreme and emergency situations with the uncertain parameters.

MOTIVATION

The energy analysis and impact assessment provide analysis on the energy consumption and the associated social, economic, and environmental impacts, including human health, greenhouse gas emissions, and global climate change. Facing the challenges of emergency response to energy shortage, decision makers often encounters various uncertainties that inevitably influence the performance of a being designated energy dispatch plan. The uncertainties can upset the optimality and even the feasibility of the dispatch plan. Thus, quantitative analysis on the impact of uncertainties is of great significance for the study of energy network dispatch under emergencies. Technically, a viable approach is to conduct a full evaluation of the effects of uncertainties based on all their possibilities. This will provide decision makers a complete roadmap of the space of uncertainty parameters. Through this way, the objective function and the optimization parameters are represented as functions of uncertainty parameters (i.e., parametric programming); meanwhile, the regions in the space of the uncertainties characterized by these functions can be obtained.

From the literature survey, the reported work on local energy shortage and management problems has been studied. The contribution includes policy making of normal management(Bellarmine & Arokiaswamv, 1996) energy operation in buildings (Meier,2006), economic impact from energy shortage (Sanghvi,1991), energy shortage solution by economic lever function (Heffner, Maurer, Sarkar & Wang, 2010) typical technology proposal of renewable energy utility (Kainkwa, 1999) and energy system optimization for reduction of environmental impact (Berredo, et.al.,2011).

We will first present the application demonstration of data mining and analysis techniques on the temperature prediction. The temperature change trend is vital to the further energy network design and optimization. Next, our developed methodology for energy network optimization. Conceivably, this is not a trivial task, because it involves multiple types of energy (traditional energy and renewable energy), different energy shortage modes (e.g., short of energy source materials or incapable of energy transformation or transportation), and various energy dispatch scenarios based on the available infrastructure of local energy dispatch network.

DEMONSTRATION

Climate Prediction

The first priority and prerequisite for a region's development is appropriate climate condition because the climate can affect almost all the aspects of our life such as economy, society, culture, education, food supply or even transportation safety. For example, the frequency of traffic accident will increase definitely during the snowing or raining days; the city cannot become the economic center if it always encounter extreme weather. The city's prosperity relies heavily on the climate with high adaptation to the people who live there so that there is no need for them to worry about the unexpected conditions the extreme meteorology condition. Therefore, it is very important for us to make a prediction on the climate change trend if we want to make a decision for municipal development plan in the future. It is very necessary to investigate the climate change trend, which will let us know whether it will have a great change in the weather condition such as temperature increase. Furthermore, such kind of climate prediction result can also become the data input for the other models such as pollutant dispersion model and flight scheduling in their further evaluation and risk assessment. Up to now a lot of professional scientists have dedicated their research to meteorology simulation and modeling and their great work has helped to provide multiple model tools in microscale, mesoscale, synoptic scale and global scale. These meteorological models rely on the application of meteorological principles (boundary layer meteorology and dynamic meteorology) and typically require powerful computers to produce output on winds, temperature, and precipitation at different horizontal locations and vertical levels in the atmosphere. The high requirement of computation hardware and professional understanding of modeling language cannot always be satisfied by the communities even though they can provide relatively more accurate result. To the majority of people, a better way for common application to predict the regional climate change is a statistical tool by data regression and analysis instead of those complex system provided by national and international research laboratories and organizations. There are two major benefits for this choice: the first benefit is data availability which means the historic climate date will always be available from websites and the second benefit is tool availability which means we can even use the common software to proceed the data mining to get the prediction results. Therefore the tool derived from this study can be used by the citizens to get more understanding of their regional climate conditions(NWS and NCEP, 2013).

As Dr. Steve Running, Climate Change Studies Program Director, and a lead author on the Nobel Prize winning Intergovernmental Panel on Climate Change said, "The climate change topic is rapidly evolving from only an earth science issue to a technological, economic and sociological issue." (Climate Change Studies Program,2013).

Climate change describes the change trend of average pattern of weather over the long term. In the previous millions of years, the earth's climate has been warmed and cooled, even long before our appearance on the earth. Even though climate change isn't new, the study of how the climate change is. The exploration of climate change encompasses many fields of study, including physics, chemistry, biology, geology, meteorology, oceanography, and even sociology.

The scientists study natural phenomena of climate change through evidence gathering, theory test, and conclusion generating. There are several general methodologies to study the climate change: simulation experiment, historical data analog, field observation, numerical modeling and computer simulation.

- **Simulation Experiment:** The procedures in order are carried out to achieve the goal of verifying, refuting, or establishing the validity of a hypothesis of climate change. Experiments provide insight into cause-and-effect between multiple natural and anthropogenic factors and the result of climate change. For example this method is used to study the responses of grassland plants to experimentally simulated climate change depend on land use and region (Bütof, et.al., 2012).

- **Historical Data Analog:** Historical recorded data is processed to be in a form to identify its similarity of its original structure of climate change trend in the spatial and temporal distribution. It has been used to conduct multi-field analog prediction of short-term climate fluctuations by the adoption of a climate state vector (Barnett & Preisendorfer, 1978).

- **Field Observation:** Climate field observation provides long-term or short-term, high quality, timely, observational data, information and products in support of climate and weather research communities, forecasters, and other service providers and users. It has included climate observing system according to climate monitoring principles, time-series indicators of climate variability and change. The observation result will be used to develop and maintain standard data sets for initialization and evaluation of climate forecast models, assessments of climate change, and informed risk management. It will be further used to develop informational products, diagnostics, and assessments of observed climate variability and change on different scales. This method has been used in many studies such as indirect radiative forcing of climate change through ozone effects on the land-carbon sink (Sitch, Cox, Collins, & Huntingford, 2007).

- **Numerical Modeling:** The results of a numerical model consist of numbers, which represent particular "cases" or "realizations." There are particular examples of what the (model) atmosphere can do: for example, we can "run" a numerical model to create a weather forecast, which consists of a large set of numbers. The application of numerical modeling for climate change has been introduced in a lot of books, such as atmosphere circulation, meteorology dynamics and three dimensional climate modeling (Chang, 1977; Durran, 1999; Haltiner & Williams, 1980; Kalnay, 2003; Manabe, 1985; Mesinger & Arakawa, 1976; Randall, 2000; Washington & Parkinson, 1986).

- **Computer Simulation:** It is a computer program which is run on a single computer, or a network of computers in order to simulate a particular system of climate. For example, the Weather Research and Forecasting (WRF) model(UCAR, 2010) is a specific computer program with a dual use for forecasting and research. It was created through a partnership that includes the National Oceanic and Atmospheric Administration(NOAA), the National Center for Atmospheric Research(NCAR), and more than 150 other organizations and universities in the United States and abroad(NCAR, 2006; Wikipedia, 2013; NCDC & NOAA, 2013).

The section will present the data analysis results based on the statistical processing of the historical temperature monitor results. During data analysis, several years of records have been summarized to characterize the climate so that a large data record of long time period will help to achieve a relatively stable change trend and statistical results. During the seasonal analysis, four seasons with respective to months are defined as below: spring (March ~ May), summer (June ~ August), autumn (September ~ November) and winter (December ~ February).

The section will present the linear regression for the above data analysis results of seasonal and annual average temperatures of Cincinnati. In the linear regression model, the independent variable will be the year, t and the dependent variable will be the temperature, Y_t. The linear regression will generate the linear function expression with respective to the year, t. The linear equation which is used in our regression is $Y_t = m + k * t$. The methodology of least square will be used to get the linear regression results, which is the value of coefficient of the above equations: k and m. Here, k is the slope which represents the trend rate of temperature change by time interval (year or decade) and m is the intercept which is a constant term. The change tendency can be identified by the sign of slope k: if the slope k is larger than zero, there will be a rising upward trend of average temperature; if the slope k is less than zero, there will be a descending downward trend of average temperature; if the slope k is equal to zero, there will be no change trend of average temperature. The absolute value of slope k will reflect the increased or decreased degree. The linear regression model for annual average temperature is constructed based on available dataset. The trend analysis plot for annual temperature has also been provided.

Energy Network Optimization

Based on the predicted temperature change trend, the energy network can be optimized to satisfy the peak energy demand. In an energy network composed of three locations (P, Q, and R), the infrastructure of node P got partially damaged and is currently experiencing energy shortage. The other two locations (Q and R) are not affected by the event and thus are able to provide energy to support place P. The initial conditions are summarized in Table 2, which gives all the parameters used in the optimization model.

Table 1. Summary of monthly mean temperature(1973-2012)

Year/Month	Jan	Feb	Mar	Apr	May	Jun	Jul	Aug	Sep	Oct	Nov	Dec
1973	0.8	1.0	10.5	11.2	15.7	23.3	24.4	23.6	21.0	15.2	8.8	2.1
1974	2.9	1.8	8.5	13.4	17.5	20.4	24.2	23.4	17.0	11.8	7.5	2.6
1975	2.6	3.0	4.9	10.3	19.8	22.8	24.1	25.0	17.8	13.5	9.5	3.0
1976	-1.4	6.4	10.4	13.0	16.6	22.3	24.0	21.9	18.0	9.9	3.4	-1.3
1977	-9.0	-0.2	9.3	14.2	20.8	21.8	26.0	23.6	21.3	11.9	8.5	-0.2
1978	-5.8	-5.9	3.8	12.8	16.6	22.8	23.9	23.1	21.5	11.3	8.0	2.4
1979	-4.4	-4.4	8.2	11.1	16.9	21.8	22.9	23.0	19.1	12.7	6.8	2.8
1980	0.3	-2.4	4.0	10.8	18.2	21.4	25.7	25.5	21.0	11.6	6.1	1.8
1981	-2.6	1.7	5.7	15.3	15.7	23.3	24.4	22.8	18.9	12.8	6.9	0.0
1982	-3.4	-0.1	6.8	10.2	20.2	20.1	24.7	21.6	18.7	13.9	8.6	6.2
1983	0.5	2.3	7.4	10.7	15.9	22.2	26.3	25.9	20.3	14.0	7.9	-2.6
1984	-3.0	4.3	2.8	11.3	16.2	24.1	23.0	23.6	18.5	16.3	5.7	5.9
1985	-3.8	-1.1	8.6	15.1	18.6	21.3	24.4	23.1	20.3	15.5	10.6	-1.4
1986	0.1	2.7	7.8	13.6	19.1	23.3	25.8	22.6	21.5	14.1	6.9	1.8
1987	0.1	3.2	7.4	12.1	20.6	23.9	24.9	24.3	20.3	10.3	9.3	3.6
1988	-1.3	0.6	6.3	12.2	18.5	23.0	25.9	25.5	19.8	9.7	7.6	1.8
1989	3.6	0.0	7.2	11.7	15.9	21.8	24.6	22.9	18.7	12.4	6.6	-5.1
1990	4.4	5.1	8.9	11.9	16.4	22.5	24.2	23.0	20.3	13.1	9.0	4.1
1991	0.3	3.2	8.1	14.1	21.3	23.7	25.0	23.3	20.0	14.2	6.2	3.6
1992	1.2	4.5	6.8	12.6	16.4	20.6	23.9	21.3	18.7	12.0	7.7	2.7
1993	2.2	-0.6	5.1	11.7	18.0	21.7	26.0	24.4	18.9	12.4	7.1	1.7
1994	-3.6	1.0	6.5	13.9	15.9	23.8	24.4	22.7	18.6	13.4	10.2	4.1
1995	0.8	0.0	7.8	12.3	17.3	22.7	25.1	26.0	18.2	13.7	4.3	-0.3
1996	-1.2	1.0	3.6	10.9	17.6	22.2	22.9	23.2	19.1	13.6	4.2	4.2
1997	-1.0	4.3	8.1	10.4	15.3	21.2	24.7	22.5	18.9	12.9	5.9	2.3
1998	4.0	4.8	7.1	11.8	19.2	22.4	23.9	23.8	21.5	13.1	7.5	4.1
1999	1.1	3.7	4.1	13.7	18.2	23.1	27.0	23.2	19.4	12.6	9.0	2.3
2000	-0.6	4.8	8.9	11.8	19.2	22.5	23.0	22.2	18.3	13.9	6.2	-3.4
2001	-0.3	3.6	5.0	14.9	17.9	20.9	23.4	23.5	17.4	12.3	8.9	4.2
2002	2.4	2.6	5.9	13.1	15.6	22.6	25.4	24.3	20.9	12.1	5.7	1.5
2003	-3.3	-1.4	7.1	12.7	16.8	19.9	23.1	23.1	18.0	12.3	9.2	2.0
2004	-1.9	1.0	7.8	12.4	19.7	21.8	23.0	21.4	19.6	13.2	8.9	1.4
2005	1.7	3.2	4.3	13.0	15.5	23.3	24.9	24.7	20.7	13.0	7.9	-0.1
2006	5.6	1.8	5.9	13.9	16.4	20.8	24.6	24.8	17.6	11.7	7.5	4.8
2007	3.1	-3.9	9.9	11.4	19.4	23.0	23.1	26.7	21.7	16.0	7.5	3.3
2008	0.3	1.3	5.7	12.8	15.8	22.8	23.9	23.3	20.5	12.6	5.6	2.1
2009	-2.3	2.7	8.9	13.2	18.1	22.5	21.3	22.1	19.1	11.0	7.8	1.4
2010	-1.8	-1.9	7.4	14.4	19.0	23.8	25.0	24.6	20.4	13.7	6.6	-2.0
2011	-2.1	2.7	7.1	14.0	17.1	22.3	26.5	23.8	18.2	12.0	9.4	4.5
2012	2.3	3.8	12.8	12.5	19.9	22.5	26.4	23.0	18.6	11.9	4.7	4.6

Figure 1. Change trend analysis for annual temperature

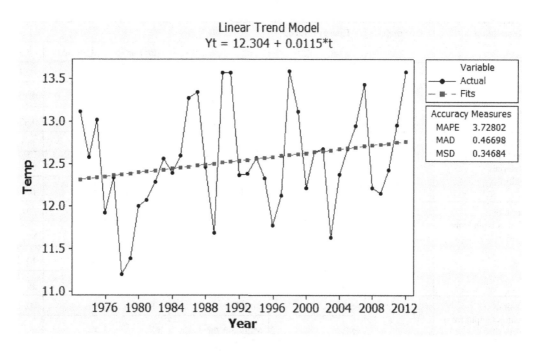

Figure 2. Residue plot for annual average temperature

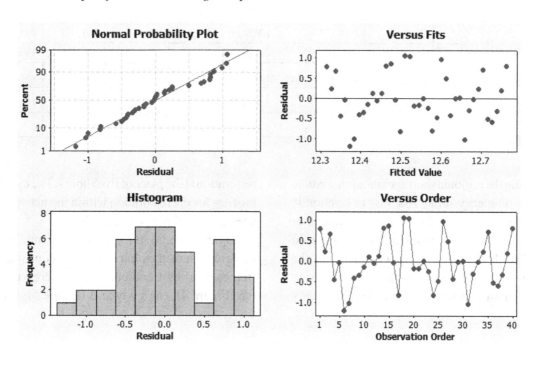

Table 2. Given data of the case study

Description	Parameter	Energy Source	Unit	i / j		
				P/Q or R	Q/R or P	R/P or Q
Electricity Conversion Efficiency from Other Energy Sources (*k*: electricity)	$\eta_{i,l,k}$	*l*: A	MWh/Barrel	0.45	0.36	0.54
		l: B	MWh/Million ft³	0.32	0.25	0.20
		l: C	MWh/Short Ton	0.80	0.70	0.60
Hourly Electricity Generation Limit from Source Materials (*k*: electricity)	$EG^u_{i,l,k}$	*l*: A	MWh/hr	250	230	280
		l: B	MWh/hr	900	600	800
		l: C	MWh/hr	80	90	100
Hourly Limit of Transportation Input from City *j* to City *i*	$EI^u_{j,i,k}$	*k*: A	Barrel/hr	20	20	20
		k: B	Million ft³/hr	8	8	8
		k: C	Short Ton/hr	40	40	40
		k: D	MWh/hr	30	30	30
Hourly Limit of Transportation Output from City *i* to City *j*	$EO^u_{i,j,k}$	*k*: A	Barrel/hr	20	20	20
		k: B	Million ft³/hr	8	8	8
		k: C	Short Ton/hr	40	40	40
		k: D	MWh/hr	30	30	30
Required Energy Inventory Amount for City *i*	$RE_{i,k}$	*k*: A	Barrel	300	220	300
		k: B	Million ft³	400	600	500
		k: C	Short Ton	400	240	300
		k: D	MWh	800	600	700
Hourly Energy Supply for City *i*	$S_{i,k,t}$	*k*: A	Barrel/hr	55	45	35
		k: B	Million ft³/hr	250	350	450
		k: C	Short Ton/hr	45	35	45
		k: D	MWh/hr	0	0	0

During the regional shortage situation, assume all types of energy suffer 10% loss in location P, meanwhile there is no loss damage to the other cities. Note that the optimization is performed to deal with an MILP problem. Based on the developed model, the optimization result shows that the minimum recovery time for this energy restoration at the place of P is 5 hours. The dynamic profiles for the restoration within the network are presented in Figures 4 through 7.

Figures 4 through 7 show the dynamic inventory (represented by bar chart) and consumption (represented by trend curves) of energy type A (see Figure 4), energy type B (Figure 5), energy

Figure 3. Residue plot for annual average temperature

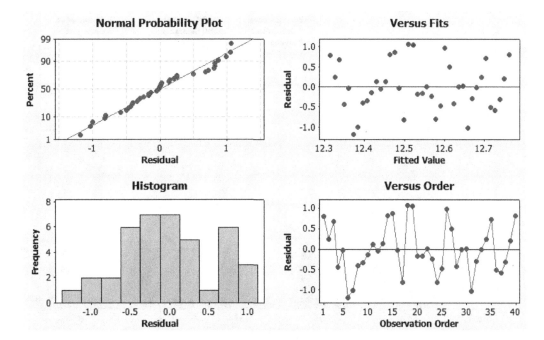

Figure 4. Dynamic profiles of energy A inventory and consumption in different places

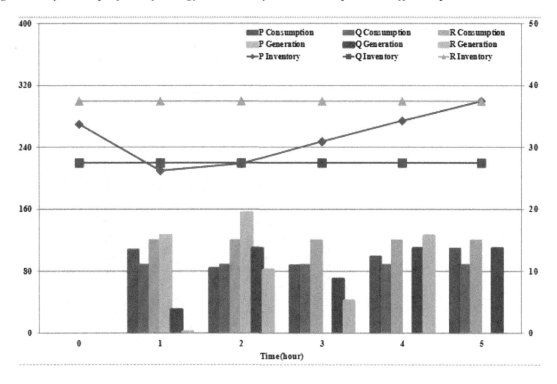

Figure 5. Dynamic profiles of energy B inventory and consumption in different places

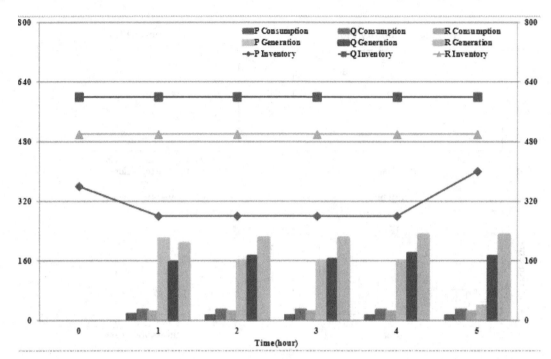

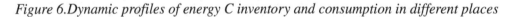

Figure 6.Dynamic profiles of energy C inventory and consumption in different places

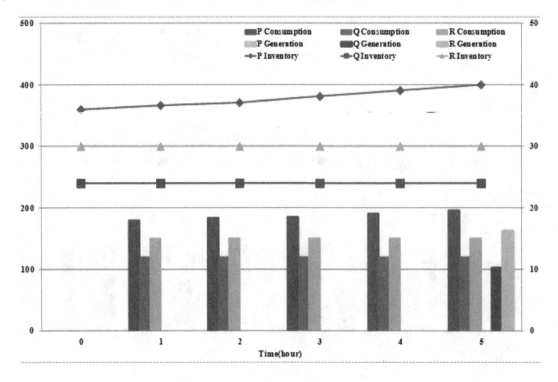

Figure 7.Dynamic profiles of energy D inventory and consumption in different places

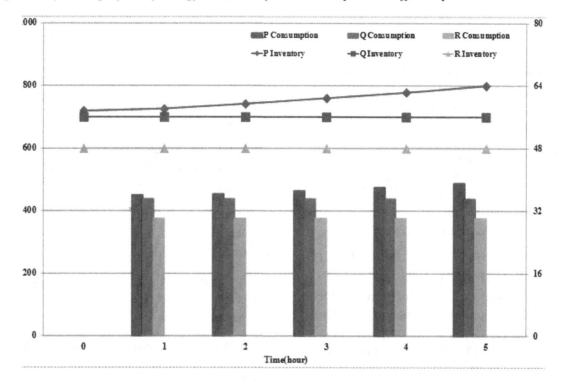

type C (Figure 6), and energy type D (Figure 7) in different places during the period. Figures 4 through 7 indicate that the energy sources of A, B, and C in the place of P have reached the required quantity within 5 hours.

From Figures 4 through 7, energy quantity profiles in Q and R only experience small upsets during the restoration period; while those of P change a lot because it suffers from shortage. Especially from Figures 4 through 7, the source consumption of energy A, B and C for D generation in P changes dramatically. This is because P needs to use the most efficient and available sources to generate energy, so as to accomplish restoration as soon as possible.

CONCLUSION

This chapter has presented data mining and analysis techniques with the implementation procedures to demonstrate the application of curve fitting for renewable energy network design and optimization which has the capability to handle the restoration during the extreme and emergency situations with the uncertain parameters. It can help to solve the diversity of energy supply with a complex network system involving energy generation, energy transformation, energy transportation, and energy consumption. It has taken advantage of inherent tolerance of the imprecision and uncertainty to obtain tractability, robustness and low solution-cost.

REFERENCES

Barnett, T. P., & Preisendorfer, R. W. (1978). Multifield analog prediction of short-term climate fluctuations using a climate state vector. *Journal of the Atmospheric Sciences, 35,* 1771–1787. doi:10.1175/1520-0469(1978)035<1771:MAPOST>2.0.CO;2

Bellarmine, G. T., & Arokiaswamv, N. S. S. (1996). Energy management techniques to meet power shortage problems in India. *Energy Conversion and Management, 37*(3), 319–328. doi:10.1016/0196-8904(95)00181-6

Berredo, R. C., Ekel, P. Y., Martini, J. S. C., Palhares, R. M., Parreiras, R. O., & Pereira, J. G. (2011). Decision making in fuzzy environment and multi-criteria power engineering problems. *International Journal of Electrical Power & Energy Systems, 33*(3), 623–632. doi:10.1016/j.ijepes.2010.12.020

Bütof, A., von Riedmatten, L. R., Dormann, C. F., Scherer Lorenzen, M., Welk, E., & Bruelheide, H. (2012). The responses of grassland plants to experimentally simulated climate change depend on land use and region. *Global Change Biology, 18*(1), 127–137. doi:10.1111/j.1365-2486.2011.02539.x

Cai, T., Zhao, C., & Xu, Q. (2012). Energy network dispatch optimization under emergency of local energy shortage. *Energy, 42*(1), 132–145. doi:10.1016/j.energy.2012.04.001

Chang, J. (1977). General circulation models of the atmosphere. *Meth. Comp. Phys., 17.*

Climate Change Studies Program. (n.d.). Retrieved from http://www.cfc.umt.edu/CCS/

Durran, D. R. (1999). *Numerical methods for wave equations in geophysical fluid dynamics.* Berlin: Springer. doi:10.1007/978-1-4757-3081-4

Eia, U. (2013). *Energy information administration, annual energy outlook 2013, AEO 2013 early release overview.* Washington, DC: Department of Energy.

Fayyad, U., Piatetsky-Shapiro, G., & Smyth, P. (1996). From data mining to knowledge discovery in databases. *AI Magazine, 17*(3), 37.

Fayyad, U. M., Piatetsky-Shapiro, G., Smyth, P., & Uthurusamy, R. (1996). *Advances in knowledge discovery and data mining.* Academic Press.

Haltiner, G. J., & Williams, R. T. (1980). *Numerical prediction and dynamic meteorology.* Hoboken, NJ: J. Wiley and Sons.

Han, J., Kamber, M., & Pei, J. (2006). *Data mining: Concepts and techniques.* San Francisco: Morgan Kaufmann.

Hand, D. J. (2007). Principles of data mining. *Drug Safety, 30*(7), 621–622. doi:10.2165/00002018-200730070-00010 PMID:17604416

Heffner, G., Maurer, L., Sarkar, A., & Wang, X. (2010). Minding the gap: World Bank's assistance to power shortage mitigation in the developing world. *Energy, 35*(4), 1584–1591. doi:10.1016/j.energy.2009.05.027

Kainkwa, R. R. (1999). Wind energy as an alternative source to alleviate the shortage of electricity that prevails during the dry season: A case study of Tanzania. *Renewable Energy, 18*(2), 167–174. doi:10.1016/S0960-1481(98)00801-5

Kalnay, E. (2003). *Atmospheric modeling, data assimilation, and predictability.* Cambridge, UK: Cambridge Univ. Press.

Manabe, S. (Ed.). (1985a). Issues in atmospheric and oceanic modeling, part A: Climate dynamics. *Adv. Geophys., 28.*

Manabe, S. (Ed.). (1985b). Issues in atmospheric and oceanic modeling, part B: Weather dynamics. *Adv. Geophys., 28.*

Meier, A. (2006). Operating building during temporary electricity shortage. *Energy and Building, 38*(11), 1296–1301. doi:10.1016/j.enbuild.2006.04.008

Mesinger, F., & Arakawa, A. (1976). Numerical methods used in atmospheric models. *GARP Publ. Ser., 17.*

NCDC and NOAA. (n.d.). Retrieved from http://www.ncdc.noaa.gov/cdo-Web/

NWS (National Weather Service) and NCEP. (National Centers for Environmental Prediction). (n.d.). *NOAA.* Retrieved from http://mag.ncep.noaa.gov/

Randall, D. A. (Ed.). (2000). *General circulation model development: Past, present, and future.* Academic Press.

Sanghvi, A. P. (1991). Power shortages in developing countries: Impacts and policy implications. *Energy Policy, 19*(5), 425–440. doi:10.1016/0301-4215(91)90020-O

Sitch, S., Cox, P. M., Collins, W. J., & Huntingford, C. (2007). Indirect radiative forcing of climate change through ozone effects on the land-carbon sink. *Nature, 448*(7155), 791–794. doi:10.1038/nature06059 PMID:17653194

UCAR. (2000, October). Planning a new paradigm: The future of high-end modeling at NCAR. *Staff Notes Monthly.* NCAR. (2006, August). *Weather forecast accuracy gets boost with new computer model.* NCAR.

Washington, W. M., & Parkinson, C. L. (1986). *An introduction to three-dimensional climate modeling.* Mill Valley, NY: University Science Books.

Wikipedia. (n.d.). Retrieved from http://en.wikipedia.org/wiki/Climate_model#Research_and_development

ADDITIONAL READING

Agrawal, R., Gehrke, J., Gunopulos, D., & Raghavan, P. (1998). Automatic subspace clustering of high dimensional data for data mining applications: Vol. 27. *No. 2* (pp. 94–105). ACM.

Bang, H. K., Ellinger, A. E., Hadjimarcou, J., & Traichal, P. A. (2000). Consumer concern, knowledge, belief, and attitude toward renewable energy: An application of the reasoned action theory. *Psychology and Marketing, 17*(6), 449–468. doi:10.1002/(SICI)1520-6793(200006)17:6<449::AID-MAR2>3.0.CO;2-8

Berry, M. J., & Linoff, G. (1997). *Data mining techniques: For marketing, sales, and customer support.* John Wiley & Sons, Inc.

Berson, A., & Smith, S. J. (1997). *Data warehousing, data mining, and OLAP.* McGraw-Hill, Inc.

Chen, M. S., Han, J., & Yu, P. S. (1996). Data mining: an overview from a database perspective. *Knowledge and data Engineering. IEEE Transactions on, 8*(6), 866–883.

Cios, K. J., Pedrycz, W., & Swiniarsk, R. M. (1998). Data mining methods for knowledge discovery. Neural Networks. *IEEE Transactions on, 9*(6), 1533–1534.

Dalton, G. J., Lockington, D. A., & Baldock, T. E. (2009). Feasibility analysis of renewable energy supply options for a grid-connected large hotel. *Renewable Energy, 34*(4), 955–964. doi:10.1016/j.renene.2008.08.012

Fayyad, U., Piatetsky-Shapiro, G., & Smyth, P. (1996). From data mining to knowledge discovery in databases. *AI Magazine*, *17*(3), 37.

Han, J., Kamber, M., & Pei, J. (2006). *Data mining: concepts and techniques*. Morgan kaufmann.

Hand, D. J. (2007). Principles of data mining. *Drug Safety*, *30*(7), 621–622. doi:10.2165/00002018-200730070-00010 PMID:17604416

Haralambopoulos, D. A., & Polatidis, H. (2003). Renewable energy projects: structuring a multi-criteria group decision-making framework. *Renewable Energy*, *28*(6), 961–973. doi:10.1016/S0960-1481(02)00072-1

Jiawei, H., & Kamber, M. (2001). Data mining: concepts and techniques. San Francisco, CA, itd: Morgan Kaufmann, 5.

Johansson, T. B., & Burnham, L. (Eds.). (1993). *Renewable energy: sources for fuels and electricity*. Island press.

Koutroulis, E., & Kalaitzakis, K. (2003). Development of an integrated data-acquisition system for renewable energy sources systems monitoring. *Renewable Energy*, *28*(1), 139–152. doi:10.1016/S0960-1481(01)00197-5

Leijon, M., Bernhoff, H., Berg, M., & Ågren, O. (2003). Economical considerations of renewable electric energy production—especially development of wave energy. *Renewable Energy*, *28*(8), 1201–1209. doi:10.1016/S0960-1481(02)00157-X

Painuly, J. P. (2001). Barriers to renewable energy penetration, a framework for analysis. *Renewable Energy*, *24*(1), 73–89. doi:10.1016/S0960-1481(00)00186-5

Pehnt, M. (2006). Dynamic life cycle assessment (LCA) of renewable energy technologies. *Renewable Energy*, *31*(1), 55–71. doi:10.1016/j.renene.2005.03.002

Söderholm, P., & Sundqvist, T. (2007). Empirical challenges in the use of learning curves for assessing the economic prospects of renewable energy technologies. *Renewable Energy*, *32*(15), 2559–2578. doi:10.1016/j.renene.2006.12.007

Srivastava, J., Cooley, R., Deshpande, M., & Tan, P. N. (2000). Web usage mining: Discovery and applications of usage patterns from Web data. *ACM SIGKDD Explorations Newsletter*, *1*(2), 12–23. doi:10.1145/846183.846188

Westphal, C., & Blaxton, T. (1998). Data mining solutions: methods and tools for solving real-world problems.

KEY TERMS AND DEFINITIONS

Artificial Neural Network: In computer science and related fields, artificial neural networks are computational models inspired by animal central nervous systems (in particular the brain) that are capable of machine learning and pattern recognition. They are usually presented as systems of interconnected "neurons" that can compute values from inputs by feeding information through the network.

Data Analysis: Analysis of data is a process of inspecting, cleaning, transforming, and modeling data with the goal of discovering useful information, suggesting conclusions, and supporting decision making. Data analysis has multiple facets and approaches, encompassing diverse techniques under a variety of names, in different business, science, and social science domains.

Data Mining: Data mining is the analysis step of the "Knowledge Discovery in Databases" process, or KDD), an interdisciplinary subfield of computer science, is the computational process of discovering patterns in large data sets involving methods at the intersection of artificial intelligence, machine learning, statistics, and database systems.

Design: Design is the creation of a plan or convention for the construction of an object or a system (as in architectural blueprints, engineering drawings, business processes, circuit diagrams and sewing patterns).

Optimization: In mathematics, computer science, or management science, mathematical optimization (alternatively, optimization or mathematical programming) is the selection of a best element (with regard to some criteria) from some set of available alternatives.

Renewable Energy: Renewable energy is a socially and politically defined category of energy sources. Renewable energy is generally defined as energy that comes from resources which are continually replenished on a human timescale such as sunlight, wind, rain, tides, waves and geothermal heat.

Uncertainty: Uncertainty is a term used in subtly different ways in a number of fields, including philosophy, physics, statistics, economics, finance, insurance, psychology, sociology, engineering, and information science.

Chapter 3
Visualizing the Bug Distribution Information Available in Software Bug Repositories

N. K. Nagwani
National Institute of Technology, India

S. Verma
National Institute of Technology, India

ABSTRACT

Software repositories contain a wealth of information that can be analyzed for knowledge extraction. Software bug repositories are one such repository that stores the information about the defects identified during the development of software. Information available in software bug repositories like number of bugs priority-wise, component-wise, status-wise, developers-wise, module-wise, summary-terms-wise, can be visualized with the help of two- or three-dimensional graphs. These visualizations help in understanding the bug distribution patterns, software matrices related to the software bugs, and developer information in the bug-fixing process. Visualization techniques are exploited with the help of open source technologies in this chapter to visualize the bug distribution information available in the software bug repositories. Two-dimensional and three-dimensional graphs are generated using java-based open source APIs, namely Jzy3d (Java Easy 3d) and JFreeChart. Android software bug repository is selected for the experimental demonstrations of graphs. The textual bug attribute information is also visualized using frequencies of frequent terms present in it.

There is a magic in graphs. The profile of a curve reveals in a flash a whole situation — the life history of an epidemic, a panic, or an era of prosperity. The curve informs the mind, awakens the imagination, convinces. - Henry D. Hubbard in Brinton

INTRODUCTION

Data visualization techniques use visual objects (images) to represent the data effectively. It helps in understanding the knowledge patterns, and is widely accepted in the field of data analysis for results representation. Visual data exploration

DOI: 10.4018/978-1-4666-6086-1.ch003

supports integrating the human in the data exploration process, applying its perceptual abilities to the large data sets. The idea behind visual data exploration is to present the data in visual form. The visualized data can help the humans to get insight into the data and make useful conclusions. The users can directly interact with the data. Visual data mining techniques have proven to be of high value in exploratory data analysis and they also have a high potential for exploring large databases. The visualizations of the data allow the user to expand insight into the data and come up with new propositions.

With the help of visual data exploration the users can be directly associated with the data and at the same time get several advantages of it in terms of handling heterogeneous and noisy data. One of the major advantage is the visual data exploration requires no understanding of complex mathematical or statistical algorithms or parameters (Keim, 2002).

Visualization of data allows a faster data exploration and provides better results and their understanding. Visual data analysis provides higher degree of confidence in terms of findings the behavior of data and its variations. Visualizations along with the machine learning and statistical analysis can be combined together for developing advanced models for analyzing the bigger and complex data. Visualization techniques can also be used for getting overview of the data, and gives a choice to the users to explore interesting subsets. Recently, visualization techniques are popularly used for analyzing the large data sets. Data visualization has a high potential and many applications such as fraud detection and data mining will use information visualization technology for an enhanced data analysis.

VISUAL ANALYTICS AND VISUAL DATA MINING

Information is increasing drastically and is a well-known observable fact of the information age. Computing techniques are also becoming advanced day by day to collect and store the data. However, performing data analysis on this huge amount data is a critical problem and is the need of the day. It is one of the primary activity of knowledge workers is to extract the knowledge and useful patterns from the vast amount of data. A number of software tools exist for this purpose using which knowledge can be retrieved from the high volume of data. Although the numbers of software tools exist, still there is a major challenge of performing data analysis in handling the high volume of data. To bridge this gap visual analytics is introduced as one of the smart and quick way of analysis over the huge amount of data. Visual analytics uses graphs, charts and other visual objects to represent the information which allows an intelligent mechanism for direct interaction of users to perform data analysis and make fruitful conclusions in faster manners. The basic concept of visual analytics is information present in one graph is equivalent to information present in number of files (Keim et al., 2006).

In general, visual analytics can be described as "the science of analytical reasoning facilitated by interactive visual interfaces". Visual analytics is consisting of a number of steps, some of the common steps in visual analytics are information collection, preprocessing of data, knowledge representation, user interaction, and decision making. Visual analytics is more than just visualization and can rather be seen as an integrated approach combining visualization, human factors and data analysis. Visual analytics consumes the techniques from knowledge discovery in databases (KDD), statistics and mathematics to derive the data analysis and uses various visualization capabilities to represent the conclusions, results and outcome of data analysis techniques in terms of user understandable visual objects like graph, charts etc. Visualization and visual analysis play important roles in discovering, analyzing and presenting vast amount of data. A survey of applying the visualization techniques over multi-faceted data like spatio-temporal and multi-variate are discussed by (Kehrer et al., 2013).

Visual analytics is the science of analytical processing using interactive visual objects and interfaces. Visual analytics integrates new computational and theory-based tools with innovative interactive visual interfaces and visual representations to enable in understanding complex information by human (Kehrer et al., 2013; Educause, 2007). Visual analytics supports people like analysts, emergency management and response staff for working under time pressure environment. An effective visual representation technique helps in understanding information more easily (Thomas et al., 2005). Challenges related to applying visual analytics for handling massive, heterogeneous, and dynamic volumes of information through user interactions and visual representations in the analysis process are discussed by Keim et al. (2006).

Due to the generation of massive data sets and the need to extract inherent information from these data sets, data mining has been recently combined with the statistical graphics which results in Visual Data Mining (VDM). VDM leads to insights the relationships between the complex data sets. Data Visualization provides graphical analysis and display for data, documents, and structures, comprehension and manipulation which becomes useful for knowledge workers. Data visualization is "the science of visual representation of 'data', which has been abstracted in some schematic form, including attributes or variables for the units of information" (Friendly, 2008). Visual Data Mining gives faster result with an effective and smarter way of human interactions in the knowledge discovery. VDM it is intuitive and requires less understanding of complex mathematical and computational background than automatic data mining (Costagliola et al., 2009). Visual mining can provide a qualitative overview of the data and allow unexpectedly detected phenomena to be pointed out and explored using further quantitative analysis (Keim et al., 2004). Data Visualization has many graphic types like from bar graphs to pie-chart, from tables to diagrams etc. Data Visualization has many applications in various fields such as in the Medical Diagnosis, Online Tests, Daily newspaper, Neural Networks, Artificial Intelligence, Educational System, Fraud Detection, etc.

Chen et al. (2009) uses the visualization technique to transform the symbolic data into geometric image which enables the researchers to observe their simulations and computations. The visualization process is mapped to a search process in the proposed work, where interaction provides the primary means for reducing the search space in visual exploration. Costagliola et al. (2009) presents an approach of tutors monitor to identify the learner's strategy during online tests by using data visualization technique. Data Visualization is used to discover the characteristics of the data for monitoring online tests by exploiting the learner's strategy in order to assess the relevant patterns of the test quality. Visualization helps in E-learning by structuring the learning material, usage of 3D animation graphics in educational activities and visualizes data regarding social, cognitive, and behavioral factors of the learning process.

As data visualization, frequently used in daily newspapers makes the complicated and uninteresting data more understandable, comprehensible, memorable and remarkable with an effective visualization (Inanc et al., 2012). Data visualization in newspaper is used to list out statistical data like election or survey results, weather forecast data, and data about scientific or financial topics and to make analysis by taking people's perception abilities. Data mining and visualization techniques are used to handle the system messages for condition monitoring purpose. Condition monitoring is a major challenge for operators of complex technical systems. Classic histogram representation along with Gantt chart is used by Uhlmann et al. (2013), to illustrate the temporal dependencies between interval data and for finding reoccurring patterns in large data sets.

SOFTWARE REPOSITORIES

Software repositories are the central storage systems, where the information about the software development is stored centrally, so that it can be accessed by the developers and team members across the world. These repositories maintains the data at various stages i.e., at requirement analysis stage, at coding stage to keep the source code available at the current stage accessible by all the developers, at testing stage to keep track of all the software bug information and at documentation stage to provide all the updated document centrally at a single location.

Software bug repositories are generally on-line databases, which contains the software bug records for a particular software or module of software. Since these repositories are online, any user involved in the project can get the data out of it using Internet, provided user has permission on that repositories. Bug tracking systems are the tool by which the bug repositories are maintained. Software repositories contains information in the HTML (Hypertext Markup Language) or XML (eXtensible Markup Language) form through Web interface. Software repositories are becoming area of focus in data mining since it contains lot of useful patterns related to software development.

The bug supervision of large projects is usually done with the facility of bug tracking tools like Bugzilla (http://www.bugzilla.org), JIRA (http://www.altassian.com/software/jira), Trac (http://trac.edgewall.org), Perforce (http://www.perforce.com), MatisBT (http://www.mantisbt.org) etc. These bug tracking tools offers various interfaces to log new bugs, access bug information and update it, and hence handle the software bugs in online software bug repositories. An example of online software bug repository is Mozilla, the URL of this repository is https://bugzilla.mozilla.org, and another example is Eclipse Bug Repository, which is available at - https://bugs.eclipse.org/bugs/.

Software bug repositories are huge source of information and this information can also be visualized for analysis. Software bug repositories contain the information about the software bugs, which can be describe using the number of attributes.

SOFTWARE BUG AS DATA

A bug indicates the wrong implementation of specified software requirements, or occasionally it may be due to some of the technical restrictions also. A software bug can be characterized using number of attributes like bug title (or summary), bug description, bug-id (a unique id for a software bug), date-of-reporting (date on which the bug is reported.), assigned-to (team member to whom the software bug is assigned.), reported-by (team member or tester by whom the bug is reported into the system.) etc.

For example, the Android bug structure available in the Android bug repository is shown in the Figure 1. An Android bug is consisting of number of attributes like Bugid, title, description, status, priority, component, stars, owner, closed-on, type, reported-by, and opened-date. One bug is consisting of a number of comments, entered by various users. The comment field is composed of three

Figure 1. The Android bug structure

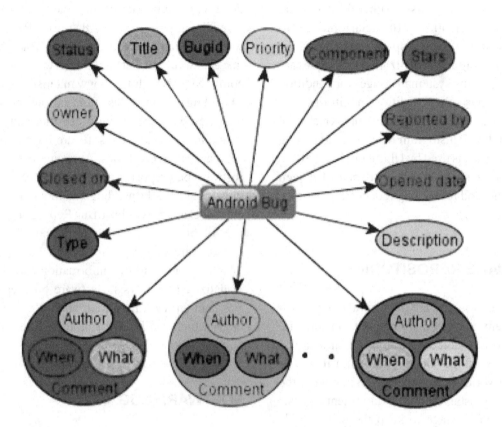

fields – Author, When and What. An "Author" is the person, who is entering the comments for the bugs, "When" is the time at which the comment is entered, and "What" specifies the actual comment text.

SOFTWARE BUG STATES

A software bug enters into the various states for its resolution. A general bug state diagram is shown in the Figure 2 (Nagwani et al., 2010). The boxes indicate various bug states and arrow indicates the transition between the states. The most common and simple path which a bug follow is Open → In-Progress → Resolved → Closed. When a bug

is identified by a tester or by a quality engineers its summary, description and related information's are entered into the bug tracking system and during this action item every bug gets one unique id number. As soon as the bug is created it enters into the "Open" state. And it is assigned to one of the developer for fixation. Once it is assigned to a developer and he or she start working for the resolution, the bug enters into the "In-Progress" state, after fixation of the bug developer mark that bug as "Resolved," which is the "Resolved" state and it is assigned back to the tester or quality engineer for verification. Once the bug is verified by tester or quality engineer and found ok then it is marked as "Closed".

Figure 2. General lifecycle of a software bug (Nagwani et al., 2010)

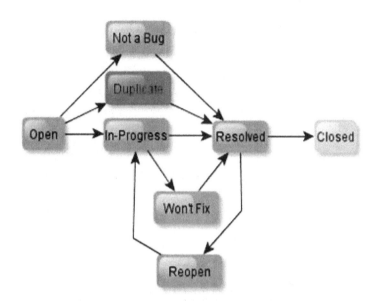

Example Snapshots of a Software Bug

An example of online software bug available in Mozilla bug repository is shown in the Figure 3. The bug record with the bug id 340535 is shown in the figure. Various attributes of the bug are presented. From the Figure 3 it can be observed that the important bug information is described using textual attributes summary and description.

Visualization techniques are the effective way of representing the data and information, which helps the better and faster ways of data assimilation and understanding. Visualization is not a new concept; it has been applied and proven best to so many fields of real life applications and engineering. Visualization has also been applied to data and Web engineering for better representation and understanding of the information available on repositories and Web.

SOFTWARE REPOSITORIES MINING

Software repositories are vast source of data related to the development of any software, data mining techniques can be applied on these repositories for useful and knowledgeable pattern identification. Data mining can be applied over any kind of database for valuable patterns identification. Data mining is a process of knowledge discovery in databases (KDD), in which the useful patterns are identified in the databases by applying various analytical methods. Data mining include three major categories of operations, i.e. association rule discovery, classification and clustering (Nagwani, 2013).

Data mining is a general term of extracting the knowledge and useful pattern from any database. When the data is specific to software bug repositories, then it is known as software bug mining. By mining these software bug repositories various

Figure 3. A snapshot of Firefox Mozilla software bug

useful patterns can be extracted. Majority of the work in mining software bug repositories includes predicting expert developers, predicting bugs, identifying duplicate bug reports, and classifying the change requests.

Bug classification is one such popular pattern in which bug's categories are identified and bugs are mapped to these categories. Software bug classification is the procedure of categorizing the software bugs into predefined bug categories. Because of a number of advantages of software bug classification, numerous works have been reported recently. Some of the foremost advantages of software bug classification are: effective team management, cost effectiveness, faster bug resolution, identifying the strength and weakness of software modules (Nagwani, 2013).

VISUAL DATA ANALYSIS OF SOFTWARE BUG REPOSITORIES

As mentioned in the previous sections that visual data analysis helps users to unerstand the useful pattern and behavior of data without much computations. The visual objects like graphs, charts etc. gives fair idea about the data in just a look. Concluding results and patterns from visual object is the most simple activities and hence the visual analytics or visual data mining is getting more and more popular. Visualization, generally can be applied to any of the data repositories and software bug repositories are not the exceptions. By applying the visualization to software bug repositories useful knowledge about the software bugs can be identified.

Work related to visualizing the software repositories is carried out of several researchers, some of the relevant work is presented here in brief. Two visualization techniques to render the software bugs are proposed by Ambros and Lanza (2007), the proposed techniques assumes the software bugs as the first level entities in the software bug repositories. The problems and experiences in porting visualization tools to the Web are presented by Ambros et al. (2011), a number of other work is also reported in visualization in the work. Carrot search circles is an interactive visualization of hierarchical data structures, such as groups of documents or network domains and is designed in terms of circles for representing groups of data items. A number of methods have been explored by Swayne et al. (1998) to visually link related components in a user interface and a tool named XGobi is presented. The proposed system uses color coding and brushing to represents the associations in various types of high dimensional data. A conceptual framework is proposed by Wood et al. (1996) for developing system architecture to extend the single-user dataflow model of visualization toolkits to support multiple users.

A visualization tool named VisGets, is proposed by Dork et al. (2008), which organize RSS feeds along three dimensions: time, location, and tags. VisGets supports the browsing through faceted interface. It was assumed that the feed items have titles and descriptions, time of creations, locations, and tags. It provides the visual overviews of Web resources and presents a way to visually filter the data and facilitates the construction of dynamic search queries that combine filters from more than one data dimension. A java based data visualization software named, Mondrian is proposed by Theus (2002), which is capable of visualizing the standard plots like histograms, bar charts, and scatter plots. Mondrian offers advanced plots for high dimensional categorical and continuous data; it also provides the linking between the plots with various interaction techniques. Brodlie et al.

(2004) present an overall review of distributed and collaborative visualization technique along with the overview of a number of visualization tools.

Fisher et al. (2010) present a framework called WebCharts, which is a Web based visualization solution, and enables users do visualization locally. New visualizations can be updated and generated using the WebCharts API from related websites. The WebCharts framework is implemented by hosting java script from within an application and providing a standard data and events interchange. Using this technique, applications can be extended dynamically, with a wide variety of visualizations. A number of visualization toolkits have been developed to help developers more rapidly create visualizations. Jazz is such a system proposed by Bederson et al. (2000), which provide libraries for common tasks such as zooming and object models. Dork et al. (2010) present a time oriented visualization used as a backchannel for events discussed on micro blogs. A system named, TwitInfo is proposed by Marcus et al. (2011), to visualize and summarize the events on Twitter, using which users can browse the collection of tweets using a timeline-based display, which highlights peaks of high tweet activity. An event summarization dashboard is generated by TwitInfo.

VISUALIZATION PROCESS

This work focuses on visualizing the software bug information available on software bug repositories. The visualization of software bug repositories is performed in three stages - pre-processing, query interface implementation and visualization interface implementation.

Data Source and Pre-Processing

Software repository of Android is selected for the present work. Android is an operating system for mobile devices, and is Linux based. Software bug records are available online and publically at http:// code.google.com/p/android/issues/. First of all the software bugs from the software bug repository is retrieved using URL programming in java, from the source URL. The URL of the android software bug repository URL is http://code.google.com/p/ android/issues/detail?id=bugno, where bugno is the bug id for which the bug information is required.

All the bugs are retrieved as individual files; the bug attributes are extracted by parsing tokens from these files. The parsed values are stored to the local database with locally defined schema for the software bugs. Now the software bugs are available on the local database, from where these values are selected for pre-processing. The pre-processing work for textual attributes includes two major tasks stopping and stemming. In stopping the words (basic text elements) which are not relevant are removed and stemming the words is transformed to their root form for effective analysis of textual data.

Query Interface

The query interface provides the implementation of aggregate information required for visualization. The aggregate measures include the aggregate functions like sum, min, max, count and average. Appropriate query is generated at runtime, based upon the user's choice selection of visualization parameters. Two examples of query generation interfaces are explained below.

Android component-wise distribution example - If the user wishes to create visualization of component-wise distribution of software bugs (on the basis of opened by date) then the user selects the appropriate parameters from the create visualization GUI (Graphical User Interface) and the query for this example will be "select opened-date, component, count(*) from androidbugs where openeddate like "month%year%" group by component" (The output of the query is fed

into the visualization interface, where the output shown in the Figure 6 is generated).

Android priority-wise distribution example - If the user has selected the priority as the bug attribute, and month as the granular time level with aggregate function as count, then the output is shown in the Figure 7. The graph is showing that Medium priority bugs are maximum across all the months. The query for this case will be, "select openeddate, priority, count(*) from androidbugs where openeddate like "month%year%" group by priority".

Visualization Interfaces

Once the query is generated and output of the query is retrieved from the local database, the result is transferred to the visualization interface. If the data is two dimensional, JFreeChart API is used to create the charts etc, for three dimensional data Jzy3d API is used.

The Android bug's visualization process is explained in the Figure 4. It starts with retrieving the bugs from the online bug repository in the html file format. Parsing is performed to extract the bug attributes. After parsing the parsed fields are stored in the local database schema separately for bugs and comments data. The data is fetched from local database now and pre-processed using various techniques like elimination of stop words, stemming etc.

With the help of Query Interface, a user can specify the bug attributes for visualization. The result of query interface along with the some logically derived data is transferred to the visu-alization interface. The visualization interface is consisting of two separate implementation of 2D (2-Dimensional) and 3D (3-Dimensional) visual-ization. The 2D implementation is done with the help of popular java API named JFreeChart and 3D implementation of bug data is performed using the open source API named jzy3d.

Figure 4. Android bugs visualization process

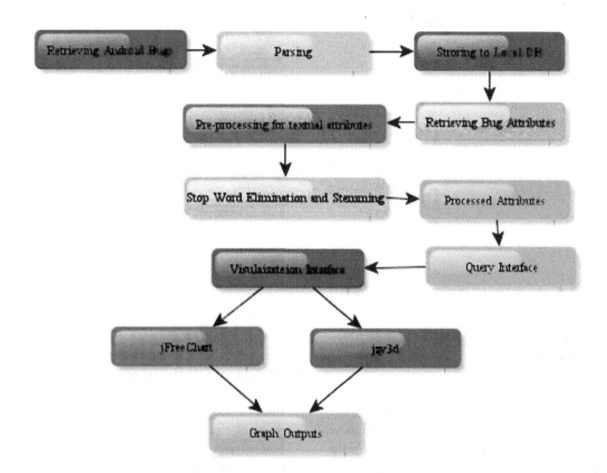

IMPLEMENTATION

A Java based tool is implemented for visualization of software bug repositories. Two open source API's are used for creating the two and three dimensional graphs, which are Jzy3d and JFreeChart respectively. Jzy3d stands for Java Easy 3d, and allows a rapid display of 3d scientific data. It is a java library for scientific 3d plotting. JFreeChart is a free Java chart library that makes it easy for developers to display professional quality charts in their applications. JFreeChart API is consist of number of features including - well-documented API, supporting a wide range of chart types, a flexible design that is easy to extend, and support for many output types, including Swing components, image files, and vector graphics file formats. The GUI of the tool is presented in the Figure 5, for Android software bug repository. To generate the visualization from the software bug repositories, user needs to specifies six parameters - (i) time level at which user want the analysis (ii) time period for the analysis (iii) time attribute - reported-on when closed-on (iv) output type: 2D or 3D (v) Bug attribute and Comments information frequent number of terms for textual attributes and (vi) aggregate functions.

Figure 5. Java based Android analysis tool

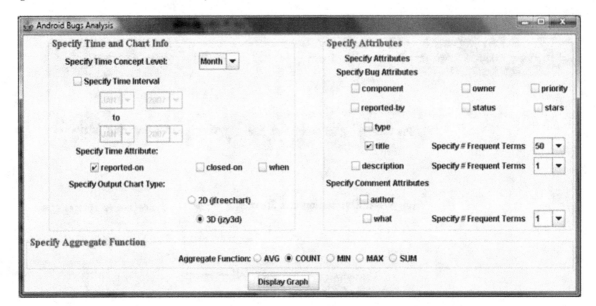

SOME VISUALIZATIONS ILLUSTRATIONS

Some examples of visualizations generated from the tool are given in this section as illustration. The monthly, component-wise distribution of Android bugs visualization is generated from the tool and is shown in the Figure 6. This graph is the example of 3D visualization. The time values and component names are represented in X and Y-axis respectively, whereas the number of bugs for the combination of X and Y values i.e. the number of bugs at a particular month for a particular component is represented in Z-axis. Various graph parameters like axis-labels, axis-intervals, and chart title are customizable (user supplied). From the Figure 6, it observed that for most of the bugs in Android bug repository, the component names are not mentioned, however for the components "Application" and "Framework," number of bugs exists between August-November 2009.

Next examples are priority-wise and status-wise distribution of bugs, which are generated by the tool and are shown in the Figure 7 and figure 8

respectively. Just like the previous example (Figure 6), here also the time values are plotted in X-axis, priority/status values are plotted in Y-axis and the number of bugs for any combination of X and Y values i.e. total bugs for a particular month and a particular priority/status is plotted in Z-axis. These graphs will also helps in understanding the timely distribution of software bugs priority and status wise.

The graphs can be generated for different time levels, for example the status-wise distribution of Android bugs for the time interval Oct-2010 to Sep-2011 is plotted in the Figure 9, which is a variation of the output shown in the Figure 8. In the Figure 8 the status-wise distribution was shown for the time interval Oct-2007 to Nov-2011. This example illustrates that the distribution analysis can be made for smaller as well as bigger time intervals.

The monthly distribution of frequent terms present in software bug title attribute is generated and presented in the Figure 10, where the top frequent 50 terms after the text pre-processing is shown in the figure. The text pre-processing

Figure 6. Android component wise distribution

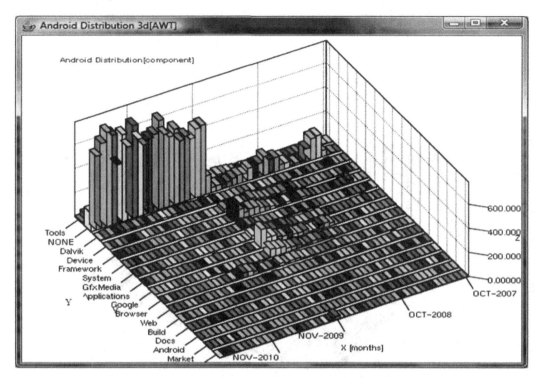

Figure 7. Android priority wise distribution

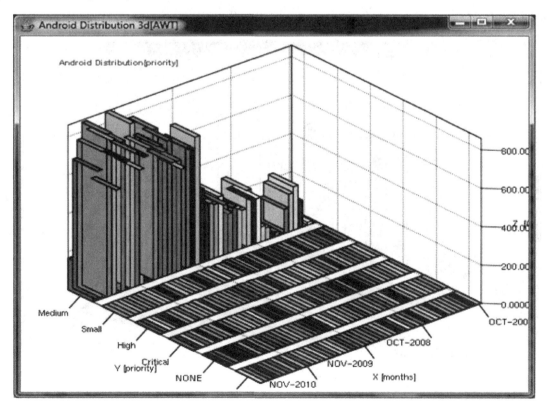

Figure 8. Android status wise distribution

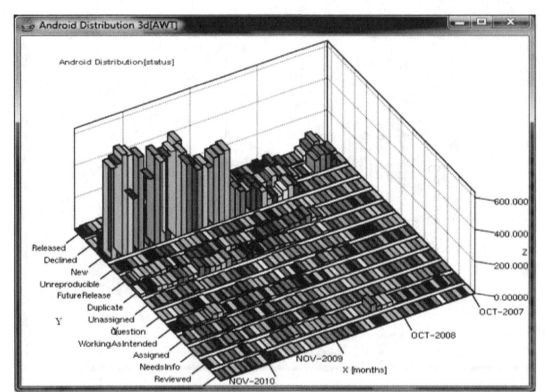

Figure 9. Android status wise distribution for Oct-2010 to Sep-2011

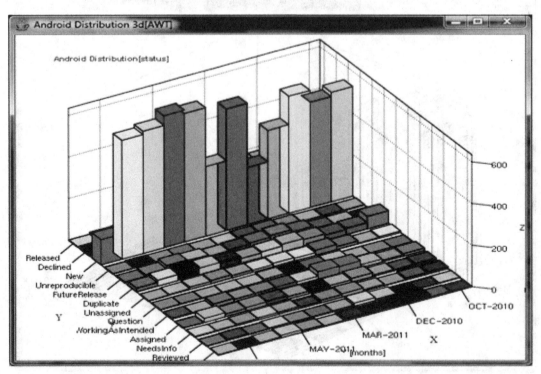

Figure 10. Android bug title frequent terms distribution

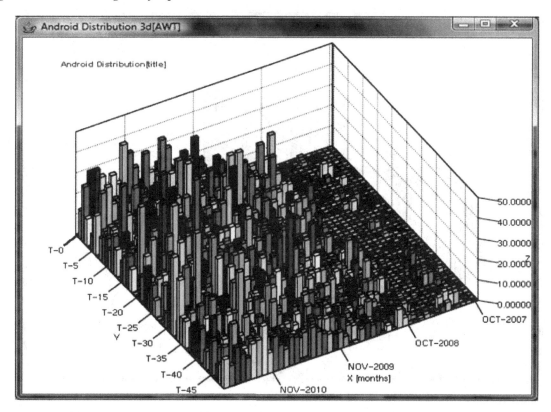

includes stopping and stemming of terms. User can specify the any number of frequent terms in the visualization GUI. The frequency of each term present in bug title is calculated their corresponding frequencies are plotted in the graph. In the figure, the X and Y values are indicating the month and the frequent terms (annotated by T0, T1 …T50) and the Z values are indicating the frequencies of these terms (Y-values) at a particular month (X-values). Top most frequent terms plays an important role in text analysis. The monthly distribution of frequent terms present in bug title for a year i.e. from October 2010 to September 2011 is presented in the Figure 11.

The sample of two dimensional analyses of software bugs is shown in the Figure 12. The figure indicates the comparison of distribution of number of bugs reported monthly versus the number of comments given per months for the bugs. The time period of analysis is selected from Jan 2008 to July 2011. The graphs indicates that earlier the number of reported bugs and comments were less, but after July 2009, there is a huge involvement of user comments in the bugs of android, This indicates that the user understanding and involvement in Android has started very actively from this month. After July 2009 bugs the average number of comments per bug has increased and because of it, more participation of users in terms of comments and bug reported has been increased.

The above examples are presented as the reference and sample graphs generated by the tool. User and select any attribute and time level by for visualizing the bug distribution for any bug repository.

Figure 11. Android bug title frequent terms distribution for Oct-2010 to Sep-2011

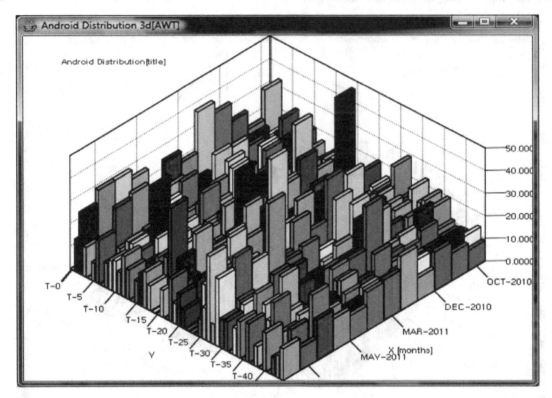

Figure 12. Reported vs commented Android bugs

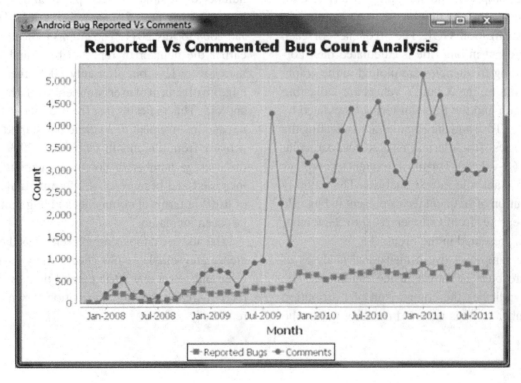

APPLICATIONS OF VISUALIZING THE SOFTWARE BUG REPOSITORIES

A graph will not only show trend and variations, but also reveals any uncommon observations or outliers that do not appear to be consistent with rest of the data. The graph will show up important features such as trend, outliers and discontinuity. The graph is useful for both clustering the data and helping in formulating the sensible model for analysis. Visualizing software bug repository has significant practical implications. There are a number of applications of visualizing the software repository data, some of the major applications are discussed here in brief.

Software Bug Analysis

Although there are plenty of applications of visualizing the information from the software bug repositories, the primary application is analysis of software bugs present in the software bug repository. Common bug patterns identification can be identified by visualizing the software bug repository data. Most affected modules (in terms of bugs) can be identified and nature of common problems in software development can be derived from the visual objects generated from the software bug repositories. One of the bug attribute is component mentioned in the software bug repositories, but the bug distribution for components can be generated, then looking at the tendencies of the graph most and least affected components (modules) of a software bugs can be identified.

Time Oriented Analysis

Software bug repositories maintains various time attributes of a software bug, e.g. reporting time of a bug, bug assigning time to a developer, time when a bug marked as fixed etc. Using these time attributes, over the period of time bug distribution analysis can be made. Analysis like how many newly bugs are reported monthly, what amount of bugs are getting fixed weekly etc. can be performed by visualizing the bug repository data using the time attributes. The analysis can be performed on different time level like weekly, monthly, quarterly or yearly.

Priority and Severity Wise Analysis

A bug can have several priority and severity level depending upon the kind of attention given to it. Most of the bug repositories maintain the five priorities and severity level. P1, P2, P3, P4, and P5 (Most of the bigger projects like Mozilla, MySql, JBoss etc. have five priority levels). The standard severity levels are typically the "Critical," "Major," "Normal," "Enhancement," "Trivial" and "Minor". Bug distribution analysis on the basis of priority and severity can be performed.

Developer, Team Member Wise Involvement in Bug Repositories

Developers and team members related graphs can be generated for visualizing the involvement of various users participating in software development through the software bug repositories. Some of the example queries are given here as reference:

How many bugs are fixed (resolved) by a particular developer over a period of time in a software bug repository?

How many new bugs are identified by the testers or quality engineers in recent one year?

How many critical bugs are fixed (resolved) by a developer in last six months?

Title and Description Tag Analysis

Term Frequency (TF) analysis is a major text mining technique which is commonly used to analyze the text documents. Summary (or title) and description are the textual attributes of a software bug, where text mining techniques can be applied for knowledge discovery. Frequent term computation can be performed on the summary and description of the bugs and the term frequencies can be visualized over the period of time to identify the bug patterns using the effective keywords available of these attributes.

Developing Classification and Prediction Models

By analyzing the visual objects generated from a software bug repositories proper feature selection can be made for knowledge discovery in software bug repositories and an effective model can be finalized for classification and prediction related tasks. In knowledge discovery from software bug repositories, prediction is used for predicting the expert developers for newly reported bugs, predicting the estimation of bugs and predicting the priorities / severities of the bugs.

CONCLUSION

Information available in the Android software bug repositories are visualized with the help of java based API's. Three dimensional graphs are generated using the Jzy3d (Java Easy 3d) and two dimensional graphs are generated using the JFreeChart API. These visualization helps in understanding the distribution of the software bugs over certain time granular levels, developer wise, module or component wise etc.

The objective of the presented chapter was to give an overview of the visualization and its importance particularly in the area of software repositories; however, the visualization can be applied to any kind of data. The work presented in the direction of identifying the data for visualization and then with the help of latest technologies how one can visualize the identified data. The future scope of the work may pertain to the integrating the statistical and data mining technique over the visual objects (graphs) for enhance pattern discovery from the data.

REFERENCES

Ambros, M. D., & Lanza, M. (2007). A bug's life visualizing a bug database. In *Proceedings of 4th IEEE International Workshop on Visualizing Software for Understanding and Analysis, VIS-SOFT 2007*. Alberta, Canada: IEEE.

Ambros, M. D., Lanza, M., Lungu, M., & Robbes, R. (2011). On porting software visualization tools to the Web. [STTT]. *International Journal on Software Tools for Technology Transfer*, *13*(2), 1–19.

Android Bug Repository. (n.d.). Retrieved October 1, 2011, from http://code.google.com/p/android/issues

Bederson, B. B., Meyer, J., & Good, L. (2000). Jazz: an extensible zoomable user interface graphics toolkit in Java. In *Proceedings of the 13th Annual ACM Symposium on User interface Software and Technology, UIST '00*. San Diego, CA: ACM.

Brodlie, K. W., Duce, D. A., Gallop, J. R., Walton, J. P. R. B., & Wood, J. D. (2004). Distributed and Collaborative Visualization. *Computer Graphics Forum*, *23*(2), 223–251. doi:10.1111/j.1467-8659.2004.00754.x

Bugzilla, bug tracking used by the mozilla projects. (n.d.). Retrieved October 1, 2011 from http://www.bugzilla.org

Carrot Search Circles. (n.d.). Retrieved from http://carrotsearch.com/circles-overview.html

Chen, M., Ebert, D., Hagen, H., Laramee, R. S., Liere, R. V., & Ma, K.-L. et al. (2009). Data Information and Knowledge in Visualization. *IEEE Computer Graphics and Applications*, 12–19. doi:10.1109/MCG.2009.6 PMID:19363954

Costagliola, G., Fuccella, V., Giordano, M., & Polese, G. (n.d.). Monitoring online tests through data visualization. *IEEE Transactions on Knowledge and Data Engineering*, *21*(6), 773-784.

Dork, M., Carpendale, S., Collins, C., & Williamson, C. (2008). VisGets: Coordinated Visualizations for Web-based Information Exploration and Discovery. *IEEE Transactions on Visualization and Computer Graphics*, *14*(6), 1205–1212. doi:10.1109/TVCG.2008.175 PMID:18988965

Dork, M., Gruen, D., Williamson, C., & Carpendale, S. (2010). A visual backchannel for large-scale events. *IEEE Transactions on Visualization and Computer Graphics*, *16*, 1129–1138. doi:10.1109/TVCG.2010.129 PMID:20975151

Eclipse Bug Repository. (n.d.). Retrieved October 1, 2011 from https://bugs.eclipse.org/bugs/

EDUCAUSE Learning Initiative. (2007). *7 things you should know about. twitter*. EDUCAUSE, Tech. Rep. Retrieved from http://connect.educause.edu/Library/ELI/7ThingsYouShouldKnowAbout

Fisher, D., Drucker, S., Frenandez, R., & Ruble, S. (2010). Visualizations everywhere: A multi-platform infrastructure for linked visualizations. *IEEE Transactions on Visualization and Computer Graphics*, *16*(6), 1157–1163. doi:10.1109/TVCG.2010.222 PMID:20975154

Friendly, M. (2011). Milestones in the history of thematic cartography, statistical graphics, and data visualization. *Retrieved*, *5*(11), 1–79.

Inanc, B., & Dur, U. (2012). Analysis of data visualizations in daily newspapers in terms of graphic design. *Procedia- Social and Behavioral Sciences*, 278-283.

JFreeChart. (n.d.). Retrieved October 1, 2011 from http://www.jfree.org/jfreechart/

JIRA. (n.d.). *A configurable project tracking tool*. Retrieved October 1, 2011, from http://www.atlassian.com/software/jira/

jzy3d. (n.d.). Retrieved October 1, 2011, from http://www.jzy3d.org/

Kehrer, J., & Hauser, H. (2013). Visualization and visual analysis of multi-faceted scientific data: A survey. *IEEE Transactions on Visualization and Computer Graphics*, *19*(3), 495–513. doi:10.1109/TVCG.2012.110 PMID:22508905

Keim, D. A. (2002). Information Visualization and Visual Data Mining. *IEEE Transactions on Visualization and Computer Graphics*, *7*(1), 100–107.

Keim, D. A., Mansmann, F., Schneidewind, J., & Ziegler, H. (2006). Challenges in visual data analysis. In *Proceedings of the IEEE Tenth International Conference on In Information Visualization*. IEEE.

Keim, D.A., Panse, C., Sips, M., & North, S.C. (n.d.). Pixel Based Visual Data Mining of Geo-Spatial Data. *Computer & Graphics*, *28*(3), 327-344.

Mantis, B. T. (n.d.). *A free Web-based bug tracking system*. Retrieved October 1, 2011, from www.mantisbt.org/

Marcus, A., Bernstein, M. S., Badar, O., Karger, D. R., Madden, S., & Miller, R. C. (2011). Twitinfo: aggregating and visualizing microblogs for event exploration. In *Proceedings of the 2011 annual conference on Human factors in computing systems, ACM CHI '11*. ACM.

Mozilla Bug Repository. (n.d.). Retrieved October 1, 2011, from https://bugzilla.mozilla.org/

Nagwani, N. K. (2013). *On Classification and Similarity Detection of Software Bugs Using Bug Database Mining*. (PhD Thesis). National Institute of Technology Raipur, India.

Nagwani, N. K., & Verma, S. (2010). Predictive Data Mining Model for Software Bug Estimation Using Average Weighted Similarity. In *Proceedings of the IEEE 2nd International Advance Computing Conference (IEEE IACC 2010)*. IEEE.

Nagwani, N. K., & Verma, S. (2012a). Rank-Me: A Java tool for ranking team members in software bug repositories. *Journal of Software Engineering and Applications*, *5*(4), 255–261. doi:10.4236/jsea.2012.54030

Nagwani, N. K., & Verma, S. (2012b). Predicting Expert Developers for Newly Reported Bugs Using Frequent Terms Similarities of Bug Attributes. In *Proceedings of the IEEE 9th International Conference on ICT and Knowledge Engineering 2011 Conference*. IEEE.

Perforce, a Commercial, Proprietary Revision Control System. (n.d.). Retrieved October 1, 2011, from http://www.perforce.com/

Swayne, D. F., Cook, D., & Buja, A. (1998). Xgobi: Interactive dynamic data visualization in the x window system. *Journal of Computational and Graphical Statistics*, *7*, 113–130.

Theus, M. (2002). Interactive data visualization using Mondrian. *Journal of Statistical Software*, *7*(11), 1–9.

Thomas, J. J., & Cook, K. A. (Eds.). (2005). *Illuminating the path: The research and development agenda for visual analytics*. IEEE Computer Society Press.

Trac, Project Management and Bug Tracking System. (n.d.). Retrieved October 1, 2011, from http://trac.edgewall.org/

Twitter. (n.d.). Retrieved October 1, 2011, from https://twitter.com

Uhlmann, E., Geisert, C., Hohwieler, E., & Altmann, I. (2013). Data Mining and Visualization of Diagnostic Messages for Condition Monitoring. *Procedia CIRP Elsevier*, *11*, 225–228. doi:10.1016/j.procir.2013.07.045

Wood, J., Brodlie, K., & Wright, H. (1996). Visualization over the World Wide Web and its application to environmental data. In *Proceedings of the 7th Conference on Visualization, VIS '96*. Los Alamitos, CA: VIS.

Chapter 4
Applications of Data Mining in Software Development Life Cycle:
A Literature Survey and Classification

Naveen Dahiya
MSIT, India

Manjeet Singh
YMCAUST, India

Vishal Bhatnagar
AIACT&R, India

Neeti Sangwan
MSIT, India

ABSTRACT

Data mining has proven to be an important technique in terms of efficient information extraction, classification, clustering, and prediction of future trends from a database. The valuable properties of data mining have been put to use in many applications. One such application is Software Development Life Cycle (SDLC), where effective use of data mining techniques has been made by researchers. An exhaustive survey on application of data mining in SDLC has not been done in the past. In this chapter, the authors carry out an in-depth survey of existing literature focused towards application of data mining in SDLC and propose a framework that will classify the work done by various researchers in identification of prominent data mining techniques used in various phases of SDLC and pave the way for future research in the emerging area of data mining in SDLC.

1. INTRODUCTION

Nowadays, computers have gained importance in every domain of life. It is not possible to think of a life without computers. The working on a computer system is widely affected by the software running on it. Development of the software is very complex task. There exists a step by step procedure for building software. This procedure is well defined by software development life cycle. SDLC explains all aspects of software development beginning from the need of software, the aims of software, design of software, cost of software, time to develop the software, testing of software till its maintenance. Several SDLC

DOI: 10.4018/978-1-4666-6086-1.ch004

models have been proposed namely evolutionary model, waterfall model, spiral model, iterative model, incremental model and prototype model. From the study of all the models the authors identified four major phases or steps of software development: Requirement gathering, Design & development, Testing, Maintenance.

To develop efficient software in terms of cost and space, several techniques have been studied by the authors. One such technique that is most important and emerging is Data mining (DM). DM is an approach to extract the relevant, previously unknown information from the data. Data mining finds application in each phase of SDLC process, gives relevant insight into the related data/requirements for software development, aid in the development process and reduce the effort and time spend on each phase of the process. DM is based on clustering, classification and association analysis. The main focus of the authors in this chapter is towards the study of software development and the role played by DM in each phase of software development. The authors have conducted a literature on applications of DM in software development life cycle. Then classification framework is presented to show the use of various DM techniques in each phase of software development life cycle.

The organization of chapter is as follows: section 2 briefs the research methodology followed by authors and the various factors that motivated the authors to carry out this study. Section 3 gives the introduction of software development life cycle. Various phases and the functionality of each phase are presented in this section. Section 4 gives introduction to DM and associated techniques. Section 5 presents the classification framework and describes the methods based on the DM techniques to improve the whole process software development. Section 6 describes the implications of our work to research domain. Section 7 shows limitations of study and finally section 8 conclude the research work and highlights some future enhancements.

2. RESEARCH METHODOLOGY

Software development is the basic and most important field for anyone (researcher, academician, scientist, business analyst, developer) who deals with software of any kind for developing new applications or refinement of existing applications. Several approaches and techniques have been proposed for development of efficient software but the basic developmental phases remain same. The continuous and rigorous study of the literature in the field of SDLC tempted the authors to look for new emerging techniques for efficient development of software. The most effective and emerging technique, identified by authors, playing a vital role in all phases of software development is DM. This urged the authors to search for an exhaustive literature on applications of DM in SDLC. As the search domain is vast and ever expanding in nature, the relevant material was found to be spread in different journals and conferences. Following journals and conferences database have been searched regarding the literature on application of DM in SDLC:

1. IEEE Publication.
2. Inderscience Publication.
3. Springer Publication.
4. Science Direct Publication.
5. ACM Publication.
6. Wiley Inderscience Publication.
7. IGI Global Publication.
8. Sage Publication.
9. World Scientific Publication.

Each research paper was extensively reviewed and classified based on SDLC phases (identified as Requirement, Design & Development, Testing and Maintenance) and DM techniques (Association rules, Classification, Clustering) incorporated in various SDLC phases. This study of literature provides a base for understanding the role of DM in SDLC.

The research roadmap leading to the study and classification of literature on role of DM in SDLC is shown in Figure 1. The research roadmap shows the path followed by authors that led them to conduct the extensive study and literature review. The research approach followed by authors started with study of software, various aspects of software, Software development models together with the identification of new emerging technique

(DM) playing a vital role in all phases of software development and concluded with a detailed literature on applications of DM in SDLC.

3. INTRODUCTION TO SDLC

Software development life cycle is a way to plan, design, develop, test and maintain the software

Figure 1. Research roadmap

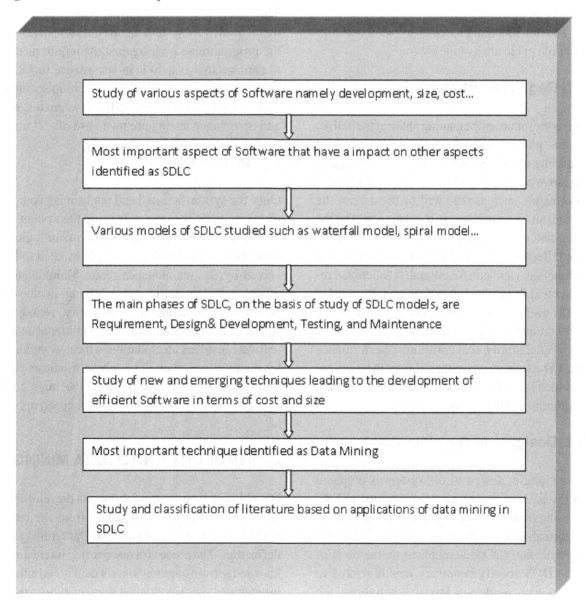

system. Faridi et al. (2012) defines SDLC as a summarized model that describes the various stages, starting from planning through maintenance for the development of the system.

SDLC involves a sequential step by step approach towards building of software. These steps constitute various phases of SDLC starting from requirement analysis, design and development, testing to maintenance. The output of each phase acts as input to next phase. There are various SDLC models namely waterfall model, incremental model, spiral model, evolutionary model, iterative model and prototype model.

The fundamental phases of software development life cycle are as follows:

3.1. Requirement Analysis

This is the initial and beginning phase of the SDLC. In this phase, analysts focus on planning and gathering of requirements from the users regarding software system to be developed. Additional information such as who will be the user of the system and how will he use it, what should be the input and output of the system, is also incorporated. Requirements from the user are classified as functional and non functional. A functional requirement shows the desired functionality needed by the user. Non functional requirements are the expectations of client from the product in terms of QoS, reliability, scalability, cost, performance etc. The requirements gathered from the users are recorded formally in a document called Software Requirement Specification (SRS).

3.2. Design and Development

In this phase, design of the system is prepared on the basis of requirements mentioned in SRS by using data flow diagrams, use case diagrams. A formal document called Design Document Specification (DDS) is prepared on the basis of SRS. DDS specify necessary details related to design such as design layout highlighting the

sequential steps to be followed along with tools and techniques required in each step, the time considerations for completion of design step, the expenses in terms of cost/effort, specification of code generated for each step and finally the results of implementation of designed code. To generate the code, developers use the coding guidelines along with the programming tools and high level programming languages.

3.3. Testing

This phase plays an important role in development of software system. In this phase, testers test the programming code against the requirements to confirm that system is in accordance to SRS. During this phase, various testing techniques such as unit testing, integration testing, system testing and acceptance testing are made use of.

3.4. Maintenance

Once the system is tested and ready, it is given to the user. When the user start using the system in the real time environment, some errors or logical problems may come. These problems need to be solved by the maintenance team. Maintenance phase copes up with ever evolving needs of customers and maintain extensibility, reusability, dynamicity of the software. Maintenance of software involves up gradation to the new version by maintenance team. This phase monitors the performance of system, rectifies the bugs and changes requested by the users are focused upon.

4. INTRODUCTION TO DATA MINING

Data Mining is an approach to extract the relevant, previously unknown information from the data in the form of rules and patterns. Data mining is defined as "The process of discovering interesting knowledge from large amounts of data stored either in databases, data warehouses, or other information repositories" (Han and Kamber (2001)). Witten and Frank (2002) defines data mining as "The extraction of implicit, previously unknown, and potentially useful information from data". Hand et al. (2001) defines data mining as "The analysis of (often large) observational data sets to find unsuspected relationships and to summarize the data in novel ways that are both understandable and useful to the data owner".

Data mining is used in variety of areas including:

- Finance,
- Healthcare,
- Retail,
- Marketing organizations,
- Banks and Insurance company,
- Web Applications,
- Telecommunication Industry,
- Medical.

There are three basic techniques of data mining which are as follows:

4.1. Clustering

Clustering is the process in which similar data objects are grouped together and dissimilar data is grouped in different clusters. Similar data is grouped together on the basis of similar values for attributes (Han and Kamber (2001)). There are various measures of similarity such as distance function, density-based, number of expected clusters. Major clustering methods includes

- **Partition Clustering:** This method is implemented using K-mean algorithm. Initially K number of clusters is formed, and then iterative relocation takes place by shifting objects from one group to another based on the mean of the objects in the cluster.
- **Hierarchical Clustering:** In this clustering, data objects are grouped in the form of

tree of the clusters. This clustering is categorized in two categories: Agglomerative clustering and Divisive Clustering. In Agglomerative clustering, atomic clusters merged into larger clusters. In Divisive clustering, data objects grouped in a single cluster and then further divided into sub clusters.

- **Density Based Clustering:** It is used to discover clusters with arbitrary shape. It clusters objects on the basis of distance between the objects. Regions with sufficiently high density form the clusters.

4.2. Classification

"Classification is the process of finding a model (or function) that describes and distinguishes data classes or concepts, for the purpose of being able to use the model to predict the class of objects whose class label is unknown" (Han and Kamber, 2001). It analyzes a set of training data whose class label (class to which it belongs) is known. On the basis of training data, a model is prepared which is used for further classification of data. Forming Classification model involves two steps. In learning step, model is constructed using predetermined set of classes on the basis of which classification rules are represented. After forming classification rules, some small data i.e. test data is checked against the rules constructed to see the accuracy of the model. If model is accepted, then these rules are used to classify data whose class is not known. Classification includes techniques such as decision tree, neural network, genetic algorithm, memory based reasoning etc.

- Decision tree is a classification tree whose each internal node denotes a test on an attribute. Each branch denotes the outcome of the test and leaf nodes represents the classes.
- Neural network is the classification technique in which network is prepared on the

basis of training data set and learning is applied to generalize the patterns for further classification.

4.3. Association Rules

It is the process of finding the relationships among the data set in the form of rules showing the attributes that occur frequently together. There are two parts that indicate strength of the association. These are support (i.e. the probability of having the two attributes together) and confidence (i.e. probability of having one attribute after having other one). A rule is strong if it satisfies the threshold i.e. minimum support (minimum frequency of occurrence of an item set) and minimum confidence (minimum frequency of occurrence of an item set relative to other item set), on the basis of which frequent patterns are mined. Association analysis is used to discover associations, sequence patterns and similar time sequences. Basic algorithm for association analysis includes Apriori Algorithm, FP-growth algorithm etc.

5. CLASSIFICATION FRAMEWORK

The framework is based on application of data mining techniques to the SDLC process. Software development life cycle process becomes efficient due to enrichment of each phase of SDLC using data mining techniques. The framework is shown in Figure 2. The framework describes the involvement of the various data mining techniques in each phase of the SDLC. The framework is explained in detail in following section.

5.1. Requirement Analysis

5.1.1. Clustering in Requirement Analysis

- Huang and Mobasher (2008) discussed the various clustering algorithms namely divi-

sive hierarchical algorithm, agglomerative algorithm, K-means algorithm to cluster the emerging themes from stakeholder's needs. These clustering techniques cluster similar kinds of needs together and dissimilar kinds of needs are placed in different clusters on the basis of the tree structure of attributes using distance function.

- Kesavan and Algarsamy (2011) discussed probabilistic clustering by combining the requirement analysis phase of SDLC with DM clustering approach. In probabilistic clustering, data is taken from user's objectives of several probability distributions. In probabilistic clustering, area around the mean of distribution forms a cluster. This approach gives better results in terms of missed requirements, accuracy and remembrance as compared to the performance of human analysis.

5.1.2. Classification in Requirement Analysis

- Huang and Mobasher (2008) state self-organizing maps i.e. neural network model based on unsupervised learning to represent the multidimensional data in the two dimensions. The model classifies data without knowing the class label of input data. It helps the analyzer to visualize the complex interaction between data and class labels.

5.1.3. Association Rule in Requirement Analysis

- Huang and Mobasher (2008) described a predictive model based on existing, organizational data to predict interest of user. The predictive model gives results on the basis of 3 way categorization. First is a content-based system which provides guidance on the basis of semantic content present in

Figure 2. Classification framework

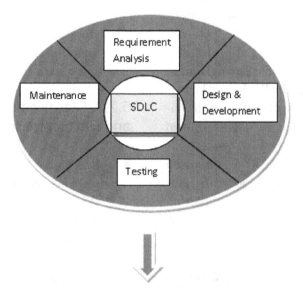

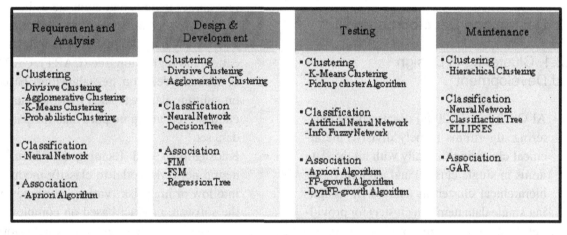

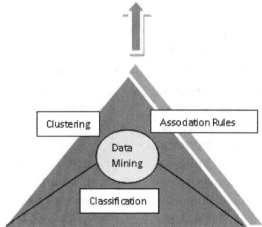

the data, second is a collaborative filtering system that provides the recommendations by checking interactions of the user with the system in the past and also identifies other stakeholders that are having similar type of interests and finally there is knowledge based system which guides on the basis of user's knowledge and predetermined heuristics.

- Selvakumar and Rajaram(2011), discussed various data mining techniques like prediction using associations and clustering to automate SDLC, to decrease time and labour, to identify non-functional requirements present in business requirements and to speed up the performance of the system.

5.2. Design and Development

5.2.1. Clustering in Design and Development

- Al-Otaiby et al. (2005) discussed the clustering algorithms namely divisive hierarchical clustering (initially with all the data items in single cluster) and agglomerative hierarchical clustering (started by assigning single data item in a cluster) for providing the method of software modularization to get a good initial design. In this chapter, authors describe how various requirements can be arranged into clusters so that requirement scenarios which are in the same clusters are functionally similar to each other and dissimilar to the scenarios in other clusters to modularize the system into manageable and less dependent sub systems. This methodology follows a three step approach. The first step is scenario requirement phase in which objects involved in requirement analysis are identified. Secondly, there is scenario analysis phase which determines the relationship between various requirement statements

and produce a scenario dependency graph and finally in scenario clustering phase, the graph produced in second step is used as input for clustering technique to form the sub systems.

5.2.2. Classification in Design and Development

- Pendharkar and Subramanian (2005) suggested bayesian probabilistic model, a classification model used to predict software development effort, to handle missing data, for learning causal relationship, to combine prior knowledge and data. Bayesian model permits the managers to generate probability bounds and combine estimates to improve the software effort predictions. The Bayesian model makes use of classification and regression tree (CART). CART is a binary decision tree algorithm based on splitting data sets such that the data in child subsets are more pure than the parent data set.
- Khoshgoftaar and Lanning (1995) used neural network model to classify modules into low or high risk. Various attributes of the software product based on complexity metrics are used to train the neural network which further predicts the class labels to know the modules with the low risks or high risks.
- Khoshgoftaar et al. (1997) described the use of neural network towards prediction of number of faults in software module. In this software product attributes based on the size metrics and complexity metrics are used to train the network and then network is used for further predictions on the software modules.
- Selby and Porter (1988) stated classification trees as a means to identify software with high number of faults and development effort. The identification is made us-

ing software metrics that are based on attributes of the software modules. Positive instances of the classification represents the modules which are likely to have fault and helps the software developers to identify the modules that consume high time, effort and other resources.

5.2.3. Association Rule in Design and Development

- Husain et al. (2011) described frequent pattern mining based on Frequent Item Mining (FIM) and Frequent Sequence Mining (FSM). FIM is used to tell the relevance of the elements in the source code. This technique mines the frequency of the program elements and find out the rules which are used to detect fault or bug in the program. By using these rules, fault-free software can be developed in the future which have similar kind of the requirements. FIM is based on principle that for frequent item set all of its subsets must be frequent. FSM is used for dynamic or run time traces or paths during the execution of program and identify the frequently occurring sequences, patters and flaws in the design which are responsible for degradation of system performance.

5.3. Testing

5.3.1. Clustering in Testing

- Muthyala and Naidu (2011) discussed K-mean algorithm and Pick-up K-mean algorithm for efficient reduction of test suite to optimize testing process. In this, K-mean clustering algorithm clusters the test cases. Test cases with similar behavior exist in same cluster. As test cases in same cluster have same behavior, so it would be redundant if different test cases from same cluster are tested because they will give same results. For this purpose, pick-up cluster algorithm is used to select one test case from each cluster and covers the whole system without any redundancy.

- Xie et al. (2009) stated that clustering is used to cluster bug reports for detection of duplicate bug reports. Clustering is also used to assign these reports to the specific developer for detection and fixation of bugs. Further assignment of the bug report to the developers can be done on the basis of the past assignments of the reports.

- Ilkhani and Abaee (2011) discussed data mining methods for software testing that helps in predicting test cases so that cost of testing phase is reduced.

5.3.2. Classification in Testing

- Last (2005) described artificial neural network, single target info-fuzzy network and multi target info-fuzzy network which are used to extract functional requirements from training of test cases that are randomly generated, the attributes relevant to the single output or many outputs and the set of non redundant test cases.

- Punitha and Chitra (2013) introduced neural networks for testing phase to improve the accuracy of the classification by application of fuzzy technique in the hidden layer of neural network. They have applied SVM (Support Vector Machine), a supervised learning algorithm for data classification.

- Naidu and Geethanjali (2013) proposed a system to identify and classify various defects using decision tree based defect classification technique. After the classification the defect patterns are measured by employing pattern mining technique.

The defect classification is based on the five attribute values such as Volume, Program length, Difficulty, Effort and Time Estimator.

5.3.3. Association Rule in Testing

- Association analysis is done to find the root cause of defects in the software system. To find link between data sets, Apriori Algorithm, FP-growth algorithm and Dyn FP-growth algorithm can be used which are based on the associations between the attributes of the software. FP-growth algorithm allows discovery of frequent item set without candidate item set generation. It is a two step approach in which data structure known as FP-tree is build and then frequent item sets are extracted from the FP-tree.
- Sharma and Sharma (2011) discussed the implementation of data mining for automation in extraction of functional requirements from data and to retrieve missing and incomplete specifications and to assess the correctness of software outputs.

5.4. Maintenance

5.4.1. Clustering in Maintenance

- Mendonca and Sunderhaft (1999) described hierarchical clustering to identify software changes that may be grouped together, take similar type of actions for the changes belonging to the same cluster. This technique forms the cluster on the basis of binary distance. Each cluster contains the objects with similar types of changes. The objects with dissimilar changes are batched in the different clusters. Clustering is also used for software maintenance planning and to estimate software reliability.

5.4.2. Classification in Maintenance

- Alvarez and Mata (1994) described 'ELLIPSES' a classification algorithm based on supervised learning which discovers most suitable region for rule discovery. The perfect region is determined by number of instances present in the region and volume of the region. It is also depends on the instances of the majority class, class of the region, instances of the other class and the instances of the class which are covered by other rules previously.

5.4.3. Association Rule in Maintenance

- Alvarez and Mata (1994) described an association algorithm GAR based on unsupervised learning for generation of management rules to help the project manager. GAR is an association analysis algorithm to discover association rules for data having the numeric attributes. It finds perfect intervals for each attribute to form the rule. Rule consists of the attributes, minimum and maximum values of the intervals. Acceptance of the rule is determined by the factors such as support, confidence, cases so that rules different from the cases considered previously can be searched, along with the number of attributes directly affecting the quality of the association rules.

6. RESEARCH IMPLICATIONS

In this chapter, the authors have presented a literature survey on the application of DM in SDLC. The implication of the research is as follows:

1. The literature review will help the researchers to gain an insight of the ways and methods

for efficient software development using data mining techniques. The classification of software development is presented through an approach starting from requirement gathering to design and development, testing and maintenance.

2. The current research will form the basis for identification of new approaches and techniques towards building of efficient software.

3. The classification of software development will enable the researchers to carry on further research work related to redesign and refinement of each phase.

4. A research roadmap to enumerate the need of studying the role of data mining in SDLC shown by Figure 1.

5. Several data mining techniques have been identified from various research journals and classified in accordance to their use in software development in the form of a classification framework. The framework at a glance is capable enough to give research insights to researchers pursuing work in the software development domain regarding existing research work and paves the way for future work related to the domain.

6. The research framework presented in the chapter can be extended by researchers to include ever-evolving newer techniques of data mining used in software development.

7. LIMITATIONS

The authors have provided a literature survey on the role of data mining in Software development by detailed study of various journals. The literature study has encountered certain limitations. Some of which are as follows:

1. **Ever Expanding Domain:** In the literature study, the authors have studied and presented various factors related to software development and data mining domain. The continu-

ous and progressive development in this field restrict as there exists the possibility that some related aspects of software development and data mining techniques might be left out.

2. **Accessibility of Journals:** The authors have accessed all the related material of the role of data mining in SDLC, from various international journals. It is probable enough that some papers might have been left out as all the journals do not have open access.

3. **Expansion Possibility of Classification Framework:** The authors have targeted on the general issues showing the role of data mining in software development. There is possibility of expansion of framework based on more deep study of the role of DM in SDLC.

4. **Scope of Elaboration of Development Phases:** The authors have presented a phase wise classification of software development. Further categorization of the software development phases is still possible based on nature and situation of the domain to which it is applied.

8. CONCLUSION

In the chapter, the authors have performed a literature survey on the application of DM in SDLC. The authors have come out with a classification framework showing the role of DM techniques (clustering, classification and association rule) in each of the phases of SDLC (requirement analysis, design and development, testing and maintenance). The framework will provide a base to researchers in understanding the role of data mining in SDLC and create platform towards the identification of newer techniques in building of efficient software. The authors have tried to include maximum possible information from various journals, still there exists scope of expansion of literature review and classification framework due to limitations discussed.

REFERENCES

Al-Otaiby, T. N., AlSherif, M., & Bond, W. P. (2005). *Toward software requirements modularization using hierarchical clustering techniques.* Paper presented at ACMSE '05. Kennesaw, GA.

Alvarez, J. L., & Mata, J. (1994). Data mining for the management of software development process. *International Journal of Software Engineering and Knowledge Engineering.*

Faridi, M. S., Mustafa, T., & Jan, F. (2012). Human Persuasion Integration in Software Development Lifecycle (SDLC). *International Journal of Computer Science, 9*(3), 65–68.

Han, J., & Kamber, M. (2001). *Data Mining: Concepts and Techniques.* Morgan Kaufmann.

Hand, D., Mannila, H., & Smyth, P. (2001). *Principles of Data Mining.* MIT Press.

Huang, J. C., & Mobasher, B. (2008). Using Data Mining and Recommender Systems to Scale up the Requirements Process. In *Proceedings of ULSSIS'08.* Leipzig, Germany: ACM.

Husain, W., Low, P. V., Ng, L. K., & Ong, Z. L. (2011). Application of Data Mining Techniques for Improving Software Engineering. In *Proceedings of ICIT 2011, 5th International Conference on Information Technology.* ICIT.

Ilkhani, A., & Abaee, G. (2011). Extracting Test Cases by Using Data Mining, Reducing the Cost of Testing. *International Journal of Computer Information Systems and Industrial Management Applications, 3,* 730–737.

Kesavan, S., & Alagarsamy, K. (2011). Data mining approach in software analysis. *International Journal of Computer & Organization Trends, 1*(2), 9–12.

Khoshgoftaar, T. M., Allen, E. B., Hudepohl, J. P., & Aud, S. J. (1997). Neural Networks for Software Quality Modeling of a Very Large Telecommunications System. *IEEE Transactions on Neural Networks, 8*(4), 902–909. doi:10.1109/72.595888 PMID:18255693

Khoshgoftaar, T. M., & Lanning, D. L. (1995). A Neural Network Approach for Early Detection of Program Modules Having High Risk in the Maintenance Phase. *Journal of Systems and Software, 29*(1), 85–91. doi:10.1016/0164-1212(94)00130-F

Last, M. (2005). Data mining for software testing. In *Data Mining and Knowledge Discovery Handbook 2005* (pp. 1239–1248). Academic Press.

Mendonca, M., & Sunderhaft, N. L. (1999). *Mining Software Engineering Data: A Survey.* A DACS (data & analysis center for software) state-of-the-art report.

Muthyala, K., & Naidu, R. (2011). A novel approach to test suite reduction using data mining. *Indian Journal of Computer Science and Engineering, 2*(3), 500–505.

Naidu, M. S., & Geethanjali, N. (2013). Classification of defects in software using decision tree Algorithm. *International Journal of Engineering Science and Technology, 5*(6), 1332–1340.

Pendharkar, P. C., Subramanian, G. H., & Rodger, J. A. (2005). A Probabilistic Model for Predicting Software Development Effort. *IEEE Transactions on Software Engineering, 31*(7), 615–624. doi:10.1109/TSE.2005.75

Punitha, K., & Chitra, S. (2013). Software defect prediction using software metrics - A survey. In *Proceedings of International Conference on Information Communication and Embedded Systems* (ICICES), (pp. 555-558). ICICES.

Selby, R. W., & Porter, A. A. (1988). Learning from Examples: Generation and Evaluation of Decision Trees for Software Resource Analysis. *IEEE Transactions on Software Engineering, 14*(12), 1743–1757. doi:10.1109/32.9061

Selvakumar, J., & Rajaram, M. (2011). Performance Evaluation of Requirements Engineering Methodology for Automated Detection of Non Functional Requirements. *International Journal on Computer Science and Engineering, 3*(8), 2991–2995.

Sharma, S., & Sharma, A. (2011). Amalgamation of Automated Testing and Data Mining: A Novel Approach in Software Testing. *International Journal of Computer Science Issues, 8*(2), 195–199.

Witten, I. H., & Frank, E. (2002). *Data Mining: Practical Machine Learning Tools and Techniques with Java Implementations*. Morgan Kaufmann.

Xie, T., Thummalapenta, S., Lo, D., & Liu, C. (2009). *Data mining for software engineering*. IEEE Computer Society.

ADDITIONAL READING

Han, J., & Kamber, M. (2001). *Data Mining: Concepts and Techniques*. San Francisco, CA: Morgan Kaufmann.

Hand, D., Mannila, H., & Smyth, P. (2001). *Principles of Data Mining*. Cambridge, CA: MIT Press.

Last, M. (2005). *Data mining for software testing*. Data Mining and Knowledge Discovery Handbook.

Witten, I. H., & Frank, E. (2002). *Data Mining: Practical Machine Learning Tools and Techniques with Java Implementations*. San Francisco, CA: Morgan Kaufmann.

Xie, T., Thummalapenta, S., Lo, D., & Liu, C. (2009). *Data mining for software engineering*. IEEE Computer Society.

KEY WORDS AND DEFINITIONS

Classification: Classification is the process of finding a model (or function) that describes and distinguishes data classes or concepts, for the purpose of being able to use the model to predict the class of objects whose class label is unknown (Han and Kamber, 2001).

Clustering: Clustering is the process that groups the data objects that are similar to one another within the same cluster and are dissimilar to the objects in other clusters. Similar data is grouped together on the basis of similar values for attributes (Han and Kamber, 2001).

Data Mining: Data mining is defined as "the process of discovering interesting knowledge from large amounts of data stored either in databases, data warehouses, or other information repositories" (Han and Kamber, 2001).

Software Development Life Cycle: SDLC is an abstract model used in project management that describes the stages concerned in a system development, from an planning through maintenance of the desired application (Faridi et al., 2012).

Chapter 5
Determination of Pull Out Capacity of Small Ground Anchor Using Data Mining Techniques

Pijush Samui
VIT University, India

ABSTRACT

The determination of pull out capacity (Q) of small ground anchor is an imperative task in civil engineering. This chapter employs three data mining techniques (Genetic Programming [GP], Gaussian Process Regression [GPR], and Minimax Probability Machine Regression [MPMR]) for determination of Q of small ground anchor. Equivalent anchor diameter (D_{eq}), embedment depth (L), average cone resistance (q_c) along the embedment depth, average sleeve friction (f_s) along the embedment depth, and Installation Technique (IT) are used as inputs of the models. The output of models is Q. GP is an evolutionary computing method. The basic idea of GP has been taken from the concept of Genetic Algorithm. GPR is a probabilistic non-parametric modelling approach. It determines the parameter from the given datasets. The output of GPR is a normal distribution. MPMR has been developed based on the principal mimimax probability machine classification. The developed GP, GPR, and MPMR are compared with the Artificial Neural Network (ANN). This chapter also gives a comparative study between GP, GPR, and MPMR models.

INTRODUCTION

The determination of pullout capacity (Q) of small ground anchor is an imperative task in civil engineering. Due to temporary use of small ground anchor, engineers do not put much effort for collecting engineering properties of soils for designing small ground anchor. Researchers use different methods for determination of Q of small ground anchor(Meyerhof and Adams, 1968; Meyerhof, 1973; Rowe and Davis, 1982a; Rowe and Davis, 1982b; Murray and Geddes, 1987; Subba Rao and Kumar, 1994; Basudhar and Singh, 1994; Koutsabeloulis and Griffiths, 1989; Vesic, 1971;

DOI: 10.4018/978-1-4666-6086-1.ch005

Das and Seeley, 1975; Das, 1978; Das, 1980; Das, 1987; Vermeer and Sutjiadi, 1985; Dickin, 1988; Sutherland, 1988). Shahin and Jaksa (2006) successfully adopted Artificial Neural Network (ANN) for determination of Q of small ground anchor. But, ANN has some limitations such as black box approach, arriving at local minima, low generalization capability, overtraining, etc (Park and Rilett, 1999; Kecman, 2001).

This chapter examines three data mining techniques {Gaussian Process Regression (GPR), Genetic Programming (GP), Minimax Probability Machine Regression (MPMR)} for prediction of Q of small ground anchor based on soil properties and geometry of small ground anchor. GPR is formulated as a Bayesian estimation problem. Researchers have successfully used GPR for solving different problems in engineering (Stegle *et al.*, 2008; Sciascio and Amicarelli, 2008; Yuan *et al.*, 2008; Pal and Deswal, 2010; Zhao et al., 2012; Chen et al., 2013). GP is a non-parametric method. It has been successfully applied to a large number of difficult problems (Hernández and Coello, 2004; Guven et al.,2009, Guven and Kisi, 2011; Azamathulla and Zahiri, 2012; Garg and Jothiprakash, 2013). MPMR is developed based on the principal mimimax probability machine classification (Lanckriet et al.,2002). It has been successfully applied for solving different problems (Sun, 2009; Sun et al., 2011; Yu et al., 2012; Zhou et al., 2013). This chapter uses the database collected by Shahin and Jaksa (2006). The dataset contains information about equivalent anchor diameter (D_{eq}), embedment depth (*L*), average cone resistance (q_c) along the embedment depth, average sleeve friction (f_s) along the embedment depth and installation technique (*IT*). This chapter has the following aims.

- To examine the capability of GPR, GP, and MPMR for prediction of Q of small ground anchor.
- To develop equation for prediction of Q of small ground anchor.

- To make a comparative study between the developed GPR,GP, MPMR and ANN models(Shahin and Jaksa, 2006).

DETAILS OF GPR

This section will describe GPR for prediction of Q of small ground anchor. In GPR, the relation between input(x) and output(y) is given by

$$y = f\left(x\right) + \varepsilon \qquad (1)$$

where ε is Gaussian noise with zero mean and variance σ2. In this chapter, Deq, qc,fs, L and IT have been used as input. The output of GPR is Q. So,

$$x = \left[D_{eq}, q_c, f_s, L, IT\right]$$

and $y = \left[Q\right]$.

GPR treats f(x) as random variables.

The distribution of output y_{N+1} for a new input (x_{N+1}) is given by

$$\begin{pmatrix} y \\ y_{N+1} \end{pmatrix} \sim N\left(0, K_{N+1}\right) \qquad (2)$$

with covariance matrix

$$K_{N+1} = \begin{bmatrix} K & K\left(x_{N+1}\right) \\ K\left(x_{N+1}\right)^T & k\left(x_{N+1}\right) \end{bmatrix}$$

where $K(x_{N+1})$ is covariances between training inputs and the test input and $k(x_{N+1})$ is the auto-covariance of the test input and T is transpose.

The distribution of y_{N+1} is Gaussian with mean and variance:

$$\mu = K\left(x_{N+1}\right)^T K^{-1} y \qquad (3)$$

$$\sigma = k\left(x_{N+1}\right) - K\left(x_{N+1}\right)^{T} K^{-1} K\left(x_{N+1}\right) \qquad (4)$$

The hyperparameters of the GPR and their optimal value for a particular data set can be derived by maximizing the log marginal likelihood using common optimization procedures.

To develop GPR, 83 datasets have been uses as training dataset. The remaining 36 datasets have been utilized as testing dataset. Testing datasets have been used to verify the developed GPR model. The datasets are normalized between 0 and 1. Radial basis function has been used as a covariance function. The program of GPR has been developed by MATLAB.

DETAILS OF GP

The concept of GP is developed based on the principle of 'survival of the fittest'. In GP, the random population of equation is created. The fitness value of each equation is evaluated. "Parents" are selected from the random population of equation. In generation, "offspring's" are formed through the process of reproduction, mutation and crossover. The details of reproduction, mutation and crossover is given by Koza(1992). The best computer program that appeared in any generation is the solution of the problem. GP uses the same training dataset and testing dataset as used by the GPR model. The program of GP has been constructed by using MATLAB.

DETAILS OF MPMR

MPMR uses the following equation for prediction output(y)

$$y = \sum_{i=1}^{N} \beta_{i} K\left(x_{i}, x\right) + b \qquad (5)$$

Where $K(x_i,x)$ is kernel function, x is input, β_i and b are outputs of the MPMR. In this chapter, D_{eq}, q_c, f_s, L and IT have been used as input. The output of MPMR is Q. So,

$$x = \left[D_{eq}, q_c, f_s, L, IT\right]$$

and $y = \left[Q\right]$.

MPMR is constructed by a dichotomy classifier (Strohmann and Grudic, 2002). One data set is obtained by shifting all of the data +ε along the output variable. The other dataset is obtained by shifting all of the regression data -ε along the output variable. The classification boundary between these two classes is called regression surface. MPMR uses the same training dataset, testing dataset and normalization technique as used by the GPR model. Radial basis function has been used as kernel function. MATLAB has been adopted to develop the MPMR model.

RESULTS AND DISCUSSION

For developing GPR, the design values of width(s) of radial basis function and ε have been determined by trial and error approach. The developed GPR gives best performance at s=0.3 and ε=0.002. The performance of GPR has been assessed in terms of Coefficient of Correlation(R). For a good model, the value of R should be close to one. Figure 1 depicts the performance of training and testing datasets. It is observed from Figure 1 that the value of R is close to one. Therefore, the developed GPR proves his ability for prediction of Q of small ground anchor.

For GP, the number of population is kept to 600. The number of generation is set to 200. The developed GP gives best performance at mutation frequency =80 and crossover frequency =60 percent. Figure 2 illustrates the performance of

Figure 1. Performance of GPR model

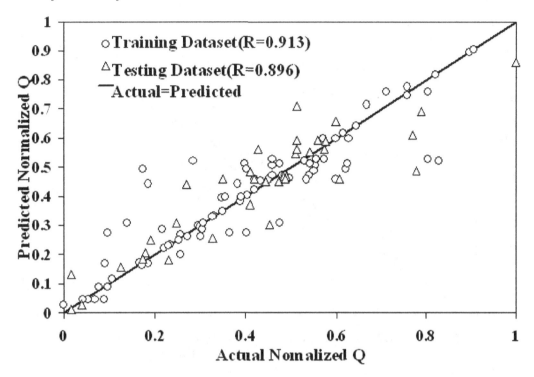

Figure 2. Performance of the GP model

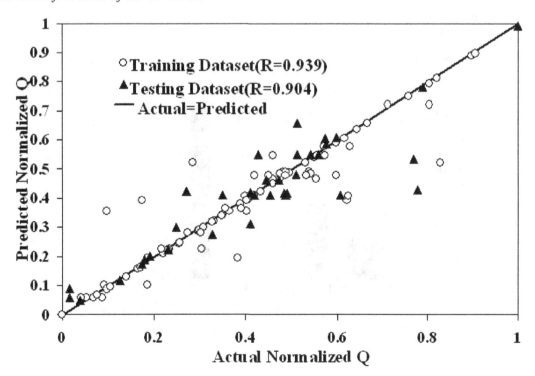

Figure 3. Performance of the MPMR

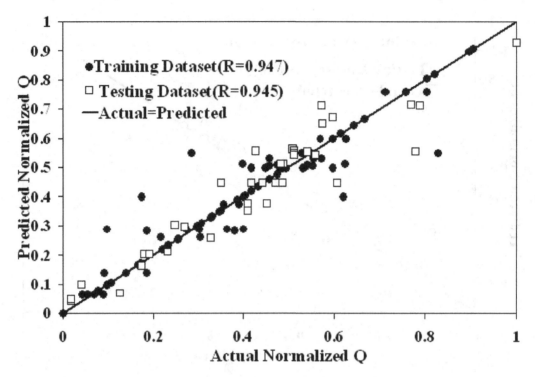

Figure 4. Histogram of variance

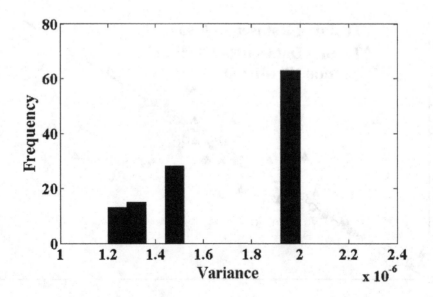

Box 1.

$$Q = 0.22L - 0.11q_c - 0.11f_s - 0.11\exp\left(f_s - D_{eq}\right) + \frac{7.57\exp\left(\exp\left(D_{eq} + IT\right)\right)}{10^5} -$$
$$0.003\exp\left(\exp\left(f_s + IT\right)\right) - 2.43\exp\left(f_s - 1.20\right)^2 + 4.75\left(2f_s - 1.06\right)^2 - 0.12\left(L - D_{eq}\right)^4 + 5.07$$
(6)

(6)

training and testing datasets. The value of R is close to one for training as well as testing datasets. The developed GP gives the following expression for prediction of Q of small ground anchor.

For MPMR, trial and error approach has been adopted to determine the design values of s and ε. The developed MPMR gives best performance at s=0.6 and ε=0.007. The performance of training and testing dataset has been shown in Figure 3. It can be seen from Figure 3 that the value of R is close to one.

A comparative has been carried out between the developed GP, GPR, MPMR and ANN models (Shahin and Jaksa, 2006). The performance of GPR and ANN is almost same. The developed GP and MPMR give better performance than the ANN model. The developed GPR gives the variance of the predicted Q. Figure 4 shows the histogram of variance.

CONCLUSION

This chapter examines the capability of GPR, GP and MPMR for prediction of Q of small ground anchor. The performance of GPR, GP and MPMR is encouraging. The developed GP gives an equation for prediction of Q of small ground anchor. The predicted variance can be used to determine uncertainty. The developed GPR, GP and MPMR have been compared with the ANN model. The performance of MPMR is best. This chapter proves the predictive ability of GP, GPR and MPMR for prediction of Q of small ground anchor.

REFERENCES

Azamathulla, H. M., & Zahiri, A. (2012). Flow discharge prediction in compound channels using linear genetic programming. *Journal of Hydrology (Amsterdam)*, *454-455*, 203–207. doi:10.1016/j.jhydrol.2012.05.065

Basudhar, P. K., & Singh, D. N. (1994). A generalized procedure for predicting optimal lower bound break-out factors of strip anchors. *Geotech*, *44*(2), 307–318. doi:10.1680/geot.1994.44.2.307

Chen, J., Chan, L. L. T., & Cheng, Y. C. (2013). Gaussian process regression based optimal design of combustion systems using flame images. *Applied Energy*, *111*, 153–160. doi:10.1016/j.apenergy.2013.04.036

Das, B. M. (1978). Model tests for uplift capacity of foundations in clay. *Soil and Foundation*, *18*(2), 17–24. doi:10.3208/sandf1972.18.2_17

Das, B. M. (1980). A procedure for estimation of ultimate uplift capacity of foundations in clay. *Soil and Foundation*, *20*(1), 77–82. doi:10.3208/sandf1972.20.77

Das, B. M. (1987). *Developments in geotechnical engineering*. Elsevier.

Das, B. M., & Seeley, G. R. (1975). Breakout resistance of horizontal anchors. *Journal of the Geotechnical Engineering Division*, *101*(9), 999–1003.

Dickin, E. A. (1988). Uplift behaviour of horizontal anchor plates in sand. *Journal of the Geotechnical Engineering Division, 114*(11), 1300–1317. doi:10.1061/(ASCE)0733-9410(1988)114:11(1300)

Garg, V., & Jothiprakash, V. (2013). Evaluation of reservoir sedimentation using data driven techniques. *Applied Soft Computing Journal, 13*(8), 3567–3581. doi:10.1016/j.asoc.2013.04.019

Guven, A., Azamathulla, H. M., & Zakaria, N. A. (2009). Linear genetic programming for prediction of circular pile scour. *Ocean Engineering, 36*(12-13), 985–991. doi:10.1016/j.oceaneng.2009.05.010

Guven, A., & Kişi, O. (2011). Daily pan evaporation modeling using linear genetic programming technique. *Irrigation Science, 29*(2), 135–145. doi:10.1007/s00271-010-0225-5

Hernández Aguirre, A., & Coello, C. A. C. (2004). Using genetic programing and multiplexers for the synthesis of logic circuits. *Engineering Optimization, 36*(4), 491–511. doi:10.1080/03052150410001686503

Kecman, V. (2001). *Learning and Soft Computing: Support Vector Machines, Neural Networks, and Fuzzy Logic Models*. Cambridge, MA: The MIT Press.

Koutsabeloulis, N. C., & Griffiths, D. V. (1989). Numerical modeling of the trap door problem. *Geotech, 39*(1), 77–89. doi:10.1680/geot.1989.39.1.77

Koza, J. R. (1992). *Genetic programming: on the programming of computers by means of natural selection*. Cambridge, MA: MIT Press.

Lanckriet, G. R. G., Ghaoui, L. E., Bhattacharyya, C., & Jordan, M. I. (2002). *Minimax probability machine*. Cambridge, MA: MIT Press.

Meyerhof, G. G. (1973). Uplift resistance of inclined anchors and piles. In *Proc., 8th Int. Conf. on Soil Mechanics and Foundation Engg* (pp. 167-172). Moscow: Academic Press.

Meyerhof, G. G., & Adams, J. I. (1968). The ultimate uplift capacity of foundations. *J. Canadian Geotec., 5*(4), 225–244. doi:10.1139/t68-024

Murray, E. J., & Geddes, J. D. (1987). Uplift of anchor plates in sand. *Journal of the Geotechnical Engineering Division, 113*(3), 202–215. doi:10.1061/(ASCE)0733-9410(1987)113:3(202)

Pal & Deswal. (2010). Modelling pile capacity using Gaussian process regression. *Computers and Geotechnics, 37*, 942–947. doi:10.1016/j.compgeo.2010.07.012

Park, D., & Rilett, L. R. (1999). Forecasting freeway link ravel times with a multi-layer feed forward neural network. *Computer Aided Civil and Infra Structure Engrg, 14*, 358–367.

Rowe, R. K., & Davis, E. H. (1982a). The behaviour of anchor plates in clay. *Geotech, 32*(1), 9–23. doi:10.1680/geot.1982.32.1.9

Rowe, R. K., & Davis, E. H. (1982b). The behaviour of anchor plates in sand. *Geotech, 32*(1), 25–41. doi:10.1680/geot.1982.32.1.25

Sciascio, F., & Amicarelli, A. N. (2008). Biomass estimation in batch bio-technological processes by Bayesian Gaussian process regression. *Computers & Chemical Engineering, 32*, 3264–3273. doi:10.1016/j.compchemeng.2008.05.015

Shahin, M. A., & Jaksa, M. B. (2006). Pullout capacity of small ground anchors by direct cone penetration test methods and neural networks. *J. Canadian Geotech., 43*, 626–637. doi:10.1139/t06-029

Shahin, M. A., & Jaksa, M. B. (2006). Pullout capacity of small ground anchors by direct cone penetration test methods and neural networks. *J. Canadian Geotech, 43*, 626–637. doi:10.1139/t06-029

Stegle, O., Fallert, S. V., MacKay, D. J., & Brage, S. (2008). Gaussian process robust regression for noisy heart rate data. *IEEE Transactions on Bio-Medical Engineering, 55*(9), 2143–2151. doi:10.1109/TBME.2008.923118 PMID:18713683

Strohmann, T. R., & Grudic, G. Z. (2002). A Formulation for minimax probability machine regression. In *NIPS) 14*. Advances in Neural Information Processing Systems Cambridge, MA: MIT Press.

Subba Rao, K. S., & Kumar, J. (1994). Vertical uplift capacity of horizontal anchors. *Journal of the Geotechnical Engineering Division, 120*(7), 1134–1147. doi:10.1061/(ASCE)0733-9410(1994)120:7(1134)

Sun, J. (2009). Modelling of chaotic time series using minimax probability machine regression. In *Proceedings - 2009 WRI International Conference on Communications and Mobile Computing, CMC, 4797010*, (pp. 321-324). WRI.

Sun, J., Bai, Y., Luo, J., & Dang, J. (2009). Modelling of a chaotic time series using a modified minimax probability machine regression. *The Chinese Journal of Physiology, 47*(4), 491–501.

Sutherland, H. B. (1988). Uplift resistance of soils. *Geotech, 38*(4), 473–516.

Vermeer, P. A., & Sutjiadi, W. (1985). The uplift resistance of shallow embedded anchors. In *Proc. 11th Int. Conf. Soil Mech., & Found. Engrg*, (vol. 3, pp. 1635–1638). San Francisco, CA: Academic Press.

Vesic, A. S. (1971). Breakout resistance of objects embedded in ocean bottom. *Journal of the Soil Mechanics and Foundations Division, 96*(SM4), 1311–1334.

Yu, M., Naqvi, S. M., Rhuma, A., & Chambers, J. (2012). One class boundary method classifiers for application in a video-based fall detection system. *IET Computer Vision, 6*(2), 90–100. doi:10.1049/iet-cvi.2011.0046

Yuan, J., Wang, K., Yu, T., & Fang, M. (2008). Reliable multi-objective optimization of high-speed WEDM process based on Gaussian process regression. *International Journal of Machine Tools & Manufacture, 48*, 47–60. doi:10.1016/j.ijmachtools.2007.07.011

Zhao, X., Wang, B., & Yu, J. (2012). Color constancy via Gaussian process regression. *Journal of Information and Computational Science, 9*(15), 4663–4671.

Zhou, Z., Wang, Z., & Sun, X. (2013). Face recognition based on optimal kernel minimax probability machine. *Journal of Theoretical and Applied Information Technology, 48*(3), 1645–1651.

KEY TERMS AND DEFINITIONS

Artificial Neural Network: Artificial Neural Networks are computational models inspired by central nervous systems (in particular the brain) that are capable of machine learning and pattern recognition. They are usually represented as systems of interconnected "neurons" that can compute values from inputs by feeding information through the network.

Gaussian Process Regression: A Gaussian process is a generalization of the Gaussian probability distribution. Whereas a probability distribution describes random variables which are scalars or vectors (for multivariate distributions), a stochastic process governs the properties of functions.

Genetic Programming: A genetic programming is a heuristic process that mimics the process of natural selection. Genetic algorithms belong to the larger class of evolutionary algorithms (EA), which generate solutions to optimization problems using techniques inspired by natural evolution, such as inheritance, mutation, selection, and crossover.

Minimax Probability Machine Regression: The problem of constructing a regression model can be posed as maximizing the minimum probability of future predictions being within some bound of the true regression function. Hence we refer to this regression framework as Minimax Probability Machine Regression (MPMR).

Prediction: Prediction is the process of making something to be known in advance, especially on the basis of special knowledge.

Probability: Probability is the chance that something will happen i.e. how likely it is that some event will happen.

Small Ground Anchor: A ground anchor is a device that is designed to support structures and is used in geotechnical and construction applications. It can also be referred to as an earth anchor, percussion driven earth anchor or mechanical anchor.

Chapter 6
Rules Extraction using Data Mining in Historical Data

Manish Kumar
IIIT, Allahabad, India

Shashank Srivastava
IIIT, Allahabad, India

ABSTRACT

Rules are the smallest building blocks of data mining that produce the evidence for expected outcomes. Many organizations like weather forecasting, production and sales, satellite communications, banks, etc. have adopted this mode of technological understanding not for the enhanced productivity but to attain stability by analyzing past records and preparing a rule-based strategy for the future. Rules may be extracted in different ways depending on the requirements and the dataset from that has to be extracted. This chapter covers various methodologies for extracting such rules. It presents the impact of rule extraction for the predictive analysis in decision making.

INTRODUCTION

Data mining has become the most prominent and assuring methodology for decision making. It can be used for extracting various rules in any historical data set and present them as an approach for efficient predictions. Rule extraction using data mining approaches is a tool for efficient decision making where preprocessed historical records like weather reports, healthcare data, geospatial data, sales records etc. act as an input for training and generating the rules through analysis. Based upon generating rules, predictions and decision making can be done in the respective areas. The whole process of rule extraction is divided into various

phases (Mishra, Addy, Roy, & Dehuri, 2011), which can be customized accordingly. There are different paradigms of rule extraction including association rule extraction such as Apriori algorithm (Agrawal & Srikant, 1994), decision tree (Apté & Weiss, 1997), hypothesis testing, rough set rules and many other algorithms. Apriori algorithm has several application areas like educational data mining (Yang & Hu, 2011) that helps arranging courses, quality education and educational model. Other application areas include medical domain (Yuguang & Chunyan, 2011), Electric Multiple unit fault data analysis (Zhang, Xie, Zhang, Li, & Liu, 2011), Electronic Commerce (Yang, 2012). Rule extraction using classification has become

DOI: 10.4018/978-1-4666-6086-1.ch006

a very promising technique in various domains for bringing innovative touches including speech recognition (Zhou, Kang, Fan, & Zhang, 2011), real estate development scheme optimization (Wang, 2013) and fraud detection (Zou, Sun, Yu, & Liu, 2012) etc. Especially decision tree has vast applications including economical statistical data processing (Jinguo & Chen, 2011), electric power marketing (Meng & Yang, 2012) etc. It is being used in several other application domains like market segmentation, prediction, fraud detection, weather forecasting, trend analysis, time series analysis and interactive marketing etc. Various rule extraction tools are available in accordance with the requirements, which are categorized according to different approaches (Laender, Ribeiro-Neto, da Silva, & Teixeira, 2002) like natural language processing tools, modeling and ontology based tools etc.

Our world is full of records and facts. There is a bit difference between facts and records. All records are not facts; we have to extract facts from records. These facts only help to reach a decision in different areas. Thus keeping this extraction of fact from records several models have been proposed but most of them lack implementation. The major reason behind their failure was the lack of transparency. Transparency is nothing but a measure of quality of rules extraction. Intelligent and efficient process of discovering and extracting the logical rules out of records is known as *Rules Extraction*. Decision making is predictive in nature. Facts are discovered using the rule extraction and these facts motivate us to reach a prediction of a decision. Therefore there exists a direct relation between rules extraction and prediction, if the rules are extracted efficiently then our predictions will also be efficient.

The rules can be extracted in two ways:

1. Top down extraction.
2. Bottom up extraction.

Rule extraction starts from the top level and then extract rules for sub modules, such mode of top to down rule extraction is known as top-down extraction while extracting rules for individual sub modules first and then aggregate them to form a composite rule set, it is known as bottom-up extraction. Extracting the facts from the bulk of the records, particular data set is used as a reference for extracting certain rules, this is known as *Training Set* or *Trained Data set*. Once the rules are discovered from the training set, another data set is used to apply those discovered rules on it and perform the predictions; this data set is called Test *Set* (Han, Kamber, & Pei, 2011).

PHASES OF RULES EXTRACTION

Figure 1 shows the phases of rule extraction (Mishra et al., 2011):

- **Rule Requirement:** It covers the rule's requirement for the class generation.
- **Rule Generation:** Based on the requirements and domain constraint rules are generated.
- **Rule Coverage:** It ensures that all the required rules are generated and also all the generated rules are required.
- **Rule Selection:** This is the final phase where all the selected rules are listed and applied to the available dataset to test the accuracy.

PARADIGM OF RULE EXTRACTION

Associative Rule Extraction

This paradigm deals with the extraction of the rules on the basis of the observable associative relationship between the attributes which can

Figure 1. Phases of rule extraction

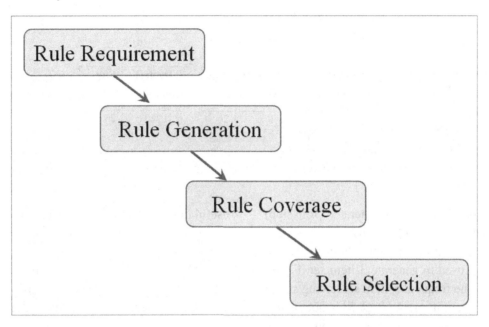

facilitate the efficient and profitable decision making. Association rules are generated in the following form:

$$A \rightarrow B$$

Part '*A*' is antecedent and '*B*' is consequent. An association rule is a pattern that states when the antecedent occurs, consequent occurs with certain probability. Association between different attributes is based on two factors i) *Support* ii) *Confidence*. *Support* is a measure of what fraction of the population i.e. no of tuples in the given transaction dataset satisfies both the antecedent and the consequent of the rule. The rule holds with support *sup* in the transaction data set *T*, if *the sup* % of transactions contain $A \cup B$.

$$sup = P\ (A\ B)$$

Confidence is a measurement of how often the consequent is true, when it is given that the antecedent is true. The rule holds in *T* with confidence *conf if conf*% of transactions that contain *A*, contain *B* too.

$$conf = P(B|A)$$

The process of extracting association rules is divided into two steps (Haberstroh, 2008); selecting frequent item sets and generating association rules between them. Apriori (Agrawal & Srikant, 1994) is the most traditional association rule mining algorithm, which uses an iterative search in the available item sets. Following example illustrates the apriori algorithm. Figure 2(a) shows transactions of different items *P, Q, R, S, T* and size of dataset *D* is |*D*|=5. Let's assume that the minimum transaction support (min *sup*) is 40% and confidence is 60%. Support count for each item is calculated, as shown in Figure 2 (b) and compared with the minimum transaction support count. Itemset with support value less than 2 is removed (pruning step)as shown in Figure 2(c).

Figure 2. (a) Transactional Database. (b) Transaction support count for each item. (c) Frequent 1- item set (FS₁). (d) Frequent 2- item set (FS₂). (e) Frequent 3- item set (FS₃).

(a)			(b)			(c)			(d)			(e)	

Tran ID	Itemset
T1	PQST
T2	QS
T3	QR
T4	PQS
T5	PR

Itemset	Sup
{P}	3
{Q}	4
{R}	2
{S}	3
{T}	1

Itemset	Sup
{P}	3
{Q}	4
{R}	2
{S}	3

Itemset	Sup
{P, Q}	2
{Q, S}	3
{P, S}	2

Itemset	Sup
{P, Q, S}	2

After pruning, 2-item set is generated (Join step) with output set as *{{P, Q}, {P, R}, {P, S}, {Q, R}, {Q, S}, {R,S}}*. Figure 2(d) shows the pruned item-set which is used to generate 3-item set. Figure 2(e) shows the frequent 3-item set having *sup ≥* 2. Thus frequent item set *{P, Q, S}* is obtained.

Based on the frequent itemset, some of the generated rules are: *Rule 1: P-> Q; Rule 2: Q-> S; Rule 3: P-> QS* etc. Considering confidence value to be 60%, only rule 2 will be selected.

Apriori is found to be more accurate and less complex than other rule based mining algorithms like PART (Partial Decision Tree) (Mazid, Ali, & Tickle, 2009) But it requires long scanning time for accessing databases repetitively. Later, boolean algebra compression technique (Anekritmongkol & Kasamsan, 2010) was proposed to reduce the scanning time and file size.

Extracted rules might be redundant and incon-sistent with the actual situation. Moreover some rules might be too general or too detailed that may not fulfill user requirements. A new framework was proposed by Xiong, Fan, and Lei (2010) combining the field knowledge with association rule mining and considering customer requirements for group-ing and pruning of the rules. Objective methods (based on statistical and machine learning) and subjective evaluation methods (that integrates user participation and domain knowledge) are combined to evaluate rule quality. Quality index is proposed to quantify multilevel association rule quality on the basis of domain ontology. It can be useful in redundancy treatment and rule analysis, whether it is fulfilling the customer requirement or not (Xiong et al., 2010). Negative Association Rule (NAR) mining is gaining more attention. These rules are important in decision making analysis by identifying the items that comple-ments or conflict each other (Kadir, Bakar, & Hamdan, 2011).

Classification

Han et al. (2011) categorized learning as *super-vised learning* where the set of possible classes is known in advance and u*nsupervised learning* where the possible classes are not known in advance. Clustering algorithms are examples of unsupervised learning. Classification is the super-vised task of data mining where data objects are classified into a labeled class. Rules are extracted during the training of the dataset and the class of test data set is predicted.

Phases of Classification:

- **Model Construction:** It is a learning phase where each tuple is assumed to belong to a predefined class, as marked by the class label attribute. The set of samples used in model construction is known as *training set* (given data). The model is represented in the form of classification rules or math-ematical formulae.

- **Model Usage:** It is a classification phase where accuracy of the constructed model is evaluated. The known label of test samples is compared with the classified result from the model; accuracy rate is the percentage of test set samples that are correctly classified by the model.

Classification vs. Prediction

Given a dataset where each record has attributes $X_1,..., X_n$. A function f such that:

$$f : \left(X_1,...,X_n \right) \to Y$$

whereas the prediction given input record ($X_1,..., X_n$). Depending upon the type of attribute Y *classification* or *prediction is* chosen. *Classification* is when *is* a discrete attribute, called the class label. *Prediction* is when *is* a continuous attribute. Thus it is a supervised learning, because true labels (Y-values) are known for the initially provided data.

DECISION RULE ALGORITHM

Decision tree learning is one of the most appropriate methodologies for rule extraction. It includes the generation of a decision tree (Han et al., 2011), where at every non leaf node certain conditions are applied and based upon the outcome, optimal decisions are predicted. The training set data are used as an input for the generation of decision trees. Once the tree is generated, test data is applied to get the optimal prediction. It maps the observations about an item to conclusions about the item's target value. The decision tree is also known as *classification trees* or *regression trees*. Decision tree act as a classifier in the form of a tree structure, where each node is either a *leaf node* (indicates the target class value) or a *decision node* (indicates test to be carried out on any attribute), having branches and sub-trees for every possible

outcome of the test. The values of the input variables are represented by the path from the root to the leaf, i.e. considering the values of all the attribute in the path. A decision tree can be used to classify a data by starting from the root of the tree and moving through it by making decisions at each internal node, until a leaf node is reached.

As shown in the Figure 3, a dataset is having a categorical attribute $Attr_1 = \{black, white\}$, a continuous attribute $Attr_2 = \{0, 1..., 10\}$ and a discrete attribute $Attr_3 = \{true, false\}$. K is a class label having values $\{Class_1, Class_2\}$. Using rule extraction in the decision tree algorithm, several rules are extracted such as:

Rule 1: If ($Attr_1 ==$ Black) AND ($Attr_2 < 3$) then $K = Class_1$.

Rule 2: If ($Attr_1 ==$ White) AND ($Attr_2 >= 6$) AND ($Attr_3 = false$) then $K = Class_2$.

Similarly three more rules will be generated as a tree has three more paths from root to leaf. Assume a new test data $\{Attr_1 = black, Attr_2 = 7$ and $Attr_3 = false\}$ have to be classified. The dataset will be classified into class $K = Class_2$. As shown above, a rule may be constructed by tracking every test that occurs on the path from root to a leaf and apply conjunction. A collection of all such rules generated by traversing a path from root to leaf is a corresponding rule- based solution for classification (Apté & Weiss, 1997).

Many more techniques are proposed like rule based decision tree (RBDT-1) which builds the decision tree on the basis of a set of declarative rules that covers the dataset instead of the dataset itself. This method enables the on demand construction of short and accurate decision tree from static as well as dynamically changing rules (Abdelhalim & Traore, 2009). Pruning methods like reduced error pruning (REP) is proposed (Mohamed, Salleh, & Omar, 2012) to overcome the problem of large size tree and try to reduce the complexity and maintaining the accuracy of

Figure 3. Decision tree example

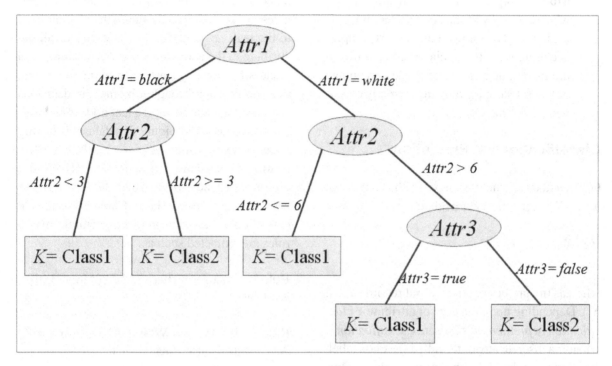

decision tree. In case of large databases, C4.5 has been improved to handle scalability issues. Attribute oriented induction, relevance analysis, AVL trees are combined with the knowledge of concept hierarchy to construct decision tree considering attribute priorities along with multilevel mining (Ali & Rajamani, 2012). To overcome the problem of having sharp decision boundaries, fuzzy supervised learning in the quest (SLIQ) decision tree (FS-DT) is proposed to create a fuzzy decision boundary rather than crisp decision boundaries. Gasification provides higher accuracy and lesser storage requirement (Chandra & Varghese, 2008).

REGRESSION

Regression (Aiken & West, 1991) literally means the analysis or a measure of the association between a dependent and an independent variable. It holds the same meaning in data mining also. It is an another important function of data mining that predicts a value of an attribute such as age, weight, temperature, distance, income, or sales. The independent attributes which are used for predicting an unknown value are known as *predictors* while the attribute that unknown value is to be predicted is known as a *target*. E.g. a regression model used for predicting children's height may involve the tracking of age, height and family history. Here, the height would be the *target* and the other attributes would be acting like *predictors*, and the data about each child would constitute a case (Haberstroh, 2008).

The main aim of regression analysis (Han et al., 2011) is to determine the values of parameters for the function that causes the function to fit a set of data observations optimally. The following equation expresses that regression is the process of estimating the value of a continuous target (Y) as a function (F) of predictors (X_1, X_2, ..., X_n), parameters (θ_1, θ_2, ..., θ_n), and error (e).

$$Y = F\left(X, \theta\right) + e$$

The process of training a regression model involves the identification of best parameter values with minimum errors. Single predictor regression techniques are of two types:

Linear Regression: It is the simplest form of regression used to visualize a linear relation with a single predictor. This technique is used when the relationship between X and Y can be approximated with a straight line as shown in Figure 4(a).

$$Y = mX + c$$

where m is the *slope* and c is the *coefficient.*

Nonlinear Regression: Sometimes the relationship between X and Y cannot be approximated with a straight line. Thus, in this case a nonlinear regression technique may be used. Instead of a straight line we get a curve to plot. Figure 4(b) shows the nonlinear regression.

HYPOTHESIS TESTING ALGORITHM

In Hypothesis testing (Hastie, Tibshirani, Friedman, & Franklin, 2005), each generated rule or pattern is tested for significance against some statistical hypothesis. Data mining can generate patterns for even a random data set. Statistical significance testing is applied to select some surprising patterns that are not clearly visible. Special

monitoring is done to avoid the probability of falsely declaring a pattern significant (Gerstman, 2006). This algorithm follows following four steps:

Step 1: Null and alternative hypothesis.

The initial step of hypothesis testing is the conversion of research question into *Null Hypothesis* (H_0) (i.e. Same as research question) or *Alternative Hypothesis* (H_1) (i.e. Contradictory to research question*)*. These hypotheses do not refer to observed statistics instead it refers only to the population values.

Step 2: Test statistic.

This step includes the calculation of different types of test statistics from the given data. Larger the statistics larger is the deviation from the expected values i.e. higher probability for the occurrence of alternative hypothesis in comparison to null.

Step 3: p Value and conclusion.

This step includes the evaluation of conditional probability from the statistics known as *p-value.* The *p- value* significantly answers the accuracy of the null hypothesis. The conventions followed as shown in Table 1.

Figure 4. (a) Linear Regression. (b) Nonlinear Regression.

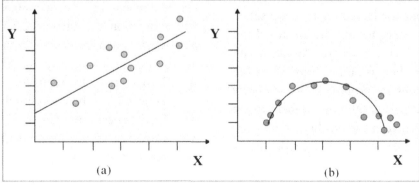

Table 1. Conventions for different range of p-value

p-value	Observed Difference
p value > .10	not significant
p value ≤ .10	marginally significant
p value ≤ .05	Significant
p value ≤ .01	highly significant

Step 4: Decision (optional)

This is the final step where threshold is provided for decision, X such that if $p\text{-}value \leq X$, the null hypothesis is rejected.

ROUGH SET RULES

Every object is associated with some data and may or may not with some knowledge. These objects are classified on the basis of the similarity in the information i.e. objects providing similar information are classified in the same group or elementary set (Pawlak, 1997).

The union of these elementary sets is known as a *crisp* (precise) set; else the set is known as *rough* (imprecise) set. Every rough set is associated with two operations *lower approximation* and *upper approximation as* shown in Figure 5. The lower approximation includes the objects that surely belongs to the set while the upper approximation includes the objects that possibly belong to the set. The difference between the lower and upper approximation forms the boundary of the rough set.

Rough Sets are used for attribute subset selection where irrelevant attributes are identified and removed. The problem of finding a relevant set with no irrelevant attribute is an *NP-Hard*, therefore various algorithms are proposed, *Discernibility matrix* (Yao & Zhao, 2009) is one of them where the difference between the attribute values are stored and used later for removing redundancy (Han et al., 2011).

Need of Data Mining in Rule Extraction

Data mining is the machine-assisted process of digging through and analyzing enormous sets of data and extracting the information out of it. This technology can generate new business opportunities (Alexander, 1997) as:

- **Trends Prediction:** Data mining identifies the predictive information in a large database. Traditional questions that use to require extensive hands-on analysis can now be directly answered through this approach. It increases the foresightedness of the business domain being applied to. Therefore it is a prospective and pro-active in nature.
- **Unknown Pattern Discovery:** This approach is also used to identify previously hidden patterns. This is the reason why it is also known as a heuristic approach since it analyses the past records to identify the unique hidden patterns.

Impact of Rule Extraction

Rule extraction has laid a tremendous impact on the processing capacity of the organizations and optimized the art of decision making. The mastercraftrule extraction workbench is introduced for mapping business rules and introducing an extraction platform for it applications such as portfolio rationalization, transformation & migration projects and managing reverse engineering projects. Rule extraction has many beneficiary traits such as (Securities and Exchange Commission, 2012):

- Introduction to repository of technical knowledge of business application.
- Easy traceability of changes.
- Providing a business definition to the application.

Figure 5. Rough set approximation for class C with Lower Approx(L) and Upper Approx(U)

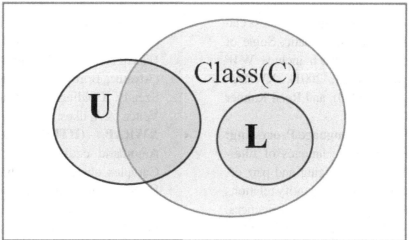

- Detailed, consistent and accurate documentation for easy and efficient task relevant data extraction.

RESEARCH METHODOLOGIES

1. Rule extraction is a basic approach of data mining which can be used with ANN, SVM, Decision Tree and other clustering and classification techniques where compact and summarized rules can be generated. Also, extracted rules can be used in the formation of better equations and intervals in bulky datasets.

2. Biology oriented research work is a prominent application area of data sciences where Combined Rule Extraction and Feature Elimination (CRF) can be used for better predictions and interpretations for multi class data.

3. Data mining is not only applicable for predicting the outcome or decision. It can also be used for predicting and uprooting the certain anomalies. Therefore, rule extraction can be used with supervised learning approaches for robust detection and eradicating the anomalies or outliers.

4. Heuristic rule evaluation technique is an another emerging branch of rule extraction where rule induction processes can be improved by selecting the optimal heuristic rule learning functions in order to obtain a good rule set.

5. The rule extraction technique can also be used for black box models by practicing pedagogical approaches which enable active learning without lending to architectural details.

TOOLS FOR RULE EXTRACTION

Data extraction from Web sources is one of the emerging challenges in the field of rule extraction. There are several techniques and approaches which are being used to meet the requirements, including machine learning, natural language processing, ontology etc. Based on different approaches, tools can be categorized as (Laender, Ribeiro-Neto, da Silva, & Teixeira, 2002):

- **Tools for Data Extraction from Web Sources:** These tools work on the structural feature of HTML (*Hyper Text Markup*

Language) documents for extracting data. The extraction process is based upon tree type of structure and the whole process can be automatic or semi-automatic. Some of the tools on this approach include W4F (Sahuguet & Azavant, 2001), XWRAP (Liu, Pu, & Han, 2000), and Road Runner (Freitag, 2000).

- **Tools for Natural Language Processing:** These tools use the techniques of filtering, lexical semantic tagging and part of-speech tagging in order to identify relations among different elements of sentences. They follow both *semantic* and *syntactic constraints* for extracting the relevant data. Some of the tools of this category are RAPIER (Califf & Mooney, 1999), SRV (Freitag, 2000), and WHISK (Soderland, 1999).

- **Wrapper Induction Tools:** It includes the delimiter based extraction tools. Unlike to NLP based tools these tools do not depend upon the linguistic constraints rather than these tools follow the constraints of format structure while extracting the data. This category includes tools like WIEN (Kushmerick, 2000), SoftMealy (Hsu & Dung, 1998), and STALKER (Muslea, Minton, & Knoblock, 2001).

- **Modeling-Based Tools:** Based upon the different modeling primitive structures of object are defined, these tools are used to identify such objects from the Web sources. Tools adopting this approach include NoDoSE (Adelberg, 1998) and DEByE (Laender, Ribeiro-Neto, & da Silva, 2002).

- **Ontology-Based Tools:** These tools work differently from all other approaches as they focus on *non-variant* and *constant* items rather than focusing on structural implementations. Based on this approach Brigham Young University proposed a new tool named Data Extraction Group (Embley, Campbell, Jiang, Liddle, Lonsdale, Ng, & Smith, 1999).

Characteristics of Different Tools

- **Minerva (Languages Tool):** Manual, coding based tool, partially supports Non-HTML sources and generates XML output (Alvarez, Borowsky, Go, Romer, Becker-Szendy, Golding, Merchant, Spasojevic, Veitch, & Wilkes, 2001).

- **XWRAP (HTML- Aware Tool):** Automatic coding based tool, supports Complex objects, partially supports Non-HTML sources and generates XML output (Liu et al., 2000).

- **SRV (NLP- Based):** Semi automated tool, supports Non- HTML sources, easy to use (Freitag, 2000).

- **Stalker (Induction):** Semi automated tool, partially supports Non- HTML sources, and supports complex objects, easy to use (Muslea et al., 2001).

- **NoDoSE (Modeling Based):** Semi-automated tool, partial support for Non-HTML sources and XML- output, supports complex objects, more convenient to use (Adelberg, 1998).

- **BYU (Ontology Based):** Manual, coding based tool, supports Non- HTML sources (Laender, Ribeiro-Neto, da Silva, & Teixeira, 2002).

An Example of Rule Extraction: A Case Study

Plastic cards are the utility through which financial firms provide their customers with credits. In other words, it is a provision that enables individuals to pay their expenses even when they are out of money. The individuals are given a fixed period of time in which they are suppose to return the credit amount with the relevant taxes back to the firms. It is a mutual bond between two bodies where one gets the credit for a time period while the other get the interest. Due to some unsocial nature of some individuals, firms are coming across the frauds where individuals deny paying back the money. Therefore, it has become quite essential for the firms to predict the nature and status of the customers based on the customer's history. Data mining comes into picture to reduce the fraudulent opportunities and reduce the risk of the financial firms. A credit card company (Hofmann, 1994) having 1000 instances of 20 attributes is analyzed where various details of the customers are observed. Mining algorithm is applied to classify the customer either as *good or bad*. Table 2 provides the details of the attributes with their types and number of values. The class attribute is defined with two values (*yes or no*) to classify the customers either in the class of *good or bad*.

ATTRIBUTE SELECTION MEASURE

Information Gain: Information gain is one of the popular attribute selection measures(Han et al., 2011). It is based upon the "information content" of the attribute. The attribute with the highest information gain is chosen as the splitting attribute. It is calculated by subtracting the expected information needed to classify the current dataset and the expected information needed to classify

all the subsets, obtained after splitting dataset by the corresponding attribute.

The expected information (Han et al., 2011), needed to classify a tuple in dataset *DS*, is given by

$$Info(DS) = \sum_{i=1}^{m} p_i \log_2(p_i)$$

where p_i is the nonzero probability that a tuple in *DS* belongs to class CL_i and given by

$$p_i = \frac{|CLi, DS|}{|DS|}$$

$$Info_A(DS) = \sum_{j=1}^{v} \frac{|DS_j|}{|DS|} x \, Info(DS_j)$$

$|DS_j|$ denotes the number of tuples in jth partition. $Info(DS_j)$ is the expected information needed to classify a tuple in partition DS_j.

$$Information\,Gain\,(A) = Info(DS) - Info_A(DS)$$

Table 2. Attribute tables

Sr. No.	Attribute Name	Attribute Type	Sr. No.	Attribute Name	Attribute Type
1*	Status of existing checking account	Qualitative	11	Present residence since	Numerical
2*	Duration in month	Numerical	12	Property	Qualitative
3*	Credit history	Qualitative	13	Age in years	Numerical
4	Purpose	Qualitative	14	Other installment plans	Qualitative
5	Credit amount	Numerical	15	Housing	Qualitative
6	Savings account/bonds	Qualitative	16	Number of existing credits at this bank	Numerical
7	Present employment since	Qualitative	17	Job	Qualitative
8	Installment rate in percentage of disposable income	Numerical	18	Number of maintenance account	Numerical
9	Personal status and sex	Qualitative	19	Telephone	Qualitative
10	Other debtors / guarantors	Qualitative	20	Foreign worker	Qualitative

Information gain of all 20 attributes is calculated and based upon the values 3 attributes with highest information gain values are selected as shown in Table 3.

All the attributes are arranged in increasing order according to their information gain values as: *1,3,2,6,4,5,12,7,15,13,14,9,20,10,17,19,18,8, 11,16*. With a threshold information gain value as 0.30000, the attributes checking status, credit history and duration are selected. Now, decision trees using J48 and REP tree algorithms are constructed and the customers are classified in either a *good or bad* class.

J48: It is an implementation of the Quinlan (1993) C4.5 algorithm for generating with pruned or without pruned decision tree. J48 constructs the decision tree from a set of attributes using the concept of information gain. It uses the attribute with highest information gain as root node of the tree, smaller the value of information gain higher is the depth of the node (attribute). Figure 6(a) shows the decision tree constructed using J48 implementation using WEKA 3.7.

Rule Generation: Based upon the constructed tree, many rules can be generated which can lead to decision making and can help to predict that whether the customer lies in the class of *good or bad*.

Rule 1: If *checking status*< 0 AND *credit history* = 'delayed previously' AND *duration*> 18 months then the customer is *bad*.
Rule 2: If *checking status*>=200 then the customer is good.

REPTree: Reduced error pruning is an efficient risk minimization algorithm (Witten & Frank, 2005), which is used to prune out (remove) the noise or error from the decision tree. It is a dynamic approach which may even show better results than J48 depending on the validation schemes. Figure 6(b) Represents the REP tree implemented using WEKA 3.7.

Rule Generation: With reference to Figure 6(b), some of the rules generated are:

Rule 1: If *checking status*< 0 AND *credit history* = 'delayed previously' then customer is *bad*.
Rule 2: If checking *status*>=200 then the customer is good.

The total number of rules that can be generated is equal to the number of leaf nodes i.e.15 rules in Figure 6(a) and 11 rules in Figure 6(b). Table 4 compares both the approaches, which are constructed on the basis of the evaluation summary shown in Figure 7.

Table 3. Information gain of attributes

Rank	Attribute	Information Gain Value
1	Checking Status	0.094739
2	Credit History	0.043618
3	Duration	0.03290
4	Savings Status	0.028115
5	Purpose	0.024894
.	.	.
.	.	.
.	.	.
20	Installment Commitment	0

Figure 6. Decision tree generated by (a) J48 and (b) REPTree algorithms

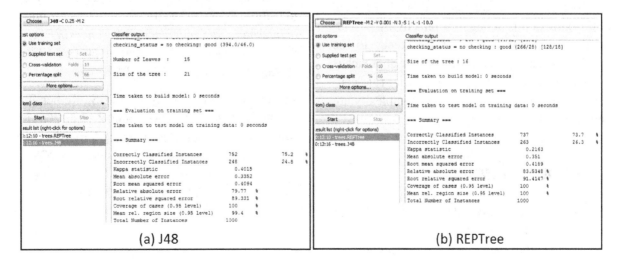

(a) J48

(b) REPTree

Table 4. Comparison of J48 and REPTree

	J48	REP Tree
Size of the tree	21	16
Correctly Classified Instances	75.2 %	73.7 %
Incorrectly Classified Instances	24.8 %	26.3 %

Figure 7. Evaluation Summary on dataset generated by WEKA 3.7 (a)J48 (b)REPTree

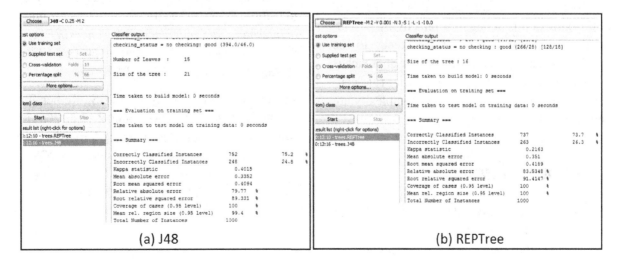

(a) J48

(b) REPTree

REMARKS

The study of above examples shows the efficiency of the rule extraction with J48 and REPTree implementation of decision tree which generates rules that can classify the customer in *good or bad* category. In Table 3, it can be observed that J48 (=21) generates tree with higher number of nodes compare to REPTree (=16). Also, the correctly classified instances in J48 are greater than REPTree. J48 may be preferable for the given example but it is not certain that J48 will always give a better result than REPTree. It is always advisable to carry a comparative study of different algorithms before implementation.

CONCLUSION

Data mining is a vast application area with rule extraction as a very small part. Data mining has always been an evolving area where every algorithm reaches its limitations after a period of time. In the current scenario, rule extraction is not only applicable for historical data but also in other field of studies involving decision making. Rule extraction plays an important role in the analysis and decision making of historical data. Several data mining techniques (such as SVM, ANN, random forests) lack comprehensibility. The domains where comprehensibility is required, rule extraction is acting as a remedy by providing comprehensibility and transparency to the decisions. The developments of new approaches and algorithms that can provide better rule generation and predictions with low complexity are encouraged.

ACKNOWLEDGMENT

We would like to acknowledge and bestow our regards to all the authors of research papers, books, and other sources whose contents are part of this work. We extend sincere thanks to Ms. Amrit Kalsi (IIIT Allahabad) for her valuable suggestions and help.

REFERENCES

Abdelhalim, A., & Traore, I. (2009). A new method for learning decision trees from rules. In *Proceedings of International Conference on Machine Learning and Applications* (pp. 693-698). Miami Beach, FL: IEEE.

Adelberg, B. (1998). NoDoSE—a tool for semi-automatically extracting structured and semistructured data from text documents. *SIGMOD Record, 27*(2), 283–294. doi:10.1145/276305.276330

Agrawal, R., & Srikant, R. (1994). Fast algorithms for mining association rules. In *Proceedings of 20th Internation Conference on Very Large Data Bases* (pp. 487-499). Santigo, Chile: Morgan Kaufmann Publishers Inc.

Aiken, L. S., & West, S. G. (1991). *Multiple regression: Testing and interpreting interactions.* Sage Publications.

Alexander, D. (1997). *Data Mining.* Retrieved May 22, 2013 from http://www.laits.utexas.edu/~anorman/BUS.FOR/course.mat/Alex

Ali, M. M., & Rajamani, L. (2012). Decision tree induction: Priority classification. In *Proceedings of International Conference on Advances in Engineering, Science and Management* (pp. 668-673). Nagapattinam, Tamil Nadu: IEEE.

Alvarez, G. A., Borowsky, E., Go, S., Romer, T. H., Becker-Szendy, R., & Golding, R. et al. (2001). Minerva: An automated resource provisioning tool for large-scale storage systems. [TOCS]. *ACM Transactions on Computer Systems, 19*(4), 483–518. doi:10.1145/502912.502915

Anekritmongkol, S., & Kasamsan, M. K. (2010). The Comparative of boolean algebra compress and apriori rule techniques for new theoretic association rule mining model. In *Proceedings of 6th International Conference on Advanced Information Management and Service* (pp. 216-222). Seoul: IEEE.

Apté, C., & Weiss, S. (1997). Data mining with decision trees and decision rules. *Future Generation Computer Systems*, *13*(2-3), 197–210. doi:10.1016/S0167-739X(97)00021-6

Califf, M. E., & Mooney, R. J. (1999). Relational learning of pattern-match rules for information extraction. In *Proceedings of the sixteenth national conference on Artificial intelligence and the eleventh Innovative applications of artificial intelligence conference innovative applications of artificial intelligence* (pp. 328-334). Orlando, FL: American Association for Artificial Intelligence.

Chandra, B., & Varghese, P. P. (2008). Fuzzy SLIQ decision tree algorithm. *IEEE Transactions on Systems, Man, and Cybernetics. Part B, Cybernetics*, *38*(5), 1294–1301. doi:10.1109/TSMCB.2008.923529 PMID:18784012

Embley, D. W., Campbell, D. M., Jiang, Y. S., Liddle, S. W., Lonsdale, D. W., Ng, Y. K., & Smith, R. D. (1999). Conceptual-model-based data extraction from multiple-record Web pages. *Data & Knowledge Engineering*, *31*(3), 227–251. doi:10.1016/S0169-023X(99)00027-0

Freitag, D. (2000). Machine learning for information extraction in informal domains. *Machine Learning*, *39*(2-3), 169–202. doi:10.1023/A:1007601113994

Gerstman, B. (2006). *Introduction to Hypothesis Testing*. Retrieved May 16, 2013 from http://www.sjsu.edu/faculty/gerstman/StatPrimer/hyptest.pdf

Haberstroh, R. (2008). *Oracle® data mining tutorial for Oracle Data Mining 11g Release 1*. Oracle.

Han, J., Kamber, M., & Pei, J. (2011). *Data Mining: Concepts and Techniques*. Morgan Kaufmann Publishers.

Hastie, T., Tibshirani, R., Friedman, J., & Franklin, J. (2005). The elements of statistical learning: data mining, inference and prediction. *The Mathematical Intelligencer*, *27*(2), 83–85. doi:10.1007/BF02985802

Hofmann, H. (1994). *Website*. Retrieved May 28, 2013 from http://archive.ics.uci.edu/ml/machine-learning-databases/statlog/german/

Hsu, C. N., & Dung, M. T. (1998). Generating finite-state transducers for semi-structured data extraction from the web. *Information Systems*, *23*(8), 521–538. doi:10.1016/S0306-4379(98)00027-1

Jinguo, X., & Chen, X. (2011). Application of decision tree method in economic statistical data processing. In *Proceedings of International Conference on E-Business and E-Government* (pp. 1-4). Shanghai, China: IEEE.

Kadir, A. S. A., Bakar, A. A., & Hamdan, A. R. (2011). Frequent absence and presence itemset for negative association rule mining. In *Proceedings of 11th International Conference on Intelligent Systems Design and Applications* (pp. 965-970). Cordoba: IEEE.

Kushmerick, N. (2000). Wrapper induction: Efficiency and expressiveness. *Artificial Intelligence*, *118*(1-2), 15–68. doi:10.1016/S0004-3702(99)00100-9

Laender, A. H., Ribeiro-Neto, B., & da Silva, A. S. (2002). DEByE–data extraction by example. *Data & Knowledge Engineering*, *40*(2), 121–154. doi:10.1016/S0169-023X(01)00047-7

Laender, A. H., Ribeiro-Neto, B. A., da Silva, A. S., & Teixeira, J. S. (2002). A brief survey of Web data extraction tools. *SIGMOD Record*, *31*(2), 84–93. doi:10.1145/565117.565137

Liu, L., Pu, C., & Han, W. (2000). XWRAP: An XML-enabled wrapper construction system for Web information sources. In *Proceedings of 16th International Conference on Data Engineering* (pp. 611-621). San Diego, CA: IEEE.

Mazid, M. M., Ali, A. S., & Tickle, K. S. (2009). A comparison between rule based and association rule mining algorithms. In *Proceedings of Third International Conference on Network and System Security* (pp. 452-455). Gold Coast, Australia: IEEE.

Meng, J., & Yang, Y. (2012). The application of improved decision tree algorithm in the electric power marketing. In *Proceedings of World Automation Congress*. Academic Press.

Mishra, B. S. P., Addy, A. K., Roy, R., & Dehuri, S. (2011). Parallel multi-objective genetic algorithms for associative classification rule mining. In *Proceedings of International Conference on Communication, Computing & Security* (pp. 409-414). Rourkela, India: ACM.

Mohamed, W., Salleh, M. N. M., & Omar, A. H. (2012). A comparative study of Reduced Error Pruning method in decision tree algorithms. In *Proceedings of International Conference on Control System, Computing and Engineering* (pp. 392-397). Penang: IEEE.

Muslea, I., Minton, S., & Knoblock, C. A. (2001). Hierarchical wrapper induction for semistructured information sources. *Autonomous Agents and Multi-Agent Systems, 4*(1-2), 93–114. doi:10.1023/A:1010022931168

Pawlak, Z. (1997). Rough set approach to knowledge-based decision support. *European Journal of Operational Research, 99*(1), 48–57. doi:10.1016/S0377-2217(96)00382-7

Quinlan, J. R. (1993). *C4. 5: programs for machine learning* (Vol. 1). Morgan Kaufmann.

Sahuguet, A., & Azavant, F. (2001). Building intelligent Web applications using lightweight wrappers. *Data & Knowledge Engineering, 36*(3), 283–316. doi:10.1016/S0169-023X(00)00051-3

Securities and exchange Commission, 17 CFR Parts 240 and 249, [Release No. 34-67717, File No. S7-42-10], RIN 3235-AK85, Disclosure of Payments by Resource Extraction Issuers.

Soderland, S. (1999). Learning information extraction rules for semi-structured and free text. *Machine Learning, 34*(1-3), 233–272. doi:10.1023/A:1007562322031

Wang, Z. (2013). Application of Decision Making Tree Method in the Real Estate Development Scheme Optimization. In *Proceedings of Third International Conference on Intelligent System Design and Engineering Applications* (pp. 365-368). Hong Kong: Kluwer Academic Publishers.

Witten, I. H., & Frank, E. (2005). *Data Mining: Practical machine learning tools and techniques*. San Francisco: Morgan Kaufmann.

Xiong, X. S., Fan, L., & Lei, Z. (2010). Ontology-Based Association Rule Quality Evaluation Using Information Theory. In *Proceedings of International Conference on Computational and Information Sciences* (pp. 170-173). Chengdu: IEEE.

Yang, Q., & Hu, Y. (2011). Application of Improved Apriori Algorithm on Educational Information. In *Proceedings of Fifth International Conference on Genetic and Evolutionary Computing* (pp. 330-332). Xiamen: IEEE.

Yang, S. (2012). Research and Application of Improved Apriori Algorithm to Electronic Commerce. In *Proceedings of 11th International Conference on Distributed Computing and Applications to Business, Engineering & Science* (pp. 227-231). Guilin: IEEE.

Yao, Y., & Zhao, Y. (2009). Discernibility matrix simplification for constructing attribute reducts. *Information Sciences: An International Journal*, *179*(7), 867–882. doi:10.1016/j.ins.2008.11.020

Yuguang, Y., & Chunyan, W. (2011). Application of the Model Multi Based on Apriori Algorithm in Supporting System of Medical Decision. In *Proceedings of Third International Conference on Measuring Technology and Mechatronics Automation* (pp. 566-569). Shangshai: IEEE.

Zhang, C., Xie, D., Zhang, N., Li, H., & Liu, F. (2011). The improvement of Apriori algorithm and its application in fault analysis of CRH EMU. In *Proceedings of Third International Conference on Service Operations, Logistics, and Informatics* (pp. 543-547). Beijing: IEEE.

Zhou, D., Kang, J., Fan, Z., & Zhang, W. (2011). The application of improved Apriori algorithm in continuous Speech Recognition. In *Proceedings of Second International Conference on Mechanic Automation and Control Engineering* (pp. 756-758). Hohhot: IEEE.

Zou, K., Sun, W., Yu, H., & Liu, F. (2012). ID3 decision tree in fraud detection application. In *Proceedings of International Conference on Computer Science and Electronics Engineering* (pp. 399-402). Hangzhou: IEEE.

ADDITIONAL READING

Borg, C., Rosner, M., & Pace, G. J. (2010, May). Automatic Grammar Rule Extraction and Ranking for Definitions. In LREC.

Fung, G., Sandilya, S., & Rao, R. B. (2005, August). Rule extraction from linear support vector machines. *In Proceedings of the eleventh ACM SIGKDD international conference on Knowledge discovery in data mining* (pp. 32-40). Chicago, IL, USA: ACM.

Green P.E., Carmone F. J., & Smith S. M. (Nov 1, 2011). Cluster Analysis revision of Multidimensional Scaling, section five: dimension reducing methods and cluster analysis, Addison Wesley, 1989.

Hamida, A. M. D. O. U. N. I., & Mohsen, G. M. (2011, May). Algorithms of association rules extraction: State of the art. *In Proceedings of Third 3rd International Conference on Communication Software and Networks* (pp. 333-339). Xi'an: IEEE.

Hanneman, G., Burroughs, M., & Lavie, A. (2011, June). A general-purpose rule extractor for SCFG-based machine translation. *In Proceedings of the Fifth Workshop on Syntax, Semantics and Structure in Statistical Translation* (pp. 135-144). Portland, Oregon, USA: Association for Computational Linguistics.

Johansson, U., König, R., & Niklasson, L. (2010, July). Genetic rule extraction optimizing brier score. *In Proceedings of the 12th annual conference on Genetic and evolutionary computation* (pp. 1007-1014). Portland, Oregon, USA: ACM

Liu, S., Patel, R. Y., Daga, P. R., Liu, H., Fu, G., & Doerksen, R. J. et al. (2012). Combined rule extraction and feature elimination in supervised classification. *IEEE Transactions on Nanobioscience*, *11*(3), 228–236. doi:10.1109/TNB.2012.2213264 PMID:22987128

Malone, J., McGarry, K., Wermter, S., & Bowerman, C. (2006). Data mining using rule extraction from Kohonen self-organising maps. *Neural Computing & Applications*, *15*(1), 9–17. doi:10.1007/s00521-005-0002-1

McIntosh, T., & Chawla, S. (2007). High confidence rule mining for microarray analysis. Computational Biology and Bioinformatics, IEEE/ACM Transactions on, 4(4), 611-623.

Núñez, H., Angulo, C., & Català, A. (2002, April). Rule extraction from support vector machines. In ESANN (pp. 107-112).

Podgorelec, V., Kokol, P., Stiglic, B., & Rozman, I. (2002). Decision trees: an overview and their use in medicine. *Journal of Medical Systems*, *26*(5), 445–463. doi:10.1023/A:1016409317640 PMID:12182209

Shangping, D., & Na, L. (2011, December). A Research about mining association rules based on Quantitative Concept Lattice. *In Proceedings of International Conference on Transportation, Mechanical, and Electrical Engineering* (pp. 1337-1340). Changchun: IEEE.

KEY TERMS AND DEFINITIONS

Association Rule: It is a pattern that shows the association between two objects.

Confidence: It is a measurement of how often the consequent is true, when it is given that the antecedent is true.

Data Mining: Data Mining is the analysis of data to convert it into useful information. It is used to analyze the data in different aspects and criteria, formerly known as dimensions.

Fuzzification: The Process of transforming crisp values into grades of membership for linguistic terms of fuzzy sets.

Information Gain: Information needed to classify the current dataset from the other subsets.

Support: It is a measure of what fraction of the population i.e. no of tuples in the given transaction dataset satisfies both the antecedent and the consequent of the rule.

Test Set: Data used to test the discovered rules is called *Test Set*.

Training Set: Data set used as a reference for extracting rules is known as *Training Set* or *Trained Data set*.

Chapter 7
Robust Statistical Methods for Rapid Data Labelling

Jamie Godwin
University of Durham, UK

Peter Matthews
University of Durham, UK

ABSTRACT

Labelling of data is an expensive, labour-intensive, and time consuming process and, as such, results in vast quantities of data being unexploited when performing analysis through data mining. This chapter presents a new paradigm using robust multivariate statistical methods to encapsulate normal operational behaviour—not failure behaviour—to autonomously derive unsupervised classifier labels for previously collected data in a rapid, cost-effective manner. This enables traditional machine learning to take place on a much richer dataset. Two case studies are presented in the mechanical engineering domain, namely, a wind turbine gearbox and a rolling element bearing. A statistically sound and robust methodology is contributed, allowing for rapid labelling of data to enable traditional data mining techniques. Model development is detailed, along with a comparative evaluation of the metrics. Robust derivatives are presented and their superiority is shown. Example "R" code is given in the appendix, allowing readers to employ the techniques discussed. High levels of agreement between the derived statistical approaches and the underlying condition of the components can be found, showing the practical nature and benefit of this approach.

INTRODUCTION

Many data-driven algorithms require accurate labels in order to encapsulate the various conditions which correspond to their meaning. However, in many real-world applications, deriving these labels is not possible in practice or is not economically viable due to the amount of resources required.

As such, although significant quantities of data exist, exploiting this data effectively is not a trivial problem.

In this chapter, an evaluation of the performance of six multivariate distance metrics on two datasets incorporating censored data is presented. Unlike traditional methods, the techniques evaluated in this chapter provide a means

DOI: 10.4018/978-1-4666-6086-1.ch007

of autonomously deriving classifier labels in an unsupervised manner for previously collected data in a rapid, cost-effective way. This can be employed in cases where previously labelled data is either scarce, or highly imbalanced – allowing a greater amount of data to be incorporated into a traditional data mining analysis. To aid in the practicality and demonstrate the soundness of the approaches detailed, 'R' code is provided at all stages of the analysis. This allows the reader to follow the examples, as the techniques are presented on publicly available data for tutorial purposes.

The remainder of this book chapter is organized as follows. Motivation and context for this work is presented in the "background to the problem" section, along with the issues of data scarcity and data imbalance. Next, traditional techniques utilised are presented in the "data intensive techniques" section. The datasets and degradation models used are given in the "dataset description." In total, 6 multivariate distance metrics are introduced and comparatively evaluated on both datasets for their robustness and merit in performing condition assessment; three Minkowski distances (Manhattan, Euclidean and Chebyshev), the Penrose distance and two forms of the Mahalanobis distance are looked at in depth. Multivariate normality testing is then covered. After this, two case studies are presented in the "case study" sections, showing how the metrics can be employed for rapid labelling of data to enable traditional data mining approaches. Conclusions are then presented, with references and 'R' code in the appendices.

BACKGROUND TO THE PROBLEM

Motivation

Data mining can be thought of as an enabler of next generation maintenance techniques within the realm of reliability engineering due to the ability to generate significant cost savings. It is substantially cheaper to perform maintenance before an asset fails (preventive maintenance), rather than after a failure has occurred (corrective maintenance). As the cost of data acquisition technology and storage has reduced significantly, the quantity of data available for analysis has risen substantially. This provides many benefits, however, these are yet to be fully realised.

For instance, by utilising previously collected data in association with data mining techniques, it is possible to determine the current level of wear (or degradation) on an asset such as a turbine or a bearing. This enables preventive maintenance (Iung et al., 2009) to be performed at a significantly reduced cost (Wu & Clements-Croome, 2006) and thus provides a competitive edge to the corporation utilising these techniques (Leger et al., 1999).

However, the uptake of these techniques within the domain of reliability engineering has been slower than expected (Moore & Starr, 2006). This is due to many factors. For example:

- "Black box" expert systems which lack the necessary transparency,
- The financial outlay required to install the infrastructure to enable the data acquisition,
- Inherent uncertainty and varying accuracy present within data-driven processes and techniques,
- Staff training costs,
- No proven track record of the systems in similar domains.

Potentially the largest cause of uncertainty in these systems is caused due to inadequate labelling of the data, required in many cases to extract condition information using traditional data mining techniques. In many real world applications is not possible to know the required information for each data point (for instance, the size of the crack in a rotor shaft or the level of corrosion in a jet engine). Inspection of the equipment can provide this information but fundamentally changes the expected behaviour of the component due to the intervention which takes place. As such, data is often collected and stored in an unlabelled state with a note or other informal meta-data specifying the final condition information of the asset when it was removed, replaced, repaired or serviced.

In conjunction to this, very little run to failure data is available. This is due to the significant costs associated with allowing equipment to fail in industry. For instance, a catastrophic failure of a wind turbine gearbox can cost over US $5M to replace (Hatch, 2004), the cost of which would otherwise be significantly reduced by performing preventive maintenance (Djurdjanovic, et al. 2003). It is simply not economically viable to allow a failure to occur purely as an exercise in data collection. This can be seen as an issue with corporate culture as the department responsible for maintenance is often regarded as a "cost-centre" providing little benefit rather than a "profit-centre" which enables the organisation. This is because it is trivial to quantify the cost of a maintenance action, but increasingly difficult to quantify the benefit (Marais & Saleh, 2009).

There are many economic incentives for solving these issues. Hameed et al (2009) presents 5 key benefits of utilising data for reliability engineering. They are:

- Helping to avoid premature failures,
- Reducing the overall maintenance cost,
- Enabling remote diagnosis,
- Increasing production,
- Optimised future equipment designs.

The synergistic nature of these benefits provides substantial economic benefit to those organisations that are willing to implement an effective maintenance strategy based upon next generation maintenance strategies (such as Niu et al (2010) or Muller et al. (2008)) which are empowered by machine learning technologies.

This is especially true within the renewable energy industry. Up to 25% of the total cost of a wind turbine can be directly related to main-tenance costs, with up to 75% of these costs due to unscheduled maintenance (WWEA, 2012). As such it is imperative that the uptake of these techniques into industry is increased to ensure the viability of wind energy into the future.

Data Scarcity and Imbalance

Due to the infeasibility of collecting failure data, new approaches are needed to encapsulate operational conditions through the data which is currently available. This requires two distinct approaches; firstly, data balancing (through sampling or synthetic data creation) and secondly, employing censored data for analysis.

Data balancing is required to remove bias from the majority class (Batista, 2004). Within the wind energy domain, the ratio of normal operational behaviour to abnormal (or failure) data can be as high as 1000:1 (Verma & Kusiak, 2011). As this is coupled with an imperfect SCADA (supervisory control and data acquisition) system which suffers from erroneous, missing, duplicate and implausible data (Sainz et al., 2009): robust techniques are required to ensure that not only is the data accurately reflecting operational behaviour, but also that the data can be effectively employed by machine learning algorithms to learn the rare failure conditions which are occur.

Various algorithms and techniques exist to balance data, the simplest being random sampling. This causes many issues, namely over-fitting if used to increases a class size, and removing valuable information if used to reduce it. Repeated random sampling is one possible way to avoid these issues. Other techniques such as SMOTE (Chawla et al. 2002), MSMOTE (Hu et al., 2009) FSMOTE (Zhang et al., 2011), Tomek links (Tomek, 1976) and Hart's condensed nearest neighbour rule (Hart, 1968) (amongst others) exist for data balancing. Readers should refer to Batista (2004) for details of these algorithms.

However, these balancing techniques often require pre-existing labels to be associated with the data in order to more accurately represent the dataset. As discussed above, in practice this information is often not available, and as such, a new paradigm is required.

This paradigm aims to use normal operational behaviour – rather than failure data – in order to perform the machine learning. This is possible due to the much richer data source available. Whereas the data imbalance problem is a concern when employing traditional data mining techniques, it becomes the greatest strength in this new paradigm, opening up vast quantities of data for analysis. This allows stronger encapsulation of the standard operational behaviour of the system, enabling more accurate identification and quantification when it deviates from these norms.

Similar techniques have been applied in the literature and show strong promise. Work done by Heng et al. (2009) utilises artificial neural networks (ANN) with Kaplan-Meier survival estimation to determine the condition of a centrifugal pump, and find that suspended data increases the quality of the prognosis. Tian et al. (2010) utilise both failure data and suspended data from bearings in order to train ANNs, and similarly gain stronger results due to the inclusion of suspended data. Widodo et al. (2011) uses suspended data for the prognosis of a bearing for prediction of the remaining useful life via a support vector machine (SVM) in conjunction with survival probability. A more accurate prediction is achieved due to the inclusion of the suspended data.

DATA INTENSIVE ANALYTICAL TECHNIQUES IN RELIABILITY ENGINEERING

Wind Turbine Gearbox Diagnosis and Prognosis Techniques

Many techniques exist for the monitoring of wind turbine gearboxes, with the majority of techniques employing high frequency condition monitoring

system (CMS) data. This data is typically recorded at over 20 KHz, and varies between CMS systems. There are a range of CMS systems available for wind turbines; work done by Crabtree (2010) reviews these systems. Most of the techniques which look at the wind turbine gearbox employ techniques in the frequency domain, using vibration data. Specifically, the use of fast Fourier transforms (FFT) and power spectrum (PS) is widely explored. Sideband analysis from the FFT provides key insights to degradation behaviour and is utilised by Zappalá et al. (2013) for condition monitoring. Similarly, PS analysis can be used to monitor wind turbines for degradation by utilising SVM for pattern recognition, as performed by Zhang et al., (2012).

In addition to the frequency domain, the time-frequency domain is studied often with the use of wavelets. Mohanty & Kar (2006) use wavelets transforms and FFTs for their analysis, Yang et al. (2010) use the continuous wavelet transform (CWT). Techniques in the time domain do exist, such as utilising oil debris monitoring (ODM) sensors as in Feng et al. (2011), using ANN for online condition monitoring as discussed in Yang et al, 2008, wavelet neural networks (WNN) as per Huang et al (2008) and multi-agent systems (MAS) as in Zaher et al. (2009). Reviews of the techniques employed on wind turbine CMS systems can be found in both Lu et al. (2009) and Hameed et al. (2009). Although vibration data is the most common form of CMS data, acoustic emission (AE) data also exists and can be employed for health monitoring. Work done by Soua et al (2013) uses AE data collected from a wind turbine gearbox to determine damage and provides an overview of the literature in this area.

Bearing Diagnosis and Prognosis Techniques

Bearings have been studied extensively over many years, and as a result there is a large body of literature available for interested readers. For a review of many of the techniques employed, readers can consult Jardine et al. (2006) which details many of the techniques available. As per gearboxes, high frequency data is studied more readily than low frequency data. Papers dealing with the analysis of bearing data can perform their analysis on publically available data in order to verify and benchmark the techniques presented. NASA has provided a high frequency bearing data set collected from their prognostic laboratory (Lee et al., 2007) which is publicly available.

Wavelets are one of the most common techniques applied to perform analysis of bearing data. Research done by Lin & Zuo (2003) and Rafiee et al. (2010) detail these techniques. Also as in the case of gearboxes, FFT and PS analysis are often performed also (Blankenship & Singh, 1995, Liu et al. 2004, Randall & Antoni, 2011). A variety of both statistical and data driven approaches also exist. McDonand et al. (2012) use an autoregressive (AR) model for bearing prognosis, as do Wang & Makis (2004) and Baillie & Mathew (1996). Multivariate analysis is performed by both Zimroz & Bartkowiak (2013) and Baydar et al. (2001) which employ principal component analysis (PCA) for the analysis. Both Caesarendra (2010) and Sohn et al. (2002) uses statistical techniques for bearing degradation analysis. Model based techniques also exist. For instance, those presented in Marble & Morton (2006) use mathematical models of physical behaviour to perform analysis of the data. Data intensive techniques such as ANNs are used often in bearing analysis, such as by Spoerre (1997), Samanta & Al-Balushi (2003) and Tian (2012). Time synchronous average (TSA) – a form of moving average – is used to remove noise from bearing data. A review of the TSA technique and its applications can be found in Dalpiaz et al (2000) with Siegel et al. (2012) providing recent updates. Other techniques, such as using analytical techniques from the mathematics of chaos theory can be applied, as done by Wang et al. (2001) who use singular spectrum analysis (SSA) for their

analysis, and Xia & Chen (2012) who use fuzzy set theory in conjunction with chaos theory for their analysis.

SCADA Data Analytical Techniques

Typically, data from a SCADA (supervisory control and data acquisition) system is very low frequency. Often, within the domain of wind energy, SCADA records are collected every 10 minutes (Godwin et al., 2013) or every 5 minutes (Kusiak & Li, 2011). As such, traditional techniques often employed on high frequency data discussed above (such as wavelets, Fourier transforms) cannot be utilised for analysis of this data.

Due to this, techniques relying on SCADA data are often used for analysis on sub-critical components. On a wind turbine this may be the pitch system as in Chen (2011) or Kusiak & Verma (2011). Techniques for analysing critical components with SCADA data do exist, but are typically not as extensively covered in the literature. Work done by Feng et al. (2012) utilises a physics of failure models in conjunction with SCADA data for prognosis of the wind turbine gearbox. Recently, statistical distance metrics have been used for analysis of SCADA data in Kusiak & Verma (2013) and Godwin & Matthews (2013).

DATASET DESCRIPTION

Overview

The core of this book chapter will now focus on the practical development and application of multivariate distance metrics for objective labelling of data. Six metrics will be presented and discussed, with their benefits and drawbacks elaborated on. For convenience, 'R' code has been added in the Appendix, allowing the reader to follow the presented analysis in a practical way.

Two sets of analysis will be performed. Firstly, publicly available high frequency bearing data provided by NASA (Lee et al., 2007) will be used to determine the condition of a bearing; this will allow rapid labelling to be performed so that traditional data mining techniques can be employed. Secondly, SCADA data taken from the Reliawind project (EU FP7 Project ReliaWind 212966) will provide low frequency data (<0.002Hz) – indirectly measured through temperature – which will be utilised to determine the condition of a wind turbine gearbox, and follow a similar analysis as the bearing data.

Bearing Degradation Model

The bearing data differs from the wind turbine gearbox data in that the data is collected at over 20 KHz. As such, each sampled value does not represent a "snapshot" of behaviour cannot independently represent the overall condition of the bearing. Due to this, an additional process of normalisation is required to allow the data to be effectively utilised.

In order to demonstrate that no underlying physics of failure degradation model is necessary, the model used for analysis of the bearings consists of 4 attributes which encapsulate the operational behaviour for each second of logged data. These attributes are the unbiased estimator of the 3rd moment (skewness), as defined by Cramer (1946):

$$Skewness = G = \frac{n}{(n-1)(n-2)} \sum_{i=1}^{n} \left(\frac{x_i - \bar{x}}{s} \right)^3 \tag{1}$$

where s represents the unbiased sample standard deviation, and $\bar{x}$ is the sample mean. The skewness encapsulates the asymmetry in the data; for an undamaged bearing we would hope there is no asymmetry. The second attribute utilised is the unbiased estimator of the 4th moment (Kurtosis), also defined by Cramer (1946):

$$Kurtosis = M_4 =$$
$$\frac{n(n^2 - 2n + 3)}{(n-1)(n-2)(n-3)} m_4$$
$$-3m_2^2 \frac{n(2n-3)}{(n-1)(n-2)(n-3)} \tag{2}$$

where m_2 and m_4 are defined as:

$$m_2 = \frac{1}{n} \sum_{i=1}^{n} \left(x_i - \bar{x} \right)^2 \tag{3}$$

$$m_4 = \frac{1}{n} \sum_{i=1}^{n} \left(x_i - \bar{x} \right)^4 \tag{4}$$

The kurtosis measures how peaked the data is. Damage has been shown to cause these peaks which can be measured by this attribute. The third attribute used to encapsulate the condition of the bearing is the root mean square (RMS) of the signal. For n values, this is defined as:

$$x_{rms} = \sqrt{\frac{1}{n}(x_1^2 + x_2^2 + \dots + x_n^2)} \tag{5}$$

This measures the magnitude of the signal; expected to increase with degradation. The final attribute is the crest factor (CF) of the signal and is defined in terms of the RMS:

$$C = \frac{|x|_{peak}}{x_{rms}} \tag{6}$$

This expresses how extreme the peaks are in relation to the magnitude of the signal. As such, it is useful for determining the condition of the bearing as it will encapsulate shocks or damage to the system.

These attributes are utilised in a 4-tuple $X_i = \{G, M_4, x_{rms}, C\}$ which represents the condition of the bearing at a given moment. As this 4-tuple of attributes requires a distribution of values, a 1 second sample of the data (20,480 samples) is encapsulated and represented as the 4 attributes. This reduces the computational intensity of the problem, reduces the quantity of data required and allows independent domain experts to fix multivariate centres if no historical data is readily available.

Wind Turbine Gearbox Degradation Model

For the wind turbine gearbox analysis, data from 3 wind turbines will be used. This data was sampled every 600 seconds for a period of 28 months across 190 sensor channels. The prognostic model from Feng et al. (2012) was used as the basis for determining the level of degradation in the gearbox. This model assumes that heat generated by a gear is proportional to the work done:

$$q \propto w \propto \Delta t \tag{7}$$

where q represents heat generated, w represents work done and Δt represents the rise in temperature. With a given gear efficiency η_{gear}, the energy dissipated will be transferred as heat onto the gear, giving:

$$Q_{gear} = \left(1 - \eta_{gear}\right)\frac{1}{2}l_{gear}\omega^2_{gear} = k_{gear}\Delta t_{gear} \tag{8}$$

This can be expressed by the inefficiency as:

$$1 - \eta_{gear} = \frac{2k_{gear}\Delta t_{gear}}{l_{gear}\omega^2_{gear}} \tag{9}$$

The work done by the wind turbine can be expressed as:

$$P_{out} = W - Q_{gear} \tag{10}$$

where P_{out} represents power output, W represents work done and Q_{gear} represents the energy dissipated as heat from (2). It follows that:

$$P_{out} = \eta_{gear}\frac{1}{2}l_{gear}\omega^2_{gear} \tag{11}$$

As per Feng (2012), comparing (8) with (11) gives:

$$\frac{1 - \eta_{gear}}{\eta_{gear}} = k_{gear}\frac{\Delta t_{gear}}{P_{out}} \tag{12}$$

Or, when rearranged:

$$\Delta t_{gear} = P_{out}\frac{1}{k_{gear}}\left(\frac{1}{\eta_{gear}} - 1\right) \tag{13}$$

This shows that the temperature rise in the gearbox is proportional to the work performed by the gearbox for a fixed efficiency η_{gear}. Thus, as degradation of the gear occurs; the efficiency decreases and Δt_{gear} must increase for the same power generated by the turbine.

As such, we can use historical data to determine expected values of Δt_{gear} for normal operational behaviour. Deviations from this will then represent the degradation of the gearbox, which can be measured by the multivariate distance metrics which are presented in the following sections.

In addition to utilising Δt_{gear} for the analysis, similar degradation phenomenon is noticed in the gearbox oil temperature. This is due to the transfer of thermal energy from the gears, to the oil, due to the increased friction caused by the degradation. As such, this attribute can be used in conjunction with the gearbox temperature to further refine the model and increase the sensitivity.

MULTIVARIATE DISTANCE METRICS

Minkowski Distances

The Minkowski distance is a generalised distance metric which can be applied in the multivariate domain, to which the Euclidean, Manhattan and Chebyshev distances are specific forms. The Minkowski distance between two $n-$dimensional vectors, $(x_1, x_2 \ldots x_n)$ and $(y_1, y_2 \ldots y_n)$ is defined as (Xu & Wunsch, 2008):

$$\left(\sum_{i=1}^{n} |x_i - y_i|^P \right)^{\frac{1}{p}} \tag{14}$$

For some real-number $p \geq 1$.

Euclidean Distance

The Euclidean distance is equivalent to the Minkowski distance with $p = 2$. Thus; we define the Euclidean distance between two $n-$dimensional multivariate vectors

$$X = \left(x_1, x_2 \ldots x_n \right)$$

and

$$Y = (y_1, y_2 \ldots y_n)$$

as (Xu & Wunsch, 2008):

$$D_2(X,Y) = D_2(Y,X) =$$
$$\sqrt{(x_1 - y_1)^2 + (x_2 - y_2)^2 + \ldots + (x_n - y_n)^2}$$
$$= \sqrt{\sum_{i=1}^{n} (x_i - y_i)^2} \tag{15}$$

Thus, for some multivariate vector X we can determine the distance (or deviation) from another vector Y, which can be determined to represent a previously known state. In this instance, the vector Y will represent normal operational behaviour. Thus, increases in distance from the pre-set vector Y represent degradation present in the system.

Manhattan Distance

The Manhattan distance is also equivalent to the Minkowski distance ($p = 1$). As such, we define the Manhattan distance between two $n-$dimensional multivariate vectors

$$X = \left(x_1, x_2 \ldots x_n \right)$$

and

$$Y = (y_1, y_2 \ldots y_n)$$

as (Xu & Wunsch, 2008):

$$D_1(X,Y) = \sum_{i=1}^{n} | x_i - y_i | \tag{16}$$

This can be thought of as the optimal route between 2 points across a square 2-dimensional lattice, such as the distance between two points in the Ising model.

Chebyshev Distance

The Chebyshev distance (also known as the maximum metric) is the Minkowski distance with $p = \infty$. The distance it records is the maximum distance in a single dimension between two multivariate vectors. As such, it is defined over the multivariate vectors

$$X = (x_1, x_2 \ldots x_n)$$

and

$$Y = (y_1, y_2 \ldots y_n)$$

as (Xu & Wunsch, 2008):

$$D_\infty \left(X, Y \right) = \max_i (\left| x_i - y_i \right|)$$
$$= \lim_{p \to \infty} \left(\sum_{i=1}^{n} \left| x_i - y_i \right|^p \right)^{\frac{1}{p}} \qquad (17)$$

In the 2-dimensional plane, this metric can be thought of the minimum distance across a 2 dimensional lattice, when the 8 adjacent positions (the Moore neighbourhood) are used to determine the route taken. In this analogy, the Manhattan distance would represent the use of the von Neumann neighbourhood (the 4 adjacent cells).

Normalisation for Minkowski Metrics

As the Minkowski metrics are not scale invariant, normalisation is required before analysis in order to ensure there is no bias placed upon individual variables. In some cases, this may be desirable;

such as adding a cost to an attribute due to high false-positive. However, determining variable weights is outside the scope of this analysis.

The issue presented to the Minkowski metrics is from the differing scale of the multivariate attributes. As such, each individual attribute must be re-scaled between pre-defined values. This can be performed by applying a linear rescaling of the values known as min-max normalisation (Jain & Bhandare, 2011). This is done on a per-variable basis as follows:

$$x_i^{'} =$$
$$\left(\left(\frac{x_i - X_{min}}{X_{max} - X_{min}} \right) * \left(MAX - MIN \right) + MIN \right) \qquad (18)$$

where x_i represents the current value to be normalised, X_{min} represents the minimum value of the variable and X_{max} represents the maximum value of the variable, MAX represents the chosen new maximum value and MIN represents the chosen new minimal value. Typically, a range of 0 to 1 is sought. However changing the maximum value will allow relatively weight to be assigned to specific variables if required.

Other techniques, such as Z-score normalisation (zero-mean normalisation) are available to rescale values. In this case, the attribute value is normalised by:

$$x^{'}_i = \frac{x_i - X_\mu}{X_\sigma} \qquad (19)$$

where μ represents the attribute sample mean of and σ represents sample standard deviation.

Penrose Distance

The Penrose distance (Penrose, 1954) is an extension to the Minkowski distance metrics in that the variance of the attributes is taken into account in the calculation, thus, making the metric scale invariant. As such, min-max normalisation or Z-score normalisation is not required before employing this metric for analysis. The Penrose distance is defined by Manly (2005) as:

$$P(x) = \sum_{i=1}^{n} \left[\frac{(X - \mu)^2}{n \cdot V_i} \right] \tag{20}$$

In this case, ¼ represents the $n-$dimensional vector of attribute means, V_i represents the variance of the attribute i and x_i represents the ith (of n) attribute of x. Similarly, lower values of P represent a higher similarity to the mean vector, whereas increased values represent a higher dissimilarity to the mean vector. In the case presented in this book chapter, the mean vectors will be represent normal operational behaviour of both the wind turbine gearbox and bearings.

Setting the multivariate centres is done by utilising an independent set of historical data for determining mean attributes. However, if no historical data, a domain expert can manually define these values based upon previous experience. It should be noted that the mean is not a robust measure of central tendency (Wilcox, 2012). It is preferable in all cases to utilise the median rather than the mean to set these points, and this should be strictly adhered to when limited data is available. It should also be noted that this technique performs poorly when attributes are highly correlated as covariance is not employed in the analysis.

The Traditional Mahalanobis Distance

The Mahalanobis distance (Mahalanobis, 1936) further extends the Penrose metric by incorporating the covariance between attributes. This additional information can be utilised to enhance the quality of the metric employed, and allows varying facts regarding the distribution of the metric value to be ascertained.

The Mahalanobis is defined by De Maesschalck et al. (2000) as:

$$MD(x_i) = \sqrt{(x - \mu)^T \, \pounds^{-1}(x - \mu)} \tag{21}$$

where x is the n-dimensional vector of observations, μ in the $n-$dimensional vector of centres and $\pounds$ represents the sample covariance matrix, which is defined as a $n \times n$ matrix S with values:

$$S_{ij} = \frac{1}{N-1} \sum_{i=1}^{N} (x_{ij} - \overline{x}_k)(x_{ik} - \overline{x}_k) \tag{22}$$

where $\overline{x}$ represents the sample mean, defined as:

$$\overline{x} = \frac{1}{N} \sum_{i=1}^{N} x_i \tag{23}$$

In the cases that the covariance matrix is equal to the identity matrix, the Mahalanobis distance is simply the Euclidean distance. However, it is unlikely that this would occur in practice. Similarly, if the covariance matrix $\pounds$ is diagonal (i.e. all entries outside the top-left to bottom-right diagonal are zero), this distance becomes a normalised Euclidean distance.

It should be worth noting that the characteristics of the distribution of the Mahalanobis value are well understood. There are three possible distributions of the Mahalanobis distance depending upon how centres and covariance are determined, and if the data used to determine these values are required as observations (Hardin & Rocke, 2005). The distribution of the Mahalanobis distance can either be a Chi-square distribution, a Beta distribution, or a Fisher distribution, with varying degrees of freedom and can be determined as follows:

If the true population mean and covariance are known, the Mahalanobis has a Chi-square distribution with p degrees of freedom (where p represents the dimensionality of the data):

$$MD^2 \sim \varsigma_p^2 \qquad (24)$$

If the estimated mean and covariance are utilised, and the observations used to estimate these are being calculated for the MD value, there is a Beta distribution with:

$$\frac{n(MD^2)}{(n-1)^2} \sim {}_2\left(\frac{p}{2}, \frac{(n-p-1)}{2}\right) \qquad (25)$$

In the case that an independent dataset is utilised to derive the estimated attribute means and covariance, it is the case that we have a $F-$ distribution with the characteristics:

$$\left(\frac{nMD^2(n-p)}{p(n-1)(n-2)}\right) \sim F(p, n-p) \qquad (26)$$

A Robust Mahalanobis Distance

It should be noted that the mean and covariance employed in the traditional Mahalanobis distance are highly sensitive to noise and as such, have low breakdown points (Hardin & Rocke, 2005). As such, robust techniques should be utilised to ensure that contamination of data does not significantly affect the analysis performed. One potential way of removing these sensitive elements is to employ the minimum covariance determinant (MCD) as a robust estimation of the attribute covariance (Rousseeuw & Leroy, 1987). This algorithm determines a robust subset of points from which to determine the multivariate vector centres and at-

tribute covariance. As such, this robust derivation of the Mahalanobis distance can be defined as:

$$\mathrm{RMD}_i = \sqrt{\left[x_i - \hat{\mu}\right]^T \pounds_\delta^{'-1} (x_i - \hat{\mu})} \qquad (27)$$

where $\pounds'_\delta$ represents the robust estimation of covariance based upon the MCD utilising an independent set of data δ, and μ represents the robust multivariate vector of centres based upon the set of points used to determine the covariance.

This is required due to the effects of masking and swamping (Rousseeuw & Driessen, 1999). Masking is when centres are moved away from normal (inlier) data, closer to degraded (outlier) behaviour; making degraded behaviour harder to identify. Swamping is when centres are moved away from this normal data, meaning that normal operational behaviour is quantified closer to degraded behaviour, potentially causing normal data to be regarded as degraded behaviour. As such, utilising a robust method to determine the attribute centres and covariance is essential so that this does not happen. As in this case the MCD algorithm utilises a subset of the dataset to determine the attribute centres and covariance, we have a $F-$ distribution with the characteristics:

$$\frac{c(m-p+1)}{pm} RMD_{\pounds'}^2(X_i, \overline{X'}) \sim F_{p,m-p+1} \qquad (28)$$

where $\overline{X}'$ and $\pounds'$ are the MCD mean and covariance (respectively). The proof of which can be followed in Hardin & Rocke (2005). However, this requires the use of two constants – c and m – which must be estimated. The techniques used to determine these parameters through Monte-Carlo simulation are detailed in Hardin & Rocke (2005).

This is required so that statistical properties of the distribution can be employed to infer additional information regarding the state of the system based upon the RMD_i value. Once the distribution parameters are known, we can determine statistically sound thresholds for the RMD_i value based upon the p value of the observation. By bounding the result to the associated p value, we obtain a finite range of values (from 0 to 1). The $1 - p$ value represents the likelihood that this observation is significantly different (at a given p level) than the data used to robustly determine attribute covariance and centres. As such, repeated instances of a 99.9% ($p = .001$) likelihood, would strongly suggest that the current operational behaviour was significantly dissimilar to the normal operational behaviour as defined by the multivariate centres and robustly determined centres.

This provides a means to automatically classify the data, identify leverage points, quantify behavioural characteristics and also (in our case studies) retrospectively determine the relative condition of the wind turbine gearbox and bearing.

Multivariate Normality Testing

For the result found in Hardin & Rocke (2005) to hold, the assumption of multivariate normality is required in order to derive the $F -$ disitribution. As such the underlying model must be multivariate normal in order for the levels derived from the distribution to hold. Some literature does not worry about normality for large sample size ($n > 1000$) due to the central limit theorem (Anderson & Amemiya, 1988, Amemiya & Anderson, 1990). However, I would recommend the analysis is performed regardless, not only to assist in understanding the underlying properties of the data, but also as data may not be normal regardless of sample size.

There are many ways to check for multivariate normality. One example is given by Holgersson (2006). Typically, it is necessary to ensure univariate normality of each of the underlying model variables individually. This can be done by any of the traditional methods (Q-Q plots, Shapiro-Wilk statistic, histogram, or Kolmogorov-Smirnov statistic).

Once this has been established, or the data transformed so that this is held, we can continue. As univariate normality of all underlying variables does not imply or guarantee multivariate normality, we often move the analysis into the bivariate domain. All linear combinations of multivariate normal attributes are normal, thus, all bivariate distribution must be bivariate normal. This can easily be checked with a scatter plot with shape and scatter estimates. Although this step is not essential, it is often useful in practice. Once this has been performed, multivariate normality tests can be performed. Typically, Mardias' Skewness and Kurtosis (Mardia, 1970), Henze-Zirklers' T statistic (Henze & Zirkler, 1990) and Roystons' H statistic (Royston, 1983) can be used. Kollo (2008) discusses some potential issues with Mardias' Skewness and Kurtosis, and I would refer interested readers to this work for details. The code detailing the use of the above 4 statistics is given in Appendix 1.

For readers interesting in multivariate normality analysis, attention should be drawn to the multivariate BHEP test statistic (discussed by Henze & Wagner, 1997) which is affine invariant, computationally tractable for any sample size and dimensionality, consistent against each fixed non-normal alternative distribution and also has asymptotic power against local alternatives of order $n^{-1/2}$ (Henze & Wagner, 1997). Although this is not currently available in the R statistics library packages, interested readers may wish to refer this statistic whilst performing multivariate normality analysis.

CASE STUDY - NASA BEARING DATA

For the analysis on already pre-processed, with each file being condensed to a 4-tuple as described in the bearing degradation model section. Code for this is available in Appendix 2.

Experiment 1

In this experiment, all 3 bearings are employed for the analysis. Of these bearings, 2 do not degrade over the length of the data collection (Bearing 2 and 3), whereas the final bearing (Bearing 1) does. All 3 bearings are used to determine the multivariate centres: this is done as in practical applications; we may not know the condition of the bearings as data is collected and it is possible that failure data is contaminating the normal operational behaviour. Code to run this experiment is given in Appendix 3.

Experiment 2

In this experiment, we use a bearing (bearing 2) which was known to not degrade substantially over the period to set the multivariate centres of the data. The metrics are then validated on an independent bearing which is known to have degraded (Bearing 1). As failure data is often unavailable in practice, this experiment examines the case when only known normal operational behaviour data is utilised (such as after maintenance, repair or servicing), and determines if it is possible to develop strong techniques to identify artefacts within the data. Code to run this experiment is given in Appendix 4.

Experiment 3

In this experiment, data from a single bearing is employed for the full analysis; bearing 1. As this bearing failed during the data collection process, the experiment is designed to detail the robust-

ness of each metric. Stronger metrics will be less influenced by the degradation process and as such, should still provide strong encapsulation of the operational behaviour without requiring additional data (such as normal operational behaviour), and without artificially adding noise to the metric. Code to run this experiment is given in Appendix 5.

the NASA bearing data (Lee et al., 2007), 3 experiments are performed in order to demonstrate the robustness to noise and quantity of data available. These experiments are detailed below.

The experiments were carried out on dataset 2 with bearings 1, 2 and 3. Bearings 2 and 3 did not fail over the data collection period, whereas bearing 1 did. This knowledge allows us to design the experiments with varying contamination to assess various aspects of the multivariate metrics. Data is assumed to be

Results

The results of each of the experiments are detailed below. For convenience, the first 650 of 984 observations are removed from the time series as in each case they contribute little to the analysis performed. The three Minkowski distances are noisy in comparison to the Penrose, Mahalanobis and robust Mahalanobis distances. We found that, in these cases, the Minkowski distances are dominated by noise and it is difficult to use the signal to perform classification. This can be seen by comparing Figures 1 (a, b and c) and Figure 2 (a, b and c): the three Minkowski metrics are highly sensitive to the data used to determine the multivariate vector centres.

As can be seen in Figure 1 (representing experiment 1), the three Minkowski distances (1(a), 1(b) and 1(c)) have a large quantity of noise in both the degraded bearing (bearing 1, black line), and also in the bearing which did not fail (bearing 2, grey line). The metrics which incorporated attribute variance and covariance were much more robust to this: the Penrose, Mahalanobis and robust Mahalanobis values for the 2nd bearing remaining

Figure 1. Metric values displayed as a time series, showing failed (black) and healthy (grey) bearings

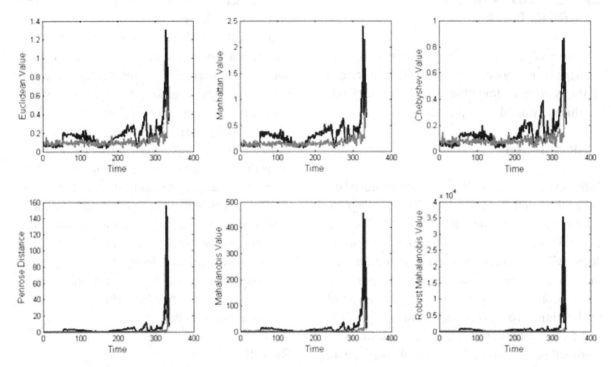

Figure 2. Metrics validated on a failed (black) and healthy (grey) bearing, with another healthy bearing used to define normality

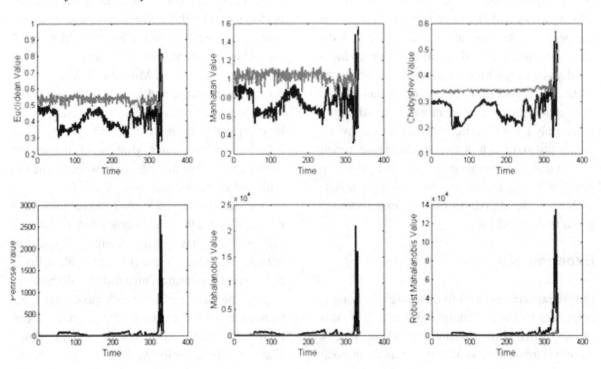

stable in comparison to the failed bearing. As three bearings were used to set the multivariate centres, this is to be expected. With more data available, Minkowski metrics will become more reliable; however, they will still be sensitive to slight deviations, resulting in noise in the signal.

Figure 2 (representing experiment 2) shows the sensitivity of the Minkowski distances to setting the multivariate vector centres. In this case, each of the 3 Minkowski distances show the bearing which did not fail (the grey line) as having more damage than the failed bearing (black line). This is unacceptable and if used for classification would cause a substantial number of false-positive classification errors. Again, the normal bearing is relatively stable when exposed to the 3 metrics which incorporate attribute variance and covariance.

Finally, Figure 3 (representing experiment 3) shows the analysis performed on a single bearing; bearing 1 (the failed bearing). This was used to set the multivariate vector centres and also used

for the analysis. Again, the Minkowski distances have more noise than the other metrics, and also do not have the sensitivity present in the other metrics. In this case, the noise in the Chebyshev metric is interesting. After time step 100, strong signals are seen which may provide information as to when damage occurred as soon after this happens, the values rise and the bearing fails.

In addition to looking at the time series, derivation of the $F-$distribution was performed through Monte-Carlo simulation as given in Hardin & Rocke (2005). A $F_{(4,108)}$ distribution was created, with critical values of <3.498 ($\alpha > .01$) representing normal operational behaviour, < 4.99 ($\alpha > .001$) representing possible degradation and values ≥ 4.99 ($\alpha \leq .001$) representing damage to the bearing. As such, Table 1 shows the classification for each of these labels for two of the bearings during experiment 1.

As can be seen in Table 1, there are significantly more instances of damage occurring in bearing 1

Figure 3. Metrics showing bearing failure over time with only failure data used to determine normality

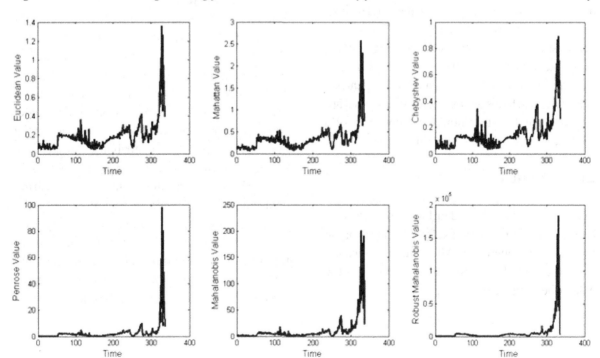

Table 1. Class distribution of labelled bearing data through robust Mahalanobis metric

	Bearing 1	Bearing 2
Normal	646 (65.65%)	913 (92.78%)
Potential Damage	8 (0.81%)	8 (0.81%)
Damage	330 (33.54%)	63 (6.41%)
Total	984 (100%)	984 (100%)

than bearing 2. This is to be expected given the failure which occurred. Bearing 2 operates in normal behaviour over 92% of the time; this is also expected as normal operational behaviour of the bearing accounts for the majority of the data collection period. The data is now in a format which traditional data mining techniques can be employed for further analysis.

CASE STUDY – WIND TURBINE GEARBOX

For the analysis of the wind turbine gearbox, a bivariate model was created as in the wind turbine gearbox degradation model section. In order to demonstrate the consistency of the metrics, the 3 experiments performed on the NASA bearing data were also performed on the wind turbine gearbox data. This also helps demonstrate the universal applicability of these techniques to many real-world applications across many domains.

Experiment 1

In this experiment, 3 wind turbines are employed for the analysis. Of these, 1 suffered a catastrophic failure during operation. All 3 wind turbines are used to define the multivariate centres as in the NASA bearing experiment 1.

Experiment 2

In this experiment, 1 wind turbine (which did not fail over the period) was employed to set the multivariate centres of the data. The metrics are then validated on the independent wind turbine which catastrophically failed. As failure data is often unavailable in practice, this experiment demonstrates the robustness of the approaches under real world conditions of data availability.

Experiment 3

Finally, in the last experiment, only 1 wind turbine is analysed. The gearbox of this wind turbine failed during operation. Metric centre points, variance and covariance should not be influenced by degradation which will be inherently present in the data, and should simultaneously provide strong encapsulation of the operational behaviour. This experiment looks to explore this.

Results

To enhance the readability of Figures 4 – 6, the data has been averaged on a daily basis. This reduces 126,864 data points per wind turbine to the 881 days during the data collection period. The results of this case study are similar to those of the NASA bearing data; however, particular attention should be paid to the Penrose distance. The model employed was selected in this instance due to the high covariance between attributes. As such, the Penrose distance performs relatively poorly in comparison to the results attained on the bearing dataset. As can be seen in Figure 4, all of the signals are noisier than those of the bearing data. This is due to many factors, such as: the aggregation of the data, the transient states of the wind turbine and the non-stationary nature of signals the underlying model attempts to encapsulate.

Figure 4. Metric values displayed as a time series, showing failed (black) and healthy (grey) gearboxes when normality is defined by data taken from 3 gearboxes

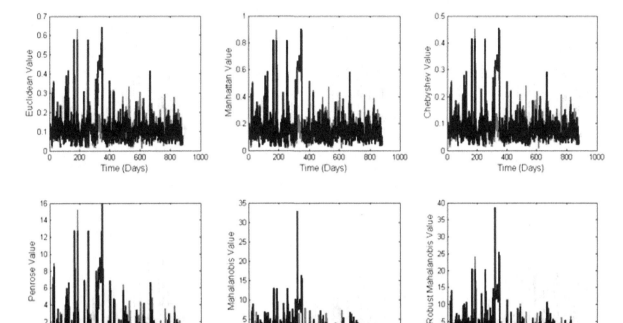

The noise in the Penrose distance is interesting; there are instances of the healthy gearbox being deemed further from normal than the damaged gearbox. This is an artefact of the redundancy caused by high attribute covariance. The Mahalanobis and robust Mahalanobis figures are similar, but it can be seen that the robust Mahalanobis metric is more sensitive to variations than its traditional counterpart.

Figure 5 provides the clearest signature of the operational behaviour through the Mahalanobis distance. The robust Mahalanobis value has more noise than the original; this is due to data from a single wind turbine being used to set the multivariate centres. If this turbine had its own operational characteristics or was subject to differing external conditions, this would be encapsulated in the metric and explain this phenomena. As such, it is always beneficial to include in the data used to determine the multivariate vector centres the largest range of operational conditions available.

Figure 6 shows similar characteristics to Figure 2, however, the increased sensitivity is more apparent once again in the robust Mahalanobis distance. Whilst the Penrose distance does look promising, due to the issues it encountered during experiment 1, the values generated should undergo further scrutiny, with analysis of another wind turbine added to provide context.

In order to derive meaningful data labels from these values, the $F-$ distribution based upon the robust Mahalanobis value was again created. Monte-Carlo simulation provided the parameters c and m for determining the necessary parameters. A $F_{(2,102)}$ distribution was derived based upon the Monte-Carlo simulation. As such, normal operational behaviour was assessed as being below the 4.81 ($\alpha > .01$) threshold, with damage occurring above the 7.40 ($\alpha \leq .001$) threshold. Intermediate values between these were deemed as "light damage" to the bearing.

Figure 5. Metrics validated on a failed (black) and healthy (grey) gearbox, with normality defined by an independent gearbox (which didn't fail)

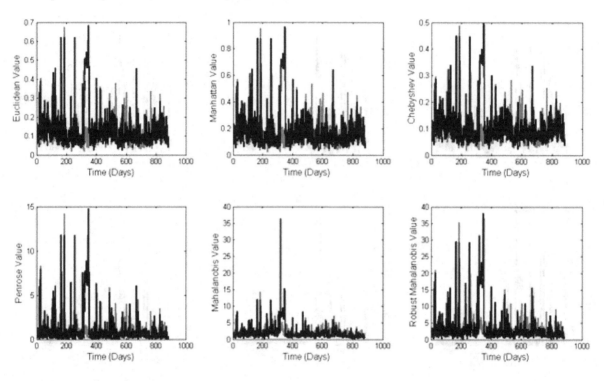

Figure 6. Gearbox failure over time with only the failed gearbox data used to determine normality

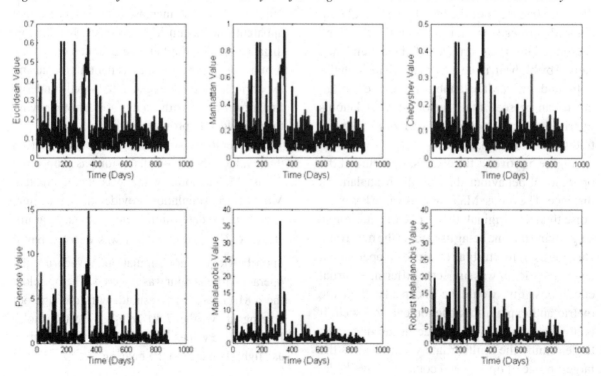

As can be seen in Table 2, the metric deemed the wind turbine gearbox to be operating under normal operational conditions for a majority of the time. In this case, wind turbine 2 represents the wind turbine gearbox which suffered the catastrophic failure. Furthermore, as can be observed in Table 2, this preliminary analysis and labelling can be used to create meta-data. In this case, simply knowing that wind turbine 2 is regarded as damaged twice as often as wind turbine 1 enables further analysis to be performed to determine the cause of this. This can be useful if the underlying data mining task aims to understand certain behavioural aspects of the system (such as gearbox degradation, system memory usage etc.)

As can be seen consistently through Figures 1 through 6, there is high correlation between the six metrics in many cases. For the Minkowski distances, there was high correlation ($r > .9$) between each of the three metrics for each of the 6 experiments. The benefits of utilising the Minkowski metrics are in the ease of the implementation and also setting of the multivariate centres. It is straight forward to use expert knowledge to determine a multivariate vector of centres, should historical data be unavailable or limited. For instance, in the case of the bearing, skewness should be close to zero for a symmetrical distribution and kurtosis should be close to 3 for a Mesokurtic distribution, and as such, these values can be used to fix the multivariate centres quantifying normal operational behaviour. However,

these metrics are sensitive to noise, require normalisation and do not account for attribute correlation or covariance. The Penrose metric provides a stronger measure than the Minkowski metrics as it is much more sensitive to deviations in the attributes. However, usage of this metric in the literature is very weak, and highly correlated variables do not perform well as covariance is not considered. As such, some developed models are unsuited for this metric. The Mahalanobis metric does take covariance into account, and sensitivity of the metric is increased substantially over the Penrose metric as a result. As the statistical underpinnings of the Mahalanobis metric are well understood, this should typically be the starting point when using these techniques for rapid labelling of data. Although the metric is more computationally complex than the other techniques, it is computationally tractable for all practical applications. However, although determining multivariate centres is possible, accurately determining attribute covariance may not be feasible in practice. The robust Mahalanobis metric is the recommended choice for rapid labelling of data due to strong statistical underpinning, robustness and well established algorithms for the computation. Whilst it is significantly more computationally intensive (especially deriving distribution parameters), the most sensitive and statistically sound metric is found. These benefits and drawbacks are summarised in Table 3.

FUTURE RESEARCH DIRECTION

Future research into these techniques aims to focus on utilising other statistical measures, such as cosine similarity, Pearson's' correlation similarity and the Bray Curtis dissimilarity statistic along with other distance measure (such as the Canberra distance) to assess their statistical properties to allow for rapid data labelling. Future work also

Table 2. Class distribution of labelled wind turbine gearbox data through robust Mahalanobis metric

	Wind turbine 1	Wind turbine 2
Normal	862 (97.72%)	827 (93.78%)
Potential Damage	11 (1.25%)	36 (4.08%)
Damage	9 (1.03%)	19 (2.14%)
Total	882 (100%)	882 (100%)

Table 3. Benefits and drawbacks of the six presented metrics

	Benefits	Drawback
Euclidean	Readily available, easy to determine attribute centres	Requires data normalisation, sensitive to noise
Manhattan	Easy to implement, can be used in real-time due to simplicity	Requires data normalisation, also sensitive to noise
Minkowski	Useful when vectors represent many forms of degradation	Not intuitive; only uses maximal difference of any attributes
Penrose	Takes into account attribute variance	Poor performance when attributes are correlated highly
Mahalanobis	Takes into account attribute covariance	Covariance matrix is sensitive to data contamination
Robust Mahalanobis	Robust, Strong statistical underpinning	More computationally intensive, requires multivariate normality

aims to look to at the MCD algorithm, in order to assess the subset utilised to determine covariance. Various algorithms are available for this, employing different heuristics; as such, quantifying the trade-off between these algorithms would be interesting to observe. Similarly, other robust techniques for determining attribute covariance, such as the minimum volume ellipsoid (MVE) and M or S estimators exist but a comparative evaluation for the purposes of rapid labelling of data to enable data mining has yet to be undertaken in the literature.

CONCLUSION

Throughout this book chapter, an emphasis has been placed on the practical application of distance metrics for the rapid labelling of data for the purposes of applying traditional data mining algorithms. Two case studies have been presented, with 6 different multivariate distance metrics compared in each analysis.

Three Minkowski-form distance metrics, (the Euclidean, Manhattan and Chebyshev distances), along with the Penrose distance, Mahalanobis distance and a robust derivation of the Mahalanobis distance were compared. In each case, the

Minkowski metrics were found to be highly erratic and as such, contained substantial amounts of noise which could lead to potential misclassification when employed for data labelling. The Penrose distance performed better in the case studies, however, due to high attribute covariance when assessing the wind turbine gearboxes, various issues arose. The Mahalanobis distance performed well in both cases, however, is typically not suitable in practice due to the high levels of contamination in real world data which manipulates the sample covariance matrix causing swamping and masking to occur.

As such, it is recommended that a robust estimation of the attribute covariance is employed in conjunction with the Mahalanobis distance. Due to the nature of the minimum covariance determinant algorithm and the fast implementations which are freely available, this technique is currently recommended, along with Monte-Carlo estimation of the F − distribution parameters.

Analysis was performed on freely available open-source data, using the open-source software 'R'. Code has been attached in the appendices assist the reader with following the techniques presented.

REFERENCES

Amemiya, Y., & Anderson, T. W. (1990). Asymptotic chi-square tests for a large class of factor analysis models. *Annals of Statistics*, *3*, 1453–1463. doi:10.1214/aos/1176347760

Anderson, T. W., & Amemiya, Y. (1988). The asymptotic normal distribution of estimates in factor analysis under general conditions. *Annals of Statistics*, *16*, 759–771. doi:10.1214/aos/1176350834

Baillie, D. C., & Mathew, J. (1996). A comparison of autoregressive modeling techniques for fault diagnosis of rolling element bearings. *Mechanical Systems and Signal Processing*, *10*(1), 1–17. doi:10.1006/mssp.1996.0001

Batista, G. E., Prati, R. C., & Monard, M. C. (2004). A study of the behavior of several methods for balancing machine learning training data. *ACM Special Interest Group on Knowledge Discovery and Data Mining*, *6*(1), 20–29.

Baydar, N., Chen, Q., Ball, A., & Kruger, U. (2001). Detection of incipient tooth defect in helical gears using multivariate statistics. *Mechanical Systems and Signal Processing*, *15*(2), 303–321. doi:10.1006/mssp.2000.1315

Blankenship, G., & Singh, R. (1995). Analytical solution for modulation sidebands associated with a class of mechanical oscillators. *Journal of Sound and Vibration*, *179*(1), 13–36. doi:10.1006/jsvi.1995.0002

Caesarendra, W., Widodo, A., & Yang, B. S. (2010). Application of relevance vector machine and logistic regression for machine degradation assessment. *Mechanical Systems and Signal Processing*, *24*(4), 1161–1171. doi:10.1016/j.ymssp.2009.10.011

Chawla, N. V., Hall, L. O., Bowyer, K. W., & Kegelmeyer, W. P. (2002). SMOTE: Synthetic Minority Oversampling Technique. *Journal of Artificial Intelligence Research*, *16*, 321–357.

Chen, B., Qiu, Y., Feng, Y., Tavner, P., & Song, W. (2011). Wind turbine scada alarm pattern recognition. In *Proceedings of the IET Conference on Renewable Power Generation*. IET Press.

Crabtree, C.J. (2010). *Survey of Commercially Available Condition Monitoring Systems for Wind Turbines*. SuperGen Wind Techical report.

Cramer, H. (1946). *Mathematical models of statistics*. Princeton University Press.

Dalpiaz, G., Rivola, A., & Rubini, R. (2000). Effectiveness and sensitivity of vibration processing techniques for local fault detection in gears. *Mechanical Systems and Signal Processing*, *14*(3), 387–412. doi:10.1006/mssp.1999.1294

De Maesschalck, R., Jouan-Rimbaud, D., & Massart, D. L. (2000). The mahalanobis distance. *Chemometrics and Intelligent Laboratory Systems*, *50*(1), 1–18. doi:10.1016/S0169-7439(99)00047-7

Djurdjanovic, D., Lee, J., & Ni, J. (2003). Watchdog agentaninfotronics-based prognostics approach for product performance degradation assessment and prediction. *Advanced Engineering Informatics*, *17*(3), 109–125. doi:10.1016/j.aei.2004.07.005

Feng, Y., Qiu, Y., Crabtree, C., Long, H., & Tavner, P. (2011). Use of SCADA and CMS signals for failure detection and diagnosis of a wind turbine gearbox. In *Proceedings of the Conference of the European Wind Energy Association*. Brussels, Belgium: European Wind Energy Association.

Feng, Y., Qiu, Y., Crabtree, C., Long, H., & Tavner, P. (2012). Monitoring wind turbine gearboxes. *Wind Energy (Chichester, England)*, *16*(5), 728–740. doi:10.1002/we.1521

Godwin, J. L., Matthew, P., & Watson, C. (2013). Classification and detection of electrical control system faults through SCADA data analysis. *Chemical Engineering Transactions*, *33*(1), 985–991.

Godwin, J. L., & Matthews, P. (2013). Prognosis of wind turbine gearbox failures by utilising robust multivariate statistical techniques. In *Proceedings of the IEEE Conference on Prognosis and Health Management (PHM)*. Gaithersburg, VA: IEEE.

Hameed, Z., Hong, Y., Cho, Y., Ahn, S., & Song, C. (2009). Condition monitoring and fault detection of windturbines and related algorithms: A review. *Renewable & Sustainable Energy Reviews, 13*(1), 1–39. doi:10.1016/j.rser.2007.05.008

Hardin, J., & Rocke, D. M. (2005). The distribution of robust distances. *Journal of Computational and Graphical Statistics, 14*(4), 928–946. doi:10.1198/106186005X77685

Hart, P. E. (1968). The Condensed Nearest Neighbor Rule. *IEEE Transactions on Information Theory, 14*, 515–516. doi:10.1109/TIT.1968.1054155

Hatch, C. (2004). Improved wind turbine condition monitoring using acceleration enveloping. GE Energy. *Journal of Electrical Systems, 3*(1), 26–38.

Heng, A., Tan, A. C., Mathew, J., Montgomery, N., Banjevic, D., & Jardine, A. K. (2009). Intelligent condition-based prediction of machinery reliability. *Mechanical Systems and Signal Processing, 23*(5), 1600–1614. doi:10.1016/j.ymssp.2008.12.006

Henze, N., & Wagner, T. (1997). A new approach to the BHEP tests for multivariate normality. *Journal of Multivariate Analysis, 62*(1), 1–23. doi:10.1006/jmva.1997.1684

Henze, N., & Zirkler, B. (1990). A class of invariant consistent tests for multivariate normality. *Communications in Statistics Theory and Methods, 19*(10), 3595–3617. doi:10.1080/03610929008830400

Holgersson, H. E. T. (2006). A graphical method for assessing multivariate normality. *Computational Statistics, 21*(1), 141–149. doi:10.1007/s00180-006-0256-9

Hu, S., Liang, Y., Ma, L., & He, Y. (2009). MS-MOTE: improving classification performance when training data is imbalanced. *Proceedings of Computer Science and Engineering, 2*, 13–17.

Huang, Q., Jiang, D., Hong, L., & Ding, Y. (2008). Application of wavelet neural networks on vibration fault diagnosis for wind turbine gearbox. In *Advances in Neural Networks*. Springer. doi:10.1007/978-3-540-87734-9_36

Iung, B., Levrat, E., Marquez, A. C., & Erbe, H. (2009). Conceptual framework for e-maintenance: Illustration by e-maintenance technologies and platforms. *Annual Reviews in Control, 33*(2), 220–229. doi:10.1016/j.arcontrol.2009.05.005

Jain, Y. K., & Bhandare, S. K. (2011). Min Max Normalization Based Data Perturbation Method for Privacy Protection. *International Journal of Computer & Communication Technology, 2*(8), 45–50.

Jardine, A. K., Lin, D., & Banjevic, D. (2006). A review on machinery diagnostics and prognostics implementing condition-based maintenance. *Mechanical Systems and Signal Processing, 20*(7), 1483–1510. doi:10.1016/j.ymssp.2005.09.012

Kollo, T. (2008). Multivariate skewness and kurtosis measures with an application in ICA. *Journal of Multivariate Analysis, 99*(10), 2328–2338. doi:10.1016/j.jmva.2008.02.033

Kusiak, A., & Li, W. (2011). The prediction and diagnosis of wind turbine faults. *Renewable Energy, 36*(1), 16–23. doi:10.1016/j.renene.2010.05.014

Kusiak, A., & Verma, A. (2011). A data-driven approach for monitoring blade pitch faults in wind turbines. *IEEE Transactions on Sustainable Energy, 2*(1), 87–96.

Kusiak, A., & Verma, A. (2013). Monitoring Wind Farms With Performance Curves. *IEEE Transactions on Sustainable Energy*, *4*(1), 192–199. doi:10.1109/TSTE.2012.2212470

Lee, J., Qiu, H., Yu, G., Lin, J., & Rexnord Technical Services. (2007). 'Bearing Data Set', IMS, University of Cincinnati. *NASA Ames Prognostics Data Repository*. NASA Ames.

Leger, J., Iung, B., Beca, A. F. D., & Pinoteau, J. (1999). An innovative approach for new distributed maintenance system: Application to hydro power plants of the remafex project. *Computers in Industry*, *38*(2), 131–148. doi:10.1016/S0166-3615(98)00114-6

Lin, J., & Zuo, M. (2003). Gearbox fault diagnosis using adaptive wavelet filter. *Mechanical Systems and Signal Processing*, *17*(6), 1259–1269. doi:10.1006/mssp.2002.1507

Liu, Z., Yin, X., Zhang, Z., Chen, D., & Chen, W. (2004). Online rotor mixed fault diagnosis way based on spectrum analysis of instantaneous power in squirrel cage induction motors. *IEEE Transactions on Energy Conversion*, *19*(3), 485–490. doi:10.1109/TEC.2004.832052

Lu, B., Li, Y., Wu, X., & Yang, Z. (2009). A review of recent advances in wind turbine condition monitoring and fault diagnosis. In *Proceedings of Power Electronics and Machines in Wind Applications*. IEEE. doi:10.1109/PEMWA.2009.5208325

Mahalanobis, P. C. (1936). On the generalized distance in statistics. *Proceedings of the National Institute of Sciences (Calcutta)*, *2*, 49–55.

Manly, B. F. J. (2005). *Multivariate statistical methods: a primer* (3rd ed.). Chapman and Hall/CRC Press.

Marais, K. B., & Saleh, J. H. (2009). Beyond its cost, the value of maintenance: An analytical framework for capturing its net present value. *Reliability Engineering & System Safety*, *94*(2), 644–657. doi:10.1016/j.ress.2008.07.004

Marble, S., & Morton, B. P. (2006). Predicting the remaining life of propulsion system bearings. In *Proceedings of the IEEE Aerospace Conference*. IEEE.

Mardia, K. V. (1970). Measures of multivariate skewness and kurtosis with applications. *Biometrika*, *57*(3), 519–530. doi:10.1093/biomet/57.3.519

McDonald, G. L., Zhao, Q., & Zuo, M. J. (2012). Maximum correlated Kurtosis deconvolution and application on gear tooth chip fault detection. *Mechanical Systems and Signal Processing*, *33*, 237–255. doi:10.1016/j.ymssp.2012.06.010

Mohanty, A., & Kar, C. (2006). Fault detection in a multistage gearbox by demodulation of motor current waveform. *IEEE Transactions on Industrial Electronics*, *53*(4), 1285–1297. doi:10.1109/TIE.2006.878303

Moore, W., & Starr, A. (2006). An intelligent maintenance system for continuous cost-based prioritisation of maintenance activities. *Computers in Industry*, *57*(6), 595–606. doi:10.1016/j.compind.2006.02.008

Muller, A., Marquez, A. C., & Iung, B. (2008). On the concept of e-maintenance: Review and current research. *Reliability Engineering & System Safety*, *93*(8), 1165–1187. doi:10.1016/j.ress.2007.08.006

Niu, G., Yang, B.-S., & Pecht, M. (2010). Development of an optimized condition-based maintenance system by data fusion and reliability-centered maintenance. *Reliability Engineering & System Safety*, *95*(7), 786–796. doi:10.1016/j.ress.2010.02.016

Oppenheimer, C. H., & Loparo, K. A. (2002). Physically based diagnosis and prognosis of cracked rotor shafts. In *Component and Systems Diagnostics, Prognostics, and Health Management II* (Vol. 4733). Academic Press. doi:10.1117/12.475502

Penrose, L. S. (1954). Distance, size and shape. *Annals of Eugenics*, *18*(4), 337. PMID:13149002

Rafiee, J., Rafiee, M., & Tse, P. (2010). Application of mother wavelet functions for automatic gear and bearing fault diagnosis. *Expert Systems with Applications, 37*(6), 4568–4579. doi:10.1016/j.eswa.2009.12.051

Randall, R. B., & Antoni, J. (2011). Rolling element bearing diagnostics—A tutorial. *Mechanical Systems and Signal Processing, 25*(2), 485–520. doi:10.1016/j.ymssp.2010.07.017

Rouseeuw, P. J., & Leroy, A. M. (1987). *Robust regression and outlier detection*. Wiley. doi:10.1002/0471725382

Rousseeuw, P. J., & Driessen, K. V. (1999). A fast algorithm for the minimum covariance determinant estimator. *Technometrics, 41*(3), 212–223. doi:10.1080/00401706.1999.10485670

Royston, J. P. (1983). Some techniques for assessing multivarate normality based on the shapiro-wilk W. *Applied Statistics, 32*(2), 121–133. doi:10.2307/2347291

Sainz, E., Llombart, E., & Guerrero, J. (2009). Robust filtering for the characterization of wind turbines: Improving its operation and maintenance. *Energy Conversion and Management, 50*(9), 2136–2147. doi:10.1016/j.enconman.2009.04.036

Samanta, B., & Al-Balushi, K. R. (2003). Artificial neural network based fault diagnostics of rolling element bearings using time-domain features. *Mechanical Systems and Signal Processing, 17*(2), 317–328. doi:10.1006/mssp.2001.1462

Siegel, D., Al-Atat, H., Shauche, V., Liao, L., Snyder, J., & Lee, J. (2012). Novel method for rolling element bearing health assessment—A tachometer-less synchronously averaged envelope feature extraction technique. *Mechanical Systems and Signal Processing, 29*, 362–376. doi:10.1016/j.ymssp.2012.01.003

Sohn, H., Worden, K., & Farrar, C. (2002). Statistical damage classification under changing environmental and operational conditions. *Journal of Intelligent Material Systems and Structures, 13*(9), 561–574. doi:10.1106/104538902030904

Soua, S., Van Lieshout, P., Perera, A., Gan, T. H., & Bridge, B. (2013). Determination of the combined vibrational and acoustic emission signature of a wind turbine gearbox and generator shaft in service as a pre-requisite for effective condition monitoring. *Renewable Energy, 51*, 175–181. doi:10.1016/j.renene.2012.07.004

Spoerre, J. (1997). Application of the cascade correlation algorithm (CCA) to bearing fault classification problems. *Computers in Industry, 32*(3), 295–304. doi:10.1016/S0166-3615(96)00080-2

Tian, Z. (2012). An artificial neural network method for remaining useful life prediction of equipment subject to condition monitoring. *Journal of Intelligent Manufacturing, 23*(2), 227–237. doi:10.1007/s10845-009-0356-9

Tian, Z., Wong, L., & Safaei, N. (2010). A neural network approach for remaining useful life prediction utilizing both failure and suspension histories. *Mechanical Systems and Signal Processing, 24*(5), 1542–1555. doi:10.1016/j.ymssp.2009.11.005

Tomek, I. (1976). Two Modifications of CNN. *IEEE Transactions on Systems Management and Communications, 6*, 769–772.

Verma, A., & Kusiak, A. (2011). Predictive Analysis of Wind Turbine Faults: A Data Mining Approach. In *Proceedings of the 2011 Industrial Engineering Research Conference*. Reno, NV: Academic Press.

Wang, W., Chen, J., Wu, X., & Wu, Z. (2001). The application of some non-linear methods in rotating machinery fault diagnosis. *Mechanical Systems and Signal Processing, 15*(4), 697–705. doi:10.1006/mssp.2000.1316

Wang, X., & Makis, V. (2009). Autoregressive model-basedgear shaft fault diagnosis using the Kolmogorov–Simonov test. *Journal of Sound and Vibration*, *327*(3), 413–423. doi:10.1016/j.jsv.2009.07.004

Widodo, A., & Yang, B. S. (2011). Machine health prognostics using survival probability and support vector machine. *Expert Systems with Applications*, *38*(7), 8430–8437. doi:10.1016/j.eswa.2011.01.038

Wilcox, R. R. (2012). *Introduction to robust estimation and hypothesis testing*. Academic Press.

Wu, S., & Clements-Croome, D. (2005). Preventive maintenance models with random maintenance quality. *Reliability Engineering & System Safety*, *90*(1), 99–105. doi:10.1016/j.ress.2005.03.012

WWEA. (2012). Quarterly bulletin. *World Wind Energy Association Bulletin*, *3*, 1–40.

Xia, X., & Chen, L. (2012). Fuzzy chaos method for evaluation of nonlinearly evolutionary process of rolling bearing performance. *Measurement*, *46*(3), 1349–1354. doi:10.1016/j.measurement.2012.11.003

Xu, R., & Wunsch, D. (2008). *Clustering* (Vol. 10). Wiley. doi:10.1002/9780470382776

Yang, S., Li, W., & Wang, C. (2008). The intelligent fault diagnosis of wind turbine gearbox based on artificial neural network. In *Proceedings of Condition Monitoring and Diagnosis*. IEEE.

Yang, W., Tavner, P. J., Crabtree, C. J., & Wilkinson, M. (2010). Cost-effective condition monitoring for wind turbines. *IEEE Transactions on Industrial Electronics*, *57*(1), 263–271. doi:10.1109/TIE.2009.2032202

Zaher, A. S. A. E., McArthur, S. D. J., Infield, D. G., & Patel, Y. (2009). Online wind turbine fault detection through automated SCADA data analysis. *Wind Energy (Chichester, England)*, *12*(6), 574–593. doi:10.1002/we.319

Zappalà, D., Tavner, P., Crabtree, C., & Sheng, S. (2013). Sideband Algorithm for Automatic Wind Turbine Gearbox Fault Detection and Diagnosis. In *Proceedings of the Conference of the European Wind Energy Association*. Vienna, Austria: European Wind Energy Association.

Zhang, D., Liu, W., Gong, X., & Jin, H. (2011). A novel improved SMOTE resampling algorithm based on fractal. *Journal of Computer Information Systems*, *7*(6), 2204–2211.

Zhang, Z., Verma, A., & Kusiak, A. (2012). Fault Analysis and Condition Monitoring of the Wind Turbine Gearbox. *IEEE Transactions on Energy Conversion*, *27*(2), 526–535. doi:10.1109/TEC.2012.2189887

ADDITIONAL READING

Bae, Y. H., Lee, S. H., Kim, H. C., Lee, B. R., Jang, J., & Lee, J. (2006). A real-time intelligent multiple fault diagnostic system. *International Journal of Advanced Manufacturing Technology*, *29*, 590–597. doi:10.1007/s00170-005-2614-0

Barata, J., Soares, C., Marseguerra, M., & Zio, E. (2002). Simulation modelling of repairable multi-component deteriorating systems for on condition maintenance optimisation. *Reliability Engineering & System Safety*, *76*(3), 255–264. doi:10.1016/S0951-8320(02)00017-0

Bartelmus, W., & Zimroz, R. (2009). A new feature for monitoring the condition of gearboxes in non-stationary operating conditions. *Mechanical Systems and Signal Processing*, *23*(5), 1528–1534. doi:10.1016/j.ymssp.2009.01.014

Caesarendra, W., Niu, G., & Yang, B.-S. (2010). Machine condition prognosis based on sequential monte carlo method. *Expert Systems with Applications*, *37*, 2412–2420. doi:10.1016/j.eswa.2009.07.014

Campos, J. (2009). Development in the application of ict in condition monitoring and maintenance. *Computers in Industry, 60*(1), 1–20. doi:10.1016/j.compind.2008.09.007

Derigent, W., Thomas, E., Levrat, E., & Iung, B. (2009). Opportunistic maintenance based on fuzzy modelling of component proximity. *CIRP Annals - Manufacturing Technology, 58 (1)*, pp. 29 - 32.

Elangovan, M., Devasenapati, S. B., Sakthivel, N., & Ramachandran, K. (2011). Evaluation of expert system for condition monitoring of a single point cutting tool using principle component analysis and decision tree algorithm. *Expert Systems with Applications, 38*(4), 4450–4459. doi:10.1016/j.eswa.2010.09.116

Garcia, M. C., Sanz-Bobi, M. A., & del Pico, J. (2006). Simap: Intelligent system for predictive maintenance: Application to the health condition monitoring of a windturbine gearbox. *Computers in Industry, 57*(6), 552–568. doi:10.1016/j.compind.2006.02.011

Gasperin, M., Juricic, D., Boskoski, P., & Vizintin, J. (2011). Model-based prognostics of gear health using stochastic dynamical models. *Mechanical Systems and Signal Processing, 25*(2), 537–548. doi:10.1016/j.ymssp.2010.07.003

Han, T., & Yang, B. S. (2006). Development of an e-maintenance system integrating advanced techniques. *Computers in Industry, 57*, 569–580. doi:10.1016/j.compind.2006.02.009

Heng, A., Zhang, S., Tan, A. C., & Mathew, J. (2009). Rotating machinery prognostics: State of the art, challenges and opportunities. *Mechanical Systems and Signal Processing, 23*(3), 724–739. doi:10.1016/j.ymssp.2008.06.009

Jacobs, F. R., Weston. (2007). Enterprise resource planning (ERP) - a brief history. *Journal of Operations Management, 25*(2), 357–363. doi:10.1016/j.jom.2006.11.005

Khashei, M., & Bijari, M. (2010). An artificial neural network (p,d,q) model for timeseries forecasting. *Expert Systems with Applications, 37*, 479–489. doi:10.1016/j.eswa.2009.05.044

Kim, K., Parthasarathy, G., Uluyol, O., Sheng, W. F. S., & Fleming, P. (2011). Use of scada data for failure detection in wind turbines. Vol. 11. *Presented at the 2011 Energy Sustainability Conference and Fuel Cell Conference*, 7-10 August 2011, 26 Washington, D.C: IEEE.

Komonen, K. (2002). A cost model of industrial maintenance for profitability analysis and benchmarking. *International Journal of Production Economics, 79*(1), 15–31. doi:10.1016/S0925-5273(00)00187-0

Lee, J. (2003). E-manufacturing - fundamental, tools, and transformation. *Robotics and Computer-integrated Manufacturing, 19*(6), 501–507. doi:10.1016/S0736-5845(03)00060-7

Lee, J., Ni, J., Djurdjanovic, D., Qiu, H., & Liao, H. (2006). Intelligent prognostics tools and e-maintenance. *Computers in Industry, 57*(6), 476–489. doi:10.1016/j.compind.2006.02.014

Lofsten, H. (2000). Measuring maintenance performance in search for a maintenance productivity index. *International Journal of Production Economics, 63*(1), 47–58. doi:10.1016/S0925-5273(98)00245-X

Loutas, T., Roulias, D., Pauly, E., & Kostopoulos, V. (2011). The combined use of vibration, acoustic emission and oil debris on-line monitoring towards a more e ective condition monitoring of rotating machinery. *Mechanical Systems and Signal Processing, 25*(4), 1339–1352. doi:10.1016/j.ymssp.2010.11.007

Mahamad, A. K., Saon, S., & Hiyama, T. (2010). Predicting remaining useful life of rotating machinery based artificial neural network. *Computers & Mathematics with Applications (Oxford, England), 60*(4), 1078–1087. doi:10.1016/j.camwa.2010.03.065

Moghaddam, K. S., & Usher, J. S. (2011). Sensitivity analysis and comparison of algorithms in preventive maintenance and replacement scheduling optimization models. *Computers & Industrial Engineering, 61,* 64–75. doi:10.1016/j.cie.2011.02.012

Niu, G., & Yang, B.-S. (2010). Intelligent condition monitoring and prognostics system based on data-fusion strategy. *Expert Systems with Applications, 37*(12), 8831–8840. doi:10.1016/j.eswa.2010.06.014

Pan, Z., & Balakrishnan, N. (2011). Reliability modeling of degradation of products with multiple performance characteristics based on gamma processes. *Reliability Engineering & System Safety, 96*(8), 949–957. doi:10.1016/j.ress.2011.03.014

Parida, C. (2007). Development of a multi-criteria hierarchical framework for maintenance performance measurement (MPM). *Journal of Quality in Maintenance Engineering, 13*(3), 241–258. doi:10.1108/13552510710780276

Roe, S., & Mba, D. (2009). The environment, international standards, asset health management and condition monitoring: An integrated strategy. *Reliability Engineering & System Safety, 94*(2), 474–478. doi:10.1016/j.ress.2008.05.007

Selvik, J., & Aven, T. (2011). A framework for reliability and risk centered maintenance. *Reliability Engineering & System Safety, 96*(2), 324–331. doi:10.1016/j.ress.2010.08.001

Shi, D., & Gindy, N. N. (2007). Tool wear predictive model based on least squares support vector machines. *Mechanical Systems and Signal Processing, 21*(4), 1799–1814. doi:10.1016/j.ymssp.2006.07.016

Sikorska, J., Hodkiewicz, M., & Ma, L. (2011). Prognostic modelling options for remaining useful life estimation by industry. *Mechanical Systems and Signal Processing, 25*(5), 1803–1836. doi:10.1016/j.ymssp.2010.11.018

Wachla, D., & Moczulski, W. A. (2007). Identification of dynamic diagnostic models with the use of methodology of knowledge discovery in databases. *Engineering Applications of Artificial Intelligence, 20*(5), 699–707. doi:10.1016/j.engappai.2006.11.002

Wang, H. (2002). A survey of maintenance policies of deteriorating systems. *European Journal of Operational Research, 139*(3), 469–489. doi:10.1016/S0377-2217(01)00197-7

Yam, R. C. M., Tse, P., Li, L., & Tu, P. (2001). Intelligent predictive decision support system for condition-based maintenance. *International Journal of Advanced Manufacturing Technology, 17,* 383–391. doi:10.1007/s001700170173

APPENDIX 1

Algorithm 1. NASA Data pre-processing 'R' code

```
# - This assumes the NASA data has been extracted to the C:\ directory
library(moments)
infiles <- list.files("C:/bearing_IMS/2nd_test/2nd_test," pattern="*.*," full.
names=TRUE)
RMS <- function(b){  sqrt(sum(b^2)/length(b)) }
processthe.files <- function(file, i){
data <- read.table(file, header=FALSE, sep="\t," row.names=NULL)
bearing <- as.vector(data[,i])
RMSVal <- RMS(bearing)
CF <- if (abs(max(bearing)) >= abs(min(bearing))) {
        (abs(max(bearing))/RMSVal)
} else {
        (abs(min(bearing))/RMSVal)
}
cat(skewness(bearing), kurtosis(bearing), RMSVal, CF,"\n")
return (NULL)
}
sink("C:/bearing1.txt")
invisible(lapply(infiles, processthe.files, i=1))
sink()
sink("C:/bearing2.txt")
invisible(lapply(infiles, processthe.files, i=2))
sink()
sink("C:/bearing3.txt")
invisible(lapply(infiles, processthe.files, i=3))
sink()
```

APPENDIX 2

Algorithm 2. Multivariate Normality Tests

```
#Assuming files are located in the C:/ directory
library(MVN)
b1 <- read.table("C:/bearing1.txt," header=FALSE, sep=", " row.names=NULL)
b1 <- b1[,1:4]
mardia.test(b1)
HZ.test(b1)
royston.test(b1)
```

APPENDIX 3

Algorithm 3. Experiment 1

```
# This assumes the bearing files from Appendix 1 are in the C:\ directory.
library(moments)
library(robustbase)
b1 <- read.table("C:/bearing1.txt," header=FALSE, sep=", " row.names=NULL)
b2 <- read.table("C:/bearing2.txt," header=FALSE, sep=", " row.names=NULL)
b3 <- read.table("C:/bearing3.txt," header=FALSE, sep=", " row.names=NULL)
col1 <- c(b1[,1], b2[,1], b3[,1])
col2 <- c(b1[,2], b2[,2], b3[,2])
col3 <- c(b1[,3], b2[,3], b3[,3])
col4 <- c(b1[,4], b2[,4], b3[,4])
dataset <- cbind(col1,col2,col3,col4)
col1Norm <- ((col1-min(col1))/(max(col1)-min(col1)))
col2Norm <- ((col2-min(col2))/(max(col2)-min(col2)))
col3Norm <- ((col3-min(col3))/(max(col3)-min(col3)))
col4Norm <- ((col4-min(col4))/(max(col4)-min(col4)))
meansNorm <- c(median(col1Norm), median(col2Norm), median(col3Norm),
median(col4Norm))
means <- c(median(col1), median(col2), median(col3), median(col4))
Sx <- cov(dataset)
res <- covMcd(x = dataset)
var <- c(var(col1), var(col2), var(col3), var(col4))
b1Norm <- cbind(col1Norm[1:984],col2Norm[1:984],col3Norm[1:984],col4Norm[1:984])
b2Norm <- cbind(col1Norm[985:1968],col2Norm[985:1968],col3Norm[985:1968],col4No
rm[985:1968])
b3Norm <- cbind(col1Norm[1969:2952],col2Norm[1969:2952],col3Norm[1969:2952],col4No
rm[1969:2952])
sink("C:/Euclidean1.txt")
for (x in 1:984)
{
Bearing1Euclidean <- sqrt(sum((b1Norm[x,] - meansNorm)^2))
Bearing2Euclidean <- sqrt(sum((b2Norm[x,] - meansNorm)^2))
Bearing3Euclidean <- sqrt(sum((b3Norm[x,] - meansNorm)^2))
cat(Bearing1Euclidean,"\t","Bearing2Euclidean,"\t","Bearing3Euclidean,"\n")
}
sink()
sink("C:/Manhattan1.txt")
for (x in 1:984)
{
Bearing1Manhattan <- sum(abs(b1Norm[x,] - meansNorm))
```

Continued on following page

Algorithm 3. Continued

```
Bearing2Manhattan <- sum(abs(b2Norm[x,] - meansNorm))
Bearing3Manhattan <- sum(abs(b3Norm[x,] - meansNorm))
cat(Bearing1Manhattan,"\t,"Bearing2Manhattan,"\t,"Bearing3Manhattan,"\n")
}
sink()
sink("C:/Chebyshev1.txt")
for (x in 1:984)
{
Bearing1Chebyshev <- max(abs(b1Norm[x,] - meansNorm))
Bearing2Chebyshev <- max(abs(b2Norm[x,] - meansNorm))
Bearing3Chebyshev <- max(abs(b3Norm[x,] - meansNorm))
cat(Bearing1Chebyshev,"\t,"Bearing2Chebyshev,"\t,"Bearing3Chebyshev,"\n")
}
sink()
sink("C:/Penrose1.txt")
for (x in 1:984)
{
Bearing1Penrose <- sum(((b1[x,] - means)^2/(var*length(var))))
Bearing2Penrose <- sum(((b2[x,] - means)^2/(var*length(var))))
Bearing3Penrose <- sum(((b3[x,] - means)^2/(var*length(var))))
cat(Bearing1Penrose,"\t,"Bearing2Penrose,"\t,"Bearing3Penrose,"\n")
}
sink()
Bearing1Mahalanobis <- mahalanobis(b1,means,Sx)
Bearing2Mahalanobis <- mahalanobis(b2,means,Sx)
Bearing3Mahalanobis <- mahalanobis(b3,means,Sx)
toPrint <- cbind(Bearing1Mahalanobis,Bearing2Mahalanobis,Bearing3Mahalanobis)
sink("C:/Mahalanobis1.txt")
for (i in 1:984)
{
cat(toPrint[i,1],"\t," toPrint[i,2],"\t,"toPrint[i,3],"\n")
}
sink()
Bearing1MCD <- res$mah[1:984]
Bearing2MCD <- res$mah[985:1968]
Bearing3MCD <- res$mah[1969:2952]
toPrint2 <- cbind(Bearing1MCD,Bearing2MCD,Bearing3MCD)
sink("C:/RobustMahalanobis1.txt")
for (i in 1:984)
{
cat(toPrint2[i,1],"\t," toPrint2[i,2],"\t,"toPrint2[i,3],"\n")
}
sink()
```

APPENDIX 4

Algorithm 4. Experiment 2

```
library(moments)
library(robustbase)
b1 <- read.table("C:/bearing1.txt," header=FALSE, sep=", " row.names=NULL)
b2 <- read.table("C:/bearing2.txt," header=FALSE, sep=", " row.names=NULL)
b3 <- read.table("C:/bearing3.txt," header=FALSE, sep=", " row.names=NULL)
b1 <- b1[,1:4]
b2 <- b2[,1:4]
b3 <- b3[,1:4]
col1 <- c(b2[,1])
col2 <- c(b2[,2])
col3 <- c(b2[,3])
col4 <- c(b2[,4])
dataset <- cbind(col1,col2,col3,col4)
col1Norm <- ((col1-min(col1))/(max(col1)-min(col1)))
col2Norm <- ((col2-min(col2))/(max(col2)-min(col2)))
col3Norm <- ((col3-min(col3))/(max(col3)-min(col3)))
col4Norm <- ((col4-min(col4))/(max(col4)-min(col4)))
meansNorm <- c(median(col1Norm), median(col2Norm), median(col3Norm),
median(col4Norm))
means <- c(median(col1), median(col2), median(col3), median(col4))
Sx <- cov(dataset)
res <- covMcd(x = dataset)
var <- c(var(col1), var(col2), var(col3), var(col4))
col1 <- c(b1[,1], b2[,1], b3[,1])
col2 <- c(b1[,2], b2[,2], b3[,2])
col3 <- c(b1[,3], b2[,3], b3[,3])
col4 <- c(b1[,4], b2[,4], b3[,4])
col1Norm <- ((col1-min(col1))/(max(col1)-min(col1)))
col2Norm <- ((col2-min(col2))/(max(col2)-min(col2)))
col3Norm <- ((col3-min(col3))/(max(col3)-min(col3)))
col4Norm <- ((col4-min(col4))/(max(col4)-min(col4)))
b1Norm <- cbind(col1Norm[1:984],col2Norm[1:984],col3Norm[1:984],col4No
rm[1:984])
b2Norm <- cbind(col1Norm[985:1968],col2Norm[985:1968],col3Norm[985:1968],col4No
rm[985:1968])
b3Norm <- cbind(col1Norm[1969:2952],col2Norm[1969:2952],col3Norm[1969:2952],col
4Norm[1969:2952])
sink("C:/Euclidean2.txt")
for (x in 1:984)
```

Continued on following page

Algorithm 4. Continued

```
{
Bearing1Euclidean <- sqrt(sum((b1Norm[x,] - meansNorm)^2))
Bearing2Euclidean <- sqrt(sum((b2Norm[x,] - meansNorm)^2))
Bearing3Euclidean <- sqrt(sum((b3Norm[x,] - meansNorm)^2))
cat(Bearing1Euclidean,"\t,"Bearing2Euclidean,"\t,"Bearing3Euclidean,"\n")
}
sink()
sink("C:/Manhattan2.txt")
for (x in 1:984)
{
Bearing1Manhattan <- sum(abs(b1Norm[x,] - meansNorm))
Bearing2Manhattan <- sum(abs(b2Norm[x,] - meansNorm))
Bearing3Manhattan <- sum(abs(b3Norm[x,] - meansNorm))
cat(Bearing1Manhattan,"\t,"Bearing2Manhattan,"\t,"Bearing3Manhattan,"\n")
}
sink()
sink("C:/Chebyshev2.txt")
for (x in 1:984)
{
Bearing1Chebyshev <- max(abs(b1Norm[x,] - meansNorm))
Bearing2Chebyshev <- max(abs(b2Norm[x,] - meansNorm))
Bearing3Chebyshev <- max(abs(b3Norm[x,] - meansNorm))
cat(Bearing1Chebyshev,"\t,"Bearing2Chebyshev,"\t,"Bearing3Chebyshev,"\n")
}
sink()
sink("C:/Penrose2.txt")
for (x in 1:984)
{
Bearing1Penrose <- sum(((b1[x,] - means)^2/(var*length(var))))
Bearing2Penrose <- sum(((b2[x,] - means)^2/(var*length(var))))
Bearing3Penrose <- sum(((b3[x,] - means)^2/(var*length(var))))
cat(Bearing1Penrose,"\t,"Bearing2Penrose,"\t,"Bearing3Penrose,"\n")
}
sink()
Bearing1Mahalanobis <- mahalanobis(b1,means,Sx)
Bearing2Mahalanobis <- mahalanobis(b2,means,Sx)
Bearing3Mahalanobis <- mahalanobis(b3,means,Sx)
toPrint <- cbind(Bearing1Mahalanobis,Bearing2Mahalanobis,Bearing3Mahalanobis)
sink("C:/Mahalanobis2.txt")
for (i in 1:984)
{
cat(toPrint[i,1],"\t," toPrint[i,2],"\t,"toPrint[i,3],"\n")
}
sink()
```

Continued on following page

Algorithm 4. Continued

```
Bearing1MCD <- mahalanobis(b1, res$center, res$cov)
Bearing2MCD <- mahalanobis(b2, res$center, res$cov)
Bearing3MCD <- mahalanobis(b3, res$center, res$cov)
toPrint2 <- cbind(Bearing1MCD,Bearing2MCD,Bearing3MCD)
sink("C:/RobustMahalanobis2.txt")
for (i in 1:984)
{
cat(toPrint2[i,1],"\t," toPrint2[i,2],"\t,"toPrint2[i,3],"\n")
}
sink()
```

APPENDIX 5

Algorithm 5. Experiment 3

```
library(moments)
library(robustbase)
b1 <- read.table("C:/bearing1.txt," header=FALSE, sep=", " row.names=NULL)
b1 <- b1[,1:4]
col1 <- c(b1[,1])
col2 <- c(b1[,2])
col3 <- c(b1[,3])
col4 <- c(b1[,4])
dataset <- cbind(col1,col2,col3,col4)
col1Norm <- ((col1-min(col1))/(max(col1)-min(col1)))
col2Norm <- ((col2-min(col2))/(max(col2)-min(col2)))
col3Norm <- ((col3-min(col3))/(max(col3)-min(col3)))
col4Norm <- ((col4-min(col4))/(max(col4)-min(col4)))
meansNorm <- c(median(col1Norm), median(col2Norm), median(col3Norm),
median(col4Norm))
means <- c(median(col1), median(col2), median(col3), median(col4))
Sx <- cov(dataset)
res <- covMcd(x = dataset)
var <- c(var(col1), var(col2), var(col3), var(col4))
b1Norm <- cbind(col1Norm[1:984],col2Norm[1:984],col3Norm[1:984],col4No
rm[1:984])
sink("C:/Euclidean3.txt")
for (x in 1:984)
{
Bearing1Euclidean <- sqrt(sum((b1Norm[x,] - meansNorm)^2))
cat(Bearing1Euclidean,"\n")
```

Continued on following page

Algorithm 5. Continued

```
}
sink()
sink("C:/Manhattan3.txt")
for (x in 1:984)
{
Bearing1Manhattan <- sum(abs(b1Norm[x,] - meansNorm))
cat(Bearing1Manhattan,"\n")
}
sink()
sink("C:/Chebyshev3.txt")
for (x in 1:984)
{
Bearing1Chebyshev <- max(abs(b1Norm[x,] - meansNorm))
cat(Bearing1Chebyshev,"\n")
}
sink()
sink("C:/Penrose3.txt")
for (x in 1:984)
{
Bearing1Penrose <- sum(((b1[x,] - means)^2/(var*length(var))))
cat(Bearing1Penrose,"\n")
}
sink()
Bearing1Mahalanobis <- mahalanobis(b1,means,Sx)
toPrint <- cbind(Bearing1Mahalanobis)
sink("C:/Mahalanobis3.txt")
for (i in 1:984)
{
cat(toPrint[i,1],"\n")
}
sink()
Bearing1MCD <- res$mah[1:984]
toPrint2 <- cbind(Bearing1MCD)
sink("C:/RobustMahalanobis3.txt")
for (i in 1:984)
{
cat(toPrint2[i,1],"\n")
}
sink()
```

APPENDIX 6

Key Terms and Definitions

- G : Empirical Skewness (symmetry of the data).
- $M4$: Empirical Kurtosis (peakedness of the data).
- RMS : Root Mean Square (magnitude of the data).
- C : Crest factor (extremeness of peaks with context).
- q : Heat generated.
- w : Work done.
- ” t : Rise in temperature.
- η_{gear} : Inefficiency of gear N (expressed as a decimal).
- P_{out} : Power output.
- D_1 : Manhattan distance (Minkowski $p = 1$).
- D_2 : Euclidean distance (Minkowski $p = 2\,0$).
- D_∞ : Chebyshev distance (Minkowski $p = \infty$).
- x' : Normalisation of vector x.
- P : Penrose distance.
- MD : Mahalanobis distance.
- RMD : A Robust Mahalanobis distance.
- $\bar{x}$: Sample mean of vector x.
- χ_p^2 : Chi-square distribution with p degrees of freedom.
- $F_{(a,b)}$: Fisher distribution with a, b degrees of freedom.
- $\beta_{(a,b)}$: Beta distribution with a, b degrees of freedom.
- μ : True (population) attribute centres.

- $\hat{\mu}$: Estimation of population attribute centres.
- £ : Attribute covariance matrix (empirically estimated from data).
- £' : Attribute covariance (empirically estimated from the MCD algorithm).
- n : Sample size.

Chapter 8
Mathematical Statistical Examinations on Script Relics

Gábor Hosszú
Budapest University of Technology and Economics, Hungary

ABSTRACT

This chapter presents statistical evaluations of script relics. Its concept is exploiting mathematical statistical methods to extract hidden correlations among different script relics. Examining the genealogy of the graphemes of scripts is necessary for exploring the evolution of the writing systems, reading undeciphered inscriptions, and deciphering undeciphered scripts. The chapter focuses on the cluster analysis as one of the most popular mathematical statistical methods. The chapter presents the application of the clustering in the classification of Rovash (pronounced "rove-ash," an alternative spelling: Rovas) relics. The various Rovash scripts were used by nations in the Eurasian Steppe and in the Carpathian Basin. The specialty of the Rovash paleography is that the Rovash script family shows a vital evolution during the last centuries; therefore, it is ideal to test the models of the evolution of the glyphs. The most important Rovash script is the Szekely-Hungarian Rovash. Cluster analysis algorithms are applied for determining the common sets among the significant Szekely-Hungarian Rovash alphabets. The determined Rovash relic ties prove the usefulness of the clustering methods in the Rovash paleography.

INTRODUCTION

The computational paleography belongs to the applied computer science and deals with the use of mathematical methods in exploring the meaning and the ties of various old inscriptions. The chapter focuses on the cluster analysis as one of the most popular mathematical statistical method. The chapter presents the fundamental concepts of the computational paleography, several earlier approaches to applying the mathematical tools for exploring the ties of the old orthographies, and the basics of the clustering methods and applied metrics. The clustering is applied to an ancient script, the Szekely-Hungarian Rovash (pronounced "rove-ash," an alternative spelling: Rovas). The chapter presents the application of the clustering in the classification of Rovash relics. Cluster analysis algorithms are used for determining the ties among the significant Szekely-Hungarian Rovash alphabets.

DOI: 10.4018/978-1-4666-6086-1.ch008

BACKGROUND

Mathematical statistical tools as the cluster analysis are useful in various scientific fields, including the computational paleography. The chapter deals with computational paleography that means modeling and analyzing methods to explore links among graphemes, deciphering ancient inscriptions, representing various glyphs in digital form by using mathematical algorithms and software tools. The applied mathematical statistical tools may accelerate the research time and provide more accurate results through the automatic process for exploring the genealogical ties among the various branches of a script.

The *writing system* is a symbolic representation of a language described in terms of linguistic units (Malatesha & Aaron, 2006). The *script* is a writing system, some examples of the scripts are the following: Aramaic, Arabic, Armenian, Brahmi, Carpathian Basin Rovash, Chinese, Cyrillic, Devanagari, Ethiopic, Georgian, Greek, Hebrew, Kannada, Kharoshthi, Latin, Runic, Szekely-Hungarian Rovash, Telugu, Umbrian, Venetic, etc.

The *grapheme* is a minimally distinctive unit in a writing system. The *symbol* is a distinct unit of an inscription, the inscriptions are composed of a series of symbols. *Grapheme* is the abstraction of a symbol. Graphemes can be letters, ligatures, numerical digits, or punctuation marks. The grapheme has the following properties: *(i)* the script belonging into, *(ii)* its glyphs, *(iii)* its sound values, *(iv)* periods of use. The *glyph* is the shape of the grapheme with topological information. One grapheme has usually more glyphs. The symbol in an inscription is an implementation of a glyph.

The *orthography* is the visual representation of a language, which uses graphemes belonging to a certain script, and it is determined by the features of a language. A script is used for different orthographies. For instance, the Latin script is used for several orthographies, including the French, German, English, Hungarian,

etc. orthographies. The orthography of a spoken language changes periodically (Rogers, 1999). The changes can occur as changing set of graphemes, which encompasses the shape transformation of a glyph. A cause of writing system alteration is the establishment of more advanced writing media or instruments. The advanced writing technology introduces new writing technique, which impacts the glyphs of a grapheme.

The *script family* is a group of scripts, which are closely related to each other. The Rovash (pronounced "rove-ash") script family includes the Proto-Rovash, the Early Steppean Rovash, the Carpathian Basin Rovash, the Steppean Rovash, and the Szekely-Hungarian Rovash scripts (Hosszú, 2013a, 2013b). The history and the genealogical ties of the Rovash scripts have been the subject of heavy research efforts from the past until today (Hosszú, 2012). It is a difficult task to determine the accurate genealogy and timelines of the Rovash scripts (Hosszú, 2012). The various Rovash scripts gradually differentiated after the geographical isolation of their users. Carpathian Basin Rovash was in use in the Carpathian Basin by Hungarians mainly, the others were used by nations and tribes of the Eurasian Steppe up to the 10th/13th centuries. Most of the Rovash scripts became extinct in the Medieval Times; however, the Szekely-Hungarian Rovash continued to be used since the 9th century throughout history until the present by the Szekelys—an organized border guard subgroup of the Hungarians.

The studies related to graphemes are challenging topics for paleographers and archaeologists, including deciphering undeciphered glyph discovered through excavation, reading patterns in glyphs transformation, etc. The mathematical statistical methods can be used in the computational paleography in different fields. Due to the significant need to decipher the inscriptions of the various archaeological finds, serious research efforts are carried out worldwide. A part of them deals with modeling the graphemes (Pardede et al., 2012). Quantitative aspects can be measured by automated means and the results can be subjected to automated clustering techniques (Ciula, 2005). Ciula used the hierarchical clustering for creating the groups of the morphologically similar glyphs of a grapheme. Wolf et al. dealt with digitalizing the historical manuscripts and used the paleographic classification to match a given document to a large set of paleographic samples (Wolf et al., 2011). Cloppet et al. introduced numerical tools that have been developed to automate the study of medieval writing samples in the context of the Graphem project, which is intended to explore, analyze and categorize medieval scripts (Cloppet et al., 2011). Further researches are dedicated to explore the genealogical relationship of different writing systems (Hosszú, 2010).

CLUSTER ANALYSIS AS TOOL OF THE COMPUTATIONAL PALEOGRAPHY

Divisive and Agglomerative Clustering

The mathematical statistical tools can be used for exploring the ties among graphemes and scripts. One of the most efficient data mining method is the cluster analysis, which connects objects to form clusters based on their distance. We concentrate on the *hierarchical cluster analysis*, also known as *connectivity based clustering*. In case of the hierarchical clustering, the number of clusters is not set in advance. Moreover, these algorithms do not generate a unique partitioning of the objects, but a hierarchy from which the user can choose appropriate clusters according to the possible interpretation of the obtained results.

A cluster hierarchy can be generated both top-down and bottom-up direction. The top-down clustering algorithms are the so-called *divisive clustering* methods, which are also called *flat clustering*, since this kind of clustering creates a flat set of clusters without any explicit structure

that would relate clusters to each other. In the case of the divisive clustering methods, the procedure starts at the top with all documents in one cluster. The cluster is split using a flat clustering method. This procedure is applied recursively until each object is in its own singleton cluster. Oppositely, the bottom-up clustering, which is also called *agglomerative clustering*, starts with single objects and aggregates them into clusters. There is evidence that divisive algorithms produce more accurate hierarchies than bottom-up algorithms in some circumstances. Bottom-up methods make clustering decisions based on local patterns without initially taking into account the global distribution. However, top-down clustering benefits from complete information about the global distribution when making top-level partitioning decisions.

The series of possible clustered structure of a set of objects can be visualized by *dendrogram* in the function of a distance at which the clusters merge. The dendrogram, gives the graphical representation of the cluster structures in the function of various metrics in a rooted tree diagram to illustrate the arrangement of the clusters produced by clustering.

The divisive hierarchical cluster analysis (Hastie et al., 2009) is carried out based on the distance matrix. In its procedure, all objects started in a single cluster of size n, where n is the number of objects. Then splits are performed recursively as an S_{min} Minimal Similarity is increased until all clusters are singletons. In this manner, at each step of the divisive algorithm, clusters are partitioned into a pair of daughter clusters, selected to maximize the distance between each daughter.

The agglomerative clustering starts out with all objects in clusters of size 1. Then, at each step of the algorithm, the pair of clusters with the shortest distance are combined into a single cluster. The procedure ends when all objects are combined into a single cluster of size n, where n is the number of objects. There are several different agglomerative clustering methods depending on the applied linkage criterion, which gives the distance between two clusters. Some of them are presented in the following.

The linkage criterion of the *single-linkage clustering* is defined with the expression (1), where the distance between two clusters C_1 and C_2 is the minimum distance between objects x_i and x_j in each cluster (Legendre & Legendre 2012). Single-linkage clustering is susceptible to chaining, in which there is a tendency to repeatedly add new individuals onto a single cluster rather than making several separate clusters. The chaining may lead to impractically heterogeneous clusters.

$$\min\left\{d\left(x_i, x_j\right) : x_i \in C_1, x_j \in C_2\right\} \qquad (1)$$

Another method is the *complete linkage clustering*, which is given in expression (2). In this case, the distance between two clusters C_1 and C_2 is the maximum distance between objects x_i and x_j in each cluster (Everitt et al. 2001).

$$\max\left\{d\left(x_i, x_j\right) : x_i \in C_1, x_j \in C_2\right\} \qquad (2)$$

The single-linkage and the complete-linkage clustering methods distort the data, since the distances between clusters are calculated on outlying points rather than the properties of the whole cluster.

The *average linkage clustering* (Sokal & Michener 1958) also known as the *Unweighted Pair-Group Method using Arithmetic averages* (UPGMA), the latter name was introduced by Sneath & Sokal (1973). The method is unweighted, since all pairwise distances contribute equally, and pair-group, since groups are combined in pairs. In the UPGMA method at each step, the nearest two clusters are joined into a higher-level cluster. In this method, the pairwise distances of each group are mean distances to all members of that group. The average distance between any two clusters C_1 and C_2 is taken to be the average of all distances between pairs of objects x_i in C_1 and x_j in C_2, that is, the average distance (arithmetic mean) between objects in each cluster is presented in expression (3).

$$\left|C_1\right|^{-1}\left|C_2\right|^{-1}\sum_{x_i \in C_1}\sum_{x_j \in C_2} d\left(x_i, x_j\right), \qquad (3)$$

where $\left|C_1\right|$ and $\left|C_2\right|$ means the number of objects in C_1 and C_2, and $d\left(x_i, x_j\right)$ is the distance between the object x_i of C_1 and the object x_j of C_2. The expression (3) is a linkage criterion, which determines the distance between groups of objects as a function of the pairwise distances between objects.

Metrics

There are several metrics, which are used to describe the similarity or dissimilarity among objects. In mathematics, the metric has three axioms (Duda et al., 2001), see Box 1.

Box 1.

$\alpha)$	$d\left(x_i, x_j\right) = d\left(x_j, x_i\right)$	$(symmetry),$
$\beta)$	$d\left(x_i, x_j\right) \geq 0 \wedge \left(d\left(x_i, x_j\right) = 0 \Leftrightarrow x_i = x_j\right)$	$(nonnegativity\ and\ zero\ property),$ (4)
$\gamma)$	$d\left(x_i, x_j\right) \leq d\left(x_i, x_k\right) + d\left(x_k, x_j\right)$	$(triangle\ inequality),$

where x_i, x_j, and x_k are different objects and $d\left(x_i, x_j\right)$ is the distance between objects x_i and x_j.

The axiom α expresses that a metric must be symmetric. The axiom β means that the metric is positive except when the objects are identical, in this case it is zero. The zero property is also called *reflexivity*. The axiom γ expresses that the straightforward way is the shortest path between two objects. The triangle inequality is not satisfied some measures of distance; in which cases, it is possible to obtain a route from x_i to an object x_k and then from x_k to x_j, which is shorter than from object x_i to object x_j directly. The distance, which satisfies only the axioms α and β but not the γ is called *dissimilarity* instead of *metric*. Although having the properties of a metric is desirable, a dissimilarity measure can be effective without being a metric (Goshtasby, 2012).

In case of categorical data, the distance of the objects is related to the number of matching attributes of the objects. In our case, each attribute of the objects has two categories, namely presence or absence. In calculating the distance of objects x_i and x_j, four cases are usually taken into account: f_{10} is the number of attributes where x_i contains certain values of the attributes (presence) and x_j does not contain them (absence); f_{00} is the number of attributes where neither x_i nor x_j contain certain values of the attributes; f_{01} is the number of attributes where x_i does not contains certain values of the attributes and x_j contains them; and finally f_{11} is the number of attributes where both x_i and x_j contain certain values of the attributes. The *Jaccard similarity index* is the number of co-presences over the number of attributes, as equation (5) presents.

$$s_J\left(x_i, x_j\right) = \frac{f_{11}}{f_{11} + f_{10} + f_{01}}, i, j \in \left\{1, ..., n\right\}, \tag{5}$$

where *n* is the number of objects. Based on (2), the *Jaccard distance* is given by equation (6). The

Jaccard distance is a proper metric (Levandowsky & Winter 1971).

$$d_J\left(x_i, x_j\right) = 1 - s_J\left(x_i, x_j\right) = \frac{f_{10} + f_{01}}{f_{11} + f_{10} + f_{01}}, i, j \in \left\{1, ..., n\right\} \tag{6}$$

Another metric is the *Simple Matching Coefficient* (SMC) distance metric, which counts the number of same attributes in both objects (Sokal & Michener, 1958). It is the ratio of the total number of matches to the total number of attributes, see equation (7). Oppositely to the Jaccard distance, this metric involves the total number of matches, independently whether the attribute of two objects has a certain value (positive match) or it has not a certain value (negative match). It is particularly useful when it is considered that a positive match conveys the same amount of information as a negative match (Dunn & Everitt 1982).

$$d_{SMC}\left(x_i, x_j\right) = \frac{f_{11} + f_{00}}{f_{11} + f_{00} + f_{10} + f_{01}}, i, j \in \left\{1, ..., n\right\} \tag{7}$$

Sometimes the absence of an attribute cannot be evaluated; therefore, a third category is necessary to be introduced besides the "presence" and the "absence." If the positive match (presence) is denoted with '1' in the data matrix of the objects, and the negative match (absence) is denoted with '-1' in the data matrix, the '0' can represent that case, when a certain attribute cannot be judged. For instance, this case occurs, if the attribute means the presence of a certain grapheme in a script relic. If the voice represented by a grapheme was not used in that speech what was recorded by a script relic, that grapheme would not be used in that relic; however, this grapheme could exist in the brain of the writer of the relic. In this case, a metric is useful, which increases the importance of the definite positive and the definite negative matches (represented with '1' and '-1', respectively) to the indefinite values (represented with '0'). For this purpose, the following metrics can be applied.

The *Squared Euclidean* distance is calculated based on (8), which is the sum of the squared differences in value for each object, where n is the total number of objects, i and j represent two rows of the data matrix, k represents the column (object), and x_{ik} is the element in the kth column of row i.

$$d_{SE}\left(x_i, x_j\right) = \sum_{k=1}^{n}\left(x_{ik} - x_{jk}\right)^2 \qquad (8)$$

Another distance metric, the *Manhattan distance* is calculated by (9). Manhattan distance is also known as *city block distance, taxicab distance* or *rectilinear distance* (Krause, 1987).

$$d_M\left(x_i, x_j\right) = \sum_{k=1}^{n}\left|x_{ik} - x_{jk}\right|, \qquad (9)$$

MAIN FOCUS OF THE CHAPTER

Issues and Controversies

A large amount of efforts are dedicated to explore the development of the various Rovash scripts. However, difficulties of the rovash research is that only a small number and seemingly incoherent writing relics were preserved. Therefore, the exploration of the geographic and historical distribution of the use of Rovash scripts is only possible if the relations in the shape, style and grapheme set of the script relics are examined by statistical methods taking into account the characteristics of each grapheme. Moreover, due

to the relatively small number of survived relics, determining the exact genealogy of the various rovash orthographies needs mathematical statistical methods.

Problems

In the followings, a computational paleographic method is presented, in which the cluster analysis is applied to detect the fine-grained kinship relationships of the rovash relics. The Szekely-Hungarian Rovash alphabets are known in the rovash paleography; however, the genealogical relationships among them were previously unexplored. The method described in this chapter, of course, can be used for the relics of other writing systems, too.

The main problem of exploring the genealogy of the graphemes is that a grapheme can have several glyphs, which are different in a lot of cases. Moreover, different graphemes may have identical glyph variants. Another problem arises due to the time: *(i)* the use of a grapheme can be changed during the time, *(ii)* the applied glyphs of the grapheme changed in different periods, *(iii)* the sound values of a grapheme changed in several cases, etc. In such a way, describing the genealogy of the graphemes is a complex modeling problem.

Cluster Analysis of the Significant Rovash Relics

In the elaborated examination, twelve Szekely-Hungarian Rovash relics were involved. These inscriptions were made between the 15th and the 18th centuries (Hosszú, 2011), see *Table 1* and *Figure 1, 2, 3, & 4*.

The majority of the survived rovash alphabets differ in the applied glyphs of the graphemes. Based on the comparison of the graphemes of the rovash alphabets, the difference and naturally

Table 1. The examined Szekely-Hungarian Rovash relics with their abbreviations

Abbreviation	Name of the Rovash Relic	Date of the Inscription
AAK	Ancient Alphabet and Sentences by Kájoni	1673
AKR	Alphabet of Kájoni based on the Rudimenta	1673
BOD	Rovash inscriptions of Péter Bod	1739
BOL	Bologna Rovash Calendar	ca. 15th c. (17th century copy)
CON	Constantinople Inscription	1515
CSI	Csíkszentmiklós Inscription	1501
MIS	Two alphabets of István Miskolczi Csulyak	between 1610 and 1645
DES	Alphabet of Dési	1753
MAR	Alphabet found in the manuscript of Marsigli	17th century
NIK	Nikolsburg Alphabet	ca. 15th century
PAT	Patakfalvi Bible	between 1776 and 1785
RUD	Ioannis Thelegdi: Rudimenta	1598/1994

the similarity of the rovash alphabets can be defined. Consequently, a 12x12 data matrix can be calculated, which describes the distance between the rovash alphabets (as objects) in the sense of the difference of their glyphs. Since in this case, both presence of a certain glyph in two objects (alphabets) and the absence that glyph in both objects carried more-or-less equal information,

Figure 1. The Ancient Alphabet and Sentences by J. Kájoni, denoted with AAK in Table 1 (Sebestyén, 1909)

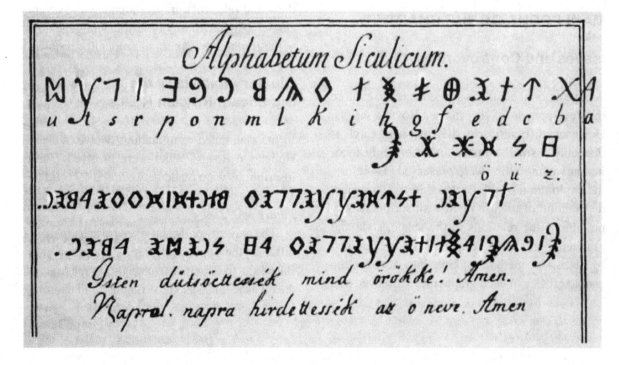

Figure 2. The Nikolsburg Alphabet, denoted with NIK in Table 1 (Jakubovich, 1935)

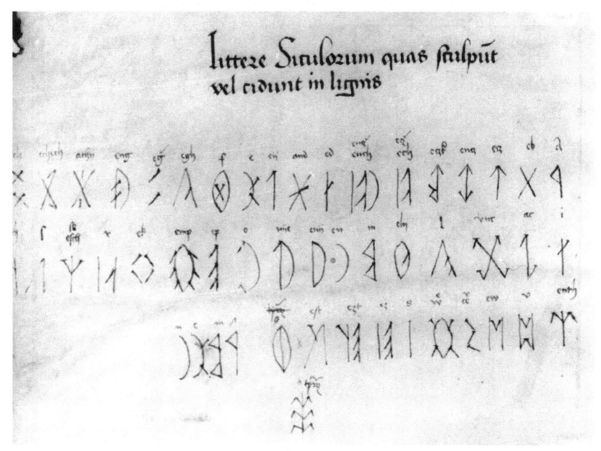

the SMC is more suitable metric than the Jaccard distance for this case. Therefore, in calculating the distance matrix, the SMC distance metric was used, see *Table 2*.

A divisive hierarchical cluster analysis was carried out based on the distance matrix, see *Table 3*, where the S_{min} denotes the *Minimal Similarity*. S_{min} means the error threshold and it is the arithmetic mean of the distances of the objects belonging to the appropriate cluster. The applied hierarchical cluster analysis was *divisive*, which means that all objects started in one cluster, and splits were performed recursively as S_{min} was increased. Depending on the actual value of the S_{min} error threshold, the objects are clustered differently as it is presented in *Table 3*.

Figure 3. The alphabet found in the manuscript of Marsigli, denoted with MAR in Table 1 (Veress, 1906)

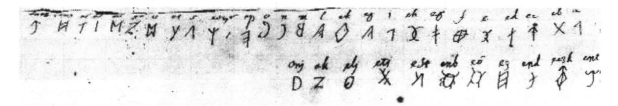

Figure 4. The Two Alphabets of I. Miskolczi Csulyak, denoted with MIS in Table 1 (Jakubovich, 1935)

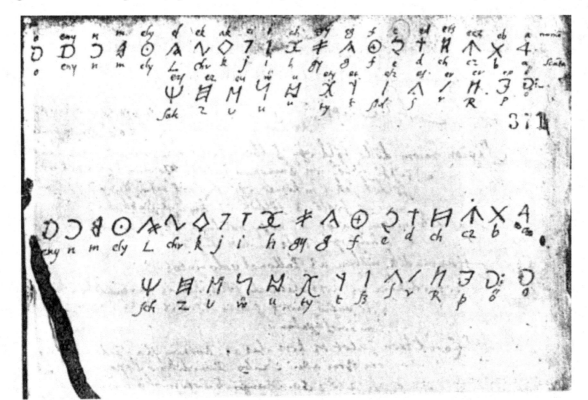

Table 2. The distance matrix of the examined Rovash relics by using the modified SMC metric

Relic	NIK	MAR	BOL	RUD	CSI	CON	MIS	AAK	AKR	BOD	DES	PAT
NIK												
MAR	56%											
BOL	47%	31%										
RUD	50%	29%	38%									
CSI	45%	32%	45%	18%								
CON	36%	27%	56%	9%	0%							
MIS	38%	33%	48%	0%	21%	14%						
AAK	61%	61%	57%	57%	68%	100%	52%					
AKR	40%	30%	39%	7%	14%	0%	5%	61%				
BOD	43%	33%	43%	3%	14%	0%	5%	61%	3%			
DES	53%	33%	43%	3%	18%	11%	0%	52%	11%	7%		
PAT	12%	65%	53%	59%	53%	33%	59%	65%	53%	53%	59%	

Table 3. The result of the cluster analysis of the Szekely-Hungarian Rovash relics depending on the actual value of the S_{min} Minimal Similarity

S [%]	Cluster 1	Cluster 2	Cluster 3	Cluster 4	Cluster 5
80%	AAK	NIK, PAT (88%)	MAR, BOL, RUD, CSI, CON, MIS, AKR, BOD, DES (80%)	-	-
86%	AAK	NIK, PAT (88%)	MAR, RUD, CSI, CON, MIS, AKR, BOD, DES (86%)	BOL	-
88%	AAK	NIK, PAT (88%)	RUD, CSI, CON, MIS, AKR, BOD, DES (92%)	BOL	MAR

By modifying the S_{min} error threshold, the number of clusters changes. The E square error is defined as (10).

$$E = \left(1 - S_{min}\right)^2 \qquad (10)$$

Each S_{min} error threshold is accepted, which gives an interpretable cluster structure. However, to obtain the optimal number of clusters it is useful to represent the function $E(N)$, where the N is the number of clusters, see *Figure 5*.

The slope of the curve in *Figure 5* has a significant change between the number of clusters 3 and 4. If the number of clusters is smaller than 3, the square error is increasing strongly. Oppositely, if the number of clusters is higher than 4, the significance of the clustering is decreasing. Therefore, the optimal number of clusters is be-

tween 3 and 4—if these cluster structures can be interpreted paleographically.

In an alternative examination, the agglomerative clustering was applied to analyze the objects of script relics. The UPGMA method with Squared Euclidean metric was used, the calculations were elaborated by the MVSP software (2012). *Table 4* presents the distance matrix of the relics calculated with the Squared Euclidean distance metric and *Figure 6* gives the dendrogram of the clustered rovash relics with Squared Euclidean metric calculated with different random input orders of the objects.

Table 5 presents the distance matrix of the relics calculated with the Manhattan metric and *Figure 7* gives the dendrogram of the clustered rovash relics with Manhattan metric.

The results of *Figure 6* and *Figure 7* are largely similar to each other. As the hierarchical cluster structures demonstrate, the results of the

Figure 5. The E square error in function of N number of clusters

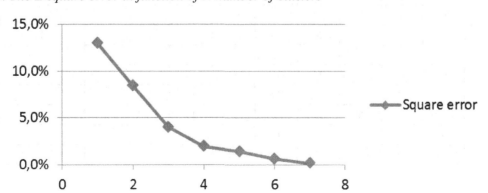

Table 4. The distance matrix of the examined Rovash relics using the Squared Euclidean distance metric

Relic	NIK	MAR	BOL	RUD	CSI	CON	MIS	AAK	AKR	BOD	DES	PAT
NIK												
MAR	76											
BOL	62	42										
RUD	68	40	50									
CSI	52	40	50	28								
CON	39	35	41	31	15							
MIS	45	41	51	13	21	26						
AAK	67	67	61	63	59	52	46					
AKR	52	40	50	12	20	23	13	63				
BOD	56	44	54	8	20	23	13	63	4			
DES	68	44	54	8	24	31	9	55	16	12		
PAT	25	61	51	57	41	24	44	50	49	49	53	

UPGMA with different metrics and the result of the divisive hierarchical clustering method *(Table 3)* are very close to each other. Based on these hierarchical cluster structures, several consequences can be drawn. One of them is that besides the dominant tradition of the Rudimenta rovash textbook (Thelegdi, 1598/1994) denoted with RUD, there were other, independent versions of the Szekely-Hungarian Rovash in Szekelyland, see the cluster of the Nikolsburg Alphabet (NIK) and the Patakfalvi Bible (PAT). The studies carried out proved the usefulness of the cluster analysis

Table 5. The distance matrix of the examined Rovash relics using the Manhattan distance metric

Relic	NIK	MAR	BOL	RUD	CSI	CON	MIS	AAK	AKR	BOD	DES	PAT
NIK												
MAR	38											
BOL	32	22										
RUD	34	20	26									
CSI	32	26	32	20								
CON	31	29	33	27	15							
MIS	29	27	31	13	13	22						
AAK	39	39	35	37	33	34	24					
AKR	28	22	28	8	14	21	11	35				
BOD	30	24	30	6	14	21	11	35	2			
DES	36	24	30	6	16	27	9	33	10	8		
PAT	21	39	33	37	25	20	24	28	31	31	33	

Figure 6. The dendrogram of the clustering of the rovash relics with Squared Euclidean distance metric calculated with different (random) input orders of the objects

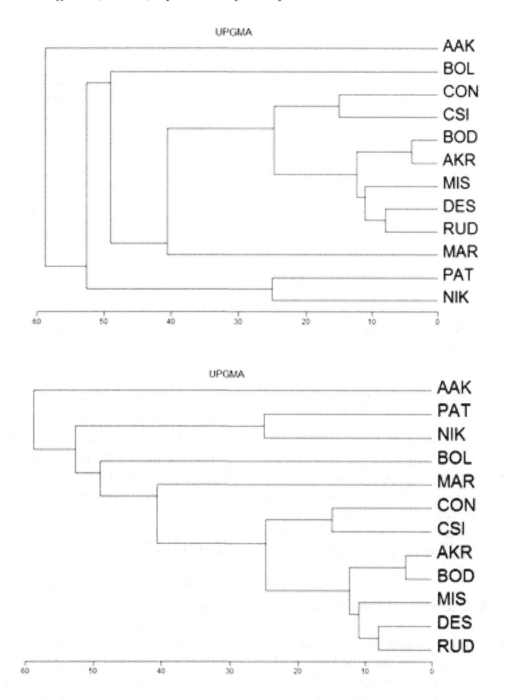

Figure 7. The dendrogram of the clustering of the Rovash relics with Manhattan metric

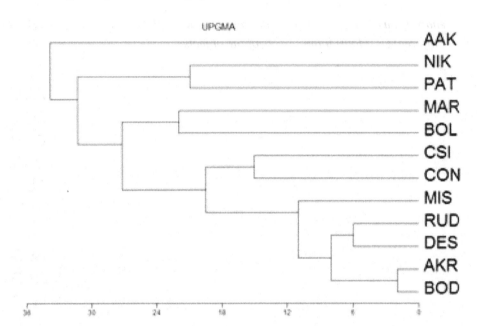

in exploring the genealogical relationships among the rovash alphabets.

ADVANTAGES AND LIMITATIONS

The advantage of applying the cluster analysis for exploring the relations of the script relic is the objective comparison of various alphabets. However, the result of this analysis depends on the interpretation of each signs of the relics. Therefore, careful paleographical analysis is necessary for obtaining realistic ties among the script relics.

FUTURE RESEARCH DIRECTIONS

Besides the readable rovash alphabets and longer rovash inscriptions, there are several rovash relics, which have been undeciphered. Deciphering unreadable inscriptions has a large importance due to the increasing number of uncovered archaeological finds. There rovash relics surely contain

significant historical and linguistic information; therefore, their deciphering is a very important task. The reconstruction of the evolution of the Rovash scripts can help in identifying the signs of the currently undeciphered rovash relics.

The results presented in the chapter proved that the cluster analysis is a useful mathematical tool in exploring the ties of various script relics. Therefore, the clustering is necessary in the computational paleographical research.

CONCLUSION

The different kinds of the cluster analysis being important in the field of the computational paleography are detailed. Moreover, some recent research directions in this field are summarized. The chapter presented applied cluster analysis methods for exploring of the evolution of the Szekely-Hungarian Rovash script. The proposed clustering-based method uses the set of graphemes called alphabets as objects, which are grouped by the topological properties of their glyphs. The alphabets are considered to be cognate, if they belong into the same cluster. The interpretation of the obtained cluster structure demonstrated the efficiency of the proposed method in the field of the rovash paleography. The research works reported in this chapter can become more efficient if larger number of paleographic relics will be included into the examinations.

ACKNOWLEDGMENT

The work reported in this chapter has been developed in the framework of the project "Talent care and cultivation in the scientific workshops of BME." This project is supported by the grant *TÁMOP - 4.2.2.B-10/1--2010-0009.*

REFERENCES

Ciula, A. (2005). Digital palaeography: using the digital representation of medieval script to support palaeographic analysis. *Digital Medievalist, 1.*

Cloppet, F., Daher, H., Églin, V., Emptoz, H., Exbrayat, M., Joutel, G., … Vincent, N. (2011). New Tools for Exploring, Analysing and Categorising Medieval Scripts. *Digital Medievalist, 7.*

Duda, R. O., Hart, P. E., & Stork, D. G. (2001). *Pattern Classification.* New York, NY: Wiley-Interscience.

Dunn, G., & Everitt, B. S. (1982). *An introduction to mathematical taxonomy.* Cambridge, UK: Cambridge University Press.

Everitt, B. S., Landau, S., & Leese, M. (2001). *Cluster Analysis.* London: Arnold.

Goshtasby, A. A. (2012). *Image Registration.* Springer-Verlag London Limited. doi:10.1007/978-1-4471-2458-0

Hastie, T., Tibshirani, R., & Friedman, J. (2009). *The Elements of Statistical Learning: Data mining, Inference, and Prediction.* New York: Springer. doi:10.1007/978-0-387-84858-7

Hosszú, G. (2010). Az informatika írástörténeti alkalmazásai. [Applications of information science in paleography]. In L. Cserny (Ed.), *Conference on the Modern Technics of the Information Science IKT 2010* (pp. 5–21). Dunaújváros, Hungary: College of Dunaújváros.

Hosszú, G. (2011). *Heritage of Scribes: The Relation of Rovas Scripts to Eurasian Writing Systems.* Budapest, Hungary: Rovas Foundation. Retrieved August 15, 2012 from http://books.google.hu/books?id=TyK8azCqC34C&pg=PA1

Hosszú, G. (2012). Rovás paleográfia: Dinamikus vagy statikus? [Rovash paleography: Dynamic or static?]. *Nyelv és tudomány.* [Language and Science]. Retrieved August 15, 2012 from http://www.nyest.hu/hirek/rovaspaleografia-dinamikus-vagy-statikus

Hosszú, G. (2013a). *Rovásatlasz* [Rovash Atlas]. Budapest, Hungary: Milani.

Hosszú, G. (2013b). The Rovas: A special script family of the central and eastern European languages. *Acta Philologica, 44,* 91–102.

Jakubovich, E. (1935). A székely rovásírás legrégibb ábécéi. [The oldest alphabets of the Szekely Rovash script]. *Magyar Nyelv, 31*(1–2), 1–17.

Krause, E. F. (1987). *Taxicab Geometry: An adventure in non-Euclidean geometry.* New York: Dover.

Legendre, P., & Legendre, L. (2012). *Numerical Ecology* (3rd ed.). Amsterdam: Elsevier.

Levandowsky, M., & Winter, D. (1971). Distance between sets. *Nature, 234*(5), 34–35. doi:10.1038/234034a0

Malatesha Joshi, R., & Aaron, P. G. (Eds.). (2006). *Handbook of Orthography and Literacy*. Mahwah, NJ: Lawrence Erlbaum Associates.

MVSP. (2012). *A MultiVariate Statistical Package, Version 3.1*. Pentraeth, UK: Kovach Computing Services.

Pardede, R. E. I., Tóth, L. L., Hosszú, G., & Kovács, F. (2012). Glyph Identification Based on Topological Analysis. In *Proceedings of Scientific Workshop organized by the PhD school on Computer Science in the framework of the project TÁMOP-4.2.2/B-10/1-2010-0009* (pp. 99-103). Budapest, Hungary: Budapest University of Technology and Economics.

Rogers, H. (1999). Sociolinguistic factors in borrowed writing systems. *Toronto Working Paper in Linguistics, 17*, 247-262.

Sebestyén, G. (1909). *Rovás és rovásírás* [Rovash and Rovash writing]. Budapest, Hungary: Hungarian Academy of Sciences.

Sneath, P. H. A., & Sokal, R. R. (1973). *Numerical Taxonomy*. San Francisco, CA: W.H. Freeman and Company.

Sokal, R. R., & Michener, C. D. (1958). A statistical method for evaluating systematic relationships. *The University of Kansas Scientific Bulletin, 38*, 1409–1438.

Thelegdi, I. (1994). *Rudimenta, Priscae hunnorum linguae brevibus quaestionibus ac responcionibus comprehensa opera et studio*. Budapest, Hungary: Ars Libri.

Veress, E. (1906). A bolognai Marsigli-iratok magyar vonatkozásai. [Hungarian connections of the Marsigli-documents of Bologna]. *Magyar Könyvszemle, 14*.

Wolf, L., Potikha, L., Dershowitz, N., Shweka, R., & Choueka, Y. (2011). Computerized Paleography: Tools for Historical Manuscripts. In *Proceedings of 18th IEEE International Conference on Image Processing (ICIP)* (pp. 3545–3548). Brussels, Belgium: IEEE Signal Processing Society.

ADDITIONAL READING

Bhowmik, T. K., van Oosten, J.-P., & Schomaker, L. (2011). *Segmental K-Means Learning with Mixture Distribution for HMM Based Handwriting Recognition* (pp. 432-439). Ser.: Pattern Recognition and Machine Intelligence. *Lecture Notes in Computer Science, 6744*.

Bulacu, M., & Schomaker, L. R. B. (2005). A comparison of clustering methods for writer identification and verification, *Proceedings of 8th International Conference on Document Analysis and Recognition (ICDAR 2005)* (pp. 1275-1279). Seoul, Korea: IEEE Computer Society.

Heller, M., & Vogeler, G. (2005). Modern Information Retrieval Technology for Historical Documents. In *Humanities, Computers and Cultural Heritage: Proceedings of the XVIth International Conference of the Association for History and Computing* (pp. 143-148). Amsterdam: Royal Netherlands Academy of Arts and Sciences.

Knight, K., & Yamada, K. (1999). A computational approach to deciphering unknown scripts. In *Proceedings of the ACL Workshop on Unsupervised Learning in Natural Language Processing* (pp. 37-44). ACL Anthology ID: W99-0906.

Levy, N., Wolf, L., Dershowitz, N., & Stokes, Peter (2012). Estimating the distinctiveness of graphemes and allographs in palaeographic classification. In J.C. Meister et al. (Ed.), *Digital Humanities: Conference Abstracts* (pp. 264-267). Hamburg: University of Hamburg.

Papadopoulos, A. (2004). *Metric Spaces, Convexity and Nonpositive Curvature*. Zürich: European Mathematical Society. doi:10.4171/010

Rollston, C. (2009). Writing and writing materials. [Nashville, Abingdon.]. *The New Interpreters Dictionary of the Bible, 5*, 937–938.

Schlapbach, A., & Bunke, H. (2008). Off-line Writer Identification and Verification Using Gaussian Mixture Models. Machine Learning in Document Analysis and Recognition (pp. 409-428). Series: Studies in Computational Intelligence, 90.

Smit, J. (2011). The Death of the Paleographer? Experiences with the Groningen Intelligent Writer Identification System (GIWIS). In Archiv für Diplomatik. Schiftgeschichte Siegel-und Wappenkunde. Begründet durch: Edmund E. Stengel (pp. 413-424). Herausgegeben von: Walter Koch & Theo Kölzer, 57, Köln, Weimar & Wien: Böhlau Verlag.

Stokes, P. (2008). Paleography and image processing: some solutions and problems. *Digital Medievalist, 3*.

Stokes, P. (2009). Computer-aided paleography, present and future. In Kodikologie und Palläographie im digitalen Zeitalter - Codicology and Paleography in the Digital Age (pp. 309-338). Schriften des Instituts für Dokumentologie und Editorik, 2. BoD, Norderstedt.

Stokes, P. (2012). Modeling medieval handwriting: A new approach to digital palaeography. J.C. Meister et al. (Ed.), Digital Humanities: Conference Abstracts (pp. 382-385). Hamburg: University of Hamburg.

Stokes, P.A. (2007). Palaeography and image processing: some solutions and problems. *Digital Medievalist*, 3.

Tan, P.-N., Steinbach, M., & Kumar, V. (2005). *Introduction to Data Mining*. Harlow, UK: Pearson Education Limited.

Vuurpijl, L., & Schomaker, L. (1997). Coarse writing-style clustering based on simple stroke-related features. In A. C. Downton, & S. Impedovo (Eds.), *Progress in Handwriting Recognition* (pp. 37–34). London: World Scientific.

Vuurpijl, L., & Schomaker, L. (1997). Finding structure in diversity: A hierarchical clustering method for the categorization of allographs in handwriting. In *Proceedings of the Fourth International Conference on Document Analysis and Recognition* (pp. 387-393). Piscataway, NJ: IEEE Computer Society.

Zinger, S., Nerbonne, J., Schomaker, L., & van Schie, H. (2007). Content-based text line comparison for historical document retrieval, Computational Phonology workshop. In *Recent Advances in Natural Language Processing Conference: RANLP-2007* (pp. 79-84). Borovets, Bulgaria: Bulgarian Academy of Sciences.

KEY TERMS AND DEFINITIONS

Agglomerative Clustering: A cluster hierarchy is created bottom-up direction. It starts with single objects and aggregates them into clusters.

Cluster Analysis: It is grouping a set of objects in such a manner that objects in the same cluster are more similar according to a certain similarity metric to each other than to those in other clusters.

Computational Paleography: Modeling and analyzing methods to explore links among graphemes, deciphering ancient inscriptions, representing various glyphs in digital form by using mathematical algorithms and software tools, applying computational algorithms in the study of ancient writings and inscriptions such as optimization or mathematical statistical methods.

Distance Matrix: Its elements measure pairwise distinction between objects.

Divisive Clustering: A cluster hierarchy is created top-down direction. It creates a flat set of clusters without any explicit structure that would relate clusters to each other.

Glyph: The shape of the grapheme with topological information.

Grapheme: A minimally distinctive unit in a writing system. Grapheme is the abstraction of a symbol. Graphemes can be letters, ligatures, numerical digits, or punctuation marks.

Rovash Scripts: A script family, which were used in the Eurasian Steppe by different nations and tribes up to the 10th/13th century, and in the Carpathian Basin mainly by Hungarians up to present time. The Rovash (pronounced "rove-ash") script family has five members, the Proto-Rovash, the Early Steppean Rovash, the Carpathian Basin Rovash, the Steppean Rovash, and the Szekely-Hungarian Rovash.

Script: A writing system, which includes different orthographies. E.g., the Latin script has several orthographies, including the French, German, English, Hungarian, etc. orthographies.

Symbol: The minimal individual visual unit of the inscription. Typically, the symbol is a realized grapheme.

Chapter 9
Rough Set on Two Universal Sets Based on Multigranulation

D. P. Acharjya
VIT University, India

Mary A. Geetha
VIT University, India

ABSTRACT

The fundamental concept of crisp set has been extended in many directions in the recent past. The notion of rough set by Pawlak is noteworthy among them. The rough set philosophy is based on the concept that there is some information associated with each object of the universe. There is a need to classify objects of the universe based on the indiscernibility relation among them. In the view of granular computing, rough set model is researched by single granulation. It has been extended to multigranular rough set model in which the set approximations are defined by using multiple equivalence relations on the universe simultaneously. However, in many real life scenarios, an information system establishes the relation with different universes. This gave the extension of multigranulation rough set on single universal set to multigranulation rough set on two universal sets. This chapter defines multigranulation rough set for two universal sets U and V. In addition, the algebraic properties, measures of uncertainty and topological characterization that are interesting in the theory of multigranular rough sets are studied. This helps in describing and solving real life problems more accurately.

INTRODUCTION

Information technology revolution in the recent past has brought radical change in the way data are collected or generated for ease of decision making. The huge data collected has no relevance unless it provides certain meaningful information pertaining to the interest of an organization. Therefore, the real challenge lies in converting huge data into knowledge. This leads to classification and clustering. The earliest to handle classification is classical set. In addition, knowledge associated with classical set is very limited and it fails to process ill-posed objects. But, the objects associated in the information system contains uncertainties and are imprecise in nature. Therefore, the rudimentary concept of classical sets has been extended in many directions as far as modeling of real life situations

DOI: 10.4018/978-1-4666-6086-1.ch009

is concerned. The earliest is the notion of Fuzzy set by L. A. Zadeh (1965) that captures impreciseness in information. On the other hand rough sets of Z. Pawlak (1982, 1991) capture indiscernibility among objects to model imperfect knowledge. The basic philosophy is that human knowledge about a universe depends upon their capability to classify its objects. So, classification of a universe and indiscernibility relations defined on it are known to be interchangeable notions. The basic idea of rough set is based upon the approximation of sets by pair of sets known as lower approximation and upper approximation. Here, the lower and upper approximation operators are based on equivalence relations. However, the requirement of equivalence relations is a restrictive one and failure in many real life situations. In order to achieve this, rough set is generalized to binary relations (Yao, 1998; Kondo, 2006; Pawlak & Skowron, 2007a), fuzzy proximity relations (Tripathy & Acharjya (2008, 2010)), intuitionistic fuzzy proximity relations (Tripathy, 2006; Tripathy & Acharjya (2009, 2011)), Boolean algebras (Liu, 2005; Pawlak & Skowron, 2007b), fuzzy lattices (Liu, 2008), completely distributive lattices (Chen et. al., 2006) and neighborhood systems (Lin, 1989). Development of these techniques and tools is studied under different domains like knowledge discovery in database, computational intelligence, knowledge representation, granular computing etc. (Saleem Durai et al., 2012; Acharjya et al. (2011, 2012); Tripathy et al., 2011).

Granular computing is an upcoming conceptual and computing pattern of information processing. It has been strongly encouraged by the urgent need for processing practical data in an intelligent manner (Pedrycz, 2007; Pedrycz et al, 2002). Such processing need is now commonly available in vast quantities into a humanly manageable abstract knowledge. On the contrary, granular computing offers a platform to transit from the current machine-centric to human-centric approach to gather information and knowledge. Granular computing as opposed to numeric computing is

knowledge oriented. Numeric computing is data oriented. The origin of granular computing is in the context of fuzzy sets (Zadeh, 1965). But, there are many other theories like interval analysis, rough set theory and probabilistic approach, which follow this approach.

In principles of programming, a granule can be a program module. In general, information granules are collections of entities that usually arranged together due to their similarity, functional or physical adjacency etc. On contrary, information granulation involves partitioning a class of objects into granules, with a granule being a bunch of objects which are drawn together by similarity or functionality. It encourages an approach to data that recognizes and makes use of the knowledge present in data at various levels. It includes all methods which provide flexibility and adaptability in the resolution at which knowledge or information is extracted and represented. A granule can be either simple or composite. A simple granule either cannot be further decomposed or formed by other granules, whereas a composite granule consists of group of its interconnected and interacting granules. A granule can be considered as an entire one when it is viewed as a part of another granule. A granule is considered to be a group of interconnected and interacting granules when some other granules are viewed as its parts. In addition, granules can be differentiated by a minimum set of properties such as internal, external, emergent, and contextual.

The internal properties of a granule generally deal with its organizational structures, its relationships and the interaction among the elements whereas the external properties of a granule reveal its interaction with other granules. The emergent properties of a granule may be viewed as one type of external property. But, both the internal and external properties of a granule were found to have certain dynamic changes with its related environment. The contextual properties of a granule show its relative existence in a particular environment. All the above said types of properties together give us a better understanding towards the notion of granule (Yao, 2001, 2004). The knowledge obtained based on granules although approximate but may be good enough for practical uses.

Granular computing is more a theoretical perspective that encourages an approach to data that recognizes the knowledge present in data at various levels of resolution or scales. This provides flexibility and adaptability in the resolution at which knowledge is extracted and represented. However, granular computing can also be studied based on a conceptual triarchic model consisting of the philosophy of structured thinking, the methodology of structured problem solving, and the computation of structured information processing (Yao, (2001, 2004, 2006)). The triarchic model of granular computing that provides systematic, natural way to analyze, understand, and represent is shown in Figure 1.

According to philosophy of structured thinking, granular computing focuses on modelling human perception of the reality and cognitive process. It unifies two complementary philosophical views about the complexity of real world problems. These are reduction thinking and the systems thinking. It

also stresses the importance of conscious efforts in thinking in terms of hierarchical structures.

The methodology perspective focuses on methods and strategies for finding structured solutions. In this perspective, granular computing promotes systematic approaches and practical strategies. An important issue is the exploration of granular structures and the methodology is inspired by human problem solving. The basic tasks that it involves are constructing granular structures, working within a particular level of the architecture, and switching between levels.

In computation perspective, granular computing focuses on the implementation of computer based systems. As a paradigm of structured information processing (Bargiela & Pedrycz, 2002), the two notions need to be discussed are representations and processes (Marr, 1982). A representation is a formal description and specification of entities in information systems whereas a process can be interpreted as the computational actions occurred in information processing. The two basic processes of granular computing are information granulation and computation with granules.

Figure 1. Triarchic model of granular computing

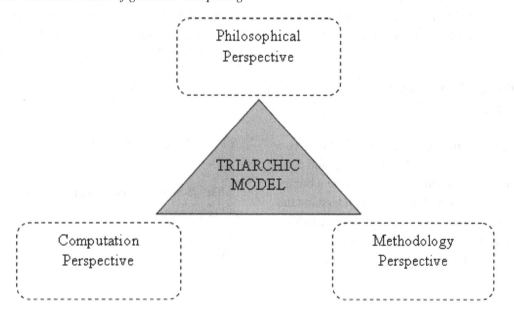

In the view of granular computing, a general concept described by a set is always characterized by lower and upper approximations under static granulation. It indicates that the concept is depicted by means of single equivalence relation on the universe. However, in many real life situations, many concepts are described by using multi equivalence relations. Therefore, basic rough set model has been extended to rough set on multigranulations (Qian et al., (2006, 2007)) in which the set approximations are defined by using multi-equivalences on the universe. On the other hand, rough set models on two universal sets are generalized with generalized approximation spaces and interval structure (Wong et al., 1993). Here, the equivalence relation is generalized to binary relation. Geetha et al (2013) further extended rough set on two universal sets to rough set on two universal sets based on multigranulation. This chapter discusses rough set on two universal sets based on multigranulations, where the set approximations are defined by using multi binary relations on the universes. The main objective of the chapter is to investigate mathematical properties; measures of uncertainty, topological characterization of rough set on two universal sets based on multigranulation have been inquired thoroughly with theorems, corollaries and relevant examples. In addition, real life examples are provided to explain the concepts developed.

ROUGH SET ON TWO UNIVERSAL SETS

The rough set model is generalized using two universal sets by G. Liu (2010). Let U and V be two universal sets and $R \subseteq (U \times V)$ be a binary relation. By a knowledge base, we understand the relational system (U, V, R) and approximation space. For an element $x \in U$, the right neighborhood or the R-relative set of U, $r(x)$ as,

$$r(x) = \cup \{y \in V : (x, y) \in R\} \qquad (1)$$

Similarly for an element $y \in V$, the left neighborhood or the R-relative set of y in V, $l(y)$ as,

$$l(y) = \cup \{x \in U : (x, y) \in R\} \qquad (2)$$

For any two elements $x_1, x_2 \in U$, x_1 and x_2 are equivalent if $r(x_1) = r(x_2)$. Therefore, $(x_1, x_2) \in E_U$ if and only if $r(x_1) = r(x_2)$, where E_U denote the equivalence relation on U. Hence, E_U partitions the universal set U into disjoint subsets and is denoted as U / E_U. Similarly for any two elements $y_1, y_2 \in V$, y_1 and y_2 are equivalent if $l(y_1) = l(y_2)$. Thus, $(y_1, y_2) \in E_V$ if and only if $l(y_1) = l(y_2)$, where E_V denotes the equivalence relation on V and partitions the universal set V into disjoint subsets. Therefore for the approximation space (U, V, R), it is clear that

$$E_V \circ R = R = R \circ E_V,$$

where $E_V \circ R$ is the composition of R and E_V.

For any $Y \subseteq V$ and the binary relation R, two subsets $\underline{R}Y$ and $\overline{R}Y$ called the R-lower and R-upper approximations of Y respectively are associated, which are given by:

$$\underline{R}Y = \cup \{x \in U : r(x) \subseteq Y\} \qquad (3)$$

$$\overline{R}Y = \cup \{x \in U : r(x) \cap Y \neq \phi\} \qquad (4)$$

The R-boundary of Y is denoted as $BN_R(Y)$ and is given as

$$BN_R(Y) = \overline{R}Y - \underline{R}Y.$$

The pair $(\underline{R}Y, \overline{R}Y)$ is called as the rough set of $Y \subseteq V$ if $\underline{R}Y \neq \overline{R}Y$ or equivalently $BN_R(Y) \neq \phi$. Further, if U and V are finite sets, then the binary relation R from U to V can be represented as $R(x, y)$, where

$$R(x,\ y) = \begin{cases} 1 & \text{if } (x,y) \in R \\ 0 & \text{if } (x,y) \notin R \end{cases}$$

The characteristic function of $X \subseteq U$ is defined for each $x \in U$ as follows:

$$X(x) = \begin{cases} 1 & \text{if } x \in X \\ 0 & \text{if } x \notin X \end{cases}$$

Therefore, the R-lower and R-upper approximations can be also presented in an equivalent form as shown below, where $\wedge$ and $\vee$ denote minimum and maximum operators respectively.

$$(\underline{R}Y)x = \bigwedge_{y \in V} ((1 - R(x,y)) \vee Y(y)) \qquad (5)$$

$$(\overline{R}Y)x = \bigvee_{y \in V} (R(x,y) \wedge Y(y)) \qquad (6)$$

Further research of rough set on two universal sets has been carried out by Tripathy & Acharjya (2012*a*, 2012*b*, 2013) and Tripathy et al. (2012).

ROUGH SET ON TWO UNIVERSAL SETS BASED ON MULTIGRANULATION

The basic idea of rough set on two universal sets (Liu, 2010) depends upon the notion of binary relation from U to V. In view of granular computing, it leads to static (single) granulation though some real life applications are discussed by Acharjya

& Tripathy (2012*a*, 2012*b*). However, in many real life situations, one often need to describe the concept through multi-relations from U to V. Therefore, Geetha et al has made efforts to define rough set on two universal sets based on multi-granulation, i.e., the target concept is described by more than one granulation spaces. However, to make the analysis simple it is restricted to two granulation spaces.

Definition 1: Let $(U, V, \Re)$ be a knowledge base, $\Re$ be a family of binary relations from U to V. Let $P \subseteq (U \times V)$ and $Q \subseteq (U \times V)$ be two binary relations from U to V. With the approximation space $(U, V, \Re)$, for $Y \subseteq V$, the lower and upper approximation operators are defined as:

$$\underline{P+Q}Y = \cup\{x \in U : r_P(x) \subseteq Y \text{ or } r_Q(x) \subseteq Y\} \qquad (7)$$

$$\overline{P+Q}Y = [\underline{P+Q}Y^c]^c \qquad (8)$$

The $(P+Q)$ boundary of Y is denoted as $BN_{P+Q}(Y)$ and is defined as

$$BN_{P+Q}(Y) = \overline{P+Q}Y - \underline{P+Q}Y.$$

The set Y is said to be rough with respect to $(P+Q)$ if and only if

$$\underline{P+Q}Y \neq \overline{P+Q}Y,$$

or equivalently $BN_{P+Q}(Y) \neq \phi$. The target set Y is said to be $(P+Q)$ definable if and only if

$$\underline{P+Q}Y = \overline{P+Q}Y$$

or $BN_{P+Q}(Y) = \phi$.

In the following example, the rough set on two universal sets based on multi-granulations is illustrated. Also, the difference between the rough set on two universal sets and the rough set on two universal sets based on multigranulations is shown.

Example 1. Let

$$U = \{x_1, x_2, x_3, x_4, x_5, x_6, x_7, x_8\}$$

and

$$V = \{y_1, y_2, y_3, y_4, y_5\}.$$

Consider the relations P and Q given by its Boolean matrix:

$$P = \begin{pmatrix} 1 & 1 & 0 & 0 & 1 \\ 0 & 0 & 1 & 0 & 1 \\ 0 & 0 & 1 & 0 & 1 \\ 0 & 1 & 0 & 1 & 0 \\ 0 & 0 & 1 & 0 & 1 \\ 0 & 0 & 1 & 0 & 1 \\ 1 & 1 & 0 & 0 & 1 \\ 0 & 0 & 0 & 1 & 0 \end{pmatrix} \quad Q = \begin{pmatrix} 1 & 0 & 0 & 1 & 1 \\ 0 & 1 & 0 & 1 & 0 \\ 0 & 0 & 1 & 0 & 1 \\ 1 & 1 & 0 & 0 & 0 \\ 0 & 0 & 1 & 0 & 1 \\ 0 & 0 & 1 & 0 & 1 \\ 0 & 1 & 1 & 0 & 1 \\ 1 & 0 & 0 & 1 & 0 \end{pmatrix}$$

From the above relations P and Q it is clear that

$$r_P(x_1) = \{y_1, y_2, y_5\};$$

$$r_P(x_2) = \{y_3, y_5\}\ ; \qquad r_P(x_3) = \{y_3, y_5\}\ ;$$
$$r_P(x_4) = \{y_2, y_4\}\ ; \qquad r_P(x_5) = \{y_3, y_5\}\ ;$$
$$r_P(x_6) = \{y_3, y_5\};$$

$$r_P(x_7) = \{y_1, y_2, y_5\};$$

$$r_P(x_8) = \{y_4\};$$

$$r_Q(x_1) = \{y_1, y_4, y_5\};$$

$$r_Q(x_2) = \{y_2, y_4\}\ ; \qquad r_Q(x_3) = \{y_3, y_5\}\ ;$$
$$r_Q(x_4) = \{y_1, y_2\}\ ; \qquad r_Q(x_5) = \{y_3, y_5\}\ ;$$
$$r_Q(x_6) = \{y_3, y_5\};$$

$$r_Q(x_7) = \{y_2, y_3, y_5\};$$

$$r_Q(x_8) = \{y_1, y_4\}.\text{Therefore,}$$

$$U / E_P = \{\{x_1, x_7\}, \{x_2, x_3, x_5, x_6\}, \{x_4\}, \{x_8\}\}$$

$$U / E_Q = \{\{x_1\}, \{x_2\}, \{x_3, x_5, x_6\}, \{x_4\}, \{x_7\}, \{x_8\}\}$$

$$U / E_{P \cap Q} =$$
$$\{\{x_1\}, \{x_2\}, \{x_4\}, \{x_3, x_5, x_6\}, \{x_7\}, \{x_8\}\}$$

Let us consider the target set $Y = \{y_1, y_2, y_5\}$. Therefore,

$$\underline{P + Q}\, Y = \{x_1, x_7, x_4\};$$

$$\overline{P + Q}\, Y = \{x_1, x_2, x_3, x_4, x_5, x_6, x_7\};$$

$$\underline{P \cap Q}\, Y = \{x_1, x_2, x_4, x_7\};$$

$$\overline{P \cap Q}\, Y = \{x_1, x_3, x_4, x_5, x_6, x_7\}.$$

From the above computation, it is clear that

$$\underline{P+Q}\,Y \neq \underline{P \cap Q}\,Y$$

and

$$\overline{P+Q}\,Y \neq \overline{P \cap Q}\,Y .$$

ALGEBRAIC PROPERTIES OF ROUGH SETS ON TWO UNIVERSAL SETS BASED ON MULTIGRANULATION

This section studies the algebraic properties of lower and upper approximation operators of rough set on two Universal sets based on multigranulation as established by Geetha et al (2013). The results obtained provide a better understanding of rough set on two Universal sets. These properties are derived from the definition of lower and upper approximations defined in earlier section.

Definition 2: Let U and V be two universal sets and $\Re$ be a family of binary relations from U to V. Let $P, Q \in \Re$. If $x \in U$ and $r_p(x) = \phi$, then x is a solitary element with respect to P. The set of all solitary elements with respect to the family $\Re$ is called the solitary set and is denoted as S, *i.e.*,

$$S = \{x \mid r_p(x) = \phi \text{ or } r_Q(x) = \phi\} \qquad (9)$$

Proposition 1. Let $\Re$ be a family of arbitrary binary relations from U to V and S be a solitary set with respect to $\Re$. Then the lower and upper approximation operators defined as in equation (7) and (8) satisfy the following properties: For subsets Y, Y_1 and Y_2 in V,

(a) $\underline{P+Q}\,\phi = S; \quad \overline{P+Q}\,\phi = \phi$

(b) $\underline{P+Q}\,V = U; \quad \overline{P+Q}\,V = S^c,$

where S^c denotes the complement of S in U.

(c) $S \subseteq \underline{P+Q}\,Y; \quad \overline{P+Q}\,Y \subseteq S^c$

(d)
$$\underline{P+Q}(Y^c) = (\overline{P+Q}\,Y)^c; \quad \overline{P+Q}\,Y^c = (\underline{P+Q}\,Y)^c$$

(e) $\underline{P+Q}\,Y - S \subseteq \overline{P+Q}\,Y$

(f) If $S \neq \phi$, then

$$\underline{P+Q}\,Y \neq \overline{P+Q}\,Y$$

for all $Y \in P(V)$; where $P(V)$ is the power set of V.

(g) $\underline{P+Q}\,Y = U$ if and only if

$$\underset{x \in U}{\cup}\, r_P(x) \subseteq Y \text{ or } \underset{x \in U}{\cup}\, r_Q(x) \subseteq Y .$$

(h) $\overline{P+Q}\,Y = \phi$ if and only if

$$Y \subseteq (\underset{x \in U}{\cup}\, r_P(x))^c \text{ and } Y \subseteq (\underset{x \in U}{\cup}\, r_Q(x))^c .$$

(i) If $Y_1 \subseteq Y_2$, then

$$\underline{P+Q}\,Y_1 \subseteq \underline{P+Q}\,Y_2 .$$

(j) If $Y_1 \subseteq Y_2$, then

$$\overline{P+Q}\,Y_1 \subseteq \overline{P+Q}\,Y_2 .$$

Proposition 2. Let $\Re$ be a family of arbitrary binary relations from U to V. Let the relational system $K = (U, V, \Re)$ be an approximation space. Let $Y, Y_1, Y_2 \subseteq V$, $P, Q \in \Re$. The lower and upper approximation operators hold the following properties. These properties are established to discover the relationship between the approximation of a single set and the approximation of two sets described by two granulations.

(a) $\underline{P+Q}\,Y = \underline{P}Y \cup \underline{Q}Y$;
$\overline{P+Q}\,Y = \overline{P}Y \cap \overline{Q}Y$

(b) $\underline{P+Q}\,Y = \underline{Q+P}\,Y$;
$\overline{P+Q}\,Y = \overline{Q+P}\,Y$

(c) $\underline{P+Q}(Y_1 \cap Y_2) \subseteq \underline{P+Q}Y_1 \cap \underline{P+Q}Y_2$

(d) $\underline{P+Q}(Y_1 \cup Y_2) \supseteq \underline{P+Q}Y_1 \cup \underline{P+Q}Y_2$

(e) $\overline{P+Q}(Y_1 \cup Y_2) \supseteq \overline{P+Q}Y_1 \cup \overline{P+Q}Y_2$

(f) $\overline{P+Q}(Y_1 \cap Y_2) \subseteq \overline{P+Q}Y_1 \cap \overline{P+Q}Y_2$

GENERALIZATION OF ALGEBRAIC PROPERTIES

This section generalizes some of the algebraic properties established in the previous section. Rough set model based on multigranulation is extended to rough set model on two universal sets based on multi-granulation, where the set approximations are defined by using multiple binary relations. The generalized definition is presented below.

Definition 3: Let $K = (U, V, \Re)$ be a knowledge base, $\Re$ be a family of binary relations from U to V. Let

$$P_i \subseteq (U \times V); \ 1 \le i \le n$$

be a family of binary relations from U to V. With the approximation space $K = (U, V, \Re)$, for $Y \subseteq V$, the lower and upper approximation operators are defined as,

$$\underline{\sum P_i}\,Y = \cup \{x \in U : r_{P_i}(x) \subseteq Y, 1 \le i \le n\} \tag{10}$$

$$\overline{\sum P_i}\,Y = (\underline{\sum P_i}\,Y^c)^c, 1 \le i \le n \tag{11}$$

Directly from the definition of lower and upper approximations the following generalized properties of the lower and upper approximations are derived. The proof of these properties is straight forward.

Proposition 3: Let the relational system $K = (U, V, \Re)$ be an approximation space. Let

$$P_i \subseteq (U \times V); \ 1 \le i \le n$$

be a family of binary relations from U to V. Let $Y, Y_1, Y_2, Y_3, \cdots, Y_m \subseteq V$. The lower and upper approximation operators hold the following properties for $1 \le i \le n$.

(a) $\underline{\sum P_i}\,Y = \cup \underline{P_i}Y$; $\overline{\sum P_i}\,Y = \cap \overline{P_i}Y$.

(b) $\underline{\sum P_i}\,Y^c = \left(\overline{\sum P_i}\,Y\right)^c$;
$\overline{\sum P_i}\,Y^c = \left(\underline{\sum P_i}\,Y\right)^c$

(c) If $Y_1 \subseteq Y_2 \subseteq Y_3 \subseteq \cdots \subseteq Y_m$, then

$$\underline{\textstyle\sum P_i}\, Y_1 \subseteq \underline{\textstyle\sum P_i} Y_2 \subseteq \cdots \subseteq \underline{\textstyle\sum P_i}\, Y_m$$

(d) If $Y_1 \subseteq Y_2 \subseteq Y_3 \subseteq \cdots \subseteq Y_m$, then

$$\overline{\textstyle\sum P_i}\, Y_1 \subseteq \overline{\textstyle\sum P_i}\, Y_2 \subseteq \cdots \subseteq \overline{\textstyle\sum P_i}\, Y_m$$

(e) $\underline{\textstyle\sum P_i}\left(\bigcap_{j=1}^{m} Y_j\right) \subseteq \bigcap_{j=1}^{m}\left(\underline{P_i}\, Y_j\right)$

(f) $\underline{\textstyle\sum P_i}\left(\bigcup_{j=1}^{m} Y_j\right) \supseteq \bigcup_{j=1}^{m}\left(\underline{\textstyle\sum P_i}\, Y_j\right)$

(g) $\overline{\textstyle\sum P_i}\left(\bigcup_{j=1}^{m} Y_j\right) \supseteq \bigcup_{j=1}^{m}\left(\overline{\textstyle\sum P_i}\, Y_j\right)$

(h) $\overline{\textstyle\sum P_i}\left(\bigcap_{j=1}^{m} Y_j\right) \subseteq \bigcap_{j=1}^{m}\left(\overline{\textstyle\sum P_i}\, Y_j\right)$

KNOWLEDGE REPRESENTATION

This section of the chapter, considers a real world example for two universal sets based on multigranulation to impart complete understanding of the concepts developed. In a city there are many hospitals and people decide to walk into various hospitals depending upon various parameters like specialization of the doctors, qualification of the doctors, nearby hospitals, medical facilities available at the hospital, service provided by the medics etc. Therefore, to design this scenario, more than one relation on two sets is needed. To put forward this application in our concept, let us consider a small universe U of 8 persons,

$$U = \{x_1, x_2, x_3, x_4, x_5, x_6, x_7, x_8\}\ .$$

Let V be the set of hospitals available, let us consider 5 hospitals,

$$V = \{y_1, y_2, y_3, y_4, y_5\}\,.$$

Let P portrays the persons selecting the hospital based on the medical facilities available and Q expose the persons opted for the hospital according to the service provided by the medics. The row one of the relation P represents the person one's i.e., x_1's choice of hospitals based on medical facilities available, which is $\{y_1, y_2, y_5\}$ which gives us the relation,

$$\{(x_1, y_1), (x_1, y_2), (x_1, y_5)\}\,.$$

The same x_1 chooses $\{y_1, y_4, y_5\}$ when it comes to service of the medics.

Let

$$U = \{x_1,\, x_2,\, x_3,\, x_4,\, x_5,\, x_6,\, x_7,\, x_8\}$$

and

$$V = \{y_1, y_2, y_3, y_4, y_5\}\,.$$

Consider the relations P and Q given by its Boolean matrix:

$$P = \begin{pmatrix} 1 & 1 & 0 & 0 & 1 \\ 0 & 0 & 0 & 0 & 0 \\ 0 & 0 & 1 & 0 & 1 \\ 0 & 1 & 0 & 1 & 0 \\ 0 & 0 & 1 & 0 & 1 \\ 0 & 0 & 1 & 0 & 1 \\ 1 & 1 & 0 & 0 & 1 \\ 0 & 0 & 0 & 1 & 0 \end{pmatrix} \quad Q = \begin{pmatrix} 1 & 0 & 0 & 1 & 1 \\ 0 & 1 & 0 & 1 & 0 \\ 0 & 0 & 1 & 0 & 1 \\ 1 & 1 & 0 & 0 & 0 \\ 0 & 0 & 1 & 0 & 1 \\ 0 & 0 & 1 & 0 & 1 \\ 0 & 1 & 1 & 0 & 1 \\ 1 & 0 & 0 & 1 & 0 \end{pmatrix}$$

From the above relations P and Q it is clear that

$r_P(x_1) = \{y_1, y_2, y_5\};$

$r_P(x_2) = \{\} \quad ; \qquad r_P(x_3) = \{y_3, y_5\} \quad ;$

$r_P(x_4) = \{y_2, y_4\};$

$r_P(x_5) = \{y_3, y_5\}; r_P(x_6) = \{y_3, y_5\};$

$r_P(x_7) = \{y_1, y_2, y_5\};$

$r_P(x_8) = \{y_4\};$

$r_Q(x_1) = \{y_1, y_4, y_5\};$

$r_Q(x_2) = \{y_2, y_4\}; r_Q(x_3) = \{y_3, y_5\};$

$r_Q(x_4) = \{y_1, y_2\};$

$r_Q(x_5) = \{y_3, y_5\}; r_Q(x_6) = \{y_3, y_5\};$

$r_Q(x_7) = \{y_2, y_3, y_5\}; r_Q(x_8) = \{y_1, y_4\}.$

Therefore,

$U / E_P = \{\{x_1, x_7\}, \{x_2\}, \{x_3, x_5, x_6\}, \{x_4\}, \{x_8\}\};$

$U / E_Q = \{\{x_1\}, \{x_2\}, \{x_3, x_5, x_6\}, \{x_4\}, \{x_7\}, \{x_8\}\}$

Examples to show the validity of various propositions established earlier are discussed. This is as follows:

Proposition 1(a). By definition of lower approximation,

$$\underline{P+Q}\,\phi = \cup\{x \in U : r_P(x) \subseteq \phi$$

or $r_Q(x) \subseteq \phi\}$. It indicates that

$$\underline{P+Q}\,\phi = \{x_2\} = S.$$

Similarly, by definition of upper approximation,

$$\overline{P+Q}\,\phi = [\underline{P+Q}\,\phi^C]^C =$$
$$[\underline{P+Q}\{y_1, y_2, y_3, y_4, y_5\}]^C$$

$$= \{x_1, x_2, x_3, x_4, x_5, x_6, x_7, x_8\}^C = \phi.$$

Therefore, it is clear that $\underline{P+Q}\,\phi = S$; and

$\overline{P+Q}\,\phi = \phi.$

(b) By definition of lower approximation,

$$\underline{P+Q}\,V = \cup\{x \in U : r_P(x) \subseteq V \text{ or } r_Q(x) \subseteq V\}.$$

It indicates that

$$\underline{P+Q}\,V = \{x_1, x_2, x_3, x_4, x_5, x_6, x_7, x_8\} = U.$$

Similarly, by definition of upper approximation,

$$\overline{P+Q}\,V = [\underline{P+Q}V^C]^C = [\underline{P+Q}\phi]^C = \{x_2\}^C$$

$$= \{x_1, x_3, x_4, x_5, x_6, x_7, x_8\} = S^C.$$

Therefore, it is clear that $\underline{P+Q}\,V = U$; and

$\overline{P+Q}\,V = S^c.$

(c) By definition of lower approximation,

$$\underline{P+Q}\,Y = \cup\{x \in U : r_P(x) \subseteq Y \text{ or } r_Q(x) \subseteq Y\}.$$

It indicates that

$$\underline{P+Q}Y = \{x_1, x_2, x_4, x_7\},$$

where $S = \{x_2\}$, it is clear that $S \subseteq \overline{P+Q}\,Y$. Similarly, $\overline{P+Q}\,Y \subseteq S^c$ can also be verified.

(d) By definition of lower approximation,

$$\underline{P+Q}\,Y^C = \cup\{x \in U : r_P(x) \subseteq Y^C \text{ or } r_Q(x) \subseteq Y^C\}.$$

Let $Y = \{y_1, y_2, y_5\}$, so $Y^C = \{y_3, y_4\}$, which leads to

$$\underline{P+Q}(Y^c) = \{x_2, x_8\}.$$

Again, by definition of upper approximation,

$$(\overline{P+Q}\,Y)^c = [[\underline{P+Q}Y^C]^C]^C$$
$$= \{\{x_2, x_8\}^C\}^C = \{x_2, x_8\}$$

Therefore, it is clear that $\underline{P+Q}(Y^c) = (\overline{P+Q}\,Y)^c$. Similarly,

$$\overline{P+Q}\,Y^c = (\underline{P+Q}\,Y)^c$$

can also be verified.

(e) Let $Y = \{y_1, y_2, y_5\}$, by definition of lower approximation,

$$\underline{P+Q}\,Y = \cup\{x \in U : r_P(x) \subseteq Y$$

or $r_Q(x) \subseteq Y\}$. Thus,

$$\underline{P+Q}\,Y = \{x_1, x_2, x_4, x_7\},$$

then

$$\underline{P+Q}\,Y - S = \{x_1, x_4, x_7\}.$$

By definition of upper approximation,

$$\overline{P+Q}Y = \{x_1, x_3, x_4, x_5, x_6, x_7\}.$$

It is clear that

$$\underline{P+Q}\,Y - S \subseteq \overline{P+Q}\,Y.$$

(f) Let $Y = \{y_1, y_2, y_5\}$. By definition of lower approximation,

$$\underline{P+Q}\,Y = \cup\{x \in U : r_P(x) \subseteq Y$$

or $r_Q(x) \subseteq Y\}$. Thus we get,

$$\underline{P+Q}\,Y = \{x_1, x_2, x_4, x_7\}.$$

According to the definition of upper approximation,

$$\overline{P+Q}Y = \{x_1, x_3, x_4, x_5, x_6, x_7\}.$$

Thus, it is clear that

$$\underline{P+Q}\,Y \neq \overline{P+Q}\,Y,$$

since $S = \{x_2\}$.

(g) Since

$$\bigcup_{x \in U} r_P(x) = \{\{y_1, y_2, y_5\}$$

$$\cup \{y_3, y_5\} \cup \{y_3, y_4\} \cup \{y_3, y_5\} \cup \{y_3, y_5\}$$
$$\cup \{y_1, y_2, y_5\} \cup \{y_4\}\}$$

$$= \{y_1, y_2, y_3, y_4, y_5\}$$

and $\bigcup_{x \in U} r_Q(x)$

$$= \{\{y_1, y_4, y_5\} \cup \{\{y_2, y_4\} \cup \{y_3, y_5\}$$

$\cup \{y_1, y_2\} \cup \{y_3, y_5\} \cup$

$\{y_3, y_5\} \cup \{y_2, y_3, y_5\} \cup \{y_1, y_4\}\}$

$= \{y_1, y_2, y_3, y_4, y_5\}$,

it is clear that $\bigcup_{x \in U} r_P(x) \subseteq Y$ or $\bigcup_{x \in U} r_Q(x) \subseteq Y$.
Let

$Y = \{y_1, y_2, y_3, y_4, y_5\}$.

By definition of lower approximation,

$\underline{P + Q}\,Y = \cup\{x \in U : r_P(x) \subseteq Y$

or $r_Q(x) \subseteq Y\}$. Thus,

$\underline{P + Q}\,Y = \{x_1, x_2, x_3, x_4, x_5, x_6, x_7, x_8\}$.

Thus, it is clear that $\underline{P + Q}\,Y = U$ if and only if $\bigcup_{x \in U} r_P(x) \subseteq Y$ or $\bigcup_{x \in U} r_Q(x) \subseteq Y$.

(h) Refer to Box 1.

(i) Let $Y_1 = \{y_1, y_2\}$ and $Y_2 = \{y_1, y_2, y_5\}$.

Therefore, by definition of lower approximation, so

$\underline{P + Q}Y_1 = \{x_2, x_4\}$

and

$\underline{P + Q}Y_2 = \{x_1, x_2, x_4, x_7\}$.

This clears that

$\underline{P + Q}\,Y_1 \subseteq \underline{P + Q}\,Y_2$,

if $Y_1 \subseteq Y_2$.

(j) Let $Y_1 = \{y_1, y_2\}$ and $Y_2 = \{y_1, y_2, y_5\}$. By definition of upper approximation, $\overline{P + Q}\,Y_1 =$

$[\underline{P + Q}Y_1^C]^C = [\underline{P + Q}\{y_3, y_4, y_5\}]^C = \{x_1, x_4, x_7\}$

and

$\overline{P + Q}\,Y_2 = \{x_1, x_3, x_4, x_5, x_6, x_7\}$.

This clears that

Box 1.

Since $\bigcup_{x \in U} r_P(x) = \{\{y_1, y_2, y_5\} \cup \{y_3, y_5\} \cup \{y_3, y_4\} \cup \{y_3, y_5\} \cup \{y_3, y_5\} \cup \{y_1, y_2, y_5\} \cup \{y_4\}\} = \{y_1,$
$y_2, y_3, y_4, y_5\}$, Thus, $(\bigcup_{x \in U} r_P(x))^c = \phi$. Again, $\bigcup_{x \in U} r_Q(x) = \{\{y_1, y_4, y_5\} \cup \{\{y_2, y_4\} \cup \{y_3, y_5\} \cup \{y_1, y_2\} \cup$
$\{y_3, y_5\} \cup \{y_3, y_5\} \cup \{y_2, y_3, y_5\} \cup \{y_1, y_4\}\} = \{y_1, y_2, y_3, y_4, y_5\}$. Thus, $(\bigcup_{x \in U} r_Q(x))^c = \phi$. Since the
assumption is $Y \subseteq (\bigcup_{x \in U} r_P(x))^c$ and $Y \subseteq (\bigcup_{x \in U} r_Q(x))^c$, it is clear that $Y \subseteq \phi$. It indicates that $Y = \phi$. Thus by
definition of upper approximation, $\overline{P + Q}\,Y = \overline{P + Q}\,\phi = [\underline{P + Q}\phi^C]^C = [\underline{P + Q}\{y_1, y_2, y_3, y_4, y_5\}]^C$
$= \{x_1, x_3, x_4, x_5, x_6, x_7, x_8\}^C = \phi$. Thus it is clear that, $\overline{P + Q}\,Y = \phi$. Similarly, the converse part can also be
proved through the given example.

$\overline{P+Q}\,Y_1 \subseteq \overline{P+Q}\,Y_2$.

Proposition 2 (a). Let $Y = \{y_1, y_2, y_5\}$. Therefore, by definition of lower approximation on two universal sets based on multiple granulation,

$$\underline{P+Q}Y = \{x_1, x_2, x_4, x_7\}.$$

Again, by definition of two universal sets based on single granulation, we have $\underline{P}Y = \{x_1, x_2, x_7\}$ and $\underline{Q}Y = \{x_4\}$. Therefore,

$$\underline{P}Y \cup \underline{Q}Y = \{x_1, x_2, x_4, x_7\}$$

and hence

$$\underline{P+Q}\,Y = \underline{P}Y \cup \underline{Q}Y.$$

Similarly, it can also be verified that

$$\overline{P+Q}\,Y = \overline{P}Y \cap \overline{Q}Y.$$

(b) Let $Y = \{y_1, y_2, y_5\}$. Therefore, by definition of lower approximation,

$$\underline{P+Q}Y = \{x_1, x_2, x_4, x_7\} =$$

$\underline{Q+P}Y$ and thus

$$\underline{P+Q}\,Y = \underline{Q+P}\,Y.$$

Similarly, it can also be verified that

$$\overline{P+Q}\,Y = \overline{Q+P}\,Y.$$

(c) Let $Y_1 = \{y_1, y_2, y_3\}$ and $Y_2 = \{y_1, y_2, y_5\}$, and so

$$Y_1 \cap Y_2 = \{y_1, y_2\}.$$

By definition of lower approximation,

$$\underline{P+Q}\,(Y_1 \cap Y_2) = \{x_2, x_4\}.$$

Similarly,

$$\underline{P+Q}\,(Y_1) = \{x_2, x_4\}$$

and $\underline{P+Q}\,(Y_2) = \{x_1, x_2, x_4, x_7\}$. It indicates that,

$$\underline{P+Q}\,Y_1 \cap \underline{P+Q}\,Y_2 = \{x_2, x_4\}$$

and hence

$$\underline{P+Q}(Y_1 \cap Y_2) \subseteq$$

$$\underline{P+Q}\,Y_1 \cap \underline{P+Q}\,Y_2.$$

(d) Let $Y_1 = \{y_1, y_2, y_3\}$ and $Y_2 = \{y_1, y_2, y_5\}$, and so

$$Y_1 \cup Y_2 = \{y_1, y_2, y_3, y_5\}.$$

By definition of lower approximation,

$$\underline{P+Q}\,(Y_1 \cup Y_2) = \{x_1, x_2, x_3, x_4, x_5, x_6, x_7\},$$

$$\underline{P+Q}\,(Y_1) = \{x_2, x_4\}$$

and $\underline{P+Q}\,(Y_2) = \{x_1, x_2, x_4, x_7\}$. It indicates that,

$$\underline{P+Q}\,Y_1 \cup \underline{P+Q}\,Y_2 = \{x_1, x_2, x_4, x_7\}$$

and hence

$$\underline{P+Q}\,(Y_1 \cup Y_2) \supseteq$$

$$\underline{P+Q}\,Y_1 \cup \underline{P+Q}\,Y_2.$$

(e) Let $Y_1 = \{y_1, y_2\}$ and $Y_2 = \{y_1, y_2, y_3\}$, and so

$$Y_1 \cup Y_2 = \{y_1, y_2, y_3\}.$$

By definition of upper approximation,

$$\overline{P+Q}\,(Y_1 \cup Y_2) = [\underline{P+Q}(Y_1 \cup Y_2)^C]^C$$
$$= \{x_2, x_8\}^C = \{x_1, x_3, x_4, x_5, x_6, x_7\}$$

Similarly,

$$\overline{P+Q}\,Y_1 = \{x_1, x_4, x_7\}$$

and

$$\overline{P+Q}Y_2 = \{x_1, x_3, x_4, x_6, x_7\}.$$

Therefore,

$$\overline{P+Q}\,Y_1 \cup \overline{P+Q}\,Y_2 = \{x_1, x_3,$$

$x_4, x_5, x_6, x_7\}$. It indicates that

$$\overline{P+Q}\,(Y_1 \cup Y_2) \supseteq \overline{P+Q}\,Y_1 \cup \overline{P+Q}\,Y_2.$$

(f) Let $Y_1 = \{y_1, y_2\}$ and $Y_2 = \{y_1, y_2, y_5\}$, and so

$$Y_1 \cap Y_2 = \{y_1, y_2\}.$$

By definition of upper approximation,

$$\overline{P+Q}\,(Y_1 \cap Y_2) = [\underline{P+Q}(Y_1 \cap Y_2)^C]^C = \{x_1, x_4, x_7\},$$

$$\overline{P+Q}\,Y_1 = \{x_1, x_4, x_7\}$$

and

$$\overline{P+Q}\,Y_2 = \{x_1, x_3,$$

$x_4, x_5, x_6, x_7\}$. Therefore,

$$\overline{P+Q}\,Y_1 \cap \overline{P+Q}\,Y_2 = \{x_1, x_4, x_7\}$$

and hence

$$\overline{P+Q}(Y_1 \cap Y_2) \subseteq \overline{P+Q}\,Y_1 \cap \overline{P+Q}\,Y_2.$$

MEASURES OF UNCERTAINTY AND ROUGHNESS

Uncertainty of a set is due to the existence of boundary line objects. The greater the boundary line objects of a set, the lower is the accuracy of the set. In order to express this idea, accuracy and roughness measure of employing the family of binary relations are introduced. The accuracy and roughness of set employing the family of binary relations are defined as follows:

Definition 4: Let the relational system $K = (U, V, \Re)$ be a knowledge base. Let $Y \subseteq V, Y \neq \phi$,

$$P_i \subseteq (U \times V); 1 \leq i \leq n$$

be a family of binary relations from U to V. Let $|Y|$ denotes the cardinality of set Y. The accuracy measure of $Y \subseteq V$ that capture the degree of completeness of our knowledge about the set $Y \subseteq V$ when classifying objects employing the family of relations $\Re$ is defined as:

$$\alpha_{\Re}(Y) = \frac{\left| \sum_{i=1}^{n} \underline{P_i} \, Y \right|}{\left| \sum_{i=1}^{n} \overline{P_i} \, Y \right|}; \quad \forall \ P_i \in \Re, 1 \leq i \leq n \tag{12}$$

Definition 5: Let the relational system $K = (U, V, \Re)$ be a knowledge base. Let $Y \subseteq V, Y \neq \phi,$

$$P_i \subseteq (U \times V); 1 \leq i \leq n$$

be a family of binary relations from U to V. The roughness of $Y \subseteq V$ which express the degree of inexactness of the set $Y \subseteq V$ when classifying objects employing the family of relations $\Re$ is defined as:

$$\rho_{\Re}(Y) = 1 - \alpha_{\Re}(Y) \tag{13}$$

PROPERTIES OF MEASURES OF COMPLETENESS AND ROUGHNESS

This section studies the properties of completeness and roughness of rough set on two universal sets based on multigranulation. Results show that approximation measure of a concept enlarges as the number of granulations for describing the concept.

Theorem 1. Let the relational system $K = (U, V, \Re)$ be a knowledge base. Let $Y \subseteq V$,

$$\Re = \{P_i : 1 \leq i \leq n\}$$

be a family of binary relations from U to V. Let $\Re' \subseteq \Re$ a subset of $\Re$. The accuracy measure holds the following property.

$$\alpha_{\Re}(Y) \geq \alpha_{\Re'}(Y) \geq \alpha_{P_i}(Y)$$

$$\forall \quad P_i \in \Re; \ 1 \leq i \leq n$$

Proof: Considering that $\Re' \subseteq \Re$ a subset of $\Re$, from definition of classical set theory and definition 3 that

$$\bigcup_{i=1}^{n} \underline{P_i} \, Y \supseteq \bigcup_{P_i \in \Re'} \underline{P_i} \, Y$$

and

$$\bigcap_{i=1}^{n} \overline{P_i} \, Y \subseteq \bigcap_{P_i \in \Re'} \overline{P_i} \, Y.$$

Therefore, it is clear that

$$\left| \bigcup_{i=1}^{n} \underline{P_i} \, Y \right| \geq \left| \bigcup_{P_i \in \Re'} \underline{P_i} \, Y \right|$$

and

$$\left| \bigcap_{i=1}^{n} \overline{P_i} \, Y \right| \leq \left| \bigcap_{P_i \in \Re'} \overline{P_i} \, Y \right|.$$

Hence, by definition of accuracy measure,

$$\alpha_{\Re}(Y) = \frac{\left| \sum_{i=1}^{n} \underline{P_i} \, Y \right|}{\left| \sum_{i=1}^{n} \overline{P_i} \, Y \right|} = \frac{\left| \bigcup_{i=1}^{n} \underline{P_i} \, Y \right|}{\left| \bigcap_{i=1}^{n} \overline{P_i} \, Y \right|}$$

$$\geq \frac{\left| \bigcup_{P_i \in \Re'} \underline{P_i} Y \right|}{\left| \bigcap_{P_i \in \Re'} \overline{P_i} Y \right|} = \frac{\left| \sum_{P_i \in \Re'} \underline{P_i} Y \right|}{\left| \sum_{P_i \in \Re'} \overline{P_i} Y \right|}$$

$$= \alpha_{\Re'}(Y)$$

Similarly, it can be proved that $\alpha_{\Re'}(Y) \geq \alpha_{P_i}(Y)$ for all

$$P_i \in \Re; \ 1 \leq i \leq n \ .$$

Thus, the inequality

$$\alpha_{\Re}(Y) \geq \alpha_{\Re'}(Y) \geq \alpha_{P_i}(Y)$$

holds for arbitrary $\Re' \subseteq \Re$ and for every $P_i \in \Re$; $1 \leq i \leq n$.

Theorem 2. Let the relational system $K = (U, V, \Re)$ be a knowledge base. Let $Y \subseteq V$,

$$\Re = \{P_i : 1 \leq i \leq n\}$$

be a family of binary relations from U to V with $P_1 \preceq P_2 \preceq P_3 \preceq \cdots \preceq P_n$. The lower and upper approximation operators hold the following property.

$$\sum_{i=1}^{n} \underline{P_i} Y = \underline{P_1} Y$$

and

$$\overline{\sum_{i=1}^{n} P_i} Y = \overline{P_1} Y$$

$$\forall \quad P_i \in \Re; \ 1 \leq i \leq n$$

Proof: Suppose that $1 \leq j < k \leq n$, and $P_j \preceq P_k$. From the definition of order relation $\preceq$, it is clear that $r_{P_i}(x) \subseteq r_{P_k}(x)$ for all $x \in U$. Again, if $r_{P_k}(x) \subseteq Y$, then

$$r_{P_i}(x) \subseteq r_{P_k}(x) \subseteq Y$$

and thus $r_{P_i}(x) \subseteq Y$. In addition to that $r_{P_i}(x) \subseteq Y$ does not imply $r_{P_k}(x) \subseteq Y$. Therefore,

$$\{x \in U : r_{P_j}(x) \subseteq Y\} \supseteq \{x \in U :$$

$r_{P_k}(x) \subseteq Y\}$. Thus by definition of lower approximation, $\underline{P_j} Y \supseteq \underline{P_k} Y$. Therefore,

$$\underline{P_j + P_k} Y = \cup \{x \in U : r_{P_j}(x) \subseteq Y \text{ or } r_{P_k}(x) \subseteq Y\}$$

$$= \{x \in U : r_{P_j}(x) \subseteq Y\} \cup \{x \in U : r_{P_k}(x) \subseteq Y\}$$

$$= \underline{P_j} Y \cup \underline{P_k} Y = \underline{P_j} Y$$

Since

$$P_1 \preceq P_2 \preceq P_3 \preceq \cdots \preceq P_n,$$

one can have that

$$\sum_{i=1}^{n} \underline{P_i} Y = \bigcup_{i=1}^{n} \underline{P_i} Y = \underline{P_1} Y$$

Similarly, by definition of upper approximation it can be obtained as

$$\overline{P_j + P_k} Y = \left(\underline{P_j + P_k} Y^c \right)^c = \left(\underline{P_j} Y^c \right)^c = \overline{P_j} Y$$

Therefore,

$$P_1 \preceq P_2 \preceq P_3 \preceq \cdots \preceq P_n,$$

one can have that

$$\overline{\sum_{i=1}^{n} P_i}\, Y = \bigcap_{i=1}^{n} \overline{P_i}\, Y = \overline{P_1}\, Y$$

This completes the proof.

EXAMPLE FOR COMPUTING COMPLETENESS AND ROUGHNESS

This section provides an example to compute the completeness and roughness of a set. On continuing with the example mentioned in the previous section, the completeness and roughness is discussed below.

Let us consider $Y = \{y_1,\, y_2,\, y_5\}$. Therefore, by definition of lower and upper approximation on two universal sets based on multiple granulation,

$$\underline{P+Q}\, Y = \{x_1,\, x_2,\, x_4,\, x_7\}$$

and $\overline{P+Q}Y = \{x_1,\, x_3,\, x_4,\ x_5,\, x_6,\, x_7\}$. Thus, completeness and roughness is given as:

$$\alpha_{\Re}(Y) = \frac{\left|\underline{P+Q\,Y}\right|}{\left|\overline{P+Q\,Y}\right|} = \frac{2}{3}$$

and

$$\rho_{\Re}(Y) = 1 - \alpha_{\Re}(Y) = \frac{1}{3}$$

The completeness measure is intended to capture the accuracy of our knowledge about the set Y. It is also clear that, $0 \leq \alpha_{\Re}(Y) \leq 1$ for every family of relations $\Re$ and $Y \subseteq V$. The set Y is said to be $(P+Q)$-definable, if $\alpha_{\Re}(Y) = 1$ and in this case it do not have any boundary line region of Y. If $\alpha_{\Re}(Y) < 1$, the set Y is called as $(P+Q)$-undefinable. Roughness is opposite to completeness and represents the degree of incompleteness of knowledge $\Re$ about the set Y. In probability theory or fuzzy sets, the numerical value of imprecision is not pre-assumed. However in rough computing, it is calculated on the basis of approximations which are the fundamental concepts to express imprecision of knowledge. This is of great value in many practical applications.

TOPOLOGICAL CHARACTERIZATION

This section introduces an interesting topological characterization of rough set on two universal sets based on multigranulation employing the notion of the lower and upper approximation. It results four important and different types of rough sets on two universal sets as shown below:

Type 1: If $\underline{\Sigma P_i Y} \neq \phi$ and $\overline{\Sigma P_i Y} \neq U$, then Y is *roughly ΣP_i- definable* on two universal sets.

Type 2: If $\underline{\Sigma P_i Y} = \phi$ and $\overline{\Sigma P_i Y} \neq U$, then Y is *internally ΣP_i-undefinable* on two universal sets.

Type 3: If $\underline{\Sigma P_i Y} \neq \phi$ and $\overline{\Sigma P_i Y} = U$, then Y is *externally ΣP_i-undefinable* on two universal sets.

Type 4: If $\underline{\Sigma P_i Y} = \phi$ and $\overline{\Sigma P_i Y} = U$, then Y is *totally ΣP_i-undefinable* on two universal sets.

FUTURE RESEARCH DIRECTIONS

This chapter extends the concept of rough set based on multigranulation to rough set on two universal sets based on multigranulation. Future work will be carried out on the study of topological properties defined in this chapter by finding out the types of the union, intersection and complement of such sets. These results will be verified for both complete and incomplete information systems. Further approximation of classification in the settings of rough set on two universal sets based on multigranulation is to be studied.

CONCLUSION

This chapter extends the study of rough set based on multigranulation to rough set on two universal sets based on multigranulation, where the approximations of sets are defined by using a family of binary relations defined over $(U \times V)$.

These multiple binary relations are chosen according to user requirements for solving real life problems. Algebraic properties of rough set on two universal sets based on multigranulation are also studied. In addition, two important measures such as completeness and roughness by using multigranulations which is always better than by using single granulation is defined. The completeness measure is not pre-assumed and will be used to express exactness of concepts and is of great value in many real life applications. Also, the topological characterization of rough set on two universal sets based on multigranulation is defined. The main objective of this approach appears to be well suited for data mining applications. Further research is planned to evaluate the proposed model in comparison to rough set on two universal sets.

REFERENCES

Acharjya, D. P., & Ezhilarasi, L. (2011). A knowledge mining model for ranking institutions using rough computing with ordering rules and formal concept analysis. *International Journal of Computer Science Issues*, 8(2), 417–425.

Acharjya, D. P., Roy, D., & Rahaman, M. A. (2012). Prediction of missing associations using rough computing and Bayesian classification. *International Journal of Intelligent Systems and Applications*, 4(11), 1–13. doi:10.5815/ijisa.2012.11.01

Acharjya, D. P., & Tripathy, B. K. (2008). Rough sets on fuzzy approximation spaces and applications to distributed knowledge systems. *International Journal of Artificial Intelligence and Soft Computing*, 1(1), 1–14.

Acharjya, D. P., & Tripathy, B. K. (2009). Rough sets on intuitionistic fuzzy approximation spaces and knowledge representation. *International Journal of Artificial Intelligence and Computational Research*, 1(1), 29–36.

Acharjya, D. P., & Tripathy, B. K. (2012). Intuitionistic fuzzy rough set on two universal sets and knowledge representation. *Mathematical Sciences International Research Journal*, 1(2), 584–598.

Acharjya, D. P., & Tripathy, B. K. (2013). Topological characterization, measures of uncertainty and rough equality of sets on two universal sets. *International Journal of Intelligent Systems and Applications*, 5(2), 16–24. doi:10.5815/ijisa.2013.02.02

Bargiela, A., & Pedrycz, W. (2002). *Granular computing: an introduction*. Boston: Kluwer Academic Publishers.

Chen, D., Zhang, W., Yeung, D., & Tsang, E. C. C. (2006). Rough approximations on a complete completely distributive lattice with applications to generalized rough sets. *Information Sciences, 176*, 1829–1848. doi:10.1016/j.ins.2005.05.009

Geetha, M. A., Acharjya, D. P., & Iyengar, N. C. S. N. (2013). Algebraic properties and measures of uncertainty in rough set on two universal sets based on multigranulation. In *Proceedings of the ACM Compute 2013*. ACM Digital Library.

Geetha, M. A., Acharjya, D. P., & Iyengar, N. C. S. N. (n.d.). Algebraic properties of rough set on two universal sets based on multigranulation. *International Journal of Rough Sets and Data Analysis*.

Kondo, M. (2006). On the structure of generalized rough sets. *Information Sciences, 176*, 589–600. doi:10.1016/j.ins.2005.01.001

Lin, T. Y. (1989). Neighborhood systems and approximation in database and knowledge base systems. In *Proceedings of the 4th International Symposium on Methodologies of Intelligent Systems* (pp. 75–86). Academic Press.

Liu, G. (2010). Rough set theory based on two universal sets and its applications. *Knowledge-Based Systems, 23*, 110–115. doi:10.1016/j.knosys.2009.06.011

Liu, G. L. (2005). *Rough sets over the Boolean algebras*. New York: Springer-Verlag.

Liu, G. L. (2008). Generalized rough sets over fuzzy lattices. *Information Sciences, 178*, 1651–1662. doi:10.1016/j.ins.2007.11.010

Marr, D. (1982). *Vision, a computational investigation into human representation and processing of visual information*. New York: Henry Holt and Co.

Pawlak, Z. (1982). Rough sets. *International Journal of Computer Information Science, 11*, 341–356. doi:10.1007/BF01001956

Pawlak, Z. (1991). *Rough sets: Theoretical Aspects of Reasoning about Data*. Kluwer Academic Publishers. doi:10.1007/978-94-011-3534-4

Pawlak, Z., & Skowron, A. (2007a). Rough sets: Some extensions. *Information Sciences, 177*(1), 28–40. doi:10.1016/j.ins.2006.06.006

Pawlak, Z., & Skowron, A. (2007b). Rough sets and Boolean reasoning. *Information Sciences, 177*(1), 41–73. doi:10.1016/j.ins.2006.06.007

Pedrycz, W. (2007). Granular computing: The emerging paradigm. *Journal of Uncertain Systems, 1*(1), 38–61.

Qian, Y. H., & Liang, J. Y. (2006). Rough set method based on multigranulations. In *Proceedings of the 5th IEEE International Conference on Cognitive Informatics* (pp. 297-304). IEEE Xplore.

Qian, Y. H., Liang, J. Y., & Dang, C. Y. (2007). MGRS in incomplete information systems. In *Proceedings of the IEEE International Conference on Granular Computing* (pp. 163-168). IEEE Xplore.

Saleem, D. M. A., Acharjya, D. P., Kannan, A., & Iyengar, N. C. S. N. (2012). An intelligent knowledge mining model for kidney cancer using rough set theory. *International Journal of Bioinformatics Research and Applications, 8*(5-6), 417–435. PMID:23060419

Tripathy, B. K. (2006). Rough sets on intuitionistic fuzzy approximation spaces. In *Proceedings of the 3rd International IEEE Conference on Intelligent Systems (IS06)* (pp.776-779). IEEE Xplore.

Tripathy, B. K., & Acharjya, D. P. (2010). Knowledge mining using ordering rules and rough sets on fuzzy approximation spaces. *International Journal of Advances in Science and Technology, 1*(3), 41–50.

Tripathy, B. K., & Acharjya, D. P. (2011). Association rule granulation using rough sets on intuitionistic fuzzy approximation spaces and granular computing. *Annals Computer Science Series, 9*(1), 125–144.

Tripathy, B. K., & Acharjya, D. P. (2012). Approximation of classification and measures of uncertainty in rough set on two universal sets. *International Journal of Advanced Science and Technology, 40*, 77–90.

Tripathy, B. K., Acharjya, D. P., & Cynthya, V. (2011). A framework for intelligent medical diagnosis using rough set with formal concept analysis. *International Journal of Artificial Intelligence & Applications, 2*(2), 45–66. doi:10.5121/ijaia.2011.2204

Tripathy, B. K., Acharjya, D. P., & Ezhilarasi, L. (2012). Topological characterization of rough set on two universal sets and knowledge representation. In P. V. Krishna, M. R. Babu, & E. Ariwa (Eds.), *Communications in Computer and Information Science* (pp. 68–81). Springer-Verlag. doi:10.1007/978-3-642-29216-3_9

Wong, S. K. M., Wang, L. S., & Yao, Y. Y. (1993). Interval structure: A framework for representing uncertain information. In *Proceedings of the 8th Conference on Uncertainty in Artificial Intelligence* (pp. 336 –343). Academic Press.

Yao, Y. Y. (1998). Constructive and algebraic methods of the theory of rough sets. *Information Sciences, 109*, 21–47. doi:10.1016/S0020-0255(98)00012-7

Yao, Y. Y. (2001). Information granulation and rough set approximation. *International Journal of Intelligent Systems, 16*, 87–104. doi:10.1002/1098-111X(200101)16:1<87::AID-INT7>3.0.CO;2-S

Yao, Y. Y. (2004). A partition model of granular computing. *LNCS Transactions on Rough Sets, 3100*, 232–253.

Yao, Y. Y. (2006). Three perspectives of granular computing. *Journal of Nanchang Institute of Thchnology, 25*, 16–21.

Zadeh, L. A. (1965). Fuzzy sets. *Information and Control, 8*, 338–353. doi:10.1016/S0019-9958(65)90241-X

ADDITIONAL READING

Geetha Mary, A., Acharjya, D. P., & Iyengar, N. Ch. S. N. (2013). Algebraic properties and measures of uncertainty in rough set on two universal sets based on multigranulation. In *Proceedings of the ACM Compute 2013*, ACM Digital Library, Vellore, India.

Geetha, Mary A., Acharjya, D. P., & Iyengar, N. Ch. S. N. (Communicated). Measures of Uncertainty and Topological Characterization in Rough Set on Two Universal Sets based on Multigranulation. *Information Resources Management Journal.*

Kryszkiewicz, M. (1998). Rough set approach to incomplete information systems. *Information Sciences, 112*, 39–49. doi:10.1016/S0020-0255(98)10019-1

Liang, J. Y., & Li, D. Y. (2005). *Uncertainty and Knowledge Acquisition in Information Systems.* Beijing, China: Science Press.

Liang, J. Y., & Qian, Y. H. (2006). Axiomatic approach of knowledge granulation in information system. *Lecture Notes in Artificial Intelligence, 4304*, 1074–1078.

Qian, Y. H., & Liang, J. Y. (2006). Rough Set Method Based on Multi-Granulations. In *Proceedings of 5th IEEE International Conference on Cognitive Informatics ICCI 2006* (pp. 297-304). IEEE Xplore, Beijing, China.

Qian, Y. H., Liang, J. Y., & Dang, C. Y. (2007). MGRS in Incomplete Information Systems. In *Proceedings of IEEE International Conference on Granular Computing GRC 2007* (pp. 2-4). IEEE Xplore, California.

Yao, Y. Y. (2000). Granular computing: basic issues and possible solutions. In *Proceedings of 5th Joint Conference on Information Sciences JCIS* (pp. 186-189), New Jersey.

Yao, Y. Y. (2005). Perspectives of Granular Computing. In *Proceedings of IEEE International Conference on Granular Computing* (pp. 85-90), IEEE Xplore, Beijing, China.

Zhan, J., & Tsau Young Lin. (2008). Granular computing in privacy-preserving data mining. In *Proceedings of IEEE International Conference on Granular Computing GrC 2008,* (pp. 86-92). IEEE Xplore, Hangzhou, China.

KEY TERMS AND DEFINITIONS

Accuracy: Accuracy measure captures the degree of completeness of our knowledge about the set when classifying objects employing the family of relations.

Algebraic Properties: The properties of objects in sets with or without giving prominence on the properties of the set as a whole.

Granule: The smallest addressable unit of knowledge in any application.

Multigranulation: The granulation of knowledge obtained by taking two or more granulations at a time.

Rough Set: A model, proposed by Pawlak to capture imprecision in data through boundary approach.

Roughness: The roughness of a set expresses the degree of inexactness of the set when classifying objects employing the family of relations.

Solitary Element: The object of the one universe which has no relation with any other object of another universe.

Solitary Set: The set of all solitary elements is termed as solitary set.

Topological Properties: The properties of sets taken as a whole without considering the properties of individual objects.

Chapter 10
Rule Optimization of Web-Logs Data Using Evolutionary Technique

Manish Kumar
IIIT, Allahabad, India

Sumit Kumar
IVY Comptech Pvt. Ltd., India

ABSTRACT

Web usage mining can extract useful information from Weblogs to discover user access patterns of Web pages. Web usage mining itself can be classified further depending on the kind of usage data. This may consider Web server data, application server data, or application level data. Web server data corresponds to the user logs that are collected at Web servers. Some of the typical data collected at Web server are the URL requested, the IP address from which the request originated, and timestamp. Weblog data is required to be cleaned, condensed, and transformed in order to retrieve and analyze significant and useful information. This chapter analyzes access frequent patterns by applying the FP-growth algorithm, which is further optimized by using Genetic Algorithm (GA) and fuzzy logic.

1. INTRODUCTION

Web mining is a data mining task to discover and retrieve useful information from large dataset. Web mining can be divided into: Web usage mining, Web content mining and Web structure mining. Web usage mining is a process of extracting useful information from Web-server logs i.e. user's history. Web content mining is the process to discover useful information from text, image, audio or video data and Web structure mining is the process to analyze the connection and node structure of a Web site. The phases involved in Web usage mining are data preprocessing, pattern discovery and pattern analysis. Preprocessing phase involves removal of unusual data like sound, image, graphics files and several server error codes. Pattern discovery extracts useful patterns from user sessions applying association rule mining and FP-growth (Han and Kamber, 2006). FP-growth algorithm is used for generating association rules. The two important approaches for the optimization of the association

DOI: 10.4018/978-1-4666-6086-1.ch010

rule: genetic algorithm (Agrawal, Lad and Manish, 2004; Pardasani, Parveen and Virendra, 2010) is applied with fuzzy logic (Jaisankar, Kannan and Veeramalai, 2010).

2. RELATED WORKS

Web usage mining consists of three phases: preprocessing, pattern discovery, and pattern analysis. B. Santhosh and Rukmani(2010) worked on 'Implementation of Web Usage Mining by using Apriori and FP-growth Algorithms'. Authors used Apriori algorithm to generate association rules that identifies the usage pattern of the client for a particular website. The output of the system is in term of memory usage and speed of producing association rules. Iyakutty and Sujatha (2010) proposed a new framework for Web usage data clustering for user's session. Web clustering involves grouping of the similar object and dissimilar object in different group. The initial clusters are selected based on statistical model to allow the iterative algorithm to converge to a better local minima and improving cluster quality using genetic algorithm based refinement. The method is scalable and can be coupled with a scalable clustering algorithm to address the large-scale clustering problems in Web mining. Biwei Li and Cunlai Chai (2010) presented a GA-based method to derive the fuzzy sets from a set of given transactions. Genetic algorithms provide efficient search algorithms to select a model, from mixed media data, based on preference criterion and objective function. It combines the strengths of rough set theory and genetic algorithm. Arslan et al. (2006) proposed method to find sequential accesses from weblog files using genetic algorithm. Weblog transaction, whether completed or not, is recorded and stored unstructured. Analyzing these log files is one of the important research areas of Web mining. Gyenesei (2000) presented methods for mining

fuzzy quantitative association rules; namely without normalization and with normalization. The results showed that the numbers of large itemset and interesting rules found by fuzzy method are larger than the discrete method (Agrawal and Srikant, 1999). Hadzic and Hecker, (2011) presented an approach where a tree structured data is converted into flat represenattion for preserving the structural and attribute value information, thus enabling a wider range of data mining and analysis techniques. Luan et al. (2012) introduced an association rule algorithm for Web log mining that reduces the search range and avoids the problem of combinatorial explosion. Nithya and Sumathi (2012) focused on data cleaning by removing the noise. Weber et al. (2012) suggested an approach where data blogs can be used to visualize political issues covering various sub issues. In Mele (2013), Author focused on improving the search engine performance by using static caching and recommending the interesting Web pages, articles and blogs.

3. OBJECTIVE

Web contains large amount of incredible information. Though it is tough to deal with vast information with user's perspective, Web service provider's perspective and business analyst's perspective because of its high complexities. Web service providers want to predict the user's behavior to design the website according to user's perspective and also to reduce the traffic load. Analysis can be done on the user's history from weblog patterns to retrieve useful information. This information can be used in different forms and places in e-business, website designing, market campaigns, measuring the success of marketing efforts, customer-company behavior and many more applications.

4. PROPOSED SOLUTION

The quality and effectiveness of the association rules highly depends on the type of the data used. When a user hits a URL in a domain, the information related to that access is stored in the form of a record in weblog file. These records have following attributes:

1. Time stamp,
2. Number of bytes transmitted,
3. User's IP Address,
4. Protocol version and status code by the server,
5. Size of the file accessed,
6. Request method (GET or POST),
7. URL of the page accessed,
8. User Agent's version number,
9. Type of the file (text/html/image etc.).

The proposed solution consists of three steps:

4.1 Preprocessing

The data present in the Weblogs cannot be directly used for mining the information. Preprocessing of the data is required for mining the important information. During preprocessing, noise is removed. Preprocessing involves following steps:

- **Data Cleaning:** Unwanted entries are removed from weblog data. It considered images, graphics and multimedia file entries and the client error code (Grace, Maheswari and Nagamalai, 2011) as the unwanted entries. The size of the weblog file reduces up to a greater extent after data cleaning.
- **User-Session or Session Identification:** This is done by the timestamping of the user access with the Web-server. Session is the total time for which the particular user accesses the Web-server. For a particular user, the user-session is recorded between its first timestamp and the last timestamp.
- **Data Transformation:** Weblog data is converted into required format for the pattern extraction. Cleaned weblog data is transformed into the form of transactions that are considered as the input to the FP-growth algorithm to generate the frequent itemsets pattern.

4.2 Pattern Discovery

User id is used for discovering the frequent patterns by FP-growth algorithm. Pattern discovery entails frequent itemset mining followed by association rule generation.

4.2.1 Generation of Association Rules from Frequent Itemset Patterns (Han et al. (2006))

Once the frequent patterns of itemsets from the set of transactions are generated, the association rule is generated using confidence and support count as:

$$confidence \ (S => T) = P(T \mid S) =$$
$$support\_count(S \cup T) \ / \ support\_count(S)$$

$$(1)$$

where,

$$confidence \ (S => T)$$

represents the conditional probability $P(T \mid S)$ that a transaction having itemset S also contains itemset T, which is expressed in terms of itemset support count whereas

$$support\_count(S \cup T)$$

is the number of transactions containing both the itemsets S and T, and

$$support\_count(S)$$

is the number of transactions containing the itemset S

Using (1), association rules is generated in the following two steps:

Step 1: For each frequent itemset A, generate all nonempty proper subsets of A. As in the case when A itself is considered, the either one of the antecedent or consequent part of the association rule will be null.

Step 2: For every nonempty subset s of A, rule "$s => (A - s)$" is generated, if

$$support\_count(A) \, / \\ support\_count(s) \geq min\_conf$$

where min_conf is the minimum confidence threshold provided by the user and

$$support\_count(A)$$

and

$$support\_count(s)$$

is the number of transactions containing the itemset A and s respectively. For rule "$s => (A - s)$," s represents the antecedent part of the rule and $(A - s)$ represents the consequent part of the rule that are present in the itemset A but not in the itemset s.

4.3 Pattern Analysis

4.3.1 Genetic Algorithm (Agrawal et al. (2004); Ali and Marghny (2005))

An attempt to optimize the rules generated by FP-growth by applying GA is made. GA was developed by John Holland. It is a stochastic, directed and evolutionary algorithm based on the natural selection of the population, which underlines biological evolution. It is a multi-iterative algorithm. GA processes generations by generating new populations from the old population. Populations are generally input to GA in the form of encoded string which may be binary or real etc. This study has considered real strings of population as the input to the GA. Standard GA apply genetic operators which are *selection, crossover* and *mutation,* on an initially generated random population, in order to generate the new population from the old population for the next iteration of GA. The probability of an individual reproducing is proportional to its fitness value which is computed by fitness function (Pardasani, Parveen and Virendra, 2010). So, the quality of the solution increases per iteration of GA. The GA process is terminated when optimal or acceptable solutions are found. The operators of GA are as follows:

- **Selection:** The fitness function value of the individuals in the population deals by this operator. It selects the individuals with high fitness function value in each iteration and eliminates the low fitted individuals.
- **Crossover:** This operator deals with the way of the combination of the two individuals or parents, to form a new crossover child for the next iteration.
- **Mutation:** This operator alters the new solutions to add stochasticity for better solutions. This is the chance that an individual

is removed or add (i.e. flipped) within a chromosome to get the complete solution space.

4.3.1.1 Fitness Function

The efficiency of GA is directly depending on the accuracy of the fitness function. The fitness function is the primary sink in a genetic algorithm. The general structure of the rule is as follows:

If antecedent then consequent.

Let a rule be of the form: $IF\ X\ THEN\ Y$, where X is the antecedent and Y is the consequent part of the rule. The confusion matrix is used (Pardasani, Parveen and Virendra, 2010), as depicted in Table 1.

Where, TP = True positive=Number of transactions satisfying itemset X and itemset Y. FP = False positive = Number of transactions not satisfying itemset X and satisfying itemset Y. FN = False negative= Number of transactions satisfying itemset X and not satisfying itemset Y. TN = True negative = Number of transactions neither satisfying itemset X nor itemset Y.

Generating useful rule, the value of TP and TN must be high and the value of FP and FN should be low. Then the following factors are computed:

$$INTERESTINGNESS\ FACTOR\ (IF) = TP\ /\ (TP + FP)$$

(2)

$$COMPLETENESS\ FACTOR\ (CF) = TP\ /\ (TP + FN)$$

(3)

The fitness function is given as:

$$Fitness\ Function = w1\times(IF\times CF)+w2\times M$$

(4)

where, $w1$ and $w2$ defined the user defined weight such that $w1 + w2 = 1$ and also $w1, w2 \mathbb{C}[0,1]$. M is the simplicity of the rule, which is inversely proportional to the number of items in the antecedent part of the rule and $M \mathbb{C}[0,1]$.

4.3.1.2 Optimization Methodology

GA is applied on the association rules obtained by FP-growth. The steps are as follows:

Step 1: Create random population of transactions as chromosomes initially.

Step 2: Compute the fitness function value of each chromosome.

Step 3: Sort the chromosomes on the basis of their fitness function value in non-increasing order.

Step 4: Select the chromosomes with high value of fitness function as the chromosomes for the next iteration.

Table 1. Confusion matrix of a rule

		Actual Class	
		X	$not\ X$
Predicted Class	Y	TP	FP
	$not\ Y$	FN	TN

Step 5: Applying the crossover on the selected chromosomes with high fitness function value.

Step 6: Applying mutation to add the stochasticity to the solution space.

Step 7: Replace the old chromosomes with new chromosomes with higher fitness function value.

Step 8: Repeat Step 2 to Step 7 until it achieve a certain level of optimization or fixed number of iterations. Table 2 shows the parameters used in the implementation of genetic algorithm.

4.3.2 Optimization using GA with Fuzzy-Logic (Agrawal et al. (2004); Jaisankar, Kannan et al. (2010); Pardasani et al. (2010))

The *fitness function* (4) is modified. User-defined weights $w1$ and $w2$ are considered as triangular fuzzy numbers and taking the alpha-cut fixed value i.e. $\alpha\_cut = 0.5$ and the rest steps are same as above.

4.3.2.1 Triangular Fuzzy Number (Alexandre et al. (2005))

Generally, fuzzy triangular number N is represented as:

$$N = (p_1, p_2, p_3)$$

Table 2. Genetic algorithm parameters

Selection	Proportionate Selection
Crossover Probability	0.1
Mutation Probability	0.01
Population	No. of rules from FP-Growth

Defining the membership function $\mu_N(x)$ as follows in Figure 1.

From the equations for intervals $p_1 \leq x \leq p_2$ and $p_2 \leq x \leq p_3$ from membership function $\mu_N(x)$ definition by putting $x = p_1^{(\alpha)}$ and $x = p_3^{(\alpha)}$ respectively, following equations are obtained:

$$(p_1^{(\alpha)} - p_1) / (p_2 - p_1) = \alpha$$
$$(p_3 - p_3^{(\alpha)}) / (p_3 - p_2) = \alpha \text{ (6)} \qquad (5)$$

From equation (5) & (6),

$$p_1^{(\alpha)} = (p_2 - p_1) + p_1$$

And

$$p_3^{(\alpha)} = -(p_3 - p_2) + p_3$$

respectively. Thus,

$$N_\alpha = \left[p_1^{(\alpha)}, p_3^{(\alpha)} \right] = \left[(p_2 - p_1) + p_1, -(p_3 - p_2) + p_3 \right]$$

Defuzzification: Centre of area (COA) method (Alexandre et al., 2005) is used for defuzzification, which is required for selecting the best fitted chromosomes. By defuzzification, Fuzzy number value is changed within the crisp boundary.

5. RESULTS AND DISCUSSION

Weblog files of the Web-server with $52,413$ entries considered as input for the analysis. Preprocessing is carried out and $37,617$ entries are obtained for mining the information [data is gathered from author's Institute]. FP-growth is applied with

Figure 1. Triangular Fuzzy Number $N = (p_1, p_2, p_3)$ $\pm$_**cut** *interval of Triangular Fuzzy Number interval* $N_\pm$

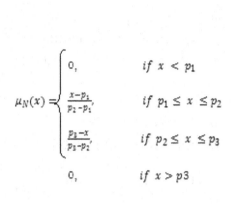

$$\mu_N(x) = \begin{cases} 0, & if \ x < p_1 \\ \frac{x-p_1}{p_2-p_1}, & if \ p_1 \leq x \leq p_2 \\ \frac{p_3-x}{p_3-p_2}, & if \ p_2 \leq x \leq p_3 \\ 0, & if \ x > p3 \end{cases}$$

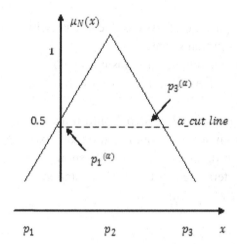

$minimum\ support(90\%)$

and

$minimum\ confidence\ (95\%)$.

Figures 2 and 3 show the run time (in seconds) and number of rules obtained using GA and GA with fuzzy logic by keeping

$minimum\ confidence$

fixed and varying the value of the minimum support respectively. Figures 4 and 5 show the run time (in seconds) and number of rules by keeping

$minimum\ support$

fixed and varying the value of minimum confidence respectively. Simulation results as depicted in Figures 2, 3, 4, and 5 clearly shows that the high value of the minimum support or minimum confidence, the run-time and number of obtained optimized rules decreases to a greater extent due to the less number of itemsets. The GA with fuzzy logic adds more useful rules and also optimizes the rules obtained from FP-growth.

6. CONCLUSION

The results show that the GA with fuzzy logic generate higher number of optimized association rules as compared to GA. The time complexity of GA with Fuzzy logic is higher as compared to GA but the tradeoff is in favour of GA with fuzzy logic in terms of optimized outcomes. Thus it is concluded that the combined approach of GA with fuzzy logic delivers refined and optimized association rules.

7. RESEARCH METHODOLOGY

Weblog mining is an open ended research field involving various level of analysis. The data stored at client as well sever are considered for analysis.

Figure 2. Minimum support vs. run time

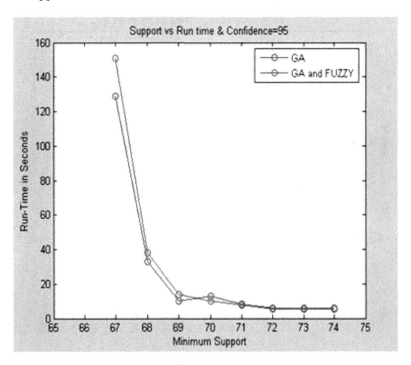

Figure 3. Minimum support vs. no. of rules

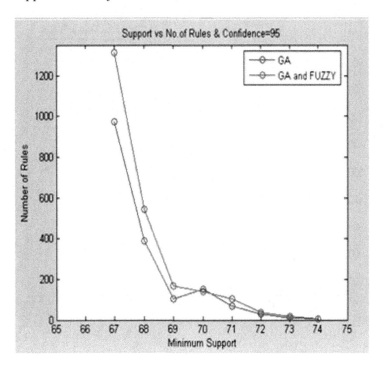

Figure 4. Minimum confidence vs. run time

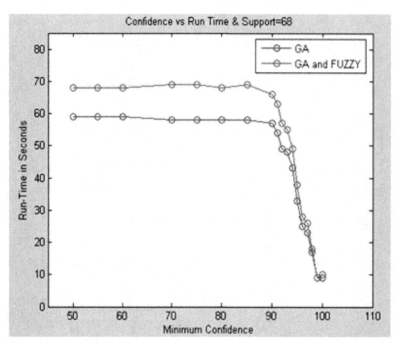

Figure 5. Minimum confidence vs. no. of rules

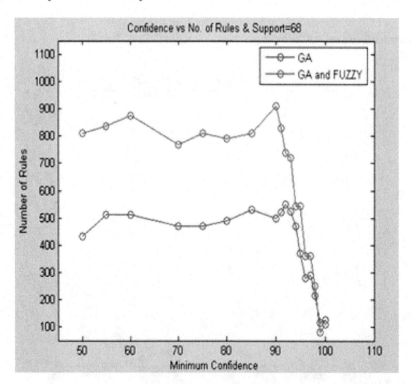

The pattern discovery, link mining, structure mining, user's behavior, user's interaction and many more are under the scope of weblog mining. Raw data analysis is difficult in weblog mining and hence opens the preprocessing activities based research. Data may be converted to required format for analysis. For example: Data may be converted into transaction data format. Each transaction is recorded in the weblog files and these files are unstructured for knowledge discovery in database techniques. Analyzing of these log files is one of the important research areas of Web mining.

REFERENCES

Agrawal, R., Imielinski, T., & Swami, A. (1993). Mining Association Rules between Sets of items in Large Databases. In *Proceedings of ACM SIGMOD Conference*. Washington, DC: ACM.

Agrawal & Srikant. (1999). Mining fuzzy quantitative association rules. In *Proceedings of IEEE International Conference on Fuzzy Systems* (pp. 99-102).Washington, DC: IEEE Computer Society.

Grace, L. K., Maheswari, V., & Nagamalai, D. (2011). Analysis of Web Logs and Web User in Web Mining. *International Journal of Network Security & Its Applications*, *3*(1).

Gyenesei, A. (2001). A fuzzy approach for mining quantitative association rules. *Acta Cybernetica*, *15*(2), 305–320.

Hadzic, F., & Hecker, M. (2011). Alternative Approach to Tree-Structured Web Log Representation and Mining. In *Proceedings of the 2011 IEEE/WIC/ACM International Conferences on Web Intelligence and Intelligent Agent Technology* (pp.235-242). Lyon, France: IEEE Computer Society.

Han, J., Kamber, M., & Pei, J. (2006). *Data mining: concepts and techniques*. San Francisco: Morgan Kaufmann.

Iyakutty, K., & Sujatha, N. (2010). Refinement of Web usage data clustering from K-means with genetic algorithm. *European Journal of Scientific Research*, *42*, 478–490.

Li, B., & Chai, C. (2010). A novel association rules method based on genetic algorithm and fuzzy set strategy for Web mining. *Journal of Computers*, *5*(9).

Luan, R., Sun, S., Zhang, J., Yu, F., & Zhang, Q. (2012). A dynamic improved apriori algorithm and its experiments in web log mining. In *Proceedings of 9th International Conference on Fuzzy Systems and Knowledge Discovery FSKD* (pp. 1261-1264). Chongqing, China: IEEE Computer Society.

Marghny, M. H., & Ali, A. F. (2005). Web mining based on genetic algorithm. In *Proceedings of AIML 05 Conference* (pp. 19-21). AIML.

Mele, I. (2013). Web usage mining for enhancing search-result delivery and helping users to find interesting web content. In *Proceedings of the sixth ACM international conference on Web search and data mining WSDM* (pp. 765-770). Rome, Italy: ACM.

Nithya, P., & Sumathi, P. (2012). Novel pre-processing technique for web log mining by removing global noise and web robots. In *Proceedings of National Conference on Computing and Communication Systems (NCCCS)* (pp. 1-5). Durgapur, West Bengal: IEEE Computer Society.

Saggar, M., Agrawal, A. K., & Lad, A. (2004). Optimization of association rule mining using improved genetic algorithms. In *Proceedings of IEEE International Conference on Systems, Man and Cybernetics 4* (pp. 3725-3729). Hague, Netherlands: IEEE Computer Society.

Sanches, A. L., Pamplona, E. D. O., & Montevechi, J. A. B. (2005). Capital budgeting using triangular fuzzy numbers. *V Encuentro Internacional de Finanzas, 19*.

Santhosh Kumar, B., & Rukmani, K. V. (2010). Implementation of Web Usage Mining Using APRIORI and FP Growth Algorithms. *International Journal of Advanced Networking & Applications, 1*(6).

Shrivastava, V. K., Kumar, D. P., & Pardasani, D. K. (2010). Extraction of Interesting Association Rules using GA Optimization. *Global Journal of Computer Science and Technology, 10*(5).

Tuğ, E., Şakiroğlu, M., & Arslan, A. (2006). Automatic discovery of the sequential accesses from web log data files via a genetic algorithm. *Knowledge-Based Systems, 19*(3), 180–186. doi:10.1016/j.knosys.2005.10.008

Veeramalai, S., Jaisankar, N., & Kannan, A. (2010). Efficient Web Log Mining Using Enhanced Apriori Algorithm with Hash Tree and Fuzzy. *International Journal of Computer Science & Information Technology, 2*(4).

Weber, I., Garimella, V. R. K., & Borra, E. (2012). Mining web query logs to analyze political issues. In *Proceedings of the 3rd Annual ACM Web Science Conference* (pp. 330-334). Evanston, IL: ACM.

ADDITIONAL READING

Adriaans, P., & Zantinge, D. (1998). *Data Mining*. Addison- Wesley.

Breiman, L., Friedman, J., Olshen, R., & Stone, C. (1984). *Classification and Regression Trees*. Wadsworth.

Brin, S., & Page, L. 1998. The anatomy of a large-scale hypertextual Web search engine. In WWW-7, 1998.

Chakrabarti, S. (2003). *Mining the Web*. Morgan Kaufman.

Cios, K., Pedrycz, W., & Swiniarski, R. (1998). *Data Mining Methods for Knowledge Discovery*. Kluwer. doi:10.1007/978-1-4615-5589-6

Coenen, F. P., Goulbourne, G., & Leng, P. Computing Association Rules Using Partial Totals. Principles of Data Mining and Knowledge Discovery. LNCS, vol. 2168, pp. 54-66. SpringerBerlin / Heidelberg, 2001.

Dasu, T., & Johnson, T. (2003). *Exploratory Data Mining and Data Cleaning*. Wiley. doi:10.1002/0471448354

Getoor, L., Link-based classification. Advanced methods for knowledge discovery from complex data (2005), 189-207.

Han, J., Pei, J., & Yin, Y. 2000. Mining frequent patterns without candidate generation. In SIGMOD, 2000.

Hastie, T., & Tibshirani, R. 1996. Discriminant Adaptive Nearest Neighbor Classification. TPAMI. 18(6)

Jiawei Han. (2011). *Micheline Kamber, and Jian Pei, Data Mining: Concepts and Techniques* (3rd ed.). Morgan Kaufmann.

Kantardzic, M. (2003). *Data Mining: Concepts, Models and Algorithms*. IEEE-Wiley.

Khan, M. S., Coenen, F., Reid, D., Tawfik, H., Patel, R., & Lawson, A. (2010). *A Sliding Windows based Dual Support Framework for Discovering Emerging Trends from Temporal Data. Research and Development in Intelligent Systems XXVII* (pp. 35–48). Springer London.

Kudo, T., Maeda, E., & Matsumoto, Y. (2004). An application of boosting to graph classification. *Advances in Neural Information Processing Systems*, *17*, 729–736.

Kuramochi, M., & Karypis, G. (2004). An Efficient Algorithm for Discovering Frequent Subgraphs. *IEEE Transactions on Knowledge and Data Engineering*, 1038–1051. doi:10.1109/TKDE.2004.33

MacQueen, J. B. Some methods for classification and analysis of multivariate observations. In Proc. 5th Berkeley Symp. Mathematical Statistics and Probability, 1967.

Pujari, A. K. (2001). *Data Mining Techniques*. Universities Press.

Quinlan, J. R. (1993). *C4.5: Programs for Machine Learning*. Morgan Kaufmann.

Rakesh Agrawal and Ramakrishnan Srikant. Fast Algorithms for Mining Association Rules. In VLDB '94.

Reddy, K. S., Varma, G., & Babu, I. R. (2012). Preprocessing the Web server logs: an illustrative approach for effective usage mining. *ACM SIGSOFT Software Engineering Notes*, *37*(3), 1–5.

Richard, O. (2001). *Duda, Peter E. Hart, and David G. Stork, Pattern Classification* (2nd ed.). New York: John Wiley & Sons.

Sampath, P., Ramesh, C., Kalaiyarasi, T., Banu, S. S., & Selvan, G. A. (2012, March). An efficient weighted rule mining for Web logs using systolic tree. In *Advances in Engineering, Science and Management (ICAESM), 2012 International Conference on* (pp. 432-436). IEEE.

Srinivasan, A., King, R. D., Muggleton, S. H., & Sternberg, M. J. E. Carcinogenesis predictions using ILP, Proc. of the 7th International Workshop on Inductive Logic Programming, volume 1297, pages 273–287. Springer-Verlag, 1997.

Vapnik, V. N. (1995). *The Nature of Statistical Learning Theory*. Springer-Verlag. doi:10.1007/978-1-4757-2440-0

Wang, C., Satuluri, V., & Parthasarathy, S. Local probabilistic models for link prediction. In *Data Mining, 2007. ICDM 2007. Seventh IEEE International Conference on* (pp. 322-331), 2007.

Weiss, S., & Indurkhya, N. (1998). *Predictive Data Mining: A Practical Guide*. Morgan Kaufmann.

Witten, I. H., & Frank, E. (2000). *Data Mining: Practical Machine Learning Tools and Techniques with Java Implementations*. Morgan Kaufmann.

Yadav, M. P., Keserwani, P. K., & Samaddar, S. G. (2012, March). An efficient Web mining algorithm for Web Log analysis: E-Web Miner. In *Recent Advances in Information Technology (RAIT), 2012 1st International Conference on* (pp. 607-613). IEEE.

KEY TERMS AND DEFINITIONS

Association: It generates relationships between data objects. It creates rules that describe how often events have occurred together. Example: "When customer buy PC, also buy CD. Such relationships are typically expressed with a support and confidence interval.

Clustering: It is the task to maximize intraclass similarity & minimizing interclass similarity. Class label is unknown. It groups data to form new classes. Example: cluster friends to find interest patterns.

Crossover: It is a genetic operator used to alter the programming of chromosome from one to another generation.

Fuzzy: It is a concept that uses approximation rather than exact values.

Mutation: It is a genetic operator that alters one or more gene values in the chromosome from its initial state.

Regression: Generate a function which models the data with the least error.

Summarization: It provides representation of the data set including visualization and also can generate reports.

Chapter 11
Machine Learning Approaches for Sentiment Analysis

Basant Agarwal
Malaviya National Institute of Technology, India

Namita Mittal
Malaviya National Institute of Technology, India

ABSTRACT

Opinion Mining or Sentiment Analysis is the study that analyzes people's opinions or sentiments from the text towards entities such as products and services. It has always been important to know what other people think. With the rapid growth of availability and popularity of online review sites, blogs', forums', and social networking sites' necessity of analysing and understanding these reviews has arisen. The main approaches for sentiment analysis can be categorized into semantic orientation-based approaches, knowledge-based, and machine-learning algorithms. This chapter surveys the machine learning approaches applied to sentiment analysis-based applications. The main emphasis of this chapter is to discuss the research involved in applying machine learning methods mostly for sentiment classification at document level. Machine learning-based approaches work in the following phases, which are discussed in detail in this chapter for sentiment classification: (1) feature extraction, (2) feature weighting schemes, (3) feature selection, and (4) machine-learning methods. This chapter also discusses the standard free benchmark datasets and evaluation methods for sentiment analysis. The authors conclude the chapter with a comparative study of some state-of-the-art methods for sentiment analysis and some possible future research directions in opinion mining and sentiment analysis.

1. INTRODUCTION

It has always been important to know what other people think. With the rapid growth of popularity and availability of online review sites, blogs, forums, and social networking sites necessity of analysing and understanding these reviews has

arisen. Companies and people can use the opinion given in these reviews for better decision making for example a user can know about pros and cons of various features of the products that can help in taking decision of purchasing items. E-commerce companies can use the users' opinion for improving their product quality and to know the current

DOI: 10.4018/978-1-4666-6086-1.ch011

trends. Opinion Mining or Sentiment Analysis is the study that analyse people's opinion, sentiment towards entities such as products, services etc. in the text (Liu, 2012). Sentiment analysis research can be categorized among Document level, Sentence level and Aspect/Feature level sentiment analysis. Document level sentiment analysis classifies a review document as positive or negative sentiment polar document. It considers a document as a single unit. Sentence level sentiment analysis takes a sentence to extract the opinion or sentiment expressed in that sentence. Aspect based sentiment analysis deals with the methods that identify the entities in the text about which an opinion is expressed (Liu, 2012). Further, the sentiments expressed about these entities are identified. Other important tasks in sentiment analysis and opinion mining research are opinion summarisation, opinion retrieval, spam review detection, etc. Solutions for the challenges incurred in these problems come from NLP, cognitive science, information retrieval, machine learning etc. Sentiment analysis research challenges and existing solutions are nicely presented in detail (Liu, 2012). Detailed survey of sentiment analysis research through various techniques is presented by Liu, (2012) and Cambria et al. (2012). However, these surveys do not discuss in detail about the machine learning approaches for sentiment analysis specifically that is the objective of this chapter. Machine learning approaches have been widely applied to sentiment classification mostly for document level sentiment classification.

There are several challenges being faced in the sentiment analysis research. Firstly, words used for expressing sentiment are domain specific. For example, word *"unpredictable"* has positive orientation in movie review domain but may be negative oriented for car review domain. Secondly, to identify the subjective portion of text from the overall review, because same words can be used in subjective and objective sentences. For example, *"author used very crude language"* and *"crude oil is extracted from sea beds"*. In this example,

same word crude is used for expressing sentiment in first sentence, however second sentence is purely objective (Verma et. al 2009). Thirdly, thwarted expectations are difficult to handle. In certain cases most of the text represent positive or negative polarity, out of sudden polarity of overall text is reversed. For example, *"This film has a great cast. It has excellent storyline and nice cinematography. However it can't hold up the audiences"*. Most of the review analysis research is based on the movie reviews and product review. Movie review sentiment classification face the challenge of handling the real facts which is generally mixed with actual review data. People generally discuss about the general traits of actors, plot of movie and relate the movie to their normal life. It is very difficult to extract the opinion from the reviews when there is a discussion of characteristics of artist and in the end overall movie is disliked. One of the biggest challenges of movie review analysis is to handle the negated opinion. Product review domain significantly differs from movie review dataset. In product reviews, reviewer generally writes both positives and negative opinion, because some features of the product are liked and some are disliked. These types of reviews are difficult to classify into positive or negative class. Generally, product review dataset contains more comparative sentences than movie review dataset, which is difficult to classify.

Main approaches for sentiment analysis can be categorized into Semantic Orientation based approaches (Turney 2002, Agarwal et al. 2013b), Knowledge based (Cambria et al. 2013) and Machine learning algorithm(Pang et al. 2002, Agarwal et al. 2013a). Sentiment orientation based approaches for sentiment analysis works in three steps. First of all sentiment-rich features are extracted. Further, semantic orientations of these sentiment-rich features are determined and finally overall semantic orientation of the document is computed by aggregating the semantic orientations of all the features in the document. Knowledge-based approaches initially use parser to extract the features, and further these features are matched in the knowledge base to the polarity value of the feature extracted. On that basis, the overall polarity of the document is determined. Knowledge based methods may perform very well only if the knowledge base is very huge. Machine Learning approaches based solution for sentiment analysis works in following phases. (1) Feature Extraction and pre-processing (2) Feature weighting schemes (3) Feature selection (4) Machine learning algorithms. Machine learning based approaches have advantages over semantic orientation based approaches and knowledge based approaches is that it only requires labelled dataset. However, semantic orientation based approaches depends on the method to determine the polarity of words, and it is quite difficult to compute the accurate polarity of a word or feature. Also, Knowledge based approaches depends on the already developed general knowledge-bases like SentiWordNet, WordNet etc. The main problem with these approaches is the coverage because most of the available knowledge-bases contain general knowledge (not affective sufficient knowledge) which is insufficient to determine the polarity of the documents. However, machine learning algorithms may learn the patterns found in the labeled dataset and can accurately determine the polarity of the testing documents.

Machine learning methods have been applied extensively for sentiment classification (Pang et al. 2002; Tan et al. 2008). Generally, Bag-of-Word (BoW) methods are used for creating feature vector for machine learning approaches. In this method, each word present in the documents is treated as a feature. Therefore, generated feature vector is of high dimensions of the order tens of thousands. Machine learning approaches face the problem of high dimensionality. For efficient sentiment classification results using machine learning algorithms, efficient features should be extracted from the text that can represent the sentiment of the user. Next, an appropriate weighting scheme is required to give the weights to each feature.

Further, prominent features should be selected from the feature vector for better classification results using efficient feature selection method. It also handles the problem of high dimensionality of feature vector. Finally, a robust and appropriate machine learning method is required for sentiment classification. For these problems, several methods have been proposed in the literature that is discussed in detail in this chapter.

This chapter covers the techniques and approaches based on machine learning algorithms that try to find the solutions of the challenges raised by sentiment analysis and opinion mining based applications. We conclude the chapter with the possible future research directions in opinion mining and sentiment analysis. This chapter is organised in following manner. Section 2 describes in detail the process of sentiment classification using machine learning methods. Section 3 presents the standard benchmark datasets for sentiment analysis research. Performance evaluation methods are discussed in the Section 4. Next, performance of some of the state-of-art methods are compared and discussed in Section 5. Further, Section 6 discusses the future research directions and finally Section 7 presents the conclusion.

2. MACHINE LEARNING APPROACHES FOR SENTIMENT ANALYSIS

Sentiment Analysis using machine learning methods is basically treated as a text classification problem. Traditional topic based text classification problem is easier than sentiment classification. Topic related keywords are the key features for classification of documents into different categories like politics, sport, etc. However, in case of sentiment classification, sentiment oriented words like good, great, amazing, etc. are important. The task of document level sentiment analysis is to classify the given review document in positive or negative based on the analysis of the text of the review. Machine learning methods have widely applied for solving sentiment classification problem mostly at document level. Therefore, in this chapter, most of the techniques and solution proposed in the literature are discussed which are based on document level sentiment classification. Machine Learning approaches based solution for sentiment analysis works in following phases.

1. Feature extraction and pre-processing.
2. Feature weighting schemes.
3. Feature selection.
4. Machine learning algorithms.

These phases are discussed in detail in subsequent sections.

2.1 Feature Extraction and Pre-Processing

Supervised machine learning methods have widely applied for sentiment classification. To improve the classification performance, it is very important to construct a feature vector that contains important features for sentiment analysis. Pang et al. (2002) is the first to use unigrams, bigrams, position based features, POS based features, adjectives, adverbs, and their combination as features for supervised document level sentiment classification. They investigated that unigram features performs best among these features. Dave et al. (2003) also applied supervised learning approach for sentiment analysis of multiple product reviews with more sophisticated features based on linguistic knowledge with feature selection and smoothing techniques. Their experimental results show that bigram and trigram can improve performance of sentiment classification under certain settings. Further, a lot of researchers have investigated various different features for better classification of review documents (Xia et al. 2011; Agarwal et al. 2013a). Many tokens or patterns that contain

syntactic and semantic information have been used as features for machine learning methods in sentiment analyses.

Matsumoto et al. (2005) has used syntactic relation between words and words sub-sequence as features for sentiment classification. Text mining techniques are applied to extract frequent word sub-sequence and dependency sub-trees from sentences to train the machine learning algorithm for sentiment classification for movie review dataset. Pak et al. (2011) extracted dependency tree subgraphs of a parsed sentence as a feature for sentiment classification. Their experimental results on movie review dataset show that sub-graphs based features with SVM classifier outperforms other bag-of-words and n-gram features. Nakagawa et al., (2010) have used the syntactic dependency trees for sentiment analysis and obtained better performance than using Bag-of-Word features. Xia et al. (2010) also investigated word relation features that incorporate the information of relation between words as effective features for sentiment classification. Gamon (2004) investigated that deep linguistic features in addition to word n-gram features improve the performance for sentiment classification on noisy data. Riloff et al. (2006) used subsumption hierarchy to formally define various types of lexical features. Joshi et al. (2009) also experimented with syntactic dependency relations based features for sentiment classification, and further proposes methods to generalize dependency features for improving opinion mining. Tu et al. (2012) proposed an approach which extracts features from the dependency forest. Dependency forest is a compact representation of multiple dependency trees. Their experimental results show improvement in the performance of sentiment classification on movie review dataset.

In many supervised sentiment classifications, adjectives are also treated as features for machine learning methods. Mejova et al. (2011), experimented the effectiveness of various POS tagged features for supervised sentiment classification. They used adjectives, adverbs and nouns in combination and individually. Experimental results showed that adjectives, adverbs, and noun in combination perform better than these features individually and Adjectives outperforms others as individual POS tagged feature. Agarwal et al. (2013a), extracted *unigram*, *bi-grams*, and Part of Speech (POS) based features (i.e. adjectives, adverbs) from the text, and used various composite features for sentiment classification on various datasets. Experimental results show that composite features perform better than other features for sentiment classification. Mullen et al. (2004) expanded the feature set based on Osgood's theory of semantic orientation (Osgood et al., 1957) and Turney's semantic orientation (Turney, 2002) for supervised sentiment classification.

Dang et al. (2010) proposed a lexicon enhanced method by combining machine learning and semantic orientation based approaches that significantly improve the performance of sentiment classification. They proposed sentiment features based on SentiWordNet lexicon in addition to content free, content specific features like unigram, bigrams. Experimental results show that rarely used sentiment features enhances the performance of sentiment classification. Whitelaw et al. (2005) proposed appraisal group based features for enhancing the performance of sentiment classification. Appraisal groups are phrases that contain word groups like *"very beautiful"*, *"extremely bad"*, etc. unlike individual words. These word groups are intensifiers or modifiers (i.e. very, extremely etc.) to opinion words (i.e. beautiful, bad etc.). These appraisal groups are used as features with Bag-of-Word features for sentiment classification, resulting into improved performance.

Text needs to be pre-processed as tokens or strings before applying machine learning models. In pre-processing, stemming (reducing words to their stem or root form) and stop word removal methods are generally used for sentiment classification. However, some studies found that stemming could not improve the classification performance. Negation word (no, not, never, didn't, don't, can't) reverses the polarity of the sentence. Therefore, it is important to handle negation for sentiment classification. Most of researchers have adopted the technique of Das et al. (2001). Pang et al. (2002) has also added the tag NOT to every word between a negation word ("not", "isn't", "didn't", etc.) and the first punctuation mark following the negation word.

2.2 Feature Weighting Schemes and Representation Methods

In machine learning based approaches, feature weighting techniques are very important for assigning values to the features for improved classification results. In sentiment analysis, many weighting schemes have been proposed in the literature such as Term Frequency (TF), Term Presence, Binary weighting scheme, Term-Frequency- Inverse Document Frequency (TF-IDF), etc. In Boolean weighting scheme, feature value is one if a term is present otherwise it is zero. In TF-IDF weighting method, weights are given to each term according to how rare these terms are in other documents. It is calculates weights by $w_{ij} = tf_{ij}*idf_i$, where tf_{ij} is the frequency of term i in document j, and idf_i is the inverse document frequency which is equal to $\log(N/n_i)$, N is total number of documents in the corpus and n_i is number of documents containing the term i.

In most of the topic based text classification tf-idf weighting scheme works well. For sentiment classification, binary weighting scheme performs better than frequency based schemes (Pang et al. 2002). One possible reason for this observation is that people tend to use different sentiment words in writing reviews. For example, when people write review about a camera, they will write like *"This Nikon camera is great. Picture quality is clear and it looks nice*". It is very unlikely that people will write like "*this Nikon camera is great. Picture quality is great and it's looking is also great*".

Martineau et al. (2009) proposed a new feature weighting scheme namely Delta TF-IDF. Delta TF-IDF weighting scheme is proved to better than term frequency and TF-IDF weighting scheme for sentiment analysis. In Delta TF-IDF, more weights are given to the terms which are unevenly distributed among positive and negative classes. It measures the importance of a features based on the class distinguishing property of a term, As it has been proved that term frequency is not important for sentiment classification, therefore this method gives very less weights to the term which are equally distributed in positive and negative classes. The value of an evenly distributed feature is zero. The more uneven the distribution of the feature among classes, the more important a feature should be.

Dai et al. (2011) proposes a method for improving sentiment classification by highlighting the sentimental features by increasing their weights. And further, bagging is used to construct multiple classifiers on various feature spaces and finally combined them into an aggregate classifier for improved performance. Paltonglou et al. (2010) discussed a detailed study of various weighting schemes for sentiment analysis. Their experimental results show that variants of classic tf-idf scheme can improve the performance of sentiment classification. Lin et al. (2012a) proposed an improved feature weighting method, which quantifies the terms sentiment scores by mutual information, further experiments on several kinds of feature presentation methods are performed for sentiment classification. The results show that mutual information based proposed weighting method is more effective than others. Raychev et al. (2009) proposed a new language independent weighting scheme is proposed based on the word position and its likelihood of being subjective. This weighting scheme is further used by NB classifier for sentiment classification.

O' keefee et al. (2009) experimented with various feature weighting methods like Feature Frequency, Feature Presence (FP), TFIDF. Further, authors propose three other methods based on words grouped by their SentiwordNet values i.e. SWN Word Score Group (SWN-SG), SWN Word Polarity Groups (SWN-PG) and SWN Word Polarity Sums (SWN-PS).

2.3. Feature Selection Methods

A feature is relevant for the classification if performance of the classifier degrades by eliminating this feature. Irrelevant features means it is not necessary at all for the classification (Yu et al. 2004). Two features are redundant features if their values are highly correlated. In presence of thousands of features, it is very common that a large number of features are not informative due to irrelevancy or redundancy with respect to the class. Therefore, removal of these irrelevant and redundant features can improve the performance of the classification (Yu et al. 2004; Forman, 2003). Characteristics of salient features for sentiment analysis are that feature should be relevant for the classification. It should be discriminating enough so that classifier can use the information of presence of this feature in dominantly in one class. For example, if a term "excellent" occurs dominantly in positive class very frequently, than presence of this term in a new test document indicates that document belongs to positive class. In addition, if a feature is frequent in many documents of same class then that feature can help machine learning method to learn better.

Apart from using relevant features and assigning correct feature weights, the feature selection methods are very important for the performance of the machine learning algorithms. The main purpose of feature selection methods is to select the features which are relevant and discriminating for the classification. In text classification task, features are typically words from the documents. Generally, it produces large number of features of order ten thousand or more. It is intuitive that this high dimensional feature vector contains lots of noisy and irrelevant features. Performance of the machine learning methods deteriorates due to high feature vector length and inclusion of irrelevant and noisy features. Dimension of feature vector can be reduced by using any feature selection method (i.e. Information Gain, Mutual Information MI etc.) or feature transformation method (i.e. SVD etc.). Feature selection methods select the important features using some goodness of a term formula; top features are selected above some threshold criteria and other irrelevant features are dropped. Feature transformation methods convert the high dimensional feature vector onto lower dimensional feature space, and reduced feature vector contain the contribution of each feature of initial feature vector. Wang et al. (2011) applied Latent Semantic Analysis (LSA) method for dimension reduction, further reduced feature vector is used by Support Vector Machine (SVM) for improving the performance of sentiment classification. In literature, mostly feature selection techniques are used for reducing the feature vector size because it is easy to use and computationally efficient as compare to other feature transformation methods. Feature selection method select important features by eliminating the noisy and irrelevant features. Method of computing importance of a feature is different for each feature selection methods.

A variety of feature selection methods have been proposed by researchers in the literature for the sentiment analysis like IG, MI, Chi Square (CHI), Document Frequency (DF) etc. The simplest feature selection method is Document Frequency (DF) i.e. to use the most frequent occurring term in the corpus. This approach is commonly used with general text classification as well as sentiment classification (Pang et al. 2002).

Tan et al. (2008), experimented the four feature selection methods MI, IG, CHI, and DF for sentiment classification on Chinese documents, using five machine learning algorithms i.e. K- nearest neighbour, Centroid classifier, Winnow classifier, NB and SVM. Authors observed that IG performs best among all the feature selection methods and SVM gives best results among machine learning algorithms. Abbasi et al. (2008) examined that information gain or genetic algorithm improves the accuracy of sentiment classification for movie review dataset. They also proposed Entropy Weighted Genetic Algorithm (EWGA) by combining the IG and genetic algorithm for higher accuracy. Nicholls et al. (2010) proposed a new feature selection method namely Document Frequency Difference, and further compared it with other feature selection methods for sentiment classification. Agarwal et al. (2012) proposed Categorical Probability Proportion Difference (CPPD) feature selection method, which is capable of selecting the features which are relevant and capable of discriminating the class. Wang et al. (2009) proposed a new Fisher's discriminant ratio based feature selection method for text sentiment classification. Agarwal et al. (2013a) experimented with mRMR (Minimum Redundancy and Maximum Relevancy) and IG feature selection methods for sentiment classification. They investigated that by removal of redundant features can improve the performance of sentiment classification.

Forman (2003) presented comparative study of twelve feature selection methods to identify the best feature selection method for text classification. Experimental result show that Information Gain outperforms among the twelve selection methods. Duric et al. (2011) proposed a new feature selection method that uses content and syntax model to separate the entities under review and the opinion context (i.e. sentiment modifiers). By considering only subjectivity expression provides more prominent features for document level sentiment classification. Experimental results using these features with maximum entropy classifier provides competitive results with the state of art approaches.

Abbasi, (2010) proposed an intelligent feature selection method that can exploit the syntactic and semantic information from the text. The proposed approach illustrates that heterogeneous feature set coupled with appropriate feature selection method can improve the performance of sentiment classification. O' keefe et al. (2009) introduced two new feature selection methods for sentiment classification i.e. SentiWordNet Subjectivity Score (SWNSS) and SentiWordNet Proportional Difference (SWNPD). The SWNSS is able to distinguish objective and subjective terms, since only subjective terms should carry sentiment. SWNPD is able to incorporate the class discriminating ability for feature selection. Verma et al. (2005) initially pruned the semantically less important terms based on semantic score retrieved from SentiWordNet, further IG feature selection technique is used to select important features for improved classification accuracy. Pang et al. (2004) proposed a minimum cut method for elimination of objective sentences that do not convey any subjectivity in the document.

2.4. Machine Learning Algorithms

Machine learning methods have widely applied for sentiment classification problem. Reduced and optimal feature vector, generated after the feature selection method is used by machine learning algorithm. Mainly Support Vector Machine (SVM), Naïve Bayes (NB), Maximum Entropy (MaxEnt) methods has been adopted by most of the researchers for sentiment classification. Pang et al. (2002) used different machine learning algorithms like NB, SVM, and MaxEnt for sentiment analysis of movie review dataset. Their experiments show that SVM outperforms other machine learning method for sentiment classification. Tan et al. (2008) also concluded that SVM performs better than other classifiers for sentiment classification. O' keefe et

al. (2009) also used SVM and NB classifiers for sentiment analysis with various feature weighting methods and feature selection methods. They concluded that SVM classifier is better than NB classifier for sentiment analysis. Ye et al. (2009) experimented with three supervised learning algorithms namely NB, SVM and character based N-gram model into the domain of travel destination reviews. They used IG for selecting important features. They used frequency of words to give weights to the feature values; experimental results show that SVM outperforms other classifiers for sentiment analysis. Cui et al. (2006) investigated that discriminative classifiers such as SVM is more appropriate for sentiment classification as compared to other generative models and winnow classifier. However, if redundancy among features is reduced efficiently, Boolean Multinomial Naïve Bayes (BMNB) algorithm can perform better than SVM classifier with various experimental settings for sentiment classification (Agarwal et al. 2013a).

Li et al (2007) generated various classifiers on different feature sets like unigram and POS based features, then these classifiers are combined using several combination rules. It was investigated that combined classifier outperforms individual classifiers. Tsutsumi et al, (2007) also proposed an integrated classifier consisting of SVM, ME and score calculation based classifiers, resulting into improved performance of movie review classification. Lin et al. (2012b) developed a three phase framework for choosing optimal combination of classifiers based on assembling multiple classifiers. Xia et al. (2011) proposed various types of ensemble methods for various categories of features (i.e. POS based, word relation based) and classifiers (NB, SVM, Maximum Entropy) for sentiment classification. Prabowo et al. (2009) proposed hybrid classifier by combining rule-based classification, machine learning and supervised learning method to improve the classification effectiveness. Dinu et al. (2012) study the use of Naïve Bayes classifier for opinion mining applications. They experiments on various relevant feature sets for sentiment classification, and further propose two combining techniques for individually trained on different features.

3. STANDARD DATASETS

3.1. Cornell Movie-review Datasets

URL: http://www.cs.cornell.edu/people/pabo/movie-review-data/

1. This dataset known as Cornell Movie review dataset consists of the 2000 reviews containing 1000 positive and 1000 negative reviews collected from Internet Movie Dataset (Pang et al. 2004).
2. **Sentence-Level:** Sentence polarity dataset v1.0: it contains 5331 positive and 5331 negative processed sentences/ snippets.
3. **Subjectivity Dataset v1.0:** This dataset contains 5000 subjective and 5000 objective processed sentences.

3.2. Multi-Domain Sentiment Dataset

URL: http://www.cis.upenn.edu/~mdredze/datasets/sentiment/

This dataset is introduced by Blitzer et al. (2007), it contains the product reviews from 20 different categories like Book, DVD, Electronics, Kitchen appliances etc.

3.3. Customer Review Dataset

URL: http://www.cs.uic.edu/~liub/FBS/CustomerReviewData.zip

This dataset is produced by Hu et al. (), this dataset contains reviews of five electronics products taken like Canon, Nokia, Nikon etc. from Amazon and Cnet. The dataset is manually labeled as to whether an opinion is expressed and about which specific feature opinion is expressed.

3.4. MPQA Corpus

URL: http://mpqa.cs.pitt.edu/corpora/mpqa_corpus/

This dataset is produced by Wiebe et al. (2005) by University of Pittsburgh. This corpus contains 692 documents, a total of 15802 sentences. This manually labeled dataset provides the debate discussions sentences for political and product debates.

3.5. Epinion Dataset

This dataset is provided by Taboada et al. (2011), this dataset is a collection of 400 review texts are provided for sentiment analysis. The collection consists of 50 reviews each of: books, cars, computers, cookware, hotels, movies, music, and phones.

3.6. Multiple-Aspect Restaurant Reviews

URL: http://people.csail.mit.edu/bsnyder/naacl07/data/unformatted/

This dataset is produced by Snyder et al. (2007). The corpus consists of 4,488 reviews. Each review gives an explicit 1-to-5 rating for five different aspects—food, ambiance, service, value, and overall experience, along with the text of the review itself, all provided by the review author.

4. EVALUATION MECHANISM

Accuracy, Precision, Recall, and F- measure are generally used for evaluating performance of sentiment analysis model. Accuracy is the total number of correctly labeled documents out of the total number of documents. Precision for a class C is the fraction of total number of documents that are correctly labeled and total number of documents that labeled to the class C, i.e. sum of True Positives (TP) and False Positives (FP). Recall is the fraction of total number of correctly labeled documents to the total number of documents that belongs to class C i.e. sum of True Positives and False Negative (FN).

Accuracy is commonly used as a measure for categorization techniques.

$$Accuracy_i = \frac{TP_i + TN_i}{TP_i + FP_i + FN_i + TN_i} \tag{1}$$

Here,

- **TPi:** Number of documents correctly classified to the class.
- **FPi:** Number of documents incorrectly classified to the class.
- **FNi:** Number of documents not classified to the class.
- **TNi:** Number of documents not classified to the correct class.

Precision and recall for class C_i can be calculated by:

$$Precision_i = \frac{TP_i}{TP_i + FP_i} \tag{2}$$

$$Recall_i = \frac{TP_i}{TP_i + FN_i} \tag{3}$$

F –measure is the combination of both precision and recall, is given by

$$F_i = \frac{\left(1 + \beta^2\right).\ \ precision*recall}{(\beta^2*precision + recall)} \tag{4}$$

Here β is a parameter, which can be used to give the importance to any one precision or recall.

If precision is more important for the task, β should tend to zero, and if recall is more important in that case β should tend to infinity. Generally β is set to 1, to give the equal importance to precision and recall.

5. PERFORMANCE COMPARISONS OF VARIOUS METHODS

Performances of some of the state-of-art methods for machine learning based approaches to sentiment classification with standard movie review dataset (Pang et al. 2004) are reported in Table 1. Previous literature has experimented with various sophisticated features based on dependency relations, syntactic, semantic structures etc. (Ng et al, 2006; Tu et al. 2012). With these complex features sentiment classification performance can improve, but it's computationally expensive to perform parsing. Abbasi et al. (2008) investigated that by feature selection method which is a

Table 1. Performance of various methods on movie review dataset

Paper	Approach	Best Accuracy
Pang et al. 2004	Minimum cut algorithm, SVM	87.1
Prabowo et al. 2009	Hybrid SVM	87.3
O'keefee et al. 2009	SentiWordNet based features and feature selection with SVM,NB classifier	87.15
Ng et al. 2006	SVM with various features	90.5
Agarwal et al. 2013	Boolean Multinomial Naïve Bayes with various experimental settings.	91.1
Tuet al. 2012	Dependency forest based with MaxEnt	91.6
Abbasi et al., 2008	Genetic Algorithms (GA), Information Gain (IG), IG + GA	91.7

combination of genetic algorithm and information gain improved accuracy to 91.7% for sentiment classification. The main drawback of this method is that it is highly computationally expensive. Agarwal et al. (2013) investigated the effect of various features with feature selection methods with different classifiers. The main drawback of their method is that they have used very simple features which are not able to incorporate the semantics and syntactic information. However, the main benefit of their approach is that BMNB classifier with feature reduction method may perform well for sentiment classification.

6. FUTURE RESEARCH DIRECTIONS

To summarize, there are several approaches for improving the performance machine learning methods for sentiment classification. (1) Appropriate feature extraction method should be explored for example syntactic, semantic, or dependency tree parsing pattern based features. New complex intelligent features can be explored which incorporates semantic, semantic polarity and other language dependent information, (2) Various feature weighting schemes (i.e. TF, TF-IDF etc.) has reported by the researchers in the literature. However, there is a scope of new weighting schemes which can improve the performance of machine learning methods for sentiment classification. (3) Feature selection methods are very important for the performance of machine learning methods, most of the methods reported in the literature are based of selecting the important features and dropping rest of the features, these methods are essentially based on threshold, which needs to be set manually. That may result into dropping important features, therefore, there is a need of such a dimension reduction method which is as fast as feature selection methods like IG, and can incorporate the contribution of all the features like feature transformation methods (i.e. SVD etc.).

(4) Appropriate machine learning algorithms are required for sentiment analysis that should be able to learn the pattern efficiently. New classifier may also be developed by ensemble of various other classifiers for better sentiment classification.

For shorter documents or sentence level sentiment classification machine learning methods do not perform well due to sparsity problem. A future direction can be to explore dimension reduction methods to handle it. A classifier trained for a specific domain generally does not perform well for other domain. It is due to the fact that words used for expressing sentiment can be domain specific. For example, word "*unpredictable*" can be positive orientation in movie review domain but would be negative oriented for car review domain. Therefore, Domain adaption methods are required to be explored for sentiment classification as it depends on the domain. To explore machine learning method for Cross lingual sentiment classification can be a good future research direction as not much work has been done in this.

7. CONCLUSION

Objective of this chapter is to present the existing techniques in the literature for how efficiently machine learning methods can be applied to sentiment classification problem. Problems and challenges faced in sentiment analysis are discussed in this chapter. Advantages of machine learning methods over other approaches for sentiment analysis are discussed. Machine learning based approaches are applied in various phrases for sentiment analysis namely feature extraction and pre-processing, feature weighting and representation, feature selection methods and machine learning algorithms. Each phase of machine learning based approach mostly for document level sentiment analysis is discussed in detail in this chapter. Next, list of state-of-art free available dataset for sentiment analysis are presented. Next, evaluation mechanisms for sentiment analysis are discussed. Finally, future research directions are presented in the end of the chapter.

REFERENCES

Abbasi, A. (2010). Intelligent feature selection for opinion classification. *IEEE Intelligent Systems*, 25(4), 75–79.

Abbasi, A., Chen, H. C., & Salem, A. (2008). Sentiment analysis in multiple languages: Feature selection for opinion classification in web forums. *ACM Transactions on Information Systems*, 26(3). doi:10.1145/1361684.1361685

Agarwal, B., & Mittal, N. (2012). Categorical Probability Proportion Difference (CPPD), A Feature Selection Method for Sentiment Classification. In *Proceedings of the 2nd Workshop on Sentiment Analysis where AI meets Psychology* (SAAIP). COLING.

Agarwal, B., & Mittal, N. (2013a). Optimal Feature Selection for Sentiment Analysis. In *Proceedings of 14th International Conference on Intelligent Text Processing and Computational Linguistics* (CICLing 2013), (Vol. 7817, pp. 13-24). CICLing.

Agarwal, B., Sharma, V., & Mittal, N. (2013b). Sentiment Classification of Review Documents using Phrases Patterns. In *Proceedings of the International Conference on Advances in Computing, Communications and Informatics* (ICACCI), (pp. 1577-1580). ICACCI.

Cambria, E., & Hussain, A. (2012). *Sentic Computing: Techniques, Tools, and Applications*. Dordrecht, Netherlands: Springer. doi:10.1007/978-94-007-5070-8

Cui, H., Mittal, V., & Datar, M. (2006). Comparative experiments on sentiment classification for online product reviews. In *Proceedings of the 21st national conference on Artificial intelligence*. Academic Press.

Dai, L., Chen, H., & Li, X. (2011). Improving Sentiment Classification using Feature Highlighting and Feature Bagging. In *Proceedings of 11th IEEE International Conference on Data Mining Workshops* (ICDMW), (pp. 61-66). IEEE.

Dang, Y., Zhang, Y., & Chen, H. (2010). A lexicon Enhanced method for sentiment classification: An experiment on Online Product Reviews. In *Proceedings of IEEE Intelligent System*, (pp. 46-53). IEEE.

Das, S., & Chen, M. (2001). Yahoo! For Amazon: Extracting market sentiment from stock message boards. In *Proc. of the 8th Asia Pacific Finance Association Annual Conference* (APFA 2001). APFA.

Dave, K., Lawrence, S., & Pennock, D. M. (2003). Mining the peanut gallery: Opinion extraction and semantic classification of product reviews. In *Proceedings of WWW*, (pp. 519–528). Academic Press.

Dinu, L. P., & Iuga, I. (2012). The Naive Bayes Classifier in Opinion Mining: In Search of the Best Feature Set. In *Proceedings of 13th International Conference on Intelligent Text Processing and Computational Linguistics*. CICLing.

Duric, A., & Song, F. (2011). Feature selection for sentiment analysis Based on Content and Syntax Models. In *Proceedings of the 2nd Workshop on Computational Approaches to Subjectivity and Sentiment Analysis*. ACL-HLT.

Forman, G. (2003). An extensive empirical study of feature selection metrics for text classification. *Journal of Machine Learning Research*, 1289–1305.

Gamon, M. (2004). Sentiment classification on customer feedback data: noisy data, large feature vectors, and the role of linguistic analysis. In *Proceedings of the 20th international conference on Computational Linguistics*, (pp. 841-848). Academic Press.

Hu, M., & Liu, B. (2004). Mining and summarizing customer reviews. In *Proceedings of the ACM SIGKDD Conference on Knowledge Discovery and Data Mining* (KDD), (pp. 168–177). ACM.

Joshi, M., & Penstein-Rosé, C. (2009). Generalizing dependency features for opinion mining. In *Proceedings of the Joint Conference of the 47th Annual Meeting of the Association for Computational Linguistics* (ACL), (pp. 313-316). ACL.

Li, S., Zong, C., & Wang, X. (2007). Sentiment Classification through Combining classifiers with multiple feature sets. In *Proceedings of International Conference on Natural Language Processing and Knowledge Engineering* (NLP-KE 2007). NLP-KE.

Lin, Y., Wang, X., Zhang, J., & Zhou, A. (2012b). Assembling the Optimal Sentiment Classifiers. In *Proceedings of the 13th international conference on Web Information Systems Engineering*. WISE.

Lin, Y., Zhang, J., Wang, X., & Zhou, A. (2012a). An information theoretic approach to sentiment polarity classification. In *Proceedings of the 2nd Joint WICOW/AIRWeb Workshop on Web Quality*. WICOW/AIRWeb.

Liu, B. (2012). Sentiment Analysis and Opinion Mining. In *Synthesis Lectures on Human Language Technologies*. Morgan & Claypool Publishers.

Martineau, J., & Finin, T. (2009). Delta TFIDF: An Improved Feature Space for Sentiment Analysis. In *Proceedings of the Third AAAI Internatonal Conference on Weblogs and Social Media*, (pp. 258-261). AAAI.

Matsumoto, S., Takamura, H., & Okumura, M. (2005). Sentiment classification using word sub-sequences and dependency sub-trees. In *Proceedings of the 9th Pacific-Asia conference on Advances in Knowledge Discovery and Data Mining* (PAKDD), (pp. 301-311). PAKDD.

Mejova, Y., & Srinivasan, P. (2011). Exploring Feature Definition and Selection for Sentiment Classifiers. In *Proceedings of the Fifth International AAAI Conference on Weblogs and Social Media*, (pp. 546–549). AAAI.

Mullen, T., & Collier, N. (2004). Sentiment analysis using support vector machines with diverse information sources. In *Proceedings of Conference on Empirical Methods in Natural Language Processing*, (pp. 412-418). Academic Press.

Nakagawa, T., Inui, K., & Kurohashi, S. (2010). Dependency tree-based sentiment classification using CRFs with hidden variables. In *Proceeding HLT '10 Human Language Technologies: Annual Conference of the North American Chapter of the Association for Computational Linguistics*. ACL.

Nicholls, C., & Song, F. (2010). Comparison of feature selection methods for sentiment analysis. In Canadian AI 2010 (LNCS), (vol. 6085, pp. 286–289). Springer.

O'Keefee, T., & Koprinska, I. (2009). Feature Selection and Weighting Methods in Sentiment Analysis. In *Proceedings of the 14th Australasian Document Computing Symposium*. Academic Press.

Osgood, C. E., Succi, G. J., & Tannenbaum, P. H. (1957). *The Measurement of Meaning*. University of Illinois.

Pak, A., & Paroubek, P. (2011). Text representation using dependency tree sub-graphs for sentiment analysis. In *Proceedings of DASFAA workshop*, (pp. 323-332). DASFAA.

Paltonglou, G., & Thelwallm, M. (2010). A study of Information retrieval weighting schemes for sentiment analysis. In *Proceedings of the 48th Annual Meeting of the Association for Computational Linguistics*, (pp. 1386-1395). ACL.

Pang, B., & Lee, L. (2004). A sentimental education: sentiment analysis using subjectivity summarization based on minimum cuts. In *Proceedings of the Association for Computational Linguistics (ACL)*, (pp. 271–278). ACL.

Pang, B., Lee, L., & Vaithyanathan, S. (2002). Thumbs up? Sentiment classification using machine learning techniques. In *Proceedings of the Conference on Empirical Methods in Natural Language Processing* (EMNLP), (pp. 79–86). EMNLP.

Prabowo, R., & Thelwall, M. (2009). Sentiment analysis: A combined approach. *Journal of Informetrics*, 3(2), 143–157. doi:10.1016/j.joi.2009.01.003

Raychev, V., & Nakov, P. (2009). Language-Independent Sentiment Analysis Using Subjectivity and Positional Information. In *Proceedings of International Conference RANLP 2009*. RANLP.

Riloff, E., Patwardhan, S., & Wiebe, J. (2006). Feature subsumption for opinion analysis. In *Proceedings of the Conference on Empirical Methods in Natural Language Processing*. Sydney, Australia: Academic Press.

Snyder, B., & Barzilay, R. (2007). Multiple aspect ranking using the Good Grief algorithm. In *Proceedings of the Joint Human Language Technology/North American Chapter of the ACL Conference* (HLT-NAACL), (pp. 300–307). ACL.

Taboada, M., Brooke, J., Tofiloski, M., Voll, K., & Stede, M. (2011). Lexicon-based methods for sentiment analysis. *Computational Linguistics*, 37(2), 267–307. doi:10.1162/COLI_a_00049

Tan, S., & Zhang, J. (2008). An empirical study of sentiment analysis for chinese documents. *Expert Systems with Applications*, 34, 2622–2629. doi:10.1016/j.eswa.2007.05.028

Tsutsumi, K., Shimada, K., & Endo, T. (2007). Movie Review Classification Based on a Multiple Classifier. In *Proceedings of PACLIC*, (pp. 481-488). PACLIC.

Tsytsarau, M., & Palpanas, T. (2012). Survey on mining subjective data on the web. *Data Mining and Knowledge Discovery*, 24, 478–514. doi:10.1007/s10618-011-0238-6

Tu, Z., Jiang, W., Liu, Q., & Lin, S. (2012). Dependency Forest for Sentiment Analysis. In *Proceedings of First CCF Conference, Natural Language Processing and Chinese Computing* (pp. 69-77). CCF.

Turney, P. D. (2002). Thumbs Up or Thumbs Down? Semantic Orientation Applied to Unsupervised Classification of Reviews. In *Proceedings of ACL 2002*, (pp. 417-424). ACL.

Verma, S., & Bhattacharyya, P. (2009). Incorporating semantic knowledge for sentiment analysis. In *Proceedings of ICON-09*. Hyderabad, India: ICON.

Wang, L., & Wan, Y. (2011). Sentiment Classification of Documents based on Latent Semantic Analysis. In *Proceedings of International Conference, Advanced Research on Computer Education, Simulation and Modeling* (CESM), (pp. 356-361). CESM.

Wang, S., Li, D., Song, S., Wei, Y., & Li, H. (2009). A Feature Selection Method Based on Fisher's Discriminant Ratio for Text Sentiment Classification. In *Proceeding WISM '09 Proceedings of the International Conference on Web Information Systems and Mining*, (pp. 88-97). WISM.

Whitelaw, C., Garg, N., & Argamon, S. (2005). Using appraisal groups for sentiment analysis. In *Proceedings of the 14th ACM international conference on Information and knowledge management*. Bremen, Germany: ACM.

Wiebe, J., Wilson, T., & Cardie, C. (2005). Annotating expressions of opinions and emotions in language. *Language Resources and Evaluation*, *39*(2-3), 165–210. doi:10.1007/s10579-005-7880-9

Xia, R., & Zong, C. (2010). Exploring the use of word relation features for sentiment classification. In *Proceedings of the 23rd International Conference on Computational Linguistics* (COLING), (pp. 1336-1344). COLING.

Xia, R., Zong, C., & Li, S. (2011). Ensemble of Feature Sets and Classification Algorithms for Sentiment Classification. *Journal of Information Science*, *181*(6), 1138–1152. doi:10.1016/j.ins.2010.11.023

Ye, Q., Zhang, Z., & Law, R. (2009). Sentiment classification of online reviews to travel destinations by supervised machine learning approaches. *Expert Systems with Applications*, *36*, 6527–6535. doi:10.1016/j.eswa.2008.07.035

Yu, L., & Liu, H. (2004). Efficient Feature Selection via Analysis of Relevance and Redundancy. *Journal of Machine Learning Research*, 1205–1224.

ADDITIONAL READING

Bespalov, D., Bai, B., Qi, Y., & Ali, S. (2011)., Sentiment classification based on supervised latent n-gram analysis. In the Proceeding of the ACM conference on Information and knowledge management (CIKM).

Cambria, E., Schuller, B., Xia, Y., & Havasi, C. (2013). New Avenues in Opinion Mining and Sentiment Analysis In IEEE Intelligent Systems, pp. 15-21.

Dey, L., & Haque, S. K. M. (2008). Opinion mining from noisy text data. In Proceedings of the Second Workshop on Analytics for Noisy Unstructured Text Data (AND-2008).

Liu, B. (2010). In N. Indurkhya, & F. J. Damerau (Eds.), *Sentiment Analysis and Subjectivity, Handbook of Natural Language Processing* (2nd ed., pp. 627–666). Chapman & Hall.

Pang, B., & Lee, L. (2008). Opinion mining and sentiment analysis. *Foundations and Trends in Information Retrieval*, *2*(1-2), 1–135. doi:10.1561/1500000011

Sentiment Analysis related useful material is available at http://www.cs.uic.edu/~liub/.

Soujanya, P., Gelbukh, A., Hussain, A., Das, D., & Bandyopadhyay, S. (2013). Enhanced SenticNet with affective labels for concept-based opinion mining. In IEEE Intelligent Systems.

KEY TERMS AND DEFINITIONS

Aspect/Feature Level Sentiment Analysis: Aspect based sentiment analysis model deals with the methods that identify the opinion expressed about at specific entity.

Bag-of-Word (BoW) Methods: Bag-of-word model is a simplest method to represent a text document used in NLP. In this method, a document is represented as unordered collection of words, disregarding word orders.

Document Level Sentiment Analysis: It classifies a text document into positive or negative sentiment document.

Feature Vector: Machine learning algorithm requires the input in a structured format. It is an n-dimensional vector of numerical feature values which can represent some object.

Knowledge-Base: Knowledge-base is kind of repository of information stored in a specific format.

Machine Learning: Machine learning is to construct a model which can learn the patterns from the training samples. For example: machine learning based classification model can learn the pattern of positive and negative documents to classify the new testing documents into positive or negative document.

Semantic Orientation: Semantic orientation is the measure of the strength of polarity i.e. positive or negative of a term/word.

Sentence Level Sentiment Analysis: It takes a sentence as a input and extracts the opinion expressed in that sentence.

Sentiment Analysis: Sentiment analysis is to determine the opinion expressed from the text document.

Chapter 12
Combining Semantics and Social Knowledge for News Article Summarization

Elena Baralis
Politecnico di Torino, Italy

Saima Jabeen
Politecnico di Torino, Italy

Luca Cagliero
Politecnico di Torino, Italy

Alessandro Fiori
Institute for Cancer Research at Candiolo (IRCC), Italy

Sajid Shah
Politecnico di Torino, Italy

ABSTRACT

With the diffusion of online newspapers and social media, users are becoming capable of retrieving dozens of news articles covering the same topic in a short time. News article summarization is the task of automatically selecting a worthwhile subset of news' sentences that users could easily explore. Promising research directions in this field are the use of semantics-based models (e.g., ontologies and taxonomies) to identify key document topics and the integration of social data analysis to also consider the current user's interests during summary generation. The chapter overviews the most recent research advances in document summarization and presents a novel strategy to combine ontology-based and social knowledge for addressing the problem of generic (not query-based) multi-document summarization of news articles. To identify the most salient news articles' sentences, an ontology-based text analysis is performed during the summarization process. Furthermore, the social content acquired from real Twitter messages is separately analyzed to also consider the current interests of social network users for sentence evaluation. The combination of ontological and social knowledge allows the generation of accurate and easy-to-read news summaries. Moreover, the proposed summarizer performs better than the evaluated competitors on real news articles and Twitter messages.

DOI: 10.4018/978-1-4666-6086-1.ch012

INTRODUCTION

Since large document collections (e.g., news articles, scientific papers, blogs) are nowadays easily accessible through Web search engines, digital libraries, and online communities, Web users are commonly interested in exploring easy-to-read text summaries rather than perusing tens of potentially large documents. Multi-document summarization focuses on automatically generating concise summaries of large document collections. Text summarizers can be classified as sentence- or keyword-based. Specifically, sentence-based approaches entail partitioning document(s) into sentences and selecting the most informative ones to include in the summary (Carenini et al. 2007; Goldstein et al. 2000; Wang & Li 2010; Wang et al. 2011), whereas keyword-based approaches focus on detecting salient keywords to summarize documents using either co-occurrence measures (Lin & Hovy, 2003) or Latent Semantic Analysis (Dredze et al., 2008). Summarizers can be further classified as query-based or generic. While query-based summaries are targeted at a specific user query, the generic summarization task entails producing a general-purpose summary that consists of a selection of most informative document sentences or keywords. This chapter addresses the sentence-based generic multi-document summarization problem, which can be formulated as follows: given a collection of news articles ranging over the same topic, the goal is to extract a concise yet informative summary, which consists of most salient document sentences.

To effectively address document summarization, different data mining and information retrieval techniques have been adopted. For example, clustering techniques (e.g., Wang & Li, 2010; Wang et al., 2011) have been applied to first group document sentences into homogenous clusters and then pick out the most representative one within each cluster, whereas graph-based approaches (e.g., Radev, 2004; Thakkar et al., 2010) generate graphs that represent the underlying correlations between keywords or sentences. These models are then indexed by means of established graph ranking algorithms (e.g., Brin & Page, 1998) to identify the most salient document content. Unfortunately, general-purpose summarization strategies hardly differentiate between relevant concepts and not within a specific knowledge domain. Hence, the generated summaries may not meet reader's expectations and interests. To address this issue, two promising research directions have recently been investigated:

1. The exploitation of advanced semantics-based models (e.g., ontologies, taxonomies) to drive the summarization process (Conroy et al., 2004; Hennig et al., 2008; Wu & Liu, 2003); and
2. The integration of social data analysis steps to identify the current user interest's (e.g., Yang et al., 2011; Zhu et al., 2009).

Semantics-based approaches evaluate the document content according to established semantics-based models, such as ontologies or controlled vocabularies. Integrating ontologies into document summarizers allows us to automatically and effectively differentiate between terms having different meanings in different contexts as well as map term occurrences to their actual (non-ambiguous) concepts. The parallel analysis of the User-Generated Content (UGC) acquired from social networks and online communities can significantly improve summarizer performance (Conrad et al., 2009; Saravanan & Ravindran, 2010; Sharifi et al., 2010a; Yang et al., 2011; Zhu et al., 2009). For example, highlighting the current social trends (Mathioudakis & Koudas, 2010), the subjects that are currently matter on contention on the Web (Gong et al., 2010; Miao & Li, 2010), or the context in which Web documents were published (Yin et al., 2009) can be useful for generating appealing text summaries.

Our goal is to combine the knowledge coming from semantic models and social data to improve document summarization performance. The contribution of this Chapter is twofold. Firstly, it overviews most recent research advances in document summarization and classifies the related approaches according to the adopted data mining or information retrieval strategy. Secondly, it presents *SociONewSum (Social and Ontology-based News Summarizer)*, a novel summarizer that selects a worthwhile subset of sentences from a collection of news ranging over the same topic. Sentences are evaluated and ranked according to their relevance with respect to an ontological knowledge base, i.e., Yago (Suchanek et al., 2007). To this purpose, an established Entity Recognition and Disambiguation step (Hoffart et al., 2011) is preliminary applied to identify most pertinent ontological concepts. Furthermore, the same concepts are also evaluated according to their importance in the textual messages posted on Twitter. The goal is to identify ontological concepts that are significant both in the news article collection and in the social network messages. Such information is then used to drive the generation of the summary of the document collection.

An experimental evaluation of the SociONew-Sum performance was conducted on real English-written news article collections and Twitter posts. The achieved results demonstrate the effectiveness of the proposed summarizer, in terms of different ROUGE scores (Lin & Hovy, 2003), compared to state-of-the-art open source summarizers as well as to a baseline version of the SociONewSum summarizer that does not perform any UGC analysis. Furthermore, the readability of the generated summaries has also been analyzed.

This Chapter is organized as follows. Section "Related works" overviews and classifies most relevant summarization approaches. Section "SociONewSum" presents SociONewSum and thoroughly describes its main steps. Section "Experiments" reports the results of the summarizer performance evaluation, while Sections "Future research directions" and "Conclusion" present future developments of this work and draw conclusions, respectively.

RELATED WORKS

This section overviews the most recent summarization approaches and classifies them according to the mainly adopted data mining or information retrieval technique.

Clustering-Based Summarization

Clustering is a well-established unsupervised data mining technique that has already been used to perform document summarization (e.g., Radev et al., 2004; Wang & Li, 2010; Wang et al. 2011). The goal is to group document sentences or keywords into homogenous clusters and then select the most authoritative representative within each group. For example, in Wang et al. (2011) clusters represent groups of sentences from which the best representatives (e.g., the centroids or the medoids) are selected. In contrast, Radev et al. (2004) propose a text summarizer, namely MEAD, which clusters documents instead of sentences. For each cluster, it generates a pseudo-document which consists of document terms having a high tf-idf value (Tan et al., 2006). Then, pseudo-document sentences are ranked based on (i) the similarity to the centroids, (ii) the sentence position in the document, and (iii) the sentence length.

A parallel issue addressed by clustering-based approaches is incremental summary update. Once a document is added or removed from the collection, the task is to update the summary without regenerating the whole clustering model. The authors in Wang & Li (2010) addressed the problem by integrating into the summarization process an incremental hierarchical clustering algorithm similar to the one previously proposed in Guha et al. (2000). Unlike Wang & Li (2010), this chapter does not address the issue of summary updating.

Unfortunately, clustering-based algorithms suffer from the presence of noise or outliers in the analyzed data. To make clustering algorithms robust to complex data distributions, the complexity of the mining process could relevantly increases.

Graph-Based Summarization

Graph-based strategies focus on modeling the correlations between document terms or sentences as graphs, which are then used to drive the sentence/keyword selection process (Radev, 2004; Wan & Yang, 2006; Carenini et al., 2007; Thakkar et al, 2010). Graph indexing algorithms are commonly used to identify authoritative graph nodes. For example, the summarizer proposed in Radev (2004) ranks sentences according to the eigenvector centrality computed on the sentence linkage matrix by means of the well-known PageRank algorithm (Brin & Page, 1998). To reduce the computational complexity, many approaches perform edge pruning before executing the graph indexing algorithm. For example, Wan & Yang (2006) consider both sentence novelty and information richness to reduce the model complexity and select the most representative sentences.

A parallel effort has been devoted to integrating social knowledge into the document summarization process (Zhu et al., 2009; Yang et al., 2011). Specifically, the authors in (Zhu et al., 2009) propose to enrich the document content with social tag annotations. Furthermore, a new tag ranking algorithm is proposed and adopted to reduce noise in tags. In contrast, the summarizer presented in Yang et al. (2011) combines the original documents with a graph-based social context description that was generated from a previous Twitter data analysis. Similar to Yang et al. (2011), the summarizer proposed in this chapter also integrates social data coming from Twitter. Sharifi et al. (2010a, 2010b) address microblog data summarization using graph-based strategies. For example, in Sharifi et al. (2010b) a phrase reinforcement graph is generated to automatically analyze the structure of the sentence without the need for exploiting ontology-based models. Unlike the previously proposed approach, our approach integrates ontology-based and social models into a unified framework.

Summarization Based on Supervised Techniques

Supervised data mining techniques (e.g., classification, regression) focus on predicting the values of one or more features of a given data instance based on a set of previously labeled instances. Many previous approaches adopted classification techniques to effectively address the document summarization problem (Chali et al., 2009; Kianmehr et al., 2009; Zhang et al., 2013; Atkinson & Munoz, 2013). For example, in (Chali et al., 2009) a Support Vector Machine (SVM) model is used to classify document sentences as eligible or not for being included in the text summary. The work presented in Kianmehr et al. (2009) compares the performance of summarization techniques based on SVMs and Neural Networks. More recently, the summarizer presented in (Atkinson & Munoz, 2013) assigns a rhetorical role to each sentence by means of a stochastic CRF classifier, which is trained from a collection of annotated sentences.

To summarize the textual messages posted in Twitter, the authors in Zhang et al. (2013) adopt speech act recognition, which is an established multi-class classification problem. The problem is solved by using word-based and symbol-based features that capture both the linguistic features of speech acts and the particularities of Twitter text. The recognized speech acts in tweets are then used to direct the extraction of key words and phrases to fill in templates designed for speech acts. Similarly, Liu et al. (2011) propose to explore a variety of text sources for summarizing the Twitter topics and also perform content-based optimization for Twitter topic summarization.

Itemset-Based Summarization

Frequent itemset mining is a widely exploratory unsupervised data mining technique to discover valuable correlations among data. This technique was first introduced in Agrawal et al. (1993) in the context of market basket analysis.

An appealing research issue is summarizing data by means of itemsets. Many previous approaches focus on discovering and selecting a worthwhile subset of frequent itemsets from transactional data. For example, in Brin et al. (1997) and Jaroszewicz & Simovici (2004) the authors compare the observed frequency of each itemset against some null hypothesis, i.e., they measure how the itemset support diverges from its expected value. However, since this approach is static, the discovered summaries are often redundant. More recent approaches (e.g., Kontonasios & De Bie, 2010; Tatti & Heikinheimo, 2008; Tatti & Mampaey, 2010) adopt entropy-based models to dynamically evaluate itemset interestingness. Specifically, they perform frequent itemset mining followed by post-pruning to select only a worthwhile itemset subset. A more effective and parameter-free itemset-based method for succinctly summarizing transactional data has been proposed in (Mampaey et al., 2011). It exploits a novel entropy-based heuristics to solve the maximum entropy problem. Furthermore, it pushes itemset evaluation deep into the itemset mining process.

Baralis et al. (2012) integrate the entropy-based itemset selection strategy proposed in Mampaey et al. (2011) into the sentence-based summarization process. They address the problem of summarizing English-written documents by exploiting frequent itemsets. More specifically, the authors first exploit the strategy presented in Mampaey et al. (2011) to generate succinct yet informative itemset sets. Then, document sentences are evaluated and selected according to (i) the previously generated itemset-based model and (ii) the commonly used term frequency-inverse document frequency (tf-idf) statistic (Lin & Hovy, 2003). Unlike the summarizer presented in this chapter, the approach presented in Baralis et al. (2012) does not rely neither on semantic-based nor on social models.

Summarization Based on Optimization Strategies and Latent Semantic Analysis

Linear programming strategies have also been used to address the text summarization problem (Takamura & Okumura, 2009a; Takamura & Okumura, 2009b). The key idea is to formalize the summarization task as a min-max optimization problem. The optimal problem solution is, in our context, the subset of document sentences that maximizes a certain cost function. For instance, Filatova & Hatzivassiloglou (2004) represent sentences as sets of words and formalize the summarization task as a maximum coverage problem with Knapsack constraints. Similarly, the approaches proposed by Takamura & Okumura (2009a) and Takamura & Okumura (2009b) search for linear programming solutions by also considering the relevance of each sentence within documents. The most significant limitation of the summarizers based on optimization strategies is the complexity of the system parameter setting, which often requires the intervention of a domain expert.

Gong & Liu (2002) first propose to adopt Latent Semantic Analysis in document summarization. Inspired by the latent semantic indexing, they applied the Singular Value Decomposition (SVD) to generic text summarization. More recently, the author in (Ozsoy et al., 2011) and (Yirdaw & Ejigu, 2012) the authors specialize the LSA-based analysis to Turkish and Amharic texts, respectively. A method of text summarization based on latent semantic indexing (LSI) is also proposed in (Ai et al., 2010). It uses semantic indexing to calculate the sentence similarity and improve the accuracy of sentence similarity calculations and subject delineation.

Ontology-Based Summarization

Ontologies have already been used to improve summarization performance. For example, they have been used to (i) identify the concepts that are most pertinent to a user-specified query (Kogilavani & Balasubramanie, 2009; Ping & Verma, 2006), (ii) model the context in which summaries are generated in different application domains (e.g., the disaster management domain (Li et al., 2010), business domain (Wu et al., 2003)), and (iii) enrich existent ontological models with textual content (Baxter et al., 2009).

Some attempts to exploit the Wikipedia knowledge base to improve summarization performance have been made (Nastase et al., 2008; Miao & Li, 2010). In parallel, many ontology-based strategies focus on considering the text argumentative structure during the summarization process. For example, the summarizer proposed in Hennig et al. (2008) exploits a Support Vector Machine classifier to map each sentence to a subset of taxonomy nodes. Unlike all of the above-mentioned approaches, the summarizer presented in this chapter does not rely on a supervised approach.

THE SOCIONEWSUM SYSTEM

SociONewSum is a novel news document summarizer that selects a worthwhile subset of news sentences by analyzing (i) the semantics behind the text, to highlight the key news concepts, and (ii) the on-topic textual messages that were published on the microblogging website Twitter, to discover the current user's interests. Figure 1 depicts the main architectural blocks of the proposed framework.

The summarizer takes in input a collection $D=\{d_1, ..., d_n\}$ of news documents that range over the same topic. Each document d_i consists of a set of sentences $S_i=\{S_{1}, ..., S_{ki}\}$. Beyond the original news documents, the system also analyzes the on-topic messages that were published on Twitter to discover and exploit the current interests of social network users. The Twitter content is modeled a single textual document P, which contains a set $P=\{p_1, ..., p_u\}$ of sentences. For sake of brevity, we will denote P as *social content* throughout the paper.

The analyzed news documents were crawled by submitting an (analyst-provided) query to the Google News search engine. In parallel, the Twitter

Figure 1. The SociONewSum architecture

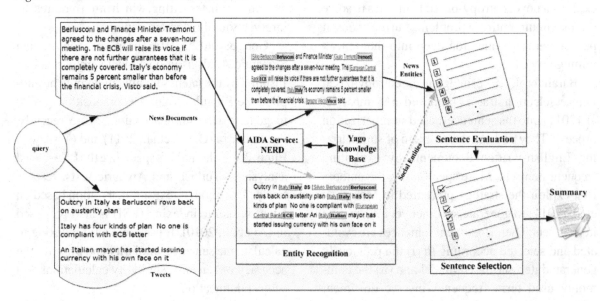

Application Programming Interfaces (APIs) were used to retrieve the corresponding set of on-topic Twitter messages (i.e., the tweets). To produce the summaries, both news and social content are processed off-line by the SociONewSum system.

The summarizer performs a three-step process. A short description of each step is given below.

- **Entity Recognition:** News documents are processed by means of an established Entity Recognition and Disambiguation step, which maps the most significant combinations of news words to non-ambiguous ontological concepts, namely the *news entities*. Furthermore, to consider the social trends about the news, the Twitter UGC is also analyzed to discover the *social entities* of topical interest.
- **Sentence Evaluation:** To evaluate news sentence relevance, each sentence is mapped to a set of news and social entities. Furthermore, a sentence relevance score is assigned to each sentence according to the importance of the corresponding news and social entities.
- **Sentence Selection:** To generate highly informative news summaries, sentences are evaluated and ranked according to the significance of the contained news and social entities. To select a worthwhile subset of document sentences, a Maximal Marginal Relevance strategy is adopted to pick out the subset of top-ranked news sentences with minimal content overlapping.

In the following the main characteristics of each step are thoroughly described.

Entity Recognition

This step focuses on discovering most relevant ontological concepts, called *entities*, which are contained either in the analyzed news collection or in the social content. This information is deemed to be worthy for summarization purposes, because an accurate news summary is expected to cover (i) all the relevant news facets and (ii) the most significant social content information. Note that, since news articles and Twitter posts range over the same topic, the two data sources are expected to share most relevant ontological concepts.

SociONewSum performs an Entity Recognition and Disambiguation step based on the Yago ontological knowledge base (Suchanek et al., 2007) from news articles and Twitter posts. Yago is a recently proposed ontological model, whose information was extracted from the Wikipedia free encyclopedia (www.wikipedia.org). Yago covers a broad range of shared concepts (e.g., more than 10 million entities and more than 120 million facts about these entities). To interface with Yago, SociONewSum exploits the APIs provided by the AIDA Web Service (Hoffart et al., 2011).

Consider a sentence composed of possibly repeated words w_1, w_2, ..., w_z that belongs either to news documents or to the social content. The Entity Recognition and Disambiguation step maps sentence words to ontological entities. Specifically, an entity could be associated with either a single word or with a combination of words. In our context, we consider names, numbers, times, and dates that occur in each sentence and we associate with each of them the corresponding entity (if any). Entity recognition for times, dates, and numbers is performed matching the word combinations with a list of regular expressions. Such procedure returns at most one single entity per word combination. For example, the expression "10 p.m." corresponds to "22:00:00", according to the standard timing notation. Conversely, named entity recognition searches for Yago entities that fit the considered words. Unfortunately, a name is frequently mapped to more than one candidate entities, because natural language expressions commonly have different meanings in different contexts. For this reason, the summarizer comprises a disambiguation step which selects, among the candidate named entities for a given word combination, the most appropriate one. For example, according to the context of use, the word "Mercury" could be mapped to the planet of the solar system, i.e., the entity Mercury(Planet), or to the chemical element, i.e., Mercury(Element).

The disambiguation process considers the following properties of a Yago entity:

- The popularity score, which indicates the frequency of usage of the entity in the Wikipedia encyclopedia,
- The set of related keywords, which describe the context of use for the given entity (e.g., {"Chemistry", "Thermometer"} for the entity Mercury(Element)),
- The numbers of incoming and outcoming Wikipedia links, which represent the entity relations with the other Wikipedia resources and, thus, measures the authority of the entity in the knowledge base.

Let $c_i \in C$ be an arbitrary document collection (either a news document $d_i \in D$ or a Twitter post P). According to the above properties, we assign a rank to an arbitrary entity ne_q in c_i, which indicates the relevance of the entity with respect to the analyzed document. Its expression is given in Box 1.

$$sim\left(cxt(ne_q), cxt(c_i)\right)$$

is the similarity between the context of use of the entity ne_q and the document c_i; it measures the contextual pertinence of the entity to the news document d_i, and it is computed by the cosine similarity between the set of related keywords of the entity and the document (Tan et al., 2006). Finally, $coh\left(ne_q, C\right)$ is the coherence of the entity with respect to all the other recognized entities for any word in the collection. When coping with a single document c_i rather than a collection of documents C (e.g.., for the Twitter posts), both similarity and coherence measures are evaluated on c_i. By following the indications reported in Hoffart et al., (2011), we set the values of θ and φ to 0.34 and 0.47, respectively. A thorough assessment of the entity recognition system performance on real data is also reported in Hachey et al. (2013). Non-named entities (i.e., numbers, times, and dates) take a fixed relevance value δ, which indicates their relative importance in the collection.

The disambiguation process for names selects the top-ranked recognized named entity according to the previously introduced entity ranking. Although the relevance scores for non-named entities are not useful for disambiguation purposes, they will be used in the following steps to evaluate news sentence relevance, as discussed in the following section.

Sentence Evaluation

To generate the summary, each sentence of the news collection is first evaluated and ranked according to the relevance of its contained entities.

To achieve this goal, each news document sentence $S_{ji} \in d_i \in D$ is modeled as the corre-

Box 1.

$$ER(ne_q, c_i) = \begin{cases} \theta \cdot popularity\left(ne_q\right) + \varphi \cdot sim\left(cxt(ne_q), cxt(c_i)\right) + \left(1 - \theta - \varphi\right) \cdot coh\left(ne_q, C\right) & \text{if } ne_q \text{ named entity} \\ \delta & \text{otherwise} \end{cases}$$

where θ, φ, and δ are user-specified parameters that take value between 0 and 1. *popularity(ne_q)* is the popularity score of the entity and measures the global relevance of the entity in the knowledge base.

sponding set E_{ji} of assigned entities. Specifically, E_{ji} contains all the entities that are mapped to any word combination in S_{ji}, which hereafter will be denoted as *news entities*. Furthermore, to evaluate sentence relevance with respect to the current social network user's interest, the Twitter UGC is modeled as the set E_p of entities, hereafter denoted as *social entities,* which are mapped to any sentence of the social content *P*.

Sentences are evaluated based on the relative importance (rank) of their contained news and social entities. A sentence rank $SR\left(S_{ji}\right)$ is associated with each sentence $S_{ji} \in d_i \in D$. Its expression is given by:

$$SR\left(S_{ji}\right) = \frac{\displaystyle\sum_{NE_q \in E_i \,|\, S_{ji} \in d_i \in D} ER\left(NE_q, d_i\right)}{\left|\left\{NE_q \in E_i \,|\, S_{ji} \in d_i \in D\right\}\right|} \, sim\left(E_{ji}, E_p\right)$$

where the first multiplication term measures the relevance of the sentence in the news collection and is expressed by the average entity rank for the news entities associated with any word combination in S_{ji}, whereas the second multiplication term indicates the relevance of the sentence with respect to the Twitter UGC. The latter term is expressed by the cosine similarity between the subset of social entities that are associated with any word combination in S_{ji} and the subset of top-*K* social entities in P (where *K* is a user-specified parameter). Note that sentences that contain many recognized news and social entities on average ranked first, whereas sentences that do not cover any significant news document topics or any potentially relevant social content facet are penalized.

Sentence Selection

This step selects a worthwhile subset of top-ranked news sentences with minimal content overlapping. Specifically, SociONewSum adopts a variant of the established iterative re-ranking strategy, called Maximal Marginal Relevance (MMR) (Carbonell & Goldstein, 1998), which has first been introduced in the context of query-based summary generation.

At each algorithm iteration, the MMR-based strategy picks out the candidate sentence that is characterized by (i) maximal relevance score and (ii) minimal similarity with respect to the previously selected sentences. The maximization function can be formulated as follows:

$$\text{maximize}_{\{S_{ji}\}} \alpha \cdot SR\left(S_{ji}\right) - \left(1-\alpha\right) \cdot sim(S_{ji}, S_{wo})$$

where $\alpha \in \left[0,1\right]$ is a user-specified parameter that weighs the impact of each summation term, S_{ji} is an arbitrary sentence not yet included in the summary, and S_{wo} is an arbitrary sentence already contained in the summary. A thorough analysis of the impact of the parameters K, δ, and α on the summarizer performance is given in Section "Parameter analysis".

EXPERIMENTS

We performed a large number of experiments to evaluate: (i) the performance of SociONewSum on real-life news articles using the ROUGE toolkit (Lin & Hovy, 2003), (ii) the readability of the generated summaries, and (iii) the impact of the input parameters on the summarizer performance.

We analyzed six different real-life news article collections. Each collection ranges over a different topic. The list of analyzed topics is given below:

- **Irene:** The Irene hurricane beats down on the U.S. East Coast.
- **Apple:** Steve Jobs resignation announcement from his role as Apple's CEO.
- **UK_riots:** The U.K. suffered widespread rioting, looting and arson in August 2011.
- **US_Open:** The U.S. Open tennis tournament held in New York City (USA) in August 2011.
- **Debt_crisis:** The ongoing crisis of the European sovereign debt.
- **Terrorism:** The fight against religious terrorism conducted by the U.S.A.

For each considered topic we collected the top-ranked news that were retrieved in August 2011 by the Google News Web search engine (http://news.google.com). Among them, we selected the top-10 news that (i) were retrieved from the most authoritative newspapers (e.g., The Guardian, BBC, Reuters, New York Post, etc.) and (ii) have length between 600 and 2,000 words.

We also retrieved and analyzed the on-topic messages that were posted on Twitter (www.twitter.com) during the same time period in which news articles were published. For Twitter data retrieval, we used the Twitter Search Application Programming Interface (API) by specifying the same news queries. The considered tweet collections consist of approximately 800 tweets each. Both the news articles and the on-topic Twitter posts are available for research purposes, upon request to the authors.

Performance Evaluation

We compared the performance of our summarizer with that of: (i) two widely used open source summarizers, i.e., the Open Text Summarizer (OTS) (Rotem, 2006) and TexLexAn (TexLexAn, 2011), and (ii) a baseline version of SociONewSum, namely Baseline, which does not consider the social content for sentence evaluation, i.e., the sentence rank depends solely on the average news entity rank.

To compare SociONewSum with other approaches, we used the ROUGE (Lin & Hovy, 2003) toolkit (version 1.5.5). ROUGE was the reference performance evaluation system[1] for the Document Understanding Conference (DUC) and the Text Analysis Conference (TAC). ROUGE measures the quality of a candidate summary by counting the unit overlaps between the summary and a set of reference summaries, which were provided by the contest organizers. Intuitively, the summarizer that achieves the highest ROUGE scores can be considered to be the most effective one.

ROUGE implements several evaluation scores (e.g., ROUGE-1, ROUGE-2, ROUGE-SU4) and measures (e.g., precision, recall, F1-measure). For the sake of brevity, we only reported, as representative scores, ROUGE-1 and ROUGE-SU4. Analogous results were achieved for the other scores. Since reference summaries (i.e., the optimal news document summaries) are not available for the news document collections, we performed, similar to (Chuang & Yang, 2000), a leave-one-out cross validation. More specifically, for each news collection we summarized nine out of ten news documents and we compared the produced summary with the remaining (not yet considered) one, which is selected as reference summary. Next, we tested all the other possible combinations by varying the reference summary and, for each summarizer, we computed the average performance results, in terms of precision (P), Recall (R), and F1-measure (F1), for both the ROUGE-1 and ROUGE-SU4 evaluation scores. Since we specifically cope with news article ranging over the same topic, the assumption that a new document is a representative summary of all the other documents in the news collection is acceptable.

Tables 1 and 2 summarize the results achieved by SociONewSum and its evaluated competitors in terms of ROUGE-1 and ROUGE-SU4 precision (Pr), recall (R), and F1-measure (F1). For OTS, TexLexAn, Baseline we reported the results that were achieved by setting the averagely best configuration setting (the same for all news collections). For SociONewSum we reported the results achieved by both a standard configuration, for which parameter values are fixed for all news collections, and a tuned configuration. For the standard configuration we set K to 10, δ to 0.2 and α to 0.7. For each collection the tuned configuration settings are reported in Tables 1 and 2. A detailed analysis of the impact of each parameter on the summarizer performance is given in Section "Parameter analysis".

Consider, as representative measure, the F1-measure, which is expressed by the harmonic average between precision and recall. SociONewSum Standard performs best on 6 out of 6 and 5 out of 6 collections in terms of ROUGE-1 and ROUGE-SU4, respectively. Furthermore, with the tuned

configuration SociONewSum outperforms all the other tested summarizers in terms of ROUGE-1 and ROUGE-SU4 F1-measure for every tested collection. Similar results were achieved for the other measures (i.e., precision and recall).

To validate the statistical significance of the achieved performance improvements, we performed the paired t-test of statistical significance (Dietterich, 1998) by setting the significance level to 95% for all the evaluated datasets and measures. Significant improvements between SociONewSum and all the other approaches for every news collection are starred in Tables 1 and 2. The results confirm the significance of the achieved performance improvements for most evaluated datasets and measures (e.g., with the standard configuration, for ROUGE-1 F1-measure 6 out of 6 against Baseline and TexLexAn, 5 out of 6 against OTS, for ROUGE-SU4 F1-measure 5 out of 6 against Baseline, 4 out 6 against OTS and TexLexAn).

In light of the above-mentioned results, the proposed approach appears to be, on average, more accurate than state-of-the-art approaches. Furthermore, based on the results of the comparison with Baseline, the integration of social

Table 1. Performance comparison in terms of ROUGE-1

Dataset (Tuned setting)	TexLexAn			OTS			Baseline			SociONewSum Standard result (Tuned result)		
	R	P	F1	R	P	F1	R	P	F1	R	P	F1
Debt Crisis (K=50, δ=0.1, α=0.6)	0.068	0.541	0.121	0.077	**0.581**	0.135	0.070	0.518	0.121	**0.081*** **(0.082*)**	0.569 **(0.582)**	**0.141*** **(0.143*)**
Irene (K=30, δ=0.1, α=0.2)	0.062	0.577	0.110	0.064	0.602	0.116	0.055	0.532	0.099	**0.066*** **(0.070*)**	**0.612*** **(0.646*)**	**0.119*** **(0.127*)**
Steve Jobs (K=40, δ=0.2, α=0.8)	0.057	0.533	0.102	0.060	0.573	0.109	0.068	0.615	0.122	**0.072*** **(0.072*)**	**0.625*** **(0.645*)**	**0.126*** **(0.128*)**
Terrorism (K=70, δ=0.1, α=0.7)	0.047	0.447	0.086	0.052	0.479	0.093	0.045	0.444	0.082	**0.055*** **(0.058*)**	**0.517*** **(0.544*)**	**0.099*** **(0.104*)**
UK riots (K=10, δ=0.1, α=0.2)	0.060	0.522	0.107	**0.065**	**0.586**	**0.117**	0.052	0.456	0.092	0.065 **(0.067)**	0.578 **(0.578)**	**0.117** **(0.120*)**
US Open (K=40, δ=0.1, α=0.5)	0.076	0.651	0.136	0.065	0.545	0.116	0.065	0.492	0.114	**0.080*** **(0.082*)**	0.654 **(0.663*)**	**0.142*** **(0.145*)**

Table 2. Performance comparison in terms of ROUGE-SU4

Dataset (Tuned setting)	TexLexAn			OTS			Baseline			SociONewSum Standard result (Tuned result)		
	R	P	F1	R	P	F1	R	P	F1	R	P	F1
Debt Crisis (K=50, δ =0.1, α =0.6)	0.021	0.175	0.038	0.024	**0.188**	0.042	0.019	0.147	0.033	**0.026*** (0.027*)	0.187 (0.199*)	**0.045*** (0.048*)
Irene (K=30, δ =0.1, α =0.2)	0.021	0.210	0.039	0.022	0.209	0.039	0.017	0.173	0.031	**0.023** (0.024*)	**0.221*** (0.230*)	**0.041** (0.043*)
Steve Jobs (K=40, δ =0.2, α =0.8)	0.018	0.173	0.032	0.021	0.203	0.037	0.024	0.225	0.043	**0.025** (0.026)	**0.232*** (0.244*)	**0.045*** (0.047*)
Terrorism (K=70, δ =0.1, 0.7)	0.015	0.147	0.028	**0.017**	**0.161**	**0.031**	0.014	0.142	0.025	0.014 (0.019*)	0.142 (0.188*)	0.025 (0.035*)
UK riots (K=10, δ =0.1, α =0.2)	0.022	0.195	0.039	0.022	0.203	0.040	0.015	0.139	0.027	**0.023** (0.024)	**0.211*** (0.211*)	**0.043*** (0.043*)
US Open (K=40, δ =0.1, α =0.5)	0.025	0.221	0.045	0.021	0.182	0.038	0.025	0.198	0.044	**0.032*** (0.034*)	**0.264*** (0.278*)	**0.056*** (0.059*)

data analysis into the summarization process is shown to relevantly improve the effectiveness of the proposed summarizer.

Summary Comparison

To validate the readability and soundness of the news summaries, we compared the results that were achieved by SociONewSum with those produced by OTS TexLexAn, and Baseline. Table 3 reports the top-3 summary sentences selected by SociONewSum and the other competitors for a representative news collection, i.e., Irene Hurricane.

The summary produced by SociONewSum appears to be sound and properly focused on the news topic. It relates the destructive tropical hurricane Irene, including the reaction of the U.S. government to the disaster. In contrast, Baseline's, OTS's and TexLexAn's summaries contain less interesting or too much detailed information (e.g., the situation in Vermont).

Since the tweets related to the Irene Hurricane collection report the announcements made by the

White House about the disaster, SociONewSum deemed the message sent by Barack Obama to be worthy for summarization purposes. Conversely, Baseline ignores the Twitter user's interests and, thus, completely disregards the official U.S. government announcements.

Parameter Analysis

We also analyzed the impact of the main input parameters on the summarizer performance. Specifically, we considered the SociONewSum standard configuration (K=10, δ=0.2, α=0.7) and we varied the value of each of the input parameter separately while keeping the value of all the other ones constant.

In Figure 2 we plotted the variation of the representative ROUGE-1 F1-measure by varying the value of α in the range [0,1] for a representative news collection (i.e., U.S. Open). The parameter α weighs the importance of the sentence rank with respect to the similarity score evaluated between the candidate sentence and the already selected ones (see Section "Sentence evaluation

Table 3. Summary examples. Irene hurricane news collection.

Summarizer	Result
SociONewSum	It's one of several towns in states such as New Jersey, Connecticut, New York, Vermont and Massachusetts dealing with the damage of torrential rain and flooding spawned by Hurricane Irene (Cleveland.com). Barack Obama, US president, has called Irene a "historic hurricane" and declared a state of emergency in New York, ordering federal aid to supplement state and local response efforts starting on Friday. Beyond deadly flooding that caused havoc in upstate New York and Vermont, the hurricane flooded cotton and tobacco crops in North Carolina, temporarily halted shellfish harvesting in Chesapeake Bay, sapped power and kept commuters from their jobs.
OTS	As emergency airlift operations brought ready-to-eat meals and water to Vermont residents left isolated and desperate, states along the Eastern Seaboard continued to be battered Tuesday by the after effects of Irene, the destructive hurricane turned tropical storm. Dangerously-damaged infrastructure, 2.5 million people without power and thousands of water-logged homes and businesses continued to overshadow the lives of residents and officials from North Carolina through New England, where the storm has been blamed for at least 44 deaths in 13 states. But new dangers developed in New Jersey and Connecticut, where once benign rivers rose menacingly high.
TexLexAn	As emergency airlift operations brought ready-to-eat meals and water to Vermont residents left isolated and desperate, states along the Eastern Seaboard continued to be battered Tuesday by the after effects of Irene, the destructive hurricane turned tropical storm. Search-and-rescue teams in Paterson have pulled nearly 600 people from flooded homes in the town after the Passaic River rose more than 13 feet above flood stage, the highest level since 1903. It's one of several towns in states such as New Jersey, Connecticut, New York, Vermont and Massachusetts dealing with the damage of torrential rain and flooding spawned by Hurricane Irene (Cleveland hurricane Katrina was a Category 5 hurricane and Hurricane Irene was a Category 1 hurricane).
Baseline	Stransky pointed out that, "because Irene tracked west of several islands including Abaco Island, which contains the third highest insured property value after New Providence and Grand Bahama it is likely that losses in the Bahamas from Hurricane Irene will be higher than those from Hurricane Floyd". US Geological Survey scientists are sampling water from six major rivers in the Northeast from the Susquehanna, which flows out of New York into the Chesapeake Bay, to Boston's Charles River for sewage contamination. In Vermont, Craig Fugate, head of the Federal Emergency Management Agency, joined the state's governor, Peter Shumlin (D).

Figure 2. Impact of α on the Rouge-1 F1-measure. U.S. Open.

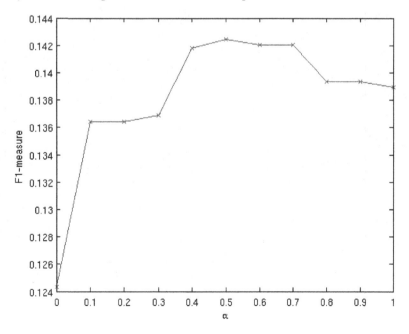

and selection"). The higher the value of α is, the more significant the selected sentence rank is. However, since the impact of the similarity score decreases, potentially redundant information could be selected as well. According to the achieved results, the best performance results were achieved by setting medium values of α, i.e., $\alpha \in [0.4, 0.7]$. Hence, a good trade-off between sentence relevance and novelty is required.

The parameter δ appears to only slightly affect the summarizer performance (see Figure 3). In most cases, setting a relatively low values of δ (e.g., 0.2) yields good summarization performance. With such parameter setting, sentences that do not contain any recognized named entity are mildly penalized, whereas sentences that contain several named entities usually achieve fairly high ranks. From a practical point of view, this is reasonable because names are most likely to contain meaningful information for summarization purposes. In contrast, higher δ values on average worsens

the quality of the result, because the scores assigned to different entity types become unevenly distributed. Since for all the analyzed collections tuning the value of δ does not produce significant performance improvements, the use of the standard parameter value (i.e., δ=0.2) is recommended.

In Figure 4 we separately analyzed the impact of the parameter *K* on the summarizer performance. During sentence selection, *K* represents the number of considered top-ranked news entities (see Section "Sentence selection"). The higher the value of *K* is, the more likely the occurrence of a news entity in a candidate sentence becomes. However, the more news entities are considered, the lower, on average, the similarity scores becomes, because a higher number of unmatched social entities is averagely considered. On the other hand, some of the low-ranked social entities may represent noisy information and, thus, should be discarded. Hence, to achieve good summarization performance medium values of

Figure 3. Impact of δ on the Rouge-1 F1-measure. U.S. Open.

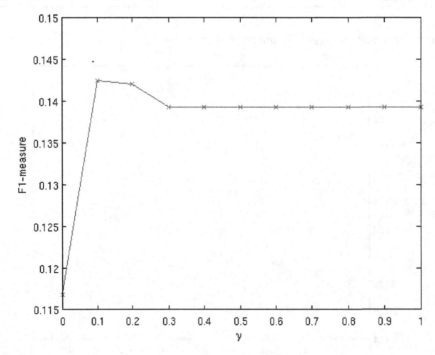

Figure 4. Impact of K on the Rouge-1 F1-measure. U.S. Open.

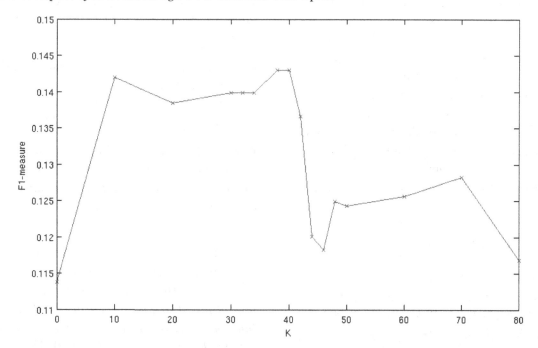

K (i.e., between 10 and 50) should be enforced. The best configuration setting actually depends on the analyzed data distribution.

FUTURE RESEARCH DIRECTIONS

Research on semantics-based news document summarization can be extended in different directions. For example, itemset-based approaches (e.g., (Baralis et al., 2012)) have recently shown fairly good performance on generic documents. Hence, the integration of ontologies with itemset-based models is a promising research direction to improve news summarization performance.

A parallel issue concerns the analysis of the evolution of news articles over time to address incremental news summary updating. For example, once a set of news articles is added to the original collection, the text summary should be updated without the need for calculating the whole data mining model. Furthermore, since SociONewSum also analyzes the Twitter UGC to generate accurate

and up-to-date news summaries, a parallel analysis of the temporal evolution of the UGC coming from social networks could further improve the performance of the proposed summarizer.

Finally, we aim integrating the proposed approach in a real-world content curation platform, in which users could select a subset of news topics of interest, create and personalize their virtual newspaper, and access to the news summaries instead of the whole article content.

CONCLUSION

This Chapter presents a novel text summarizer that focuses on extracting accurate and appealing summaries of collections of news articles ranging over the same topic. The proposed summarizer combines the use of an established semantics-based model with the analysis of the on-topic textual message published on Twitter. To identify the key news topics and also consider the current interests of social network users, news sentences are evaluated and selected according to the importance of their contained ontological concepts in the news collection and in the Twitter UGC.

The experiments, conducted on real-life news article collections and driven by on-topic Twitter posts, demonstrate the effectiveness of the proposed approach compared to other open source summarizers and the usefulness of social content for improving the summarization performance. Furthermore, the readability of the generated summaries has also been evaluated on real-life data.

REFERENCES

Agrawal, R., Imielinski, T., & Swami, A. (1993). Mining association rules between sets of items in large databases. *SIGMOD Record, 22*(2), 207–216. doi:10.1145/170036.170072

Ai, D., Zheng, Y., & Zhang, D. (2010). Automatic text summarization based on latent semantic indexing. *Artificial Life and Robotics, 15*(1), 25–29. doi:10.1007/s10015-010-0759-x

Atkinson, J., & Munoz, R. (2013). Rhetorics-based multi-document summarization. *Expert Systems with Applications, 40*(11), 4346–4352. doi:10.1016/j.eswa.2013.01.017

Baralis, E., Cagliero, L., Jabeen, S., & Fiori, A. (2012). Multi-document summarization exploiting frequent itemsets. In *Proceedings of the 27th Annual ACM Symposium on Applied Computing (SAC '12)* (pp. 782-786). New York, NY: ACM.

Baxter, D., Klimt, B., Grobelnik, M., Schneider, D., Witbrock, M., & Mladenic, D. (2009). Capturing document semantics for ontology generation and document summarization. In *Proceedings of Semantic Knowledge Management: Integrating Ontology Management, Knowledge Discovery, and Human Language Technologies* (pp. 141–154). Heidelberg, Germany: Springer. doi:10.1007/978-3-540-88845-1_11

Bird, S., Klein, E., & Loper, E. (2009). *Natural language processing with Python*. Cambridge, MA: O'Reilly Media.

Brin, S., Motwani, R., & Silverstein, C. (1997). Beyond market baskets: generalizing association rules to correlations. *SIGMOD Record, 26*(2), 265–276. doi:10.1145/253262.253327

Brin, S., & Page, L. (1998). The anatomy of a large-scale hypertextual Web search engine. In *Proceedings of the seventh international conference on World Wide Web* (pp. 107-117). New York, NY: ACM.

Carbonell, J., & Goldstein, J. (1998). The use of MMR diversity-based re-ranking for reordering documents and producing summaries. In *Proceedings of the ACM 21st Special Interest Group on Information Retrieval International Conference (SIGIR'98)* (pp. 335-336). New York, NY: ACM.

Carenini, G., Ng, R. T., & Zhou, X. (2007). Summarizing email conversations with clue words. In *Proceedings of World Wide Web Conference Series* (pp. 91–100). New York, NY: ACM.

Chali, Y., Hasan, S. A., & Joty, S. R. (2009). A SVM-based ensemble approach to multi-document summarization. In *Proceedings of the 22nd Canadian Conference on Artificial Intelligence: Advances in Artificial Intelligence (Canadian AI '09)* (pp. 199-202). Heidelberg, Germany: Springer-Verlag.

Conrad, J. G., Leidner, J. L., Schilder, F., & Kondadadi, R. (2009). Query-based opinion summarization for legal blog entries. In *Proceedings of the 12th International Conference on Artificial Intelligence and Law (ICAIL '09)* (pp. 167-176). New York, NY: ACM.

Dietterich, T. G. (1998). Approximate statistical test for comparing supervised classification learning algorithms. *Neural Computation, 10*(7), 1895–1923. doi:10.1162/089976698300017197 PMID:9744903

Dredze, M., Wallach, H. M., Puller, D., & Pereira, F. (2008). Generating summary keywords for emails using topics. In *Proceedings of the 13th international conference on Intelligent user interfaces* (pp. 199-206). New York: ACM.

Filatova, E., & Hatzivassiloglou, V. (2004). A formal model for information selection in multi-sentence text extraction. In *Proceedings of the 20th international conference on Computational Linguistics* (pp. 39-47). Stroudsburg, Germany: Association for Computational Linguistics.

Goldstein, J., Mittal, V., Carbonell, J., & Kantrowitz, M. (2000). Multi-Document Summarization By Sentence Extraction. In *Proceedings of the ANLP/NAACL Workshop on Automatic Summarization* (pp. 40-48). Stroudsburg, Germany: Association for Computational Linguistics.

Gong, S., Qu, Y., & Tian, S. (2010). Summarization using Wikipedia. In *Proceedings of Text Analysis Conference* (pp. 1-7). New York: ACM.

Gong, Y., & Liu, X. (2001). Generic Text Summarization Using Relevance Measure and Latent Semantic Analysis. In *Proceedings of the 24th annual international ACM SIGIR conference on Research and development in information retrieval*, (pp. 19-25). New York: ACM.

Guha, S., Mishra, N., Motwani, R., & O'Callaghan, L. (2000). Clustering data streams. In *Proceedings of 41st Annual Symposium on Foundations of Computer Science* (pp. 359-361). New York: ACM.

Hachey, B., Radford, W., Nothman, J., Honnibal, M., & Curran, J. R. (2013). Evaluating entity linking with Wikipedia. *Artificial Intelligence*, *194*, 130–150. doi:10.1016/j.artint.2012.04.005

Hamasaki, M., Matsuo, Y., Nishimura, T., & Takeda, H. (2008). Ontology extraction by collaborative tagging with social networking. In *Proceedings of the World Wide Web Conference (WWW'08)* (pp. 291-294). ACM.

Hennig, L., Umbrath, W., & Wetzker, R. (2008). An Ontology-Based Approach to Text Summarization. In *Proceedings of the IEEE/WIC/ACM Web Intelligence and Intelligent Agent Technology* (pp. 291-294). New York: ACM.

Hoffart, J., Yosef, M. A., Bordino, I., Fürstenau, H., Pinkal, M., Spaniol, M., et al. (2011). Robust disambiguation of named entities in text. In *Proceedings of the Conference on Empirical Methods in Natural Language Processing (EMNLP '11)* (pp. 782-792). Stroudsburg, Germany: Association for Computational Linguistics.

Jaroszewicz, S., & Simovici, D. A. (2004). Interestingness of frequent itemsets using Bayesian networks as background knowledge. In *Proceedings of the tenth ACM SIGKDD international conference on Knowledge discovery and data mining* (pp. 178-186). New York, NY: ACM.

Kianmehr, K., Gao, S., Attari, J., Rahman, M. M., Akomeah, K., Alhajj, R., et al. (2009). Text summarization techniques: SVM versus neural networks. In *Proceedings of the 11th International Conference on Information Integration and Web-based Applications & Services (iiWAS '09)* (pp. 487-491). New York, NY: ACM.

Kogilavani, A., & Balasubramanie, B. (2009). Ontology enhanced clustering based summarization of medical documents. *International Journal of Recent Trends in Engineering*, *1*(1), 546–549.

Kontonasios, K., & De Bie, T. (2010). An Information-Theoretic Approach to Finding Informative Noisy Tiles in Binary Databases. In *Proceedings of SIAM International Conference on Data Mining* (pp. 47-57). New York, NY: ACM.

Li, L., Wang, D., Shen, C., & Li, T. (2010). Ontology-enriched multi-document summarization in disaster management. In *Proceedings of the 33rd international ACM SIGIR conference on Research and development in information retrieval (SIGIR '10)* (pp. 819-820). New York, NY: ACM.

Lin, C., & Hovy, E. (2003). Automatic evaluation of summaries using N-gram co-occurrence statistics. In *Proceedings of the Conference of the North American Chapter of the Association for Computational Linguistics on Human Language Technology* (pp.71-78). Stroudsburg, Germany: Association for Computational Linguistics.

Liu, F., Liu, Y., & Weng, F. (2011). Why is SXSW trending? exploring multiple text sources for Twitter topic summarization. In *Proceedings of the Workshop on Languages in Social Media (LSM '11)* (pp. 66-75). Stroudsburg, PA: Association for Computational Linguistics.

Mampaey, M., Tatti, N., & Vreeken, J. (2011). Tell me what I need to know: succinctly summarizing data with itemsets. In *Proceedings of the 17th ACM SIGKDD Conference on Knowledge Discovery and Data Mining* (pp. 573-581). New York, NY: ACM.

Mathioudakis, M., & Koudas, N. (2010). Twitter-Monitor: trend detection over the twitter stream. In *Proceedings of the 2010 international conference on Management of data* (pp. 1155-1158). New York, NY: ACM.

Miao, Y., & Li, C. (2010). WikiSummarizer - A Wikipedia-based Summarization System. In *Proceedings of Text Analysis Conference*. Academic Press.

Nastase, V. (2008). Topic-driven multi-document summarization with encyclopedic knowledge and spreading activation. In *Proceedings of Conference on Empirical Methods on Natural Language Processing* (pp. 763-772). New York, NY: ACM.

Oberle, D., Guarino, N., & Staab, S. (2009). What is an ontology? In *Handbook on Ontologies*. Academic Press.

Ozsoy, M. G., Alpaslan, F. N., & Cicekli, I. (2011). Text summarization of Turkish texts using Latent Semantic Analysis. In *Proceedings of the 23rd International Conference on Computational Linguistics (COLING '10)* (pp. 869-876). Stroudsburg, PA: Association for Computational Linguistics.

Ping, C., & Verma, R. (2006). A query-based medical information summarization system using ontology knowledge. In *Proceedings of IEEE Computer-Based Medical Systems* (pp. 37–42). IEEE Computer Society.

Radev, D. R. (2004). Lexrank: Graph-based lexical centrality as salience in text summarization. *Journal of Artificial Intelligence Research, 22*(4), 457–479.

Radev, D. R., Jing, H., Sty, M., & Tam, D. (2004). Centroid-based summarization of multiple documents. *Information Processing & Management, 40*(6), 919–938. doi:10.1016/j.ipm.2003.10.006

Rotem, N. (2006). *Open Text Summarizer (OTS)*. Retrieved in July 2011 from http://libots.sourceforge.net

Saravanan, M., & Ravindran, B. (2010). Identification of rhetorical roles for segmentation and summarization of a legal judgment. *Artificial Intelligence and Law, 18*(1), 45–76. doi:10.1007/s10506-010-9087-7

Sharifi, B., Hutton, M.-A., & Kalita, J. (2010). Summarizing microblogs automatically. In *Proceedings of the 2010 Annual Conference of the North American Chapter of the Association for Computational Linguistics (HLT '10)* (pp. 685-688). Stroudsburg, PA: Association for Computational Linguistics.

Sharifi, B., Hutton, M.-A., & Kalita, J. (2010). Experiments in Microblog Summarization. In *Proceedings of the 2010 IEEE Second International Conference on Social Computing (SOCIALCOM '10)* (pp. 49-56). IEEE Computer Society.

Suchanek, F. M., Kasneci, G., & Weikum, G. (2007). Yago: a core of semantic knowledge. In *Proceedings of the 16th international conference on World Wide Web* (pp. 697-706). New York, NY: ACM.

Takamura, H., & Okumura, M. (2009a). Text summarization model based on maximum coverage problem and its variant. In *Proceedings of the 12th Conference of the European Chapter of the Association for Computational Linguistics* (pp. 781-789). Stroudsburg, PA: Association for Computational Linguistics.

Takamura, H., & Okumura, M. (2009b). Text summarization model based on the budgeted median problem. In *Proceeding of the 18th ACM conference on Information and knowledge management* (pp. 1589-1592). New York, NY: ACM.

Tan, P. N., Steinbach, M., & Kumar, V. (2006). *Introduction to data mining*. Boston, MA: Pearson Addison Wesley.

Tang, J., Yao, L., & Chen, D. (2009). Multi-topic based query-oriented summarization. In *Proceedings of SIAM International Conference Data Mining* (pp. 20-26). New York, NY: ACM.

Tatti, N., & Heikinheimo, H. (2008). Decomposable families of itemsets. In *Proceedings of European Conference on Machine Learning and Knowledge Discovery in Databases* (PKDD'08) (pp. 472-487). Heidelberg, Germany: Springer-Verlag.

Tatti, N., & Mampaey, M. (2010). Using background knowledge to rank itemsets. *ACM Data Mining and Knowledge Discovery.*, *21*(2), 293–309. doi:10.1007/s10618-010-0188-4

TexLexAn. (2011). *Texlexan: An open-source text summarizer*. Retrieved March 15, 2011, from http://texlexan.sourceforge.net/

Thakkar, K., Dharaskar, R., & Chandak, M. (2010). Graph-based algorithms for text summarization. In *Proceedings of Third International Conference on Emerging Trends in Engineering and Technology*, (pp. 516–519). Academic Press.

Town, C. (2006). Ontological inference for image and video analysis. *Machine Vision and Applications*, *17*(2), 94–115. doi:10.1007/s00138-006-0017-3

Wan, X., & Yang, J. (2006). Improved affinity graph based multi-document summarization. In *Proceedings of the Human Language Technology Conference of the NAACL* (pp. 181-184). Stroudsburg, PA: Association for Computational Linguistics.

Wang, D., & Li, T. (2010). Document update summarization using incremental hierarchical clustering. In *Proceedings of the 19th ACM international conference on Information and knowledge management* (pp. 279–288). New York, NY: ACM.

Wang, D., Zhu, S., Li, T., Chi, Y., & Gong, Y. (2011). Integrating Document Clustering and Multidocument Summarization. *ACM Transactions on Knowledge Discovery from Data*, *5*(3), 1–26. doi:10.1145/1993077.1993078

Wang, J., Li, Q., & Chen, Y. P. (2010). User comments for news recommendation in social media. In *Proceedings of the 33rd international ACM SIGIR conference on Research and development in information retrieval* (pp. 881-882). New York, NY: ACM.

Wu, C.-W., & Liu, C.-L. (2003). Ontology-based text summarization for business news articles. In *Computers and their Applications*. Academic Press.

Yang, Z., Cai, K., Tang, J., Zhang, L., Su, Z., & Li, J. (2011). Social Context Summarization. In *Proceedings of International ACM SIGIR Conference on Research and Development in Information Retrieval* (pp. 255-264). New York, NY: ACM.

Yin, Z., Li, R., Mei, Q., & Han, J. (2009). Exploring social tagging graph for web object classification. In *Proceedings of the 15th ACM SIGKDD international conference on Knowledge discovery and data mining* (pp. 957-966). New York, NY: ACM.

Zhang, R., Li, W., Gao, D., & Ouyang, Y. (2013). Automatic Twitter Topic Summarization With Speech Acts. *IEEE Transactions on Audio, Speech, and Language Processing*, *21*(3), 649–658. doi:10.1109/TASL.2012.2229984

Zhu, J., Wang, C., He, X., Bu, J., Chen, C., Shang, S., et al. (2009). Tag-oriented document summarization. In *Proceedings of the 18th international ACM conference on World Wide Web Conference* (pp. 1195-1196). New York, NY: ACM.

ADDITIONAL READING

Abrol, S., & Khan, L. (2010). TWinner: understanding news queries with geo-content using Twitter. In *Proceedings of the 6th Workshop on Geographic Information Retrieval* (pp. 1-8). New York, NY: ACM.

Agarwal, D., Phillips, J. M., & Venkatasubramanian, S. (2006). The Hunting of the Bump: On Maximizing Statistical Discrepancy. In *Proceedings of the seventeenth annual ACM-SIAM symposium on Discrete algorithm* (pp. 1137-1146). New York, NY: ACM.

Agrawal, R., & Srikant, R. (1994). Fast algorithms for mining association rules in large databases. In *Proceedings of the 20th Very Large DataBases conference* (pp. 487-499). San Francisco, CA: Morgan Kaufmann Publishers Inc.

Baralis, E., Garza, P., Quintarelli, E., & Tanca, L. (2007). Answering XML queries by means of data summaries. *ACM Transactions on Information Systems*, *25*(3), 10–33. doi:10.1145/1247715.1247716

Basile, P., Gendarmi, D., Lanubile, F., & Semeraro, G. (2007). *Recommending smart tags in a social bookmarking system. Bridging the Gap between Semantic Web and Web* (pp. 22–29). New York, NY: ACM.

Becker, H., Naaman, M., & Gravano, L. (2011). Selecting Quality Twitter Content for Events. In *Proceedings of the Fifth International AAAI Conference on Weblogs and Social Media.* (pp. 34-39). Palo Alto, CA: Association for the Advancement of Artificial Intelligence.

Bender, M., Crecelius, T., Kacimi, M., Michel, S., Neumann, T., Parreira, J. X., et al. (2008). Exploiting social relations for query expansion and result ranking. In *IEEE 24th International Conference on Data Engineering Workshop (pp.* 501-506). Washington DC: USA: IEEE Computer Society.

Diaz, A., & Gervas, P. (2007). User-model based personalized summarization. *Information Processing & Management*, *43*(6), 1715–1734. doi:10.1016/j.ipm.2007.01.009

Foong, O. M., Oxley, A., & Sulaiman, S. (2010). Challenges and Trends of Automatic Text Summarization. *International Journal of Information and Telecommunication Technology*, *1*(1), 34–39.

Ganesan, K., Zhai, C., & Han, J. (2010). Opinosis: A Graph-Based Approach to Abstractive Summarization of Highly Redundant Opinions. *Proceedings of the 23rd International Conference on Computational Linguistics* (pp. 340-348). Stroudsburg, USA: Association for Computational Linguistics.

Girardin, F., Calabrese, F., Fiore, F. D., Ratti, C., & Blat, J. (2008). Digital Footprinting: Uncovering Tourists with User- Generated Content. *Pervasive Computing*, *7*(4), 36–43. doi:10.1109/MPRV.2008.71

Gong, Y., & Liu, X. (2001). Generic Text Summarization Using Relevance Measure and Latent Semantic Analysis. *Proceedings of the 24th Annual International ACM SIGIR Conference on Research and Development in Information Retrieval.* (pp. 902-905). New York, NY: ACM.

Gupta, V., & Lehal, G. S. (2010). A Survey of Text Summarization Extractive Techniques. *Journal of Emerging Technologies in Web Intelligence*, *2*(3), 57–65. doi:10.4304/jetwi.2.3.258-268

Jauua, M., & Hamadou, A. B. (2003). Automatic Text Summarization of Scientific Articles Based on Classification of Extract's Population. In *Proceedings of the 4th international conference on Computational linguistics and intelligent text processing* (pp. 623-634). Stroudsburg, USA: Association for Computational Linguistics.

Kleinberg, J. (1999). Authoritative sources in a hyperlinked environment. *Journal of the ACM*, *46*(5), 604–632. doi:10.1145/324133.324140

Lappas, T., Arai, B., Platakis, M., Kotsakos, D., & Gunopulos, D. (2009). On burstiness-aware search for document sequences. In *Proceedings of the 15th ACM SIGKDD international conference on Knowledge discovery and data mining* (pp. 477-486). New York, NY: ACM.

Li, Q., Wang, J., Chen, Y. P., & Lin, Z. (2010). User comments for news recommendation in forum-based social media. *Information Sciences*, *180*(24), 4929–4939. doi:10.1016/j.ins.2010.08.044

Li, X., Guo, L., & Zhao, Y. E. (2008). Tag-based social interest discovery. In *Proceeding of the 17th international conference on World Wide Web* (pp. 675-684). New York, NY: ACM.

Lin, F., & Liang, C. (2008). Storyline-based summarization for news topic retrospection. *Decision Support Systems*, *45*(3), 473–490. doi:10.1016/j.dss.2007.06.009

Lloret, E., & Palomar, M. (2010). Challenging Issues of Automatic Summarization: Relevance Detection and Quality-based Evaluation. *Informatica*, *34*(1), 29–35.

Nagwani, N. K., & Verma, S. (2011). A Frequent Term and Semantic Similarity based Single Document Text Summarization Algorithm. *International Journal of Computers and Applications*, *17*(2), 36–40. doi:10.5120/2190-2778

Nomoto, T., & Matsumoto, Y. (2001). A new approach to unsupervised text summarization. In *Proceedings of the 24th annual international ACM SIGIR conference on Research and development in information retrieval* (pp. 26-34). New York, NY: ACM.

Ralphs, T. K., & Güzelsoy, M. (2005) The SYMPHONY Callable Library for Mixed-Integer Linear Programming. In *Proceedings of the Ninth INFORMS Computing Society Conference* (pp. 61-76). Heidelberg, Germany: Springer-Verlag.

Rambow, O., Shrestha, L., Chen, J., & Lauridsen, C. (2004). Summarizing email threads. In *Proceedings of the Human Language Technology Conference of the NAACL* (pp. 105-108). Stroudsburg, USA: Association for Computational Linguistics.

Rusu, D., Fortuna, B., Grobelnik, M., & Mladenic, D. (2009). Semantic graphs derived from triplets with application in document summarization. *Informatica: An International Journal of Computing and Informatics*, *33*(3), 357–362.

Tatti, N. (2010). Probably the best itemsets. In *Proceedings of the 16th ACM SIGKDD international conference on Knowledge discovery and data mining* (pp. 293-302). New York, NY: ACM.

Tatti, N., & Mampaey, M. (2010). Using background knowledge to rank itemsets. Data Mining and Knowledge Discovery, 1-17. Heidelberg, Germany: Springer-Verlag.

Vivaldi, J., Cunha, I. d., Moreno, J. M. T., & Velázquez-Morales, P. (2010). Automatic Summarization Using Terminological and Semantic Resources. In *Proceedings of the International Conference on Language Resources and Evaluation.* (pp. 31-35). New York, NY: ACM.

Wei, F., Li, W., Lu, Q., & He, Y. (2008). Query-sensitive mutual reinforcement chain and its application in query-oriented multi-document summarization. In *Proceedings of the 31st annual international ACM SIGIR conference on Research and development in information retrieval* (pp. 283-290). New York, NY: ACM.

Xue, Y., Zhang, C., Zhou, C., Lin, X., & Li, Q. (2008). An Effective News Recommendation in Social Media Based on Users' Preference. In *Proceedings of the 2008 International Workshop on Education Technology and Training & 2008 International Workshop on Geoscience and Remote Sensing (pp.* 627-631). New York, NY: ACM.

KEY TERMS AND DEFINITIONS

Data Mining: The process of discovering valuable information from large data sources.

Document Summarization: The process of extracting most relevant textual content from either a single document or from a document collection.

Itemset Mining: Itemset mining is a widely exploratory technique to discover relevant recurrences hidden in the analyzed data.

Ontology: Formal representation of the most peculiar concepts related to a knowledge domain and their corresponding relations.

Semantics-Based Summarization: The process of extracting document summaries with the aid of complex semantics-based models (e.g., ontologies, taxonomies).

Social Network Services: Social network services allow users to define a profile, build a network with other users (friends) and share information or user-generated media content with their friends.

Tweets: Short textual messages that Twitter users post on the microblogging website.

User-Generated Content: User-generated content (UGC) refers to various kinds of publicly available media content that are produced by end-users, such as document, photos, and videos.

ENDNOTES

[1]   The provided command is: ROUGE-1.5.5.pl -e data -x -m -2 4 -u -c 95 -r 1000 -n 4 -f A -p 0.5 -t 0 -d -a.

Chapter 13

A Layered Parameterized Framework for Intelligent Information Retrieval in Dynamic Social Network using Data Mining

Shailendra Kumar Sonkar
National Institute of Technical Teacher's Training and Research, India

Vishal Bhatnagar
Ambedkar Institute of Advanced Communication Technologies and Research, India

Rama Krishna Challa
National Institute of Technical Teacher's Training and Research, India

ABSTRACT

Dynamic social networks contain vast amounts of data, which is changing continuously. A search in a dynamic social network does not guarantee relevant, filtered, and timely information to the users all the time. There should be some sequential processes to apply some techniques and store the information internally that provides the relevant, filtered, and timely information to the users. In this chapter, the authors categorize the social network users into different age groups and identify the suitable and appropriate parameters, then assign these parameters to the already categorized age groups and propose a layered parameterized framework for intelligent information retrieval in dynamic social network using different techniques of data mining. The primary data mining techniques like clustering group the different groups of social network users based on similarities between key parameter items and by classifying the different classes of social network users based on differences among key parameter items, and it can be association rule mining, which finds the frequent social network users from the available users.

DOI: 10.4018/978-1-4666-6086-1.ch013

INTRODUCTION

In the modern era people are connected and communicate all over time using social network that span globally geographical area. Fan and Shelton (2009) defined "Social networks, which represent the relationships (such as friendship or co-authorship) among actors (such as individuals or companies), have been studied for decades". Social network is a large group of people in which an individual can communicate or interact to each other at any time throughout the world. Social network comprises of city, state, country or whole world. Information sharing among the individuals can be texts, images, and videos. Social network is represented by a social graph in which nodes or vertices represent an individual or a person of the social network and links or edges represent an interaction or communication among the individuals or persons of a social network. In social network an individual can communicate and interact to other using messages or videos. Social network can be static or dynamic. In static social network most of the information is static and a person can communicate or interact to other at a particular time and all the information about the communication is removed. Static social network is represented by a social graph (V, E) where V represents an individual or a person of social network and E represents an interaction or communication among the individual of a social network at an instant of time. Nguyen et al. (2011) defined the same as "Let Gs = (Vs, Es) be a time dependent network snapshot recorded at time s". In dynamic social network all the information continuously change, communication or interaction between two persons take place all over the time and all the information about the communication or interaction must be considered. Dynamic social network is represented by a social graph {V (t), E (t)} where V (t) represents an individual or a person of a social network and E (t) represents an interaction or communication among individuals at all the time. Dynamic social network contains billions of users, some of them may be with the same names or different names. Finding a person based on some known information in dynamic social network does not provide the relevant information all the times. It may or may not give the relevant information all the time during a search in dynamic social network. There is a need to an intelligent information retrieval that provides the relevant, filtered and timely information to the users during a search in dynamic social network. The intelligent information retrieval system takes the inputs which processes these inputs without any user intervention and produces the output as relevant, filtered and timely information to the user. The author's proposes a layered parameterized framework for intelligent information retrieval using data mining techniques in dynamic social network that provide the most relevant information to the user during a search in dynamic social network.

The organization of the chapter as follows: Section 2 discusses the background of the chapter that includes the subsections are, related research and motivation, research methodology, introduction to social network, introduction to data mining and introduction to intelligent information retrieval. Section 3 outlines the main focus of the chapter that includes the subsections are, parameters for intelligent information retrieval in dynamic social network, layered framework for intelligent information retrieval, empirical case example and advantages and disadvantages of framework and Section 4 summarizes conclusion and future research.

BACKGROUND

Related Research and Motivation

A deep study conducted on several journals article and research papers related to intelligent information retrieval. Several researchers given the different views on different approaches and techniques related to intelligent information retrieval. These are:

- An idea or concept of an intelligent information retrieval system presented by several researchers. Belkin (2006) argued an agency and its constituents based intelligent information retrieval system and an idea of an intelligent information retrieval system. Li and Huang (2005) developed a platform for an intelligent information retrieval system that generates an idea based, domain specific information retrieval and exact answer by questioning-answering in order to produce less number of irrelevant pages. Chen et al. (2002) showed three layers architecture based system that enhances the power of refining the information and gives the suitable and timely information to the users. Yong-Min and Shu (2009) discovered a prototype system based on allotting context to documents that gives the effective information to the users.
- Different researchers argued different approaches and model based on agent's concept for intelligent information retrieval in the past couple of years. Tu and Hsiang (1998) proposed an agent based framework for intelligent information retrieval with the identification of suitable characteristics of an agent, division of an agent into subagents, representation of an agent community and showed the issues related to category information. Xie et al. (2003) developed a three-layer agent structure based model and algorithms for an intelligent information retrieval in order to provides the appropriate and speedily information to the user. Wu et al. (2013) discovered an intelligent information retrieval system based on

multi agent model to retrieve the information from various sources of information and gives the advantages and disadvantages. Xiao et al. (2007) argued a multi-agent (analysis agent, feedback agent, filter agent and search agent) based model to intelligent information retrieval that gives the suitable, refined and timely information to the user. Jain (2005) showed a joint venture of multi-agent conceptual graph based approach for an intelligent information retrieval model and presented merits and demerits of this model to achieve the relevant information timely. Kavousi and Moshiri (2007) proposed the design of framework of fusion agent based intelligent information retrieval that retrieves the information from dynamic environment.

- Several researchers and scholars proposed different techniques and methods based on Web page clustering for intelligent information retrieval. Quintana (1997) argued a framework and algorithm for intelligent information retrieval based on cluster knowledge and discussed the functionality of the model. Li et al. (2006) developed a technique based on concept mining and Web page clustering that gives the appropriate Web pages to the user. Koval and Navrat (2002) discovered a model of a Web tool system that finds the appropriate information using autonomous searching, without intervention of any user and retrieves the information based on history of the previous Web pages that users visited in the past. Z. Wang, (2013) presented the performance evaluation for strategy based on auto-adapting users in cross language information retrieval and provide the better results as compared to past one. Nihei et al. (1998) proposed an intelligent information retrieval, Expert Guide developed using

Java Applet that execute with the help of World Wide Web browser and discover the relevant Web pages to the user.

- Various intelligent information retrieval system and model based on an idea of ontology has been developed by several researchers. Li et al. (2004) showed an intelligent information retrieval system based on ontology that provides the suitable and timely information to the users. Ying et al. (2007) developed an ontology based intelligent information retrieval system that provides the knowledge about the computer graphics course. Wiese et al. (2012) proposed a personal social network for dynamic and computational purpose to retrieve the information in a faster and appropriate way. Liu et al. (2008) discovered ontology based scientific document and an intelligent information retrieval system that is used in digital library. Lee and Yoo (2005) presented an intelligent information retrieval system for data repository designed based on Web and discussed the metadata and ontology helps users or application systems share product data in a virtual and distributed environment.

- A number of researchers and scholars have proposed different approaches and techniques for intelligent information retrieval using the concept of semantic Web. Li et al. (2008) proposed a semantic Web-oriented framework for intelligent information retrieval that is useful for personal purpose. Jiang et al. (2010) argued a semantic Web based model for the intelligent information retrieval which provides the facility to the computer system to understand and operate on the Web and information exchange globally. Wu et al. (2009) developed an intelligent information retrieval system based on Web, an idea of knowledge base and latent semantic indexing model. Karthik et al. (2008) argued a model for

extracting the semantic information from the text based Web document that facilitates an intelligent information algorithm for appropriate information retrieval from the RDF databases. Cesarano et al. (2003) discussed a sematic Web based prototype intelligent information retrieval system that retrieves the appropriate information from the Internet.

- Some fuzzy logic and natural language processing based algorithms and techniques have discovered by several researchers. Baranyi et al. (1998) proposed an algorithm based on fuzzy logic for intelligent information retrieval that enhance the power of refining the information and provides better result to the users. He and Feng (2005) argued a system based on variable precision rough set model by combining the rough sets and fuzzy sets that gives the appropriate, filtered and speedily information to the users. Jacobs and Rau (1988) argued an intelligent information retrieval system based on natural language processing and discussed the issues related to retrieval of information using the natural language processing. Narayanan et al. (1995) proposed a methodology and combined the technique for intelligent information retrieval in the context of Wright State University. Lim et al. (1997) discovered a term distribution based technique for an automatic query expansion that represents the sematic of information retrieval which provides the better performance to the retrieval system. Daniels and Rissland (1995) discovered a case based approach for intelligent information retrieval and described its advantages and disadvantages. Danilowicz and Nguyen (2002) presented an intelligent information retrieval system based on concept of vector that facilitates the personal information from the user profiles.

Research Methodology

Search for a particular person based on some known information does not guarantee to provide the relevant, filtered and timely information to the user of the dynamic social network. There is a need to propose a layered framework based on some specified parameters for intelligent information retrieval in dynamic social network using data mining techniques. It provides the most relevant, filtered and speedily information to the users of dynamic social network. It can be achieved through the examination of various journals and conference papers that is scattered over different electronic databases. The following journals and conference databases were searched to provide full bibliography.

- Springer,
- ACM,
- IEEE,
- IGI Global,
- Inderscience,
- Elsevier,
- World Scientific,
- Wiley Inter-Science.

The identification of the parameters for the intelligent information retrieval in dynamic social network has been done by the authors. The authors presented a layered framework based on these identified parameters for intelligent information retrieval in dynamic social network using different techniques of data mining. The following stages (see Figure 1) involved in our research methodology are:

- **Problem Discovery:** The authors have conducted a deep literature survey and studied on several journals and conference papers related to dynamic social network to identify the problem.
- **Accumulation of Appropriate Materials:** In this stage of our research methodology,

the authors have downloaded and collected the relevant journals and conference papers related to intelligent information retrieval from the different electronic databases.

- **Study and Categorization of the Papers:** Categorized the papers related to intelligent information retrieval based on different algorithms, techniques and different source of information as a result of a deep and thorough study.
- **Finding the Suitable Parameters for Intelligent Information Retrieval:** Identification of suitable parameters for intelligent information retrieval in dynamic social network using different techniques of data mining has been done by the authors.
- **Presentation of Layered Parameterized Framework:** In the final stage of our research methodology, the authors have proposes a layered framework based on identified parameters for intelligent information retrieval in dynamic social network using different techniques of data mining.

Social Networks: An Introduction

In the modern era of Internet technology a person can communicate or interact to other verbally or face-to-face using video chat facility in any social network at any time throughout the world easily. Konishi and Toyama (2008) defined "Social networks describe a structure of relationships between individuals, and interpersonal influences". Social network contains a billions of users in which an individual or a person can communicate or interact to each other throughout the world at any time. Social network can be spread over a city or a state or a country or all over the world. Sharing of information can be limited to text or it can be images or videos as well. Tantipathananandh et al. (2007) defined "Social networks are the graphs of interactions between individuals and play an important role in the dissemination of information, innovations, or diseases. Edges can represent social

Figure 1. Sequential stages of research methodology

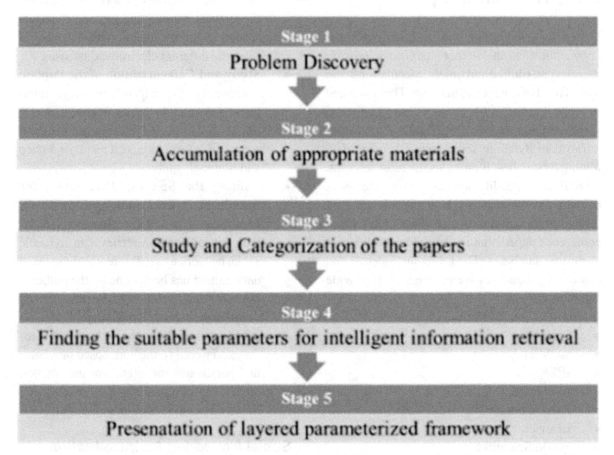

interactions, organizational structures, physical proximity, or even more abstract interactions such as hyperlinks or similarity". Social network contains billions of user in which an individual can communicate and interact to other all over the world. Yang et al. (2009) found "Social networks are usually represented by graphs where nodes represent individuals and edges represent relationships and interactions among individuals". Social network is depicted by a graph in which a node represents an individual and a link represents relationship or interaction between two persons. There are two types of social network static and dynamic. Tai et al. (2011) defined static social network as" The static social network keeps the adversary from distinguishing whether a vertex is newly added or not". In static social network all

the communication or interaction takes place at a particular time and all the information during the communication is removed. Static social network represented by a graph (V, E) in which a node (V) represents an individual and an edge (E) represents the relationship between two people at a particular time. Nguyen et al. (2011) Dynamic social network defined as "A Dynamic social network as the kind of network evolve and changes rapidly over time". In dynamic social network an individual can communicate or interact to other all over the time and all the information during communication must be preserved. Dynamic social network is depicted by a graph G (t) = {V (t), E (t)} in which a node V (t) represents an individual and an edge E (t) represents a relationship between two persons at time t.

Data Mining: An Introduction

Data mining refers to extracting or "mining" knowledge from large amounts of data. Many other terms carry a similar or slightly different meaning to data mining, such as knowledge mining from data, knowledge extraction, data/pattern analysis, data archaeology, and data dredging. Many people treat data mining as a synonym for another term, knowledge discovery from the data, or KDD (Han and Kamber, 2006). Data mining is also called knowledge discovery from databases. It is commonly defined as the process of discovering useful patterns or knowledge from data sources, e.g., databases, text, images, the Web, etc. The pattern must be valid, potentially useful, and understandable (Liu, 2007). Data mining is generic term and is used to look for hidden patterns and trends in data that is not immediately apparent from summarizing the data (Srinath and Ram).

Data miners first understand the application domain of the data mining application then they identify the suitable data sources and the target data. Data mining can be performed on data using following data mining process:

- **Pre-Processing:** In this step of mining process the data are prepared for mining. These are the following pre-processing steps:
  - **Data Cleaning:** The raw data contains the noise and abnormalities. The clean operation is applied to remove the noise and abnormalities.
  - **Data Integration:** Data integration is performed to combine the multiple data sources.
  - **Data Selection:** Data selection is applied to get the relevant data from the database for analysis task.
  - **Data Transformation:** Data transformation is performed to retrieve the appropriate form for mining.

- **Data Mining:** The processed data is then fed to the data mining algorithms or applied intelligent methods to obtain the patterns.
- **Post-Processing:** All discovered patterns are not useful to the many applications. There are two steps to discover the useful patterns. These are:
  - **Pattern Evaluation:** It is the process of to identify the truly interesting patterns representing knowledge based on some interestingness measures.
  - **Knowledge Presentation:** It is used to present the mined knowledge to the user.

There are some data mining task and concepts that help to mine the frequent item sets among the data items, group the data item based on similarities between elements and grouping the data item into different classes based on difference among data elements. These are:

- **Supervised Learning or Classification:** Classification is the technique of data mining that group the data item in to some pre-defined classes based on difference among data items that belongs to the different classes. Decision tree is one of the famous techniques of classification that form a decision tree of classes of different data items.
- **Unsupervised Learning or Clustering:** Clustering is the process of grouping of data items into different group based on the similarity between data items. In other word Clustering divide the data items into clusters or equivalence classes. The nearest neighbor algorithm is one of the famous clustering algorithms.
- **Association Rule Mining:** Association rule find all the frequent item sets from the available data items. A real life example of association rule mining is market basket

analysis that aims to extract how data items purchased in a store are associated. In other word an association is a rule of the form if X then Y and it is depicted by X→Y. Strength of an association rule is measured by support and confidence. The support of a rule X→Y is the ratio of the number of union of X and Y to the total number of occurrence of all rule. Confidence of a rule X→Y is the ratio of the number of union of X and Y to the number of occurrence of X. The Apriori Algorithm is one of the famous algorithms to mining frequent item sets and this can be used to mining association rule.

- **Neural Network (NN):** The neural network represented as a directed graph in which source as input, sink as output, and internal as hidden nodes. The input layer contains inputs, output layer contains outputs and one or more hidden layers contain internal nodes. A tuple is given to input nodes as input and the output nodes produce the possible prediction during evaluation of the data mining task.

- **Genetic Algorithm (GA):** A genetic algorithm is a computational procedure that contains five steps:
  ○ Start with the set of individuals, P.
  ○ Apply Crossover technique.
  ○ Apply Mutation algorithm.
  ○ Apply Fitness function.
  ○ To keep the best individuals in P, fitness function is applied on algorithm that applies the crossover and mutation techniques to P iteratively. Every iteration gives, the algorithm replaces a predefined number of individuals from the population and terminates when some threshold is met.

Intelligent Information Retrieval: An Introduction

A major concern to the users is that they do not get the relevant information during a search in dynamic social network that comprised of such a huge amount and continuous changing information. A search in dynamic social network retrieves the information based on key word matching and page hits algorithms. It may or may not give the relevant and timely information all the time. There is a need to perform a selection or filter the information from the available list of information to obtain the relevant information. These are the time taking process to get the relevant information. There is a need to apply an intelligent information retrieval in dynamic social network that provides the relevant and timely information to the user during a search. Li et al. (2004) stated "The objective of perfect intelligent information retrieval system are display friendly interactive search interface, create describable information of users according to their search interests, query based on instances or natural language, provide users with relational documents automatically, integrate particular retrieval with centralized browse, return query results speedily, and high precision and efficiency of information retrieval". Belkin et al. (1987) defined "an intelligent IR system was one in which the functions of the human intermediary were performed by a program, interacting with the human user." Maes (1994) defined "Intelligent IR is performed by a computer program (a so-called intelligent agent), which, acting on (perhaps minimal or even no explicit) instructions from a human user, retrieves and presents information to the user without any other interaction". The aim of the intelligent information retrieval is to provide the highly relevant and timely information to the user based on their search interest.

The existing methodology based on page ranking algorithm and cookies not based on history. It does not give the relevant and timely information to the users based on existing methodology. This layered parameterized framework based on historical information which fetch the information from the subject oriented parameterized datawarhouse. It gives the relevant and timely information to the users most of the time.

MAIN FOCUS OF THE CHAPTER

Parameters for Intelligent Information Retrieval in Dynamic Social Network

There are some parameters which control and decide the retrieval of information in dynamic social network. These are:

- **Interest:** Interest is defined as the feeling you have when you want to know more about something or somebody. Area of interest and Places of interest near the city is an example of interest. People with same interest grouping into same clusters, people with the different interest classified into different groups and people with frequent interest find using association rule mining.
- **Vicinity:** The area around a particular place is known as the vicinity. The area around Effiel Tower and the area around Tajmahal is an example of vicinity. If people lives or resides area around the same city then we can group into same clusters, if people frequently visits the area around the city then we can find frequent item set using association rule mining and if people lives area around the different city then we can classified into different groups.
- **Education:** Education is the process of teaching, training and learning, especially in school or colleges, to im- prove knowledge and develop skill. Highschool, Intermediate, Graduation, Post-Graduation, Doctorate, Engineering, Medical are example of education back- ground. Social network users with the dif- ferent education background are fed into different circles and Clustering store the same education background persons into different clusters.
- **Place:** Places are a particular position, a particular city, town, a building or an area of land used for a particular purpose. People lives or resides in the same city or town group into same cluster, people lives or resides in the different city or town clas- sified into different groups and association rule mining find the people who frequently visits a particular city or town.
- **Language:** Language is the system of communication in speech and writing that is used by people of a particular country or area. Hindi, English, Punjabi, Japanese are the languages used by the people of dif- ferent country. The same language used by the persons are group into same group, the persons who used frequent language are determined by association rule mining and the persons who used different languages are distributed into different circles.
- **Habit:** Habit is defined a thing that you do often and almost without thinking, es- pecially something that is hard to stop do- ing. An individual with the similar habit are grouping into the same circle, people who have different habits are put into dif- ferent groups and association rule mining find the persons who performed the habit frequently.
- **Course:** Course is a period of study at a college or university that leads to an exam or a qualification. Degree courses includes, B.Tech., B.E.,B.S., B.Sc.,B.Com. B.A.,BBA,BCA and Master's or post-graduate courses in-

cludes M.Tech., M.E.,M.S.,M.Sc.,M. Com.,M.A.,MBA,MCA are example of courses. People with the different courses classified into different groups and people with the same courses are group into same clusters.

- **University:** University is an institution at the highest level of education where people can study for a degree or do research. BHU, JNU, Howard University is an example of a university. An individual who completed or pursuing their degree or research with the same university are grouping into the same circles and persons who completed or pursuing their degree or research with the different university are fed into the distinct circles.

- **Community:** Community is a group of people who live in a particular area, country and share the same religion, job. Persons belongs to the distinct community distributed into the distinct groups and persons belongs to the same community are group together to create a cluster.

- **Feature:** Feature is defined as something important, interesting or typical of a place or thing. Beautiful eyes and face of a female is an example of feature of parts of body of a female. Similar feature persons are grouping into the same circles and distinct feature persons classified into distinct groups.

- **Domain:** Domain is an area of knowledge or activity for which somebody is responsible. An individual who are working on different domain distributed into the different groups and persons who are working with similar domain are grouping into the distinct circle.

- **Job:** Job is a piece of work or a particular task that people have to do and receive regular payment. People engaged with the different kind of job classified around different groups and people engaged with the same kind of job create a new cluster.

- **Working Organization:** Individual workings with the same organization are grouping into the same cluster and persons working with the different organization classified into distinct circles.

- **Relationship:** Relationship is the way in which two or more person or things related or connected to other. Friendship, Colleague, Brother, Sister are an example of relationship. Persons with the similar relationship are organized around the same cluster and persons with the distinct relationship are organized around different classes. If a person is related to a second person and second person is related to third person, then indirectly third person is also related to the first person and this can be achieved using association rule mining.

- **Time:** People which are connected to each other from long time organize or group into same cluster and people are connected to each other from different time classified into different group.

- **Duration or Status of Service:** An individual who are serving from the distinct time distributed into the distinct circles and persons who are serving together from the same time create a new circles.

The person with different age group behaves and communicates differentially to other. The authors categorized the parameters for intelligent information retrieval in dynamic social network into four age group, Youth (0-20), Adults (21-40), Seniors (41-65) and Old (66-80). These are:

- **Youth (0-20 Years):** People comes under this age group are frequently user of social network and they are interested to show their vicinity, place of residence, education, course, affiliation to colleges or university, features, habits, interest and mention community or circle to whom they belongs.

- **Adults (21-40 Years):** People comes under this age group may or may not frequent user of social network due to they may be busy or engage their work, study or business. They are interested to mentioning the general parameters (i.e. education, course, affiliation of college or university, vicinity, interest, habit and features) as well as some more important related parameters to their domain, job, working organization and relationship status.

- **Seniors (41-65 Years):** People comes under this age category are not frequent user of the social network due to they are mostly or highly busy with their family members (Take care of their child carrier, busy schedule with their parents health issues etc.), job or service. They are not interested to show their interest, habit and information related to their education. They are interested only to show their information related to living location (place and vicinity), known languages (Hindi, English etc.), affiliation to organization (Job, University), relationship status, and connections with community or group and most important is show their time of affiliation to social network.

- **Old (66-80 Years):** The old age people are not or very less frequent user of the social network. They are not showing their hobbies, interests, education etc. They are mentioning little information related to residing place, vicinity, languages know, their time duration or status of service and joining time of social network.

Layered Framework for Intelligent Information Retrieval

The authors identified as a result of rigorous study of dynamic social network most of the time users of dynamic social network do not get the relevant, filtered and timely information during a search. The authors developed a framework based on these identified parameters for intelligent information retrieval in dynamic social network using the different techniques of data mining for quick and efficient information retrieval. The effective usage of the any new development is only possible provided that we had appropriate facilities in terms of the infrastructure and other software's. This prompted the authors to clearly state the various assumptions which are needed for the successful implementation of the proposed framework. They are:

1. The availability of a well implemented data warehouse in the setup.
2. The availability of the Data mining tools and techniques for the effective analysis of the data.
3. The common and most used features already available in the social network site of the service provider.
4. The authors had assumed a basic site and tried to develop the framework with minimum features to avoid the complexity.
5. The assumption of age wise key parameters for intelligent information retrieval from dynamic social network has been done by the authors.
6. The availability of the decomposed framework into distinct logical layers for enhanced development of the framework.

The layered framework for intelligent information retrieval based on the identified parameters using different techniques of data mining (see Figure 1) is divided into three layers. They are: Parameterized Internal layer, Analytics Layer and Search layer.

- **Parameterized Internal Layer:** This layer consist of the categorization of social network users based on their age groups (e.g. 0-20, 21-40, 41-60 and 61-80) and assignment of identified parameters to these age groups due to a person behaves and communicates in different ways to other in different age groups. These assigned parameters fed to the database layer for further processing.

- **Analytics Layer:** The incoming information related to parameters must be stored in databases. The different techniques of data mining (e.g. Classification, Clustering etc.) applied on the data stored on the databases to obtain the useful pattern. People with the same interest, education and vicinity are group into same cluster whereas people with the different domain, course, and community classified into different group. If a person is related to the second person and second one is related to third then third one is indirectly related to first person and this can be determined by association rule mining. These useful patterns obtained by using the clustering, classification and association rule mining must be put in the subject oriented parameterized data warehouse. This data warehouse provides the mostly relevant, filtered and timely information to the users of the dynamic social network.

- **Search Layer:** This layer helps to the users of dynamic social network to find out a particular person to whom they want in search either globally (Wide Search) or locally (search limited to community or circle). This search is known as an intelligent search due to the users of dynamic social

network gets the mostly relevant, filtered and speedily information or gets the person to whom they want in search.

Empirical Case Example

Let us consider a scenario of service Provider Company of social networking sites. Social networking sites contain several groups, communities to education, industry, relationships etc. Modern day requires the usage of Web for effective communication which has increased the users day by day. Users wants to access the more information in lesser time and that too fruitful and targeted as desired by the user by being valid information and as per demand of the users. The growing demand of intelligent information retrieval has become an increasing need in social network also. This Filtered information will be more relevant and timely for the social network users. The social network service provider company thought of adding such a feature in their existing network which will enable the users to target the information quickly. To add this, they asked IT people of the organization to enable intelligence in the network. The IT people then come up with parameters to provide the intelligence in retrieval from social network. These parameters will be stored in the databases. The different data mining techniques will be used to identify or reveal the hidden and unknown information which will add the intelligence for future usage by the users while surfing the site. These data mining techniques are clustering, classification or association rule mining. Clustering using the algorithms like two step clustering will help to find the minimum number of required cluster/groups on the basis of similarities between user's educations backgrounds, similarities between interests, similarities between domains or more. Classification using the CHAID algorithm will help to build the decision tree that will classify the different classes based on differences among languages, courses, features, communities and relationships. The Association rule mining tech-

Figure 2. Layered parameterized framework for intelligent information retrieval in dynamic social network

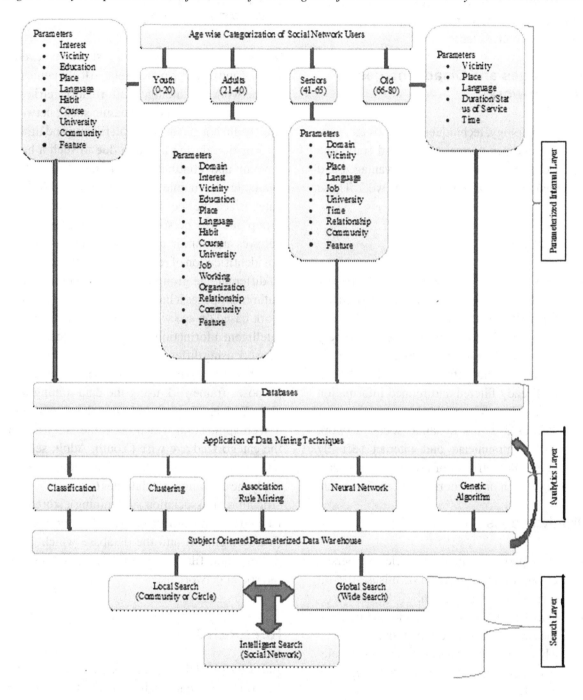

niques with GRI algorithm will help to find the key associations using the frequent users who visited the places or vicinity frequently. This will give the subject oriented parameterized information and that identified or revealed information will again be stored in the data warehouse. People or users will get the relevant, speedily and reduced amount of information during a global or local search in a much faster and targeted manner as compared to earlier method. These changes were suggested and incorporated by the IT people who enhanced the usage of the network and help in popularity of the service provider.

Advantages and Disadvantages of Framework

Every technology, techniques, methods etc. generates sometimes correct results and sometime incorrect results. There are few advantages and disadvantages of this proposed framework. These are:

Advantages

- The user of the dynamic social network mostly retrieves relevant and required information during the search.
- This framework will provide the timely and speedily information to the users of the dynamic social network due to the retrieval of already filtered and refined information during search.
- The user of the dynamic social network will communicate and interact securely due to the retrieval of relevant person during search or to whom they want in search.

Disadvantages

- An opponent can find a relevant person easily, timely and harm or misuse the information of that person.
- This framework may seem too complex to the social network service provider.
- This framework provides the mostly relevant and timely information to the user not exactly.
- This framework is based on assumptions which may be updated by someone with the addition of more key parameters.

CONCLUSION AND FUTURE RESEARCH

The authors conducted a deep study on several journal and research papers related to dynamic social network and intelligent information retrieval. They found that users of dynamic social network mostly did not get the relevant, filtered and timely information during a search due to such a huge amount and continuous changing information available on dynamic social network. The authors categorized the social network users into an age group due to a person with different age group behaves and communicates differently to others. An identification of relevant parameters assigned to different age group done by the authors. The authors proposes a layered parameterized framework based on age wise assigned parameters for intelligent information retrieval in dynamic social network using different techniques of data mining.

The future research includes the validation of proposes framework using the data mining tool and a Web application. In future, development of a Web application which takes the entry as per the categorized age wise (Youth, Adult, seniors and Old), saved these entries into the database, apply the data mining techniques (clustering, classification or association rule mining), stored the filtered information into the database and search (local or global) into the database which gives the relevant, filtered and timely information to the social network users.

REFERENCES

Ballocca, G., Politi, R., Ruffo, G., & Schifanella, R. (2003). Integrated techniques and tools for Web mining, user profiling and benchmarking analysis. In *Proceedings of CMG'03*. CMG.

Baranyi, P., Gedeon, T. D., & Koczy, L. T. (1998). Intelligent Information Retrieval Using Fuzzy Approach. In *Proceedings of IEEE International Conference on Systems, Man, and Cybernetics,* (Vol. 2, pp. 1984-1989). IEEE.

Belkin, N. J. (1996). Intelligent Information Retrieval: Who's Intelligent? In *Proceedings des 5. International Symposium for Informationswissenschaft (ISI 96),* (pp. 25-31). ISI.

Bing, L. (2007). *Web Data Mining: Exploring Hyperlinks, Contents and Usage Data.* Chicago, IL: Springer.

Cesarano, C., d'Aciemo, A., & Picariello, A. (2003). An Intelligent Search Agent System for Semantic Information Retrieval on the Internet. In *Proceedings of the 5ᵗʰ ACM international workshop on Web information and data management,* (pp. 111-117). ACM.

Chen, J., Liu, L., Song, H., & Yu, X. (2002). An Intelligent Information Retrieval System Model. In *Proceedings of the 4ᵗʰ World Congress on Intelligent Control and Automation,* (pp. 2500-2503). Academic Press.

Daniels, J. J., & Rissland, E. L. (1995). A Case-Based Approach to Intelligent Information Retrieval. In *Proceedings of the 18ᵗʰ annual International ACM SIGIR conference on Research and Development in information retrieval,* (pp. 238-245). ACM.

Danilowicz, C., & Nguyen, H. C. (2002). Using User Profiles in Intelligent Information Retrieval. *Lecture Notes in Computer Science, 2366,* 223–231. doi:10.1007/3-540-48050-1_26

Fan, Y., & Shelton, C. R. (2009). Learning continuous-Time social network dynamics. In *Proceedings of the 25ᵗʰ conference on uncertainty in artificial intelligence (UAI 2009),* (pp. 161-168). UAI.

He, M., & Feng, B.-Q. (2005). Intelligent Information Retrieval Based on the Variable Precision Rough Set Model and Fuzzy Sets. *Lecture Notes in Computer Science, 3642,* 184–192. doi:10.1007/11548706_20

Jacobs, P. S., & Rau, L. F. (1988). Natural Language Techniques for Intelligent Information Retrieval. In *Proceedings of the 11ᵗʰ annual International ACM SIGIR conference on Research and Development in information retrieval,* (pp. 85-99). ACM.

Jain, P. (2005). Intelligent Information Retrieval. In *Proceedings of 3ʳᵈ International Conference: Sciences of Electronic, Technologies of Information and Telecommunications (SETIT 2005).* SETIT.

Jiang, J., Wang, Z., Liu, C., Tan, Z., Chen, X., & Li, M. (2010). The Technology of Intelligent Information Retrieval Based on the Semantic Web. In *Proceedings of 2ⁿᵈ International Conference on Signal Processing Systems,* (pp. V2-824 – V2-827). Academic Press.

Jiawei, H., & Micheline, K. (2006). *Data Mining: Concepts and Techniques.* San Francisco, CA: Morgan Kaufmann Publishers.

Karthik, M., Marikkannan, M., & Kannan, A. (2008). An Intelligent System for Semantic Information Retrieval Information from Textual Web Documents. *Lecture Notes in Computer Science, 5158,* 135–146. doi:10.1007/978-3-540-85303-9_13

Kavousi, K., & Moshiri, B. (2007). Architecture design of an intelligent information fusion information retrieval from dynamic environment. In *Proceedings of 10ᵗʰ International Conference on Information Fusion,* (pp. 1-7). Academic Press.

Konishi, K., & Toyama, T. (2008). Community identification in dynamic social networks based on H2 norm analysis: A new approach from control theory'. In *Proceedings IEEE international* conference *on systems, Man and cybernetics (SMC 2008),* (pp. 2840-2845). IEEE.

Koval, R., & Navrat, P. (2002). Intelligent Support for Information Retrieval in the WWW Environment. *Lecture Notes in Computer Science, 2435,* 51–64. doi:10.1007/3-540-45710-0_5

Lee, H., & Yoo, S. B. (2005). Intelligent Information Retrieval for Web-Based Design Data Repository. *Lecture Notes in Computer Science, 3488,* 544–552. doi:10.1007/11425274_56

Li, F., & Huang, X. (2007). An Intelligent Platform for Information Retrieval. *Lecture Notes in Computer Science, 4429,* 45–57. doi:10.1007/978-3-540-70934-3_5

Li, F., Mehlitz, M., Feng, L., & Sheng, H. (2006). Web Pages Clustering and Concepts Mining: An approach towards Intelligent Information Retrieval. In *Proceedings of IEEE Conference on Cybernetics and Intelligent Systems,* (pp. 1-6). IEEE.

Li, W., Feng, Z., Li, Y., & Xu, Z. (2004). Ontology-Based Intelligent Information Retrieval System. In *Proceedings of Canadian Conference on Electrical and Computer Engineering,* (Vol. 1, pp. 373-376). Academic Press.

Li, W., Zhang, X., & Wei, X. (2008). Semantic Web-Oriented Intelligent Information Retrieval System. In *Proceedings of IEEE International Conference on Biomedical Engineering and Informatics,* (pp. 357-361). IEEE.

Lim, J.-H., Seung, H.-W., Hwang, J., Kim, Y.-C., & Kim, H.-N. (1997). Query Expansion for Intelligent Information Retrieval on Internet. In *Proceedings of International Conference on Parallel and Distributed Systems,* (pp. 656-662). Academic Press.

Liu, L., Wang, C., Wu, M., & He, G. (2008). Research of Intelligent Information Retrieval System Ontology-based in Digital Library. In *Proceedings of IEEE International Symposium on IT in Medicine and Education,* (pp. 375-379). IEEE.

Narayanan, S., Walchli, S. E., Reddy, N., Wood, A. L., & Reynolds, B. K. (1995). Developing intelligent information retrieval systems - issues in database organization, distributed processing, and interface design. In *Proceedings of IEEE International Conference on System, Man and Cybernetics: Intelligent Systems for the 21st Century,* (Vol. 4, pp. 3584-3589). IEEE.

Nguyen, N. P., Dinh, T. N., Xuan, Y., & Thai, M. T. (2011). Adaptive algorithms for detecting community structure in dynamic social networks. [IEEE.]. *Proceedings - IEEE INFOCOM, 2011,* 2282–2290.

Nihei, K., Tomizawa, N., Shibata, A., & Shimazu, H. (1998). ExpertGuide for help desks-an intelligent information retrieval system for WWW pages. In *Proceedings of Ninth International Workshop on Database and Expert Systems Applications,* (pp. 937-942). Academic Press.

Quintana, Y. (1997). Cognitive Approaches to Intelligent Information Retrieval. In *Proceedings of IEEE Canadian Conference on Engineering Innovation: Voyage of Discovery,* (Vol. 1, pp. 261-264). IEEE.

Revelle, M., Dit, B., & Poshyvanyk, D. (2010). Using Data Fusion and Web Mining to Support Feature Location in Software. In *Proceedings of IEEE 18th International Conference on Program Comprehension,* (pp. 14-23). IEEE.

Srinath, S., & Ram, D. J. (n.d.). *Data Mining and Knowledge Discovery.* Retrieved from http://nptel.iitm.ac.in/video.php?subjectId=106106093

Tai, C.-H., Tseng, P.-J., Yu, P. S., & Chen, M.-S. (2011). Identities anonymization in dynamic social networks. In *Proceedings 11th IEEE international conference on data mining*, (pp. 1224-1229). IEEE.

Tantipathananandh, C., Berger-Wolf, T., & Kempe, D. (2007). A framework for community identification in dynamic social networks. In *Proceedings of the 13th ACM SIGKDD international conference on knowledge discovery and data mining (KDD'07)*, (pp. 717-726). ACM.

Tu, H.-C., & Hsiang, J. (1998). An Architecture and Category Knowledge for Intelligent Information Retrieval Agents. In *Proceedings of the Thirty-First Hawaii International Conference on System Sciences,* (Vol. 4, pp. 405-414). IEEE.

Wang, Z. (2013). Performance Evaluation for Strategy Based on Auto-Adapting Users in Cross Language Information Retrieval. *International Journal of Multimedia and Ubiquitous Engineering*, 8(3), 83–92.

Wiese, J., Hong, J. I., & Zimmerman, J. (2012). Building a dynamic and computational understanding of personal social network. In *Proceedings of 1st ACM Workshop on Mobile Systems for Computational Social Science,* (pp. 5-10). ACM.

Wu, L., Feng, J., & Luo, Y. (2009). A Personalized Intelligent Web Retrieval System Based on the Knowledge-Base Concept and Latent Semantic Indexing Model. In *Proceedings of 7th ACIS International Conference on Software Engineering Research, Management and Applications,* (pp. 45-50). ACIS.

Wu, Z., Shi, C., & Lu, Y. (2013). Intelligent Information Retrieval System Based on Muti-Agent Model. In *Proceedings of the 2nd International Conference on Systems Engineering and Modeling*. Academic Press.

Xiao, Y., Xiao, M., & Zhang, F. (2007). Intelligent Information Retrieval Model Based on Multi-Agents. In *Proceedings of International Conference on Wireless Communications, Networking and Mobile Computing (WiCOM 2007),* (pp. 5464-5467). WiCOM.

Xie, S.-Y., Liu, J.-C., & Wang, H. (2003). Research of Intelligent Information Retrieval System Based on Three Layers Agent Structure. In *Proceedings of the 2nd International Conference on Machine Learning and Cybernetics*, (pp. 2329-2332). Academic Press.

Yang, T., Chi, Y., Zhu, S., Gong, Y., & Jin, R. (2011). Detecting communities and their evolutions in dynamic social networks-a Bayesian approach. *Journals on Machine Learning, 82*(2), 157–189. doi:10.1007/s10994-010-5214-7

Ying, P., Tianjiang, W., & Xueling, J. (2007). Building Intelligent Information Retrieval System Based on Ontology. In *Proceedings of the 8th International Conference on Electronic Measurement and Instruments (ICEMT'2007),* (pp. 4-612 – 4-615). ICEMT.

Yong-Min, L., & Shu, C. (2009). Artificial Intelligent Information Retrieval Using Assigning Context of Documents. In *Proceedings of IEEE International Conference on Network Security, Wireless Communications and Trusted Computing,* (pp. 592-595). IEEE.

ADDITIONAL READING

Belkin, N. J. (1996). Intelligent Information Retrieval: Who's Intelligent?' *In Proceedings des 5. International Symposium for Informationswissenschaft (ISI 96)*. 25-31. A paper on basic concepts of an intelligent information retrieval.

Daniels, J. J., & Rissland, E. L. (1995). A case-based approach to intelligent information retrieval, *Proceedings of the 18th annual international ACM SIGIR conference on Research and development in information retrieval*, 238-245. A paper to understand the concept of intelligent information retrieval based on case-based reasoning.

Jain, P. (2005). Intelligent Information Retrieval, *Third International Conference: Sciences of Electronic, Technologies of Information and Telecommunications*, 1-4. A theoretical paper to understand the basic knowledge of intelligent agent-based model for information retrieval.

Jensen, D., & Neville, J. (2002). Data mining in social network, *Papers of the Symposium on Dynamic Social Network Modeling and Analysis*, 1-14. A conceptual paper to understand the data mining techniques in social network.

Lim, J.-H., Seung, H.-W., Hwang, J., Kim, Y.-C., & Kim, H.-N. (1997). Query Expansion for Intelligent Information Retrieval on Internet, *International Conference on Parallel and Distributed System*, 656-662. A conceptual paper to understand the automatic query expansion method based on term distribution which naturally reflects semantics of retrieval terms in order to enhance the performance of information retrieval.

Schedl, M., Flexer, A., & Urbano, J. (2013). The Neglected User in Music Information Retrieval Research [A conceptual paper to understand the concept of music information retrieval.]. *Journal of Intelligent Information Systems*, 1–12.

Xu, C., & Shi, T. (2013). Research on the Model of Intelligent Pas-senger Information Service System based on Multi-Agent, *International Conference on Information, Business and Education Technology*, 195-198. A theoretical paper to understand the model of intelligent passenger information service system based on multi-agent.

KEY TERMS AND DEFINITIONS

Data Mining: Data mining is the process of extraction of useful knowledge and patterns from different sources of information like Web, text etc.

Dynamic Social Network: Dynamic social network is a network of people in which an individual can communicate or interact to other all the time and all the information about the interaction is considered.

Framework: Framework is a conceptual structure of something that expresses the judgments or decisions based on ideas and beliefs.

Intelligent Information Retrieval: An intelligent information retrieval system takes the user query, automatically performed the action and provides the filtered and user interest information that is highly probable relevant to the user.

Key Parameters: Key parameters are parameters that are highly relevant to decide and limit the intelligent information retrieval.

Keyword: Keyword is a word that expresses about the main idea or subject of something.

Social Network: Social network is network of people in which an individual can communicate or interact to other without any barrier of time or distance.

Static Social Network: Static social network is a network of people in which an individual can communicate or interact to other at an instant of time and all the information about the interaction is removed.

Chapter 14
Implementation of Mining Techniques to Enhance Discovery in Service–Oriented Computing

Chellammal Surianarayanan
Bharathidasan University, India

Gopinath Ganapathy
Bharathidasan University, India

ABSTRACT

Web services have become the de facto platform for developing enterprise applications using existing interoperable and reusable services that are accessible over networks. Development of any service-based application involves the process of discovering and combining one or more required services (i.e. service discovery) from the available services, which are quite large in number. With the availability of several services, manually discovering required services becomes impractical and time consuming. In applications having composition or dynamic needs, manual discovery even prohibits the usage of services itself. Therefore, effective techniques which extract relevant services from huge service repositories in relatively short intervals of time are crucial. Discovery of service usage patterns and associations/ relationships among atomic services would facilitate efficient service composition. Further, with availability of several services, it is more likely to find many matched services for a given query, and hence, efficient methods are required to present the results in useful form to enable the client to choose the best one. Data mining provides well known exploratory techniques to extract relevant and useful information from huge data repositories. In this chapter, an overview of various issues of service discovery and composition and how they can be resolved using data mining methods are presented. Various research works that employ data mining methods for discovery and composition are reviewed and classified. A case study is presented that serves as a proof of concept for how data mining techniques can enhance semantic service discovery.

DOI: 10.4018/978-1-4666-6086-1.ch014

INTRODUCTION

Service Oriented Architecture (SOA) is an architectural style for building business applications using existing interoperable and reusable services that are accessible over network such as the Internet. A Service is a self contained, autonomous, loosely coupled interoperable software component that implements particular business functionality. It has well defined interface to expose its functionality to its clients. Web services, a set of eXtensible Markup Language (XML) based protocols, namely, Web Service Description Language (WSDL), Simple Object Access Protocol (SOAP) and Universal Description, Discovery and Integration(UDDI)(Gottschalk, Graham, Kreger, & Snell, 2002) become de facto platform for implementing SOA. New business applications are built by assembling existing services with the help of Web services. Simple business requirements can be fulfilled by atomic services whereas complex business processes can be fulfilled by composite services which are formed by combining more than one service in a particular pattern. The process of combining more than one atomic service to achieve a composite functionality is called *service composition* (Claro, Albers, & Hao, 2006).

Services which undergo composition should be discovered based on functional characteristics prior to composition itself. Service discovery is a mandatory prerequisite for composition.

The functional characteristics of services are expressed through service name, operation name and input and output parameters of operations. Typically, service users express their needs in the form of key words or in terms of input and output parameters. To find a suitable service, the query is matched with each service description available in a service repository as in Figure 1.

Service discovery turns into difficult task due to the steady growth in number of services in the Web and other service repositories of enterprises (Rao, & Su, 2005). Despite the availability of several services, each service has a limited functionality and very frequently, a query is fulfilled by service composition. The atomic services involved in composition may originate from different as well as heterogeneous business organizations. Further services are described using different semantic service description languages such as WSDL, Semantically Annotated Web Service Description Language(SAWSDL), Web Ontology Language for Services (OWL-S), etc. In such situations, discovering required services

Figure 1. Process of service discovery

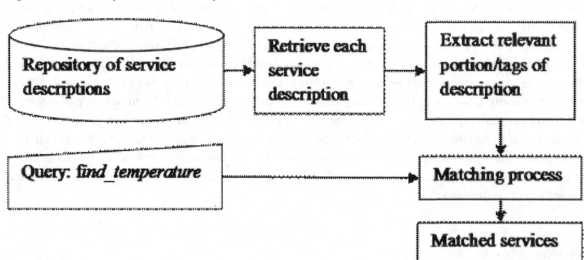

manually becomes impractical and time consuming. Business organizations look for efficient methods for choosing appropriate services from huge service repositories for composition within relatively short intervals of time. It is crucial to have a scalable infrastructure for service discovery (Nayak, 2008) which drives the need for applying some techniques to characterize, group, categorize and properly organize services. As data mining provides a collection of exploratory techniques it fits as a natural choice for resolving the issues related to discovery and composition.

In enterprises, data mining tasks are mainly employed to two kinds of data, (i) historical data which are characterized and summarized by various concept hierarchies in multiple dimensions and (ii) events or data logged at server (Web log). In the case of services, mining tasks are employed to repository of service descriptions and service execution log as in Figure 2. Applying mining methods to historical data helps in extraction of hidden knowledge such as *whether credit card can be issued to a customer or not* from huge data. In the case of services, manually discovering

Figure 2. Mining tasks employed to service descriptions and service execution log

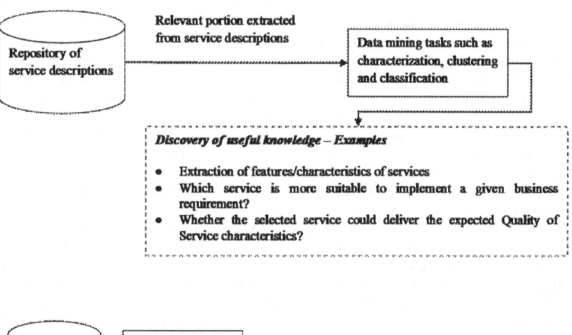

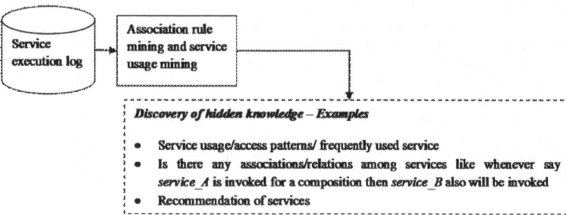

relevant and useful knowledge from huge service repositories is time consuming and becomes impractical. In practice, mining methods are used to extract useful and hidden knowledge such as *which service is more suitable to implement a given business need* from huge service repositories in short intervals of times.

From literature, it is understood that though there exists significant number of research works focusing on specific issues of discovery using data mining methods, only a few research works such as (Nayak, 2007), (Nayak, 2008) highlights an outline of how data mining methods can be applied to services.

In (Nayak, 2007) how mining techniques facilitate and improve the use of services is discussed using existing works. Also, the work highlights the growing need for further research in data mining based solutions for services. In (Nayak, 2008) applications of data mining to services have been discussed from two different perspectives, namely, *business* and *technical*. The proposed chapter describes various issues related to discovery and composition in a holistic view. It describes how various mining methods fit as natural choice to resolve various issues related to discovery and enhance service discovery and composition. Further, a case study is presented as proof of concept to exhibit how data mining methods help in enhancing discovery. In this study, a case which requires semantics based discovery is considered. The case suffers from the issue that semantics based service discovery is time consuming. The study demonstrates how clustering technique can be used to improve the performance of semantics based service discovery.

The rest of the chapter is organized as follows. In Section 2, various issues of service discovery and composition and how data mining techniques can be used to resolve those issues are described using motivating scenarios. In Section 3, some of the research works that employ data mining

techniques for discovery and composition are reviewed and classified. A case study is presented in Section 4 which deals with a specific case having semantics based discovery and explains how clustering helps in enhancing the performance of semantics based service discovery. Section 5 concludes the chapter.

ISSUES IN SERVICE DISCOVERY AND RESOLUTIONS

Service discovery is a mandatory process in any service based application. It is the process of finding matched services for a given query (from a client) from available services which are large in number. Typically the matching is found out by finding the similarity between input/output parameters of the query and that of each available service. Service client may be a human user or another program or another service. In the case of human client, browsing a repository of huge number of services for a specific functionality is tedious. It is essential to provide the information on summarization or characterization of services to facilitate the clients. This is illustrated with following scenario.

Let us consider a client who looks for an *Appointment Booking Service* which books appointment with a physician based on the other scheduled appointments and time availability of physician. Imagine that all appointment booking services will book appointment with concerned physician only when the request is made at least one week prior to the date of meeting or consultation. In case, a client tries to book an appointment later than the specified booking time, his search will become useless as there is no service which can book appointment for him. In this scenario, summarized description such as "*All Appointment booking services provide service only if the request is made at least one week in advance to the date of appointment*" can assist clients in advance planning for seeking appointments. This kind of summarization can be constructed by extracting useful features from service descriptions where data mining methods come in hand.

The process of finding matched services of a given query does not only involve matching the query with relevant services but also with irrelevant services. For example, for a query, *'flight booking service'* the discovery involves matching the query with each and every available service even though there exists many obviously irrelevant services such as *'temperature service'*, *'loan service'*, *'weather service'*, etc. This kind of irrelevancy poses a big problem while discovering services for dynamic composition.

Dynamic composition based applications demand a critical and conflicting requirement that discovery should be based on semantics as semantics enhances search accuracy(Hou, Zhang, Nayak, & Bose, 2011) and also it should be completed within short intervals of time as specified by clients. Though semantics based discovery fulfills the accuracy and compatibility requirements of service composition, it is time consuming (Mokhtar, Kaul, Georgantas, & Issarny, 2006). Semantic discovery involves the process of finding semantic relations such as *equivalent, subsumes, plugin* and *fail* (Sycara, Paolucci, Ankolekar, & Srinivasan, 2003) between concepts of services with the help of ontology reasoners such as Pellet. From (Mokhtar, Kaul, Georgantas, & Issarny, 2006) loading and classifying ontologies are found to be major time consuming tasks which lead to very high response time of 4 to 5 seconds

for performing a single semantic match between two services having typically ten concepts. When irrelevancy exists during discovery, semantics based matching has to be employed to irrelevant services also. If irrelevancy is removed by some methods, then number of services that undergo semantics based matching will be reduced. Elimination of irrelevancy will certainly improve the performance of discovery. Hence some methods are sought to eliminate the irrelevancy during service discovery.

Clustering services into known categories helps in reducing the time consumption of semantics based service discovery by eliminating the irrelevancy. It is illustrated as follows. Let all available services be clustered into known categories based on functional characteristics as given in Figure 3.

When a query is submitted for finding matched services, the query is matched with only a particular category which is most similar to the query ignoring all other categories as irrelevant. For example, to find matched services for the query, *Hotel booking service* it is sufficient to match the query with services present in *Hotel* category alone. Thus performance of discovery has been improved by reducing the number of services that undergo semantic matching from the entire pool of services to a specific category.

Service composition involves the process of discovering required services and then combining them in a particular pattern to achieve the given requirement. Further, the required services for composition may arise from different organizations as given in the following example. Consider

Figure 3. Services are clustered into known categories

a client who wants to plan a package tour to Singapore using a *Travel Plan Service*. The service query cannot be fulfilled by a single service. To implement *Travel Plan service*, services from different domains such as *Flight booking, Hotel booking* and *Cab booking* should be combined in a specific pattern say as in a typical workflow given in Figure 4.

Discovering appropriate services for composition poses an issue as the search has to be made from a large number of service combinations. The process of composition can well be improved if some methods provide information about associations or relations among services. Association rule mining facilitates efficient composition by identifying associations among services. An association rule takes the form $X \rightarrow Y$ where X and Y denote set of services accessed in a transaction. Each rule is associated with a support, s and confidence, c, both are expressed in %. Support, s of the rule $X \rightarrow Y$ indicates that $s\%$ of the entire transactions, say T contain $X \cup Y$ and confidence, c of the rule $X \rightarrow Y$ indicates that $c\%$ of T which contain X will also contain Y. Association rules are generated from frequent service sets mined from service execution log. With the help of such association rules, a composing agent can find out composable services quite easily. Let us consider an association rule, say,

$$flight\_klm \text{----} > hotel\_klm, s = 80\%, c = 75\%$$

for *Travel Plan Service*. This rule specifies that if the service *flight_klm* is invoked in a transaction then there is 75% probability for *hotel_klm* also would be invoked in the same transaction. Also, consider that the user specified threshold viz. *minimum support* be 75% and *minimum confidence* be 70%. Now the above rule becomes an interesting rule. Hence, whenever the agent discovers *flight_klm* service for a composition, it will consider *hotel_klm* also for composition without performing an exploratory search for hotel functionality.

Despite the availability of several services for use, perfect match for a query seldom exists while it is more likely to have a large number of partially matched services. For example, consider a client who is looking for *finding price of a car in US dollars*. As matching process should not fail to find any potential match, the retrieved results will be many in number which include services having low similarity(with the query) to services having high similarity. For example, the results for the above query may include services which find price of a car in *Euro* or *in some currency other than US dollar* to services which find price of a car in *US dollar*. So, browsing the results to retrieve the desired service is difficult and organizing the results in appropriate fashion is essential. In this scenario, organizing results into different clusters based on similarity as in (Skoutas, Sacharidis, Simitsis, & Sellis, 2010) would facilitate a client in choosing the desired result.

Consider another example. A novice client who looks for *wind_speed_service* which returns the speed of wind at a given location is considered. Imagine that the client is an *atmospheric dispersion modeling application* which looks for the above

Figure 4. Services involved in composite Travel Plan Service

service with an intention of modeling dispersion characteristics during cyclonic or high wind speed conditions. Hence, the client specifically looks for *wind_speed_service* with minimum response time, (QoS attribute) of 10 milli seconds. Consider that many services are available to provide the required functionality. Now, selecting an appropriate service with specific QoS from the set of several functionally similar services is time consuming. The QoS characteristics of each service should be checked for whether the service meets the expected QoS. In this situation, either the retrieved services can be clustered based on QoS to present the results in useful form or suitable service can be recommended by clustering similar users as in(Nayak, 2007).

In nut shell, a few important issues in service discovery along with their resolutions from data mining techniques are given in Table 1.

Various ways in which data mining fits as a natural choice to provide efficient solutions for service discovery and composition are given in Figure 5.

LITERATURE REVIEW

Some survey has been made in the research works which employ data mining for service discovery and composition and the reviewed literature are categorized into association rule mining in services, clustering in services, classification in services and usage mining in services.

Association Rule Mining in Services

The process of finding composable services for composition is difficult due to availability of several services. Discovery of associations among services by applying association rule mining to service execution log helps in identifying composable services easily. Different levels of mining tasks can be performed on service execution log data depending on richness of the data logged. In (Dustdar & Gombotz, 2006), how different levels of mining, namely, operation level, interaction level and workflow level can be performed with various levels of service log, namely, Standard

Table 1. Issues in service discovery and their resolutions

Issue ID	Description of Issue	Resolution
Issue-1	Browsing a repository of services to find a specific functionality is tedious	Characterization of services can be used to provide features and summarized information about services in a repository.
Issue-2	Finding matched services for a query involves matching query not only with relevant services but also with irrelevant services.	Techniques such as clustering and classification can be used to eliminate irrelevancy.
Issue-3	Service composition necessitates semantics based automatic discovery methods with high performance. But semantics based discovery is time consuming.	Clustering or categorization of services can be used to improve the performance of semantics based discovery. It helps in identifying a reduced set of candidate services for semantics based matching.
Issue-4	Finding composable services involves searching among a large number of combinations.	Association rule mining can be used to find associations and correlations among atomic services and thereby identifies composable service quickly without performing exploratory search for each service.
Issue-6	Finding the best service such as service having specific Quality of Service (QoS) is difficult	By using service usage mining, appropriate service can be recommended. Retrieved results can be clustered either by services or by users and accordingly only interested services will be presented to user.
Issue-7	The matched services for a query would be a large list of partial as well as potential matches for a query. Browsing the matched results to fetch a suitable result is tedious.	Retrieved services of discovery can be clustered based on similarity score.

Figure 5. Applications of data mining tasks towards efficient service discovery and composition

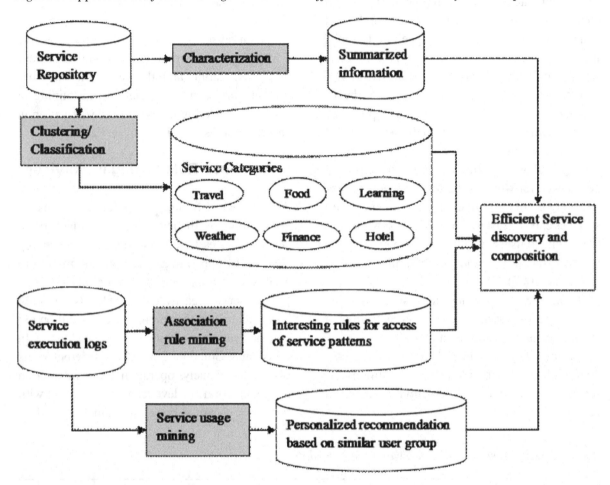

HTTP Server logging, HTTP Request-Response logging, SOAP message level logging, Client level Logging and Process level logging is presented.

In (Bayati, Nejad, Kharazmi, & Bahreininejad, 2009), association rule mining is used to find most useful services and their compositions based on user behaviors as well as processes. Data is logged at five levels similar to (Dustdar & Gombotz, 2006) and association rules for finding related services and services having best performance are constructed using Apriori algorithm. Knowledge repository is constructed using these rules which helps in predicting the best composition based on user behaviors and processes.

In (Liang, Chung, Miller, & Ouyang, 2006), association rules are constructed to find related

services for efficient template level service access. Two types of associations, namely, *interaction association* and *orthogonal association* are handled in this work. Two Services, say, S_A and S_B are said to have interaction association if they interact with each other with some dependency i.e. S_A depends on S_B or vice versa. The services are said to have orthogonal association if they are independent and they are executed either sequentially or in parallel. In this work, a set of operations (operation set) that are invoked to produce a given requirement is considered as a transaction. Transactions are found out from process descriptions and process instance execution logs. Frequent operation sets are identified. In order to guide efficient composition, association rules such as if an operation say,

S_A is invoked in a transaction, then the operation say, S_B is also likely to be invoked in the transaction having required support and confidence are generated from frequent operation sets.

In (Ritcharoenwattu & Rungworawut, 2013) a framework is presented to discover interesting service composition patterns by applying association rule mining on service execution logs. In another work (Rong, Liu, & Liang, 2008), a framework is proposed to select the most suitable matched service from several semantically equivalent matches based on the matching between provider's context and user's context. In this work, the provider's context represents a collection of services to which an advertised service is related and the user's context represents a collection of services related to the query. For each advertised service, its related services (*service dependency*) are found out using association rule mining prior to querying in offline itself. When a query is submitted, user's context is found out by finding the related services of the query. Then semantically matched services of the query are discovered. For each candidate(i.e. semantically matched service), its context is found out from its service dependency. The candidate which has highest degree of match between its context and user's context is found out as the most suitable matched service.

In (Rong, Liu, & Liang, 2009), for a particular user, his similar users are discovered using Collaborative Filtering (CF) method. The composition patterns accessed by these users are identified. These service access patterns form as the database for applying association rule mining and rules are generated for finding related services. Based on the rules, suitable services are recommended to that user. In another work (Luo, Yan, & Chen, 2008) a method is proposed to automatically discover various semantic relations, namely, *empty, equivalent, similar and cross* that can exist among Web resources such as services using existing association rules. The discovery of such semantic relations helps in efficient composition.

Clustering in Services

Clustering is used to handle various issues of discovery such as removal of irrelevancy, grouping of services into known categories, organization of retrieved services based on QoS, organization of service registries, etc.

Computing similarity among services based on desired characteristics such as functional characteristics, non-functional characteristics, etc is the pre-requisite for clustering. The accuracy of clustering is mainly determined by the way in which similarity among services is computed. Based on the accuracy requirements of applications, different types of similarity models such as syntactic similarity (WSDL based similarity), similarity based on WordNet database, similarity based on ontologies specific to concerned services, etc., are used while computing similarity. An approach presented in (Dong, Halevy, Madhavan, Nemes, & Zhang, 2004) groups services according to the heuristics that parameters which occur together frequently tend to express the same concept. In this work, the similarity among concepts is used to compute operation level similarity which in turn is used to compute similarity between services. The method presented in (Zhu, Yuan, Song, Bi, & Liu, 2010) considers different parts of WSDL and computes various similarities such as *element similarity, segment similarity, WSDL similarity and Web services similarity* along with name and documentation of services. The approach uses SCAN (Structural Clustering Algorithm for Networks) algorithm to cluster services.

The method presented in (Liang, Li, Hung, & Wu, 2009) considers both keywords and semantic information which is implicit in various structural tags of service descriptions while clustering services. This work considers that each service consists of one or more interfaces, each interface consists of one or more operations and each operation contains a set of input and output parameters. The work performs clustering in two steps. In first step, 'rough clustering' of services is performed based on the similarity among names and textual description of services using incremental K-Means clustering algorithm. In second step, semantics of structural features, namely, interface, operation, input and output of WSDL documents are used for clustering services using Bisecting K-Means algorithm.

The methods (Dong et al., 2004), (Zhu et al., 2010), (Liang et al., 2009) are syntactic based whereas (Qu, Sun, Li, Liu, & Lin, 2009), (Ren, Chen, Xiao, Song, & Li, 2008) use WordNet based similarity while clustering WSDL based services. The method proposed in (Zhang, Yu, Liu, & Wang, 2009) extends the WSDL representation of services to semantic representation while computing dissimilarity among services using Jaccard method. The method clusters services using single linkage algorithm. Similar to (Zhang et al. 2009) an extended OWL-S/UDDI matchmaker architecture presented in (Liu, Zhang, & Yu, 2009) which uses semantics-based clustering approach and *Automatic Knowledge Acquisition* (AKA) to enhance service discovery. In another work (Zhou, & Li, 2009) genetic algorithm is used to reduce the overhead and perform discovery of semantically matched services quickly. Another work (Chifu et al., 2010) clusters services using Ant's inspired clustering algorithm with ontology based semantic similarity. Similar to (Chifu et al., 2010), in (Xie, Chen, & Kou, 2011), functional similarity among services is computed based on the ontological concepts related to functional and process descriptions. The method uses K-means algorithm to cluster services. It is understood that in research works (Zhou, & Li, 2009), (Chifu et al., 2010), (Xie et al., 2011), (Wang, Si, & Hu, 2009) which use ontology based similarity computation, clustering helps in improving the performance of semantic matching.

Further, clustering is used to organize the results obtained from a service search engine. Each service has a set of input and output parameters and hence while searching matched services for a query, matching among several parameters of the query and that of available services has to be performed. This results in many matched services which vary in degree of match. In (Skoutas et al., 2010) clustering is used to present the retrieved services of a query in a useful form. The relevant services of a query obtained during matchmaking are clustered according to different trade-offs between the matched parameters of services. A method to prioritize and cluster the retrieved services using K-Means by determining dominance relationships using *multiple Parameter Degree of Match* among services is presented (Prasad, Meena, Kumar, & Kartheek, 2012). The research work presented in (Shou, & Chi, 2008) uses Star-Clustering algorithm to organize the services returned by a *Service Search Engine* as a clustered view which is more useful than the traditional ranked list.

In (Zhu, Kang, Zheng, & Lyu, 2012) a clustering-based Quality of Service (QoS) prediction framework is presented. In this framework, a set of computers which monitor and maintain real-time QoS information is taken as reference for QoS data and the QoS information is clustered using hierarchical clustering algorithm based on both users (*User Based Clustering*)and services (*Web Service Based Clustering*). Here, clustering based methods help in enhancing the QoS prediction accuracy.

Nowadays, the architecture of service registry is shifting from centralized model to distributed or de-centralized model. Clustering is found to be useful in grouping similar service registries leading to an efficient searching method. In (Sellami, Gaaloul, & Tata, 2010), an overlapping or fuzzy C-Means clustering is used to organize the service registries which are distributed at different sites. In this work, each registry is functionally represented using concepts and terms of service descriptions contained in it. Then each registry is considered as a document. The document is represented as vector using Vector Space Model (VSM). Cosine similarity measure is used to find the similarity among different registries/documents and the registries are clustered using Fuzzy clustering algorithm. With registries clustered, to find matched services for a given query, it is not necessary to search in all the registries. The query will be routed to most similar cluster and the registries present that cluster alone will be searched to find the matched services of the query.

Classification in Services

Services are classified into known categories using clustering and classification algorithms towards efficient discovery. In the approach presented in (Gao, Stucky, & Liu, 2009), WSDL description elements are converted into standard vector form with the concept of position weight from computing similarity between services. The approach uses a self-organizing neural network based learning algorithm and clustering algorithm to classify the services into known categories automatically. The method presented in (Ma, Zhang, & He, 2008) combines VSM with K-Means to classify services into known categories.

In (Yuan-jie, & Jian, 2012), a method is proposed to annotate semantics to WSDL descriptions from natural language processing and classify services using three different classification algorithms, namely, Naïve Bayes, Decision Tree and Support Vector Machine. Further, to improve the classification accuracy, the method uses multi-classifier ensemble learning method (combines the features of more than one classification algorithm) with *AdoBoost* technique. From this work, ensemble learning method is found to produce better accuracy than the individual methods with a test collection of 951 WSDL files which are classified into 19 categories.

In (Mohanty, Ravi, & Patra, 2012), a method is proposed which classifies the services based on the quality attributes such as response time, availability, throughput, successability, reliability, etc., using three different algorithms, namely, Naïve Bayesian, Markov Blanket and Tabu search. The quality attributes are used as classifying criteria. According to this work, with a test collection of 364 services Naïve Bayesian is found to outperform the other two approaches. In (Makhlughian, Hashemi, Rastegari, & Pejman, 2012) Classification Based on Association(CBA) algorithm which is based on Associative Classification is used to classify services into different QoS levels according to user's QoS requirements and preferences. Further, the method ranks the services in each class according to semantic functional matching.

Usage Mining in Services

Service usage mining refers to the discovery of service access patterns by applying mining tasks to service execution log. By mining the log data, access patterns of service usage can be analyzed with respect to services as well as users. The data can be analyzed to find information such as how frequently a service is used, how many users have accessed a particular service, how similar the users are, what are the preferences of users, etc. Suitable services can be recommended by considering user's preferences or feedback. For example, a service if frequently selected becomes *hot spot service* (Li, & Yang, 2012) and many users prefer this service. In (Li, & Yang, 2012), '*entity clustering index*' is proposed which groups services into clusters by similarity and organizes clusters in a hierarchical structure along with *hit number* which indicates how many times a service is selected. In this work, this attribute is treated as user's preference, based on which best matched service is located. In another work (Zheng, Xiong, Cui, Chen, & Han, 2012), a method is proposed to cluster users having similar interests using K-Means algorithm. The method is based on the assumption that users with similar interest will be interested in similar services. This method establishes a recommendation library to recommend appropriate services to users.

A CASE STUDY

Consider a case such as *Travel Plan* which involves composition of services from different domains. Let the case use semantics based discovery to automatically discover required services for composition. When the number of available services is large, the number of possible combinations for composition will be many. Discovery process consumes a large amount of time. Under such large search space, the performance of semantic service discovery becomes critical in deciding the performance of the entire composition. A case involving semantics based discovery (for composition) in large search space is considered for study. The case suffers from the issue that semantics based discovery consumes a large amount of time. The performance of semantic discovery process has to be optimized. The purpose of this case study is to prove how data mining techniques can address the issue effectively. More specifically, the case study uses clustering technique to address the issue.

In this study, clustering technique is used to partition the available services into groups of services having similar functional characteristics. For example, the published services are partitioned into different clusters and the clusters are labeled as *banking, financial, weather, education, travel, communication*, etc. Once the services are clustered and labeled, on the arrival of a query, it will be sufficient to employ semantic matching between the query and those services present in a cluster which is more similar to the query. For example, in the case of an incoming query, *'findEmailVerification'*, it will be sufficient to employ semantic matching to services present in the cluster *communication* alone (whereas in the case of discovery without clustering, semantic matching will be employed to all the services). All other clusters can be eliminated from semantic matching. Thus, clustering assists in optimizing the performance of discovery by providing a specific cluster containing a set of services which are more relevant to the query called *candidate services,* for semantic matching.

In this study, the clustering approach is implemented using three steps, namely, dissimilarity computation, clustering of services and identification of candidate services. The steps are carried out in sequence.

Dissimilarity Computation

In dissimilarity computation, pair-wise dissimilarity among all possible service pairs is computed and dissimilarity matrix is constructed to be given as input for clustering. Let us consider that services are described using Semantically Annotated Web Service Description Language (SAWSDL). Consider the syntactic portion of the tag *portType* of service description as relevant portion of service description for finding similarity among services.

A service is modeled as

$$S = (PN, ON, M_o, M_i)$$

where PN denotes the name of portType, ON denotes the name of *operation*, M_o denotes the *output message* of the operation and M_I denotes the *input message* of the service. The portion of SAWSDL that describes *portType* tag is given in Figure 6.

Steps involved in computing dissimilarity between two services are described in Listing given in Figure 7.

Let $s_1, s_2, s_3, ..., s_n$ denote the available services. Dissimilarity between all possible pairs of services is computed. For n available services, the dissimilarity matrix of dimension $n \times n$ is constructed as in Figure 8.

Figure 6. Portion of service description that describes portType tag

```
<wsdl:portType name="PersonbookPriceSoap">
        <wsdl:operation name="get_PRICE">
            <wsdl:input message="get_PRICERequest">
                </wsdl:input>
            <wsdl:output message="get_PRICEResponse">
                </wsdl:output>
        </wsdl:operation>
</wsdl:portType>
```

Figure 7. Steps involved in computing dissimilarity between services

Step 1: Extract contents of portType, operation, input message and output message tags from service descriptions of the pair of services for which similarity is to be found out. For each service, the extracted contents would form its *representative string*.

Step 2: Remove stop words, common words, insignificant service terms and duplicate terms from representative strings

Step 3: Find the normalized cosine similarity between the representative strings of pair of services. Let s_1 and s_2 be the pair of services for which similarity is to be computed. Let $Sim(s_1,s_2)$ denote the normalized cosine similarity between s_1 and s_2. Now, the value of $Sim(s_1,s_2)$ is computed using $Sim(s_1,s_2) = \dfrac{s_1.s_2}{\sqrt{s_1}.\sqrt{s_2}}$ where $s_1.s_2$ denote the number of common terms between s_1 and s_2 and $\sqrt{s_1}.\sqrt{s_2}$ denote the product of length of s_1 and s_2.

Step 4: Find dissimilarity or distance between the concerned services using $Dissim(s_1,s_2) = 1 - Sim(s_1,s_2)$

Example

Let a denote the representative string of s_1. Let b denote the representative string of s_2.

Let $a = \{$academic degree funding duration$\}$ Let $b = \{$academic degree lending$\}$

$ab = 2$

$\sqrt{a} \times \sqrt{b} = \sqrt{4} \times \sqrt{3}$

$Sim(s_1,s_2) = \dfrac{2}{\sqrt{4} \times \sqrt{3}} = 0.577$ and $Dissim(s_1,s_2) = 0.423$

Figure 8. Dissimilarity matrix for n services

$$\begin{pmatrix} & s_1 & s_2 & s_3 & \cdots & s_n \\ s_1 & 0 & 0.2 & 0.6 & \cdots & 0.8 \\ s_2 & 0.2 & 0 & 0.3 & \cdots & 0.6 \\ s_3 & 0.6 & 0.3 & 0 & \cdots & 0.7 \\ \cdots & \cdots & \cdots & \cdots & 0 & \cdots \\ s_n & 0.8 & 0.6 & 0.7 & \cdots & 0 \end{pmatrix}$$

Clustering of Services

In this step, the dissimilarity matrix (which is obtained in the previous step) is given as input to hierarchical agglomerative clustering algorithm. Hierarchical clustering algorithm which builds a hierarchy of clusters iteratively by merging most similar pair of clusters is used for clustering services. Hierarchical clustering does not require any input of expected number of clusters produced. Given $n \times n$ dissimilarity matrix, the hierarchical clustering algorithm clusters services using the steps given in Figure 9.

In Step 3 of clustering algorithm, the dissimilarity between clusters can be computed in different ways, namely, single-linkage, complete-linkage and average-linkage. Further, a similarity threshold is specified as stopping criterion depending upon the application requirements. When a similarity threshold is specified as stopping criterion, the clusters will get merged as long as the inter-cluster similarity between the most similar pair of clusters satisfies the specified threshold. After services are clustered, each cluster is assigned with a label. For a given cluster, the label is constructed as a string consisting of most frequently occurring key words contained in that cluster.

Identification of Candidate Services

When a query (a query is expressed as a set of key words or input/output parameters) is submitted, it is matched with label of each cluster by computing the cosine similarity between them. The cluster whose label is most similar to the query is chosen as '*relevant cluster*' of the query. The services present in the relevant cluster are identified as candidate services for the query. Now, the candidate services alone will be chosen for employing semantic matching of service capabilities.

Figure 9. Steps of hierarchical agglomerative clustering algorithm

1. Start by assigning each service to a cluster. Each cluster contains just one service. Let the dissimilarities between the clusters is same as the dissimilarities between the services.
2. Find the closest pair of clusters and merge them into a single cluster
3. Compute the dissimilarities between new cluster and each of the old clusters
4. Repeat steps 2 and 3 until the algorithm meets the stopping criterion.

The three steps of implementation are shown in Figure 10.

A test collection of 30 services (please refer to the Appendix) from 6 different domains, namely, academic, film, book, vehicle, food and camera with known internal groups among them as given in Table 2 is constructed using services from the SAWSDL test collection (http://semwebcentral. org).

Values of dissimilarity among all possible pairs of services are computed (using *Simmetrics.*

jar) and dissimilarity matrix is constructed. This matrix is given as input to hierarchical clustering algorithm with single linkage method as merging criterion. Agglomerative clustering tool from http://www.cs.umb.edu/~smimarog/agnes/agnes. html is used for clustering services.

Threshold similarity for inter-cluster merging is fixed as 0.5. This means that as long as the inter-cluster similarity of most similar pair of services is at least 0.5, the merging of clustering will be performed. Merging of clusters will be stopped

Figure 10. Implementation

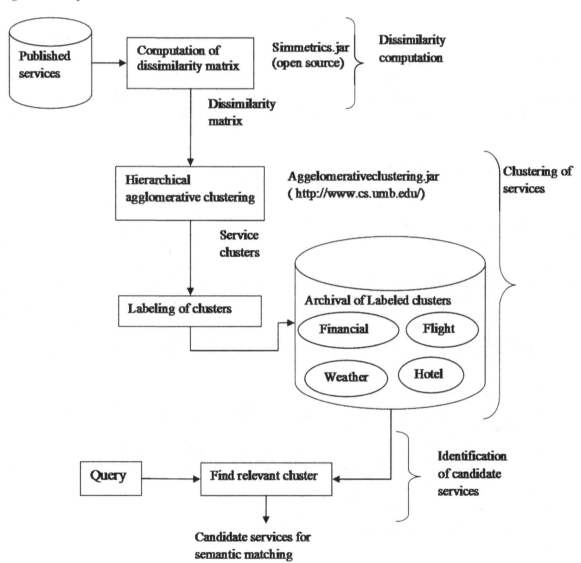

Table 2. Test data

Service Group	Number of Services
Vehicle	8
Film	3
Book	3
Hospital	5
Academic	5
Food	5
Camera	1

if the inter-cluster similarity of the most similar pair of clusters is found to be less than 0.5. The clusters produced are given in Table 3 along with labels of clusters.

Further the following example illustrates the improvement in performance obtained using clustering. Let us consider a query that belongs to 'hospital' cluster arrives. In this case, matching

will be employed only to 5 services instead of 30 services. The % of number of services that require semantic matching, denoted by '*m*' is calculated for each cluster using the formula,

$$m = \frac{number\_of\_service\_in\_relevant\_cluster}{total\_services} \times 100 \cdot$$

The value of *m* along with % of performance improvement (The value of (100-*m*) expressed as %) is given in Table 4.

Validation

The results of clustering are evaluated for correctness using an external measure, purity. To compute purity, each cluster is assigned with a class which is most frequent in that cluster. The most frequent class of a cluster is found manu-

Table 3. Service clusters produced

Cluster ID	Label of cluster	# of services	Services clustered
C_1	{person, bicycle, wheel, car, price}	8	$s_1, s_2, s_4, s_5, s_9, s_{13}, s_{15}, s_{21}$
C_2	{ book,author}	3	s_{10}, s_{19}, s_{27}
C_3	{ film, video, media }	3	s_{11}, s_{20}, s_{23}
C_4	{hospital, diagnostic, time, duration,cost}	5	$s_8, s_{12}, s_{14}, s_{18}, s_{26}$
C_5	{academic, degree,funding,lending,duration}	5	$s_7, s_{16}, s_{24}, s_{28}, s_{30}$
C_6	{food, price}	6	$s_3, s_6, s_{17}, s_{22}, s_{25}, s_{29}$

Table 4. Performance improvement for queries from different clusters

Cluster ID	*m* (%)	Performance Improvement (%)
C_1	26.6	73.4
C_2	10	90
C_3	10	90
C_4	16.7	83.3
C_5	16.7	83.3
C_6	20	80

ally. Let N number of services is partitioned into K number of clusters. Let n_{imfc} be the number of services of the most frequent class of ith cluster. The value of purity of a clustering, denoted by P is computed using $P = \frac{1}{N} \sum_{i=1}^{K} n_{imfc}$. The value of n_{imfc} for each cluster is found out as in Table 5.

The value of purity of clustering solution is computed as 96.67%. The results are analyzed to find the cause for decrease in Purity. In the cluster C_6, a camera service is found to be grouped with food cluster. Here the most frequent class is food. The reason for this grouping is due the similarity obtained with the common term 'price'. Depending upon application requirements, by fixing an appropriate similarity threshold as decided by domain expert, purity of clustering may still be improved. Further, from experimentation with a test collection of 30 services clustering technique helps to enhance the performance of semantics based matching by 83.3% (please refer Table 5). This enhancement is achieved by eliminating the obviously irrelevant services from employing semantic matching.

Thus the case study demonstrates how the Issue-3(Refer Table 1) can be resolved using clustering and how clustering enhances the performance of discovery. Similarly, all other issues can be resolved using other data mining techniques as highlighted in Section 2.

CONCLUSION

Service discovery and service composition are complex due to the availability of several services in the Web, the steady growth in number of services and constant update in service descriptions. As data mining provides a set of exploratory techniques, it fits as a natural choice in resolving the issues related to discovery and composition. In this chapter how core aspects of service discovery and compositions such as characterization of services, categorization of services, associations among services and service usage access patterns can be realized using data mining methods are discussed. Recent research works which use data mining methods in the context of service discovery and composition are reviewed and classified. A case study is presented to illustrate how clustering of services can be used as an optimization approach to enhance the performance of semantic service discovery. From implementation, with a typical test collection of 30 services, the average performance improvement obtained using clustering is found to be 83.3%.

Table 5. Number of services of most frequent class of different clusters

Cluster ID	n_{imfc}
C_1	8
C_2	3
C_3	3
C_4	5
C_5	5
C_6	5

REFERENCES

Bayati, S., Nejad, A. F., Kharazmi, S., & Bahreininejad, A. (2009). Using association rule mining to improve semantic Web services composition performance. In Proceedings of Computer, Control and Communication, (pp. 1-5). IEEE.

Chifu, V. R., Pop, C. B., Salomie, I., Dinsoreanu, M., Acretoaie, V., & David, T. (2010). An ant-inspired approach for semantic web service clustering. In *Proceedings of Roedunet International Conference (RoEduNet), 2010 9th* (pp. 145-150). IEEE.

Claro, D. B., Albers, P., & Hao, J. K. (2006). Web services composition. In Semantic Web Services, Processes and Applications (pp. 195-225). Springer US.

Dong, X., Halevy, A., Madhavan, J., Nemes, E., & Zhang, J. (2004). Similarity search for Web services. In *Proceedings of the Thirtieth international conference on Very large data bases* (vol. 30, pp. 372-383). VLDB Endowment.

Dustdar, S., & Gombotz, R. (2006). Discovering Web service workflows using Web services interaction mining. *International Journal of Business Process Integration and Management*, *1*(4), 256–266. doi:10.1504/IJBPIM.2006.012624

Gao, H., Stucky, W., & Liu, L. (2009). Web Services Classification Based on Intelligent Clustering Techniques. []. IEEE.]. *Proceedings of Information Technology and Applications*, *3*, 242–245.

Gottschalk, K., Graham, S., Kreger, H., & Snell, J. (2002). Introduction to Web services architecture. *IBM Systems Journal*, *41*(2), 170–177. doi:10.1147/sj.412.0170

Hou, J., Zhang, J., Nayak, R., & Bose, A. (2011). Semantics-based Web service discovery using information retrieval techniques. In *Comparative Evaluation of Focused Retrieval* (pp. 336–346). Springer. doi:10.1007/978-3-642-23577-1_32

Li, M., & Yang, Y. (2012). Efficient clustering index for semantic Web service based on user preference. In *Proceedings of Computer Science and Information Processing (CSIP), 2012 International Conference on* (pp. 291-294). IEEE.

Liang, Q., Li, P., Hung, P. C., & Wu, X. (2009). Clustering Web services for automatic categorization. In *Proceedings of Services Computing* (pp. 380–387). IEEE.

Liang, Q. A., Chung, J. Y., Miller, S., & Ouyang, Y. (2006). Service pattern discovery of Web service mining in Web service registry-repository. In *Proceedings of e-Business Engineering* (pp. 286–293). IEEE. doi:10.1109/ICEBE.2006.90

Liu, P., Zhang, J., & Yu, X. (2009). Clustering-Based Semantic Web Service Matchmaking with Automated Knowledge Acquisition. In *Web Information Systems and Mining* (pp. 261–270). Springer. doi:10.1007/978-3-642-05250-7_28

Luo, X., Yan, K., & Chen, X. (2008). Automatic discovery of semantic relations based on association rule. *Journal of Software*, *3*(8), 11–18. doi:10.4304/jsw.3.8.11-18

Ma, J., Zhang, Y., & He, J. (2008). Efficiently finding Web services using a clustering semantic approach. In *Proceedings of the 2008 international workshop on Context enabled source and service selection, integration and adaptation: organized with the 17th International World Wide Web Conference (WWW 2008)*. ACM.

Makhlughian, M., Hashemi, S. M., Rastegari, Y., & Pejman, E. (2012). Web service selection based on ranking of qos using associative classification. *arXiv preprint arXiv:1204.1425*.

Mohanty, R., Ravi, V., & Patra, M. R. (2012). Classification of Web Services Using Bayesian Network. *Journal of Software Engineering and Applications*, *5*(4). doi:10.4236/jsea.2012.54034

Mokhtar, S. B., Kaul, A., Georgantas, N., & Issarny, V. (2006). Towards efficient matching of semantic Web service capabilities. In *Proceedings of International Workshop on Web Services–Modeling and Testing (WS-MaTe 2006)*. WS-MaTe.

Nayak, R. (2007). Facilitating and improving the use of Web services with data mining. In *Research and trends in data mining technologies and applications* (pp. 309–327). Academic Press. doi:10.4018/978-1-59904-271-8.ch012

Nayak, R. (2008). Data mining in Web services discovery and monitoring. [IJWSR]. *International Journal of Web Services Research*, *5*(1), 63–81. doi:10.4018/jwsr.2008010104

Prasad, A. A., Meena, B., Kumar, B. U., & Kartheek, V. (2012). Efficient Retrieval of Web Services Using Prioritization and Clustering. *Computer Engineering and Intelligent Systems*, *3*(5), 8–15.

Qu, X., Sun, H., Li, X., Liu, X., & Lin, W. (2009). WSSM: A WordNet-Based Web Services Similarity Mining Mechanism. In Proceedings of Future Computing, Service Computation, Cognitive, Adaptive, Content, Patterns, (pp. 339-345). IEEE.

Rao, J., & Su, X. (2005). A survey of automated Web service composition methods. In *Semantic Web Services and Web Process Composition* (pp. 43–54). Springer. doi:10.1007/978-3-540-30581-1_5

Ren, K., Chen, J., Xiao, N., Song, J., & Li, J. (2008). Building Quick Service Query List Using Wordnet for Automated Service Composition. In *Proceedings of Asia-Pacific Services Computing Conference*, (pp. 297-302). IEEE.

Ritcharoenwattu, T., & Rungworawut, W. (2013). New Patterns Discovery for Web Services Composition from mining Execution Logs. *International Journal of Computer and Electrical Engineering*, *5*(1), 88–92. doi:10.7763/IJCEE.2013.V5.670

Rong, W., Liu, K., & Liang, L. (2008). Association rule based context modeling for Web service discovery. In *Proceedings of E-Commerce Technology and the Fifth IEEE Conference on Enterprise Computing, E-Commerce and E-Services, 2008 10th IEEE Conference on* (pp. 299-304). IEEE.

Rong, W., Liu, K., & Liang, L. (2009). Personalized Web service ranking via user group combining association rule. In *Proceedings of Web Services* (pp. 445–452). IEEE. doi:10.1109/ICWS.2009.113

Sellami, M., Gaaloul, W., & Tata, S. (2010). Functionality-driven clustering of Web service registries. In *Proceedings of Services Computing (SCC), 2010 IEEE International Conference on* (pp. 631-634). IEEE.

Shou, D., & Chi, C. H. (2008). Effective Web Service Retrieval Based on Clustering. In Proceedings of Semantics, Knowledge and Grid, (pp. 469-472). IEEE.

Skoutas, D., Sacharidis, D., Simitsis, A., & Sellis, T. (2010). Ranking and clustering Web services using multicriteria dominance relationships. *Services Computing. IEEE Transactions on*, *3*(3), 163–177.

Sycara, K., Paolucci, M., Ankolekar, A., & Srinivasan, N. (2003). Automated discovery, interaction and composition of semantic Web services. *Web Semantics: Science. Services and Agents on the World Wide Web*, *1*(1), 27–46. doi:10.1016/j.websem.2003.07.002

Wang, L., Si, J., & Hu, X. B. (2009). Research on the Clustering and Composition of P2P-Based Web Services. In Proceedings of Biomedical Engineering and Informatics, (pp. 1-5). IEEE.

Xie, L. L., Chen, F. Z., & Kou, J. S. (2011). Ontology-based semantic Web services clustering. In *Proceedings of Industrial Engineering and Engineering Management (IE&EM), 2011 IEEE 18Th International Conference on* (pp. 2075-2079). IEEE.

Yuan-Jie, L., & Jian, C. (2012). Web service classification based on automatic semantic annotation and ensemble learning. In *Proceedings of Parallel and Distributed Processing Symposium Workshops & PhD Forum (IPDPSW), 2012 IEEE 26th International* (pp. 2274-2279). IEEE.

Zhang, J., Yu, X., Liu, P., & Wang, Z. (2009). Research on Improving Performance of Semantic Search in UDDI. []. IEEE.]. *Proceedings of Intelligent Systems, 4*, 572–576.

Zheng, K., Xiong, H., Cui, Y., Chen, J., & Han, L. (2012). User Clustering-based Web Service Discovery. In *Proceedings of Internet Computing for Science and Engineering (ICICSE), 2012 Sixth International Conference on* (pp. 276-279). IEEE.

Zhou, J., & Li, S. (2009). Semantic Web Service Discovery Approach Using Service Clustering. In *Proceedings of Information Engineering and Computer Science* (pp. 1–5). IEEE. doi:10.1109/ICIECS.2009.5363051

Zhu, J., Kang, Y., Zheng, Z., & Lyu, M. R. (2012). A Clustering-Based QoS Prediction Approach for Web Service Recommendation. In *Proceedings of Object/Component/Service-Oriented Real-Time Distributed Computing Workshops (ISORCW), 2012 15th IEEE International Symposium on* (pp. 93-98). IEEE.

Zhu, Z., Yuan, H., Song, J., Bi, J., & Liu, G. (2010). WS-SCAN: A effective approach for Web services clustering. In *Proceedings of Computer Application and System Modeling (ICCASM), 2010 International Conference on* (Vol. 5, pp. V5-618). IEEE.

ADDITIONAL READING

AbuJarour, M., & Awad, A. (2011, July). Discovering linkage patterns among Web services using business process knowledge. In *Services Computing (SCC), 2011 IEEE International Conference on* (pp. 314-321). IEEE.

AbuJarour, M., & Naumann, F. (2010, December). Information Integration in Service-oriented Computing (p. 190). AlgoSyn.

Asbagh, M. J., & Abolhassani, H. (2007, November). Web service usage mining: mining for executable sequences. In *Proceedings of the 7th Conference on 7th WSEAS International Conference on Applied Computer Science* (Vol. 7, pp. 266-271).

Bose, A., Nayak, R., & Bruza, P. (2008). Improving Web service discovery by using semantic models. In *Web Information Systems Engineering-WISE 2008* (pp. 366–380). Springer Berlin Heidelberg. doi:10.1007/978-3-540-85481-4_28

Dustdar, S., Gombotz, R., & Baïna, K. (2004). *Web services interaction mining*. Technical Report TUV-1841-2004-16, Information Systems Institute, Vienna University of Technology, Wien, Austria.

Elgazzar, K., Hassan, A. E., & Martin, P. (2010, July). Clustering wsdl documents to bootstrap the discovery of Web services. In *Web Services (ICWS), 2010 IEEE International Conference on* (pp. 147-154). IEEE.

Gaaloul, W., Bhiri, S., & Godart, C. (2006). Research challenges and opportunities in Web services mining. *Proc of System and Information Service Web, INFORSID2006*.

Gaaloul, W., & Godart, C. (2005). Mining workflow recovery from event based logs. In *Business Process Management* (pp. 169–185). Springer Berlin Heidelberg. doi:10.1007/11538394_12

Gombotz, R., Baïna, K., & Dustdar, S. (2005). Towards Web services interaction mining architecture for e-commerce applications analysis. In *Proceedings of the Conference on E-Business and E-Learning*.

Gombotz, R., & Dustdar, S. (2006, January). On Web services workflow mining. In Business Process Management Workshops (pp. 216–228). Springer Berlin Heidelberg. doi:doi:10.1007/11678564_19 doi:10.1007/11678564_19

Han, J., Kamber, M., & Pei, J. (2006). *Data mining: concepts and techniques*. Morgan kaufmann.

Hepp, M., Leymann, F., Domingue, J., Wahler, A., & Fensel, D. (2005, October). Semantic business process management: A vision towards using semantic Web services for business process management. In *e-Business Engineering, 2005. ICEBE 2005. IEEE International Conference on* (pp. 535-540). IEEE.

Kokash, N. (2006). A comparison of Web service interface similarity measures. *Frontiers in Artificial Intelligence and Applications*, *142*, 220.

Liang, Q. A., Miller, S., & Chung, J. Y. (2005, August). Service mining for Web service composition. In *Information Reuse and Integration, Conf, 2005. IRI-2005 IEEE International Conference on*. (pp. 470-475). IEEE.

Liu, W., & Wong, W. (2008). Discovering homogenous service communities through Web service clustering. In Service-Oriented Computing: Agents, Semantics, and Engineering (pp. 69-82). Springer Berlin Heidelberg.

Liu, W., & Wong, W. (2009). Web service clustering using text mining techniques. *International Journal of Agent-Oriented Software Engineering*, *3*(1), 6–26. doi:10.1504/IJAOSE.2009.022944

Meng, H., Wu, L., Zhang, T., Chen, G., & Li, D. (2008, October). Mining frequent composite service patterns. In *Grid and Cooperative Computing, 2008. GCC'08. Seventh International Conference on* (pp. 713-718). IEEE.

Nayak, R., & Tong, C. (2004). Applications of data mining in Web services. In *Web Information Systems–WISE 2004* (pp. 199–205). Springer Berlin Heidelberg. doi:10.1007/978-3-540-30480-7_22

Paliwal, A. V., Adam, N. R., & Bornhovd, C. (2007, July). Web service discovery: Adding semantics through service request expansion and latent semantic indexing. In *Services Computing, 2007. SCC 2007. IEEE International Conference on* (pp. 106-113). IEEE.

Paolucci, M., Kawamura, T., Payne, T. R., & Sycara, K. (2002). Semantic matching of Web services capabilities. In The Semantic Web—ISWC 2002 (pp. 333-347). Springer Berlin Heidelberg.

Papazoglou, M. (2008). *Web Services: Principles and Technology*. Pearson Prentice Hall.

Srivastava, B., & Koehler, J. (2003, June). Web service composition-current solutions and open problems. In ICAPS 2003 workshop on Planning for Web Services (Vol. 35, pp. 28-35).

van der Aalst, W. (2012). Service Mining: Using Process Mining to Discover, Check, and Improve Service Behavior. *IEEE Transactions on Services Computing*, 1.

Wen, T., Sheng, G., Li, Y., & Guo, Q. (2011, August). Research on Web service discovery with semantics and clustering. In *Information Technology and Artificial Intelligence Conference (ITAIC), 2011 6th IEEE Joint International* (Vol. 1, pp. 62-67). IEEE.

Winkler, M., Springer, T., Trigos, E. D., & Schill, A. (2010, January). Analysing dependencies in service compositions. In Service-Oriented Computing. ICSOC/ServiceWave 2009 Workshops (pp. 123-133). Springer Berlin Heidelberg.

Wu, J., & Wu, Z. (2005, July). Similarity-based Web service matchmaking. In*Services Computing, 2005 IEEE International Conference on* (Vol. 1, pp. 287-294). IEEE.

Zheng, G., & Bouguettaya, A. (2010). Web service mining framework. In Web Service Mining (pp. 31-75). Springer US.

KEY TERMS AND DEFINITIONS

Candidate Service: A service relevant to query and considered as candidate for employing semantic matching of functional capabilities.

Relevant Cluster: The cluster whose label is most similar to the query.

Semantic Service Description Language: It is the interface of a service which describes the functionality offered by a service with explicit semantics in ontologies.

Semantic Service Discovery: The process of finding matched services for a query according to semantics of services expressed through ontologies.

Service Composition: The process of combining one or more atomic services in a particular pattern to implement a composite functionality.

Service Description: It is the interface of a service which describes the functionality offered by that service.

Service Discovery: The process of retrieving matched services for a query by computing similarity between query and functional characteristics of advertised services.

Service Usage Mining: The process of extracting useful knowledge from service execution log.

APPENDIX

Table 6. Test collection

Service ID	Representative String
s_1	{1 person bicycle 4 wheeled car, price}
s_2	{2 person bicycle 4 wheeled car price}
s_3	{food recommended price}
s_4	{3 wheeled car year price }
s_5	{1 person bicycle car price}
s_6	{camera price}
s_7	{academic degree lending duration }
s_8	{hospital diagnostic process}
s_9	{3 wheeled car price}
s_{10}	{book author book-type}
s_{11}	{film video media}
s_{12}	{hospital diagnostic process time duration}
s_{13}	{1 person bicycle car price}
s_{14}	{hospital diagnostic process}
s_{15}	{1 person bicycle car price}
s_{16}	{academic degree funding}
s_{17}	{food price physical-quantity}
s_{18}	{hospital diagnostic process cost}
s_{19}	{book author}
s_{20}	{film}
s_{21}	{3 wheeled car year recommended price}
s_{22}	{food price quantity}
s_{23}	{film}
s_{24}	{academic degree scholarship }
s_{25}	{food price}
s_{26}	{hospital biopsy}
s_{27}	{book author}
s_{28}	{academic degree funding duration}
s_{29}	{food price}
s_{30}	{academic degree lending }

Chapter 15
Overview of Business Intelligence through Data Mining

Abdulrahman R. Alazemi
Kuwait University, Kuwait

Abdulaziz R. Alazemi
Kuwait University, Kuwait

ABSTRACT

The advent of information technologies brought with it the availability of huge amounts of data to be utilized by enterprises. Data mining technologies are used to search vast amounts of data for vital insight regarding business. Data mining is used to acquire business intelligence and to acquire hidden knowledge in large databases or the Internet. Business intelligence can find hidden relations, predict future outcomes, and speculate and allocate resources. This uncovered knowledge helps in gaining competitive advantages, better customer relationships, and even fraud detection. In this chapter, the authors describe how data mining is used to achieve business intelligence. Furthermore, they look into some of the challenges in achieving business intelligence.

INTRODUCTION

The tremendous advancements made in data mining (DM) technologies have shifted thought from data collection to knowledge discovery and collection (Desikan et al., 2009). With today's powerful and relatively inexpensive hardware and network infrastructure, matched with advanced software, enterprises are adopting data mining as essential business processes. In addition, the Internet plays an integral part as networks and communications

are ubiquitous today, and data mining is carried over the world through networked databases. The vast amount of knowledge is not only consumed at the top senior management level but at all the other levels of an enterprise as well. Current data mining software utilize complex algorithms to achieve pattern recognition and forecast complex stock market activity, as example of the many usages of data mining. Currently, IBM and Microsoft are competing to dominate the data mining software market; this is also influenced by security and

DOI: 10.4018/978-1-4666-6086-1.ch015

intelligence agencies such as the FBI and CIA. Beside business intelligence, data mining acquires security-related intelligence. Many surveyors, such as Gartner group, one of the main pioneers in business intelligence, predicted that more than 5 billion dollars of business will be the net worth of e-commerce in the coming years (MineIT, 2010).

Acquiring business-oriented information through data mining is referred to as *business intelligence* (BI). BI tools are now an integral part of most enterprises' decision making and risk management. Enterprise datasets are growing rapidly every day, thanks to the use of Information Systems (IS), and data warehousing technologies. On average, investment and credit card companies usually have millions of transactions logged per year (Dorronsoro, Ginel, Sanchez, & Cruz, 1997). Datasets generated by global telecommunications operators can collect up to 100 million users' data, each generating thousands of millions of data per year (Phua, Lee, Smith, & Gayler, 2010). As these numbers mount up annually, traditional analytical processing such as OLAP and manual comprehension seems ineffective or to some extent impossible. With BI, such tasks are within

reach; according to Gartner group, "data mining and artificial intelligence are at the top five key technology areas that will clearly have a major impact across a wide range of industries within the next three to five years." This was back in a 1997 report (Lee & Siau, 2001). BI has become the stable for decision support systems in large organizations. BI has dominated many industries including retail, banking, and insurance (Ramakrishnan et al., 2011). It's worth mentioning that BI software is aimed at knowledge workers, mainly executives, analysts, middle management, and to a lesser extent operational management. Figure 1 illustrates how data today is transformed to acquire BI.

This chapter will explore how DM is used to achieve BI. First, we shall explore the background and the many developments that led to the inception of BI. And then, we shall look into the basics behind DM. afterwards, we will discuss how to achieve BI. After that, the chapter will address the problem of gaining competitive advantages through the use of BI. How the impact of BI on modern business and its effects on the return on investment (ROI) will be discussed, and then,

Figure 1. Data transforming into business intelligence

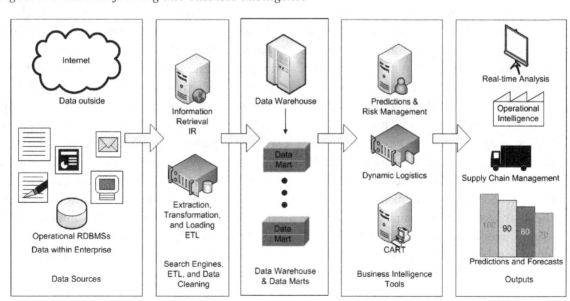

case studies highlighting BI tools usage will be discussed. Finally, the chapter discusses the future challenges in the BI field as well as touching on new trends, and then the chapter closes on the discussion and remarks to highlight key points for further readings and analysis; and then comes the conclusion, in which final remarks are given.

BACKGROUND

Many developments were made leading to the BI technologies we have today. These developments date back to early days of mathematical models and statistical analysis using regression and Bayesian methods in mid-1700s. With the advent of commercial electronic computers after World War II, large datasets were stored into magnetic tapes to automate business work. Starting from early 1960s, data stored in early commercial computers helped analyzers to answer simple predictive business questions. With the development of programming languages, specifically common business oriented language (COBOL) and rational database management systems (RDBMS), querying databases became possible. That meant more complex information and knowledge could be extracted.

Development of advanced object-oriented languages such as C++, Java, multidimensional databases, data warehousing, and online analytical processing OLAP made possible totally automated algorithmic ways of extracting patterns and knowledge from large datasets. BI tools today are more advanced and provide more than just reporting capabilities; they can discover hidden patterns, predict future outcomes, and assess risks incurred. Most of these commercial tools were developed in the early to mid-1990s, with tremendous growth with the dawn of the new millennia.

Business intelligence was achieved traditionally using manual methods, such as expert financial and market studies and analyses. Such methods were slow, inaccurate and simply inefficient; to mitigate such problems computers software such as spreadsheets and OLAP provided a new way to achieve business intelligence. Such software also had its shortcomings, such as limited functionalities, for example OLAP cannot provide forecasting analysis, they are used as a front-side analysis tools, used for day-to-day analysis. With advancements achieved in the development made in DM technologies and software, the application of such techniques provided to be the trend unto how BI is achieved; this trend began and is the de facto in the world of BI. It's worth mentioning that several techniques such as data warehousing, explained later, are also used in BI applications. DM technologies are the backbone behind BI tools used today; they provide useful information for BI (Duan & Xu 2012). At the heart of using DM for BI is the goal of achieving highly accurate predictions, known as quality business forecasts.

BI tools had developed into sophisticated software systems that provide an array of BI capabilities. The reader is encouraged to try out these systems to get a feel for acquiring and implementing BI. BI tools functions include, to name a few, dashboards, real-time analysis, future predictions, marketing and sales strategies, market forecasts, and custom-detailed analyses. IBM is one of major providers of solution-based packages, tools such as IBM's Cognos 8 solutions (IBM, 2010), provide a comprehensive set of BI tools that integrate well with most existing solutions. On the other hand Oracle, the dominant RDBMS vendor, also provides Oracle data mining, a tool that is integrated into the company's flagship RDBMS software package. SAS offers its SAS enterprise miner (Thomsen & Pedersen, 2009), a part of its enterprise solutions. A world leader in the enterprise and business software technologies is SAP; it offers the world-renown SAP Enterprise Resource Planning (ERP) solution. *ERPs* are basically automated tools that manage all different resources the enterprise has: monetary, financial, human, and industrial resources. The SAP ERP solution provides additional BI tools that are used within its ERP environment. Atos is an international information technology service provider that utilizes SAP software (Atos, 2011), to produce online, cloud-based BI services. Software giant Microsoft offers SQL server analysis services, a platform-dependent solution integrated in Microsoft SQL for Microsoft Windows server. Microsoft also provides Microsoft Dynamics (Microsoft, 2013), a full suite of ERP tools with BI tools built in. As BI is an interdisciplinary field between business, computer science and engineering, we shall focus upon the engineering aspects of BI.

DATA MINING BASICS

Let's look on the definition of DM; it's defined as data processing using certain criteria to infer hidden knowledge or information in the data. DM is widely regarded as the analysis step of the Knowledge Discovery in Databases (KDD) process (Apte, Liu, Pednault, & Smyth 2002). KDD usually has three steps, first step is data preprocessing, then data processing, which is DM, then finally data verification (Fayyad, Shapiro, & Smyth, 1996). Data mining is also known by other names including *knowledge extraction*, *data archaeology*, and *data pattern processing*. However the term data mining is the most popular. For DM used for BI, usually, but not necessarily, data must be stored in a data warehouse, will be discussed later. To process the data, or mine the data, artificial intelligence (AI) and neural network (Vellidoa, Lisboaa, & Vaughan, 1999) techniques are used most often. These techniques are nonlinear predictive models (Alexander, 2011) that learn through training; called machine learning, such a trait is used for business modeling and predictions (Fethi & Pasiouras, 2010). DM techniques include, naming a few, classifying and clustering, association rule mining, anomaly detection, summarization, regression, and sequential patterns. Most of these techniques are very useful in BI applications. As such most DM algorithms and software packages use such techniques for BI. For example, classifying and clustering, which are classifying data stored in multidimensional databases into meaningful sets, involve identifying all groups that can be found in the data set, like organizing fraudulent transactions in a separate group from legitimate transactions. Examples of classification and clustering techniques are decision trees and nearest neighbor algorithms. *Decision trees*, described in Quinlan (1986), are top-down induction rationale tools that facilitate classifying decisions into different branches. Starting from the root and stemming to the leaves, each decision branch has its risks and possibilities. Popular types of decision trees used are classification and regression trees (CART); see Figure 2. Nearest neighbor techniques on the other hand, classify records of data based on their resemblance to a specific data point or record. This technique is used to compare updated records or data to a pivotal important record; it tries to mimic the human comparison in recognizing patterns, used widely in behavioral analysis of customers.

Associations and rule inductions are basically inferring if–then relations from patterns found hidden in data. This leads to finding hidden correlations, like inferring *market baskets,* which are defined as the products bought mostly together in groups, for example, baby bottles and baby diapers. Other tasks include regression modeling or predictive modeling (Smith, 2010), that are key techniques in predicting future outcomes like ROI calculations and business forecasting. Usually, regression modeling is used for extrapolating data in mathematics; but for BI, it helps in finding a model that fits the given data set, such as sales figures, providing a systematic analysis and predictions. Another technique is sequential pattern; they are pattern manipulation algorithms working on sets of sequential data, such as monthly bills or employee records. Their goal is to find a

Figure 2. Simple CART example, "Sales Predictions"

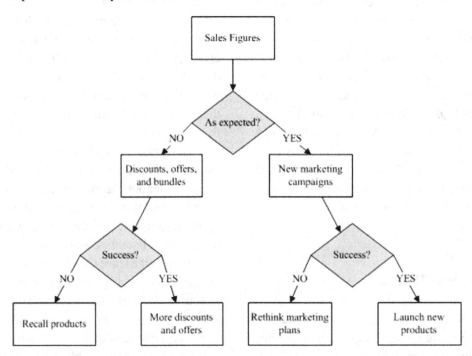

trend or pattern that happen in such sequence, for better business forecasting and risk management. Finally Figure 3 shows a clear view on what is and what is not DM.

Data Warehouses

As mentioned before, BI tools require as a prerequisite a data source, usually, but not always, a data warehouse. While it is possible to use BI without a data warehouse, the functionality is to an extent limited (IBM, 2011). *Data warehouses* (Inmon, 1996) are large, long-term data storages that transform data for analysis, mining, and aggregation. A data warehouse extracts and transforms the data from the database management system (DBMS) that organization enterprise uses for its daily use. Through the use of Extraction, Transformation, and Loading (ETL) processes (Chhillar, 2008), the data is completely transformed. ETL extracts the data from the DBMS, and then it preprocesses the datasets and finally loads it into the data warehouse.

Figure 3. What DM is and is not

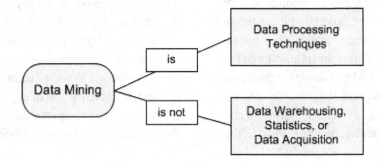

While data warehousing is considered a database oriented technology; the main purpose of implementing a data warehouse is for BI. Data in the data warehouse is further processed and cleaned, and sifted to be used by BI tools. Data warehouses are further divided into data marts. *Data marts* are subsections of the data warehouse that house specified data, like a data mart for finance and another for Human Resource. A major concern arises about data warehousing is that they are *not a DBMS*, they do not function as or overlap the job of a DBMS. A data warehouse is aggregated, consolidated, and extracted information already transformed to be used by BI tools, on long term basis, for example a BI tool may synch with the information of the data ware house on weekly basis or quarter annual basis. On the other hand DBMS are used daily for day to day activities such as querying and storage. Figure 4 illustrates the relationship between a DBMS/RDBMS, DW, DM and BI.

Data Mining in the Engineering and Manufacturing Field

Aside from BI, DM is a tool used heavily in manufacturing, engineering and software engineering. Traditionally as in business application, manufacturing and engineering application requires a sense of forecasting and dynamic planning. The planning of plant outputs, mineral and metallurgical industries quantity planning, and supply chain planning are fields were DM is used heavily. Today's manufacturing and engineering are called digital manufacturing environments (Choudhary, Harding, and Tiwari, 2008). These digital environment consist of DBMS, barcodes, wireless sensor networks, dozen thousands of data is collected, exchanged, manipulated and ultimately used to acquire competitive advantages.

With the advent of DM tools, it's obvious that the manufacturing industry such as the business industry would pick up and evolve DM tools suited for engineering and industries. As in the vein of business applications, manufacturing and engineering industries use data warehouses to store manufacturing and engineering records, where this data is further transformed to be used by DM tools. Supply chain management, material optimization, quality control, and engineering costs planning are some examples were DM techniques and tools are used to provide competitive advantages.

The challenge that faces DM in manufacturing and engineering stems from the problem of data collection, which heavily affects the quality of the results. Unlike the business industry were most data are customers' records, market data, or world trade figures, manufacturing data collection

Figure 4. RDBMS, DW, DM & BI

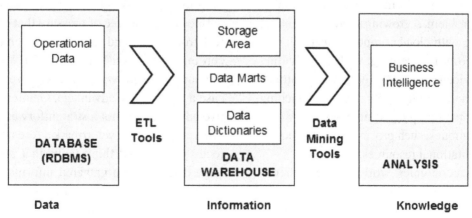

is much harder. Most data acquired in engineering filed are collected from sensors, electronic measurement devices such as transducers, wireless sensor networks and such. Such data is fuzzy and requires more cleaning. As mentioned in Huyet (2006), data mining in used in a simulated job shop environment, were DM is used to optimize the stated environment. Manufacturing defects and quality control is another area where DM tools are used, in order to understand what's common among fault products, DM tools can to a certain extent pinpoint the cause of the problem by associating the common attribute between defects. Quality control management effectively improves yield and improving manufacturing processes and increasing profits (Hou & Yang, 2006).

Business Intelligence Implementation

Implementing BI tools usually require substantial investments and careful planning. In fact such major financial investments and elaborate professional planning are main hurdles that prevent BI from penetrating mid-sized business markets. Most failure in implementing BI are credited to lack of upper management interest which cripples the financial resources needed for the success of the BI implementation or flawed planning and business modeling of the BI tools. Aside from financial and design issues, BI also need huge processing power, usually top-class computing prowess, which just one other facet of the BI implementation problem. A growing interest in combing data mining with cloud computing technologies to reduce costs is emerging, such as providing BI as a service (Mircea, Ghilic-Micu, & Stoica, 2007). BI tools usually apply number-crunching algorithms, parallel processing, neural networks and AI techniques, such processing tasks require huge computational resources.

Modern economies worldwide are driven by information technologies, becoming what is known as information-based economies (Mocanu,

Litan, Olaru, & Munteanu, 2010). In 2008, the world market for BI software reached more than 7.8 billion USD, according to Mikut and Reischl (2011). BI market had reached the 10 billion mark by 2011, with a net worth of 10.7 billion dollars with an annual growth of 9.7% (Davey, 2011). BI tools are one of the top reasons of the huge development of information technologies in business today. BI tools are integrated into most enterprise ISs such as ERP, Customer Relationship Management (CRM), supply chain management, and even some DBMSs. BI tools have become key tools for decision support processes in modern enterprises and organizations. BI tools provide many business advantages; we shall touch upon three main topics in the next section, which include competitive advantages, customer relationships management, and management of risk in investments.

COMPETITIVE ADVANTAGE THROUGH BI

The ever-so-competitive market of today's world is heavily driven by information. A *competitive advantage* is seen as a differentiation point, something that defines a product or a service; it's like a merit that other competitors lack. Enterprises and organization strive to stand out among the competition with such unique advantages. Of course, it goes without saying that the concept of acquiring a competitive advantage is heavily driven by competitive pressure. *Competitive pressure* is defined as the degree of pressure that companies feel from rivals and possible new entrants, according to Ramakrishnan et al. (2011). The said pressure is driven away by gaining an edge, in this case a competitive advantage. Gaining competitive advantages is not a straightforward process; often enterprises develop market research groups, focus groups, and think tanks that analyze the large datasets from gathered information about the competition. Such daunting endeavors are keys in acquiring insight on what possible competitive advantages might be helpful. Market research, through data mining, or technically BI, tries to find what products dominate the market, the reasons for this domination, and what sets such products apart from the others.

As an example of such research we can see that media networks use BI, in this case a media-wide search, in order to set the common factors between different audience and their programs' scheduled slots. The BBC often used to hire human experts to schedule its programs slots. Currently the BBC uses fully automated BI tools for scheduling only with human supervision; the results were better than the manual scheduling they used to have, especially as BI tools take far less time to get appropriate results (Fitzsimons, Khabaza, & Shearer, 1993). Results usually are in the form of lists of the competition's competitive advantages, such as finding the market's baskets, as mentioned before, and locating certain peculiarities and anomalies. Such results are used further by BI tools to form long-term strategies. As mentioned earlier, most competitive enterprises keep their competitive advantages a trade secret, something that is the cornerstone of the entire business model. With the aid of BI tools, such secrets are revealed to an extent. Leading competitive retail enterprises such as Wal-Mart, Costco, and K-Mart, keep their market baskets their own trade secrets for example. In the next subsections, we shall see in detail how BI helps in acquiring such an edge over the competition.

Improved Customer Relationships

Today's customers are very well informed, thanks to the Internet and free market competition; moreover, they are demanding. In a way customers are getting more and more difficult to please. For such reasons, *CRM* systems were developed to automate the process of handling the customers. CRM can be enhanced by BI tools, which can strengthen the relationships of organizations' customers through BI technology focusing on the customers' satisfaction and further development of this satisfaction, resulting in prolonged and profitable relationships (Chen & Popovich, 2003). With the advent of information systems in business since the 1980s, one of the early uses of such systems was to strengthen and to further develop their customer relationships; this was in an age where most BI tasks were manual and had little automation by such ISs. CRM used to manage customers' information, but with the introduction of BI tools in the 1990s, further and newer exploitations of such information were possible. BI can answer questions like how to keep customers satisfied. What makes a customer happy? What attracts potential customers? What do rival customers have? Such questions are further explored by the BI tools. BI tools are integrated into modern CRM systems. BI features within the CRMs include service selection, market targeting, and product evaluation, to name a few. The main consumers of BI-enhanced CRM systems are classical or conventional retailers (brick-and-mortar retailers), electronic retailers (e-tailers), service providers such as Internet service providers (ISP), and telecommunication (Phan & Vogel, 2010).

Enterprises achieve competitive advantages in providing what is known as value propositions to its customers; *value propositions* come in the form of lowest costs of ownership, special bundles and discounts, or as loyalty and partnership privileges. BI tools help in providing price transparency in the market by offering the enterprise the choice of price discrimination. *Price discrimination*, according to Phan and Vogel (2010), is defined as offering the same product with different prices for different people and regions; this of course depends on each region's economic state and culture. This trait allows enterprises to appeal to diverse customers with offers that are tailored to them specifically.

BI tools help in evaluating customers' buying and spending habits with its inductive reasoning; they can also predict sales outcomes depending on the customers. Moreover, customers' willingness to pay more for certain products differs depending on personal parameters such as hobbies, age, or culture. Enterprises try to offer prices that match the customers' expected willingness. Such tactics helps keep most customers happy. Other customers may only pay for such prices if they are given some incentives, limited-time offers, and special discounts; those customers can also be kept happy. In the end, the enterprise can create a win-win situation, a state of equilibrium with its customers. It's worth noting that very sophisticated BI techniques are employed to achieve effective price discrimination tactics. The reader is encouraged to look at Mudimigh, Saleem, Ullah, Al-Aboud (2009); the paper describes a tool that utilizers BI in CRM software through a sophisticated DM engine that mines the CRM database.

BI also helps in assessing possible switching costs of customers. Switching costs are defined as the costs incurred by the customer to switch from one vendor to another. According to Phan & Vogel (2010), high switching costs leads to lower customer satisfaction. As customers are not satisfied with being stuck or entrapped with a particular company or vendor because of such costs, it reduces their overall satisfaction. In addition, BI finds the market baskets, as stated earlier. A market basket helps analyzers to classify customers based on what market baskets they are associated with.

Through CRM data, BI tools can form known market baskets for customers or improvised market baskets for certain groups of customers that are unconventional. Amazon, eBay, and Google are among the best utilizes of customer market baskets. Market baskets can be recommendations and targeted advertisements, Google AdSense for example, discounts certain products and bundle prices. Furthermore, market baskets implemented by e-tailers are more flexible because it is more easily designed than traditional brick-and-mortar retailers, where certain physical products are hard to group together.

Derivatives of CRM are customer experience management (CEM) systems. *CEMs* basically track down the customers' experiences with a service during a period of time. Services industries rely on CEM systems because they provide services, not product, in the sense that customers experience the service over time. BI tools help find evidence of what make customers satisfied with the service and what they expect in the near future. BI is also used in CRM research to find reasons for customer churns. *Customer churn* is defined as the customers turning away, or the drop rate of customers. In most organizations, the customer churn rate is a vital enterprise health indicator. High customer churn ratings are signs of failure in the organization CRM system. Churn analysis can also show causes for such turnover, switching to rival companies, or finding substitutes for the services provided. BI in CEM systems can also help identify *alpha customers;* those are highly valued customers that must be kept satisfied, for example VIPs, celebrities, tycoons, or authority figures.

Better Logistics and Inventory Management

A *supply chain* is defined as the process of moving a product or service from the suppliers to customers. Supply chain management systems such as warehouse management systems (WMS) and inventory management systems (IMS) (Chen, Huang, Chen, & Wu, 2005) are software systems that provide automated control and management of supply chains. These systems can achieve logistics and production efficiencies such as high distributions rates, on-demand supplies, and quick response to inventory levels. Logistics industries depend on the efficiency of their supply chain managements systems. BI tools help support supply chain management; enterprises have predictive management tools over their supplies. BI in WMS or IMS, finds patterns of shortages, possible overproduction, and underproduction. Most importantly it provides quick response to demand spikes, which are extremely important to catch very early on.

Traditionally, tedious, time-consuming, and complex mathematical models were used for supply chain management and logistical predictions. Those slow methods effected inventories in the form of underflows or overflows. Specifically during spikes in demand, failures to respond in the right time resulted in losses. Forecasting was also unreliable and was always late. The logistics industry resolved such problems with order batching methods. *Order batching* basically batches many items to as many different locations as possible (Van den Berg, 1999). Another problem that spun out was batched orders routing. Using DM techniques such as association rules and clustering, BI helps in effectively routing batched orders in a suboptimal solution; optimal routing is again the traveling salesperson's problem, which is, being on time and effective. For example a supply management company was having problems in delivering goods, and by factoring out the causes they found the causes to be either geography; schedule; or the vehicles. After using BI tools to fine-grain search the logs, geography was found the most determining factor (Partridge, 2013).

BI tools analyze current market situations, providing timely predictions on demand and supply spikes. These predictions help in managing inventories, keeping underflows and overflows at minimum. BI forecasting is a function of demand surges that are estimated through reading market history, current political events, or even rivals' reactions. Modeling, beside prediction, is another BI function used for inventory and warehouse management that corresponds to demand and supply cycles. Models help automate the replenishment processes by suggesting a certain model for each item in the inventory. It is worth noting that some sophisticated BI tools can predict market demand by segments. Such market segments are used in niche marketing; *niche markets* are small but lucrative markets dominated by small groups of enterprises. Such markets have special logistics and rules.

Utilization of BI tools has resulted in delivering timely decisions and quick respond to feedbacks. Such benefits of BI are in food supply chain networks (Li, Kramer, Beulens, & Vorst, 2010). The food industry depends on timely delivery of goods; it is critical for stocks of food supplies or livestock supplies not to rot or die during any one of the supply chain stages. Poor management and slow reactions inside supply chain results in low yields, leading to massive losses that could have been avoided. The problem of *death-on-arrival* (DOA) occurs when the livestock die during transport due to problems in the supply chain. BI tools provide early warnings that the livestock dying due to road blocks, weather, or natural disasters. This information can help in reducing the casualties or identifying the problem and rescuing the remaining livestock traveling inside the supply chain. Aside from livestock management and preservation in the supply chain, food products like milk, sugar, fruits, and other raw food items spoil if not handled in time. BI helps in dynamically routing the supplies before they rot during transportation and distribution.

One of the main users of BI in supply chain managements are third-party logistics (TPL) or 3PL. A *TPL* is an outsourced party providing logistics services to a contracting first party (Rao & Swarup, 2001). In addition to the traditional services, 3PL with BI provides new services such as detailed reports and forecasts about the delivered goods. Another additional service is the cost-benefit analysis; this service allows customers to analyze their order supplies and reevaluate their shipments dynamically. Another service powered by BI tools is supply chain visibility, allowing customers to track their supplies online dynamically and in real time, ideal for sensitive shipments. BI has been seen as an essential part of the supply chain industry, and many transportation management solution vendors notice the customers' need of it. BI provides a sense of safety to the whole operation, by providing dynamic real-time reporting and dashboards, and benchmarking (Amy Roach, 2013).

Anomalies and Fraud Detection

BI tools sift capabilities and locate certain hidden patterns found in daily transactions. These patterns are used to detect possible fraudulence and anomalies. *Fraud and anomaly detection* is defined as detection of deceptive transactions or strange and unusual transactions that need further inspection. BI tools are one of the main tools used in forensics against fraudulence. Most credit, insurance, and telecommunication companies use fraud detection daily. Those businesses are plagued by fraudulence and anomalies in their transactions, according to Phua et al. (2010). Other techniques used are: Artificial Intelligence, Fuzzy logic, and Data Mining (which is BI in the business and industrial engineering field) (Raj & Portia, 2011).

In telecommunications and credit industries, it is hard to manually detect such fraudulence. Fraudulence is deliberate; its goal is to acquire money or free services. While on the other hand, anomalies are not deliberate like fraudulence. They are unusual behaviors that may manifest in normal data for unknown reasons, due to corrupted data or glitches, or from network errors in transmissions. If not identified correctly, anomalies can lead to a shift and divergence in the data, making fraudulence even harder to spot. Anomalies must be detected so as to leave out the surge or upheavals these anomalies bring in datasets.

Fraudulence, however deliberate the actions are, is usually conducted for monetary gain and is usually carried out by white-collar criminals, such as insiders, high-profile technology criminals, and computer hackers. Usually, credit companies try to find certain patterns used in its CRM of charging and billing its customers. For example, usually, stolen credit cards result in erroneous behaviors and transactions. These transactions usually happen in short periods, where huge sums of figures are spent in numerous transactions in matter of hours.

Fraud detection isn't limited to fraudulent customers but also fraud within the company, as in fraudulent reports and predictions. BI tools detect suspected behaviors over periods of time, providing what user accounts and individuals that require special intention. BI is also used in financial crimes like money laundering, through sifting records of individuals, and *insider trading*, which is defined as trading upon secret inside information. Much like spam detection, BI tries to find fraudulence and gives warnings. Finally, we should mention the main problems with such tools: false positives, wrong detection of genuine transactions, miss rates, and undetected fraud transactions that may have legal and monetary consequences.

Global Economics and Enterprise Resource Planning

BI tools that are integrated in the company's ERP system allow for more functionalities and productivities from the ERP's components. Components may include a data warehouse or CRM. BI tools give higher management the ability to view the whole company seamlessly and in multiple views, such as functional or structural (Chaudhuri & Narasayya, 2011). Reports from HR, finance, and other departments can be viewed live in order to manage tactical and strategic plans as well as calculating Key Performance Indicators (KPIs) on daily basis. These functionalities can be real-time feeds, dashboards, charts, or reports. BI tools are also essential for global economic analysis made a company; the techniques may include trend analysis, time-variant, multi-variant, and qualitative analysis (Kahraman, Kaya, Ulukan, & Ucal, 2010).

Because BI tools can also be fed from outside sources, such as third-party market analyst, that may be local or global. This provides compa-

Table 1. BI benefits in acquiring competitive advantages

Competitive Advantage	BI Features	Advantages
CRM	• Market research. • Price discrimination. • Market baskets. • Customers satisfaction.	• Finding rivals' competitive advantages. • Worldwide appeal. • Better marketing and advertisements. • Assessing switching costs, customer churn rates, and satisfaction rates.
Logistics	• Manufacturing optimization. • Supply chain scheduling. • Forecasting.	• Prevent over- and underproduction. • Dynamic view of the supply chain. • Dynamic reaction to demand spikes. • Production forecast.
Fraudulence and Anomalies	• Fraud detection. • Anomaly removal.	• Stop fraudulence. • Prevent illegal transactions. • Clean data from glitches, anomalies, and other sources of errors.
ERP and Global Economics	• Global view of the company. • Live data feeds, dashboards, and KPIs. • Global indexes and trends. • Transparency.	• Helps in evaluating a company's tactical and strategic plans. • Integrating social responsibility into the BI strategy to increase sustainability through global metrics.

nies, especially large global companies such as automobile or logistics companies, with global market trends, feeds, and global metrics, such as stock and currency values. These have paved the way for a more transparent business environment that affected inter-company relationships as well as a company and its environment and its social responsibility, which must be integrated in its BI projects planning (Petrini & Pozzebon, 2009). The Dow Jones sustainability indexes, for example, are one such set of global indexes that show the financial performance of companies that focus on sustainability worldwide through integrating social responsibility in their BI strategies. This set of indexes provides BI with global metrics. Of course, other negative effects could affect the company through globalization; these include the rise of protectionism in some regions, economic crises, or state and private global laws affecting the company's business strategies (*The Economist,* 2009).

IMPACT OF BUSINESS INTELLIGENCE ON MODERN BUSINESS

BI tools are integrated within most enterprises' ISs, which are a multitude of many other subsystems and components. A BI tool can operate on analytical and operational data, given it is processed, preprocessed, or even sometimes unstructured data as well, such as graphs or charts (SAS, 2013). The integration of most BI tools is nearly universal in today's large sized business. The substantial investments needed for implementing BI initiatives and projects is largely rationalized the impact that these projects and their integration into the business eco system, specifically the ROI. The ROI is an essential stat for any project the enterprise invests in, and utilizing an efficient BI tool to help the company maintain a competitive edge is no exception. ROI represents the time and costs for a project to return or justify its investing budget under constraints of a limited budget or a given time window. A project that cannot have a feasible ROI is rejected, and given the fact the cost of installing BI tools, whether whole ERPs or just the BI tool, is substantial, careful ROI planning is needed.

Engineering projects, such as industrial, civil, or any other engineering projects usually have predictable ROI rates. For example, in a civil engineering project, the staff of engineers and finance people can estimate the initial costs, time for the construction, and overall maintenance and added costs, and finally the operation costs, as well as estimating revenues. This sums up good and predictable ROI values (King & O'Shea, 2003; Schweighardt, 2010). For BI installations, however, studies show an average ROI of 112% percent over five years with a budget of $2 million (Negash, 2004). As mentioned earlier, BI market had already reached the 10.7 billion in 2011, with an annual growth of 9.7%. (Davey, 2011), being the one of the most fast spreading trends in modern business practices.

The key reasons for ROI being elusive on BI installations can be summed up in the nature of such tools. First, as with most of the high-end decision support and management systems (e.g. ERPs, data warehouses, and CRMs), they have high initial costs, high installation costs, and high maintenance operational costs as well, according to experts in the field. Initial costs are for the BI environment itself and the software. The environment usually requires a data warehouse, whether local or from a third-party vendor, a sophisticated data center with cooling and security measures; IT people are quite aware of such costs in such centers (DTEK, 2011).

Software costs for BI are high as well in terms of tens of thousands in US dollars (Negash, 2004). Some BI tools require subscriptions to BI data providers to provide live feeds and feedback. Also, for the operators there are costs for training and maintaining the individuals and systems. These individuals can be occupied solely for analyzing

BI output and are hired specifically for BI usages. Second, the efficiency of a BI tool's results is very dependent on many factors, such as the input from the various other systems, the quality and freshness of the input, and the skill of the BI tool user. Poor input or usage of the tools would yield low benefits, such as slow forecasting or wrong forecasting (BARC, 2013).

While the relationship between ROI and BI tools is hard to predict, several companies invest in BI tools not to gain improvements in future costs or time slots but to forecast market trends and hopefully be the first to take advantage of these trends quicker than competitors. This leads to huge profits when a new trend is successfully exploited. This also reflects back on the engineering R&D departments, predicting what and when to develop. Other factors that contribute to BI projects are the managers' attitudes toward extra investment. For example, in software engineering, if careful system engineering is to be made for software projects, extra costs will be induced. Some managers will see this as degrading the overall ROI of the project, but actually, system engineering will prevent future undesirable costs, such as missing requirement, inaccurate functionalities, and extra costs in implementation, and so increasing ROI instead of decreasing it (Boehm Valerdi, & Honour, 2008). This logic can be applied to BI tool strategies as well.

CASE STUDY: JAEGER LOCATES LOSSES WITH BI

Jaeger is a midsized, privately owned British chain cloth retailer in the UK (Hedfield, 2009) with hundreds of outlets located throughout the UK. During the 2008 recession in the UK, shoplifting was on the rise. Retail giants such as Marks and Spencer were accumulating losses with a rate that was at least two times higher than the previous three years. According to the center for retail research, shoplifters stole approximately more than £1.6 billion, while employees stole £1.3 billion, and suppliers took more than £209 million in fraudulent transactions.

Current technologies to defend against such theft and shoplifting are closed-circuit televisions (CCTV) surveillance systems and electronic article surveillance (EAS). However, even with these technologies implemented, many losses can't be estimated. With new innovations in BI technologies, this made it possible for these tools to help in locating the loss sources. Jaeger, in 2008, implemented a BI application to identify its losses. The new application was centralized, used to process data collected from all the other outlets to try to make sense of the information.

The BI application Jaeger created was called LossManager, provided by IDM software. The software used feeds from Jaeger's other ISs, such as the electronic point of sales (EPOS) system. It was meant to monitor the employees' behavior as well to monitor EPOS systems throughout Jaeger's outlets. Jaeger's employees were capable of doing fraud transactions by using unauthorized discounts. Jaeger had another BI software before LossManager, but it was far too cumbersome, and it did not integrate well with Jaeger's other ISs.

LossManager was developed with the current systems in mind to provide possible integration. Jaeger's main aim with LossManager wasn't to detect shoplifters, as CCTV and EAS systems were aimed for that purpose. LossManager's aim was to spot loss coming from theft from employees through fraudulent transactions, unknown loss in inventories, and marginal losses from unnecessary work practices. The Jaeger audit team was in charge of reading the reports generated from LossManager. The team analyzed the reports to identify possible dishonest employees and to locate sources of loss. However, the reports generated by LossManager had false positives; to overcome this, the audit team used these reports as a starting point for further investigations, a double-check process.

LossManager reduced losses to less than those accumulated from theft in the last year. Jaeger already expected an ROI in its first year of using this system. Managers did have concerns regarding the double-checking process that the audit team took in every step. Major findings were that losses from employee theft comprised a very small portion of total losses. In addition, LossManager found out many erroneous transactions; not all were identified as fraud, though. The system also helped Jaeger in better managing its inventory, reducing loss gained from stock going off-season, or missing items from the other outlets' inventories.

Jaeger's experience with LossManager proved that the BI tool, which was meant for fraud and theft detection, did manage to be useful in inventory stock management as well. LossManager helped in keeping losses generated from fraudulence at a minimum. LossManager did show a significant relation between outlets with high lose figures and frequent EAS breakdowns. It worth noting that the main difficulty faced came from the integration with the current systems at Jaeger. The DM tool, LossManager, was implemented in C++, using a Microsoft Development Environment to interface with other systems. The feeds from the EPOSs and EASs were challenging as they were the sources of information. In addition, the system being centralized made the data collection time-consuming.

CASE STUDY: KFC/PIZZA HUT FIND A BETTER BI TOOL

KFC/Pizza Hut Singapore (Zap Tech, 2010), have more than 120 outlets distributed all over Singapore, with a workforce of no less than 5000 employees. As a global fast food franchise, they deliver fast food and beverages to customers through outlets, drive-throughs, and home delivery services. To deal with the workload, KFC/Pizza Hut have used a BI tool; this tool was growing increasingly inefficient quickly over time. The tool did not meet with the time requirements to deliver business reports. It also had issues with performance benchmarking, as it was not a straight forward tool, plus daily reports across multiple systems was very tedious and time consuming. KFC/Pizza Hut most important daily operation was calculating payments needed for daily paid workers, such as the deliver staff. Using current BI tool, the managers would take hours and had to work extra hours to sum up pay correctly. Finally, the old BI reporting was slowing down KFC/Pizza Hut ability to match and adapt to current and rapid changes, with business reports taking days to be ready.

The solution was to find another BI tool that was modern, cost effective, and surpasses the issues with the current BI tool. KFC/Pizza Hut contracted with Zap Tech, a BI vendor, using their product Zap Business Intelligence. The new solution was Web based; it was also linked to other external sources online. Such external sources proved quite useful in enriching the functionality of this new BI solution. The corporate data warehouse was completely remodeled as to include the point of sales (POS), marketing, HR, and the corporate very own supply chain. In September 2009, after two month of testing the new BI tool, KFC/Pizza Hut went live with the new BI tool. The employees and managers were generally happy with it. As it was Web based, and it offered modern BI capabilities like dashboards, instant report generation, key performance indicators KPI benchmarking, scoreboards, and had a very user-friendly interface.

The benefits of the new tool were very significant to KFC/Pizza Hut. The improvement included optimized market spending, through the use of live updates; KFC/Pizza Hut immediately responded and adjusted its marketing campaigns and offers. Restaurant planning and outlet location managements were based on results from the new BI tool, to cope with KFC/Pizza Hut strategy of being ever close to its customers. Customer service was highly improved, especially the home delivery service, as the new BI tool accurately captured the parameters of such deliveries to optimize the delivery process. In addition, the POS integration

into the data warehouse allowed KFC/Pizza Hut to manage its deals and optimize the offers per outlet; different customers at different locations had very varied demands.

Finally, the new BI tool, Zap Business Intelligence, had an expected ROI within 12 months of deployment, as the staff members were reduced down, and daily time wasted on reporting was cut to minutes. Workforce efficiency increased and managers didn't have to work for extra hours. The major cost reduction came from the lessened reliance on the IT staff. The new tool was Web based and very intuitive and friendly to use, as most of the operations were carried over to the servers situated at KFC/Pizza Hut's central IT center. Little IT provision was needed on the different outlets, and fewer staff could manage the new BI tool. The new BI tool proved that a modern BI tool, which is carefully planned and designed, can help not only improve profits but also day-to-day business activities as well.

FUTURE CHALLENGES

The DM field alone has its set of challenges that had barred it from reaching its full potential. We can view these challenges in three sets: technical, legal and ethical. The DM tools used for BI are considered to be elaborate, expensive, and sophisticated. They are mostly integrated into yet larger and more complex systems, such as ERP systems.

In terms of the first, technical, we see that DM tools are yet still expensive are not used unless careful ROI is calculated to justify their need; as DM tools are a set of elaborate hardware and software tool, and as these systems will be ran partly by human operators, these individuals are expected to be experts and have a considerable knowledge of the field due to its complexity (Shapiro, Brachman, & Khabaza, 1996).

Legal and ethical challenges arise from privacy laws for individuals in government. Basically, one of the uses of DM tools in BI is to sift through data to extract facts, such as market trends. Sometimes, these sets of data are of individuals (e.g., customers), which can be combined with other sources of data to produce more facts concerning these individuals (e.g., average age, gender, location, hobbies, addresses, income). From an engineering perspective, these uses are essentials for R&D teams because they can forecast what R&D should focus on, which can benefit ROI on future projects. However, these sources of data have impacted the privacy of individuals; public awareness groups have noticed and effectively worked against these practices, resulting in acts like the Health Insurance Portability and Accountability Act (HIPAA) in the United States; the act states that an individual must be informed about what his or her private data will be used for. And as such, laws to make the data anonymous are set to protect individuals (Taipale, 2003). For example, if the company uses its customer's personal information or sensitive data, processes to make the data anonymous are often employed to comply with these regulations.

This process either destroys or makes it hard for the DM tool to be useful in BI because DM tools can still de-anonymize some data. Another issue in the legal field is data quality. When a BI provider provides data to a company, the level of the data completeness, authenticity, and freshness determines its quality (Rodríguez, Daniel, Casati, & Cappiello, 2010). Misleading data leads to inaccurate DM and BI tool results (Laundon & Laundon, 2011).

Several midsized to small sized companies that find the costs of ERP, DM, and DW tools to be too high find the cloud an alternative. Although the cloud can provide DM as well as BI tools to companies, several pitfalls and challenges lurk as well. The cloud provides lesser costs for DM and BI tools. It provides expert data analysts to provide services to a company without being part of it (outsourcing). This is mostly true for small-sized companies that lack any financial or human resources. These services are known as infrastructure-as-service (IAS) (Inmon, 1994;

Ballard et al., 1998; Hedfield, 2009). Some issues with cloud computing are dependency and privacy. Dependency issues are how a company will be bound to a third-party vendor with potentially different views and loyalties in the market. This limits the company BI tools by having their data and tools at the vendor. Now if a network problem occurs, or the vendor is out of reach for any reason, BI tools will be offline. Another dependency issue includes moving from one BI solution vendor to another. Because it is outsourced, difficult negotiations might ensue. The privacy issue follows that an IAS provider has access to a company's data.

While regulations might prevent the vendor from taking advantage of the data, several privacy issues are still possible. For example, through the network used to transmit data, the vendor may use the company's data under the binding laws of agreement, such as providing it as BI feed data to regional markets or abusing or misusing the data in any form that causes confidentiality risks.

New trends and challenges in the BI field are Hadoop and Big data. First, what are Hadoop and Big data? *Hadoop* is open source software for clusters of servers to enable distributed computing in a scalable and easy-to-manage manner, and its benefits are managed scalability and distributed computing, which allows for real-time, ad hoc *unstructured* data processing, such as MapReduce (Elliott, 2011). Hadoop enables huge amounts of data, such as terabytes to petabytes of data, to be processed in real time (e.g., weather data, GPS data, and data from orbiting satellites), which are unstructured data and are part of the *Big data*, and that makes Hadoop adopted in many companies. So if companies already have data warehouse, DM, and BI tools to handle their data, why use Hadoop? The answer lies in the source of the data itself. While data warehouses handle structured data, Hadoop handles the unstructured data, and so BI tools should adapt to newer ad-hoc algorithms for that (Kobielus, 2011; Vijayan, 2011). This is true because data warehouses get their information from the ETL tools which take the data from relational databases that houses structured data. Structured data is data with is identified as records with known fields, types, and names. Databases' data is stored and committed and handled atomically (e.g. when handling such data its size and types are known prior to processing). While unstructured data have no specific fields, or types, and instead is being fetched from a live source. This data can be weather information, or GPS data. The size of each piece of data is variable; its type is also variable. For example a string of unstructured data may be the following 37 Celsius, Trend: Microsoft, Picture: the new ford. These pieces of data cannot be stored and committed in a database since we have no prior knowledge of its size and types because it is coming live from a source. And so the technology in Hadoop allows these pieces to be handled, transformed, and queried in real-time. And so, data warehouses handle structured data that was stored in a database prior to the ETL stage. Hadoop difficulties lie in its need for expert programmers and analysts to handle real-time ad hoc and raw data processing.

For *Big data*, we can define it as the processes, tools, and procedures that enable the handling and manipulation of large unstructured data (in terabytes and petabytes). The sources of this large data have been stated: weather data, energy company supplies, and medical drug testing. Because Big data sources are rapid and need processing daily, they are unstructured, and hence, the use of tools such as Hadoop are needed to handle them. Big data enables raw data that may not be needed to be stored in its current state to be processed, and results can be yielded and saved from it (IBM, 2013). Hadoop and Big data, alongside traditional RDBMS and DW, all allow for a BI environment that is dynamic, quick, and accurate.

DISCUSSION AND REMARKS

From the material we've seen so far, we have introduced a many applications and definitions

in which Data Mining is used. We know now that BI is the use of special Data Mining software that uses special libraries in order to produce business-oriented information. In this section we shall discuss key terms and definition, and give answers and questions for further readings and discussion.

• What are data, information, and knowledge?

Understanding the difference is essential in the study of data mining in business. Data is raw source of pieces. These can be numbers, text, or pictures among many other types. Information is useful, or data that is understood by the handler. Knowledge is the most elusive form of data. Knowledge is *the* summation of a history of information that allows and gives the handler the wisdom needed to forecast and predict current and future trends and changes.

• What impact did Data Mining tools have on the engineering field?

Before the emergence and availability of Data Mining tools to the engineering field, expert human professionals, and even expert systems were used instead. These forms were based on heuristics that needed time, resources, and have had questionable results. With the availability of Data Mining techniques, data marts (specific and critical forms of queried data) which are produced from RDBMs, BI can be produced with high accuracy and less time. Industrial and manufacturing engineering fields benefit from Data Mining, in the form of planning, supply chain management, customer relationship, and future trends forecasting.

• What vendors provide DM for BI tools, and what are their costs ranges?

Providers include computing technology giants such as IBM and Microsoft. These types of software have very high costs and require a full-fledged IT environment, which have ETL tools, DWs, ERPs. Some vendors do provide DM tools for free using APIs for specific websites on the Internet and for limited academic use only. An example is Waikato Environment for Knowledge Analysis WEKA (Hall, M., Frank, E., Holmes, G., Pfahringer, B., Reutemann, P., & Witten, I. 2009).

- In the business field, what have BI tools introduced to the implementer?

BI tools allow for a dashboard that outputs statistics, charts, KPIs, as well as market trends for management and technical auditing. These outputs are the main inputs in developing strategies and day-to-day tactics of the business. BI output is determined by many factors, these include the quality of the data source, data marts, and the ETL tools among many others.

- Besides the future trends and challenges mentioned in this chapter, what further new trends and challenges await DM and BI?

The chapter discussed privacy, outsourcing, and handling unstructured data as future concerns as well as trends. Indeed marketing strategies and big business companies do involve the use of sensitive data to determine their user base and reach potential customers through spam. *But how much is too much?* What if the use was in the medical field, in order to produce drugs, using private and sensitive data? DM tools do pose a threat for individuals' privacy, since even surfing the Web, a DM tool can sift through the browser information to identify certain individuals through their surfing trends (access time, IP, visited websites, and search key-words).

Trends in DM tools in BI include real-time data processing using Hadoop, and since the data is live its types and sizes are variable, newer DM algorithms are indeed needed. Data Visualization

techniques are also incorporated into DM tools. Visualization allows BI output to be displayed live as graphs, charts, and as complex 3D models. Challenges in DM/BI tools and Visualization tools include interactivity and response levels in outputs during real-time analysis; quality of data sources; the efficiency of the algorithms used in the ETL and BI tools; and reliability of unstructured data processing.

CONCLUSION

Competitiveness today is the main driver for the use of BI tools. Organizations achieve competitiveness through the use of extensive BI tools highly integrated into their workflow. The software developments, along with hardware development, have made it possible more commercially available BI tools to be found and used. Revolution in the field of information brought in by the Internet and information technologies (DBMS, auditing and logging tools) have made a paradigm shift in how business works. BI utilizing these vast amounts of data can help in achieving competitive advantages through producing liable strategies; better customer relationships; effective resource planning; and fraudulence detection. BI tools have good ROI on engineering projects; although it takes considerable time to regain the investment. But the benefits are critical, such as predicting new market trends and innovations to occupy R&D activities. BI tools are heavily used in the engineering field, the usage range from supply chain management, to resource planning in industrial engineering. BI tools are usually found in big companies' environments since they require an elaborate IT environment, which include ETL tools, data mart schemes, DW, and ERPs. Providing such environment is usually costly.

Many challenges hinder the further development of such tools. The challenges are technological, ethical, and legislative. The more dependent we are on such tools, more obstacles must be dealt with in order to progress further ahead. Today, we see more development and innovation coming into the BI field, such as the cloud, Hadoop, and Big data. Cloud computing has been around for some time, and its perks and blessings are well known. BI tools can be provided through the cloud, which widens the user base for BI. Hadoop and Big data are relative newcomers that also allow for complementary roles in the BI environment. Hadoop systems can process Big data, which is a collection of large, unstructured, potentially varied forms of data. What can BI deduce from such data? As opposed to structured data stored in DWs and mined using DM, and analyzed using BI tools, Big data will definitely provide newer sources for BI tools that are capable of analyzing such sets. BI tools integrated into the IS and ERPs of companies will form the backbone for any business conducted in future years.

REFERENCES

Al-Mudimigh, A., Saleem, F., Ullah, Z., & Al-Aboud, F. (2009). Implementation of Data Mining Engine on CRM, Improve Customer Satisfaction. *International Conference on Information and Communication Technologies ICICT '09, 1*(2), 193–197.

Alexander, D. (2011). *Data Mining*. Retrieved March 7, 2012, from https://dea@tracor.com

Apte, C., Liu, B., Pednault, E., & Smyth, P. (2002). Business applications of data mining. *Communications of the ACM, 45*(8), 49–53. doi:10.1145/545151.545178

Atos. (2011). *Business Intelligence Solutions: Decisions That Are Better-Informed Leading to Long-Term Competitive Advantage*. Retrieved April 12, 2012, from https://atos.com

Ballard, C., Herreman, D., Schau, D., Bell, R., Kim, E., & Valencic, A. (1998). *Data Modeling Techniques for Data Warehousing*. Retrieved November 16, 2011, from www.redbooks.ibm.com/redbooks/pdfs/sg242238.pdf

BARC. (2013). *The BI Survey 12*. Retrieved April 24, 2013, from www.bi-survey.com/index.php?id=35

Boehm, B., Valerdi, R., & Honour, E. (2008). The ROI of Systems Engineering: Some Quantitative Results for Software-Intensive Systems. *Systems Engineering*, 1–14.

Chaudhuri, S., & Narasayya, V. (2011). New Frontiers in Business Intelligence. In *Proceedings of 37th International Conference on Very Large Data Bases* (pp. 1502–1503). Seattle, WA: Academic Press.

Chen, I., & Popovich, K. (2003). Understanding customer relationship management (CRM), people, process and technology. *Business Process Management Journal, 9*, 672–688. doi:10.1108/14637150310496758

Chen, M., Huang, C., Chen, K., & Wu, H. (2005). Aggregation of orders in distribution centers using data mining. *Expert Systems with Applications, 28*(3), 453–460. doi:10.1016/j.eswa.2004.12.006

Chhillar, R. (2008). Extraction Transformation Loading, a Road to Data Warehouse. In *Proceedings of Second National Conference Mathematical Techniques: Emerging Paradigms for Electronics and IT Industries* (pp. 384–388). Academic Press.

Choudhary, Harding, & Tiwari. (2008). Data Mining in Manufacturing: a Review Based on the Kind of Knowledge. *Journal of Intelligent Manufacturing*. ISSN: 0956-5515.

Desikan, P., Delong, C., Mane, S., Beemanapalli, K., Hsu, K., & Sriram, P. ... Venuturumilli, V. (2009). Web Mining for Business Computing. In Handbooks in Information Systems, (vol. 3). Emerald Group.

Dorronsoro, J., Ginel, F., Sanchez, C., & Cruz, C. (1997). Neural Fraud Detection in Credit Card Operations. *IEEE Transactions on Neural Networks*, 8(4), 827–834. doi:10.1109/72.595879 PMID:18255686

DTEK. (2011). *Utility firm will cut downtime by 20 percent and boost agility with Microsoft and SAP.* Retrieved April 23, 2013, from www.microsoft.com/casestudies/Microsoft-SQL-Server-2008-R2-Enterprise/DTEK/Utility-Firm-Will-Cut-Downtime-by-20-Percent-and-Boost-Agility-with-Microsoft-and-SAP/4000009335

Duan, L., & Da Xu, L. (2012). Business intelligence for enterprise systems: A survey. *IEEE Transactions on Industrial Informatics*, 8(3), 679–687. doi:10.1109/TII.2012.2188804

Economist. (2009). Globalization stalled: How global economic upheaval will hit the business environment [Special Report]. *The Economist*, pp. 1–37.

Elliott, T. (2011). *Hadoop, Big Data, and Enterprise Business Intelligence.* Retrieved April 21, 2013, from http://timoelliott.com/blog/2011/09/hadoop-big-data-and-enterprise-business-intelligence.html

Fayyad, U., Shapiro, G., & Smyth, P. (1996). From data mining to knowledge discovery in databases. *AI Magazine*, 17(3), 37–54.

Fethi, M., & Pasiouras, F. (2010). Assessing bank efficiency and performance with operational research and artificial intelligence techniques: A survey. *European Journal of Operational Research*, 204(2), 189–198. doi:10.1016/j.ejor.2009.08.003

Fitzsimons, M., Khabaza, T., & Shearer, C. (1993). The application of rule induction and neural networks for television audience prediction. In *Proceedings of Symposium on Information Based Decision Making in Marketing ESOMAR/EMAC/AFM* (pp. 69–82). Paris, France: ESOMAR/EMAC/AFM.

Hall, M., Frank, E., Holmes, G., Pfahringer, B., Reutemann, P., & Witten, I. (2009). The WEKA data mining software: an update. *Special Interest Group on Knowledge Discovery and Data Mining SIGKDD Explorer News*, 11(1), 10–18.

Hedfield, W. (2009). *Case study: Jaeger uses data mining to reduce losses from crime and waste.* Retrieved December 13, 2012, from http://www.computerweekly.com/feature/Case-study-Jaeger-uses-data-mining-to-reduce-losses-from-crime-and-waste

Hou, J. L., & Yang, S. T. (2006). Technology Mining Model Concerning Operation Characteristics of Technology and Service Providers. *International Journal of Production Research*, 44(16), 3345–3365. doi:10.1080/00207540500490996

Huyet, A. L. (2006). Optimization and analysis aid via data-mining for simulated production system. *European Journal of Operational Research*, 173, 827–838. doi:10.1016/j.ejor.2005.07.026

IBM. (2010). Great Canadian gaming corporation leverages IBM [Software Group Case Study]. *Cognos 8: Solutions for Financial Consolidation and Reporting Standardization.* Retrieved April 8, 2012, from http://www-01.ibm.com/software/success/cssdb.nsf/softwareL2VW?OpenView&Count=30&RestrictToCategory=cognos_Cognos8BusinessIntelligence&cty=en_us

IBM. (2011). *Forward view: Business intelligence breakthrough, no data warehouse required.* Retrieved April 6, 2012, from http//ibm.com/businesscenter/forwardview.com

IBM. (2013). *What Is Big Data?* IBM. Retrieved April 21, 2013, from www-01.ibm.com/software/data/bigdata/

Inmon, W. H. (1994). *Building the data warehouse.* J. Wiley & Sons.

Inmon, W. H. (1996). The data warehouse and data mining. *Communications of the ACM, 39*(11), 49–50. doi:10.1145/240455.240470

Kahraman, C., Kaya, I., Ulukan, H., & Ucal, I. (2010). Economic forecasting techniques and their application. In Business Intelligence in Economic Forecasting: Technologies and Techniques (pp. 19-44). IGI Global.

King, C., & O'Shea, D. (2003). *Estimating Return-on-Investment (ROI) for Texas Workforce Development Boards: Lessons Learned and Next Steps.* Paper presented at Texas Workforce Leadership of Texas. Austin, TX.

Kobielus, J. (2011). *Hadoop: What Is It Good For? Absolutely... Something.* Retrieved April 23, 2013, from blogs.forrester.com/james_kobielus/11-06-06-hadoop_what_is_it_good_for_absolutely_something

Laundon, K., & Laundon, J. (2011). *Management Information Systems: Managing the Digital Firm.* Pearson Education.

Lee, S., & Siau, K. (2001). A review of data mining techniques. *Industrial Management & Data Systems, 101*(1), 41–46. doi:10.1108/02635570110365989

Li, Y., Kramer, M., Beulens, A., & Vorst, J. (2010). A framework for early warning and proactive control systems in food supply chain networks. *Computers in Industry, 61*(9), 852–862. doi:10.1016/j.compind.2010.07.010

Microsoft. (2013). *Microsoft Dynamics.* Retrieved December 13, 2012, from www.microsoft.com/dynamics.com

Mikut, R., & Reischl, M. (2011). Data mining tools. *Wiley Interdisciplinary Reviews: Data Mining and Knowledge Discovery, 1*(5), 431–443.

Mine, I. T. (2010). *Web Mining, the E-Tailers' Holy Grail?* Retrieved November 23, 2012, from www.mineit.com

Mircea, M., Ghilic-Micu, B., & Stoica, M. (2007). Combining business intelligence with cloud computing to delivery agility in actual economy. *Journal of Economics, 2011,* 39–54.

Mocanu, A., Litan, D., Olaru, S., & Munteanu, A. (2010). Information systems in the knowledge based economy. *WSEAS Transactions on Business and Economics, 7*(1), 11–21.

Negash, S. (2004). Business intelligence. *Communications of the Association for Information Systems, 13,* 177–195.

Partridge, A. (2013). Business intelligence in the supply chain. *Inbound Logistics.* Retrieved September 6, 2013, from http://www.inboundlogistics.com/cms/article/business-intelligence-in-the-supply-chain/

Petrini, M., & Pozzebon, M. (2009). Managing Sustainability with the Support of Business Intelligence: Integrating Socio-Environmental Indicators and Organizational Context. *The Journal of Strategic Information Systems, 18*(4), 178–191. doi:10.1016/j.jsis.2009.06.001

Phan, D., & Vogel, D. (2010). A Model of Customer Relationship Management and Business Intelligence Systems for Catalogue and Online Retailers. *Information & Management, 47*(2), 69–77. doi:10.1016/j.im.2009.09.001

Phua, C., Lee, V., Smith, K., & Gayler, R. (2010). A Comprehensive Survey of Data Mining-Based Fraud Detection Research. *Cornell University Library.* Retrieved November 10, 2012, from http://arxiv.org/abs/1009.6119

Quinlan, J. (1986). Induction of Decision Trees. *Readings in Machine Learning*, *1*(1), 81–106. doi:10.1007/BF00116251

Raj, S., & Portia, A. (2011). Analysis on Credit Card Fraud Detection Methods. In *Proceedings of International Conference on Computers, Communication and Electrical Technology ICCCET* (pp. 152-156). Tamilnadu, India: ICCCET.

Ramakrishnan, T., Jones, M., & Sidorova, A. (2011). Factors Influencing Business Intelligence and Data Collection Strategies: An Empirical Investigation. *Decision Support Systems*, *52*(2), 486–496. doi:10.1016/j.dss.2011.10.009

Rao, S., & Swarup, S. (2001). Business Intelligence and Logistics. *Wipro Technologies*. Retrieved November 5, 2012, from http://idii.com/wp/bilogistics.pdf

Rodríguez, C., Daniel, F., Casati, F., & Cappiello, C. (2010). Toward Uncertain Business Intelligence: The Case of Key Indicators. *IEEE Internet Computing*, *14*(4), 32–40. doi:10.1109/MIC.2010.59

SAS. (2013). SAS business intelligence software. *SAS*. Retrieved April 22, 2013, from http://www.sas.com/technologies/bi/index.html

Schweighardt, C. (2010). *Calculating ROI to Realize Project Value*. Retrieved April 24, 2013, from www.isixsigma.com/operations/finance/calculating-roi-realize-project-value/

Shapiro, G., Brachman, R., & Khabaza, T. (1996). An Overview of Issues in Developing Industrial Data Mining and Knowledge Discovery Applications. In *Proceedings of Knowledge Discovery and Data Mining KDD-96 Proceedings* (pp. 89–95). ACM.

Smith, D. (2010). Using Data and Text Mining to Drive Innovation. SAS. *PhUSE 2010*. Retrieved December 10, 2012, from http://www.phusewiki.org/docs/2010/2010%20PAPERS/SP02%20Paper.pdf

Taipale, K. (2003). Data Mining and Domestic Security: Connecting the Dots to Make Sense of Data. *Columbia Science and Technology Law Review*, *5*(2), 83.

Thomsen, C., & Pedersen, T. B. (2009). A survey of open source tools for business intelligence. *International Journal of Data Warehousing and Mining*, *5*(3), 56–75. doi:10.4018/jdwm.2009070103

Van den Berg, J. P. (1999). A Literature Survey on Planning and Control of Warehousing Systems. *LIE Transactions*, *31*(8), 751–762.

Vellidoa, A., Lisboaa, P. J. G., & Vaughan, J. (1999). Neural Networks in Business: A Survey of Applications (1992–1998). *Expert Systems with Applications*, *17*(1), 51–70. doi:10.1016/S0957-4174(99)00016-0

Vijayan, J. (2011). *Hadoop finds niche alongside conventional database systems*. Retrieved April 22, 2013, from www.computerworld.com/s/article/358164/Hadoop_Works_Alongside_RDBMS

Zap Technology. (2010). *KFC/Pizza Hut makes efficiency gains with Zap Business Intelligence: Businesses become more agile, responsive and performance-focused, a case study*. Retrieved April 6, 2012, from http//www.zaptechnology.com

ADDITIONAL READING

Abello, A., & Romero, O. (2011). *Service-oriented business intelligence*. Berlin/Heidelberg, Germany: Springer-Verlag GmbH.

Abraham, A. (2003). Business Intelligence from Web Usage Mining. *Journal of Information & Knowledge Management*, 2(4), 375–390. doi:10.1142/S0219649203000565

Atsalakis, G. S., Valavanis, K. P., Zopounidis, C. D., & Nezis, D. (2010). Time Series Based House Sale Value Market Forecasting Using Genetically Evolved Neural Networks. In J. Wang, & S. Wang (Eds.), *Business Intelligence in Economic Forecasting: Technologies and Techniques* (pp. 265–282). United States of America: IGI Global. doi:10.4018/978-1-61520-629-2.ch014

Davey, N. KnowledgeBoard, (2011). Productivity Concerns Driving Business Intelligence Growth. Retrieved April 8, 2012, from http://www.knowledgeboard.com/item/3119/23/5/3

Fayyad, U., Piatetsky-Shapiro, G., & Smyth, P. (1996). From Data Mining to Knowledge Discovery in Databases. *AI Magazine. American Association for Artificial Intelligence AAAI*, 17(3), 37–54.

Girdzijauskas, S., & Streimikiene, D. (2010). Logistic Analysis of Business Cycles, Economic Bubbles and Crises. In J. Wang, & S. Wang (Eds.), *Business Intelligence in Economic Forecasting: Technologies and Techniques* (pp. 45–64). doi:10.4018/978-1-61520-629-2.ch003

Grabova, O., Darmont, J., Chauchat, J., & Zolotaryova, I. (2010). Business Intelligence for Small and Middle-Sized Enterprises. *Special Interest Group on Management of Data SIGMOD Record*, 39(2), 39–50.

Inmon, W. H. (1996). The Data Warehouse and Data Mining. *Communications of the ACM*, 39(11), 49–50. doi:10.1145/240455.240470

Kolker, A. (2012). *Business Intelligence and Data Mining*. New York: Springer.

Lahrmann, G., Marx, F., Winter, R., & Wortmann, F. (2011). Business Intelligence Maturity: Development and Evaluation of a Theoretical Model. *44th Hawaii International Conference on System Sciences HICSS* (pp. 1–10). Hawaii, United States of America.

Larson, D. (2012). Agile Methodologies for Business Intelligence. In A. Rahman El Sheikh, & M. Alnoukari (Eds.), *Business Intelligence and Agile Methodologies for Knowledge-Based Organizations: Cross-Disciplinary Applications* (pp. 101–119). United States of America: IGI Global.

Laundon, K., & Laundon, J. (2011). *Management Information Systems: Managing the Digital Firm*. Canada: Pearson Education.

Lawyer, J., & Chowdhury, S. (2004). Best Practices in Data Warehousing to Support Business Initiatives and Needs. *37th Annual Hawaii International Conference on System Sciences* (pp. 5–7). Hawaii, United States of America.

Liautaud, B. (2000). *E-Business Intelligence: Turning Information into Knowledge into Profit*. New York: McGraw-Hill.

Loshin, D. (2013). *Business Intelligence: The Savvy Manager's Guide*. United States of America: Morgan Kaufmann.

Lynn, K. (2012). *Search Fuels Business Intelligence for Decision Making. TNR Global*. Retrieved March 20, 2012, from http://www.tnrglobal.com/blog/tag/business-intelligence/

Martin, A., Manjula, M., & Venkatesan, V. P. (2011). A Business Intelligence Model to Predict Bankruptcy Using Financial Domain Ontology with Association Rule Mining Algorithm. *International Journal of Computer Science IJCSI*, 8(3), 3–2.

Mazón, J., Zubcoff, J. J., Garrigós, I., Espinosa, R., & Rodríguez, R. (2012). Open Business Intelligence: On The Importance of Data Quality Awareness in User-Friendly Data Mining. *Proceedings of the 2012 Joint EDBT/ICDT Workshops,* ACM (pp. 144–147). New York, United States.

Negash, S. (2004). Business Intelligence. *Communications of the Association for Information Systems, 13,* 177–195.

Olszak, C. M., & Ziemba, E. (2012). Critical Success Factors for Implementing Business Intelligence Systems in Small and Medium Enterprises on the Example of Upper Silesia, Poland. *Interdisciplinary Journal of Information, Knowledge, and Management, 7,* 129–150.

Seah, M., Hsieh, M. H., & Weng, P. (2010). *International Journal of Information Management, 30*(4), 368–373. doi:10.1016/j.ijinfomgt.2010.04.002

Vitt, E. Luckevich, & M., Misner, S. (2010). Business Intelligence. *Microsoft Press Books.* Retrieved March 22, 2012, from www.microsoft.com/mpress

Watson, H. J. (2009). Tutorial: Business Intelligence—Past, Present, and Future. *Communications of the Association for Information System.* Retrieved September 16, 2013, from http://aisel.aisnet.org/cais/vol25/iss1/39

Williams, S., & Williams, N. (2003). The Business Value of Business Intelligence. *Business Intelligence Journal, 2*(1), 38–42.

Williams, S., & Williams, N. (2007). *The Profit Impact of Business Intelligence.* United States of America: Morgan Kaufmann Publishing.

Yeoh, W. (2010). *Critical Success Factors for Business Intelligence Systems: Case Studies in Engineering Enterprises.* Germany: VDM Verlag Dr. Müller.

KEY TERMS AND DEFINITIONS

BI Software: Sophisticated enterprise level systems that provide BI capabilities.

Business Intelligence (BI): Acquiring business-oriented information through data mining.

Competitive Advantage: A differentiation point, a merit that other competitors lack.

Customer Experience Management (CEM): Systems that track customers' experiences during a period of time.

Customer Relationship Management (CRM): Systems that automate the process of handling customers.

Data Warehouse: Large, long-term data storage that transform data for analysis, mining and aggregation.

Enterprise Resource Planning (ERP): Software that manages all the different resources that an enterprise has: monetary, financial, human, and industrial resources.

Extraction, Transformation, and Loading (ETL): Process of transforming data to be kept in the data warehouse.

Information Economies: Economies driven by information technologies.

Supply Chain: The process of moving a product or service from the suppliers to customers.

Chapter 16
Population–Based Feature Selection for Biomedical Data Classification

Seyed Jalaleddin Mousavirad
University of Kashan, Iran

Hossein Ebrahimpour-Komleh
University of Kashan, Iran

ABSTRACT

Classification of biomedical data plays a significant role in prediction and diagnosis of disease. The existence of redundant and irrelevant features is one of the major problems in biomedical data classification. Excluding these features can improve the performance of classification algorithm. Feature selection is the problem of selecting a subset of features without reducing the accuracy of the original set of features. These algorithms are divided into three categories: wrapper, filter, and embedded methods. Wrapper methods use the learning algorithm for selection of features while filter methods use statistical characteristics of data. In the embedded methods, feature selection process combines with the learning process. Population-based metaheuristics can be applied for wrapper feature selection. In these algorithms, a population of candidate solutions is created. Then, they try to improve the objective function using some operators. This chapter presents the application of population-based feature selection to deal with issues of high dimensionality in the biomedical data classification. The result shows that population-based feature selection has presented acceptable performance in biomedical data classification.

INTRODUCTION

Data mining or knowledge discovery is a computational process of extracting hidden knowledge in large databases. The goal of data mining process is to extract useful information from a dataset. Figure 1 illustrates the phases of a data mining

process. The first step in data mining process is to understanding of the problem. In the next step, data collect and prepare. In this step, data is cleaned from outlier instances or missing data and dataset reduces to only variables that are useful in a given data mining process. In the third step, a mining model or model is built. The quality of a model

DOI: 10.4018/978-1-4666-6086-1.ch016

Figure 1. The data mining process

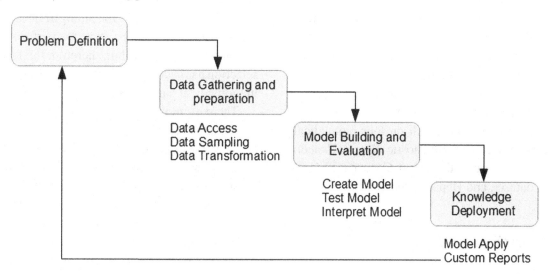

can evaluate using a number of the techniques. The last step in the data mining process is to deploy the models to a real environment.

Data mining techniques have been successfully used in various biomedical domains, for example the detection of tumors, the diagnosis of cancers and other diseases. One of the main challenge in biomedical data mining and analysis is the so called "curse of dimensionality". Especially the biomedical data are presented by relatively few instances and exhibited in a high dimensional feature space(Peng, Wu, & Jiang, 2010). Feature selection, a process in data transformation phase, reduces the number of features, removes irrelevant, redundant and misleading features, which leads to expediting learning algorithm and improves predictive performance. Feature selection algorithms are divided into three categories: wrapper methods that uses the learning algorithms to evaluate the usefulness of features, filter methods that evaluate features according to the statistical characteristics of the data, and embedded methods that feature selection embed in the learning algorithm. Population based metaheuristics such as genetic algorithm, particle swarm optimization, Imperialist competitive algorithm, artificial bee

algorithm, Ant colony optimization, and leap frog optimization have been considered as effective wrapper feature selection approach. These metaheuristics are based on a population of solutions and an iterative procedure. At each iteration, they try to find a better solution than previous solutions using some operators. Feature selection algorithms have been successfully applied in various biomedical domains. A. Antoniadis et al, (2003) presented a statistical feature reduction approach for the classification of tumors. I. Guyan et al, (2002) address the problem of selection of a small subset of genes from broad patterns of gene expression data, recorded on DNA micro-arrays. Using available training examples from cancer and normal patients, they build a classifier suitable for genetic diagnosis, as well as drug discovery. In another work, wrapper approaches was applied for gene selection(Blanco, Larrañaga, Inza, & Sierra, 2004). Y. Peng et al. (2010) presents a novel feature selection approach to deal with issues of high dimensionality in biomedical data classification. The approach proposed in this paper integrated filter and wrapper methods into a sequential search procedure with the aim to improve the classification performance of the features selected. In this chapter, we focus on application of population based feature selection algorithms for biomedical data classification. To this purpose, four population based metaheuristics are considered: genetic algorithm, particle swarm optimization, artificial bee algorithm, and imperialist competitive algorithm. We also analyze the efficiency of this approach on four biomedical dataset: Wisconsin Diagnostic Breast Cancer, Wisconsin Prognostic Breast Cancer, SPECTF heart dataset, and Hepatitis diagnosis.

FEATURE SELECTION

Data mining techniques have been successfully applied in various biomedical domains such as the diagnosis of disease and the detection of tumors. A major problem associated with biomedical data mining and analysis is the so-called "curse of dimensionality". Curse of dimensionality refers to the rapid increase in volume of the space associated with adding extra dimensions to a space(Abraham, Grosan, & Pedrycz, 2008). Peaking phenomenon illustrates that for a given sample size, there is a maximum number of features which there can be

before the performance of classification algorithm starts to reduce (Figure 2). Excluding irrelevant and redundant features can promote the performance of classification algorithm, therefore the feature selection has become one of the main sub-domain in biomedical data mining

There is more than one reason for feature selection(Theodoridis S., 2008):

First, the use of more features may not always improve the performance, it can even increase computational complexity. Sometimes, many features are available, but because of high mutual correlation, these features are not independent. An inappropriate feature extremely reduce the performance of classification algorithm. Thus, it may increases complexity without increase in performance.

Second, a large number of features is directly associated into a large number of classifier parameters (e.g., weights in a neural network). According to the minimum description length (MDL) principle(Barron, Rissanen, & Yu, 1998) a simple model is better than a complex model. A complex model may overfit the training data and its performance on test data reduce. Thus, it may reduce good generalization capabilities.

Figure 2. Peaking phenomenon

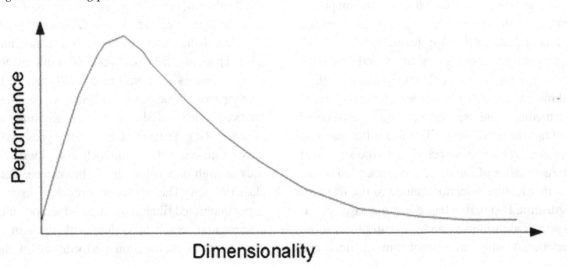

Third, fewer features can decrease the computational costs. It is important for real time applications.

Finding the appropriate features with N number of features need to evaluate 2^N possible subset. For example, selecting the best features out of 25 means that 33554432 feature sets must be considered. Therefore, we must regard methods of searching through the space of features so that reduce the amount of computations.

There are three general strategies for feature selection:

1. Filter strategies: In this strategy, features are ranked according to a scoring function, and the highest ranked features are selected. They are independent of learning algorithm (Figure 3.a).
2. Wrapper strategies: Learning algorithms is used as a main part of this strategy. Wrapper

methods are generally more accurate than filter methods but it is more computationally expensive (Figure 3.b).

3. Embedded strategies: In this strategy, feature selection process not be separated from the learning process such as decision trees.

Sequential forward selection (SFS) and Sequential backward selection (SBS) are one of the most popular search algorithm for feature selection. SFS starts with an empty selection of features. At each step, a feature add to selected feature set that it maximize objective function when combine with the previous selected features. SBS works in the opposite direction of SFS. SBS algorithm starts from the full set of features, then at each step, a feature which results in the smallest decrease in the value of fitness function is removed. Notice that removal of a feature may lead to an increase in the objective function.

Figure 3. a. Filter method. b. Wrapper method.

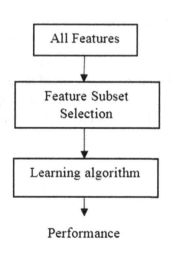

a

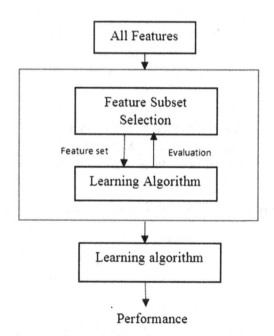

b

POPULATION BASED METAHEURISTICS

Metaheuristics are a branch of optimization in computer science which is design to solve approximately optimization problems. They employ some degree of randomness to find optimal solutions(Luke, 2010). Application of Metaheuristics falls into a large number of research areas and industries such as engineering design, system modeling, and planning in routing problems. In designing a Metaheuristic, two conflicting criteria must be taken: exploration of the search space that its goal the generation of new solutions in untested regions of the search space and exploitation of the search space that concentrate on the search in the vicinity of good solutions(Talbi, 2009). A metaheuristic will be successful on a given optimization problem if it can provide a tradeoff between the exploitation and the exploration. These algorithms can be divided into two categories(Talbi, 2009):

- Single solution based Metaheuristics (S-Metaheuristics): these algorithms (e.g., simulated annealing, tabu search) starts with a single initial solution and move away from it. These Metaheuristics are exploitation oriented and allow better intensification the search in local regions.
- Population based Metaheuristics (p-metaheuristics): these algorithms (e.g., evo-

lutionary algorithms, swarm intelligence) deal with a set of solutions rather than a single solution. They are exploration oriented and make a better diversification in the whole search space.

Population based metaheuristics can be seen as an iterative process in a population of candidate solutions. First, a population of solutions is initialized. Then, a new population is iteratively generated using some operators. In the next step, this new population is integrated into the current one using some selection operators. The search space is stopped when a termination condition is satisfied. Algorithms such as genetic algorithm (GA), particle swarm optimization (PSO), ant colony optimization (ACO), artificial immune systems (AIS), and imperialist competitive algorithm (ICA) belong to this category of metaheuristics. Figure 4 presents the general scheme of p- metaheuristics. In this chapter, four p- metaheuristics is considered: genetic algorithm, particle swarm optimization, artificial bee algorithm, and imperialist competitive algorithm.

GENETIC ALGORITHM

Genetic algorithm (GA) is a population based metaheuristic that mimics the process of neutral selection. This algorithm has been developed by J.Holland in the 1970. This metaheuristic exten-

Figure 4. The general scheme of population based metaheuristics

Begin
    INITIALIZE population with random candidate solutions ($p = p_0$);
    EVALUATE each candidate;
    T=0;
    REPEAT UNTIL (*TERMINATION CONDITION* is satisfied) *DO*
        GENERATE a new population ($p_t^{'}$);
        SELECT new population ($p_{t+1} = select\_population(p_t \cup p_t^{'})$);
        T=T+1;
    End
End

sively is applied in different scientific fields such as bioinformatics, computational science, engineering, and economics. GA encodes the problem variables into strings. Each string, called individual or chromosome, represents a candidate solution. The initial population of chromosomes randomly is created. Then, chromosomes are evaluated with a fitness function. Fitness function determines the quality of each candidate solution. Chromosomes with more fitness function are selected from the current population and each chromosome is modified to form a new generation using crossover and mutation operators. Crossover operator exchanges and combines selected parent chromosomes to create new offspring. Mutation randomly changes offspring resulted from crossover. It increases the exploration of the GA. This process continue until a termination condition is satisfied. Figure 5 shows the flowchart of the GA.

PARTICLE SWARM OPTIMIZATION

Particle swarm optimization (PSO) is a population based optimization inspired by the movement and intelligence of swarms. It was developed by James Kennedy and Russell Eberhart in 1995.

This algorithm combine self-experience with social experience. Similar to GA, it starts with a population of candidate solution called particle. Unlike GA, PSO has no evolution operator such as crossover and mutation. The particles fly through the problem space by following the current optimum particles. Each particle then determines its movement through the search space by combining some aspect of the history of its own current and best (best-fitness) locations with those of one or more members of the swarm, with some random perturbations. The next iteration takes place after all particles have been moved. Eventually the swarm as a whole, like a flock of birds collectively foraging for food, is likely to move close to an optimum of the fitness function(Poli, Kennedy, & Blackwell, 2007). Figure 6 shows the flowchart of the PSO.

ARTIFICIAL BEE ALGORITHM

Artificial bee algorithm(ABA) is a new population based algorithm developed in 2005(Karaboga, 2005; Pham et al., 2006). It mimics the food foraging behavior of swarms of honey bees. In its basic version, the algorithm performs a kind

Figure 5. The flowchart of GA

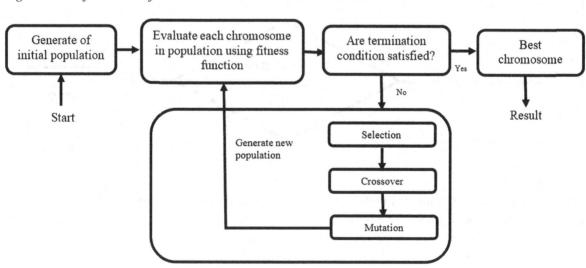

Figure 6. The flowchart of PSO

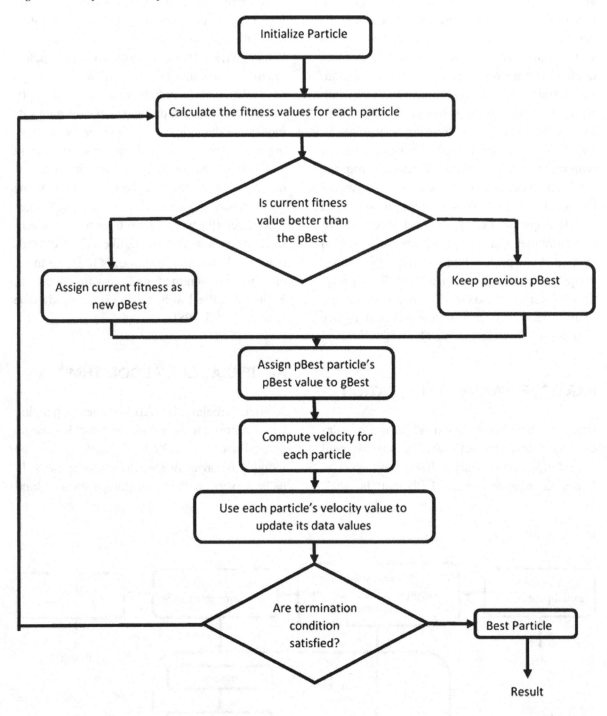

of neighborhood search combined with random search. A colony of honey bees can extend itself over long distances and in multiple directions simultaneously to exploit a large number of food sources. In principle, flower patches with plentiful amount of nectar or pollen that can be collected with less effort should be visited by more bees, whereas, patches with less nectar or pollen should receive fewer bees. The foraging process begins in a colony by scout bees being sent out to search for promising flower patches. Scout bees move randomly from one patch to another. During the harvest season, a colony continuous its exploration, keeping a percentage of population as scout bees. When the scout bees return to the hive, those that found a patch which is rated above a certain quality threshold (measured as a combination of some constituents, such as sugar content) deposit their nectar or pollen and go to the "dance floor" to perform a dance known as "waggle dance". The waggle dance is essential for colony communication, and contains three pieces of information regarding a flower patch:

- The direction in which it will be found.
- Its distance from the hive.
- Its quality rating (or fitness)

This information helps the colony to send its bees to flower patches precisely, without using guides or maps. After the waggle dance on the dancing floor, the dances (i.e. scout bee) goes back to the flower patch with follower bees that are waiting inside the hive. More follower bees are sent to more promising patches(Pham et al., 2006). Figure 7 shows the pseudo code for this algorithm.

IMPERIALIST COMPETITIVE ALGORITHM

Imperialist competitive algorithm (ICA) is a novel population based optimization method that has recently been introduced for dealing with different kinds of optimization problem(Atashpaz-Gargari & Lucas, 2007; Gargari, Hashemzadeh, Rajabioun, & Lucas, 2008). This algorithm is based on sociopolitical process of imperialist competition. Similar other population based algorithms, it starts with a set of candidate random solutions in the search space called countries. Some of the best initial countries become imperialists and the rest form the colonies of these imperialists. Figure 8 shows the initial population of each empire.

After dividing colonies between imperialists, each empire try to improve the economy, culture and political situations of their colonies. According to this policy, colonies move toward their related imperialist countries. This movement is based on assimilation policy. In ICA, revolution is a sudden change in the position of some countries in the search space. It increases the exploration of the algorithm. The total power of an empire depends on both the power of the imperialist country and the power of its colonies. Imperialist competition among empires forms the basis of ICA. According to the imperialist competition, the most powerful

Figure 7. The pseudo code for bee algorithm (Pham et al., 2006)

1. Initialize population with random solutions.

2. Evaluate fitness of the population.

3. While (stopping criterion not met).

4. Select sites for neighborhood search.

5. Recruit bees for selected sites (more bees for best e sites) and evaluate finesses.

6. Select the fittest bee from each patch.

7. Assign remaining bees to search randomly and evaluate their finesses.

8. End While.

Figure 8. Generating the initial empires

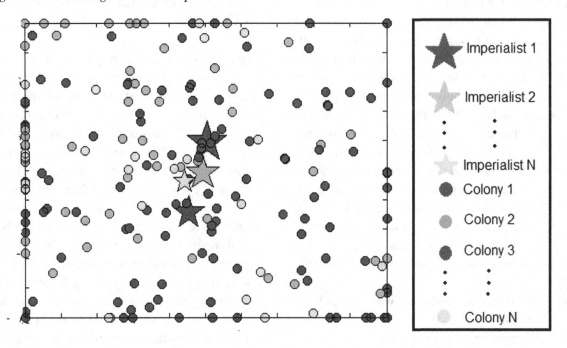

empires tend to increase their power while weak empires collapse. In imperialist competition, all empires try to take possession of colonies of other empires and control them. This is modeled by just picking some of the weakest colony of the weakest empires and making a competition among all empires to possess these colonies. Figure 9 shows a picture of the modeled imperialist competition.

Algorithm continues until a termination condition is satisfied such as just one imperialist will remain. Figure 10 shows the flowchart of the ICA.

POPULATION BASED FEATURE SELECTION

The goal of feature selection is to optimize the number of features so it can be said that Feature selection is an optimization problem. Therefore, different optimization methods can be applied for feature selection. One of the optimization methods is population based metaheuristics. In this chapter, population based metaheuristics is used for feature selection in biomedical data classification. For this purpose, GA, PSO, ABA, and ICA as population based metaheuristics are employed for feature selection.

The Structure of Feature Selection Problem in Population Based Optimization

In the GA, each chromosome represents the possible solutions in the search space. They are explained by a $1 \times N_{var}$ dimension array. These arrays are defined by:

$$chromosome = [p_1, p_2, ..., p_{N_{var}}]$$

In this problem, each chromosome is a string of binary numbers. When value of a cell of array is 1, the corresponding feature is selected and when it is 0, it is not selected. Figure 11 demonstrates

Figure 9. Imperialist competition. The more powerful empire will possess the weakest colony of the weakest empire.

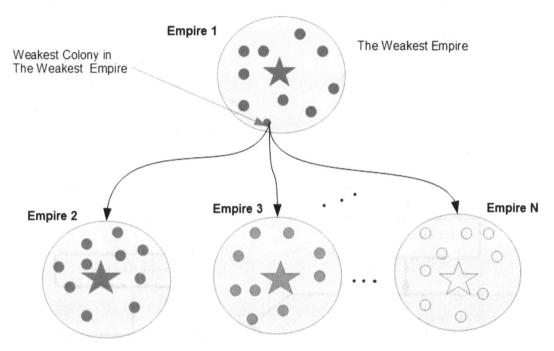

the chromosome representation in this problem. Countries in ICA, particles in PSO, and food sources in ABA are similar to chromosomes in GA.

Cost (Fitness) Function

The fitness value of a chromosome is defined as the classification error of support vector machine (SVM). It is defined as follows:

$$Cost(Fitness) = 1 - \frac{\text{Number of correctly classified samples}}{\text{Total number of samples}}$$

SVM is a supervised learning algorithm which is used for pattern classification. The basic idea of SVM is to construct a hyperplane as decision line. There are many hyperplanes that might classify the instances. The distance from the hyperplane to the closest instances determines the margin of the classifier. SVM choose the maximum margin

hyperplane. Cost function in ICA, and fitness in PSO and ABA correspond to fitness function in GA.

GA Based Feature Selection

The steps of the GA based feature selection are demonstrated in details in the following subsections.

Step 1: Initialization of the parameters of GA.

First, some parameters of GA are initialized such as the population size POP_{Size}, the mutation probability pr_{mu}, the crossover probability pr_{cr}, and the maximum itertation max_{itr}. The current iteration with Itr is denoted.

Step 2: Generating of the initial population.

In the beginning, an initial population of size POP_{Size} is randomly created.

Figure 10. The flowchart of ICA

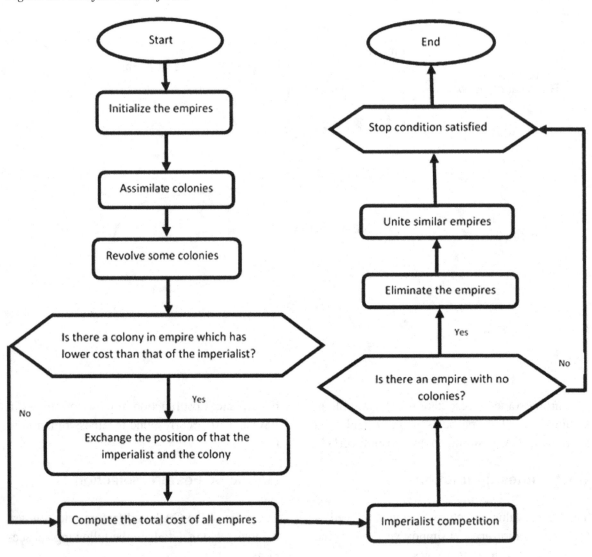

Figure 11. An example of country (chromosome) representation in the feature selection problem

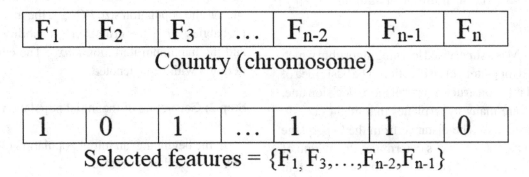

Step 3: Evaluation of each chromosome in the population using the fitness function.

Step 4: Parent Selection.

In this step, the better chromosomes become parents. Parent selection is typically probabilistic. Chromosomes with the better fitness get a higher chance to become parents than the lower fitness. The simplest method of parent selection is the roulette wheel algorithm. The pseudo code of this algorithm is shown in the Figure 12.

Step 5: Crossover.

In this step, two parents combine and two children create using crossover operator. One point crossover is used for this chapter. It works by choosing a random number in the range $[0, n-1]$ (n is the length of chromosome), then both parents are split at this point and two children are created by exchanging the tails. This process is shown in Figure 13.

Step 6: Mutation.

This operator increases the exploration of genetic algorithm. Mutation allows each bit to flip with a small probability pr_{mu}. An example of this operator is shown in Figure 14.

Step 7: Evaluation of new candidates.

Step 8: Selection of chromosomes for the next generation based on fitness function.

Step 10: Increasing of Itr variable ($Itr++$).

Step 11: If Itr parameter is greater than max_{itr} parameter ($Itr > max_{Itr}$) Algorithm is finished, otherwise go to the step 4.

PSO Based Feature Selection

The steps of the PSO based feature selection are demonstrated in details in the following subsections.

Step 1: Initializing of the parameters of PSO

First, some parameters of PSO are initialized such as population size (POP_{size}), maximum velocity of particles (Max_v), maximum iteration (Max_{itr}). In addition, Pbest(i)=0 and Gbest=0. The current iteration with Itr is denoted.

Step 2: Generating of the population of size POP_{size}.

Step 3: Evaluation of particles with fitness function.

Step 4: Compare the performance of each particles to its best performance thus far: if current

Figure 12. The pseudo code of roulette wheel algorithm

```
For all chromosomes of population
    Sum+=fitness of this chromosome
End for
For all chromosomes of population
    Probability=sum of probabilies + (fitness/sum)
    Sum of probability += probability
End for
    rand_number=a rand number between 0 and 1
For each chromosome i
    If rand_number> probability
        Return i
    End if
End for
```

Figure 13. One-point crossover

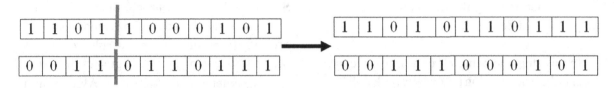

Figure 14. Bitwise mutation

value is better than Pbest, then assign Pbest value equal to the current value and the Pbest location equal to the current location:

```
If (Fitness(i)>Pbest(i))
            {
Pbest(i)=Fitness(i);  x_{Pbest} = x_i(t)  }
```

Step 5: Compare the performance of each particles with the population's overall previous best thus far (Gbest):

```
            If (Fitness(i)>Gbest(i))
            { Gbest(i)=Fitness(i);
x_{Gbest} = x_i(t)  }
```

Step 6: Update particles and position according to the below equations:

$$v_i(t+1) =$$

$$v_i(t) + \rho_1 \left(\overrightarrow{x_{Pbest_i}} - \overrightarrow{x(t)} \right) + \rho_2 \left(\overrightarrow{x_{Gbest}} - \overrightarrow{x(t)} \right)$$

$$\overrightarrow{x_i}(t+1) = \overrightarrow{x_i}(t) + \overrightarrow{v}(t+1)$$

Step 7: Increase *Itr* variable (*Itr* ++)

Step 8: If *Itr* parameter is greater than Max_{itr} parameter ($Itr > max_{Itr}$) Algorithm is finished, otherwise go to the step 3.

ABA Based Feature Selection

Step 1: Initializing of the parameters of ABA.

First, some parameters of ABA algorithm are initialized such as Maximum Iteration (Max_{itr}), number of scout bees(N_{scout}), number of sites selected out of N_{scout} visited sites(N_{site}), number of bees recruited for best N_{site} sites($\text{N}_{recruited}$). The current iteration with *Itr* is denoted.

Step 2: Initialize population with random solutions (N_{scout}).

Step 3: Evaluate fitness of the population with fitness function.

Step 4: Select sites for neighborhood search (N_{site}): bees that have the highest fitness are chosen as "selected bees" and sites visited by them are chosen for neighborhood search.

Step 5: Recruit bees for selected sites (more bees for best e sites) and evaluate fitness.

Step 6: Select the fittest bee from each patch: For each patch, only the bee with the highest fitness will be selected to form the next bee population.

Step 7: Assign remaining bees to search randomly and evaluate their finesses.

Step 8: Increase Itr variable ($Itr++$).

Step 9: If Itr parameter is greater than Max_{itr} parameter ($Itr > max_{Itr}$) Algorithm is finished, otherwise go to the step 3.

ICA Based Feature Selection

The steps of the imperialist competition based feature selection are demonstrated in details in the following subsections.

Step1: Initialization of the parameters of ICA.

First, some parameters of ICA are initialized such as the population size (POP_{size}), the number of the countries *NumOfCountries,* the number of imperialists *NumOfImp*, and the number of colonies *NumOfCol,* which satisfy the condition as follows:

$$NumOfCountries = NumOfImp + NumOfCol$$

The maximum iteration max_{Dec} and the current iteration with Dec are denoted. The starting iteration $Dec = 1$ are initialized.

Step 2: Generating of the countries.

In the beginning, an initial population of size POP_{size} is randomly created. The cost value of a country is defined as the classification error of SVM classifier. These countries (*NumOfCoun-*

tries) is divided into imperialists and colonies. Imperialists (*NumOfImp)* are countries with lower value of cost function (the best countries), and the remaining countries are colonies.

Step 3: Generating the initial empires.

To form the initial empires, the colonies are distributed among the imperialists with respect to the power of each imperialist. For this purpose, the normalized cost of an imperialist is defined by:

$$C_n = c_n - \max_i\{c_i\}$$

where c_n is the cost of nth imperialist and C_n is its normalized cost. Finally, the normalized power for each imperialists is defined by

$$P_n = \frac{|C_n|}{\left|\sum_{i=1}^{NumOfImp} C_i\right|}$$

The normalized power of an imperialist represents the approximate of number of initial colonies that this imperialists possess, and it is given by:

$$N.C._n = round(p_n.NumOfCol)$$

where $N.C._n$ is the initial number of colonies of the nth empire.

Step 4: Movement of colonies toward the imperialist (Assimilation)

In the assimilation step, all colonies in the same empire move toward their corresponding imperialists. Original ICA operates on continuous optimization problems but feature selection is a discrete problem. Therefore, a new assimilation operator is applied which is suitable for discrete problems. This operator is demonstrates in Figure 15. In this operator, the city block distance is used. The city block distance between two points, *a* and *b*, with *k* dimensions is calculated as:

$$\sum_{j=1}^{k} | a_j - b_j |$$

Step 5: Revolution.

Revolution is a sudden change in the position of some countries in the search space. This process can be helpful in escaping local optima. It increases the exploration of the ICA. In this operator, for each colony a random number between 0 and 1 is generated in each iteration. Then, this value is compared with revolution probability (P_R). If random number is lower than P_R, revolution operator is performed.

Step 6: Imperialist movement.

In the original ICA, imperialists never change and this fixed situation can lead to lose global optima or prevent to achieve better solutions. Imperialist movement is a new operator which is increased the exploitation of the ICA. In this approach, a random movement is assumed for each imperialist in each iteration and the cost of this new position is calculated. If the cost of new position is less than the cost of previous one,

the imperialists move to new position(Soltani-Sarvestani & Lotfi, 2012).

Step 6: Exchanging position of the colony and its imperialist.

After assimilation for all colonies and revolution for some them, a colony might reach a position with lower cost than the imperialist. In such a case, the imperialist and the colony switch their position. Then algorithm continue by the new imperialist.

Step 7: Computing total cost of an empire.

Total power of an empire depends on the power of imperialists and its colonies. But the main power in one empire is imperialist power and colonies power has lower impact. The equation of total cost is defined as follows:

$$T.C._n = Cost\{imperialist_n\}$$
$$+\xi mean\{Cost\{colonies\ of\ empire_n\}\}$$

where $T.C._n$ is the total cost of the *n*th empire and ξ is a positive number which is considered to be less than 1.

Step 8: *Imperialist Competition.*

This step forms the basis of the ICA. Imperialist competition is modeled by just picking one of the weakest colonies of the weakest empire and mak-

Figure 15. The used assimilation operator

For each imperialist and their colonies **do**
- Calculate city block distance (*D*) between each colony and their imperialist
- Create an array of binary string (*S*) of length *N* with initial value of zero
- Assign 1 to some array cells proportional to *D*.
- Copy the cells from the imperialist correspond to location of the '1's in the *S* to the same position in the colony.

End

ing a competition among all empires to possess this colony. To start the competition, the weakest colony of the weakest empire is chosen and then, the possession probability of each empire based on its total power is calculated. The normalized total cost of an empire is simply obtained by

$$N.T.C._n = T.C._n - \max_i\{T.C._i\}$$

where $T.C._n$ and $N.T.C._n$ are the total cost and the normalized total cost of the n empire, respectively. The possession probability of each empire is given by:

$$P_{emp_n} = \left| \frac{N.T.C._n}{\sum_{i=1}^{N_{imp}} N.T.C._n} \right|$$

To divide the mentioned colonies among empires vector P is formed as following

$$P = [P_{p_1}, P_{p_2}, ..., P_{p_{NumOfImp}}]$$

Then the vector R with the same size as P whose elements are uniformly distributed random number is created

$$R = [r_1, r_2, ..., r_{NumOfEmp}]$$

$$r_1, r_2, ..., r_{NumOfImp} \sim U(0,1)$$

The vector D is formed by subtracting R form P

$$D = P - R = [D_1, D_2, ..., D_{NumOfImp}]$$
$$= [P_{p_1} - r_1, P_{p_2} - r_2, ..., P_{p_{NumOfImp}} - r_{NumOfImp}]$$

Finally, Referring to vector D the mentioned colony is given to an empire whose relevant index in D is maximized.

Step 9: Eliminating the weak empires.

In this step, empires without colony is eliminated.

Step 10: Increase Dec variable ($Dec++$).
Step 11: If Dec parameter is greater than $\max_{Dec}$ parameter ($Dec > max_{Dec}$) Algorithm is finished, otherwise go to the step 4.

APPLICATION TO BIOMEDICAL DATA CLASSIFICATION

In this section, the results of some experiments on biomedical data classification is presented to evaluate the effectiveness of the population based feature selection methods. All of the used datasets are obtained from the machine learning data repository of the University of California(Merz, Murphy, & Aha, 2012). In all experiments, k fold cross validation is used. In the k fold cross validation, the dataset is randomly partitioned into k equally size segment (fold). One segment is retained as the test dataset, and the remaining k-1 segment are used as training dataset. The cross validation process is then repeated k times, where one of segments becomes test dataset each time. The average of k results are used as estimation of the accuracy. The accuracy measure employed for evaluating of the efficiency of feature selection methods.

Wisconsin Diagnostic Breast Cancer

Wisconsin Diagnostic Breast Cancer Data Set (WDBC) is created by William H.wolberg at university of Wisconsin. The goal of this dataset is the diagnosis of breast cancer diseases. In this dataset, extracted Features are computed from digitized images of fine needle aspirate (FNA) of breast masses. They describe characteristics of the cell nuclei present in the image(Merz et al., 2012). Figure 16 shows a sample of these images. This data set contains 569 observations among which 357 are benign cases and 212 are malignant cases. In this dataset, 10 real valued features for each cell nucleus is extracted:

1. Radius (mean of distances from center to points on the perimeter),
2. Texture (standard deviation of gray-scale values),
3. Perimeter,
4. Area,
5. Smoothness (local variation in radius lengths),
6. Compactness ($\frac{(perimeter)^2}{(area - 1)}$),
7. Concavity (severity of concave portions of the contour),
8. Concave points (number of concave portions of the contour),
9. Symmetry,
10. Fractal dimension (coastline approximation - 1).

Then, mean, standard error, and worst mean these features are computed. This process resulted in 30 features for each image.

Extracted features include a range of different values. Features with large values may have a large influence in the objective function than features with small values. Feature values lie within similar ranges by normalizing features. One of the straightforward normalization techniques is the estimates of mean and variance.

This technique is defined by:

$$\overline{x}_k = \frac{1}{N}\sum_{i=1}^{N} x_{ik}, \qquad k = 1, 2, ..., l$$

$$\sigma_k^2 = \frac{1}{N-1}\sum_{i=1}^{N}(x_{ik} - \overline{x}_k)$$

$$\widehat{x}_{ik} = \frac{x_{ik} - \overline{x}_k}{\sigma_k}$$

where x_{ik} is the kth feature of ith instance, N is the number of features, x_k is the mean of kth feature, σ_k^2 is variance, and $\widehat{x}_{ik}$ is the normalized

Figure 16. Fine noodle biopsies of breast. a. Malignant and b. benign breast tumors.

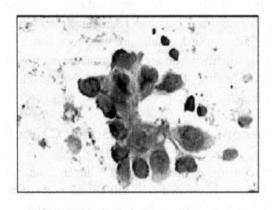

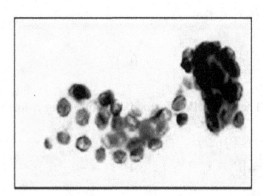

a

b

features. After feature normalization, all features will have zero mean and unit variance.

After feature extraction and normalization, the best features is selected. The population based feature selection approaches are applied to feature selection process. These methods are described in the previous section. An example of the process of the population based feature selection searching for optimal solutions for WDBC Data Set is given in Figure 17 and 18. In the Figure 17, the mean classification error at each iteration are presented. Figure 18 presents the minimum classification error at each iteration. Figure 19 shows the evolution of the search for the best number of features.

In order to show the accuracy and efficiency of the population based feature selection, the performance of these algorithms are compared with SFS and SBS feature selection. Table 1

shows the result of classification of WDBC dataset using all features. The results of feature selection are presented in the Table 2. According to these tables, all algorithms were used to select features considerably increase the performance of classification. In addition, ICA based feature selection is presented the better mean accuracy and the lower standard deviation compare with the other methods used.

Wisconsin Prognostic Breast Cancer

Similar to WDBC dataset, Wisconsin Prognostic Breast Cancer (WPBC) dataset is the result of the effort made at the university of Wisconsin hospital for the prognosis of breast tumors based on FNA test. The WPBC dataset consists of 198 instance which each instance represents follow up

Figure 17. Average classification error for each iteration in the WDBC dataset

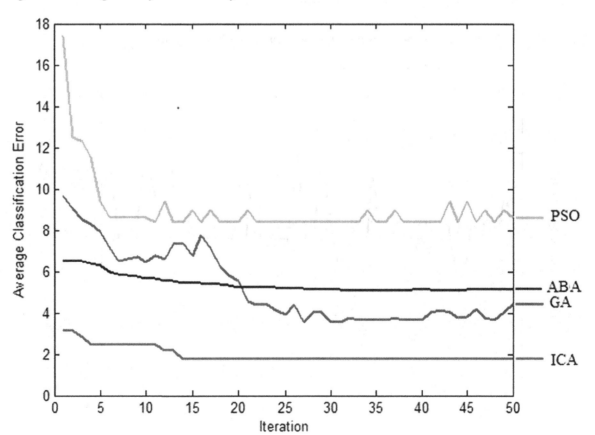

Figure 18. Minimum classification error for each iteration in the WDBC dataset

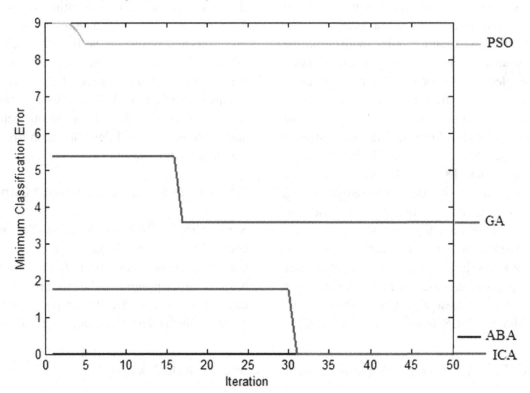

Figure 19. The Best number of features for each iteration in the WDBC dataset

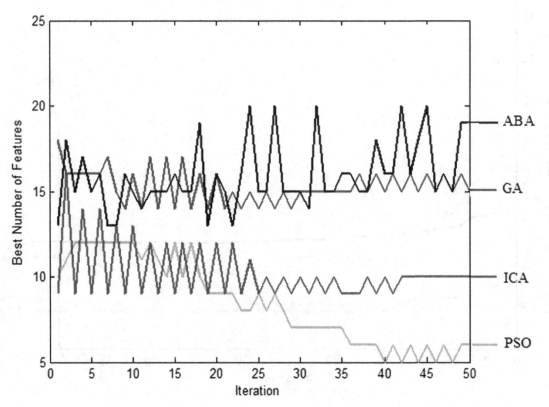

Table 1. Classification results using all features on WDBC dataset

Method	Classification Accuracy							
	Training Set				Test Set			
	Mean	Std. Dev.	Max.	Min.	Mean	Std. Dev.	Max.	Min.
SVM without feature selection	83.62	6.63	91.26	76.17	76.32	7.71	79.63	68.45

Table 2. Classification results using selected features on WDBC dataset

Method	Classification Accuracy							
	Training Set				Test Set			
	Mean	Std. Dev.	Max.	Min.	Mean	Std. Dev.	Max.	Min.
GA-FS	99.45	0.45	100	98.80	98.25	2.08	100	95.64
PSO_FS	94.36	0.23	97.85	95.89	91.72	0.43	92.38	91.21
ABA_FS	98.65	0.34	100	98.04	97.02	2.48	100	92.98
ICA_FS	99.96	0.02	99.98	99.91	99.95	0.04	100	99.89
SFS	98.64	0.86	99.20	97.22	97.54	1.61	99.1	95.98
SBS	98.83	0.76	99.00	97.81	98.24	1.92	99.34	95.74

data for on breast cancer case. Each instance has 34 attribute. The first two attribute corresponds to the prognosis status (recur/non-recur) and the recurrence time (Time to recur-TTR). The last two attributes are the diameter of the excised tumor (in cm) and the number of positive axillary lymph nodes observed at time of surgery(Merz et al., 2012). The rest of attributes are similar to the above mentioned 30 features in WDBC dataset. In this dataset, lymph node values is missing in 4 instance.

Handling Missing Value

Depending on objective in data mining, instances with missing values must be removed or replaced by some estimates. In this chapter, k nearest neighbor imputation are used. In this method, missing values replace (impute) with the corresponding values calculated from the k nearest neighbor in Euclidean distance. The Euclidean distance is defined as follows:

$$E(a,b) = \sqrt{\sum_{i \in D} (x_{ai} - x_{bi})^2}$$

where $E(a,b)$ is the Euclidean distance between the two instance a,b, x_{ai} and x_{bi} are the values of feature i in instances a and b, respectively, and D is set of features with non-missing values in both instances. For example, the dataset shown in table 3 is considered. The goal is replacing missing values with some estimates. First, the distance between instance 1 and 3 is calculated. When calculating the distance between these

Table 3. A sample dataset

	Feature 1	Feature 2	Feature 3	Feature 4	Feature 5
Instance 1	2	3	4	2	2
Instance 2	2	2	3	1	3
Instance 3	-	-	3	2	4
Instance 4	1	3	3	3	1

instances, the features for which both have values are feature 3, 4 and 5. Thus, D= {feature 3, feature 4, feature 5}. The distance between these two instances is equal

$$D_{1,3} = \sqrt{(3-4)^2 + (2-2)^2 + (4-2)^2} = \sqrt{5}$$

Similarly, we have:

$$D_{2,3} = \sqrt{(3-3)^2 + (2-1)^2 + (4-3)^2} = \sqrt{2}$$

$$D_{2,4} = \sqrt{(3-3)^2 + (1-3)^2 + (3-1)^2} = \sqrt{8}$$

When k nearest neighbor have been found, a replacement value to substitute for the missing value must be estimated. For example in the mentioned dataset, feature 1 and 2 in instance 3 is replaced with 2 and 2 using 1-nearest neighbor method, respectively, because the distance between these two instances is minimum.

Feature Selection and Classification

After replacing missing values with some estimates, the best features are selected using the population based feature selection. Then, the selected features are fed to SVM. An example of the evolution of the algorithms for the WPBC dataset is presented in figure 20 and 21. In fig-

ure 20, the average of classification error for all solutions at each iteration is presented. Figure 21 demonstrates the minimum classification error at each iteration. In Figure 22, the evolution of the search for the best number of features is shown. Table 4 presents the accuracy using all features in both training sets and the test set. The result of population based feature selection is shown in Table 5. The ABA based feature selection is presented the best mean classification accuracy on test dataset.

SPECTF Heart Dataset

SPECTF heart dataset describes cardiac single proton emission computed Tomography (SPECT) images. Each of the patients are classified two categories: normal and abnormal. This dataset consists of 276 instances which is extracted from Tomography images. 44 continues features are created for each patient(Merz et al., 2012).

In the first step, the features are normalized using method described in the classification of WDBC dataset. Then, the best normalized features is selected using population based feature selection. In Figure 23 and 24, an example of the evolution of the algorithm tours is shown for this dataset. In Figure 25, the evolution of the search for the best features cardinality is presented for one of the runs of the population based feature selection. Table 6 presents the accuracy statistics using all features in both training and test set. The results of feature selection is shown in Table 7.

Figure 20. Average classification error for each iteration in the WPBC dataset

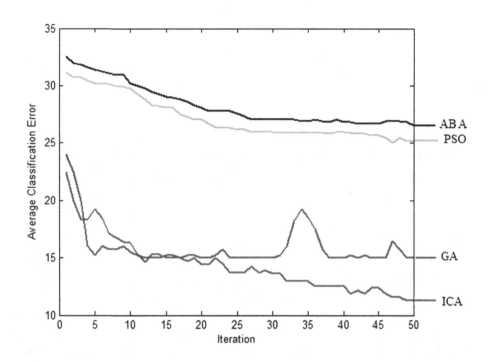

Figure 21. Minimum classification error for each iteration in the WPBC dataset

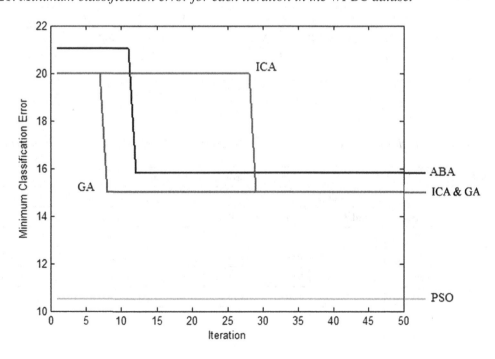

Table 4. Accuracy statistics using all features in training and test sets on WPBC dataset

Method	Classification Accuracy							
	Training Set				Test Set			
	Mean	Std. Dev.	Max.	Min.	Mean	Std. Dev.	Max.	Min.
SVM without feature selection	75.79	11.75	81.87	62.87	76.32	6.95	84.21	68.42

Table 5. Accuracy statistics using selected features in training and test sets on WPBC dataset

Method	Classification Accuracy							
	Training Set				Test Set			
	Mean	Std. Dev.	Max.	Min.	Mean	Std. Dev.	Max.	Min.
GA-FS	77.29	2.32	79.53	74.42	78.87	8.83	88.88	70.37
PSO-FS	84.42	3.96	93.82	84.83	80.64	6.32	89.47	70.00
ABA-FS	91.23	2.64	98.31	92.69	89.42	4.47	100	84.21
ICA_FS	85.5	3.69	90.00	80.00	82.57	2.48	85.47	76.54
SFS	76.79	2.22	78.21	73.74	76.37	11.77	81.48	66.66
SBS	77.32	3.11	80.44	75.41	77.34	11.38	85.18	74.07

Table 6. Accuracy statistics using all features in training and test sets on SPECTF heart dataset

Method	Classification Accuracy							
	Training Set				Test Set			
	Mean	Std. Dev.	Max.	Min.	Mean	Std. Dev.	Max.	Min.
SVM without feature selection	84.15	1.71	86.72	81.33	78.07	2.64	81.48	74.07

Table 7. Accuracy statistics using selected features in training and test sets on SPECTF heart dataset

Method	Classification Accuracy							
	Training Set				Test Set			
	Mean	Std. Dev.	Max.	Min.	Mean	Std. Dev.	Max.	Min.
ICA_FS	89.13	1.43	91.70	87.14	78.44	3.77	85.19	74.07
GA-FS	94.07	3.58	100	88.89	78.14	2.10	81.48	74.07
ABA_FS	96.68	2.33	100	92.91	93.69	4.28	100	85.19
PSO_FS	93.23	4.51	95.83	88.75	88.64	1.58	91.25	86.30
SFS	86.96	4.25	90.72	81.85	77.63	3.93	82.14	71.42
SBS	87.21	3.23	90.32	84.67	77.84	3.63	85.71	75.00

Figure 22. The Best number of features for each iteration in the WPBC dataset

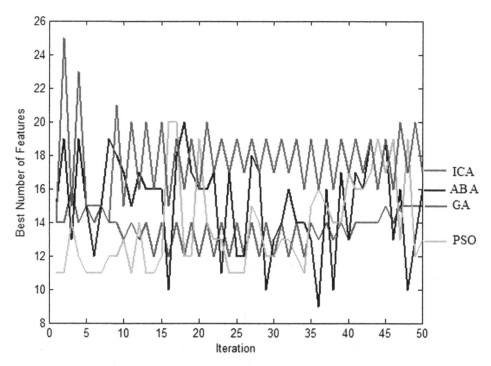

Figure 23. Average classification error for each iteration in the SPECTF heart dataset

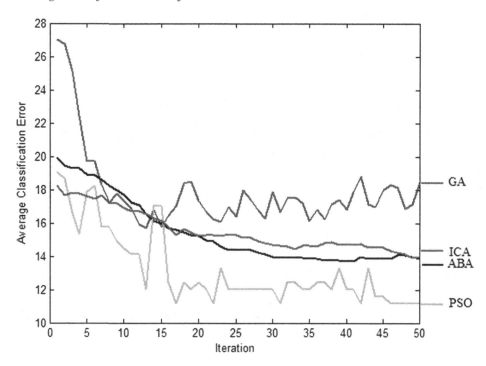

Figure 24. Minimum classification error for each iteration in the SPECTF heart dataset

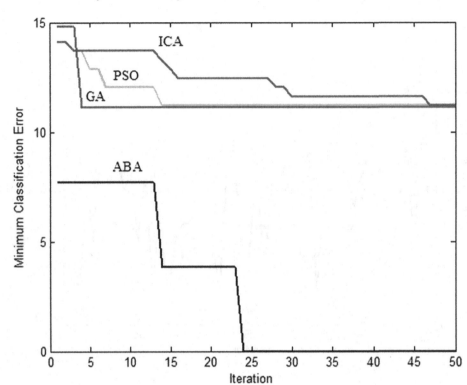

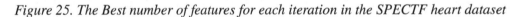

Figure 25. The Best number of features for each iteration in the SPECTF heart dataset

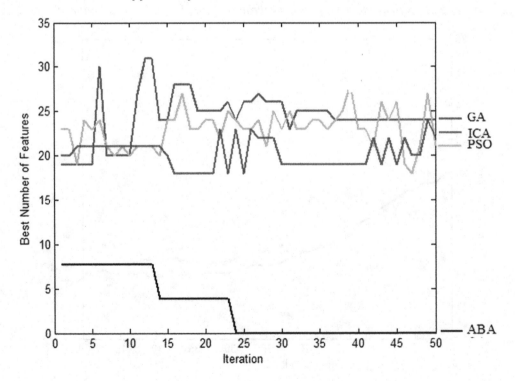

Hepatitis Diagnosis

The purpose of this dataset is to predict the presence or absence of hepatitis disease given the results of various medical tests conducted on a patient. This dataset contains 155 instance in total 75 of them having missing values. All instance have 19 feature that are shown as follows:

1. Age: 10, 20, 30, 40, 50, 60, 70, 80,
2. Sex: male, female,
3. Steroid: no, yes,
4. Antivirals: no, yes,
5. Fatigue: no, yes,
6. Malaise: no, yes,
7. Anorexia: no, yes,
8. Liver big: no, yes,
9. Liver firm: no, yes,
10. Spleen palpable: no, yes,
11. Spiders: no, yes,
12. Ascites: no, yes,
13. Varices: no, yes,
14. Bilirubin: 0.39, 0.80, 1.20, 2.00, 3.00, 4.00,
15. Alkaline phosphate: 33, 80, 120, 160, 200, 250,
16. Sgot: 13, 100, 200, 300, 400, 500,
17. Albumin: 2.1, 3.0, 3.8, 4.5, 5.0, 6.0,
18. Protime: 10, 20, 30, 40, 50, 60, 70, 80, 90,
19. Histology: no, yes.

Similar to WPBC dataset, this dataset includes missing values. Therefore first, a similar missing value handling method (k nearest neighbor imputation) is applied on this dataset. Then, obtained features are normalized using method described in the classification of WDBC dataset. In the next step, the best features are selected using population based feature selection. In figure 26 and 27, an example of the evolution of the algorithms tour for the hepatitis diagnosis dataset is demonstrated, where the average classification error and the minimum classification error at each iteration are

Figure 26. Average classification error for each iteration in the Hepatitis diagnosis dataset

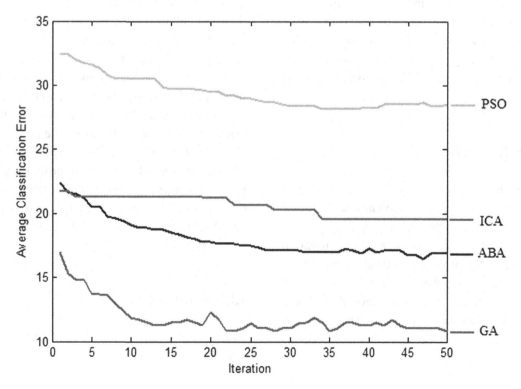

Figure 27. Minimum classification error for each iteration in the Hepatitis diagnosis dataset

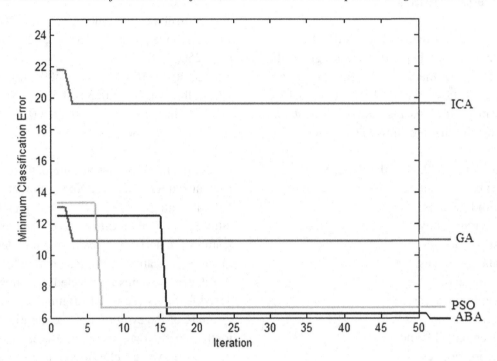

shown. In figure 28, the evolution of the search for the best feature cardinality is presented. Table 8 presents the accuracy statistics using all features in both training and test set. The results of feature selection is shown in Table 9. According to the results, The PSO based feature selection presents the higher performance compared with other used methods.

CONCLUSION

One of the main challenge in biomedical data mining is the existing of redundant and irrelevant features. The selection of appropriate features can improve the performance of classification algorithm. One of the methods of feature selection is based on population metaheuristics. These methods maintain and improve several candidate solutions. In this chapter, population based feature selection is considered in biomedical data. For this purpose, four population metaheuristic is used for feature selection: genetic algorithm, particle swarm optimization, artificial bee algorithm, and imperialist competitive algorithm. To fulfil the requirements of biomedical data classification and enhance the reliability of the selected features, population based feature selection approach uses the accuracy with cross-validation. Experiments on various biomedical data set show that population based feature selection has acceptable performance. In addition, appropriate feature selection algorithm depends on the data set; for example, ICA presents the highest performance in WDBC dataset, while it did not provided a good result in hepatitis diagnosis. These results clearly demonstrates the great potential of the population based feature selection in the classification of biomedical data.

ACKNOWLEDGMENT

Authors are grateful to council of University of Kashan for providing financial support to undertake this work.

Figure 28. The Best number of features for each iteration in the Hepatitis diagnosis dataset

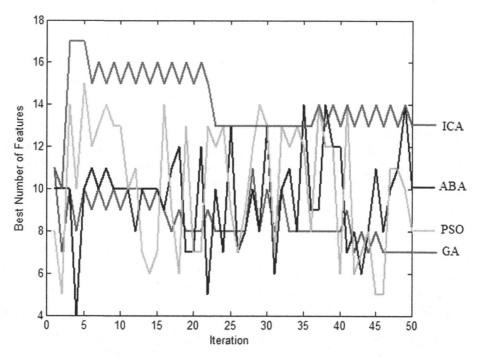

Table 8. Accuracy statistics using all features in training and test sets on WPBC dataset

Method	Classification Accuracy							
	Training Set				Test Set			
	Mean	Std. Dev.	Max.	Min.	Mean	Std. Dev.	Max.	Min.
SVM without feature selection	80.79	0.92	79.29	82.14	78.91	1.05	78.26	80.43

Table 9. Accuracy statistics using selected features in training and test sets on WPBC dataset

Method	Classification Accuracy							
	Training Set				Test Set			
	Mean	Std. Dev.	Max.	Min.	Mean	Std. Dev.	Max.	Min.
ICA-FS	84.12	3.42	87.32	81.56	82.12	1.19	84.32	79.85
GA-FS	81.15	0.95	83.12	79.65	89.13	1.12	80.43	78.26
PSO-FS	94.39	3.21	98.56	90.64	92.95	4.72	100	86.66
ABA-FS	93.65	4.43	96.40	86.33	91.16	6.10	100	81.25
SFS	84.65	3.48	87.91	80.32	83.35	4.23	85.22	77.49
SBS	85.11	4.85	87.46	80.73	83.65	5.17	85.16	77.23

REFERENCES

Abraham, A., Grosan, C., & Pedrycz, W. (2008). *Engineering Evolutionary Intelligent Systems* (Vol. 82). Springer. doi:10.1007/978-3-540-75396-4_1

Antoniadis, A., Lambert-Lacroix, S., & Leblanc, F. (2003). Effective dimension reduction methods for tumor classification using gene expression data. *Bioinformatics (Oxford, England)*, *19*(5), 563–570. doi:10.1093/bioinformatics/btg062 PMID:12651713

Atashpaz-Gargari, E., & Lucas, C. (2007). *Imperialist competitive algorithm: an algorithm for optimization inspired by imperialistic competition.* Paper presented at the Evolutionary Computation, 2007. New York, NY.

Barron, A., Rissanen, J., & Yu, B. (1998). The minimum description length principle in coding and modeling. *Information Theory. IEEE Transactions on*, *44*(6), 2743–2760.

Blanco, R., Larrañaga, P., Inza, I., & Sierra, B. (2004). Gene selection for cancer classification using wrapper approaches. *International Journal of Pattern Recognition and Artificial Intelligence*, *18*(8), 1373–1390. doi:10.1142/S0218001404003800

Gargari, E. A., Hashemzadeh, F., Rajabioun, R., & Lucas, C. (2008). Colonial competitive algorithm: a novel approach for PID controller design in MIMO distillation column process. *International Journal of Intelligent Computing and Cybernetics*, *1*(3), 337–355. doi:10.1108/17563780810893446

Guyon, I., Weston, J., Barnhill, S., & Vapnik, V. (2002). Gene selection for cancer classification using support vector machines. *Machine Learning*, *46*(1-3), 389–422. doi:10.1023/A:1012487302797

Karaboga, D. (2005). *An idea based on honey bee swarm for numerical optimization.* Techn. Rep. TR06, Erciyes Univ. Press, Erciyes.

Luke, S. (2010). *Essentials of Metaheuristics. 2009.* Retrieved from http://cs.gmu.edu/~sean/book/metaheuristics

Merz, C., Murphy, P., & Aha, D. (2012). *UCI Repository of Machine Learning Databases.* Department of Information and Computer Science, University of California.

Peng, Y., Wu, Z., & Jiang, J. (2010). A novel feature selection approach for biomedical data classification. *Journal of Biomedical Informatics*, *43*(1), 15–23. doi:10.1016/j.jbi.2009.07.008 PMID:19647098

Pham, D., Ghanbarzadeh, A., Koc, E., Otri, S., Rahim, S., & Zaidi, M. (2006). *The bees algorithm–a novel tool for complex optimisation problems.* Paper presented at the Proceedings of the 2nd Virtual International Conference on Intelligent Production Machines and Systems (IPROMS 2006). New York, NY.

Poli, R., Kennedy, J., & Blackwell, T. (2007). Particle swarm optimization. *Swarm Intelligence*, *1*(1), 33–57. doi:10.1007/s11721-007-0002-0

Soltani-Sarvestani, M., & Lotfi, S. (2012). QCA & CQCA: Quad Countries Algorithm and Chaotic Quad Countries Algorithm. *Journal of Theoretical and Applied Computer Science*, *6*(3), 3–20.

Talbi, E.-G. (2009). *Metaheuristics: from design to implementation* (Vol. 74). John Wiley & Sons. doi:10.1002/9780470496916

Theodoridis, S. K. K. (2008). *Pattern recognition.* Academic Press.

ADDITIONAL READING

Akay M.F. (2009), support vector machines combined with feature selection for breast cancer diagnosis, expert systems with applications, 36(2), 3240-3247

Carugo, O., & Eisenaber, F. (2010). *Data Mining Techniques for the life science*. Humana Press. doi:10.1007/978-1-60327-241-4

Chen, H., Yang, B., Liu, J., & Liu, D. (2011). a support vector machine classifier with rough set based feature selection for breast cancer diagnosis. *Expert Systems with Applications*, *38*(7), 9014–9022. doi:10.1016/j.eswa.2011.01.120

Ding, C. (2005). Minimum redundancy feature selection from microarray gene expression data. *Journal of Bioinformatics and Computational Biology*, *3*(2). doi:10.1142/S0219720005001004 PMID:15852500

Gheyas I.A., L.S. smith. (2010), Feature Subset selection in large dimensionality domains, pattern recognition, 43(1), 5-13

Guyon I., & Elisseeff. (2003), an introduction to variable and feature selection, the journal of machine learning research, volume 3, 1157-1182

Huang, M. L., Hung, Y. H., & Chen, W. Y. (2010). neural network classifier with entropy based feature selection on breast cancer diagnosis. *Journal of Medical Systems*, *34*(5), 865–873. doi:10.1007/s10916-009-9301-x PMID:20703622

Jerez-Aragonés, J. M., Gómez-Ruiz, J. A., Ramos-Jiménez, G., Muñoz-Pérez, J., & Alba-Conejo, E. (2003). a combined neural network and decision trees model for prognosis of breast cancer relapse. *Artificial Intelligence in Medicine*, *27*(1), 45–63. doi:10.1016/S0933-3657(02)00086-6 PMID:12473391

Leardi, R., Boggia, R., & Terrile, M. (1992). genetic algorithm as a strategy for feature selection. *Journal of Chemometrics*, *6*(5), 267–281. doi:10.1002/cem.1180060506

Look S. (2011), Essentials of metaheuristics, publisher: lulu.com

Maglogiannis, I., Zafiropoulos, E., & Anagnostopoulos, I. (2009). An intelligent system for automated breast cancer diagnosis and prognosis using SVM classifiers. *Applied Intelligence*, *30*(1), 24–36. doi:10.1007/s10489-007-0073-z

Mousavirad S.J. Akhlaghian F., & Mollazade K. (2012). Application of imperialist competitive algorithm for feature selection: A case study on bulk rice classification, International journal of computer application, 40(16)

Mousavirad, S. J., & Ebrahimpur-Komleh, H. (2013). Feature selection using modified imperialist competitive algorithm, 3rd international Conference on Computer and Knowledge Engineering, ICKKE 2013, Iran

Polat K. Sahan S. Kodaz H., & Gunes S. (2005). A new classification method for breast cancer diagnosis: feature selection artificial immune recognition system, Advances in neural computations (vol 3611), 830-838

Sacha, J. (1999), New Synthesis of Bayesian network classifiers and cardiac SPECT image interpretation, Unpublished doctoral dissertation, University of Toledo

Talbi E. (2009), metaheuristics: from design to implementation, Wiley publisher Eiben A.E. (1999), Evolutionary computation, los pr inc publishing

Tan, K. C., Yu, Q., Heng, C. M., & Lee, T. H. (2003). Evolutionary computing for knowledge discovery in medical diagnosis. *Artificial Intelligence in Medicine, 27*(2), 129–154. doi:10.1016/S0933-3657(03)00002-2 PMID:12636976

Yang J., & Honaver V. (1998), feature subset selection using a genetic algorithm, the springer international series in engineering and computer science (Vol 453), 117-136

Yurong, H.., D. Lixin, x. Datong, w. Shenwen. (2012). A Novel Discrete Artificial Bee Colony Algorithm for Rough Set-based Feature Selection. *International Journal of Advancements in Computing Technology, 4*(6).

KEY TERMS AND DEFINITIONS

Artificial Bee Colony: It is a population based metaheuristic based on the intelligent foraging behavior of honey bee swarm.

Data Mining: It is computational process of discovering hidden knowledge in the large datasets.

Feature Selection: It is a process to remove redundant and irrelevant features without reducing the classification accuracy.

Genetic Algorithm: It is a population based metaheuristic that mimics the process of natural selection.

Imperialist Competitive Algorithm: It is a population based metaheuristic based on inspired by imperialist competition.

Particle Swarm Optimization: It is a population based metaheuristic based on the movement and intelligence of swarms.

Population Based Feature Selection: A feature selection approach based on population based metaheuristics.

Chapter 17
A Comparative Study on Medical Diagnosis Using Predictive Data Mining:
A Case Study

Seyed Jalaleddin Mousavirad
University of Kashan, Iran

Hossein Ebrahimpour-Komleh
University of Kashan, Iran

ABSTRACT

Medical diagnosis is a most important problem in medical data mining. The possible errors of a physician can reduce with the help of data mining techniques. The goal of this chapter is to analyze and compare predictive data mining techniques in the medical diagnosis. To this purpose, various data mining techniques such as decision tree, neural networks, support vector machine, and lazy modelling are considered. Results show data mining techniques can considerably help a physician.

INTRODUCTION

Data mining techniques have been successfully employed in the various biomedical domains. Diagnosis of disease is one of the most important issues in this domain. Medical diagnosis is a difficult and visual task which is often carried out by an expert. An expert commonly takes decisions by evaluating the current test results of a patient or the expert compares the patient with other patients with some condition by referring to the previous decisions(Polat & Güneş, 2006). Therefore, medical diagnosis is a very difficult task for an expert. For this reason, in recent years, data mining techniques have been considered to design automated medical diagnosis systems. With the help of automated medical diagnosis systems, the possible error experts can dramatically reduce.

Data mining is a computational process to find hidden patterns in large datasets. One of the main steps in data mining is model building using predictive data mining techniques. Predictive data

DOI: 10.4018/978-1-4666-6086-1.ch017

mining techniques learn from past experience and apply it to future situations. Classification is a method of predictive data mining. Classification algorithms build a model to predict class labels in the given data. There are various algorithms to classification such as support vector machine, neural networks, decision tree, and nearest neighbor classifier. Performance of classification algorithms depend on the characteristics of the data. There is no classification algorithm that works best on all problems (no-free-launch principle). Various empirical tests should be done to find the best classification algorithm on a dataset.

The goal of this chapter is to analysis and compare various classification algorithms on medical diagnosis. For this purpose, a case study on diagnosis of breast cancer is considered. Breast cancer is a type of cancer originating from breast tissues. It is reported that breast cancer was the second one among the most diagnosis cancers and includes 22.9% of all cancers in women(Moftah et al., 2013). It is one of the major causes of death all over the world and more than 1.2 million women will be diagnosed with breast cancer each year worldwide(Tondini, Fenaroli, & Labianca, 2007). Such a disease needs effective and accurate diagnosis to ensure quick and effective treatment.

In this study, various classification algorithms with various parameters are compared for diagnosis of breast cancer. The rest of this chapter is organized as follows: first, various classification algorithms is considered. Then, a general configuration for medical diagnosis will be introduced. In this configuration, after feature extraction, features are reduced with feature selection and reduction algorithms then, a classification algorithm is applied on new feature subset.

LITERATURE REVIEW

This chapter is referred to the application of data mining in medical diagnosis, in particular predictive data mining methods. Data mining methods have been applied to a variety of medical diagnosis in order to improve the process of medical diagnosis. Artificial neural networks (ANN) such as Multilayer perceptron (MLP), Probabilistic Neural Network (PNN), Radial Basis function (RBF), and learning vector quantization (LVQ) have been widely used in disease diagnosis. Temurtas (2009) compared MLP, PNN and LVQ for thyroid disease diagnosis. In another work, MLP was applied for diagnosis of hepatitis disease(Bascil & Temurtas, 2011); in the subsequent work, these authors used PNN for hepatitis diagnosis(Bascil & Oztekin, 2012). PNN has also been used to Mesothelioma's disease(Er, Tanrikulu, Abakay, & Temurtas, 2012). In addition, evolutionary neural networks and ensemble of neural networks have been applied in some works(Abbass, 2002; Das, Turkoglu, & Sengur, 2009b).

Support vector machine is another classifier which was frequently used for disease diagnosis such as Thyroid(Dogantekin, Dogantekin, & Avci, 2011), hepatitis(Çalişir & Dogantekin, 2011; Chen, Liu, Yang, Liu, & Wang, 2011; Sartakhti, Zangooei, & Mozafari, 2011), breast cancer(Chen, Yang, Liu, & Liu, 2011), and heart disease(Yan & Shao, 2003). In addition, tree based classification algorithms and discriminant analysis can be seen in the literature(Jerez-Aragonés, Gómez-Ruiz, Ramos-Jiménez, Muñoz-Pérez, & Alba-Conejo, 2003; Kabari & Nwachukwu, 2012; Pandey, Pandey, Jaiswal, & Sen, 2013; Vlahou, Schorge, Gregory, & Coleman, 2003).

Fusion of classifiers is one method to improve the classification performance. These methods were applied to disease diagnosis. Das et al. (2009b) applied ensemble of neural networks for heart disease. In another works, the same authors used ensemble of neural networks for valvular heart disease (Das, Turkoglu, & Sengur, 2009a). Ozcift (2012) employed forest ensemble to improve computer-aided diagnosis of Parkinson disease.

Table 1 provides a review on data mining applications in medical diagnosis.

Table 1. An overview of data mining applications in medical diagnosis

Disease Type	Methods	References
Thyroid Diseases	Combination of Generalized Discriminant Analysis and SVM	(Dogantekin et al., 2011)
	LDA	(Coomans, Jonckheer, Massart, Broeckaert, & Blockx, 1978)
	MLP	(Temurtas, 2009)
	PNN	(Temurtas, 2009)
	LVQ	(Temurtas, 2009)
Hepatitis	Combination of SVM and Simulated Annealing (SVM_SA)	(Sartakhti et al., 2011)
	Local Fisher Discriminant Analysis and SVM	(Chen, Liu, et al., 2011)
	Least Square Support Vector Machine(LSSVM)	(Çalişir & Dogantekin, 2011)
	PNN	(Bascil & Oztekin, 2012)
	MLP	(Bascil & Temurtas, 2011)
Mesothelioma	PNN	(Er et al., 2012)
Breast Cancer	LSSVM	(Polat & Güneş, 2007)
	Evolutionary Neural Network	(Abbass, 2002)
Diabetes	GRNN	(Kayaer & Yıldırım, 2003)
	RBF	(Venkatesan & Anitha, 2006)
Heart	KNN	(Shouman, Turner, & Stocker, 2012)
	SVM	(Yan & Shao, 2003)
	Ensemble of ANN	(Das et al., 2009b)
Parkinson	Forest Ensemble	(Ozcift, 2012)

PREDECTIVE DATA MINING TECHNIQUES

This section investigates some of the classification algorithms as a predictive data mining technique. These algorithms predict a target value. The goal of predictive data mining in the medical diagnosis is to drive models that can diagnose the diseases. Some of predictive data mining models are demonstrates in the following subsections.

Discriminant Analysis

Linear discriminant analysis (LDA) and Quadratic discriminant analysis (QDA) are two classic classifiers (classification algorithms) in the medical field with a linear and quadratic decision surface, respectively.

LDA can learn linear boundaries while QDA can learn quadratic boundaries. The LDA works as follows:

LDA tries to find a linear combination of features which separates two or more classes of instances. LDA projects the features to a lower dimensional vector space(Ye, Janardan, & Li, 2004). The goal of LDA is to obtain a univariate sample by projecting the multivariate sample X into a line so that this line maximize the seperability of the instances.

$$y = w^T x \quad where \quad x = \begin{bmatrix} x_1 \\ . \\ . \\ . \\ x_n \end{bmatrix}, w = \begin{bmatrix} w_1 \\ . \\ . \\ . \\ w_n \end{bmatrix}$$

Figure 1 demonstrates a two class problem mapping to a line. In the Figure 1.a, the two classes are not well separated when projection into line while line in the Figure 1.b can separate two class separately.

For each class, the scatter matrix are given by

$$S_i = \sum_{x \in w_i} (x - \overline{x_i})(x - \overline{x_i})^T$$

where $x_i = \dfrac{1}{n_i} \sum_{x \in w_i} X$ and n_i is the number of instances in w_i. It is a measure of variability within the two classes w_i after projection on a line. The total intra class scatter matrix is given by

$$S_w = S_1 + S_2$$

Fisher suggested the linear function $w^T x$ to maximum the following criterion:

$$J(w) = \frac{| \overline{x_1} - \overline{x_2} |^2}{S_1 + S_2}$$

According to this criterion, LDA tries to provide a projection where instances from the same class are projected close to each other, and the projected means to be far apart as possible.

QDA works in a similar way. for more information about LDA and QDA, please see the additional reading list at the end of this chapter.

Decision Tree

Decision Tree (DT) is another classification algorithm which is used in the medical field. A DT is a hierarchical tree which each inner node corresponds to one feature of the instances and each leaf is associated with one of the classes. For classification, the feature values of a new instance are tested beginning with root. At each node, the tree is traced along the path of successful tests until a leaf is visited. Figure 2 illustrates a typical DT. There are various algorithms for

Figure 1. A two class problem mapping two a line

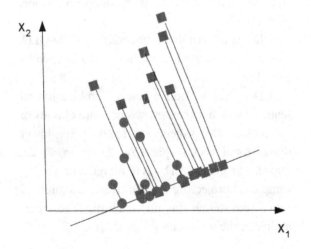
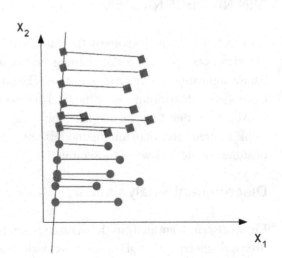

constructing DTs. These algorithms construct a DT in a top down recursive divide-and-conquer manner. These algorithms usually partition the training set recursively by selecting a feature. The best splitting feature is determined with a quality criterion. The quality criterion provides a ranking for each feature. The feature having the best score is chosen as the splitting feature. Examples of such quality criteria are information gain, gain ratio, gini index and accuracy.

Information Gain

This criterion reflects expected reduction in entropy caused by partitioning the instances according to a feature. The feature with the highest information gain is chosen as the splitting feature(Mitchell, 1997).

In order to define information gain precisly, first, entropy is defined. Entropy determines the randomness or impurity of a collection of instances. The entropy the collection of instances S is given by

$$Entropy(S) = -\sum_{i=1}^{m} p_i \log_2(p_i),$$

where p_i is the probability that an arbitary instance in S belongs to class w_i.

Information gain, *Gain(S, F)* of an feature *F*, relative to a collection of examples S, is defined by

$$Gain(S, F) =$$
$$Entropy(S) - \sum_{j=1}^{v} \frac{|S_j|}{|S|} \times Entropy(S_j)$$

where v is the set of all possible values for feature F, and S_j contains instances in S that feature A has value v (Mitchell, 1997).

Gain Ratio

Some of the features in feature set such as *Date* have a very large number of possible values. These features have the highest information gain of any of the features but constructed DT is poor for clas-

Figure 2. A Decision Tree

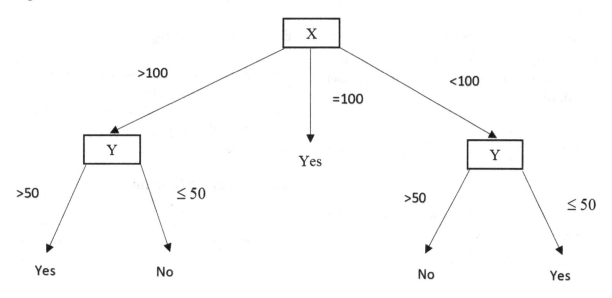

sification. Gain ratio is a variant of information gain which reduces its bias on high branch features such as *Date(Russell, Norvig, Canny, Malik, & Edwards, 1995)*. It is defined as

$$GainRatio(A) = \frac{Gain(A)}{SplitInfo_A(D)}$$

Which $SplitInfo_A(D)$ is "split information". It is large when data is spread over all branches and is small when all data belong to one branch. $SplitInfo_A(D)$ is given by

$$SplitInfo_A(S) = -\sum_{j=1}^{v} \frac{|S_j|}{|S|} \times \log_2(\frac{|S_j|}{|S|})$$

Gini Index

Gini index is an another sensible quality criterion. If dataset D contains from n classes, Gini index is defined by

$$Gini(\mathrm{D}) = 1 - \sum_{i=1}^{m} p_i^2$$

where p_i is the probability that a instance in D belongs to class w_i. After splitting D into two subsets D_1 and D_2, the gini index of the split data is defined as

$$Gini_A(D) = \frac{|D_1|}{|D|} \times Gini(D_1) + \frac{|D_2|}{|D|} \times Gini(\mathrm{D}_2)$$

The feature providing smallest $Gini_A(D)$ is chosen to split the node.

Accuracy

In this quality criterion, a feature is selected for splitting feature that maximize the accuracy of whole tree.

Random Forest

Random forest is an ensemble classifier for classification. This classifier has been used for medical applications such as acute appendicitis(Hsieh et al., 2011) and Alzheimer's disease(Ramírez et al., 2010). Ensemble classifiers do not learn a single classifier but learn a set of classifier. Random forest constructs many classification trees. To classify a new instance, it is applied to each of the trees in the forest. Each tree produces a classification result. The new instance assign to a class with the most votes. The overal algorithm is described in follows:

1. Sample M samples.
2. Train M different tree classifiers on these samples.
3. For a new instance, all classifiers predict and assign the new instance to a class with the most vote(majority vote).

Bayesian Modeling

These models classify an instance based on a statistical approach called Bayes therom. Two category of these classification algorithms are explained in this chapter: Naïve bayes classifier and bayesian belief network.

Naïve Bayes Classifier

Naïve Baye classifier is a statistical classifier based on bayes theorm. This classifier assumes that feature values are mutually independent. Let T be a training set of instances and their associated class labels. There are k classes, $W_1, W_2...,W_k$. each instance is represented by a n-dimensional vector, $X = \{x_1,...,x_n\}$. given a instance X, the naïve bayes classifier will predict that X belongs to the class having the highest probabilities, conditoned on X or the class that maximize $P(W_i \mid X)$. by Bayes' theorem:

$$P(W_i \mid X) = \frac{P(X \mid W_i)P(W_i)}{P(X)}$$

Because $P(X)$ is constant for all classes, it is enough to maximize $P(X \mid W_i)P(W_i)$.

Bayesian Belief Networks

Bayesian Belief Networks(BBN) are probabilistic graphical models representing a set of random variables. unlike naïve bayesian classifier, BBNs allow the representation of dependencies among subsets of features via a directed acyclic graph(DAG). Each node corresponds to a feature (random variable) and the edges between the nodes represent probabilistic dependencies among the corresponding features. Each BBN has one conditional probability table(CPT) for each variables. The CPT for a variable X specifies the conditional distribution P(X|parents(X)). Figure 3 shows a BBN inspired by the discipline of medical diagnosis where S is smoker, L is lung cancer,

Figure 3. A sample BBN

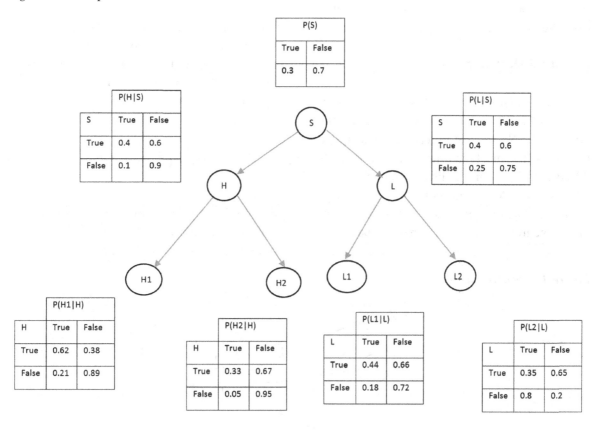

and H is heart disease. L1 and L2 are lung disease medical tests, and H1 and H2 are cancer medical tests. The CPT values are not real.

Training of BNN consists of two parts. The first is to learn the network topology. It may be constructed by human expert or inferred from data. This problem is a optimization problem. one of the topology learning algorithm is local score metric. In this method, network topology learning considers as an optimization problem where a quality measure needs to be maximized. The quality measure can be based on bayesian approach, minimum discription length, and other criteria. The several search algorithms such as hill climbing, simulated annealing, and genetic algorithm can be used for local score metrics. for more solutions, please see the additional reading list at the end of this chapter. Once the topology has been constructed, the unknown parameters such as conditional probabilities are estimated from the training data.

Artificial Neural Networks

Artificial Neural Networks (ANNs) are processing elements that is inspired from biological nervous systems. ANNs are able to learn and generalize from data. The most important characteristics of ANNs is their learning ability from input output relationships. ANNs are composed of a large number of highly interconnected processing elements (neurons) that can compute values from

inputs by feeding data through the network. Each neuron receives a number of inputs and produce an output to other nodes. Each node performs a simple computations by its activation function. Figure 4 shows a general neuron model.

An ANN is determined by:

1. **Neuron Model:** The processing elements of the ANN.
2. **An Architecture:** A set of neurons and links connecting neurons. Each connection link has a weight.
3. **A Learning Algorithm:** Learning in an ANN is performed by examples. This process is also called training. The process of learning in ANN is to adjust weights of interconnections so that error between the actual output of an ANN and the desired correct output is minimized.

Perceptron is a simple ANN that is used to classify its input into one of two classes. The perceptron can only model linearly separable classes. Activation function of perceptron is a step function as follows:

$$\phi(s) = \begin{cases} +1 \text{ if } s \geq 0 \\ -1 \text{ if } s < 0 \end{cases}$$

where s is weighted sum of its input and ϕ is output of perceptron.

Figure 4. A general neuron model

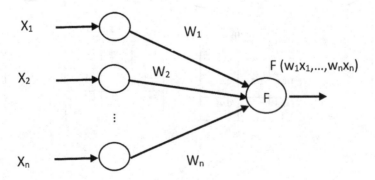

A learning algorithm called the "perceptron learning algorithm" can be used to obtain the weights of perceptron. This algorithm is presented as follows:

- Initially assign randomly chosen weights (w_0).
- Training data is presented to perceptron and its output is computed.
- If output is incorrect, the weights are adjusted using following formula.

$$w_{i+1} = w_i + \eta.x.e$$

where 'e' is error and η is learning rate.

A multilayer feedforward neural network (MLF) is consists of an input layer, one or more hidden layers and an output layer. An example of MLF with one hidden layer is shown in Figure 5. It is a feedforward neural network because none of the links come back to a previous layer. Each neuron in the input and the hidden layers is connected to all neurons in the next layer by weight links. Except for the input layer, each neuron in the other layers is a processing element with a nonlinear activation function. The sigmoid function is a common choice of activation function. It is defined as:

$$\phi(s) = \frac{1}{1 + e^{-s}}$$

The neurons of the hidden layers compute weighted sum of their inputs and add a threshold (bias). Then, the result apply to an activation function. This process is defined as follows:

$$v_j = \sum_{i=1}^{p} w_{ji} x_i + \theta_j$$
$$y_i = f(v_j)$$

Figure 5. A MLF

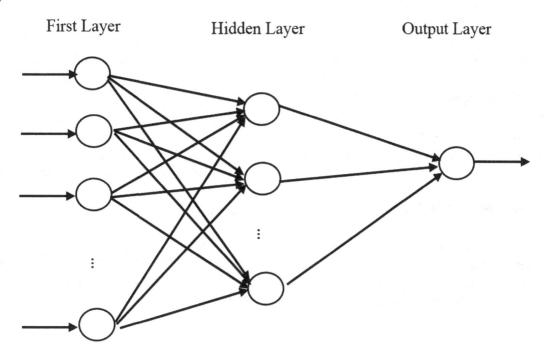

First Layer   Hidden Layer   Output Layer

where v_j is the linear combination of $x_1, ..., x_n$, w_{ji} is the link weight between the input x_i and the neuron j, θ_j is threshold, and f is activation function.

The backpropagation algorithm (BP) is one of the most frequently used technique for MLF neural network which is based on gradient descent. This algorithm for a MLF with one hidden layer is summarized in Figure 6. BP algorithm has disadvantages because of using gradient descent. It often gets into the local minimum of the error function. One approach to overcome the gradient descent problems is adapting Evolutionary algorithms. One of the latest these algorithms is cuckoo optimization algorithm (COA)(Rajabioun, 2011). It is inspired by the lifestyle of a species of bird called cuckoo. Unordinary egg laying and breeding of cuckoo is the fundamentals of COA. In this algorithm each solution is shown by an array. This array is defined by

Habitat=$[x_1, x_2, ..., x_N]$

where x_i is the variable that to be optimized.

In this method, each habitat is a string of floating point numbers which is shown weights of a structure. Figure 7 demonstrates the weights representation as a habitat from the initial cuckoos(Ebrahimpour-Komleh & Mousavirad, 2013).

For more information about this method, please see the additional reading list at the end of this chapter.

Support Vector Machine

Support vector machine (SVM) is a method for linear and nonlinear classification. It transforms the original training data into a higher dimension. Within this new dimension, it searches for the linear optimal hyperplane. Suppose that the data set is a linearly separable two class problem. There are an infinite number of hyperplane for separating of data. Figure 8 illustrates a linearly separable two class problem with three hyperplane.

Figure 9 shows two possible hyperplane and their associated margin. Both hyperplane able to classify the data correctly, but hyperplane with the large margin to be more accurate at classifying new instance than the hyperplane with the small margin. SVM searches maximum marginal hyperplane as best hyperplane.

Let us consider a binary classification problem:

$$\left\{x_i, y_i\right\}, \ i = 1, 2, ..., L, \ y_i = \left\{-1, +1\right\}$$

where x_i are the feature vectors of training set and y_i are the corresponding labels. The goal is to design a hyperplane that classifies correctly all the training vectors. This separating hyperplane can be written as

$$\overline{w}.\overline{x} + b = 0$$

where $\overline{w}$ is a n dimensional weight vector and b is bias. For each training example (x_i, y_i)

$$\overline{w}.\overline{x} + b \leq 0 \ \ \text{if} \ y_i = -1$$
$$\overline{w}.\overline{x} + b \geq 0 \ \ \text{if} \ y_i = +1$$

Combining the above two inequality, we get

$$y_i(\overline{w}.\overline{x} + b) \geq 1 \ \ \forall i$$

Support vectors are the closet training data to separating hyperplane. For each support vector, the above inequality is an equality. In Figure 10,

Figure 6. Back propagation algorithm

BackPropagation Algorithm
Input:
  D: a dataset consists of training examples and their associated target values
  η : learning rate
Output: a trained MLF neural network
Method:
 Initialize all weights and biases in the network
 While mean square error is unsatisfactory
 {
   For each input pattern in D
   {
     For each hidden or output layer neuron j
       {
         //propagate the input forward.

$$net_j = \sum_i w_{ij} o_i + \theta_j \quad \text{// compute the net input of neuron } j \text{ with respect to the}$$
$$\text{previous layer } i.$$

$$O_j = \frac{1}{1+e^{-net_j}} \quad \text{//compute the output of each neuron } j$$

//backpropagate the errors
 for each neuron j in the output layer
$$error_j = o_j(1-o_j)(T_j - o_j) \text{ // compute the error for each neuron } j \text{ in the}$$
$$\text{hidden layers}$$
 for each neuron j in the hidden layers

$$error_j = O_j(1-O_j)\sum_k error_k w_{jk} \quad \text{// compute the error with respect to next}$$
$$\text{higher layer } k$$

//weight updating
   For each weight w_{ij} in MLF {
       $$\Delta w_{ij} = \eta.error_j.O_i$$
       $$w_{ij} = w_{ij} + \Delta w_{ij} \}$$
   For each bias in MLF {
       $$\Delta \theta_j = \eta.error_j$$
       $$\theta_j = \theta_j + \Delta \theta_j ; \}$$
   }
  }
 }

Figure 7. a) An Feedforward ANN Structure. b) Its habitat in the COA algorithm.

a)

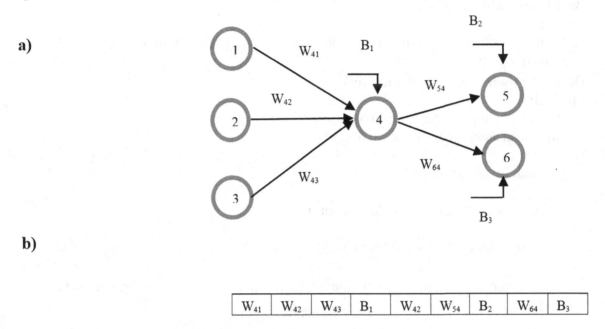

b)

W_{41}	W_{42}	W_{43}	B_1	W_{42}	W_{54}	B_2	W_{64}	B_3

Figure 8. An example of linearly separable two class problem with three hyperplane

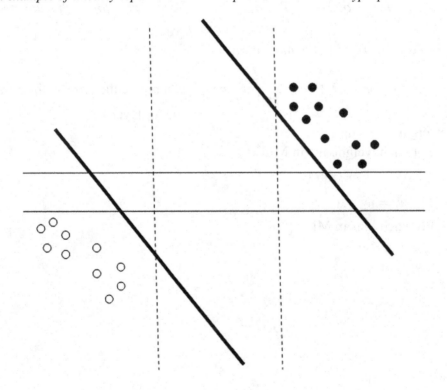

Figure 9. Two hyperplane and their associated margin. Hyperplane with large margin has greater generalization than small margin.

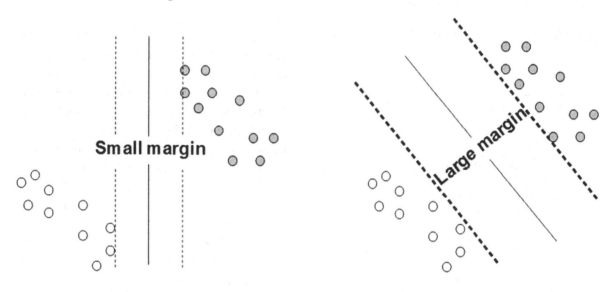

Figure 10. Support vectors

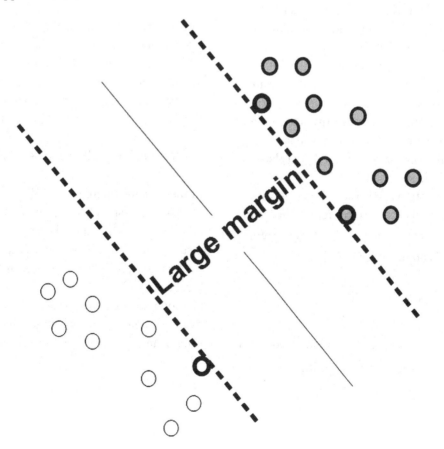

the support vectors are shown encircled with a thicker border. The distance between x_s and the hyperplane is $\dfrac{1}{\|w\|}$ where $\|w\|$ is the Euclidean norm of w, that is

$$\sqrt{w_1^2 + w_2^2 + \dots + w_n^2}\ .$$

Therefore, the maximum margin is $\dfrac{2}{\|w\|}$. The task can be summarized as:

$$\text{minimize}\quad g(w) = \frac{1}{2}\|w\|^2$$
$$\text{subject to } y_i(w.x + b) \geq 1$$

This is a nonlinear optimization task subject to a set of linear inequality constraints. This task can be solve using Karush-Kuhn-Tucker (KKT) conditions. Details can be found in the additional reading list at the end of this chapter.

In order to extend the linear SVMs with nonlinear cases, an extended SVM algorithm is introduced as follows. There are two main steps, first, the original feature vector transforms into a higher dimension space using a non-linear mapping. In the next step, a linear separating hyperplane in the new space is searched.

The computation cost in the training algorithm is very heavy and costly. To overcome this problem, a kernel function, $K(X_i, X_j)$, to the original input vector is applied. That is

$$K(X_i, X_j) = \phi(X_i).\phi(X_j)$$

In other words, $K(X_i, X_j)$ is replaced with $\phi(X_i).\phi(X_j)$ in the training algorithm.

Lazy Modelling

The classification algorithms discussed so far in this chapter - discriminant analysis, decision tree, Bayesian modelling, artificial neural networks, and support vector machine- are all examples of eager classification algorithms. Edger classification algorithms construct a classification model before receiving new instance to classify. A lazy classification model simply store the training examples and construction of classification model is delayed until we want to classify a new instance. Lazy classification algorithms make less time in training but more time in prediction(Han, Kamber, & Pei, 2006). In this section, we look at three examples of lazy classification algorithms: default model, k nearest neighbor classifier, and k* classifier.

Default Model

This classification algorithm generates a model that predicts a specified and constant value for the label in all examples. This type of classification model often cannot be used for actual classification problems but it can be used as a criterion for comparison with other classification algorithms.

K-Nearest Neighbor Classifiers

In the *k*-nearest neighbor (*KNN*) classifier, each instance corresponds to a point in n-dimensional space and classification is delayed until a new instance arrived. When a new instance is given, *KNN* classifier searches in the instance space for the *k* training instances that are closest to the unknown test. Closest is defined with a suitable distance metric such as Euclidean distance. The Euclidean distance between two instances,

$$X_1 = (x_{11}, x_{12}, ..., x_{1n})$$

and

$$X_2 = (x_{21}, x_{22}, ..., x_{2n})$$

is defined as:

$$dist(X_1, X_2) = \sqrt{\sum_{i=1}^{n} (x_{1i} - x_{2i})^2}$$

Figure 11 shows the *KNN* classifier for the case where instances are points in two dimensional space. Training instances from class 1 and class 2 are shown by "+" and "-," respectively. Note that the 1-nearest neighbor algorithm classifies test instances as an instance from class 1, whereas 5- nearest neighbor algorithm classifies it as an instance from class 2.

K* Classifier

K* is a lazy classifier that the class of a test instance is determined by training instances similar to it. It is similar to k-nearest neighbor but it uses an entropy based distance function. In other words, in this method, the distance between instances be defined as the complexity of transforming one instance into another(Cleary & Trigg, 1995).

COMBINATION OF CLASSIFICATION ALGORITHMS

The main motivation for combining of different classifiers is accuracy improvement. Different classifiers use different biases for generalizing from examples and different representations of the knowledge, therefore they tend to error on different parts of the instance space (Xu, Krzyzak, & Suen, 1992). Figure 12 illustrates the basic

Figure 11. K- nearest neighbor

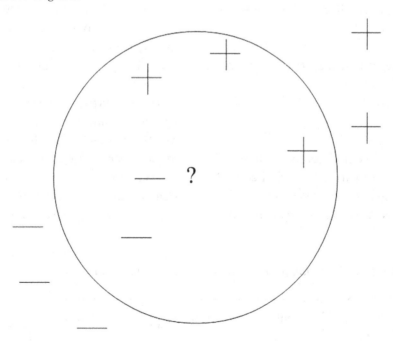

Figure 12. Basic framework for combination of classifiers

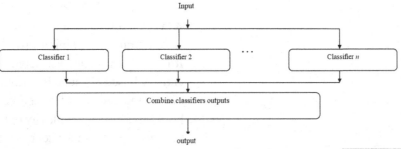

framework for combination of classifiers. In this section, two approach of combination of classifiers is described: bagging and voting.

Bagging

Bagging or bootstrap aggregating is a classification technique that can be used with many classification algortihms to improve classification perfroamnce. This method create classifiers using training sets that are bootstrapped. Given a training set D. In this algorithm, in each iteration, a new trainign set D_i is created by sampling from D randomly and with replacement. This kind of training data is known as a bootstrap data. Then, m classification algorithm are fitted using M bootstrap data and combined with voting.

Voting

Voting is another method for combining of classifiers. In this method, the output of several classifiers are computed. The class with the most votes is selected as the final classification result.

MEDICAL DIAGNOSIS USING PREDICTIVE DATA MINING

In this section, the results of medical diagnosis using several predictive data mining techniques are evaluated in three data mining environment: rapidminer, weka and matlab. Rapidminer is an open source software for data mining. It is ranked second in data mining tools used for real project in 2013("Data Mining / Analytic Tools Used Poll,"). Weka is a popular open source for machine learning and data mining developed at the University of Waikato, NewZealand. Matlab is a numerical computations environment developed by mathworks. Figure 13 shows the general medical diagnosis configuration using data mining techniques.

To this purpose, a case study is considered. Wisconsin Diagnostic Breast Cancer Data Set (WDBC) is a dataset which its goal is diagnosis of breast cancer disease(Frank & Asuncion, 2010). In this dataset, extracted Features are computed from digitized images of fine needle aspirate (FNA) of breast masses. They describe characteristics of the

Figure 13. A general configuration for medical diagnosis using data mining techniques

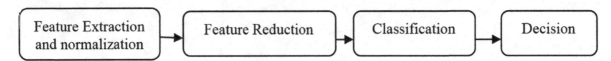

cell nuclei present in the image. Figure 14 shows a sample of these images. This data set contains 569 instances among which 357 are benign cases and 212 are malignant cases. In this dataset, ten features are computed for each cell nucleus. These features are listed as follows:

1. Radius (mean of distances from center to points on the perimeter),
2. Texture (standard deviation of gray-scale values),
3. Perimeter,
4. Area,
5. Smoothness (local variation in radius lengths),
6. Compactness ($\frac{(perimeter)^2}{(area - 1)}$),
7. Concavity (severity of concave portions of the contour),
8. Concave points (number of concave portions of the contour),
9. Symmetry,
10. Fractal dimension (coastline approximation - 1).

After feature extraction, mean, standard error, and worst mean these features are calculated. This process resulted in 30 features for each image.

Feature Normalizing

Extracted features have different measurement units. Features with large values may dominant features with small values. To help avoid dependence on the choice of measurement units, the features are normalized. In the feature normalization process, features are transformed into a common range such as [-1, +1]. One of the straightforward normalization techniques is the estimates of mean and variance. In this technique, features are mapped to features with zero mean and unit variance. This technique is defined by:

$$\overline{x}_k = \frac{1}{N} \sum_{i=1}^{N} x_{ik}, \qquad k = 1, 2, ..., l$$

$$\sigma_k^2 = \frac{1}{N-1} \sum_{i=1}^{N} (x_{ik} - \overline{x}_k)$$

$$\widehat{x}_{ik} = \frac{x_{ik} - \overline{x}_k}{\sigma_k}$$

where x_{ik} is the kth feature of ith instance, N is the number of features, x_k is the mean of kth feature, σ_k^2 is variance, and $\widehat{x}_{ik}$ is the normalized features.

Figure 14. Image taken using the FNA test. a. Benign and b. Malignant breast tumors.

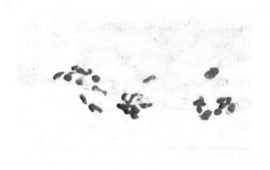

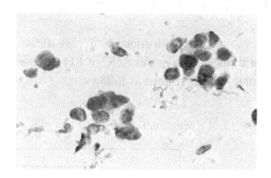

a

b

Principal Component Analysis

Principal component analysis (PCA) is an unsupervised method that reduces the features. PCA is transformed a set of correlated features to a set of uncorrelated features. In this method, features are combined for creating an alternative and smaller set of features. The basic procedure is as follows:

1. Compute the K orthonormal vectors: these vectors are unit vectors that each point in a direction perpendicular to the others. These vectors are called principal components (PCs).
2. Sort the PCs in order of decreasing: the PCs are a new set of axes for the data. In the sorted axes, first axes shows the most variance among the data, the second axes shows the next highest variance, and so on.
3. Eliminate the weaker components: it is obtained a good approximation of the original data using the strongest PCs.

After feature normalization on the breast cancer dataset, PCA is used to reduce the dimensionality and the first five principal are extracted components (this number is obtained by trial and error or expert knowledge). The five principal components values are: 98.62, 1.26, 0.07, 0.03, and 0.01. In other words, the first two PCs account for more than 98% information of data.

Classification Algorithms

To evaluate the performance of classification algorithms, accuracy and AUC of ROC is used. Accuracy is determined as follows:

$$Accuracy = \frac{Number\ of\ Correctly\ Classified\ Samples}{Total\ Number\ of\ Samples}$$

Confusion matrix is a specific table which each column of the matrix represents the instances in a predicted class while each row represents the instances in an actual class. A confusion matrix for a problem with two classes is shown in Figure 15.

Precision is a measure of the accuracy which is defined by the following equation:

$$precision = tp\ /\ (tp + fp),$$

Recall is another criterion which represents the ability of a classifier to select instances of a specific class. It is defined as:

$$recall = tp\ /\ (tp + fn)$$

Receiving operating characteristics curve (ROC) is a two dimensional curve in which TP is plotted on the Y axes and FP is plotted on the X axes. A ROC curve for a given classification model presents the tradeoff between the true positive rate and the false positive rate. The area under the ROC curve (AUC) is a measure of the accuracy of the classification algorithm. Threshold in ROC curve refers to the confidence value of the prediction. For more information, please see the additional reading lists at the end of this chapter.

To evaluate the different classification methods, Hold out method is employed on the data set. In this method, the given dataset are randomly

Figure 15. A confusion matrix for a two class problem

		Predicted Class	
		Yes	No
Actual Class	Yes	True Positive(TP)	False Negative(FN)
	No	False Positive(FP)	True Negative(TN)

portioned into two subsets, a training set and test set. Usually, two-third of the data are assigned to the training set, and the remaining one-third is assigned to the test set. Hold out method can be more reliable by repeating the process k times with different subsamples (random subsampling). In this study, hold out methods repeated 10 times.

Diagnosis Using Discriminant Analysis

The performance results of diagnosis using linear and quadratic discriminant analysis are presented in Table 2. The confusion matrix of LDA and QDA classifier for the case of maximum accuracy is presented in the Table 3. The ROC curve for this case is presented in Figure 16.

Diagnosis Using DT

The performance results of diagnosis of breast cancer disease using DT are shown in Table 4. Based on the results, information gain criterion is presented the highest mean accuracy using DT (93.98) with the lowest standard deviation (1.07). Confusion matrix and ROC plot for the case of maximum accuracy is shown in Table 5 and Figure 17.

Two main parameters in random forest are number of trees and quality criteria. The classification results using random forest with different parameters are presented in Table 6. According to the results, the best mean accuracy is obtained when the number of trees are 13 and quality criterion is information gain. In the all experiments

Table 2. The results of LDA and QDA classifiers

Learning Method	Criteria	Min	Max	Std.	Mean
LDA	Accuracy	88.30	94.73	2.33	91.29
	AUC of ROC	0.450	0.584	0.128	0.542
QDA	Accuracy	90.64	95.32	1.51	92.63
	AUC of ROC	0.532	0.592	0.136	0.583

Table 3. Confusion matrix obtained from the evaluation for the case of the highest accuracy using a. LDA and b. QDA classifier

	Predict 1	Predict 2	precision
Class 1	52	2	96.30
Class 2	7	110	94.02
recall	88.14	98.21	

(a)

	Predict 1	Predict 2	precision
Class 1	55	2	96.49%
Class 2	6	108	94.74%
recall	90.16%	98.18%	

(b)

Table 4. The results of DT for diagnosis of breast cancer using various quality criteria

Quality Criteria	Accuracy			
	Min	Max	Std.	Mean
Information Gain	92.40	95.91	1.07	93.98
Gain Ratio	89.47	95.91	2.04	93.45
Gini Index	91.23	95.32	1.58	92.98
Accuracy	87.72	95.32	2.26	91.99

Figure 16. The roc curve for a. LDA and b. QDA classifiers

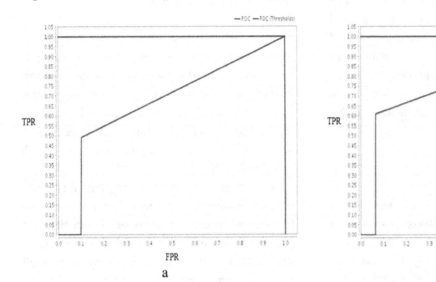

a   b

Table 5. Confusion matrix for DT classifier

	Predict 1	Predict 2	Precision
Class 1	52	0	100
Class 2	7	112	94.12
Recall	88.14	100	

Table 6. The performance of random forest

Number of Trees	Quality Criteria	Accuracy				AUC of ROC			
		Min	Max	Std.	Mean	Min	Max	Std.	Mean
5	Information Gain	82.46	94.15	3.98	90.23	0.877	0.976	0.0317	0.9422
	Gain Ratio	67.84	93.57	7.94	87.77	0.794	0.969	0.0526	0.8996
	Gini Index	84.21	92.98	2.45	88.54	0.895	0.966	0.0224	0.9380
	Accuracy	72.51	92.40	6.40	84.97	0.801	0.908	0.0332	0.8584
7	Information Gain	87.13	97.66	2.88	90.70	0.935	0.979	0.0168	0.9558
	Gain Ratio	78.36	97.47	4.86	88.58	0.710	0.974	0.0769	0.9008
	Gini Index	82.46	94.15	3.68	90.29	0.845	0.972	0.0424	0.9387
	Accuracy	74.85	92.98	5.77	87.66	0.779	0.917	0.5453	0.8651
13	Information Gain	89.47	97.08	2.92	92.40	0.954	0.991	0.0123	0.9783
	Gain Ratio	80.70	95.92	4.33	89.09	0.973	0.988	0.0052	0.982
	Gini Index	80.07	92.40	4.16	88.12	0.973	0.988	0.0052	0.9822
	Accuracy	80.70	92.40	4.04	88.19	0.948	0.990	0.0125	0.9781

Figure 17. ROC curve for DT classifier

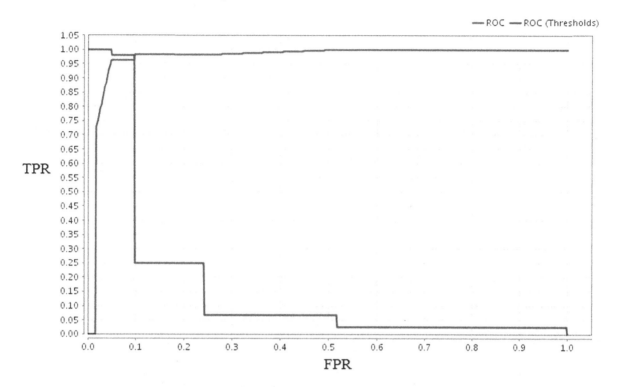

with several number of trees, information gain is presented the highest mean accuracy and mean AUC. The lowest performance is provided by accuracy quality criterion in the all experiments. The confusion matrix for the case that has the highest accuracy is presented in Table 7. The ROC curve associated to this case is shown in Figure 18. It is possible to achieve better accuracy with the change of number of trees.

Table 7. Confusion matrix for Random Forest

	Predict 1	Predict 2	Precision
Class 1	50	4	92.59
Class 2	9	108	92.31
Recall	84.75	96.43	

Diagnosis using Bayesian Modelling

Results of diagnosis of breast cancer disease by NB classifier are shown in Table 8. The confusion matrix for one run with maximum accuracy and its ROC curve are shown in Table 9 and Figure 19. The type of learning process is very important in BBNs because the performance of BBNs highly dependents on this parameter. In this study, four methods including K2, Hillclimbing, simulated annealing, and tabu search were applied in the learning stage of BBNs. The results of learning stage of BBN using above search methods are shown in Table 10. Results indicated the Hill climbing technique is given better results because it presented higher mean accuracy and mean AUC. Confusion matrix for one run with the highest

Figure 18. ROC curve for Random Forest classifier

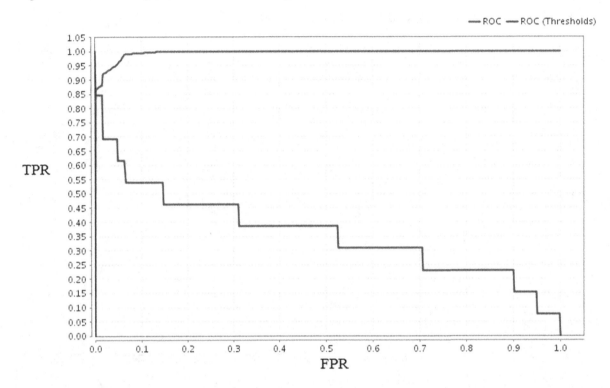

Table 8. The results of NB classifier

	Min	Max	Std.	Mean
Accuracy	88.30	95.91	2.29	91.81
AUC of ROC	0.9580	0.9980	0.0113	0.9750

Table 9. Confusion matrix for NB

	Predict 1	Predict 2	Precision
Class 1	53	1	98.15
Class 2	6	111	94.87
Recall	89.83	99.11	

accuracy is shown in Table 11. ROC curve associated with this run is presented in Figure 20.

Diagnosis with ANNs

Network structure is one of the main factors in designing ANNs, because network structure has a significant influence on the final performance. The number of hidden layers and their neurons are two main factor for designing MLF networks. The number of neurons in the first layer is equal to the number of selected components in PCA (the number of input patterns vector). The number of neurons in the output layer is two since this dataset has two classes. The number of hidden layers and their neurons depends on the complexity of the problem. In general, ANN with too few hidden neurons will not have a sufficient capability for training of input patterns and too many hidden neurons leads to overfitting on the input patterns. Hence, specifying the number of layers and their neurons is a critical step in the designing the networks. In this chapter, one hidden layer are used and several combinations of the number of

Figure 19. ROC curve for NB classifier

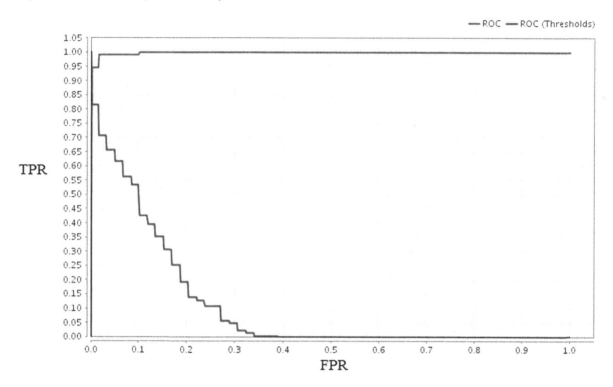

Table 10. The results of BBN with various learning methods

Learning Method	Criterion	Min	Max	Std.	Mean
K2(Cooper & Herskovits, 1992)	Accuracy	90.64	95.32	1.50	91.88
	AUC of ROC	0.9530	0.9890	0.0098	0.9708
Hill Climbing(Cheng & Greiner, 1999)	Accuracy	91.23	95.91	1.51	93.53
	AUC of ROC	0.9760	0.9900	0.0056	0.9840
Simulated annealing(Bouckaert, 1995)	Accuracy	91.23	95.91	1.40	91.23
	AUC of ROC	0.9740	0.9920	0.0061	0.9830
Tabu Search(Bouckaert, 1995)	Accuracy	91.23	95.91	1.45	93.45
	AUC of ROC	0.961	0.988	0.0098	0.9773

Table 11. Confusion matrix for BBN

	Predict 1	Predict 2	Precision
Class 1	53	2	96.36
Class 2	5	111	95.69
Recall	91.38	98.23	

Figure 20. ROC curve for BBN

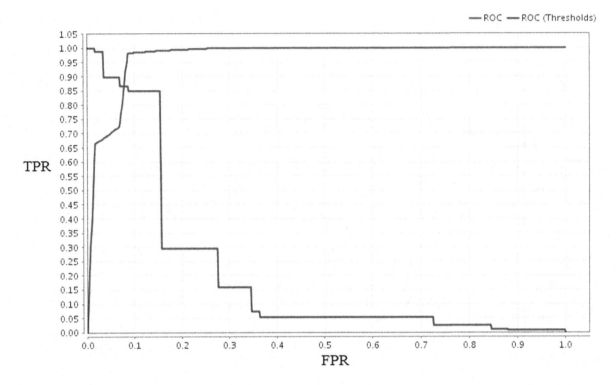

neurons in hidden layer are examined by train and error. In the experiments, the number of neurons changed from 2 to 20. According to the Figure 21, hidden layer with 12 neurons and COA learning has the highest accuracy and AUC of ROC. Confusion matrix for one run with highest accuracy is shown in Table 12 and its ROC curve is shown in Figure 22.

Diagnosis with SVM

Kernel function is a technique to solve nonlinear problems in the SVM classifier. In this technique, the original feature vector maps into a higher dimension space. In practice, predefined kernel function is applied. The choice of a suitable kernel function in SVM can be compared with determin-

Figure 21. Variation of selection crieteria with the different combination of neurons in hidden layer, and BP and COA learning algorithms

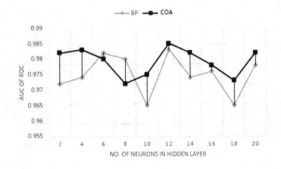

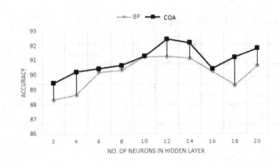

Table 12. Confusion matrix for a run using ANN

	Predict 1	**Predict 2**	**Precision**
Class 1	47	2	95.92
Class 2	9	113	92.62
Recall	83.93	98.26	

ing the optimal structure of neural networks. In this study, four commonly chosen kernel functions were applied. These kernel functions are defined as follows:

- **Dot Kernel:** The dot kernel is defined by:

$$k(x, y) = x * y$$

- **Radial Basis Function Kernel (RBF):** The RBF kernel is defined as:

$$K(x, x') = \exp(\frac{-\parallel x - x' \parallel^2}{2\delta^2})$$

where $\parallel x - x' \parallel^2$ is the squared Euclidean distance between the two feature vector and δ is a free parameter.

- **Polynomial Kernel:** This kernel is defined as:

$$K(x, x') = (x^T.x' + 1)^d$$

where d is the degree of polynomial.

- **Anova Kernel:** This kernel is a type of RBF kernel. It is given by the following equation:

Figure 22. ROC curve for ANN

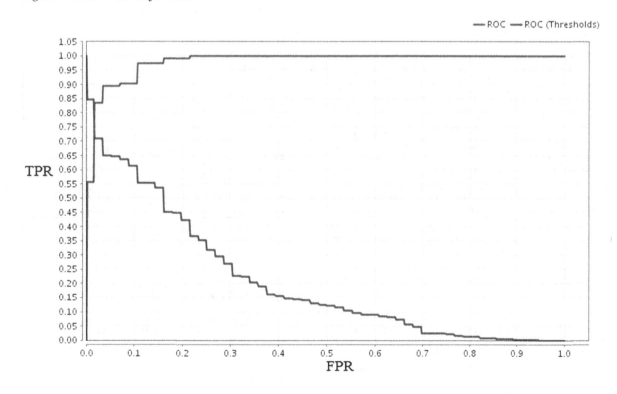

351

$$K(x,x^{'}) = \sum_{k=1}^{n} \exp(-\gamma(x_i - x_i^{'}))^d$$

In the above equation, the shape of kernel is controlled by the parameter γ (gamma) and d (degree).

Table 13 shows the results of breast cancer diagnosis using SVM with the above kernel functions. Results showed Anova kernel function has the highest mean accuracy and AUC of ROC. So, this kernel was selected as the best one for breast cancer diagnosis. The confusion matrix for SVM with Anova kernel function is shown in Table 14. In addition, its ROC curve is presented in Figure 23.

Diagnosis with Lazy Modelling

A default value use for all labels in the default model. In this study, median, mode, and average of label values were used as the default value. All three methods is offered 1 as the default class for all datasets so their results is similar together. This method is not used in practice. According to the Table 15, the efficiency of this method is not suitable and is often used for comparison with other methods. The confusion matrix for the best accuracy is presented in Table 16 and its ROC curve is shown in Figure 24.

The most important factor in the KNN is the K value. This value can be determined experimentally. A small value of K means that noise will have a higher influence on the performance. A large value of K make it computationally expensive and it is in contrast with the basic philosophy behind KNN (that feature vectors that are near might have similar classes). According to the Figure 25, the value of 9 for k has the highest mean accuracy and mean AUC of ROC. Confusion matrix and its AUC of ROC is shown in Table 17 and Figure 26, respectively. One of version of KNN is K* classifier. Table 17 shows result of diagnosis with this classifier. In this problem, $k*$ presented the lower performance compared with KNN classifier.

Table 13. The results of diagnosis using SVM with various kernel types

Kernel Type	Criterion	Min	Max	Std.	Mean
Dot	Accuracy	93.57	97.66	1.16	95.20
	AUC of ROC	0.986	0.995	0.0028	0.9900
RBF	Accuracy	93.57	96.49	1.11	95.03
	AUC of ROC	0.972	0.995	0.0057	0.9830
Polynomial	Accuracy	78.34	89.47	3.10	82.81
	AUC of ROC	0.867	0.952	0.0245	0.9015
Anova	Accuracy	93.57	97.66	1.36	95.61
	AUC of ROC	0.982	0.999	0.0056	0.9914

Table 14. Confusion matrix for SVM with Anova kernel

	Predict 1	Predict 2	Precision
Class 1	59	3	95.16
Class 2	1	108	99.08
Recall	98.33	97.30	

Table 15. The results of default model

	Min	Max	Std.	Mean
Accuracy	56.14	66.08	3.39	62.97
AUC of ROC	0.5	0.5	0	0.5

Figure 23. ROC curve for SVM with Anova kernel

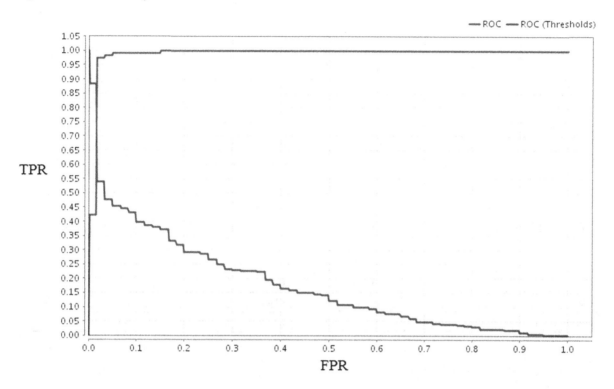

Figure 24. ROC curve for Default model

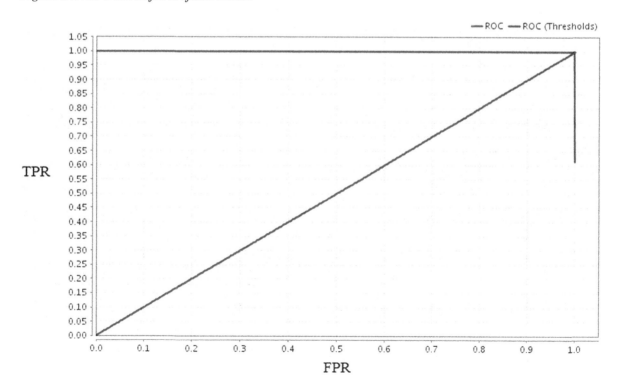

Figure 25. Variation of selection criteria with different K values

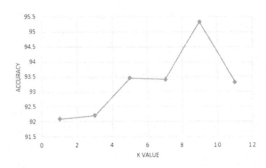 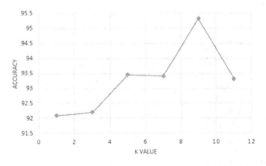

Table 16. Confusion matrix for Default model

	Predict 1	Predict 2	Precision
Class 1	0	0	0.00%
Class 2	58	113	66.08%
Recall	0.00%	100%	

Table 17. Confusion matrix for KNN classifier

	Predict 1	Predict 2	Precision
Class 1	57	4	93.44
Class 2	4	106	96.36
Recall	93.44	96.36	

Figure 26. ROC curve for KNN classifier

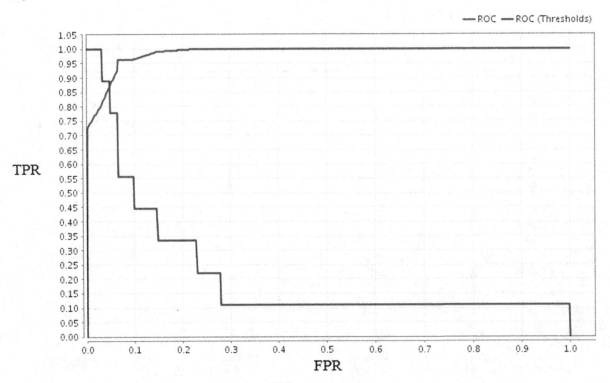

Diagnosis with Combination of Classifiers

In this section, two experiments have been performed: Bagging of KNN and voting on five classifiers. Table 19 shows results of these two experiments. In the first experiment, the base classifier is KNN. In the second experiment, result of five classifier is combined. These classifiers are: ANN, SVM, KNN, LDA and QDA. The confusion matrix for the best accuracy is presented in Table 20 and its ROC curve is shown in Figure 27. According to the result, combination of classifiers can be improved the classification performance. According to the results, voting method improve the classification results.

CONCLUSION

At present, various data mining techniques have been successfully applied to medical diagnosis for automated medical diagnosis systems. These systems can assist to a physician as a partner.

Table 18. The results of k* classifier

	Min	**Max**	**Std.**	**Mean**
Accuracy	81.87	8479	3.22	82.32
AUC of ROC	0.853	0.902	0.123	0.873

Table 19. The results of Bagging of KNN and voting method

Method		**Min**	**Max**	**Std.**	**Mean**
Bagging of KNN	Accuracy	89.47	96.49	3.34	95.89
	AUC of ROC	0.929	0.968	0.162	0.936
Voting	Accuracy	96.49	99.42	1.21	97.32
	AUC of ROC	0.983	0.999	0.006	0.994

Table 20. Confusion matrix for voting method

	Predict 1	**Predict 2**	**Precision**
Class 1	62	0	100
Class 2	1	108	99.08
Recall	98.41	100	

Figure 27. ROC curve for voting method

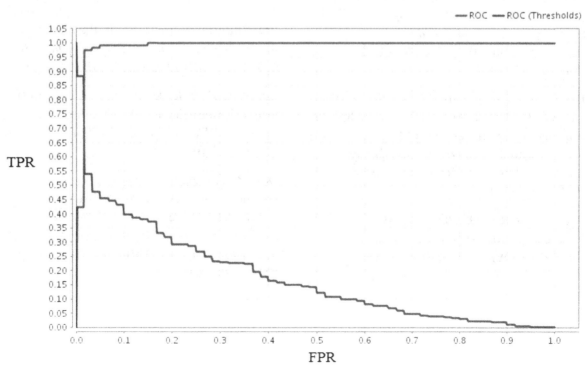

The possible errors of physician can be reduced with the help of these systems. Classification is a step in data mining process. There are various classification algorithms for classification. According to the no-free-launch principle, there is no classification algorithm that work best for all problems. In this chapter, various predictive data mining techniques for medical diagnosis is analyzed and compared.

ACKNOWLEDGMENT

Authors are grateful to council of University of Kashan for providing financial support to undertake this work.

REFERENCES

Abbass, H. A. (2002). An evolutionary artificial neural networks approach for breast cancer diagnosis. *Artificial Intelligence in Medicine*, *25*(3), 265–281. doi:10.1016/S0933-3657(02)00028-3 PMID:12069763

Bascil, M. S., & Oztekin, H. (2012). A study on hepatitis disease diagnosis using probabilistic neural network. *Journal of Medical Systems*, *36*(3), 1603–1606. doi:10.1007/s10916-010-9621-x PMID:21057884

Bascil, M. S., & Temurtas, F. (2011). A study on hepatitis disease diagnosis using multilayer neural network with Levenberg Marquardt Training Algorithm. *Journal of Medical Systems*, *35*(3), 433–436. doi:10.1007/s10916-009-9378-2 PMID:20703548

Bouckaert, R. R. (1995). *Bayesian belief networks: from construction to inference*. Universiteit Utrecht, Faculteit Wiskunde en Informatica.

Çalişir, D., & Dogantekin, E. (2011). A new intelligent hepatitis diagnosis system: PCA–LSSVM. *Expert Systems with Applications*, *38*(8), 10705–10708. doi:10.1016/j.eswa.2011.01.014

Chen, H.-L., Liu, D.-Y., Yang, B., Liu, J., & Wang, G. (2011). A new hybrid method based on local fisher discriminant analysis and support vector machines for hepatitis disease diagnosis. *Expert Systems with Applications*, *38*(9), 11796–11803. doi:10.1016/j.eswa.2011.03.066

Chen, H.-L., Yang, B., Liu, J., & Liu, D.-Y. (2011). A support vector machine classifier with rough set-based feature selection for breast cancer diagnosis. *Expert Systems with Applications*, *38*(7), 9014–9022. doi:10.1016/j.eswa.2011.01.120

Cheng, J., & Greiner, R. (1999). *Comparing Bayesian network classifiers*. Paper presented at the Proceedings of the Fifteenth conference on Uncertainty in artificial intelligence. New York, NY.

Cleary, J. G., & Trigg, L. E. (1995). *K^*: An Instance-based Learner Using an Entropic Distance Measure*. Paper presented at the ICML. New York, NY.

Coomans, D., Jonckheer, M., Massart, D., Broeckaert, I., & Blockx, P. (1978). The application of linear discriminant analysis in the diagnosis of thyroid diseases. *Analytica Chimica Acta*, *103*(4), 409–415. doi:10.1016/S0003-2670(01)83105-6

Cooper, G. F., & Herskovits, E. (1992). A Bayesian method for the induction of probabilistic networks from data. *Machine Learning*, *9*(4), 309–347. doi:10.1007/BF00994110

Das, R., Turkoglu, I., & Sengur, A. (2009a). Diagnosis of valvular heart disease through neural networks ensembles. *Computer Methods and Programs in Biomedicine*, *93*(2), 185–191. doi:10.1016/j.cmpb.2008.09.005 PMID:18951649

Das, R., Turkoglu, I., & Sengur, A. (2009b). Effective diagnosis of heart disease through neural networks ensembles. *Expert Systems with Applications*, *36*(4), 7675–7680. doi:10.1016/j.eswa.2008.09.013

Data Mining / Analytic Tools Used Poll. (2013). Retrieved from http://www.kdnuggets.com/polls/2013/analytics-big-data-mining-data-science-software.html

Dogantekin, E., Dogantekin, A., & Avci, D. (2011). An expert system based on Generalized Discriminant Analysis and Wavelet Support Vector Machine for diagnosis of thyroid diseases. *Expert Systems with Applications*, *38*(1), 146–150. doi:10.1016/j.eswa.2010.06.029

Ebrahimpour-Komleh, H., & Mousavirad, S. J. (2013). *Cuckoo Optimization Algorithm for Feedforward neural network training*. Paper presented at the 21th Iranian Conference on Electrical Engineering. Mashhad, Iran.

Er, O., Tanrikulu, A. C., Abakay, A., & Temurtas, F. (2012). An approach based on probabilistic neural network for diagnosis of Mesothelioma's disease. *Computers & Electrical Engineering*, *38*(1), 75–81. doi:10.1016/j.compeleceng.2011.09.001

Frank, A., & Asuncion, A. (2010). *UCI machine learning repository*. Academic Press.

Han, J., Kamber, M., & Pei, J. (2006). *Data mining: concepts and techniques*. Morgan Kaufmann.

Hsieh, C.-H., Lu, R.-H., Lee, N.-H., Chiu, W.-T., Hsu, M.-H., & Li, Y.-C. J. (2011). Novel solutions for an old disease: diagnosis of acute appendicitis with random forest, support vector machines, and artificial neural networks. *Surgery*, *149*(1), 87–93. doi:10.1016/j.surg.2010.03.023 PMID:20466403

Jerez-Aragonés, J. M., Gómez-Ruiz, J. A., Ramos-Jiménez, G., Muñoz-Pérez, J., & Alba-Conejo, E. (2003). A combined neural network and decision trees model for prognosis of breast cancer relapse. *Artificial Intelligence in Medicine*, *27*(1), 45–63. doi:10.1016/S0933-3657(02)00086-6 PMID:12473391

Kabari, L., & Nwachukwu, E. (2012). *Neural Networks and Decision Trees For Eye Diseases Diagnosis*. Academic Press.

Kayaer, K., & Yıldırım, T. (2003). *Medical diagnosis on Pima Indian diabetes using general regression neural networks*. Paper presented at the international conference on artificial neural networks and neural information processing (ICANN/ICONIP). New York, NY.

Mitchell, T. M. (1997). *Machine learning*. Burr Ridge, IL: McGraw Hill.

Moftah, H. M., Azar, A. T., Al-Shammari, E. T., Ghali, N. I., Hassanien, A. E., & Shoman, M. (2013). Adaptive k-means clustering algorithm for MR breast image segmentation. *Neural Computing & Applications*, 1–12.

Ozcift, A. (2012). SVM feature selection based rotation forest ensemble classifiers to improve computer-aided diagnosis of Parkinson disease. *Journal of Medical Systems*, *36*(4), 2141–2147. doi:10.1007/s10916-011-9678-1 PMID:21547504

Pandey, A. K., Pandey, P., Jaiswal, K., & Sen, A. K. (2013). A Heart Disease Prediction Model using Decision Tree. *International Journal of Engineering Mathematics and Computer Sciences*, *1*(3).

Polat, K., & Güneş, S. (2006). Hepatitis disease diagnosis using a new hybrid system based on feature selection (FS) and artificial immune recognition system with fuzzy resource allocation. *Digital Signal Processing, 16*(6), 889–901. doi:10.1016/j.dsp.2006.07.005

Polat, K., & Güneş, S. (2007). Breast cancer diagnosis using least square support vector machine. *Digital Signal Processing, 17*(4), 694–701. doi:10.1016/j.dsp.2006.10.008

Rajabioun, R. (2011). Cuckoo optimization algorithm. *Applied Soft Computing, 11*(8), 5508–5518. doi:10.1016/j.asoc.2011.05.008

Ramírez, J., Górriz, J., Segovia, F., Chaves, R., Salas-Gonzalez, D., López, M., & Padilla, P. (2010). Computer aided diagnosis system for the Alzheimer's disease based on partial least squares and random forest SPECT image classification. *Neuroscience Letters, 472*(2), 99–103. doi:10.1016/j.neulet.2010.01.056 PMID:20117177

Russell, S. J., Norvig, P., Canny, J. F., Malik, J. M., & Edwards, D. D. (1995). *Artificial intelligence: a modern approach* (Vol. 74). Prentice Hall.

Sartakhti, J. S., Zangooei, M. H., & Mozafari, K. (2011). Hepatitis disease diagnosis using a novel hybrid method based on support vector machine and simulated annealing (SVM-SA). In *Computer methods and programs in biomedicine*. Academic Press.

Shouman, M., Turner, T., & Stocker, R. (2012). *Applying k-Nearest Neighbour in Diagnosing Heart Disease Patients*. Paper presented at the 2012 International Conference on Knowledge Discovery (ICKD 2012) IPCSIT. New York, NY.

Temurtas, F. (2009). A comparative study on thyroid disease diagnosis using neural networks. *Expert Systems with Applications, 36*(1), 944–949. doi:10.1016/j.eswa.2007.10.010

Tondini, C., Fenaroli, P., & Labianca, R. (2007). Breast cancer follow-up: just a burden, or much more? *Annals of Oncology, 18*(9), 1431–1432. doi:10.1093/annonc/mdm380 PMID:17761702

Venkatesan, P., & Anitha, S. (2006). Application of a radial basis function neural network for diagnosis of diabetes mellitus. *Current Science, 91*(9), 1195.

Vlahou, A., Schorge, J. O., Gregory, B. W., & Coleman, R. L. (2003). Diagnosis of ovarian cancer using decision tree classification of mass spectral data. *BioMed Research International,* (5), 308-314.

Xu, L., Krzyzak, A., & Suen, C. Y. (1992). Methods of combining multiple classifiers and their applications to handwriting recognition. *Systems, Man and Cybernetics. IEEE Transactions on, 22*(3), 418–435.

Yan, W.-W., & Shao, H.-H. (2003). Application of support vector machines and least squares support vector machines to heart disease diagnoses. *Control and Decision, 18*(3), 358–360.

Ye, J., Janardan, R., & Li, Q. (2004). *Two-dimensional linear discriminant analysis*. Paper presented at the Advances in Neural Information Processing Systems. New York, NY.

ADDITIONAL READING

Çakı, A., & Demirel, B. (2011). A software tool for determination of breast cancer treatment methods using data mining approach. *Journal of Medical Systems, 35*(6), 1503–1511. doi:10.1007/s10916-009-9427-x PMID:20703767

Cios, K. J., & Kacprzyk, J. (2001), Medical data mining and knowledge discovery, PA: Physica-Verlag New York, NY

Curtis, A. (2005), Classification using LDA, QDA and logistic regression, Mech learn, Vol. 3, 1-23,

Ebrahimpour, H., & Kouzani, A. (2007), Face Recognition with bagging KNN, International Conference on Signal Processing and Communication Systems (ICSPCS'2007) Australia, Gold Coast, 17-19

Ebrahimpour-Komleh, H., & Mousavirad, S. J. (2013), Cuckoo Optimization Algorithm for Feedforward neural network training, Paper presented at the 21th Iranian Conference on Electrical Engineering, Mashhad, Iran

Fawcett T. (2006), An introduction to ROC analysis, pattern recognition letters, 27(8), 861-874

Hagan, M. T., & Menhaj, M. B. (1994). Training feedforward networks with the Marquardt algorithm, Neural Networks. *IEEE Transactions on, 5*(6), 989–993.

Han, J., Kamber, M., & Pei, J. (2006), data mining:concept and techniques, PA:Morgan Kaufmann

Koh, H., & Tan, G. (2011). Data mining applications in healthcare. *Journal of Healthcare Information Management, 19*(2). PMID:15869215

Li, T., Zhu, S., & Pgihara, M. (2006). Using discriminant analysis for multi-class classification: an experimental investigation. *Knowledge and Information Systems, 10*(4), 453–742. doi:10.1007/s10115-006-0013-y

Maria-Luiza A., Osmar Z., Alexandru C. (2001), Application of Data Mining Techniques for Medical Image Classification, MDM/KDD, 94-101

Markus, B., & Wolfgang, B. (2001). A comparison of linear genetic programming and neural networks in medical data mining. *IEEE Transactions on Evolutionary Computation, 5*(1), 17–26. doi:10.1109/4235.910462

Mousavirad S.J., Akhlaghian F., & Mollazade k,(2011), Classification of rice variaties Using optimal color and texture features and BP neural networks, 7th iranian conferences on machine vision and image processing, tehran, iran

Nanni, L. (2006). an ensemble of classifiers for the diagnosis of erythemato-squamous diseases. *Neurocomputing, 69*(7), 842–845. doi:10.1016/j.neucom.2005.09.007

Prather, J. C., Lobach, D. F., Goodwin, L. K., Hales, J. W., Hage, M. L., & Hammond, W. E. (1997), Medical data mining: knowledge discovery in a clinical data warehouse, Proceedings of the AMIA Annual Fall Symposium, PA: American Medical Informatics Association

Ruggeri, F., Faltin, F., & Kenett, R. (2007). Bayesian Networks. In F. Ruggeri, F. Faltin, & R. Kenett (Eds.), *Encyclopedia of Statistics in Quality & Reliability*. PA: Wiley & Sons.

Sebastian, M., Gunnar, R., Jason, W., Bernhard, S., & Mullers, K. R. (1999), Fisher Discriminant analysis with kernels, IEEE conference on Neural Networks for Signal Processing, Madison, WI

Shen, H., & Chou, K. (2006). Ensemble classifier for protein fold pattern recognition. *Bioinformatics (Oxford, England), 22*(14), 1717–1722. doi:10.1093/bioinformatics/btl170 PMID:16672258

Wu, D., Warwick, K., Ma, Z., Gasson, M. N., Burgess, J., Pan, S., & Aziz, T. Z. (2010). Prediction of Parkinson's disease tremor onset using a radial basis function neural network based on particle swarm optimization. *International Journal of Neural Systems, 20*(02), 109–116. doi:10.1142/S0129065710002292 PMID:20411594

Yao, X. (1993). A review of evolutionary artificial neural networks. *International Journal of Intelligent Systems, 8*(4), 539–567. doi:10.1002/int.4550080406

KEY TERMS AND DEFINITIONS

Artificial Neural Network: This model is a classification algorithm inspired from biological nervous systems.

Bayesian Modelling: This approach is a classification algorithm based on Bayes theorem.

Combination of Classifiers: This method combine the results of different classifiers to improve classification performance.

Data Mining: It is computational process of discovering hidden knowledge in the large datasets.

Decision Tree: It is a classification algorithm that uses a tree-like model of decisions.

Discriminant Analysis: It is a classification algorithm based on linear and quadratic decision surface.

Lazy Modelling: In this method, construction of classification model is delayed until we want to classify a new instance.

Medical Diagnosis: It is process of trying to discover and identify a possible disease.

Principal Component Analysis: It is a statistical method for feature reduction in feature set.

Support Vector Machine: A classifier based on maximum margin hyperplane.

Compilation of References

Abbasi, A. (2010). Intelligent feature selection for opinion classification. *IEEE Intelligent Systems*, *25*(4), 75–79.

Abbasi, A., Chen, H. C., & Salem, A. (2008). Sentiment analysis in multiple languages: Feature selection for opinion classification in web forums. *ACM Transactions on Information Systems*, *26*(3). doi:10.1145/1361684.1361685

Abbass, H. A. (2002). An evolutionary artificial neural networks approach for breast cancer diagnosis. *Artificial Intelligence in Medicine*, *25*(3), 265–281. doi:10.1016/S0933-3657(02)00028-3 PMID:12069763

Abdelhalim, A., & Traore, I. (2009). A new method for learning decision trees from rules. In *Proceedings of International Conference on Machine Learning and Applications* (pp. 693-698). Miami Beach, FL: IEEE.

Abraham, A., Grosan, C., & Pedrycz, W. (2008). *Engineering Evolutionary Intelligent Systems* (Vol. 82). Springer. doi:10.1007/978-3-540-75396-4_1

Acharjya, D. P., & Ezhilarasi, L. (2011). A knowledge mining model for ranking institutions using rough computing with ordering rules and formal concept analysis. *International Journal of Computer Science Issues*, *8*(2), 417–425.

Acharjya, D. P., Roy, D., & Rahaman, M. A. (2012). Prediction of missing associations using rough computing and Bayesian classification. *International Journal of Intelligent Systems and Applications*, *4*(11), 1–13. doi:10.5815/ijisa.2012.11.01

Acharjya, D. P., & Tripathy, B. K. (2008). Rough sets on fuzzy approximation spaces and applications to distributed knowledge systems. *International Journal of Artificial Intelligence and Soft Computing*, *1*(1), 1–14.

Acharjya, D. P., & Tripathy, B. K. (2009). Rough sets on intuitionistic fuzzy approximation spaces and knowledge representation. *International Journal of Artificial Intelligence and Computational Research*, *1*(1), 29–36.

Acharjya, D. P., & Tripathy, B. K. (2012). Intuitionistic fuzzy rough set on two universal sets and knowledge representation. *Mathematical Sciences International Research Journal*, *1*(2), 584–598.

Acharjya, D. P., & Tripathy, B. K. (2013). Topological characterization, measures of uncertainty and rough equality of sets on two universal sets. *International Journal of Intelligent Systems and Applications*, *5*(2), 16–24. doi:10.5815/ijisa.2013.02.02

Adelberg, B. (1998). NoDoSE—a tool for semi-automatically extracting structured and semistructured data from text documents. *SIGMOD Record*, *27*(2), 283–294. doi:10.1145/276305.276330

Agarwal, B., & Mittal, N. (2012). Categorical Probability Proportion Difference (CPPD), A Feature Selection Method for Sentiment Classification. In *Proceedings of the 2nd Workshop on Sentiment Analysis where AI meets Psychology* (SAAIP). COLING.

Agarwal, B., & Mittal, N. (2013). Optimal Feature Selection Methods for Sentiment Analysis. In *Proceedings of 14th International Conference on Intelligent Text Processing and Computational Linguistics* (CICLing 2013), (Vol. 7817, pp. 13-24). CICLing.

Agarwal, B., Sharma, V., & Mittal, N. (2013). Sentiment Classification of Review Documents using Phrases Patterns. In *Proceedings of the International Conference on Advances in Computing, Communications and Informatics* (ICACCI), (pp. 1577-1580). ICACCI.

Agrawal & Srikant. (1999). Mining fuzzy quantitative association rules. In *Proceedings of IEEE International Conference on Fuzzy Systems* (pp. 99-102).Washington, DC: IEEE Computer Society.

Agrawal, R., & Srikant, R. (1994). Fast algorithms for mining association rules. In *Proceedings of 20th International Conference on Very Large Data Bases* (pp. 487-499). Santigo, Chile: Morgan Kaufmann Publishers Inc.

Agrawal, R., Imielinski, T., & Swami, A. (1993). Mining association rules between sets of items in large databases. *SIGMOD Record*, *22*(2), 207–216. doi:10.1145/170036.170072

Ai, D., Zheng, Y., & Zhang, D. (2010). Automatic text summarization based on latent semantic indexing. *Artificial Life and Robotics*, *15*(1), 25–29. doi:10.1007/s10015-010-0759-x

Aiken, L. S., & West, S. G. (1991). *Multiple regression: Testing and interpreting interactions*. Sage Publications.

Alexander, D. (1997). *Data Mining*. Retrieved May 22, 2013 from http://www.laits.utexas.edu/~anorman/BUS. FOR/course.mat/Alex

Alexander, D. (2011). *Data Mining*. Retrieved March 7, 2012, from https://dea@tracor.com

Ali, M. M., & Rajamani, L. (2012). Decision tree induction: Priority classification. In *Proceedings of International Conference on Advances in Engineering, Science and Management* (pp. 668-673). Nagapattinam, Tamil Nadu: IEEE.

Al-Mudimigh, A., Saleem, F., Ullah, Z., & Al-Aboud, F. (2009). Implementation of Data Mining Engine on CRM, Improve Customer Satisfaction. *International Conference on Information and Communication Technologies ICICT '09*, *1*(2), 193–197.

Al-Otaiby, T. N., AlSherif, M., & Bond, W. P. (2005). *Toward software requirements modularization using hierarchical clustering techniques*. Paper presented at ACMSE '05. Kennesaw, GA.

Alvarez, G. A., Borowsky, E., Go, S., Romer, T. H., Becker-Szendy, R., & Golding, R. et al. (2001). Minerva: An automated resource provisioning tool for large-scale storage systems.[TOCS].*ACM Transactions on Computer Systems*, *19*(4), 483–518. doi:10.1145/502912.502915

Alvarez, J. L., & Mata, J. (1994). Data mining for the management of software development process. *International Journal of Software Engineering and Knowledge Engineering*.

Ambros, M. D., & Lanza, M. (2007). A bug's life visualizing a bug database. In *Proceedings of 4th IEEE International Workshop on Visualizing Software for Understanding and Analysis, VISSOFT 2007*. Alberta, Canada: IEEE.

Ambros, M. D., Lanza, M., Lungu, M., & Robbes, R. (2011). On porting software visualization tools to the Web.[STTT]. *International Journal on Software Tools for Technology Transfer*, *13*(2), 1–19.

Amemiya, Y., & Anderson, T. W. (1990). Asymptotic chi-square tests for a large class of factor analysis models. *Annals of Statistics*, *3*, 1453–1463. doi:10.1214/aos/1176347760

Anderson, T. W., & Amemiya, Y. (1988). The asymptotic normal distribution of estimates in factor analysis under general conditions. *Annals of Statistics*, *16*, 759–771. doi:10.1214/aos/1176350834

Andrew, W., Michael, V., Matthew, H., Christopher, T., & Arun, L. (2007). *A: Exploiting similarity between variants to defeat malware: Vilo method for comparing and searching binary programs*. Academic Press.

Android Bug Repository. (n.d.). Retrieved October 1, 2011, from http://code.google.com/p/android/issues

Anekritmongkol, S., & Kasamsan, M. K. (2010). The Comparative of boolean algebra compress and apriori rule techniques for new theoretic association rule mining model. In *Proceedings of 6th International Conference on Advanced Information Management and Service* (pp. 216-222). Seoul: IEEE.

Annie, H. T., & Mark, S. (2013). Chi-squared distance and metamorphic virus detection. *Journal in Computer Virology, 9*(1), 1–14.

Antoniadis, A., Lambert-Lacroix, S., & Leblanc, F. (2003). Effective dimension reduction methods for tumor classification using gene expression data. *Bioinformatics (Oxford, England), 19*(5), 563–570. doi:10.1093/bioinformatics/btg062 PMID:12651713

Apte, C., Liu, B., Pednault, E., & Smyth, P. (2002). Business applications of data mining. *Communications of the ACM, 45*(8), 49–53. doi:10.1145/545151.545178

Apté, C., & Weiss, S. (1997). Data mining with decision trees and decision rules. *Future Generation Computer Systems, 13*(2-3), 197–210. doi:10.1016/S0167-739X(97)00021-6

Asaf, S., Robert, M., Yuval, E., & Chanan, G. (2009). Detection of malicious code by applying machine learning classifiers on static features: A state-of-the-art survey. *Inf. Sec. Techn. Report, 14*(1), 16–29.

Atashpaz-Gargari, E., & Lucas, C. (2007). *Imperialist competitive algorithm: an algorithm for optimization inspired by imperialistic competition.* Paper presented at the Evolutionary Computation, 2007. New York, NY.

Atkinson, J., & Munoz, R. (2013). Rhetorics-based multi-document summarization. *Expert Systems with Applications, 40*(11), 4346–4352. doi:10.1016/j.eswa.2013.01.017

Atos. (2011). *Business Intelligence Solutions: Decisions That Are Better-Informed Leading to Long-Term Competitive Advantage.* Retrieved April 12, 2012, from https://atos.com

Attaluri, S., McGhee, S., & Stamp, M. (2009). Profile hidden Markov models and metamorphic virus detection. *Journal in Computer Virology, 5*, 151–169. doi:10.1007/s11416-008-0105-1

Aycock, J. (2006). Computer viruses and malware. *Advances in Information Security, 22*, 1–227.

Azamathulla, H. M., & Zahiri, A. (2012). Flow discharge prediction in compound channels using linear genetic programming. *Journal of Hydrology (Amsterdam), 454-455*, 203–207. doi:10.1016/j.jhydrol.2012.05.065

Baillie, D. C., & Mathew, J. (1996). A comparison of autoregressive modeling techniques for fault diagnosis of rolling element bearings. *Mechanical Systems and Signal Processing, 10*(1), 1–17. doi:10.1006/mssp.1996.0001

Baker, K. (2013). *Singular value decomposition tutorial.* Retrieved from http://www.ling.ohio-state.edu/~kbaker/pubs/Singular_Value_Decomposition_Tutorial.pdf

Ballard, C., Herreman, D., Schau, D., Bell, R., Kim, E., & Valencic, A. (1998). *Data Modeling Techniques for Data Warehousing.* Retrieved November 16, 2011, from www.redbooks.ibm.com/redbooks/pdfs/sg242238.pdf

Ballocca, G., Politi, R., Ruffo, G., & Schifanella, R. (2003). Integrated techniques and tools for Web mining, user profiling and benchmarking analysis. In *Proceedings of CMG'03.* CMG.

Baralis, E., Cagliero, L., Jabeen, S., & Fiori, A. (2012). Multi-document summarization exploiting frequent itemsets. In *Proceedings of the 27th Annual ACM Symposium on Applied Computing (SAC '12)* (pp. 782-786). New York, NY: ACM.

Baranyi, P., Gedeon, T. D., & Koczy, L. T. (1998). Intelligent Information Retrieval Using Fuzzy Approach. In *Proceedings of IEEE International Conference on Systems, Man, and Cybernetics,* (Vol. 2, pp. 1984-1989). IEEE.

BARC. (2013). *The BI Survey 12.* Retrieved April 24, 2013, from www.bi-survey.com/index.php?id=35

Bargiela, A., & Pedrycz, W. (2002). *Granular computing: an introduction.* Boston: Kluwer Academic Publishers.

Barnett, T. P., & Preisendorfer, R. W. (1978). Multifield analog prediction of short-term climate fluctuations using a climate state vector. *Journal of the Atmospheric Sciences, 35*, 1771–1787. doi:10.1175/1520-0469(1978)035<1771:MAPOST>2.0.CO;2

Barron, A., Rissanen, J., & Yu, B. (1998). The minimum description length principle in coding and modeling. *Information Theory. IEEE Transactions on, 44*(6), 2743–2760.

Bascil, M. S., & Oztekin, H. (2012). A study on hepatitis disease diagnosis using probabilistic neural network. *Journal of Medical Systems, 36*(3), 1603–1606. doi:10.1007/s10916-010-9621-x PMID:21057884

Bascil, M. S., & Temurtas, F. (2011). A study on hepatitis disease diagnosis using multilayer neural network with Levenberg Marquardt Training Algorithm. *Journal of Medical Systems, 35*(3), 433–436. doi:10.1007/s10916-009-9378-2 PMID:20703548

Basudhar, P. K., & Singh, D. N. (1994). A generalized procedure for predicting optimal lower bound break-out factors of strip anchors. *Geotech, 44*(2), 307–318. doi:10.1680/geot.1994.44.2.307

Batista, G. E., Prati, R. C., & Monard, M. C. (2004). A study of the behavior of several methods for balancing machine learning training data. *ACM Special Interest Group on Knowledge Discovery and Data Mining, 6*(1), 20–29.

Baxter, D., Klimt, B., Grobelnik, M., Schneider, D., Witbrock, M., & Mladenic, D. (2009). Capturing document semantics for ontology generation and document summarization. In *Proceedings of Semantic Knowledge Management: Integrating Ontology Management, Knowledge Discovery, and Human Language Technologies* (pp. 141–154). Heidelberg, Germany: Springer. doi:10.1007/978-3-540-88845-1_11

Bayati, S., Nejad, A. F., Kharazmi, S., & Bahreininejad, A. (2009). Using association rule mining to improve semantic Web services composition performance. In Proceedings of Computer, Control and Communication, (pp. 1-5). IEEE.

Baydar, N., Chen, Q., Ball, A., & Kruger, U. (2001). Detection of incipient tooth defect in helical gears using multivariate statistics. *Mechanical Systems and Signal Processing, 15*(2), 303–321. doi:10.1006/mssp.2000.1315

Baysa, D., & Low, R. M., & Stamp, M. (2013). Structural entropy and metamorphic malware. *Journal of Computer Virology and Hacking Techniques.*

Bederson, B. B., Meyer, J., & Good, L. (2000). Jazz: an extensible zoomable user interface graphics toolkit in Java. In *Proceedings of the 13th Annual ACM Symposium on User interface Software and Technology, UIST '00.* San Diego, CA: ACM.

Belkin, N. J. (1996). Intelligent Information Retrieval: Who's Intelligent? In *Proceedings des 5. International Symposium for Informationswissenschaft (ISI 96)*, (pp. 25-31). ISI.

Bellarmine, G. T., & Arokiaswamv, N. S. S. (1996). Energy management techniques to meet power shortage problems in India. *Energy Conversion and Management, 37*(3), 319–328. doi:10.1016/0196-8904(95)00181-6

Berredo, R. C., Ekel, P. Y., Martini, J. S. C., Palhares, R. M., Parreiras, R. O., & Pereira, J. G. (2011). Decision making in fuzzy environment and multi-criteria power engineering problems. *International Journal of Electrical Power & Energy Systems, 33*(3), 623–632. doi:10.1016/j.ijepes.2010.12.020

Bing, L. (2007). *Web Data Mining: Exploring Hyperlinks, Contents and Usage Data.* Chicago, IL: Springer.

Bird, S., Klein, E., & Loper, E. (2009). *Natural language processing with Python.* Cambridge, MA: O'Reilly Media.

Blanco, R., Larrañaga, P., Inza, I., & Sierra, B. (2004). Gene selection for cancer classification using wrapper approaches. *International Journal of Pattern Recognition and Artificial Intelligence, 18*(8), 1373–1390. doi:10.1142/S0218001404003800

Blankenship, G., & Singh, R. (1995). Analytical solution for modulation sidebands associated with a class of mechanical oscillators. *Journal of Sound and Vibration, 179*(1), 13–36. doi:10.1006/jsvi.1995.0002

Boehm, B., Valerdi, R., & Honour, E. (2008). The ROI of Systems Engineering: Some Quantitative Results for Software-Intensive Systems. *Systems Engineering*, 1–14.

Bouckaert, R. R. (1995). *Bayesian belief networks: from construction to inference.* Universiteit Utrecht, Faculteit Wiskunde en Informatica.

Brin, S., & Page, L. (1998). The anatomy of a large-scale hypertextual Web search engine. In *Proceedings of the seventh international conference on World Wide Web* (pp. 107-117). New York, NY: ACM.

Brin, S., Motwani, R., & Silverstein, C. (1997). Beyond market baskets: generalizing association rules to correlations. *SIGMOD Record, 26*(2), 265–276. doi:10.1145/253262.253327

Brodlie, K. W., Duce, D. A., Gallop, J. R., Walton, J. P. R. B., & Wood, J. D. (2004). Distributed and Collaborative Visualization. *Computer Graphics Forum, 23*(2), 223–251. doi:10.1111/j.1467-8659.2004.00754.x

Bugzilla, bug tracking used by the mozilla projects. (n.d.). Retrieved October 1, 2011 from http://www.bugzilla.org

Bütof, A., von Riedmatten, L. R., Dormann, C. F., Scherer Lorenzen, M., Welk, E., & Bruelheide, H. (2012). The responses of grassland plants to experimentally simulated climate change depend on land use and region. *Global Change Biology, 18*(1), 127–137. doi:10.1111/j.1365-2486.2011.02539.x

Caesarendra, W., Widodo, A., & Yang, B. S. (2010). Application of relevance vector machine and logistic regression for machine degradation assessment. *Mechanical Systems and Signal Processing, 24*(4), 1161–1171. doi:10.1016/j.ymssp.2009.10.011

Cai, T., Zhao, C., & Xu, Q. (2012). Energy network dispatch optimization under emergency of local energy shortage. *Energy, 42*(1), 132–145. doi:10.1016/j.energy.2012.04.001

Califf, M. E., & Mooney, R. J. (1999). Relational learning of pattern-match rules for information extraction. In *Proceedings of the sixteenth national conference on Artificial intelligence and the eleventh Innovative applications of artificial intelligence conference innovative applications of artificial intelligence* (pp. 328-334). Orlando, FL: American Association for Artificial Intelligence.

Çalişir, D., & Dogantekin, E. (2011). A new intelligent hepatitis diagnosis system: PCA–LSSVM. *Expert Systems with Applications, 38*(8), 10705–10708. doi:10.1016/j.eswa.2011.01.014

Cambria, E., & Hussain, A. (2012). *Sentic Computing: Techniques, Tools, and Applications.* Dordrecht, Netherlands: Springer. doi:10.1007/978-94-007-5070-8

Carbonell, J., & Goldstein, J. (1998). The use of MMR diversity-based re-ranking for reordering documents and producing summaries. In *Proceedings of the ACM 21ˢᵗ Special Interest Group on Information Retrieval International Conference (SIGIR'98)* (pp. 335-336). New York, NY: ACM.

Carenini, G., Ng, R. T., & Zhou, X. (2007). Summarizing email conversations with clue words. In *Proceedings of World Wide Web Conference Series* (pp. 91–100). New York, NY: ACM.

Carrot Search Circles. (n.d.). Retrieved from http://carrotsearch.com/circles-overview.html

Cesarano, C., d'Aciemo, A., & Picariello, A. (2003). An Intelligent Search Agent System for Semantic Information Retrieval on the Internet. In *Proceedings of the 5ᵗʰ ACM international workshop on Web information and data management,* (pp. 111-117). ACM.

Chali, Y., Hasan, S. A., & Joty, S. R. (2009). A SVM-based ensemble approach to multi-document summarization. In *Proceedings of the 22nd Canadian Conference on Artificial Intelligence: Advances in Artificial Intelligence (Canadian AI '09)* (pp. 199-202). Heidelberg, Germany: Springer-Verlag.

Chandra, B., & Varghese, P. P. (2008). Fuzzy SLIQ decision tree algorithm. *IEEE Transactions on Systems, Man, and Cybernetics. Part B, Cybernetics, 38*(5), 1294–1301. doi:10.1109/TSMCB.2008.923529 PMID:18784012

Chang, J. (1977). General circulation models of the atmosphere. *Meth. Comp. Phys., 17.*

Chaudhuri, S., & Narasayya, V. (2011). New Frontiers in Business Intelligence. In *Proceedings of 37th International Conference on Very Large Data Bases* (pp. 1502–1503). Seattle, WA: Academic Press.

Chawla, N. V., Hall, L. O., Bowyer, K. W., & Kegelmeyer, W. P. (2002). SMOTE: Synthetic Minority Oversampling Technique. *Journal of Artificial Intelligence Research, 16,* 321–357.

Chen, B., Qiu, Y., Feng, Y., Tavner, P., & Song, W. (2011). Wind turbine scada alarm pattern recognition. In *Proceedings of the IET Conference on Renewable Power Generation.* IET Press.

Chen, J., Liu, L., Song, H., & Yu, X. (2002). An Intelligent Information Retrieval System Model. In *Proceedings of the 4ᵗʰ World Congress on Intelligent Control and Automation,* (pp. 2500-2503). Academic Press.

Chen, D., Zhang, W., Yeung, D., & Tsang, E. C. C. (2006). Rough approximations on a complete completely distributive lattice with applications to generalized rough sets. *Information Sciences, 176,* 1829–1848. doi:10.1016/j.ins.2005.05.009

Cheng, J., & Greiner, R. (1999). *Comparing Bayesian network classifiers*. Paper presented at the Proceedings of the Fifteenth conference on Uncertainty in artificial intelligence. New York, NY.

Chen, H.-L., Liu, D.-Y., Yang, B., Liu, J., & Wang, G. (2011). A new hybrid method based on local fisher discriminant analysis and support vector machines for hepatitis disease diagnosis. *Expert Systems with Applications*, *38*(9), 11796–11803. doi:10.1016/j.eswa.2011.03.066

Chen, H.-L., Yang, B., Liu, J., & Liu, D.-Y. (2011). A support vector machine classifier with rough set-based feature selection for breast cancer diagnosis. *Expert Systems with Applications*, *38*(7), 9014–9022. doi:10.1016/j.eswa.2011.01.120

Chen, I., & Popovich, K. (2003). Understanding customer relationship management (CRM), people, process and technology. *Business Process Management Journal*, *9*, 672–688. doi:10.1108/14637150310496758

Chen, J., Chan, L. L. T., & Cheng, Y. C. (2013). Gaussian process regression based optimal design of combustion systems using flame images. *Applied Energy*, *111*, 153–160. doi:10.1016/j.apenergy.2013.04.036

Chen, M., Ebert, D., Hagen, H., Laramee, R. S., Liere, R. V., & Ma, K.-L. et al. (2009). Data Information and Knowledge in Visualization. *IEEE Computer Graphics and Applications*, 12–19. doi:10.1109/MCG.2009.6 PMID:19363954

Chen, M., Huang, C., Chen, K., & Wu, H. (2005). Aggregation of orders in distribution centers using data mining. *Expert Systems with Applications*, *28*(3), 453–460. doi:10.1016/j.eswa.2004.12.006

Chhillar, R. (2008). Extraction Transformation Loading, a Road to Data Warehouse. In *Proceedings of Second National Conference Mathematical Techniques: Emerging Paradigms for Electronics and IT Industries* (pp. 384–388). Academic Press.

Chifu, V. R., Pop, C. B., Salomie, I., Dinsoreanu, M., Acretoaie, V., & David, T. (2010). An ant-inspired approach for semantic web service clustering. In *Proceedings of Roedunet International Conference (RoEduNet), 2010 9th* (pp. 145-150). IEEE.

Chouchane, M. R., & Lakhotia, A. (2006). Using engine signature to detect metamorphic malware. In *Proceedings of the 4th ACM Workshop on Recurring Malcode*. ACM.

Choudhary, Harding, & Tiwari. (2008). Data Mining in Manufacturing: a Review Based on the Kind of Knowledge. *Journal of Intelligent Manufacturing*. ISSN: 0956-5515.

Ciula, A. (2005). Digital palaeography: using the digital representation of medieval script to support palaeographic analysis. *Digital Medievalist, 1*.

Claro, D. B., Albers, P., & Hao, J. K. (2006). Web services composition. In Semantic Web Services, Processes and Applications (pp. 195-225). Springer US.

Cleary, J. G., & Trigg, L. E. (1995). *K^*: An Instance-based Learner Using an Entropic Distance Measure*. Paper presented at the ICML. New York, NY.

Climate Change Studies Program. (n.d.). Retrieved from http://www.cfc.umt.edu/CCS/

Cloppet, F., Daher, H., Églin, V., Emptoz, H., Exbrayat, M., Joutel, G., … Vincent, N. (2011). New Tools for Exploring, Analysing and Categorising Medieval Scripts. *Digital Medievalist, 7*.

Conrad, J. G., Leidner, J. L., Schilder, F., & Kondadadi, R. (2009). Query-based opinion summarization for legal blog entries. In *Proceedings of the 12th International Conference on Artificial Intelligence and Law (ICAIL '09)* (pp. 167-176). New York, NY: ACM.

Coomans, D., Jonckheer, M., Massart, D., Broeckaert, I., & Blockx, P. (1978). The application of linear discriminant analysis in the diagnosis of thyroid diseases. *Analytica Chimica Acta*, *103*(4), 409–415. doi:10.1016/S0003-2670(01)83105-6

Cooper, G. F., & Herskovits, E. (1992). A Bayesian method for the induction of probabilistic networks from data. *Machine Learning*, *9*(4), 309–347. doi:10.1007/BF00994110

Costagliola, G., Fuccella, V., Giordano, M., & Polese, G. (n.d.). Monitoring online tests through data visualization. *IEEE Transactions on Knowledge and Data Engineering*, *21*(6), 773-784.

Crabtree, C.J. (2010). *Survey of Commercially Available Condition Monitoring Systems for Wind Turbines.* SuperGen Wind Techical report.

Cramer, H. (1946). *Mathematical models of statistics.* Princeton University Press.

Cui, H., Mittal, V., & Datar, M. (2006). Comparative experiments on sentiment classification for online product reviews. In *Proceedings of the 21st national conference on Artificial intelligence.* Academic Press.

Dahl, S. Deng, & Yu. (2013). Large-scale malware classification using random projections and neural networks. In *Proceedings of ICASSP 2013.* ICASSP.

Dai, L., Chen, H., & Li, X. (2011). Improving Sentiment Classification using Feature Highlighting and Feature Bagging. In *Proceedings of 11ᵗʰ IEEE International Conference on Data Mining Workshops* (ICDMW), (pp. 61-66). IEEE.

Dalpiaz, G., Rivola, A., & Rubini, R. (2000). Effectiveness and sensitivity of vibration processing techniques for local fault detection in gears. *Mechanical Systems and Signal Processing, 14*(3), 387–412. doi:10.1006/mssp.1999.1294

Dang, Y., Zhang, Y., & Chen, H. (2010). A lexicon Enhanced method for sentiment classification: An experiment on Online Product Reviews. In *Proceedings of IEEE Intelligent System,* (pp. 46-53). IEEE.

Daniels, J. J., & Rissland, E. L. (1995). A Case-Based Approach to Intelligent Information Retrieval. In *Proceedings of the 18ᵗʰ annual International ACM SIGIR conference on Research and Development in information retrieval,* (pp. 238-245). ACM.

Danilowicz, C., & Nguyen, H. C. (2002). Using User Profiles in Intelligent Information Retrieval. *Lecture Notes in Computer Science, 2366,* 223–231. doi:10.1007/3-540-48050-1_26

Das, S., & Chen, M. (2001). Yahoo! For Amazon: Extracting market sentiment from stock message boards. In *Proc. of the 8th Asia Pacific Finance Association Annual Conference* (APFA 2001). APFA.

Das, B. M. (1978). Model tests for uplift capacity of foundations in clay. *Soil and Foundation, 18*(2), 17–24. doi:10.3208/sandf1972.18.2_17

Das, B. M. (1980). A procedure for estimation of ultimate uplift capacity of foundations in clay. *Soil and Foundation, 20*(1), 77–82. doi:10.3208/sandf1972.20.77

Das, B. M. (1987). *Developments in geotechnical engineering.* Elsevier.

Das, B. M., & Seeley, G. R. (1975). Breakout resistance of horizontal anchors. *Journal of the Geotechnical Engineering Division, 101*(9), 999–1003.

Das, R., Turkoglu, I., & Sengur, A. (2009a). Diagnosis of valvular heart disease through neural networks ensembles. *Computer Methods and Programs in Biomedicine, 93*(2), 185–191. doi:10.1016/j.cmpb.2008.09.005 PMID:18951649

Das, R., Turkoglu, I., & Sengur, A. (2009b). Effective diagnosis of heart disease through neural networks ensembles. *Expert Systems with Applications, 36*(4), 7675–7680. doi:10.1016/j.eswa.2008.09.013

Data Mining / Analytic Tools Used Poll. (2013). Retrieved from http://www.kdnuggets.com/polls/2013/analytics-big-data-mining-data-science-software.html

Dave, K., Lawrence, S., & Pennock, D. M. (2003). Mining the peanut gallery: Opinion extraction and semantic classification of product reviews. In *Proceedings of WWW,* (pp. 519–528). Academic Press.

De Maesschalck, R., Jouan-Rimbaud, D., & Massart, D. L. (2000). The mahalanobis distance. *Chemometrics and Intelligent Laboratory Systems, 50*(1), 1–18. doi:10.1016/S0169-7439(99)00047-7

Desikan, P., Delong, C., Mane, S., Beemanapalli, K., Hsu, K., & Sriram, P. ... Venuturumilli, V. (2009). Web Mining for Business Computing. In Handbooks in Information Systems, (vol. 3). Emerald Group.

Dickin, E. A. (1988). Uplift behaviour of horizontal anchor plates in sand. *Journal of the Geotechnical Engineering Division, 114*(11), 1300–1317. doi:10.1061/(ASCE)0733-9410(1988)114:11(1300)

Dietterich, T. G. (1998). Approximate statistical test for comparing supervised classification learning algorithms. *Neural Computation, 10*(7), 1895–1923. doi:10.1162/089976698300017197 PMID:9744903

Dima, S., Robert, M., Zvi, B., Yuval, S., & Yuval, E. (2009). Using artificial neural networks to detect unknown computer worms. *Neural Computing & Applications*, *18*(7), 663–674. doi:10.1007/s00521-009-0238-2

Dinu, L. P., & Iuga, I. (2012). The Naive Bayes Classifier in Opinion Mining: In Search of the Best Feature Set. In *Proceedings of 13th International Conference on Intelligent Text Processing and Computational Linguistics.* CICLing.

Djurdjanovic, D., Lee, J., & Ni, J. (2003). Watchdog agentaninfotronics-based prognostics approach for product performance degradation assessment and prediction. *Advanced Engineering Informatics*, *17*(3), 109–125. doi:10.1016/j.aei.2004.07.005

Dogantekin, E., Dogantekin, A., & Avci, D. (2011). An expert system based on Generalized Discriminant Analysis and Wavelet Support Vector Machine for diagnosis of thyroid diseases. *Expert Systems with Applications*, *38*(1), 146–150. doi:10.1016/j.eswa.2010.06.029

Dong, X., Halevy, A., Madhavan, J., Nemes, E., & Zhang, J. (2004). Similarity search for Web services. In *Proceedings of the Thirtieth international conference on Very large data bases* (vol. 30, pp. 372-383). VLDB Endowment.

Dork, M., Carpendale, S., Collins, C., & Williamson, C. (2008). VisGets: Coordinated Visualizations for Web-based Information Exploration and Discovery. *IEEE Transactions on Visualization and Computer Graphics*, *14*(6), 1205–1212. doi:10.1109/TVCG.2008.175 PMID:18988965

Dork, M., Gruen, D., Williamson, C., & Carpendale, S. (2010). A visual backchannel for large-scale events. *IEEE Transactions on Visualization and Computer Graphics*, *16*, 1129–1138. doi:10.1109/TVCG.2010.129 PMID:20975151

Dorronsoro, J., Ginel, F., Sanchez, C., & Cruz, C. (1997). Neural Fraud Detection in Credit Card Operations. *IEEE Transactions on Neural Networks*, *8*(4), 827–834. doi:10.1109/72.595879 PMID:18255686

Dredze, M., Wallach, H. M., Puller, D., & Pereira, F. (2008). Generating summary keywords for emails using topics. In *Proceedings of the 13th international conference on Intelligent user interfaces* (pp. 199-206). New York: ACM.

DTEK. (2011). *Utility firm will cut downtime by 20 percent and boost agility with Microsoft and SAP*. Retrieved April 23, 2013, from www.microsoft.com/casestudies/Microsoft-SQL-Server-2008-R2-Enterprise/DTEK/Utility-Firm-Will-Cut-Downtime-by-20-Percent-and-Boost-Agility-with-Microsoft-and-SAP/4000009335

Duan, L., & Da Xu, L. (2012). Business intelligence for enterprise systems: A survey. *IEEE Transactions on Industrial Informatics*, *8*(3), 679–687. doi:10.1109/TII.2012.2188804

Duda, R. O., Hart, P. E., & Stork, D. G. (2001). *Pattern Classification*. New York, NY: Wiley-Interscience.

Dunn, G., & Everitt, B. S. (1982). *An introduction to mathematical taxonomy*. Cambridge, UK: Cambridge University Press.

Duric, A., & Song, F. (2011). Feature selection for sentiment analysis Based on Content and Syntax Models. In *Proceedings of the 2nd Workshop on Computational Approaches to Subjectivity and Sentiment Analysis*. ACL-HLT.

Durran, D. R. (1999). *Numerical methods for wave equations in geophysical fluid dynamics*. Berlin: Springer. doi:10.1007/978-1-4757-3081-4

Dustdar, S., & Gombotz, R. (2006). Discovering Web service workflows using Web services interaction mining. *International Journal of Business Process Integration and Management*, *1*(4), 256–266. doi:10.1504/IJBPIM.2006.012624

Ebrahimpour-Komleh, H., & Mousavirad, S. J. (2013). *Cuckoo Optimization Algorithm for Feedforward neural network training*. Paper presented at the 21th Iranian Conference on Electrical Engineering. Mashhad, Iran.

Eclipse Bug Repository. (n.d.). Retrieved October 1, 2011 from https://bugs.eclipse.org/bugs/

Economist. (2009). Globalization stalled: How global economic upheaval will hit the business environment [Special Report]. *The Economist*, pp. 1–37.

EDUCAUSE Learning Initiative. (2007). *7 things you should know about. twitter*. EDUCAUSE, Tech. Rep. Retrieved from http://connect.educause.edu/Library/ELI/7ThingsYouShouldKnowAbout

Eia, U. (2013). *Energy information administration, annual energy outlook 2013, AEO 2013 early release overview.* Washington, DC: Department of Energy.

Eitan, M., Asaf, S., Lior, R., & Yuval, E. (2009). Improving malware detection by applying multi-inducer ensemble. *Computational Statistics & Data Analysis, 53*(4), 1483–1494. doi:10.1016/j.csda.2008.10.015

Elliott, T. (2011). *Hadoop, Big Data, and Enterprise Business Intelligence.* Retrieved April 21, 2013, from http://timoelliott.com/blog/2011/09/hadoop-big-data-and-enterprise-business-intelligence.html

Embley, D. W., Campbell, D. M., Jiang, Y. S., Liddle, S. W., Lonsdale, D. W., Ng, Y. K., & Smith, R. D. (1999). Conceptual-model-based data extraction from multiple-record Web pages. *Data & Knowledge Engineering, 31*(3), 227–251. doi:10.1016/S0169-023X(99)00027-0

Er, O., Tanrikulu, A. C., Abakay, A., & Temurtas, F. (2012). An approach based on probabilistic neural network for diagnosis of Mesothelioma's disease. *Computers & Electrical Engineering, 38*(1), 75–81. doi:10.1016/j.compeleceng.2011.09.001

Eskandari, & Hashemi. (n.d.). Metamorphic malware detection using control flow graph mining. *International Journal of Computer Science and Network Security, 11*(12), 1-6.

Everitt, B. S., Landau, S., & Leese, M. (2001). *Cluster Analysis.* London: Arnold.

Fan, Y., & Shelton, C. R. (2009). Learning continuous-Time social network dynamics. In *Proceedings of the 25th conference on uncertainty in artificial intelligence (UAI 2009),* (pp. 161-168). UAI.

Faridi, M. S., Mustafa, T., & Jan, F. (2012). Human Persuasion Integration in Software Development Lifecycle (SDLC). *International Journal of Computer Science, 9*(3), 65–68.

Fayyad, U. M., Piatetsky-Shapiro, G., Smyth, P., & Uthurusamy, R. (1996). *Advances in knowledge discovery and data mining.* Academic Press.

Fayyad, U., Piatetsky-Shapiro, G., & Smyth, P. (1996). From data mining to knowledge discovery in databases. *AI Magazine, 17*(3), 37.

Feng, Y., Qiu, Y., Crabtree, C., Long, H., & Tavner, P. (2011). Use of SCADA and CMS signals for failure detection and diagnosis of a wind turbine gearbox. In *Proceedings of the Conference of the European Wind Energy Association.* Brussels, Belgium: European Wind Energy Association.

Feng, Y., Qiu, Y., Crabtree, C., Long, H., & Tavner, P. (2012). Monitoring wind turbine gearboxes. *Wind Energy (Chichester, England), 16*(5), 728–740. doi:10.1002/we.1521

Fethi, M., & Pasiouras, F. (2010). Assessing bank efficiency and performance with operational research and artificial intelligence techniques: A survey. *European Journal of Operational Research, 204*(2), 189–198. doi:10.1016/j.ejor.2009.08.003

Filatova, E., & Hatzivassiloglou, V. (2004). A formal model for information selection in multi-sentence text extraction. In *Proceedings of the 20th international conference on Computational Linguistics* (pp. 39-47). Stroudsburg, Germany: Association for Computational Linguistics.

Fisher, D., Drucker, S., Frenandez, R., & Ruble, S. (2010). Visualizations everywhere: A multiplatform infrastructure for linked visualizations. *IEEE Transactions on Visualization and Computer Graphics, 16*(6), 1157–1163. doi:10.1109/TVCG.2010.222 PMID:20975154

Fitzsimons, M., Khabaza, T., & Shearer, C. (1993). The application of rule induction and neural networks for television audience prediction. In *Proceedings of Symposium on Information Based Decision Making in Marketing ESOMAR/EMAC/AFM* (pp. 69–82). Paris, France: ESOMAR/EMAC/AFM.

Forman, G. (2003). An extensive empirical study of feature selection metrics for text classification. *Journal of Machine Learning Research,* 1289–1305.

Frank, A., & Asuncion, A. (2010). *UCI machine learning repository*. Academic Press.

Freitag, D. (2000). Machine learning for information extraction in informal domains. *Machine Learning*, *39*(2-3), 169–202. doi:10.1023/A:1007601113994

Friendly, M. (2011). Milestones in the history of thematic cartography, statistical graphics, and data visualization. *Retrieved*, *5*(11), 1–79.

Gamon, M. (2004). Sentiment classification on customer feedback data: noisy data, large feature vectors, and the role of linguistic analysis. In *Proceedings of the 20th international conference on Computational Linguistics*, (pp. 841-848). Academic Press.

Gao, H., Stucky, W., & Liu, L. (2009). Web Services Classification Based on Intelligent Clustering Techniques. []. IEEE.]. *Proceedings of Information Technology and Applications*, *3*, 242–245.

Gargari, E. A., Hashemzadeh, F., Rajabioun, R., & Lucas, C. (2008). Colonial competitive algorithm: a novel approach for PID controller design in MIMO distillation column process. *International Journal of Intelligent Computing and Cybernetics*, *1*(3), 337–355. doi:10.1108/17563780810893446

Garg, V., & Jothiprakash, V. (2013). Evaluation of reservoir sedimentation using data driven techniques. *Applied Soft Computing Journal*, *13*(8), 3567–3581. doi:10.1016/j.asoc.2013.04.019

Geetha, M. A., Acharjya, D. P., & Iyengar, N. C. S. N. (2013). Algebraic properties and measures of uncertainty in rough set on two universal sets based on multigranulation. In *Proceedings of the ACM Compute 2013*. ACM Digital Library.

Geetha, M. A., Acharjya, D. P., & Iyengar, N. C. S. N. (n.d.). On some algebraic properties of rough set on two universal sets based on multigranulation. *International Journal of Information and Communication Technology*.

Gerstman, B. (2006). *Introduction to Hypothesis Testing*. Retrieved May 16, 2013 from http://www.sjsu.edu/faculty/gerstman/StatPrimer/hyp-test.pdf

Godwin, J. L., & Matthews, P. (2013). Prognosis of wind turbine gearbox failures by utilising robust multivariate statistical techniques. In *Proceedings of the IEEE Conference on Prognosis and Health Management (PHM)*. Gaithersburg, VA: IEEE.

Godwin, J. L., Matthew, P., & Watson, C. (2013). Classification and detection of electrical control system faults through SCADA data analysis. *Chemical Engineering Transactions*, *33*(1), 985–991.

Goldstein, J., Mittal, V., Carbonell, J., & Kantrowitz, M. (2000). Multi-Document Summarization By Sentence Extraction. In *Proceedings of the ANLP/NAACL Workshop on Automatic Summarization* (pp. 40-48). Stroudsburg, Germany: Association for Computational Linguistics.

Gong, S., Qu, Y., & Tian, S. (2010). Summarization using Wikipedia. In *Proceedings of Text Analysis Conference* (pp. 1-7). New York: ACM.

Gong, Y., & Liu, X. (2001). Generic Text Summarization Using Relevance Measure and Latent Semantic Analysis. In *Proceedings of the 24th annual international ACM SIGIR conference on Research and development in information retrieval*, (pp. 19-25). New York: ACM.

Goshtasby, A. A. (2012). *Image Registration*. Springer-Verlag London Limited. doi:10.1007/978-1-4471-2458-0

Gottschalk, K., Graham, S., Kreger, H., & Snell, J. (2002). Introduction to Web services architecture. *IBM Systems Journal*, *41*(2), 170–177. doi:10.1147/sj.412.0170

Grace, L. K., Maheswari, V., & Nagamalai, D. (2011). Analysis of Web Logs and Web User in Web Mining. *International Journal of Network Security & Its Applications*, *3*(1).

Guha, S., Mishra, N., Motwani, R., & O'Callaghan, L. (2000). Clustering data streams. In *Proceedings of 41st Annual Symposium on Foundations of Computer Science* (pp. 359-361). New York: ACM.

Guven, A., Azamathulla, H. M., & Zakaria, N. A. (2009). Linear genetic programming for prediction of circular pile scour. *Ocean Engineering*, *36*(12-13), 985–991. doi:10.1016/j.oceaneng.2009.05.010

Guven, A., & Kişi, O. (2011). Daily pan evaporation modeling using linear genetic programming technique. *Irrigation Science, 29*(2), 135–145. doi:10.1007/s00271-010-0225-5

Guyon, I., Weston, J., Barnhill, S., & Vapnik, V. (2002). Gene selection for cancer classification using support vector machines. *Machine Learning, 46*(1-3), 389–422. doi:10.1023/A:1012487302797

Gyenesei, A. (2001). A fuzzy approach for mining quantitative association rules. *Acta Cybernetica, 15*(2), 305–320.

Haberstroh, R. (2008). *Oracle® data mining tutorial for Oracle Data Mining 11g Release 1*. Oracle.

Hachey, B., Radford, W., Nothman, J., Honnibal, M., & Curran, J. R. (2013). Evaluating entity linking with Wikipedia. *Artificial Intelligence, 194*, 130–150. doi:10.1016/j.artint.2012.04.005

Hadzic, F., & Hecker, M. (2011). Alternative Approach to Tree-Structured Web Log Representation and Mining. In *Proceedings of the 2011 IEEE/WIC/ACM International Conferences on Web Intelligence and Intelligent Agent Technology* (pp.235-242). Lyon, France: IEEE Computer Society.

Hall, Frank, & Holmes, Pfahringer, Reutemann, & Witten. (2009). The WEKA data mining software: An update. *SIGKDD Explorations, 11*(1). doi:10.1145/1656274.1656278

Haltiner, G. J., & Williams, R. T. (1980). *Numerical prediction and dynamic meteorology*. Hoboken, NJ: J. Wiley and Sons.

Hamasaki, M., Matsuo, Y., Nishimura, T., & Takeda, H. (2008). Ontology extraction by collaborative tagging with social networking. In *Proceedings of the World Wide Web Conference (WWW'08)* (pp. 291-294). ACM.

Hameed, Z., Hong, Y., Cho, Y., Ahn, S., & Song, C. (2009). Condition monitoring and fault detection of wind turbines and related algorithms: A review. *Renewable & Sustainable Energy Reviews, 13*(1), 1–39. doi:10.1016/j.rser.2007.05.008

Hand, D. J. (2007). Principles of data mining. *Drug Safety, 30*(7), 621–622. doi:10.2165/00002018-200730070-00010 PMID:17604416

Hand, D., Mannila, H., & Smyth, P. (2001). *Principles of Data Mining*. MIT Press.

Han, J., & Kamber, M. (2001). *Data Mining: Concepts and Techniques*. Morgan Kaufmann.

Han, J., Kamber, M., & Pei, J. (2006). *Data mining: concepts and techniques*. San Francisco: Morgan Kaufmann.

Hardin, J., & Rocke, D. M. (2005). The distribution of robust distances. *Journal of Computational and Graphical Statistics, 14*(4), 928–946. doi:10.1198/106186005X77685

Hart, P. E. (1968). The Condensed Nearest Neighbor Rule. *IEEE Transactions on Information Theory, 14*, 515–516. doi:10.1109/TIT.1968.1054155

Hastie, T., Tibshirani, R., & Friedman, J. (2009). *The Elements of Statistical Learning: Data mining, Inference, and Prediction*. New York: Springer. doi:10.1007/978-0-387-84858-7

Hastie, T., Tibshirani, R., Friedman, J., & Franklin, J. (2005). The elements of statistical learning: data mining, inference and prediction. *The Mathematical Intelligencer, 27*(2), 83–85. doi:10.1007/BF02985802

Hatch, C. (2004). Improved wind turbine condition monitoring using acceleration enveloping. GE Energy. *Journal of Electrical Systems, 3*(1), 26–38.

Hedfield, W. (2009). *Case study: Jaeger uses data mining to reduce losses from crime and waste*. Retrieved December 13, 2012, from http://www.computerweekly.com/feature/Case-study-Jaeger-uses-data-mining-to-reduce-losses-from-crime-and-waste

Heffner, G., Maurer, L., Sarkar, A., & Wang, X. (2010). Minding the gap: World Bank's assistance to power shortage mitigation in the developing world. *Energy, 35*(4), 1584–1591. doi:10.1016/j.energy.2009.05.027

He, M., & Feng, B.-Q. (2005). Intelligent Information Retrieval Based on the Variable Precision Rough Set Model and Fuzzy Sets. *Lecture Notes in Computer Science, 3642*, 184–192. doi:10.1007/11548706_20

Henchiri, O., & Japkowicz, N. (2006). A feature selection and evaluation scheme for computer virus detection. In *Proceedings of ICDM* (pp. 891-895). IEEE Computer Society.

Heng, A., Tan, A. C., Mathew, J., Montgomery, N., Banjevic, D., & Jardine, A. K. (2009). Intelligent condition-based prediction of machinery reliability. *Mechanical Systems and Signal Processing*, 23(5), 1600–1614. doi:10.1016/j.ymssp.2008.12.006

Hennig, L., Umbrath, W., & Wetzker, R. (2008). An Ontology-Based Approach to Text Summarization. In *Proceedings of the IEEE/WIC/ACM Web Intelligence and Intelligent Agent Technology* (pp. 291-294). New York: ACM.

Henze, N., & Wagner, T. (1997). A new approach to the BHEP tests for multivariate normality. *Journal of Multivariate Analysis*, 62(1), 1–23. doi:10.1006/jmva.1997.1684

Henze, N., & Zirkler, B. (1990). A class of invariant consistent tests for multivariate normality. *Communications in Statistics Theory and Methods*, 19(10), 3595–3617. doi:10.1080/03610929008830400

Hernández Aguirre, A., & Coello, C. A. C. (2004). Using genetic programing and multiplexers for the synthesis of logic circuits. *Engineering Optimization*, 36(4), 491–511. doi:10.1080/03052150410001686503

Hoffart, J., Yosef, M. A., Bordino, I., Fürstenau, H., Pinkal, M., Spaniol, M., et al. (2011). Robust disambiguation of named entities in text. In *Proceedings of the Conference on Empirical Methods in Natural Language Processing (EMNLP '11)* (pp. 782-792). Stroudsburg, Germany: Association for Computational Linguistics.

Hofmann, H. (1994). *Website*. Retrieved May 28, 2013 from http://archive.ics.uci.edu/ml/machine-learning-databases/statlog/german/

Holgersson, H. E. T. (2006). A graphical method for assessing multivariate normality. *Computational Statistics*, 21(1), 141–149. doi:10.1007/s00180-006-0256-9

Hosszú, G. (2010). Az informatika írástörténeti alkalmazásai. [Applications of information science in paleography]. In L. Cserny (Ed.), *Conference on the Modern Technics of the Information Science IKT 2010* (pp. 5–21). Dunaújváros, Hungary: College of Dunaújváros.

Hosszú, G. (2011). *Heritage of Scribes: The Relation of Rovas Scripts to Eurasian Writing Systems*. Budapest, Hungary: Rovas Foundation. Retrieved August 15, 2012 from http://books.google.hu/books?id=TyK8azCqC34C&pg=PA1

Hosszú, G. (2012). Rovás paleográfia: Dinamikus vagy statikus? [Rovash paleography: Dynamic or static?]. *Nyelv és tudomány*. [Language and Science]. Retrieved August 15, 2012 from http://www.nyest.hu/hirek/rovaspaleografia-dinamikus-vagy-statikus

Hosszú, G. (2013). *Rovásatlasz* [Rovash Atlas]. Budapest, Hungary: Milani.

Hou, J. L., & Yang, S. T. (2006). Technology Mining Model Concerning Operation Characteristics of Technology and Service Providers. *International Journal of Production Research*, 44(16), 3345–3365. doi:10.1080/00207540500490996

Hou, J., Zhang, J., Nayak, R., & Bose, A. (2011). Semantics-based Web service discovery using information retrieval techniques. In *Comparative Evaluation of Focused Retrieval* (pp. 336–346). Springer. doi:10.1007/978-3-642-23577-1_32

Hsieh, C.-H., Lu, R.-H., Lee, N.-H., Chiu, W.-T., Hsu, M.-H., & Li, Y.-C. J. (2011). Novel solutions for an old disease: diagnosis of acute appendicitis with random forest, support vector machines, and artificial neural networks. *Surgery*, 149(1), 87–93. doi:10.1016/j.surg.2010.03.023 PMID:20466403

Hsu, C. N., & Dung, M. T. (1998). Generating finite-state transducers for semi-structured data extraction from the web. *Information Systems*, 23(8), 521–538. doi:10.1016/S0306-4379(98)00027-1

Hu, M., & Liu, B. (2004). Mining and summarizing customer reviews. In *Proceedings of the ACM SIGKDD Conference on Knowledge Discovery and Data Mining (KDD)*, (pp. 168–177). ACM.

Huang, J. C., & Mobasher, B. (2008). Using Data Mining and Recommender Systems to Scale up the Requirements Process. In *Proceedings of ULSSIS'08*. Leipzig, Germany: ACM.

Huang, Q., Jiang, D., Hong, L., & Ding, Y. (2008). Application of wavelet neural networks on vibration fault diagnosis for wind turbine gearbox. In *Advances in Neural Networks*. Springer. doi:10.1007/978-3-540-87734-9_36

Hu, S., Liang, Y., Ma, L., & He, Y. (2009). MSMOTE: improving classification performance when training data is imbalanced. *Proceedings of Computer Science and Engineering, 2,* 13–17.

Husain, W., Low, P. V., Ng, L. K., & Ong, Z. L. (2011). Application of Data Mining Techniques for Improving Software Engineering. In *Proceedings of ICIT 2011, 5th International Conference on Information Technology.* ICIT.

Huyet, A. L. (2006). Optimization and analysis aid via data-mining for simulated production system. *European Journal of Operational Research, 173,* 827–838. doi:10.1016/j.ejor.2005.07.026

IBM. (2010). Great Canadian gaming corporation leverages IBM [Software Group Case Study]. *Cognos 8: Solutions for Financial Consolidation and Reporting Standardization.* Retrieved April 8, 2012, from http://www-01.ibm.com/software/success/cssdb.nsf/software L2VW?OpenView&Count=30&RestrictToCategory=cognos_Cognos8BusinessIntelligence&cty=en_us

IBM. (2011). *Forward view: Business intelligence breakthrough, no data warehouse required.* Retrieved April 6, 2012, from http//ibm.com/businesscenter/forwardview. com

IBM. (2013). *What Is Big Data?* IBM. Retrieved April 21, 2013, from www-01.ibm.com/software/data/bigdata/

Igor, S., Felix, B., Javier, N., Yoseba, P., Borja, S., Carlos, L., & Pablo, B. (2010). Idea: Opcode-sequence-based malware detection.[LNCS]. *Proceedings of Engineering Secure Software and Systems, 5965,* 35–43. doi:10.1007/978-3-642-11747-3_3

Ilkhani, A., & Abaee, G. (2011). Extracting Test Cases by Using Data Mining, Reducing the Cost of Testing. *International Journal of Computer Information Systems and Industrial Management Applications, 3,* 730–737.

Inanc, B., & Dur, U. (2012). Analysis of data visualizations in daily newspapers in terms of graphic design. *Procedia-Social and Behavioral Sciences,* 278-283.

Inmon, W. H. (1994). *Building the data warehouse.* J. Wiley & Sons.

Inmon, W. H. (1996). The data warehouse and data mining. *Communications of the ACM, 39*(11), 49–50. doi:10.1145/240455.240470

Iung, B., Levrat, E., Marquez, A. C., & Erbe, H. (2009). Conceptual framework for e-maintenance: Illustration by e-maintenance technologies and platforms. *Annual Reviews in Control, 33*(2), 220–229. doi:10.1016/j.arcontrol.2009.05.005

Iyakutty, K., & Sujatha, N. (2010). Refinement of Web usage data clustering from K-means with genetic algorithm. *European Journal of Scientific Research, 42,* 478–490.

Jacobs, P. S., & Rau, L. F. (1988). Natural Language Techniques for Intelligent Information Retrieval. In *Proceedings of the 11th annual International ACM SIGIR conference on Research and Development in information retrieval,* (pp. 85-99). ACM.

Jain, P. (2005). Intelligent Information Retrieval. In *Proceedings of 3rd International Conference: Sciences of Electronic, Technologies of Information and Telecommunications (SETIT 2005).* SETIT.

Jain, Y. K., & Bhandare, S. K. (2011). Min Max Normalization Based Data Perturbation Method for Privacy Protection. *International Journal of Computer & Communication Technology, 2*(8), 45–50.

Jakubovich, E. (1935). A székely rovásírás legrégibb ábécéi.[The oldest alphabets of the Szekely Rovash script]. *Magyar Nyelv, 31*(1–2), 1–17.

Jardine, A. K., Lin, D., & Banjevic, D. (2006). A review on machinery diagnostics and prognostics implementing condition-based maintenance. *Mechanical Systems and Signal Processing, 20*(7), 1483–1510. doi:10.1016/j.ymssp.2005.09.012

Jaroszewicz, S., & Simovici, D. A. (2004). Interestingness of frequent itemsets using Bayesian networks as background knowledge. In *Proceedings of the tenth ACM SIGKDD international conference on Knowledge discovery and data mining* (pp. 178-186). New York, NY: ACM.

Jerez-Aragonés, J. M., Gómez-Ruiz, J. A., Ramos-Jiménez, G., Muñoz-Pérez, J., & Alba-Conejo, E. (2003). A combined neural network and decision trees model for prognosis of breast cancer relapse. *Artificial Intelligence in Medicine*, *27*(1), 45–63. doi:10.1016/S0933-3657(02)00086-6 PMID:12473391

JFreeChart. (n.d.). Retrieved October 1, 2011 from http://www.jfree.org/jfreechart/

Jiang, J., Wang, Z., Liu, C., Tan, Z., Chen, X., & Li, M. (2010). The Technology of Intelligent Information Retrieval Based on the Semantic Web. In *Proceedings of 2nd International Conference on Signal Processing Systems,* (pp. V2-824 – V2-827). Academic Press.

Jinguo, X., & Chen, X. (2011). Application of decision tree method in economic statistical data processing. In *Proceedings of International Conference on E-Business and E-Government* (pp. 1-4). Shanghai, China: IEEE.

JIRA. (n.d.). *A configurable project tracking tool*. Retrieved October 1, 2011, from http://www.atlassian.com/software/jira/

Joshi, M., & Penstein-Rosé, C. (2009). Generalizing dependency features for opinion mining. In *Proceedings of the Joint Conference of the 47th Annual Meeting of the Association for Computational Linguistics* (ACL), (pp. 313-316). ACL.

jzy3d. (n.d.). Retrieved October 1, 2011, from http://www.jzy3d.org/

Kabari, L., & Nwachukwu, E. (2012). *Neural Networks and Decision Trees For Eye Diseases Diagnosis*. Academic Press.

Kadir, A. S. A., Bakar, A. A., & Hamdan, A. R. (2011). Frequent absence and presence itemset for negative association rule mining. In *Proceedings of 11th International Conference on Intelligent Systems Design and Applications* (pp. 965-970). Cordoba: IEEE.

Kahraman, C., Kaya, I., Ulukan, H., & Ucal, I. (2010). Economic forecasting techniques and their application. In Business Intelligence in Economic Forecasting: Technologies and Techniques (pp.19-44). IGI Global.

Kainkwa, R. R. (1999). Wind energy as an alternative source to alleviate the shortage of electricity that prevails during the dry season: A case study of Tanzania. *Renewable Energy*, *18*(2), 167–174. doi:10.1016/S0960-1481(98)00801-5

Kalnay, E. (2003). *Atmospheric modeling, data assimilation, and predictability*. Cambridge, UK: Cambridge Univ. Press.

Karaboga, D. (2005). *An idea based on honey bee swarm for numerical optimization*. Techn. Rep. TR06, Erciyes Univ. Press, Erciyes.

Karthik, M., Marikkannan, M., & Kannan, A. (2008). An Intelligent System for Semantic Information Retrieval Information from Textual Web Documents. *Lecture Notes in Computer Science*, *5158*, 135–146. doi:10.1007/978-3-540-85303-9_13

Kavousi, K., & Moshiri, B. (2007). Architecture design of an intelligent information fusion information retrieval from dynamic environment. In *Proceedings of 10th International Conference on Information Fusion,* (pp. 1-7). Academic Press.

Kayaer, K., & Yıldırım, T. (2003). *Medical diagnosis on Pima Indian diabetes using general regression neural networks*. Paper presented at the international conference on artificial neural networks and neural information processing (ICANN/ICONIP). New York, NY.

Kecman, V. (2001). *Learning and Soft Computing: Support Vector Machines, Neural Networks, and Fuzzy Logic Models*. Cambridge, MA: The MIT Press.

Kehrer, J., & Hauser, H. (2013). Visualization and visual analysis of multi-faceted scientific data: A survey. *IEEE Transactions on Visualization and Computer Graphics*, *19*(3), 495–513. doi:10.1109/TVCG.2012.110 PMID:22508905

Keim, D. A., Mansmann, F., Schneidewind, J., & Ziegler, H. (2006). Challenges in visual data analysis. In *Proceedings of the IEEE Tenth International Conference on In Information Visualization*. IEEE.

Keim, D.A., Panse, C., Sips, M., & North, S.C. (n.d.). Pixel Based Visual Data Mining of Geo-Spatial Data. *Computer & Graphics, 28*(3), 327-344.

Keim, D. A. (2002). Information Visualization and Visual Data Mining. *IEEE Transactions on Visualization and Computer Graphics, 7*(1), 100–107.

Kephart & Arnold. (1994). A feature selection and evaluation of computer virus signatures. In *Proceedings of the 4th Virus Bulletin International Conference*. Virus Bulletin Ltd.

Kesavan, S., & Alagarsamy, K. (2011). Data mining approach in software analysis. *International Journal of Computer & Organization Trends, 1*(2), 9–12.

Khoshgoftaar, T. M., Allen, E. B., Hudepohl, J. P., & Aud, S. J. (1997). Neural Networks for Software Quality Modeling of a Very Large Telecommunications System. *IEEE Transactions on Neural Networks, 8*(4), 902–909. doi:10.1109/72.595888 PMID:18255693

Khoshgoftaar, T. M., & Lanning, D. L. (1995). A Neural Network Approach for Early Detection of Program Modules Having High Risk in the Maintenance Phase. *Journal of Systems and Software, 29*(1), 85–91. doi:10.1016/0164-1212(94)00130-F

Kianmehr, K., Gao, S., Attari, J., Rahman, M. M., Akomeah, K., Alhajj, R., et al. (2009). Text summarization techniques: SVM versus neural networks. In *Proceedings of the 11th International Conference on Information Integration and Web-based Applications & Services (iiWAS '09)* (pp. 487-491). New York, NY: ACM.

King, C., & O'Shea, D. (2003). *Estimating Return-on-Investment (ROI) for Texas Workforce Development Boards: Lessons Learned and Next Steps*. Paper presented at Texas Workforce Leadership of Texas. Austin, TX.

Kobielus, J. (2011). *Hadoop: What Is It Good For? Absolutely... Something*. Retrieved April 23, 2013, from blogs.forrester.com/james_kobielus/11-06-06-hadoop_what_is_it_good_for_absolutely_something

Kogilavani, A., & Balasubramanie, B. (2009). Ontology enhanced clustering based summarization of medical documents. *International Journal of Recent Trends in Engineering, 1*(1), 546–549.

Kollo, T. (2008). Multivariate skewness and kurtosis measures with an application in ICA. *Journal of Multivariate Analysis, 99*(10), 2328–2338. doi:10.1016/j.jmva.2008.02.033

Kolter, J. Z., & Maloof, M. A. (2006). Learning to detect and classify malicious executables in the wild. *Journal of Machine Learning Research, 6*, 2721–2744.

Kondo, M. (2006). On the structure of generalized rough sets. *Information Sciences, 176*, 589–600. doi:10.1016/j.ins.2005.01.001

Konishi, K., & Toyama, T. (2008). Community identification in dynamic social networks based on H2 norm analysis: A new approach from control theory'. In *Proceedings IEEE international conference on systems, Man and cybernetics (SMC 2008)*, (pp. 2840-2845). IEEE.

Kontonasios, K., & De Bie, T. (2010). An Information-Theoretic Approach to Finding Informative Noisy Tiles in Binary Databases. In *Proceedings of SIAM International Conference on Data Mining* (pp. 47-57). New York, NY: ACM.

Koutsabeloulis, N. C., & Griffiths, D. V. (1989). Numerical modeling of the trap door problem. *Geotech, 39*(1), 77–89. doi:10.1680/geot.1989.39.1.77

Koval, R., & Navrat, P. (2002). Intelligent Support for Information Retrieval in the WWW Environment. *Lecture Notes in Computer Science, 2435*, 51–64. doi:10.1007/3-540-45710-0_5

Koza, J. R. (1992). *Genetic programming: on the programming of computers by means of natural selection*. Cambridge, MA: MIT Press.

Krause, E. F. (1986). *Taxicab Geometry: An Adventure in Non-Euclidean Geometry*. New York: Dover.

Kushmerick, N. (2000). Wrapper induction: Efficiency and expressiveness. *Artificial Intelligence, 118*(1-2), 15–68. doi:10.1016/S0004-3702(99)00100-9

Kusiak, A., & Li, W. (2011). The prediction and diagnosis of wind turbine faults. *Renewable Energy, 36*(1), 16–23. doi:10.1016/j.renene.2010.05.014

Kusiak, A., & Verma, A. (2011). A data-driven approach for monitoring blade pitch faults in wind turbines. *IEEE Transactions on Sustainable Energy, 2*(1), 87–96.

Kusiak, A., & Verma, A. (2013). Monitoring Wind Farms With Performance Curves. *IEEE Transactions on Sustainable Energy, 4*(1), 192–199. doi:10.1109/TSTE.2012.2212470

Laender, A. H., Ribeiro-Neto, B. A., da Silva, A. S., & Teixeira, J. S. (2002). A brief survey of Web data extraction tools. *SIGMOD Record, 31*(2), 84–93. doi:10.1145/565117.565137

Laender, A. H., Ribeiro-Neto, B., & da Silva, A. S. (2002). DEByE–data extraction by example. *Data & Knowledge Engineering, 40*(2), 121–154. doi:10.1016/S0169-023X(01)00047-7

Lanckriet, G. R. G., Ghaoui, L. E., Bhattacharyya, C., & Jordan, M. I. (2002). *Minimax probability machine.* Cambridge, MA: MIT Press.

Last, M. (2005). Data mining for software testing. In *Data Mining and Knowledge Discovery Handbook 2005* (pp. 1239–1248). Academic Press.

Laundon, K., & Laundon, J. (2011). *Management Information Systems: Managing the Digital Firm.* Pearson Education.

Lee, J., Qiu, H., Yu, G., Lin, J., & Rexnord Technical Services. (2007). 'Bearing Data Set', IMS, University of Cincinnati. *NASA Ames Prognostics Data Repository.* NASA Ames.

Lee, H., & Yoo, S. B. (2005). Intelligent Information Retrieval for Web-Based Design Data Repository. *Lecture Notes in Computer Science, 3488*, 544–552. doi:10.1007/11425274_56

Lee, S., & Siau, K. (2001). A review of data mining techniques. *Industrial Management & Data Systems, 101*(1), 41–46. doi:10.1108/02635570110365989

Legendre, P., & Legendre, L. (2012). *Numerical Ecology* (3rd ed.). Amsterdam: Elsevier.

Leger, J., Iung, B., Beca, A. F. D., & Pinoteau, J. (1999). An innovative approach for new distributed maintenance system: Application to hydro power plants of the remafex project. *Computers in Industry, 38*(2), 131–148. doi:10.1016/S0166-3615(98)00114-6

Levandowsky, M., & Winter, D. (1971). Distance between sets. *Nature, 234*(5), 34–35. doi:10.1038/234034a0

Li, F., Mehlitz, M., Feng, L., & Sheng, H. (2006). Web Pages Clustering and Concepts Mining: An approach towards Intelligent Information Retrieval. In *Proceedings of IEEE Conference on Cybernetics and Intelligent Systems*, (pp. 1-6). IEEE.

Li, L., Wang, D., Shen, C., & Li, T. (2010). Ontology-enriched multi-document summarization in disaster management. In *Proceedings of the 33rd international ACM SIGIR conference on Research and development in information retrieval (SIGIR '10)* (pp. 819-820). New York, NY: ACM.

Li, M., & Yang, Y. (2012). Efficient clustering index for semantic Web service based on user preference. In *Proceedings of Computer Science and Information Processing (CSIP), 2012 International Conference on* (pp. 291-294). IEEE.

Li, S., Zong, C., & Wang, X. (2007). Sentiment Classification through Combining classifiers with multiple feature sets. In *Proceedings of International Conference on Natural Language Processing and Knowledge Engineering (NLP-KE 2007)*. NLP-KE.

Li, W., Feng, Z., Li, Y., & Xu, Z. (2004). Ontology-Based Intelligent Information Retrieval System. In *Proceedings of Canadian Conference on Electrical and Computer Engineering,* (Vol. 1, pp. 373-376). Academic Press.

Li, W., Zhang, X., & Wei, X. (2008). Semantic Web-Oriented Intelligent Information Retrieval System. In *Proceedings of IEEE International Conference on Biomedical Engineering and Informatics,* (pp. 357-361). IEEE.

Liang, Q. A., Chung, J. Y., Miller, S., & Ouyang, Y. (2006). Service pattern discovery of Web service mining in Web service registry-repository. In *Proceedings of e-Business Engineering* (pp. 286–293). IEEE. doi:10.1109/ICEBE.2006.90

Liang, Q., Li, P., Hung, P. C., & Wu, X. (2009). Clustering Web services for automatic categorization. In *Proceedings of Services Computing* (pp. 380–387). IEEE.

Li, B., & Chai, C. (2010). A novel association rules method based on genetic algorithm and fuzzy set strategy for Web mining. *Journal of Computers*, 5(9).

Li, F., & Huang, X. (2007). An Intelligent Platform for Information Retrieval. *Lecture Notes in Computer Science*, 4429, 45–57. doi:10.1007/978-3-540-70934-3_5

Lim, J.-H., Seung, H.-W., Hwang, J., Kim, Y.-C., & Kim, H.-N. (1997). Query Expansion for Intelligent Information Retrieval on Internet. In *Proceedings of International Conference on Parallel and Distributed Systems*, (pp. 656-662). Academic Press.

Lin, C., & Hovy, E. (2003). Automatic evaluation of summaries using N-gram co-occurrence statistics. In *Proceedings of the Conference of the North American Chapter of the Association for Computational Linguistics on Human Language Technology* (pp.71-78). Stroudsburg, Germany: Association for Computational Linguistics.

Lin, T. Y. (1989). Neighborhood systems and approximation in database and knowledge base systems. In *Proceedings of the 4th International Symposium on Methodologies of Intelligent Systems* (pp. 75–86). Academic Press.

Lin, Y., Wang, X., Zhang, J., & Zhou, A. (2012b). Assembling the Optimal Sentiment Classifiers. In *Proceedings of the 13th international conference on Web Information Systems Engineering*. WISE.

Lin, Y., Zhang, J., Wang, X., & Zhou, A. (2012a). An information theoretic approach to sentiment polarity classification. In *Proceedings of the 2nd Joint WICOW/AIRWeb Workshop on Web Quality*. WICOW/AIRWeb.

Lin, D., & Stamp, M. (2011). Hunting for undetectable metamorphic viruses. *Journal in Computer Virology*, 7, 201–214. doi:10.1007/s11416-010-0148-y

Lin, J., & Zuo, M. (2003). Gearbox fault diagnosis using adaptive wavelet filter. *Mechanical Systems and Signal Processing*, 17(6), 1259–1269. doi:10.1006/mssp.2002.1507

Liu, F., Liu, Y., & Weng, F. (2011). Why is SXSW trending? exploring multiple text sources for Twitter topic summarization. In *Proceedings of the Workshop on Languages in Social Media (LSM '11)* (pp. 66-75). Stroudsburg, PA: Association for Computational Linguistics.

Liu, L., Pu, C., & Han, W. (2000). XWRAP: An XML-enabled wrapper construction system for Web information sources. In *Proceedings of 16th International Conference on Data Engineering* (pp. 611-621). San Diego, CA: IEEE.

Liu, L., Wang, C., Wu, M., & He, G. (2008). Research of Intelligent Information Retrieval System Ontology-based in Digital Library. In *Proceedings of IEEE International Symposium on IT in Medicine and Education*, (pp. 375-379). IEEE.

Liu, B. (2012). Sentiment Analysis and Opinion Mining. In *Synthesis Lectures on Human Language Technologies*. Morgan & Claypool Publishers.

Liu, G. (2010). Rough set theory based on two universal sets and its applications. *Knowledge-Based Systems*, 23, 110–115. doi:10.1016/j.knosys.2009.06.011

Liu, G. L. (2005). *Rough sets over the Boolean algebras*. New York: Springer-Verlag.

Liu, G. L. (2008). Generalized rough sets over fuzzy lattices. *Information Sciences*, 178, 1651–1662. doi:10.1016/j.ins.2007.11.010

Liu, P., Zhang, J., & Yu, X. (2009). Clustering-Based Semantic Web Service Matchmaking with Automated Knowledge Acquisition. In *Web Information Systems and Mining* (pp. 261–270). Springer. doi:10.1007/978-3-642-05250-7_28

Liu, Z., Yin, X., Zhang, Z., Chen, D., & Chen, W. (2004). Online rotor mixed fault diagnosis way based on spectrum analysis of instantaneous power in squirrel cage induction motors. *IEEE Transactions on Energy Conversion*, 19(3), 485–490. doi:10.1109/TEC.2004.832052

Li, Y., Kramer, M., Beulens, A., & Vorst, J. (2010). A framework for early warning and proactive control systems in food supply chain networks. *Computers in Industry*, 61(9), 852–862. doi:10.1016/j.compind.2010.07.010

Luan, R., Sun, S., Zhang, J., Yu, F., & Zhang, Q. (2012). A dynamic improved apriori algorithm and its experiments in web log mining. In *Proceedings of 9th International Conference on Fuzzy Systems and Knowledge Discovery FSKD* (pp. 1261-1264). Chongqing, China: IEEE Computer Society.

Lu, B., Li, Y., Wu, X., & Yang, Z. (2009). A review of recent advances in wind turbine condition monitoring and fault diagnosis. In *Proceedings of Power Electronics and Machines in Wind Applications*. IEEE. doi:10.1109/PEMWA.2009.5208325

Luke, S. (2010). *Essentials of Metaheuristics. 2009*. Retrieved from http://cs.gmu.edu/~sean/book/metaheuristics

Luo, X., Yan, K., & Chen, X. (2008). Automatic discovery of semantic relations based on association rule. *Journal of Software*, *3*(8), 11–18. doi:10.4304/jsw.3.8.11-18

Ma, J., Zhang, Y., & He, J. (2008). Efficiently finding Web services using a clustering semantic approach. In *Proceedings of the 2008 international workshop on Context enabled source and service selection, integration and adaptation: organized with the 17th International World Wide Web Conference (WWW 2008)*. ACM.

Mahalanobis, P. C. (1936). On the generalized distance in statistics. *Proceedings of the National Institute of Sciences (Calcutta)*, *2*, 49–55.

Makhlughian, M., Hashemi, S. M., Rastegari, Y., & Pejman, E. (2012). Web service selection based on ranking of qos using associative classification. *arXiv preprint arXiv:1204.1425*.

Malatesha Joshi, R., & Aaron, P. G. (Eds.). (2006). *Handbook of Orthography and Literacy*. Mahwah, NJ: Lawrence Erlbaum Associates.

Mampaey, M., Tatti, N., & Vreeken, J. (2011). Tell me what I need to know: succinctly summarizing data with itemsets. In *Proceedings of the 17th ACM SIGKDD Conference on Knowledge Discovery and Data Mining* (pp. 573-581). New York, NY: ACM.

Manabe, S. (Ed.). (1985a). Issues in atmospheric and oceanic modeling, part A: Climate dynamics. Adv. Geophys., 28.

Manabe, S. (Ed.). (1985b). Issues in atmospheric and oceanic modeling, part B: Weather dynamics. Adv. Geophys., 28.

Manly, B. F. J. (2005). *Multivariate statistical methods: a primer* (3rd ed.). Chapman and Hall/CRC Press.

Mantis, B. T. (n.d.). *A free Web-based bug tracking system*. Retrieved October 1, 2011, from www.mantisbt.org/

Marais, K. B., & Saleh, J. H. (2009). Beyond its cost, the value of maintenance: An analytical framework for capturing its net present value. *Reliability Engineering & System Safety*, *94*(2), 644–657. doi:10.1016/j.ress.2008.07.004

Marble, S., & Morton, B. P. (2006). Predicting the remaining life of propulsion system bearings. In *Proceedings of the IEEE Aerospace Conference*. IEEE.

Marcus, A., Bernstein, M. S., Badar, O., Karger, D. R., Madden, S., & Miller, R. C. (2011). Twitinfo: aggregating and visualizing microblogs for event exploration. In *Proceedings of the 2011 annual conference on Human factors in computing systems, ACM CHI '11*. ACM.

Mardia, K. V. (1970). Measures of multivariate skewness and kurtosis with applications. *Biometrika*, *57*(3), 519–530. doi:10.1093/biomet/57.3.519

Marghny, M. H., & Ali, A. F. (2005). Web mining based on genetic algorithm. In *Proceedings of AIML 05 Conference* (pp. 19-21). AIML.

Marr, D. (1982). *Vision, a computational investigation into human representation and processing of visual information*. New York: Henry Holt and Co.

Martineau, J., & Finin, T. (2009). Delta TFIDF: An Improved Feature Space for Sentiment Analysis. In *Proceedings of the Third AAAI Internatonal Conference on Weblogs and Social Media*, (pp. 258-261). AAAI.

Mathioudakis, M., & Koudas, N. (2010). TwitterMonitor: trend detection over the twitter stream. In *Proceedings of the 2010 international conference on Management of data* (pp. 1155-1158). New York, NY: ACM.

Matsumoto, S., Takamura, H., & Okumura, M. (2005). Sentiment classification using word sub-sequences and dependency sub-trees. In *Proceedings of the 9th Pacific-Asia conference on Advances in Knowledge Discovery and Data Mining (PAKDD)*, (pp. 301-311). PAKDD.

Mazid, M. M., Ali, A. S., & Tickle, K. S. (2009). A comparison between rule based and association rule mining algorithms. In *Proceedings of Third International Conference on Network and System Security* (pp. 452-455). Gold Coast, Australia: IEEE.

McDonald, G. L., Zhao, Q., & Zuo, M. J. (2012). Maximum correlated Kurtosis deconvolution and application on gear tooth chip fault detection. *Mechanical Systems and Signal Processing, 33,* 237–255. doi:10.1016/j.ymssp.2012.06.010

Md.Enamul, K., Andrew, W., & Lakhotia. (2005). Malware phylogeny generation using permutations of code. *Journal in Computer Virology, 1*(1-2), 13-23.

Meier, A. (2006). Operating building during temporary electricity shortage. *Energy and Building, 38*(11), 1296–1301. doi:10.1016/j.enbuild.2006.04.008

Mejova, Y., & Srinivasan, P. (2011). Exploring Feature Definition and Selection for Sentiment Classifiers. In *Proceedings of the Fifth International AAAI Conference on Weblogs and Social Media,* (pp. 546–549). AAAI.

Mele, I. (2013). Web usage mining for enhancing search-result delivery and helping users to find interesting web content. In *Proceedings of the sixth ACM international conference on Web search and data mining WSDM* (pp. 765-770). Rome, Italy: ACM.

Menahem, E., Rokach, L., & Elovici, Y. (2009a). Troika-An improved stacking schema for classification tasks. *Journal of Information Science, 179,* 4097–4122. doi:10.1016/j.ins.2009.08.025

Mendonca, M., & Sunderhaft, N. L. (1999). *Mining Software Engineering Data: A Survey.* A DACS (data & analysis center for software) state-of-the-art report.

Meng, J., & Yang, Y. (2012). The application of improved decision tree algorithm in the electric power marketing. In *Proceedings of World Automation Congress.* Academic Press.

Merz, C., Murphy, P., & Aha, D. (2012). *UCI Repository of Machine Learning Databases.* Department of Information and Computer Science, University of California.

Mesinger, F., & Arakawa, A. (1976). Numerical methods used in atmospheric models. *GARP Publ. Ser., 17.*

Meyerhof, G. G. (1973). Uplift resistance of inclined anchors and piles. In *Proc., 8th Int. Conf. on Soil Mechanics and Foundation Engg* (pp. 167-172). Moscow: Academic Press.

Meyerhof, G. G., & Adams, J. I. (1968). The ultimate uplift capacity of foundations. *J. Canadian Geotec., 5*(4), 225–244. doi:10.1139/t68-024

Miao, Y., & Li, C. (2010). WikiSummarizer - A Wikipedia-based Summarization System. In *Proceedings of Text Analysis Conference.* Academic Press.

Microsoft. (2013). *Microsoft Dynamics.* Retrieved December 13, 2012, from www.microsoft.com/dynamics.com

Mikut, R., & Reischl, M. (2011). Data mining tools. *Wiley Interdisciplinary Reviews: Data Mining and Knowledge Discovery, 1*(5), 431–443.

Mine, I. T. (2010). *Web Mining, the E-Tailers' Holy Grail?* Retrieved November 23, 2012, from www.mineit.com

Mircea, M., Ghilic-Micu, B., & Stoica, M. (2007). Combining business intelligence with cloud computing to delivery agility in actual economy. *Journal of Economics, 2011,* 39–54.

Mishra, B. S. P., Addy, A. K., Roy, R., & Dehuri, S. (2011). Parallel multi-objective genetic algorithms for associative classification rule mining. In *Proceedings of International Conference on Communication, Computing & Security* (pp. 409-414). Rourkela, India: ACM.

Mitchell, T. M. (1997). *Machine learning.* Burr Ridge, IL: McGraw Hill.

Mocanu, A., Litan, D., Olaru, S., & Munteanu, A. (2010). Information systems in the knowledge based economy. *WSEAS Transactions on Business and Economics, 7*(1), 11–21.

Moftah, H. M., Azar, A. T., Al-Shammari, E. T., Ghali, N. I., Hassanien, A. E., & Shoman, M. (2013). Adaptive k-means clustering algorithm for MR breast image segmentation. *Neural Computing & Applications,* 1–12.

Mohamed, W., Salleh, M. N. M., & Omar, A. H. (2012). A comparative study of Reduced Error Pruning method in decision tree algorithms. In *Proceedings of International Conference on Control System, Computing and Engineering* (pp. 392-397). Penang: IEEE.

Mohanty, A., & Kar, C. (2006). Fault detection in a multistage gearbox by demodulation of motor current waveform. *IEEE Transactions on Industrial Electronics*, *53*(4), 1285–1297. doi:10.1109/TIE.2006.878303

Mohanty, R., Ravi, V., & Patra, M. R. (2012). Classification of Web Services Using Bayesian Network. *Journal of Software Engineering and Applications*, *5*(4). doi:10.4236/jsea.2012.54034

Mokhtar, S. B., Kaul, A., Georgantas, N., & Issarny, V. (2006). Towards efficient matching of semantic Web service capabilities. In *Proceedings of International Workshop on Web Services–Modeling and Testing (WS-MaTe 2006)*. WS-MaTe.

Moore, W., & Starr, A. (2006). An intelligent maintenance system for continuous cost-based prioritisation of maintenance activities. *Computers in Industry*, *57*(6), 595–606. doi:10.1016/j.compind.2006.02.008

Moskovitch, R., Nissim, N., & Elovici, Y. (2009). Acquisition of malicious code using active learning. In *Proceedings of Privacy, Security, and Trust in KDD* (pp. 74–91). Berlin: Springer-Verlag. doi:10.1007/978-3-642-01718-6_6

Mozilla Bug Repository. (n.d.). Retrieved October 1, 2011, from https://bugzilla.mozilla.org/

Mullen, T., & Collier, N. (2004). Sentiment analysis using support vector machines with diverse information sources. In *Proceedings of Conference on Empirical Methods in Natural Language Processing*, (pp. 412-418). Academic Press.

Muller, A., Marquez, A. C., & Iung, B. (2008). On the concept of e-maintenance: Review and current research. *Reliability Engineering & System Safety*, *93*(8), 1165–1187. doi:10.1016/j.ress.2007.08.006

Murray, E. J., & Geddes, J. D. (1987). Uplift of anchor plates in sand. *Journal of the Geotechnical Engineering Division*, *113*(3), 202–215. doi:10.1061/(ASCE)0733-9410(1987)113:3(202)

Muslea, I., Minton, S., & Knoblock, C. A. (2001). Hierarchical wrapper induction for semistructured information sources. *Autonomous Agents and Multi-Agent Systems*, *4*(1-2), 93–114. doi:10.1023/A:1010022931168

Muthyala, K., & Naidu, R. (2011). A novel approach to test suite reduction using data mining. *Indian Journal of Computer Science and Engineering*, *2*(3), 500–505.

MVSP. (2012). *A MultiVariate Statistical Package, Version 3.1*. Pentraeth, UK: Kovach Computing Services.

Nagwani, N. K. (2013). *On Classification and Similarity Detection of Software Bugs Using Bug Database Mining*. (PhD Thesis). National Institute of Technology Raipur, India.

Nagwani, N. K., & Verma, S. (2010). Predictive Data Mining Model for Software Bug Estimation Using Average Weighted Similarity. In *Proceedings of the IEEE 2nd International Advance Computing Conference (IEEE IACC 2010)*. IEEE.

Nagwani, N. K., & Verma, S. (2012b). Predicting Expert Developers for Newly Reported Bugs Using Frequent Terms Similarities of Bug Attributes. In *Proceedings of the IEEE 9th International Conference on ICT and Knowledge Engineering 2011 Conference*. IEEE.

Nagwani, N. K., & Verma, S. (2012a). Rank-Me: A Java tool for ranking team members in software bug repositories. *Journal of Software Engineering and Applications*, *5*(4), 255–261. doi:10.4236/jsea.2012.54030

Naidu, M. S., & Geethanjali, N. (2013). Classification of defects in software using decision tree Algorithm. *International Journal of Engineering Science and Technology*, *5*(6), 1332–1340.

Nakagawa, T., Inui, K., & Kurohashi, S. (2010). Dependency tree-based sentiment classification using CRFs with hidden variables. In *Proceeding HLT '10 Human Language Technologies: Annual Conference of the North American Chapter of the Association for Computational Linguistics*. ACL.

Narayanan, S., Walchli, S. E., Reddy, N., Wood, A. L., & Reynolds, B. K. (1995). Developing intelligent information retrieval systems - issues in database organization, distributed processing, and interface design. In *Proceedings of IEEE International Conference on System, Man and Cybernetics: Intelligent Systems for the 21st Century,* (Vol. 4, pp. 3584-3589). IEEE.

Nastase, V. (2008). Topic-driven multi-document summarization with encyclopedic knowledge and spreading activation. In *Proceedings of Conference on Empirical Methods on Natural Language Processing* (pp. 763-772). New York, NY: ACM.

Nayak, R. (2007). Facilitating and improving the use of Web services with data mining. In *Research and trends in data mining technologies and applications* (pp. 309–327). Academic Press. doi:10.4018/978-1-59904-271-8.ch012

Nayak, R. (2008). Data mining in Web services discovery and monitoring.[IJWSR]. *International Journal of Web Services Research*, 5(1), 63–81. doi:10.4018/jwsr.2008010104

NCDC and NOAA. (n.d.). Retrieved from http://www.ncdc.noaa.gov/cdo-Web/

Negash, S. (2004). Business intelligence. *Communications of the Association for Information Systems*, 13, 177–195.

Nguyen, N. P., Dinh, T. N., Xuan, Y., & Thai, M. T. (2011). Adaptive algorithms for detecting community structure in dynamic social networks.[IEEE.]. *Proceedings - IEEE INFOCOM*, 2011, 2282–2290.

Nicholls, C., & Song, F. (2010). Comparison of feature selection methods for sentiment analysis. In Canadian AI 2010 (LNCS), (vol. 6085, pp. 286–289). Springer.

Nihei, K., Tomizawa, N., Shibata, A., & Shimazu, H. (1998). ExpertGuide for help desks-an intelligent information retrieval system for WWW pages. In *Proceedings of Ninth International Workshop on Database and Expert Systems Applications,* (pp. 937-942). Academic Press.

Nir, N., Robert, M., Lior, R., & Yuval, E. (2012). Detecting unknown computer worm activity via support vector machines and active learning. *Pattern Analysis & Applications*, 15(4), 459–475. doi:10.1007/s10044-012-0296-4

Nithya, P., & Sumathi, P. (2012). Novel pre-processing technique for web log mining by removing global noise and web robots. In *Proceedings of National Conference on Computing and Communication Systems (NCCCS)* (pp. 1-5). Durgapur, West Bengal: IEEE Computer Society.

Niu, G., Yang, B.-S., & Pecht, M. (2010). Development of an optimized condition-based maintenance system by data fusion and reliability-centered maintenance. *Reliability Engineering & System Safety*, 95(7), 786–796. doi:10.1016/j.ress.2010.02.016

NWS (National Weather Service) and NCEP. (National Centers for Environmental Prediction). (n.d.). *NOAA.* Retrieved from http://mag.ncep.noaa.gov/

O'Keefee, T., & Koprinska, I. (2009). Feature Selection and Weighting Methods in Sentiment Analysis. In *Proceedings of the 14th Australasian Document Computing Symposium.* Academic Press.

Oberle, D., Guarino, N., & Staab, S. (2009). What is an ontology? In *Handbook on Ontologies.* Academic Press.

Olivier, H., & Nathalie, J. (2006). A feature selection and evaluation scheme for computer virus detection. In *Proceedings of the Sixth International Conference on Data Mining,* (pp. 891-895). Washington, DC: IEEE Computer Society.

Open Source Machine Learning Software Weka. (n.d.). Retrieved from http://www.cs.waikato.ac.nz/ml/weka/

Oppenheimer, C. H., & Loparo, K. A. (2002). Physically based diagnosis and prognosis of cracked rotor shafts. In *Component and Systems Diagnostics, Prognostics, and Health Management II* (Vol. 4733). Academic Press. doi:10.1117/12.475502

Osgood, C. E., Succi, G. J., & Tannenbaum, P. H. (1957). *The Measurement of Meaning*. University of Illinois.

Ozcift, A. (2012). SVM feature selection based rotation forest ensemble classifiers to improve computer-aided diagnosis of Parkinson disease. *Journal of Medical Systems, 36*(4), 2141–2147. doi:10.1007/s10916-011-9678-1 PMID:21547504

Ozsoy, M. G., Alpaslan, F. N., & Cicekli, I. (2011). Text summarization of Turkish texts using Latent Semantic Analysis. In *Proceedings of the 23rd International Conference on Computational Linguistics (COLING '10)* (pp. 869-876). Stroudsburg, PA: Association for Computational Linguistics.

Pak, A., & Paroubek, P. (2011). Text representation using dependency tree sub-graphs for sentiment analysis. In *Proceedings of DASFAA workshop*, (pp. 323-332). DASFAA.

Pal & Deswal. (2010). Modelling pile capacity using Gaussian process regression. *Computers and Geotechnics, 37*, 942–947. doi:10.1016/j.compgeo.2010.07.012

Paltonglou, G., & Thelwallm, M. (2010). A study of Information retrieval weighting schemes for sentiment analysis. In *Proceedings of the 48th Annual Meeting of the Association for Computational Linguistics*, (pp. 1386-1395). ACL.

Pandey, A. K., Pandey, P., Jaiswal, K., & Sen, A. K. (2013). A Heart Disease Prediction Model using Decision Tree. *International Journal of Engineering Mathematics and Computer Sciences, 1*(3).

Pang, B., & Lee, L. (2004). A sentimental education: sentiment analysis using subjectivity summarization based on minimum cuts. In *Proceedings of the Association for Computational Linguistics* (ACL), (pp. 271–278). ACL.

Pang, B., Lee, L., & Vaithyanathan, S. (2002). Thumbs up? Sentiment classification using machine learning techniques. In *Proceedings of the Conference on Empirical Methods in Natural Language Processing* (EMNLP), (pp. 79–86). EMNLP.

Pardede, R. E. I., Tóth, L. L., Hosszú, G., & Kovács, F. (2012). Glyph Identification Based on Topological Analysis. In *Proceedings of Scientific Workshop organized by the PhD school on Computer Science in the framework of the project TÁMOP-4.2.2/B-10/1-2010-0009* (pp. 99-103). Budapest, Hungary: Budapest University of Technology and Economics.

Park, D., & Rilett, L. R. (1999). Forecasting freeway link ravel times with a multi-layer feed forward neural network. *Computer Aided Civil and Infra Structure Engrg, 14*, 358–367.

Partridge, A. (2013). Business intelligence in the supply chain. *Inbound Logistics*. Retrieved September 6, 2013, from http://www.inboundlogistics.com/cms/article/business-intelligence-in-the-supply-chain/

Pawlak, Z. (1982). Rough sets. *International Journal of Computer Information Science, 11*, 341–356. doi:10.1007/BF01001956

Pawlak, Z. (1991). *Rough sets: Theoretical Aspects of Reasoning about Data*. Kluwer Academic Publishers. doi:10.1007/978-94-011-3534-4

Pawlak, Z. (1997). Rough set approach to knowledge-based decision support. *European Journal of Operational Research, 99*(1), 48–57. doi:10.1016/S0377-2217(96)00382-7

Pawlak, Z., & Skowron, A. (2007a). Rough sets: Some extensions. *Information Sciences, 177*(1), 28–40. doi:10.1016/j.ins.2006.06.006

Pawlak, Z., & Skowron, A. (2007b). Rough sets and Boolean reasoning. *Information Sciences, 177*(1), 41–73. doi:10.1016/j.ins.2006.06.007

Pedrycz, W. (2007). Granular computing: The emerging paradigm. *Journal of Uncertain Systems, 1*(1), 38–61.

Pendharkar, P. C., Subramanian, G. H., & Rodger, J. A. (2005). A Probabilistic Model for Predicting Software Development Effort. *IEEE Transactions on Software Engineering, 31*(7), 615–624. doi:10.1109/TSE.2005.75

Peng, Y., Wu, Z., & Jiang, J. (2010). A novel feature selection approach for biomedical data classification. *Journal of Biomedical Informatics*, 43(1), 15–23. doi:10.1016/j.jbi.2009.07.008 PMID:19647098

Penrose, L. S. (1954). Distance, size and shape. *Annals of Eugenics*, 18(4), 337. PMID:13149002

Perforce, a Commercial, Proprietary Revision Control System. (n.d.). Retrieved October 1, 2011, from http://www.perforce.com/

Petrini, M., & Pozzebon, M. (2009). Managing Sustainability with the Support of Business Intelligence: Integrating Socio-Environmental Indicators and Organizational Context. *The Journal of Strategic Information Systems*, 18(4), 178–191. doi:10.1016/j.jsis.2009.06.001

Pham, D., Ghanbarzadeh, A., Koc, E., Otri, S., Rahim, S., & Zaidi, M. (2006). *The bees algorithm–a novel tool for complex optimisation problems*. Paper presented at the Proceedings of the 2nd Virtual International Conference on Intelligent Production Machines and Systems (IPROMS 2006). New York, NY.

Phan, D., & Vogel, D. (2010). A Model of Customer Relationship Management and Business Intelligence Systems for Catalogue and Online Retailers. *Information & Management*, 47(2), 69–77. doi:10.1016/j.im.2009.09.001

Phua, C., Lee, V., Smith, K., & Gayler, R. (2010). A Comprehensive Survey of Data Mining-Based Fraud Detection Research. *Cornell University Library*. Retrieved November 10, 2012, from http://arxiv.org/abs/1009.6119

Ping, C., & Verma, R. (2006). A query-based medical information summarization system using ontology knowledge. In *Proceedings of IEEE Computer-Based Medical Systems* (pp. 37–42). IEEE Computer Society.

Polat, K., & Güneş, S. (2006). Hepatitis disease diagnosis using a new hybrid system based on feature selection (FS) and artificial immune recognition system with fuzzy resource allocation. *Digital Signal Processing*, 16(6), 889–901. doi:10.1016/j.dsp.2006.07.005

Polat, K., & Güneş, S. (2007). Breast cancer diagnosis using least square support vector machine. *Digital Signal Processing*, 17(4), 694–701. doi:10.1016/j.dsp.2006.10.008

Poli, R., Kennedy, J., & Blackwell, T. (2007). Particle swarm optimization. *Swarm Intelligence*, 1(1), 33–57. doi:10.1007/s11721-007-0002-0

Prabowo, R., & Thelwall, M. (2009). Sentiment analysis: A combined approach. *Journal of Informetrics*, 3(2), 143–157. doi:10.1016/j.joi.2009.01.003

Prasad, A. A., Meena, B., Kumar, B. U., & Kartheek, V. (2012). Efficient Retrieval of Web Services Using Prioritization and Clustering. *Computer Engineering and Intelligent Systems*, 3(5), 8–15.

Punitha, K., & Chitra, S. (2013). Software defect prediction using software metrics - A survey. In *Proceedings of International Conference on Information Communication and Embedded Systems* (ICICES), (pp. 555-558). ICICES.

Qian, Y. H., & Liang, J. Y. (2006). Rough set method based on multigranulations. In *Proceedings of the 5th IEEE International Conference on Cognitive Informatics* (pp. 297-304). IEEE Xplore.

Qian, Y. H., Liang, J. Y., & Dang, C. Y. (2007). MGRS in incomplete information systems. In *Proceedings of the IEEE International Conference on Granular Computing* (pp. 163-168). IEEE Xplore.

Qu, X., Sun, H., Li, X., Liu, X., & Lin, W. (2009). WSSM: A WordNet-Based Web Services Similarity Mining Mechanism. In Proceedings of Future Computing, Service Computation, Cognitive, Adaptive, Content, Patterns, (pp. 339-345). IEEE.

Quinlan, J. (1986). Induction of Decision Trees. *Readings in Machine Learning*, 1(1), 81–106. doi:10.1007/BF00116251

Quinlan, J. R. (1993). *C4. 5: programs for machine learning* (Vol. 1). Morgan Kaufmann.

Quintana, Y. (1997). Cognitive Approaches to Intelligent Information Retrieval. In *Proceedings of IEEE Canadian Conference on Engineering Innovation: Voyage of Discovery*, (Vol. 1, pp. 261-264). IEEE.

Radev, D. R. (2004). Lexrank: Graph-based lexical centrality as salience in text summarization. *Journal of Artificial Intelligence Research*, 22(4), 457–479.

Radev, D. R., Jing, H., Sty, M., & Tam, D. (2004). Centroid-based summarization of multiple documents. *Information Processing & Management, 40*(6), 919–938. doi:10.1016/j.ipm.2003.10.006

Rafiee, J., Rafiee, M., & Tse, P. (2010). Application of mother wavelet functions for automatic gear and bearing fault diagnosis. *Expert Systems with Applications, 37*(6), 4568–4579. doi:10.1016/j.eswa.2009.12.051

Raj, S., & Portia, A. (2011). Analysis on Credit Card Fraud Detection Methods. In *Proceedings of International Conference on Computers, Communication and Electrical Technology ICCCET* (pp. 152-156). Tamilnadu, India: ICCCET.

Rajabioun, R. (2011). Cuckoo optimization algorithm. *Applied Soft Computing, 11*(8), 5508–5518. doi:10.1016/j.asoc.2011.05.008

Ramakrishnan, T., Jones, M., & Sidorova, A. (2011). Factors Influencing Business Intelligence and Data Collection Strategies: An Empirical Investigation. *Decision Support Systems, 52*(2), 486–496. doi:10.1016/j.dss.2011.10.009

Ramírez, J., Górriz, J., Segovia, F., Chaves, R., Salas-Gonzalez, D., López, M., & Padilla, P. (2010). Computer aided diagnosis system for the Alzheimer's disease based on partial least squares and random forest SPECT image classification. *Neuroscience Letters, 472*(2), 99–103. doi:10.1016/j.neulet.2010.01.056 PMID:20117177

Randall, D. A. (Ed.). (2000). *General circulation model development: Past, present, and future.* Academic Press.

Randall, R. B., & Antoni, J. (2011). Rolling element bearing diagnostics—A tutorial. *Mechanical Systems and Signal Processing, 25*(2), 485–520. doi:10.1016/j.ymssp.2010.07.017

Rao, S., & Swarup, S. (2001). Business Intelligence and Logistics. *Wipro Technologies.* Retrieved November 5, 2012, from http://idii.com/wp/bilogistics.pdf

Rao, J., & Su, X. (2005). A survey of automated Web service composition methods. In *Semantic Web Services and Web Process Composition* (pp. 43–54). Springer. doi:10.1007/978-3-540-30581-1_5

Raychev, V., & Nakov, P. (2009). Language-Independent Sentiment Analysis Using Subjectivity and Positional Information. In *Proceedings of International Conference RANLP 2009.* RANLP.

Ren, K., Chen, J., Xiao, N., Song, J., & Li, J. (2008). Building Quick Service Query List Using Wordnet for Automated Service Composition. In *Proceedings of Asia-Pacific Services Computing Conference,* (pp. 297-302). IEEE.

Revelle, M., Dit, B., & Poshyvanyk, D. (2010). Using Data Fusion and Web Mining to Support Feature Location in Software. In *Proceedings of IEEE 18th International Conference on Program Comprehension,* (pp. 14-23). IEEE.

Riloff, E., Patwardhan, S., & Wiebe, J. (2006). Feature subsumption for opinion analysis. In *Proceedings of the Conference on Empirical Methods in Natural Language Processing.* Sydney, Australia: Academic Press.

Ritcharoenwattu, T., & Rungworawut, W. (2013). New Patterns Discovery for Web Services Composition from mining Execution Logs. *International Journal of Computer and Electrical Engineering, 5*(1), 88–92. doi:10.7763/IJCEE.2013.V5.670

Robert, M., Dima, S., Clint, F., Nir, N., Nathalie, J., & Yuval, E. (2009). Unknown malcode detection and the imbalance problem. *Journal in Computer Virology, 5*(4), 295–308. doi:10.1007/s11416-009-0122-8

Rodríguez, C., Daniel, F., Casati, F., & Cappiello, C. (2010). Toward Uncertain Business Intelligence: The Case of Key Indicators. *IEEE Internet Computing, 14*(4), 32–40. doi:10.1109/MIC.2010.59

Rogers, H. (1999). Sociolinguistic factors in borrowed writing systems. *Toronto Working Paper in Linguistics, 17,* 247-262.

Rong, W., Liu, K., & Liang, L. (2008). Association rule based context modeling for Web service discovery. In *Proceedings of E-Commerce Technology and the Fifth IEEE Conference on Enterprise Computing, E-Commerce and E-Services, 2008 10th IEEE Conference on* (pp. 299-304). IEEE.

Rong, W., Liu, K., & Liang, L. (2009). Personalized Web service ranking via user group combining association rule. In *Proceedings of Web Services* (pp. 445–452). IEEE. doi:10.1109/ICWS.2009.113

Ronny, M., Tobias, H., Christian, K., & Jana, D. (2010). Statistical detection of malicious PE-executables for fast offline analysis.[LNCS]. *Proceedings of Communications and Multimedia Security, 6109*, 93–105. doi:10.1007/978-3-642-13241-4_10

Rotem, N. (2006). *Open Text Summarizer (OTS)*. Retrieved in July 2011 from http://libots.sourceforge.net

Rouseeuw, P. J., & Leroy, A. M. (1987). *Robust regression and outlier detection*. Wiley. doi:10.1002/0471725382

Rousseeuw, P. J., & Driessen, K. V. (1999). A fast algorithm for the minimum covariance determinant estimator. *Technometrics, 41*(3), 212–223. doi:10.1080/00401706.1999.10485670

Rowe, R. K., & Davis, E. H. (1982a). The behaviour of anchor plates in clay. *Geotech, 32*(1), 9–23. doi:10.1680/geot.1982.32.1.9

Rowe, R. K., & Davis, E. H. (1982b). The behaviour of anchor plates in sand. *Geotech, 32*(1), 25–41. doi:10.1680/geot.1982.32.1.25

Royston, J. P. (1983). Some techniques for assessing multivarate normality based on the shapiro-wilk W. *Applied Statistics, 32*(2), 121–133. doi:10.2307/2347291

Runwal, N., Mark, S., & Low, R. M. (2012). Opcode graph similarity and metamorphic detection. *Journal in Computer Virology, 8*(1-2), 37–52. doi:10.1007/s11416-012-0160-5

Russell, S. J., Norvig, P., Canny, J. F., Malik, J. M., & Edwards, D. D. (1995). *Artificial intelligence: a modern approach* (Vol. 74). Prentice Hall.

Saggar, M., Agrawal, A. K., & Lad, A. (2004). Optimization of association rule mining using improved genetic algorithms. In *Proceedings of IEEE International Conference on Systems, Man and Cybernetics 4* (pp. 3725-3729). Hague, Netherlands: IEEE Computer Society.

Sahuguet, A., & Azavant, F. (2001). Building intelligent Web applications using lightweight wrappers. *Data & Knowledge Engineering, 36*(3), 283–316. doi:10.1016/S0169-023X(00)00051-3

Sainz, E., Llombart, E., & Guerrero, J. (2009). Robust filtering for the characterization of wind turbines: Improving its operation and maintenance. *Energy Conversion and Management, 50*(9), 2136–2147. doi:10.1016/j.enconman.2009.04.036

Saleem, D. M. A., Acharjya, D. P., Kannan, A., & Iyengar, N. C. S. N. (2012). An intelligent knowledge mining model for kidney cancer using rough set theory. *International Journal of Bioinformatics Research and Applications, 8*(5-6), 417–435. PMID:23060419

Saleh, Mohamed, & Nabi. (2011). Eigenviruses for metamorphic virus recognition. *IET Information Security, 5*(4), 191-198.

Samanta, B., & Al-Balushi, K. R. (2003). Artificial neural network based fault diagnostics of rolling element bearings using time-domain features. *Mechanical Systems and Signal Processing, 17*(2), 317–328. doi:10.1006/mssp.2001.1462

Sanches, A. L., Pamplona, E. D. O., & Montevechi, J. A. B. (2005). Capital budgeting using triangular fuzzy numbers. *V Encuentro Internacional de Finanzas, 19*.

Sanghvi, A. P. (1991). Power shortages in developing countries: Impacts and policy implications. *Energy Policy, 19*(5), 425–440. doi:10.1016/0301-4215(91)90020-O

Santhosh Kumar, B., & Rukmani, K. V. (2010). Implementation of Web Usage Mining Using APRIORI and FP Growth Algorithms. *International Journal of Advanced Networking & Applications, 1*(6).

Santos, I., Penya, Y. K., Devesa, J., & Bringas, P. G. (2009). N-grams-based file signatures for malware detection. In J. Cordeiro, & J. Filipe (Eds.), *ICEIS* (Vol. 2, pp. 317–320). ICEIS.

Saravanan, M., & Ravindran, B. (2010). Identification of rhetorical roles for segmentation and summarization of a legal judgment. *Artificial Intelligence and Law, 18*(1), 45–76. doi:10.1007/s10506-010-9087-7

Sartakhti, J. S., Zangooei, M. H., & Mozafari, K. (2011). Hepatitis disease diagnosis using a novel hybrid method based on support vector machine and simulated annealing (SVM-SA). In *Computer methods and programs in biomedicine*. Academic Press.

SAS. (2013). SAS business intelligence software. *SAS*. Retrieved April 22, 2013, from http://www.sas.com/technologies/bi/index.html

Schultz, E. Zadok, & Stolfo. (2001). Data mining methods for detection of new malicious executables. In *Proceedings of the IEEE Symposium on Security and Privacy*, (pp. 38-49). Washington, DC: IEEE Computer Society.

Schweighardt, C. (2010). *Calculating ROI to Realize Project Value*. Retrieved April 24, 2013, from www.isixsigma.com/operations/finance/calculating-roi-realize-project-value/

Sciascio, F., & Amicarelli, A. N. (2008). Biomass estimation in batch bio-technological processes by Bayesian Gaussian process regression. *Computers & Chemical Engineering*, *32*, 3264–3273. doi:10.1016/j.compchemeng.2008.05.015

Sebestyén, G. (1909). *Rovás és rovásírás* [Rovash and Rovash writing]. Budapest, Hungary: Hungarian Academy of Sciences.

Securities and exchange Commission, 17 CFR Parts 240 and 249, [Release No. 34-67717, File No. S7-42-10], RIN 3235-AK85, Disclosure of Payments by Resource Extraction Issuers.

Selby, R. W., & Porter, A. A. (1988). Learning from Examples: Generation and Evaluation of Decision Trees for Software Resource Analysis. *IEEE Transactions on Software Engineering*, *14*(12), 1743–1757. doi:10.1109/32.9061

Sellami, M., Gaaloul, W., & Tata, S. (2010). Functionality-driven clustering of Web service registries. In *Proceedings of Services Computing (SCC), 2010 IEEE International Conference on* (pp. 631-634). IEEE.

Selvakumar, J., & Rajaram, M. (2011). Performance Evaluation of Requirements Engineering Methodology for Automated Detection of Non Functional Requirements. *International Journal on Computer Science and Engineering*, *3*(8), 2991–2995.

Seon, Y., & Ulrich, U. N. (2006). Towards establishing a unknown virus detection technique using SOM. *Journal in Computer Virology*, *2*(3), 163–186.

Shahin, M. A., & Jaksa, M. B. (2006). Pullout capacity of small ground anchors by direct cone penetration test methods and neural networks. *J. Canadian Geotech.*, *43*, 626–637. doi:10.1139/t06-029

Shapiro, G., Brachman, R., & Khabaza, T. (1996). An Overview of Issues in Developing Industrial Data Mining and Knowledge Discovery Applications. In *Proceedings of Knowledge Discovery and Data Mining KDD-96 Proceedings* (pp. 89–95). ACM.

Sharifi, B., Hutton, M.-A., & Kalita, J. (2010). Experiments in Microblog Summarization. In *Proceedings of the 2010 IEEE Second International Conference on Social Computing (SOCIALCOM '10)* (pp. 49-56). IEEE Computer Society.

Sharifi, B., Hutton, M.-A., & Kalita, J. (2010). Summarizing microblogs automatically. In *Proceedings of the 2010 Annual Conference of the North American Chapter of the Association for Computational Linguistics (HLT '10)* (pp. 685-688). Stroudsburg, PA: Association for Computational Linguistics.

Sharma, S., & Sharma, A. (2011). Amalgamation of Automated Testing and Data Mining: A Novel Approach in Software Testing. *International Journal of Computer Science Issues*, *8*(2), 195–199.

Shou, D., & Chi, C. H. (2008). Effective Web Service Retrieval Based on Clustering. In Proceedings of Semantics, Knowledge and Grid, (pp. 469-472). IEEE.

Shouman, M., Turner, T., & Stocker, R. (2012). *Applying k-Nearest Neighbour in Diagnosing Heart Disease Patients.* Paper presented at the 2012 International Conference on Knowledge Discovery (ICKD 2012) IPCSIT. New York, NY.

Shrivastava, V. K., Kumar, D. P., & Pardasani, D. K. (2010). Extraction of Interesting Association Rules using GA Optimization. *Global Journal of Computer Science and Technology, 10*(5).

Siegel, D., Al-Atat, H., Shauche, V., Liao, L., Snyder, J., & Lee, J. (2012). Novel method for rolling element bearing health assessment—A tachometer-less synchronously averaged envelope feature extraction technique. *Mechanical Systems and Signal Processing, 29*, 362–376. doi:10.1016/j.ymssp.2012.01.003

Sitch, S., Cox, P. M., Collins, W. J., & Huntingford, C. (2007). Indirect radiative forcing of climate change through ozone effects on the land-carbon sink. *Nature, 448*(7155), 791–794. doi:10.1038/nature06059 PMID:17653194

Skoutas, D., Sacharidis, D., Simitsis, A., & Sellis, T. (2010). Ranking and clustering Web services using multicriteria dominance relationships. *Services Computing. IEEE Transactions on, 3*(3), 163–177.

Smith, D. (2010). Using Data and Text Mining to Drive Innovation. SAS. *PhUSE 2010.* Retrieved December 10, 2012, from http://www.phusewiki.org/docs/2010/2010%20PAPERS/SP02%20Paper.pdf

Sneath, P. H. A., & Sokal, R. R. (1973). *Numerical Taxonomy.* San Francisco, CA: W.H. Freeman and Company.

Snyder, B., & Barzilay, R. (2007). Multiple aspect ranking using the Good Grief algorithm. In *Proceedings of the Joint Human Language Technology/North American Chapter of the ACL Conference* (HLT-NAACL), (pp. 300–307). ACL.

Soderland, S. (1999). Learning information extraction rules for semi-structured and free text. *Machine Learning, 34*(1-3), 233–272. doi:10.1023/A:1007562322031

Sohn, H., Worden, K., & Farrar, C. (2002). Statistical damage classification under changing environmental and operational conditions. *Journal of Intelligent Material Systems and Structures, 13*(9), 561–574. doi:10.1106/104538902030904

Sokal, R. R., & Michener, C. D. (1958). A statistical method for evaluating systematic relationships. *The University of Kansas Scientific Bulletin, 38*, 1409–1438.

Soltani-Sarvestani, M., & Lotfi, S. (2012). QCA & CQCA: Quad Countries Algorithm and Chaotic Quad Countries Algorithm. *Journal of Theoretical and Applied Computer Science, 6*(3), 3–20.

Soua, S., Van Lieshout, P., Perera, A., Gan, T. H., & Bridge, B. (2013). Determination of the combined vibrational and acoustic emission signature of a wind turbine gearbox and generator shaft in service as a pre-requisite for effective condition monitoring. *Renewable Energy, 51*, 175–181. doi:10.1016/j.renene.2012.07.004

Spoerre, J. (1997). Application of the cascade correlation algorithm (CCA) to bearing fault classification problems. *Computers in Industry, 32*(3), 295–304. doi:10.1016/S0166-3615(96)00080-2

Srinath, S., & Ram, D. J. (n.d.). *Data Mining and Knowledge Discovery.* Retrieved from http://nptel.iitm.ac.in/video.php?subjectId=106106093

Stegle, O., Fallert, S. V., MacKay, D. J., & Brage, S. (2008). Gaussian process robust regression for noisy heart rate data. *IEEE Transactions on Bio-Medical Engineering, 55*(9), 2143–2151. doi:10.1109/TBME.2008.923118 PMID:18713683

Strohmann, T. R., & Grudic, G. Z. (2002). A Formulation for minimax probability machine regression. In *NIPS) 14.* Advances in Neural Information Processing SystemsCambridge, MA: MIT Press.

Subba Rao, K. S., & Kumar, J. (1994). Vertical uplift capacity of horizontal anchors. *Journal of the Geotechnical Engineering Division, 120*(7), 1134–1147. doi:10.1061/(ASCE)0733-9410(1994)120:7(1134)

Suchanek, F. M., Kasneci, G., & Weikum, G. (2007). Yago: a core of semantic knowledge. In *Proceedings of the 16th international conference on World Wide Web* (pp. 697-706). New York, NY: ACM.

Sudarshan, M. S., & Mark, S. (2013). Metamorphic worm that carries its own morphing engine. *Journal in Computer Virology, 9*(2), 49–58.

Sun, J. (2009). Modelling of chaotic time series using minimax probability machine regression. In *Proceedings - 2009 WRI International Conference on Communications and Mobile Computing, CMC, 4797010*, (pp. 321-324). WRI.

Sun, J., Bai, Y., Luo, J., & Dang, J. (2009). Modelling of a chaotic time series using a modified minimax probability machine regression. *The Chinese Journal of Physiology*, *47*(4), 491–501.

Sutherland, H. B. (1988). Uplift resistance of soils. *Geotech, 38*(4), 473–516.

Swayne, D. F., Cook, D., & Buja, A. (1998). Xgobi: Interactive dynamic data visualization in the x window system. *Journal of Computational and Graphical Statistics, 7*, 113–130.

Sycara, K., Paolucci, M., Ankolekar, A., & Srinivasan, N. (2003). Automated discovery, interaction and composition of semantic Web services. *Web Semantics: Science. Services and Agents on the World Wide Web, 1*(1), 27–46. doi:10.1016/j.websem.2003.07.002

Tabish, S. M., Shafiq, M. Z., & Farooq, M. (2009). Malware detection using statistical analysis of byte-level file content. In *Proceedings of the ACM SIGKDD Workshop on Cyber Security and Intelligence Informatics* (CSI-KDD' 09), (pp. 23-31). New York, NY: ACM.

Taboada, M., Brooke, J., Tofiloski, M., Voll, K., & Stede, M. (2011). Lexicon-based methods for sentiment analysis. *Computational Linguistics, 37*(2), 267–307. doi:10.1162/COLI_a_00049

Tai, C.-H., Tseng, P.-J., Yu, P. S., & Chen, M.-S. (2011). Identities anonymization in dynamic social networks. In *Proceedings 11th IEEE international conference on data mining*, (pp. 1224-1229). IEEE.

Taipale, K. (2003). Data Mining and Domestic Security: Connecting the Dots to Make Sense of Data. *Columbia Science and Technology Law Review, 5*(2), 83.

Takamura, H., & Okumura, M. (2009a). Text summarization model based on maximum coverage problem and its variant. In *Proceedings of the 12th Conference of the European Chapter of the Association for Computational Linguistics* (pp. 781-789). Stroudsburg, PA: Association for Computational Linguistics.

Takamura, H., & Okumura, M. (2009b). Text summarization model based on the budgeted median problem. In *Proceeding of the 18th ACM conference on Information and knowledge management* (pp. 1589-1592). New York, NY: ACM.

Talbi, E.-G. (2009). *Metaheuristics: from design to implementation* (Vol. 74). John Wiley & Sons. doi:10.1002/9780470496916

Tang, J., Yao, L., & Chen, D. (2009). Multi-topic based query-oriented summarization. In *Proceedings of SIAM International Conference Data Mining* (pp. 20-26). New York, NY: ACM.

Tan, P. N., Steinbach, M., & Kumar, V. (2006). *Introduction to data mining*. Boston, MA: Pearson Addison Wesley.

Tan, S., & Zhang, J. (2008). An empirical study of sentiment analysis for chinese documents. *Expert Systems with Applications, 34*, 2622–2629. doi:10.1016/j.eswa.2007.05.028

Tantipathananandh, C., Berger-Wolf, T., & Kempe, D. (2007). A framework for community identification in dynamic social networks. In *Proceedings of the 13th ACM SIGKDD international conference on knowledge discovery and data mining (KDD'07)*, (pp. 717-726). ACM.

Tatti, N., & Heikinheimo, H. (2008). Decomposable families of itemsets. In *Proceedings of European Conference on Machine Learning and Knowledge Discovery in Databases* (PKDD'08) (pp. 472-487). Heidelberg, Germany: Springer-Verlag.

Tatti, N., & Mampaey, M. (2010). Using background knowledge to rank itemsets. *ACM Data Mining and Knowledge Discovery., 21*(2), 293–309. doi:10.1007/s10618-010-0188-4

Temurtas, F. (2009). A comparative study on thyroid disease diagnosis using neural networks. *Expert Systems with Applications, 36*(1), 944–949. doi:10.1016/j.eswa.2007.10.010

Terrell, Jeffay, Smith, Zhang, Shen, Zhu, & Nobel. (2005). Multivariate SVD analyses for network anomaly detection. In *Proceedings of ACM SIGCOMM Conference*. ACM.

TexLexAn. (2011). *Texlexan: An open-source text summarizer*. Retrieved March 15, 2011, from http://texlexan.sourceforge.net/

Thakkar, K., Dharaskar, R., & Chandak, M. (2010). Graph-based algorithms for text summarization. In *Proceedings of Third International Conference on Emerging Trends in Engineering and Technology*, (pp. 516–519). Academic Press.

Thelegdi, I. (1994). *Rudimenta, Priscae hunnorum linguae brevibus quaestionibus ac responcionibus comprehensa opera et studio*. Budapest, Hungary: Ars Libri.

Theodoridis, S. K. K. (2008). *Pattern recognition*. Academic Press.

Theus, M. (2002). Interactive data visualization using Mondrian. *Journal of Statistical Software, 7*(11), 1–9.

Thomas, J. J., & Cook, K. A. (Eds.). (2005). *Illuminating the path: The research and development agenda for visual analytics*. IEEE Computer Society Press.

Thomsen, C., & Pedersen, T. B. (2009). A survey of open source tools for business intelligence. *International Journal of Data Warehousing and Mining, 5*(3), 56–75. doi:10.4018/jdwm.2009070103

Tian, Z. (2012). An artificial neural network method for remaining useful life prediction of equipment subject to condition monitoring. *Journal of Intelligent Manufacturing, 23*(2), 227–237. doi:10.1007/s10845-009-0356-9

Tian, Z., Wong, L., & Safaei, N. (2010). A neural network approach for remaining useful life prediction utilizing both failure and suspension histories. *Mechanical Systems and Signal Processing, 24*(5), 1542–1555. doi:10.1016/j.ymssp.2009.11.005

Tomek, I. (1976). Two Modifications of CNN. *IEEE Transactions on Systems Management and Communications, 6*, 769–772.

Tondini, C., Fenaroli, P., & Labianca, R. (2007). Breast cancer follow-up: just a burden, or much more? *Annals of Oncology, 18*(9), 1431–1432. doi:10.1093/annonc/mdm380 PMID:17761702

Town, C. (2006). Ontological inference for image and video analysis. *Machine Vision and Applications, 17*(2), 94–115. doi:10.1007/s00138-006-0017-3

Trac, Project Management and Bug Tracking System. (n.d.). Retrieved October 1, 2011, from http://trac.edgewall.org/

Tripathy, B. K. (2006). Rough sets on intuitionistic fuzzy approximation spaces. In *Proceedings of the 3rd International IEEE Conference on Intelligent Systems (IS06)* (pp.776-779). IEEE Xplore.

Tripathy, B. K., & Acharjya, D. P. (2010). Knowledge mining using ordering rules and rough sets on fuzzy approximation spaces. *International Journal of Advances in Science and Technology, 1*(3), 41–50.

Tripathy, B. K., & Acharjya, D. P. (2011). Association rule granulation using rough sets on intuitionistic fuzzy approximation spaces and granular computing. *Annals Computer Science Series, 9*(1), 125–144.

Tripathy, B. K., & Acharjya, D. P. (2012). Approximation of classification and measures of uncertainty in rough set on two universal sets. *International Journal of Advanced Science and Technology, 40*, 77–90.

Tripathy, B. K., Acharjya, D. P., & Cynthya, V. (2011). A framework for intelligent medical diagnosis using rough set with formal concept analysis. *International Journal of Artificial Intelligence & Applications, 2*(2), 45–66. doi:10.5121/ijaia.2011.2204

Tripathy, B. K., Acharjya, D. P., & Ezhilarasi, L. (2012). Topological characterization of rough set on two universal sets and knowledge representation. In P. V. Krishna, M. R. Babu, & E. Ariwa (Eds.), *Communications in Computer and Information Science* (pp. 68–81). Springer-Verlag. doi:10.1007/978-3-642-29216-3_9

Tsutsumi, K., Shimada, K., & Endo, T. (2007). Movie Review Classification Based on a Multiple Classifier. In *Proceedings of PACLIC*, (pp. 481-488). PACLIC.

Tsytsarau, M., & Palpanas, T. (2012). Survey on mining subjective data on the web. *Data Mining and Knowledge Discovery, 24*, 478–514. doi:10.1007/s10618-011-0238-6

Tu, H.-C., & Hsiang, J. (1998). An Architecture and Category Knowledge for Intelligent Information Retrieval Agents. In *Proceedings of the Thirty-First Hawaii International Conference on System Sciences,* (Vol. 4, pp. 405-414). IEEE.

Tu, Z., Jiang, W., Liu, Q., & Lin, S. (2012). Dependency Forest for Sentiment Analysis. In *Proceedings of First CCF Conference, Natural Language Processing and Chinese Computing* (pp. 69-77). CCF.

Tuğ, E., Şakiroğlu, M., & Arslan, A. (2006). Automatic discovery of the sequential accesses from web log data files via a genetic algorithm. *Knowledge-Based Systems, 19*(3), 180–186. doi:10.1016/j.knosys.2005.10.008

Turney, P. D. (2002). Thumbs Up or Thumbs Down? Semantic Orientation Applied to Unsupervised Classification of Reviews. In *Proceedings of ACL 2002*, (pp. 417-424). ACL.

Twitter. (n.d.). Retrieved October 1, 2011, from https://twitter.com

UCAR. (2000, October). Planning a new paradigm: The future of high-end modeling at NCAR. *Staff Notes Monthly*. NCAR. (2006, August). *Weather forecast accuracy gets boost with new computer model*. NCAR.

Uhlmann, E., Geisert, C., Hohwieler, E., & Altmann, I. (2013). Data Mining and Visualization of Diagnostic Messages for Condition Monitoring. *Procedia CIRP Elsevier, 11*, 225–228. doi:10.1016/j.procir.2013.07.045

Van den Berg, J. P. (1999). A Literature Survey on Planning and Control of Warehousing Systems. *LIE Transactions, 31*(8), 751–762.

Veeramalai, S., Jaisankar, N., & Kannan, A. (2010). Efficient Web Log Mining Using Enhanced Apriori Algorithm with Hash Tree and Fuzzy. *International Journal of Computer Science & Information Technology, 2*(4).

Vellidoa, A., Lisboaa, P. J. G., & Vaughan, J. (1999). Neural Networks in Business: A Survey of Applications (1992–1998). *Expert Systems with Applications, 17*(1), 51–70. doi:10.1016/S0957-4174(99)00016-0

Venkatesan, P., & Anitha, S. (2006). Application of a radial basis function neural network for diagnosis of diabetes mellitus. *Current Science, 91*(9), 1195.

Veress, E. (1906). A bolognai Marsigli-iratok magyar vonatkozásai. [Hungarian connections of the Marsigli-documents of Bologna]. *Magyar Könyvszemle, 14*.

Verma, A., & Kusiak, A. (2011). Predictive Analysis of Wind Turbine Faults: A Data Mining Approach. In *Proceedings of the 2011 Industrial Engineering Research Conference*. Reno, NV: Academic Press.

Verma, S., & Bhattacharyya, P. (2009). Incorporating semantic knowledge for sentiment analysis. In *Proceedings of ICON-09*. Hyderabad, India: ICON.

Vermeer, P. A., & Sutjiadi, W. (1985). The uplift resistance of shallow embedded anchors. In *Proc. 11th Int. Conf. Soil Mech., & Found. Engrg,* (vol. 3, pp. 1635–1638). San Francisco, CA: Academic Press.

Vesic, A. S. (1971). Breakout resistance of objects embedded in ocean bottom. *Journal of the Soil Mechanics and Foundations Division, 96*(SM4), 1311–1334.

Vijayan, J. (2011). *Hadoop finds niche alongside conventional database systems*. Retrieved April 22, 2013, from www.computerworld.com/s/article/358164/Hadoop_Works_Alongside_RDBMS

Vinod, P. Jain, Golecha, Gaur, & Laxmi. (2010). MEDUSA: Metamorphic malware dynamic analysis using signature from API. In *Proceedings of the 3rd International Conference on Security of Information and Networks (SIN 2010)* (pp. 263-269). Rostov-on-Don, Russia: SIN.

Vinod, P. Laxmi, & Gaur. (2012a). Reform: Relevant features for malware analysis. In *Proceedings of 26th International Conference on Advanced Information Networking and Applications Workshops* (WAINA 2012) (pp. 738-744). Fukuoka, Japan: WAINA.

Vinod, P. Laxmi, Gaur, Kumar, & Chundawat. (2009). Static CFG analyzer for metamorphic malware code. *In Proceedings of the 2nd International Conference on Security of Information and Networks*. SIN.

Vinod, P., Laxmi, V., Gaur, M. S., & Chauhan, G. (2012b). Momentum: MetamOrphic malware exploration techniques using MSA signatures. In Proceedings of Innovations in Information Technology (IIT). IIT.

Vinod, P., Vijay, L., Manoj, S. G., Smita, N., & Parvez, F. (2013). MCF: Multi-component features for malware analysis. In *Proceedings of 27th IEEE International Conference on Advanced Information Networking and Applications* (AINA-2013). Barcelona, Spain: AINA.

Vinod, P., Laxmi, V., & Gaur, M. (2011a). Metamorphic malware analysis and detection methods. In R. Santanam, M. Sethumadhavan, & M. Virendra (Eds.), *Cyber security, cyber crime and cyber forensics: Applications and perspectives* (pp. 178–202). Hershey, PA: Information Science Reference.

Vinod, P., Laxmi, V., & Gaur, M. S. (2011b). Scattered feature space for malware analysis. In *Proceedings of Advances in Computing and Communications* (pp. 562–571). Berlin: Springer. doi:10.1007/978-3-642-22709-7_55

Vlahou, A., Schorge, J. O., Gregory, B. W., & Coleman, R. L. (2003). Diagnosis of ovarian cancer using decision tree classification of mass spectral data. *BioMed Research International,* (5), 308-314.

VX Heavens. (n.d.). Retrieved from http://vx.netlux.org/lib

Wan, X., & Yang, J. (2006). Improved affinity graph based multi-document summarization. In *Proceedings of the Human Language Technology Conference of the NAACL* (pp. 181-184). Stroudsburg, PA: Association for Computational Linguistics.

Wang, D., & Li, T. (2010). Document update summarization using incremental hierarchical clustering. In *Proceedings of the 19th ACM international conference on Information and knowledge management* (pp. 279–288). New York, NY: ACM.

Wang, J., Li, Q., & Chen, Y. P. (2010). User comments for news recommendation in social media. In *Proceedings of the 33rd international ACM SIGIR conference on Research and development in information retrieval* (pp. 881-882). New York, NY: ACM.

Wang, L., & Wan, Y. (2011). Sentiment Classification of Documents based on Latent Semantic Analysis. In *Proceedings of International Conference, Advanced Research on Computer Education, Simulation and Modeling* (CESM), (pp. 356-361). CESM.

Wang, L., Si, J., & Hu, X. B. (2009). Research on the Clustering and Composition of P2P-Based Web Services. In Proceedings of Biomedical Engineering and Informatics, (pp. 1-5). IEEE.

Wang, S., Li, D., Song, S., Wei, Y., & Li, H. (2009). A Feature Selection Method Based on Fisher's Discriminant Ratio for Text Sentiment Classification. In *Proceeding WISM '09 Proceedings of the International Conference on Web Information Systems and Mining,* (pp. 88-97). WISM.

Wang, Z. (2013). Application of Decision Making Tree Method in the Real Estate Development Scheme Optimization. In *Proceedings of Third International Conference on Intelligent System Design and Engineering Applications* (pp. 365-368). Hong Kong: Kluwer Academic Publishers.

Wang, D., Zhu, S., Li, T., Chi, Y., & Gong, Y. (2011). Integrating Document Clustering and Multidocument Summarization. *ACM Transactions on Knowledge Discovery from Data, 5*(3), 1–26. doi:10.1145/1993077.1993078

Wang, W., Chen, J., Wu, X., & Wu, Z. (2001). The application of some non-linear methods in rotating machinery fault diagnosis. *Mechanical Systems and Signal Processing, 15*(4), 697–705. doi:10.1006/mssp.2000.1316

Wang, X., & Makis, V. (2009). Autoregressive model-based gear shaft fault diagnosis using the Kolmogorov–Simonov test. *Journal of Sound and Vibration, 327*(3), 413–423. doi:10.1016/j.jsv.2009.07.004

Wang, Z. (2013). Performance Evaluation for Strategy Based on Auto-Adapting Users in Cross Language Information Retrieval. *International Journal of Multimedia and Ubiquitous Engineering, 8*(3), 83–92.

Washington, W. M., & Parkinson, C. L. (1986). *An introduction to three-dimensional climate modeling.* Mill Valley, NY: University Science Books.

Weber, I., Garimella, V. R. K., & Borra, E. (2012). Mining web query logs to analyze political issues. In *Proceedings of the 3rd Annual ACM Web Science Conference* (pp. 330-334). Evanston, IL: ACM.

Wei, J. L., Wang, K., Stolfo, S. J., & Herzog, B. (2005). Fileprints: Identifying file types by n-gram analysis. In *Proceedings of the Sixth Annual IEEE SMC 4th Virus Bulletin Conference,* (pp. 64-71). IEEE.

Whitelaw, C., Garg, N., & Argamon, S. (2005). Using appraisal groups for sentiment analysis. In *Proceedings of the 14th ACM international conference on Information and knowledge management*. Bremen, Germany: ACM.

Widodo, A., & Yang, B. S. (2011). Machine health prognostics using survival probability and support vector machine. *Expert Systems with Applications*, *38*(7), 8430–8437. doi:10.1016/j.eswa.2011.01.038

Wiebe, J., Wilson, T., & Cardie, C. (2005). Annotating expressions of opinions and emotions in language. *Language Resources and Evaluation*, *39*(2-3), 165–210. doi:10.1007/s10579-005-7880-9

Wiese, J., Hong, J. I., & Zimmerman, J. (2012). Building a dynamic and computational understanding of personal social network. In *Proceedings of 1st ACM Workshop on Mobile Systems for Computational Social Science*, (pp. 5-10). ACM.

Wikipedia. (n.d.). Retrieved from http://en.wikipedia.org/wiki/Climate_model#Research_and_development

Wilcox, R. R. (2012). *Introduction to robust estimation and hypothesis testing*. Academic Press.

Witten, I. H., & Frank, E. (2002). *Data Mining: Practical Machine Learning Tools and Techniques with Java Implementations*. Morgan Kaufmann.

Witten, I. H., & Frank, E. (2005). *Data Mining: Practical machine learning tools and techniques*. San Francisco: Morgan Kaufmann.

Wolf, L., Potikha, L., Dershowitz, N., Shweka, R., & Choueka, Y. (2011). Computerized Paleography: Tools for Historical Manuscripts. In *Proceedings of 18th IEEE International Conference on Image Processing (ICIP)* (pp. 3545–3548). Brussels, Belgium: IEEE Signal Processing Society.

Wong, S. K. M., Wang, L. S., & Yao, Y. Y. (1993). Interval structure: A framework for representing uncertain information. In *Proceedings of the 8th Conference on Uncertainty in Artificial Intelligence* (pp. 336–343). Academic Press.

Wong, W., & Stamp, M. (2006). Hunting for metamorphic engines. *Journal in Computer Virology*, *2*(3), 211–229. doi:10.1007/s11416-006-0028-7

Wood, J., Brodlie, K., & Wright, H. (1996). Visualization over the World Wide Web and its application to environmental data. In *Proceedings of the 7th Conference on Visualization, VIS '96*. Los Alamitos, CA: VIS.

Wu, L., Feng, J., & Luo, Y. (2009). A Personalized Intelligent Web Retrieval System Based on the Knowledge-Base Concept and Latent Semantic Indexing Model. In *Proceedings of 7th ACIS International Conference on Software Engineering Research, Management and Applications*, (pp. 45-50). ACIS.

Wu, Z., Shi, C., & Lu, Y. (2013). Intelligent Information Retrieval System Based on Muti-Agent Model. In *Proceedings of the 2nd International Conference on Systems Engineering and Modeling*. Academic Press.

Wu, C.-W., & Liu, C.-L. (2003). Ontology-based text summarization for business news articles. In *Computers and their Applications*. Academic Press.

Wu, S., & Clements-Croome, D. (2005). Preventive maintenance models with random maintenance quality. *Reliability Engineering & System Safety*, *90*(1), 99–105. doi:10.1016/j.ress.2005.03.012

WWEA. (2012). Quarterly bulletin. *World Wind Energy Association Bulletin*, *3*, 1–40.

Xia, R., & Zong, C. (2010). Exploring the use of word relation features for sentiment classification. In *Proceedings of the 23rd International Conference on Computational Linguistics* (COLING), (pp. 1336-1344). COLING.

Xiao, Y., Xiao, M., & Zhang, F. (2007). Intelligent Information Retrieval Model Based on Multi-Agents. In *Proceedings of International Conference on Wireless Communications, Networking and Mobile Computing (WiCOM 2007)*, (pp. 5464-5467). WiCOM.

Xia, R., Zong, C., & Li, S. (2011). Ensemble of Feature Sets and Classification Algorithms for Sentiment Classification. *Journal of Information Science*, *181*(6), 1138–1152. doi:10.1016/j.ins.2010.11.023

Xia, X., & Chen, L. (2012). Fuzzy chaos method for evaluation of nonlinearly evolutionary process of rolling bearing performance. *Measurement*, *46*(3), 1349–1354. doi:10.1016/j.measurement.2012.11.003

Xie, L. L., Chen, F. Z., & Kou, J. S. (2011). Ontology-based semantic Web services clustering. In *Proceedings of Industrial Engineering and Engineering Management (IE&EM), 2011 IEEE 18Th International Conference on* (pp. 2075-2079). IEEE.

Xie, S.-Y., Liu, J.-C., & Wang, H. (2003). Research of Intelligent Information Retrieval System Based on Three Layers Agent Structure. In *Proceedings of the 2ⁿᵈ International Conference on Machine Learning and Cybernetics*, (pp. 2329-2332). Academic Press.

Xie, T., Thummalapenta, S., Lo, D., & Liu, C. (2009). *Data mining for software engineering.* IEEE Computer Society.

Xiong, X. S., Fan, L., & Lei, Z. (2010). Ontology-Based Association Rule Quality Evaluation Using Information Theory. In *Proceedings of International Conference on Computational and Information Sciences* (pp. 170-173). Chengdu: IEEE.

Xu, L., Krzyzak, A., & Suen, C. Y. (1992). Methods of combining multiple classifiers and their applications to handwriting recognition. *Systems, Man and Cybernetics. IEEE Transactions on, 22*(3), 418–435.

Xu, R., & Wunsch, D. (2008). *Clustering* (Vol. 10). Wiley. doi:10.1002/9780470382776

Yang, Q., & Hu, Y. (2011). Application of Improved Apriori Algorithm on Educational Information. In *Proceedings of Fifth International Conference on Genetic and Evolutionary Computing* (pp. 330-332). Xiamen: IEEE.

Yang, S. (2012). Research and Application of Improved Apriori Algorithm to Electronic Commerce. In *Proceedings of 11ᵗʰ International Conference on Distributed Computing and Applications to Business, Engineering & Science* (pp. 227-231). Guilin: IEEE.

Yang, Z., Cai, K., Tang, J., Zhang, L., Su, Z., & Li, J. (2011). Social Context Summarization. In *Proceedings of International ACM SIGIR Conference on Research and Development in Information Retrieval* (pp. 255-264). New York, NY: ACM.

Yang, S., Li, W., & Wang, C. (2008). The intelligent fault diagnosis of wind turbine gearbox based on artificial neural network. In *Proceedings of Condition Monitoring and Diagnosis*. IEEE.

Yang, T., Chi, Y., Zhu, S., Gong, Y., & Jin, R. (2011). Detecting communities and their evolutions in dynamic social networks-a Bayesian approach. *Journals on Machine Learning, 82*(2), 157–189. doi:10.1007/s10994-010-5214-7

Yang, W., Tavner, P. J., Crabtree, C. J., & Wilkinson, M. (2010). Cost-effective condition monitoring for wind turbines. *IEEE Transactions on Industrial Electronics, 57*(1), 263–271. doi:10.1109/TIE.2009.2032202

Yan, W.-W., & Shao, H.-H. (2003). Application of support vector machines and least squares support vector machines to heart disease diagnoses. *Control and Decision, 18*(3), 358–360.

Yan, W., Zhang, Z., & Ansari, N. (2008). Revealing packed malware. *IEEE Security and Privacy, 6*, 65–69. doi:10.1109/MSP.2008.126

Yao, Y. Y. (1998). Constructive and algebraic methods of the theory of rough sets. *Information Sciences, 109*, 21–47. doi:10.1016/S0020-0255(98)00012-7

Yao, Y. Y. (2001). Information granulation and rough set approximation. *International Journal of Intelligent Systems, 16*, 87–104. doi:10.1002/1098-111X(200101)16:1<87::AID-INT7>3.0.CO;2-S

Yao, Y. Y. (2004). A partition model of granular computing. *LNCS Transactions on Rough Sets, 3100*, 232–253.

Yao, Y. Y. (2006). Three perspectives of granular computing. *Journal of Nanchang Institute of Thchnology, 25*, 16–21.

Yao, Y., & Zhao, Y. (2009). Discernibility matrix simplification for constructing attribute reducts. *Information Sciences: An International Journal, 179*(7), 867–882. doi:10.1016/j.ins.2008.11.020

Ye, J., Janardan, R., & Li, Q. (2004). *Two-dimensional linear discriminant analysis.* Paper presented at the Advances in Neural Information Processing Systems. New York, NY.

Ye, Q., Zhang, Z., & Law, R. (2009). Sentiment classification of online reviews to travel destinations by supervised machine learning approaches. *Expert Systems with Applications, 36*, 6527–6535. doi:10.1016/j.eswa.2008.07.035

Yin, Z., Li, R., Mei, Q., & Han, J. (2009). Exploring social tagging graph for web object classification. In *Proceedings of the 15th ACM SIGKDD international conference on Knowledge discovery and data mining* (pp. 957-966). New York, NY: ACM.

Ying, P., Tianjiang, W., & Xueling, J. (2007). Building Intelligent Information Retrieval System Based on Ontology. In *Proceedings of the 8th International Conference on Electronic Measurement and Instruments (ICEMT'2007)*, (pp. 4-612 – 4-615). ICEMT.

Yong-Min, L., & Shu, C. (2009). Artificial Intelligent Information Retrieval Using Assigning Context of Documents. In *Proceedings of IEEE International Conference on Network Security, Wireless Communications and Trusted Computing*, (pp. 592-595). IEEE.

Yuan, J., Wang, K., Yu, T., & Fang, M. (2008). Reliable multi-objective optimization of highspeed WEDM process based on Gaussian process regression. *International Journal of Machine Tools & Manufacture*, 48, 47–60. doi:10.1016/j.ijmachtools.2007.07.011

Yuan-Jie, L., & Jian, C. (2012). Web service classification based on automatic semantic annotation and ensemble learning. In *Proceedings of Parallel and Distributed Processing Symposium Workshops & PhD Forum (IPDPSW), 2012 IEEE 26th International* (pp. 2274-2279). IEEE.

Yuguang, Y., & Chunyan, W. (2011). Application of the Model Multi Based on Apriori Algorithm in Supporting System of Medical Decision. In *Proceedings of Third International Conference on Measuring Technology and Mechatronics Automation* (pp. 566-569). Shangshai: IEEE.

Yu, L., & Liu, H. (2004). Efficient Feature Selection via Analysis of Relevance and Redundancy. *Journal of Machine Learning Research*, 1205–1224.

Yu, M., Naqvi, S. M., Rhuma, A., & Chambers, J. (2012). One class boundary method classifiers for application in a video-based fall detection system. *IET Computer Vision*, 6(2), 90–100. doi:10.1049/iet-cvi.2011.0046

Zadeh, L. A. (1965). Fuzzy sets. *Information and Control*, 8, 338–353. doi:10.1016/S0019-9958(65)90241-X

Zaher, A. S. A. E., McArthur, S. D. J., Infield, D. G., & Patel, Y. (2009). Online wind turbine fault detection through automated SCADA data analysis. *Wind Energy (Chichester, England)*, 12(6), 574–593. doi:10.1002/we.319

Zap Technology. (2010). *KFC/Pizza Hut makes efficiency gains with Zap Business Intelligence: Businesses become more agile, responsive and performance-focused, a case study*. Retrieved April 6, 2012, from http//www.zaptechnology.com

Zappalà, D., Tavner, P., Crabtree, C., & Sheng, S. (2013). Sideband Algorithm for Automatic Wind Turbine Gearbox Fault Detection and Diagnosis. In *Proceedings of the Conference of the European Wind Energy Association*. Vienna, Austria: European Wind Energy Association.

Zhang, C., Xie, D., Zhang, N., Li, H., & Liu, F. (2011). The improvement of Apriori algorithm and its application in fault analysis of CRH EMU. In *Proceedings of Third International Conference on Service Operations, Logistics, and Informatics* (pp. 543-547). Beijing: IEEE.

Zhang, D., Liu, W., Gong, X., & Jin, H. (2011). A novel improved SMOTE resampling algorithm based on fractal. *Journal of Computer Information Systems*, 7(6), 2204–2211.

Zhang, J., Yu, X., Liu, P., & Wang, Z. (2009). Research on Improving Performance of Semantic Search in UDDI.[). IEEE.]. *Proceedings of Intelligent Systems*, 4, 572–576.

Zhang, R., Li, W., Gao, D., & Ouyang, Y. (2013). Automatic Twitter Topic Summarization With Speech Acts. *IEEE Transactions on Audio, Speech, and Language Processing*, 21(3), 649–658. doi:10.1109/TASL.2012.2229984

Zhang, Z., Verma, A., & Kusiak, A. (2012). Fault Analysis and Condition Monitoring of the Wind Turbine Gearbox. *IEEE Transactions on Energy Conversion*, 27(2), 526–535. doi:10.1109/TEC.2012.2189887

Zhao, X., Wang, B., & Yu, J. (2012). Color constancy via Gaussian process regression. *Journal of Information and Computational Science*, 9(15), 4663–4671.

Zheng, K., Xiong, H., Cui, Y., Chen, J., & Han, L. (2012). User Clustering-based Web Service Discovery. In *Proceedings of Internet Computing for Science and Engineering (ICICSE), 2012 Sixth International Conference on* (pp. 276-279). IEEE.

Zhou, D., Kang, J., Fan, Z., & Zhang, W. (2011). The application of improved Apriori algorithm in continuous Speech Recognition. In *Proceedings of Second International Conference on Mechanic Automation and Control Engineering* (pp. 756-758). Hohhot: IEEE.

Zhou, J., & Li, S. (2009). Semantic Web Service Discovery Approach Using Service Clustering. In *Proceedings of Information Engineering and Computer Science* (pp. 1–5). IEEE. doi:10.1109/ICIECS.2009.5363051

Zhou, Z., Wang, Z., & Sun, X. (2013). Face recognition based on optimal kernel minimax probability machine. *Journal of Theoretical and Applied Information Technology, 48*(3), 1645–1651.

Zhu, J., Kang, Y., Zheng, Z., & Lyu, M. R. (2012). A Clustering-Based QoS Prediction Approach for Web Service Recommendation. In *Proceedings of Object/Component/Service-Oriented Real-Time Distributed Computing Workshops (ISORCW), 2012 15th IEEE International Symposium on* (pp. 93-98). IEEE.

Zhu, J., Wang, C., He, X., Bu, J., Chen, C., Shang, S., et al. (2009). Tag-oriented document summarization. In *Proceedings of the 18th international ACM conference on World Wide Web Conference* (pp. 1195-1196). New York, NY: ACM.

Zhu, Z., Yuan, H., Song, J., Bi, J., & Liu, G. (2010). WS-SCAN: A effective approach for Web services clustering. In *Proceedings of Computer Application and System Modeling (ICCASM), 2010 International Conference on* (Vol. 5, pp. V5-618). IEEE.

Zou, K., Sun, W., Yu, H., & Liu, F. (2012). ID3 decision tree in fraud detection application. In *Proceedings of International Conference on Computer Science and Electronics Engineering* (pp. 399-402). Hangzhou: IEEE.

About the Contributors

Vishal Bhatnagar received the B-Tech degree in Computer Science and Engineering from Nagpur University in Nagpur, India in 1999, the M-Tech in Information Technology from Punjabi University, Patiala, India in 2005, and PhD from Shobhit University in 2010. Vishal Bhatnagar is Associate Professor in Computer Science and Engineering Department at Ambedkar Institute of Advanced Communication Technologies and Research (Govt. of Delhi), GGSIPU, Delhi, India. His research interests include database, advance database, data warehouse, and data mining. He has been in teaching for more than eight years. He has guided undergraduate and postgraduate students in various research projects in databases and data mining.

* * *

D. P. Acharjya received his Ph. D. in computer science from Berhampur University, India; M. Tech. degree in computer science from Utkal University, India in 2002; and M. Sc. from NIT, Rourkela, India. He has been awarded with Gold Medal in M.Sc. Currently, he is a professor in the school of computing sciences and engineering, VIT University, Vellore, India. He has authored many national and international journal papers and five books: *Fundamental Approach to Discrete Mathematics; Computer Based on Mathematics; Theory of Computation; Rough Set in Knowledge Representation and Granular Computing; Introduction to Information Technology and Computer Programming*. In addition, he has edited two books. He is associated with many professional bodies CSI, ISTE, IMS, AMTI, ISIAM, OITS, IACSIT, CSTA, IEEE, and IAENG. He was founder secretary of OITS Rourkela chapter. His current research interests include rough sets, formal concept analysis, knowledge representation, data mining, and granular computing.

Basant Agarwal is a doctoral candidate at Malaviya National Institute of Technology, Jaipur. He received his master in computer engineering from Malaviya National Institute of Technology, Jaipur, India. His research interest is in Natural Language Processing, Machine learning, Sentiment Analysis, and Opinion Mining.

Abdulaziz R. Alazemi earned his bachelor from Kuwait University (2008/2009) from the college of petroleum and engineering in computer engineering, followed by a master's degree in computer engineering in 2012 from Kuwait University, college of graduate studies. He is working as a computer engineer at distance learning center at Kuwait University. He's pursuing his doctoral studies abroad. His work experience includes video conferencing, interactive learning, and distance learning technologies. His projects include digital systems testing, software engineering modeling, performance optimization through GPGPU, low power wireless sensor networks, business intelligence, business strategies, IT management, and data mining. He has been published in places like the *American Journal of Networks and Communications* and *Research Notes in Information Science.*

Abdulrahman R. Alazemi earned his bachelor from Kuwait University (2008/2009) from the college of petroleum and engineering in computer engineering. It was followed by a master's degree in computer engineering in 2012 from Kuwait University. He is working now at the libraries department, the Technologies and Systems Unit at Kuwait University. The working environment has earned him experience in understanding technologies, how they reflect on each and every simple task at work, and the importance in implementing technologies to enable faster, safer, and more efficient work. His projects include performance optimization through GPGPU, enhancing leader elections, systems modeling, data warehousing, and data visualization. He has been published in places like the *International Journal of Network Security* and the *International Journal of Computer Science and Security.*

T. K. Ansari received his Bachelor in Technology from SCMS School of Engineering and Technology, Ernakulam, Kerala, India in 2013. His area of Interest is computer security and information forensics.

Sonal Ayyappan received her B.Tech in Computer Science and Engineering from Cochin University of Science and Technology, Kerala and M.Tech in Computer Science and Engineering from Bharathidasan University, Trichy, Tamilnadu. She is currently pursuing her Ph.D. from SRM University, Chennai. Presently, she is working as Associate Professor in the department of Computer Science and Engineering, SCMS School of Engineering and Technology, Ernakulam, Kerala. Her areas of interest include computer security, image processing, and computer vision.

Elena Baralis is full professor at the Dipartimento di Automatica e Informatica of the Politecnico di Torino since January 2005. She holds a Master's degree in Electrical Engineering and a Ph.D. in Computer Engineering, both from Politecnico di Torino. Her current research interests are in the field of database systems and data mining, more specifically on mining algorithms for very large databases and sensor/stream data analysis. She has published over 80 papers in international journals and conference proceedings. She has served on the program committees or as area chair of several international conferences and workshops, among which are VLDB, IEEE ICDM, ACM SAC, DaWak, ACMCIKM, and PKDD.

Luca Cagliero has been a research assistant at the Dipartimento di Automatica e Informatica of the Politecnico di Torino since March 2012. He holds a Master degree in Computer and Communication Networks and a PhD in Computer Engineering from Politecnico di Torino. His current research interests are in the fields of Data Mining and Database Systems. Specifically, he has worked on structured and unstructured data mining by means of classification and Association rule mining algorithms.

Tianxing Cai is a researcher in the Dan. F Smith Department of Chemical Engineering, Lamar University. Tianxing specialized in the research fields of modeling, simulation and optimization for the industrial operation, process safety, and environment protection. His major research is the development of optimization models (Linear Programming, Quadratic Constraint Programming, Nonlinear Programming, Mixed Integer Programming, Relaxed Mixed Integer Programming, Mixed Integer Quadratic Constraint Programming, Mixed Integer Nonlinear Programming, Relaxed Mixed Integer Quadratic Constraint Programming) to realize the synthesis of energy and water systems, manufacturing planning and scheduling, and plant wide optimization. Besides that, he also involves the software application of Aspen, HYSYS, ProII, MATLAB, and gPROMS to conduct simulation and optimization for the process design, environment impact reduction, and safety assessment.

Rama Krishna Challa received B.Tech. from JNTU, Hyderabad, M.Tech. from Cochin University of Science and Technology, Cochin, and Ph.D. from IIT, Kharagpur. Since 1996, he is working with Department of Computer Science and Engineering, National Institute of Technical Teachers' Training and Research, Chandigarh and currently holds the position of Associate Professor. His areas of research interest include Computer Networks, Wireless Networks, Cryptography and Cyber Security, and Distributed Computing.

Mostafa Chiguer, applied computer sciences engineer, received his degree in 2010 from Faculty of Sciences in Rabat and has work experience as SAP HCM consultant. His current research interest is the use of data mining techniques in software quality and routing protocols of mobile ad-hoc networks.

Naveen Dahiya received his B.E. in Computer Science and Engineering from Maharshi Dayanand University, Rohtak, Haryana, India in 2003 and M-Tech in Computer Engineering from Maharshi Dayanand University, Rohtak, Haryana, India in 2005, and is currently pursuing Ph.D from Y.M.C.A. University of Science and Technology, Faridabad, Haryana, India. He is working as an Assistant Professor in Computer Science and Engineering Department at Maharaja Surajmal Institute of Technology, C-4, Janak Puri, New Delhi, India. His research interests include database systems, data warehouse, and data mining. He has supervised various undergraduate and postgraduate students in various research projects in data warehousing and data mining.

Hossein Ebrahimpour-Komleh is currently an Assistant Professor at the Department of Electrical and Computer Engineering at the University of Kashan, Kashan, Iran. His main area of research includes computer vision, image processing, pattern recognition, biometrics, robotics, fractals, chaos theory, and applications of artificial intelligence in engineering. He received his Ph.D. degree in Computer Engineering from Queensland University of Technology, Brisbane, Australia in 2006. His Ph.D. research work was on the "Fractal Techniques for Face Recognition." From 2005 to 2007 and prior to joining the

University of Kashan, he was working as a post-doc researcher in the University of Newcastle, NSW, Australia and as a visiting scientist in CSRIO Sydney. Hossein Ebrahimpour-Komleh has B.Sc. and M.Sc. degrees both in computer engineering from Isfahan University of Technology (Isfahan, Iran) and Amirkabir University of Technology (Tehran, Iran), respectively. He has served as an editorial board member and reviewer for several journals and international and national conferences.

Alessandro Fiori received the European Ph.D. Degree from Politecnico di Torino, Italy. He is a project manager at the Institute for Cancer Research and Treatment (IRCC) of Candiolo, Italy since January 2012. His research interests are in the field of data mining, in particular bioinformatics and text mining. His activity is focused on the development of information systems and analysis frameworks oriented to the management and integration of biological and molecular data. His research activities are also devoted to text summarization and social network analysis.

Gopinath Ganapathy is a Professor in Computer Science at Bharathidasan University, India. He published around 60 research papers in international journals and conferences. He has 23 years of experience in academia, industry, research, and consultancy services. He has around 8.5 years of international experience in US and UK. His research interests include Semantic Web, auto programming, natural language processing, and text mining.

Mary A. Geetha received her M. Tech. in computer science and engineering from VIT University, Vellore, India in 2008 and B.E. from University of Madras, Tamil Nadu, India in 2004. At present, she is working at VIT University as Assistant Professor-Senior. She is currently doing her PhD at VIT University. Her field of interest spans and is not limited to computer science and health care management. Her research interests include security for data mining, databases and intelligent systems. She is associated with professional bodies IAENG and CSTA.

Jamie L. Godwin received the BSc (Hons) degree in computer science from the University of Durham, England in 2010. At present, he is working towards the degree of Doctor of Philosophy within the Department of Engineering and Computing Sciences, also at the University of Durham. He has researched areas such as SCADA data analysis and robust multivariate prognostic techniques. He has provided consultancy to various public and private entities, including 5G technologies, Northumbrian Water, various electricity distributors, and North Yorkshire Police. His current doctoral research focuses on metrics for maintenance effectiveness, SCADA data analysis, and robust multivariate statistical measures for prognosis.

Ahmed Habbani received a Ph.D. degree in 2007 from the Graduate School of Engineering, EMI, in Information and Computer Sciences. He received a HDR degree in 2012. He is currently Research Professor at the School of Computer Science and System (ENSIAS). He is working within the Wireless Sensor Networks (WSN) team of the Laboratory Electronics and Telecommunication (LEC) and the MIS (Mobile intelligent System) team of Laboratory SIME (Mobile and Embedded Information Systems) for studying ad-hoc mobile intelligent communication systems and wireless sensor networks.

Gábor Hosszú received the M.E. and the PhD degree from the Technical University of Budapest in 1985 and in 1991, respectively. In 2011, he received his MSc in Law from the Pázmány Péter Catholic University, Budapest. He joined the Technical University of Budapest in 1990 being Associate Professor on the Faculty of Electrical Engineering and Informatics from 1997. In 2013 he has been awarded the title doctor habil. in the field of Informatics, Engineering and Technology. His main activities include the VHDL based hardware modeling, Internet-based media communication, IP multicasting, P2P networks, statistical evaluation of bioelectronic signals, and computational paleography. He has published more than 200 technical papers. His additional research fields are signal processing and evaluation of data collected from distributed intelligent locations via one telemedicine system.

Saima Jabeen is a PhD student at the Dipartimento di Automatica e Informatica of the Politecnico di Torino. She has received her Master degree in Computer Science from Pakistan. Her research interests are in the field of text mining, document analysis, and in natural language processing. Her focus is on integrating semantics and social knowledge in text summarization.

Manish Kumar received his PhD from Indian Institute of Information Technology, Allahabad, India in Data Management in Wireless Sensor Networks. He is an Assistant Professor at Indian Institute of Information Technology, Allahabad, India. His research interest areas are databases, data management in sensor networks, and data mining.

Sumit Kumar received his B.Tech from Indian Institute of Information Technology, Allahabad, India. He is Software Engineer at IVY Comptech Pvt. Ltd., Hyderabad, India. His research interest areas are distributed systems, data mining, databases, and computer networks.

Jikku Kuriakose completed Bachelor of Engineering in Computer Science and Engineering from Maharaja Engineering College, Avinashi, Tamilnadu. He is pursuing his Masters of Technology in Computer Science and Engineering with specialization in Information Systems from SCMS School of Engineering and Technology, Ernakulam, Kerala affiliated to Mahatma Gandhi University. His area of Interest is computer security, information forensics, and metamorphic malware analysis.

Peter Matthews is a Lecturer in Design Informatics at the School of Engineering and Computing Sciences and holds degrees in Mathematics (1994), Computer Science (1995), and Engineering Design (2002), which were all taken at Cambridge University. He is the author or co-author of numerous books, technical papers, and EU patents. His current research interests are centred around industrial data analysis involving collecting and analysing data obtained either from production process monitoring (e.g. SCADA logs from various production machinery) or service life data (e.g. maintenance logs) and utilising Monte Carlo simulations, evolutionary algorithms, Bayesian belief networks, and interval probabilities (p-boxes) to form future design and operation decisions.

Namita Mittal has worked as an Assistant Professor for 18 years at Department of Computer Engineering, Malaviya National Institute of Technology, Jaipur, India. She is involved in teaching undergraduate and graduate courses like database management, information retrieval, data mining, natural language processing, Semantic Web, etc. She has published several research papers in reputed international conferences and journals. She has a PhD in Computer Engineering from Malaviya National Institute of Technology, Jaipur, India.

Seyed Jalaleddin Mousavirad was born in Neishabour, Iran, in 1986. He graduated from Azad University of Mashhad in 2007. He received MA degree from Kurdistan University, Iran in 2011 and started his Ph.D. at Computer Engineering Department in the University of Kashan, Iran in 2012. His main research interests are data mining, pattern recognition, and image processing. He has published about 15 research papers in national and international journals and conferences. Presently, he is working in the area of data mining and pattern recognition.

Naresh Kumar Nagwani has completed his graduation in Computer Science and Engineering in 2001 from Guru Ghasidas University, Bilaspur. He completed his post-graduation M.Tech. in Information Technology from ABV-Indian Institute of Information Technology, Gwalior in 2005 and completed the Ph.D. in Computer Science and Engineering in 2013 from National Institute of Technology Raipur, India. His area of interest is DBMS, data mining, text mining, and information retrieval. His employment experience includes SSCET Bhilai, Team Lead in Persistent Systems Limited and NIT Raipur. Presently, he is assistant professor and head at Department of Computer Science and Engineering, National Institute of Technology, Raipur.

Pijush Samui is a professor at Centre for Disaster Mitigation and Management in VIT University, Vellore, India. He obtained his B.E. at Bengal Engineering and Science University, M.Sc. at Indian Institute of Science, and Ph.D. at Indian Institute of Science. He worked as a postdoctoral fellow at University of Pittsburgh (USA) and Tampere University of Technology (Finland). He is the recipient of CIMO fellowship from Finland. Dr. Samui worked as a guest editor in *Disaster Advances* journal. He also serves as an editorial board member in several international journals. Dr. Samui is editor of *International Journal of Geomatics and Geosciences*. He is a reviewer for several journal papers. Dr. Samui is a Fellow of the International Congress of Disaster Management and Earth Science, India. He is the recipient of Shamsher Prakash Research Award for the year of 2011.

Neeti Sangwan received her B Tech. from Maharishi Dayanand University, Rohtak in 2010 and M Tech. from Banasthali University, Rajasthan in 2012. Presently, she is working as an assistant professor (C.S.E) in Maharaja Surajmal Institute of Technology, Janak Puri, New Delhi. Her research interest includes data mining, data warehousing, and database.

Sajid Shah is a PhD student at the Dipartimento di Elettronica e Telecomunicazioni of the Politecnico di Torino. He received his master degree Computer and Communication Networks from Politecnico di Torino in 2011. His research interests are in the field of databases and data mining particularly text summarization. He is currently working on developing algorithms for weather forecasting in the field of radar and remote sensing.

Manjeet Singh received his M.tech degree in Computer Science and Engineering from Guru Jhambeshwar University, Hissar, India and Ph.D from Maharshi Dayanand University, Rohtak, India in 2009. He is working as a Associate Professor in Computer Science and Engineering Department at Y.M.C.A University of Science and Technology, Faridabad, Haryana, India. His research interests include database systems, natural language processing, and compiler construction. He has supervised various undergraduate and postgraduate students in various research projects of data warehousing, data mining, and natural language processing.

Shailendra Kumar Sonkar obtained his B.Tech. in Computer Science and Engineering from Krishna Institute of Engineering and Technology Ghaziabad, Uttar Pradesh Technical University Lucknow Uttar Pradesh, India in 2006, and is pursuing M.E. in Computer Science and Engineering from National Institute of Technical Teacher's Training and Research Chandigarh, Panjab University Chandigarh, India. He is an Assistant Professor in Department of Computer Science and Engineering at Ashoka Institute of Technology and Management Varanasi, Uttar Pradesh Technical University Lucknow Uttar Pradesh, India.

Shashank Srivastava is pursuing his M.Tech from Indian Institute of Information Technology, Allahabad, India in Software Engineering. His research interest areas are data mining, databases, and data structures.

Chellammal Surianarayanan is an Assistant Professor in Computer Science at Bharathidasan University Constituent College for Women, Orathanadu, TamilNadu, India. She has 12 years of experience in research and academic services. She is a research scholar in the School of Computer Science and Engineering, Bharathidasan University, India. Her research interests include Semantic Web services, Semantic Web, and data mining.

Shrish Verma has completed his graduation in Electronics and Telecommunication Engineering and his post-graduation M.Tech. in Computer Engineering from Indian Institute of Technology, Kharagpur. He has completed his Ph.D. in Engineering from Pt. Ravi Shankar Shukla University Raipur. Presently, he is Dean Faculty Welfare and Professor at Department of Electronics and Telecommunication Engineering, National Institute of Technology, Raipur.

P. Vinod completed his Ph.D in Computer Engineering from Malaviya National Institute of Technology, Jaipur, Rajasthan, India. He received his Masters of Technology in Information Technology as well as Bachelor of Engineering in Computer Science and Engineering from Rajiv Gandhi Proudyogiki Vishwavidyalaya, Bhopal, Madhaya Pradesh. He has around 25 research publications to his credit in well-known international conferences and book chapters. In addition, he has executed a project entitled "PROSIM: Probabilistic Signature for Metamorphic Malware Detection," funded by Department of Information Technology, MCIT, New Delhi. Presently, he is working as Associate Professor in Department of Computer Science and Engineering, SCMS School of Engineering and Technology, Ernakulam, Kerala, India. His research interests are desktop and mobile malware analysis, intrusion detection, cryptography, natural language processing, and image analysis.

Index